PEOPLE AND PROPERTY IN
MEDIEVAL STAMFORD

a catalogue of title deeds from Stamford, Lincolnshire,
from the twelfth century to 1547

GW00566673

Edited by Alan Rogers

with the assistance of Colin Taylor, Robert Ball, John Hartley and others.
Index prepared by members of the Stamford Survey Group

Published 2012 by Abramis Academic Publishing

www.abramis.co.uk

ISBN 978 1 84549 548 0

Printed and bound in the United Kingdom

Abramis is an imprint of arima publishing.

arima publishing
ASK House, Northgate Avenue
Bury St Edmunds, Suffolk IP32 6BB
t: (+44) 01284 700321

www.abramis.co.uk

CONTENTS

FOREWORD

Stamford was one of the country's major urban centres for much of the Middle Ages, especially during the twelfth and thirteenth centuries and the early part of the fourteenth century. William the Conqueror found it standing as a quasi-county town – one with all the trappings except the county area of Kesteven which had been given to Lincoln to make that a double county (soon to become a triple county as the wetlands of Holland were re-colonised). It was a military centre, the castle withstanding sieges during Stephen's civil war and for nearly a century the town acting as a focal point for rebellious groups of magnates. It was an industrial centre making and distributing internationally top quality pottery and cloth. It was a religious centre with schools of national reputation. Above all, it was one of England's five great international fairs. The thirteenth century saw it at the peak of its greatness (I suspect that the start of the town's decline was the expulsion of the Jews in 1290, for as the deeds calendared here show, the Jews with their synagogue were fully embedded in the town's economic and social life) but it retained aspects of its greatness to the end of the fifteenth century and even into the first years of the sixteenth century. The death of medieval greatness came with the catastrophic dissolution of the religious establishments in the middle of the sixteenth century[1].

But despite this, the history of this town has yet to be explored, for Stamford has been all but ignored by historians of medieval towns (and later periods). And with reason, for there is so little medieval documentation available. There are no borough records at all apart from one borough minute book which does not start until 1465. Compared with the records available for Lincoln, for Nottingham and Leicester (other members of the original Five Borough Federation), Stamford fares badly. This absence of documentation has been attributed to the so-called 'sack' of the town in 1461 by the Lancastrian army as it passed through the town. I would have more sympathy for this view if the records started fully immediately after 1461 but they don't. There are no surviving chamberlains' accounts nor accounts of other officials although we know these were written up; there are no surviving freemen's rolls, virtually no estate records. I think the answer to this is simple; these records were kept by the town clerk (we know the name of only one of these officials) in their private houses just as later town clerks who were solicitors kept them in their offices rather than in the town hall and they were destroyed with the private papers of those officials. Only the Hall Book survives – probably because it is very large and obvious – but that too was not well kept. Some years apart from the election of the Alderman and the two councils, the First Twelve and the Second Twelve, there are no entries at all. Medieval Stamford was not good at creating and preserving its borough records.

There are of course other records from which the past of Stamford can be discerned: deeds; account rolls of St Michael's nunnery and of St Leonard's Priory/St Cuthbert's fee; records from Browne's Hospital and from at least one gild and one other hospital in

---

[1] See Rogers 1965; Rogers 1973

the town; a very few estate records from the dukes of York. And it was with the intention of putting into the public domain some of this material, i.e. property title deeds of the Middle Ages, so that historians can engage with this important town, that this project was commenced in association with the Stamford Survey Group in the late 1960s. It has taken many years to bring to a conclusion for which I apologise. There have been reasons for the delay but they do not need to be rehearsed here. I am only too glad that at long last this calendar can see the light of day. And the delay has brought two unexpected advantages – I have been able to digitalise the text, and through the internet I have been able to include a much wider range of title deeds held in other record offices than the Public Record Office (now The National Archive).

INTRODUCTION

Working as I was on medieval Stamford from 1960, my attention was drawn to a large collection of title deeds relating to the town held in the then Public Record Office (PRO). Most of these came from the estates of the nunnery of St Michael just outside Stamford but there were others from other religious houses – for many monasteries and other religious houses held property in Stamford in the Middle Ages[2], probably because of its fairs and markets as well as its schools, and these title deeds were stripped away by the government officials when these establishments passed through their hands on their way to private individuals.

The aim then was to calendar all the known title deeds relating to property in Stamford. One or two other documents have been included – an occasional receipt, bond, arbitration award or agreement etc – and indeed one or two documents which relate to Stamford owners but not to Stamford property, but these are very few. Most of the records come from the Public Record Office (TNA) but others come from other collections – either in their original form or in notes made of them. One large collection of medieval deeds relating to the town, from Browne's Hospital, has gone missing. They are known only from lists preserved amongst the records of the Hospital and from a partial and inaccurate set of notes in Francis Peck, *Antiquarian Annals of Stamford* (1727)[3] up to 1461 but not beyond this date. Peck's notes have been included here in summary form. I have discussed these deeds elsewhere[4].

Having started but not made much progress, in the late 1970s, when I was working at the University of Nottingham, I received a grant from the then SSRC to employ an assistant to work on the deeds in the PRO. First Colin Taylor and then later Dr Robert Ball worked for me and produced a first set of notes of almost all the Stamford deeds in the PRO and some of those in the then British Museum, now British Library. We were fortunate to obtain the support of several local archivists, especially Alan Piper at Durham who supplied us with notes of the deeds in their collection. Work was broken off in the mid-1980s when I found myself working abroad for some years; but when I resumed in the late 1990s, the internet gave access to a number of other record office collections, and I have incorporated their notes into this calendar.

The deeds listed here are thus scattered in many places - from Kent to Durham, from Exeter to Harvard in the USA. The most extensive collection is of course in the Public Record Office (now the National Archives). All the identified deeds in that office have been calendared from original sources. The only exceptions are the Stamford items

---

[2] See Hartley and Rogers 1974
[3] See Peck 1979 edition
[4] Alan Rogers, William Browne's title deeds and late medieval Stamford, *Archives* 34, 2009 pp 1-7

published in the two collections of Feet of Fines or Final Concords for Lincolnshire[5]. I have not of course seen every one of these records myself; I have had to rely on the summaries sent to me.

The deeds deal with both the urban and rural area of Stamford town. The main part of the town lay in Lincolnshire, but part of the town (Stamford Baron) lay in Northamptonshire and part (Bredcroft) lay in Rutland. The deeds relate to property in the town and fields and also to Wothorpe which is contiguous with the town on the south. I have omitted (with reluctance) Burley (now Burghley) which lay within what is now the park to Burghley House. Except exceptionally, transactions outside of Stamford which involve parties from Stamford are not included.

The period covered is from the earliest known deeds up to the end of the reign of Henry VIII. The dissolution of the religious houses had such a major impact on the land-holding structure of Stamford that it is clear that the deeds of the reigns of Edward VI, Mary and Elizabeth relate to a different set of circumstances. The date 1547 has been chosen as a cut-off point rather than 1603 as in the Public Record Office.

I cannot and do not claim that these are all the title deeds relating to Stamford from the twelfth century to the middle of the sixteenth century. More will undoubtedly turn up. The large collection in Burghley House is not yet available to scholars but when these become available (as the notes printed here drawn in part from the existing NRA lists and in part from new lists being compiled show), they will have many riches among them. But the summary list here is enough to show something of the value of this source.

Altogether there are well over 1000 documents summarised in these pages. They are all drawn from original documents or notes on original documents. Unlike many other towns, there are no enrolled deeds for Stamford unless they survive among the archives of Burghley House, although there are several endorsements which show that some deeds were enrolled in the court of the lord at the castle and in other courts such as that of the abbot of Peterborough for Stamford Baron.

One final comment is needed. Because this calendar has taken such a long time to prepare, it may be that some of the call numbers in some record offices have changed – even the PRO has changed some of its call numbers. This is particularly true of the town hall records in Stamford for the very few title deeds which they hold; these records are undergoing revision at the moment, but the deeds themselves have been identified although the call numbers may be different.

---

[5] Two volumes of Final Concords for Lincolnshire were published – *Abstracts of Final Concords temp Richard I, John and Henry III* volume I, privately printed 1896 (edited by W O Massingberd and R Boyd; this is sometimes referred to erroneously as Lincoln Record Society volume 1, for it is entitled *Lincolnshire Records* on the titlepage); and *Final Concords of the County of Lincoln* volume II edited by Canon Foster, 1920. I have not included the Stamford Final Concords from these two volumes in this collection, nor the title deeds which are enrolled on the Pipe Rolls as published by the Pipe Roll Society - only unpublished Feet of Fines.

WHAT THE DEEDS SHOW

I cannot and do not wish to provide here a full commentary on these title deeds, nor to explore their various formats and meanings[6]. Others will do that. But a few comments will help.

The key importance of this collection is for the thirteenth century when Stamford was at its greatest. This period urgently needs a full study. David Roffe has made a valuable start with his edition of the Hundred Rolls for the town and the commentary which goes with it, but this is just a beginning. These deeds add a great deal to his picture. The strength of the Jewish element in the town and their integration into the social fabric is revealed. They were followed by alien merchants (especially Flemings) who seem systematically to have bought up the debts to the Jews of residents in a manner reminiscent of contemporary banks. Terricus the German (Teutonicus) has already been studied in his international context by Natalie Fryde (1997), but we can now examine his local context also. Local dynasties such as the Apethorpes and Tyddeswell took over from the alien merchants leading to the de la Pole family making Stamford one of its main centres in the fourteenth century. The same families come up time and again. The role that the clergy played in the economic and social life of the town is now becoming clearer. The list of occupations mentioned here adds to our knowledge of Stamford's trades, industries and crafts. Religious life, especially the socio-religious gilds of the town, and pilgrimages come into sharper focus. We can see the borough Alderman (elsewhere the mayor) but few other town officers.

There is a large amount of evidence here for the topography of the town – the markets, the importance of the narrow lanes. The large number of gardens and orchards in the town centre is revealed. The river with its bridge and its mills was clearly a key element in the town's history. There is evidence here for the kinds of buildings which were being erected (and when and by whom) and maintained; the fifteenth century in particular showed signs of one larger building replacing two smaller ones even in the heart of the town. These can now be related to the extensive surviving and known architectural remains from the medieval period. There is some evidence of the kind of rents being paid. But there is surprisingly little light thrown here on the practice of borough English (the inheritance of urban property by the youngest son rather than the oldest) which we know was practised in Stamford widely.

---

[6] The best collection of medieval deeds which explain both their formats and uses is *Men of Property: an analysis of the Norwich enrolled deeds 1285-1311* by Serena Kelly, Elizabeth Rutledge and Margot Tillyard edited by Ursula Priestley published by the Centre for East Anglian Studies, University of East Anglia 1983; there are many other collections. See also M Gervers ed *Dating undated medieval charters* 2000 Boydell.

ACKNOWLEDGEMENTS

So many people have helped with this collection and over such a long time that it is impossible for me to include every name which should be included. I apologise in advance if this omission may give offence.

First of course must be the SSRC (now the ESRC); without their grant the whole project would not exist. I apologise to them for the length of time which the project has taken. I have received immense support and help from the staff of so many libraries and record offices that I am unable to list them all. The calendar was initially typed by Agnes McConway of Magee University College, Londonderry; Deirdre McGill helped to check the typescript; it was scanned into the computer by John Dawes. The members of the Stamford Survey Group over so many years have always provided help, not least with the indexing of this volume. John Hartley as ever has been a great help in searching for material and in checking some of my more extreme views. The town hall staff in Stamford and the staff of Burghley House have all played their part.

I hope the collection will interest many people and prove useful for historians, and that it will lead to a greater understanding of this important medieval town.

Alan Rogers
Honorary Research Fellow, School of History, University of Nottingham
May 2012

THE USE OF DEEDS FOR MEDIEVAL HISTORY[7]

Sciant presentes et future…

It has on occasion been alleged that medieval men and women had little real sense of history until the later fourteenth or fifteenth century; but the opening phrases of many medieval charters and property deeds and the accumulation of deeds relating to transactions in the long distant past both reveal something of a sense of change and of future development. Such documents, written witnesses to transactions already carried out, often survive in large numbers, especially for urban communities, but they have so far remained relatively unexploited on any large scale, except occasionally such as Salter's study of medieval Oxford[8].

The town of Stamford provides a good example of such a possible study. Scattered among the various Exchequer and Chancery classes of 'Ancient Deeds' in the National Archives/Public Record Office are some seven or eight hundred original deeds ranging in date from the late twelfth to the late sixteenth century[9]. Their survival there is largely accidental: it would seem that most of them belonged to corporate institutions (especially monasteries, friaries, chantries and hospitals) whose property passed through government hands at the time of the Reformation. When the property was in turn granted, leased or sold to new owners, the medieval deeds were stripped away and thus remained with the central administration[10]. Subsequent disturbance has destroyed the original archive groupings but the deeds, many complete with their seals, are still there.

A number of smaller discrete collections survive: for instance, Magdalen College, Oxford, possesses some fifty deeds relating to its property in the town; Durham Cathedral Archives possess some registered deeds relating to property managed by St Leonard's Priory; and St George's parish church has its own collection of records, including medieval deeds[11]. Other deeds of course survive in copies, especially in the

---

[7] This paper was published in *The Medieval Town in Britain*, ed P Riden, University College Cardiff, 1980 pp 1-14. It has been only slightly amended here.

[8] H.E. Salter, *Medieval Oxford* (Oxford Historical Society, 100, 1936). Salter oversimplifies the tenements which were heavily subdivided during much of the middle ages and on into the early modern period. Other published collections of urban medieval deeds are noted below: see also *Early deeds relating to Newcastle upon Tyne*, ed. A.M. Oliver (Surtees Society, 137, 1924).

[9] The main classes are PRO C146, E40, E210, E212, also E315, E326.

[10] It is probably true to say that deeds were most likely to be transferred to the new owners of former ecclesiastical lands in those cases where the new owners had already had some previous connection with the particular religious house concerned, perhaps as attorney, steward or other servant.

[11] Archives of Magdalen College, Oxford (MCO) were surveyed with the help of Dr G.L. Harriss and the College Archivist, to whom we are most grateful for access to their records; Durham Cathedral Archives were accessed with the help of Dr Alan Piper;

medieval cartularies of ecclesiastical houses[12]. A collection of nearly two hundred deeds of Stamford property belonging to William Browne, the wealthy fifteenth-century merchant, and given by him to the hospital which he founded in 1475 and which now bears his name, is summarised in scattered entries in Francis Peck's *Antiquarian Annals of Stamford* (1727)[13]. There is one collection of enrolled deeds of purely secular nature, a roll of deeds and bonds belonging to Terricus Teutonicus of Cologne, a merchant of the town in the 1230s[14]; but this is exceptional, not so much in its lay character (for after all, the deeds of Browne's Hospital or those relating to the property of Magdalen College originally belonged to laymen who gave the endowment, and the deeds, to the religious bodies which preserved the records) but in the fact that it provides a survey of much of the property held by one man at one time rather than a sequence of transactions spread over many decades.

There are thus for medieval Stamford over 1200 known deeds relating to property transactions during the medieval centuries. Compared with some towns, this number is not very large. Many must have been lost but these at least survive, most of them in groups but a few as strays. They are particularly important for the study of this town because of the relative lack of other archives. The borough of Stamford apparently did not enjoy the privilege of a court of recognizance (or registration of land transactions) until the town's charters were renewed in 1663[15]; before that time, such enrolment of deeds as did exist was apparently made in the steward's court of Stamford manor and medieval court rolls for Stamford do not survive or are as yet inaccessible[16]. The result is that, unlike Ipswich or London[17] where series of enrolled deeds survive, we cannot hope for recovery of most of the property transactions at any one time. Ipswich tells us something of the size of the original archive - 297 property deeds or associated

---

the parish chest, St George's church, Stamford, by permission of the then Rector Rev. J. Ormston (PG; these records are now in Lincolnshire Archives Office).

[12] E.g. Belvoir and Croxton cartularies, Belvoir Castle muniments; Crowland cartulary, Spalding Gentlemen's Society; Fineshade cartulary, Lambeth Palace Library; Swaffham cartulary, Peterborough Cathedral muniments; Thorney cartulary, Cambridge University Library, MS.3021; Deeping St James priory cartulary, British Library, Harl .MS. 3658, and others. The deeds of St Mary's gild survive in enrolled form in PRO C47/41/174.

[13] All the medieval deeds of Browne's Hospital, *except those referring to the town of Stamford*, survive in the hospital and have now been deposited in Lincolnshire Archives Office (LAO, BHS); a list has been compiled. See Rogers, *Archives* 2008

[14] PRO E328/16. Dr Natalie Fryde has prepared an edition of this roll for publication. The version used in this catalogue has been prepared from the originals in the PRO.

[15] For urban courts of recognizance, see G.H. Martin, 'The registration of deeds of title in the medieval borough', in *The Study of Medieval Records: Essays in Honour of Kathleen Major*, ed. D.A. Bullough and R.L. Storey (1971), pp. 151-73.

[16] See e.g. Peck, XIV. 16; and endorsement to PG deed 1 October 1 Henry VIII: 'Irrotulatur ad Curiam tentam in castro Staunford xiii die Septembris anno Regni Regis Henrici Octam quinto'.

[17] For Ipswich, see G.H. Martin (ed), *The Ipswich Recognizance Rolls 1294-1327* (Suffolk Record Society, 16, 1973); for London, see *Calendar of Wills proved and enrolled in the Court of Hustings, London, 1258—1688*, ed. R.R. Sharpe (1889-90). Deeds of medieval Bath have been calendared in *Medieval Deeds of Bath and District*, ed. D.M.M. Shorrocks (Somerset Record Society, 73, 1974).

documents such as wills were registered in a period of 33 years, a number which would lead to an estimate of some 3,500 deeds altogether for that town during the centuries prior to 1550. Nor is it easy in Stamford to study in depth the different forms of records and processes involved, for not all forms of legal process and title deeds have survived equally, although quitclaims (especially by *femmes couvertes*) seem to be common[18]. But the fact that most of the Stamford deeds are preserved in their original form rather than in enrolments is important; it adds new dimensions to the study, not least the fact that these represent the personal collections of individual landholders rather than the records of courts or corporations; and it is possible to study the seals of private individuals more intensively.

A range of questions may be asked of these deeds, and what follows is a brief attempt to assess the value of this particular source. It must be stressed that this is an interim report. The findings here are based on only a partial analysis of the corpus available; a fuller study needs to be undertaken, particularly by period. It is the process of analysis employed which is under consideration in this introduction rather than the findings, and this is likely to be valid for other places as well as for Stamford.

Anno Regni Regis Henrici filii Johannis Regis Anglie vicesimo...

Any analysis of these deeds depends upon dating them within fairly close limits. Not all of the deeds are dated within themselves. It would appear that approximately 40 per cent of the surviving Stamford deeds possess dating clauses (Table 1).

An analysis of the distribution of these dated deeds has revealed some unexpected results: dating clauses rarely occur on twelfth- or early thirteenth-century deeds, but are common from 1290 to about 1340. Most of these are expressed in regnal years but a significant number of deeds are dated by the dominical year. An almost complete gap in dated deeds occurs from 1340 into the reign of Henry V, but thereafter most deeds are dated. The regnal year however is the normal form of the dating clause, not the dominical year, at this period.

die veneris post festum sancti Dionysius...

The dating clause is of course subject to closer analysis. Most dates are given in reference to one of the church's feast days. From a cursory survey, a whole crop of dates emerges. Many different feasts are used up to the reigns of Edward II and Edward III - St Denys, St John of the Latin Gate, St James Apostle, St Matthew, St Lawrence, St Mark and St Ambrose, none of them related to any of the fourteen parish churches or the other

---

[18] There are for instance no wills or extracts from wills preserved; but then the probate history of Stamford is obscure; local wills were proved in the court of the 'dean of Stamford', an official about whom very little is known. See Rogers Wills 2008. Few fines exist; several apparent leases and releases only survive in one of the two parts of the transactions etc. The survival is partial, unlike enrolled deeds; it is not necessarily haphazard. Three main formulae survive: *Omnibus sancti matris ecclesie ... Sciant presentes et futuri ... ; Noverit universi*

religious establishments in the town[19]. Some are obscure - SS Tiburtius and Valerian (14 April) and SS Fabian and Sebastian (20 January) but these possibly reflect Exchequer usage, for London influence was still strong as far away as Stamford was from the capital. More central to the worshipping concerns of the community are St Martin, St Katherine the Virgin (one of the town's gilds), St Andrew, the decollation of St John the Baptist, SS Peter and Paul, the translation of St Thomas the Martyr (associated with one of the town's hospitals) and the nativity and assumption of the BVM. There are some surprises — the eve of midsummer, and 'the Easter after the election of Martin le Monk as abbot of Peterborough'; but secular datings are rare. A second stage is seen in the later fourteenth and early fifteenth centuries when dates are most commonly settled on the greater festivals, Easter and Michaelmas, although SS Simon and Jude, St Peter *ad vincula* and St Dunstan do occur. Late in the fifteenth century the dates are mensal, 4 July, 24 September etc (the first to occur so far is in the reign of Richard II), although St Barnabus and Epiphany also appear.

Table 1

Dating clauses in medieval Stamford deeds (sample o nly)

Class PRO	Undated	C or earlier	B or E1	E2	E3	R2	H4	H5	H6	E4	H7	H8	Total
E210	78	3	8	6	9	1	4	4	3	4	1	—	120
E212	10	1	8	1	2	—	—	1	—	—	—	—	23
E315	76	1	9	7	19	—	—	2	7	1	3	1	126

This table must be regarded as provisional until the analysis has been completed.

What may be made of this? Two things immediately seem to emerge from such an analysis. The first is that the study of a large number of deeds may lead to an assessment of the number and nature of the calendrical focal points at any one time — the sort of events which occurred most easily to the minds of those who wrote and dated their deeds. There is no other source for such a study. And secondly some assessment of the increasingly lay involvement in the writing of deeds and in the creation of such focal points may be detected within a town where ecclesiastical interests were very strong.

So much for the dating clauses: but this can only apply to those deeds (some 40 per cent of the total) which are clearly dated. What of the rest?

Most of these can be dated approximately by a study of the handwriting, by the nature of the transaction concerned or by a careful analysis of the lists of witnesses. It is unlikely that it will be possible to detect the hands of particular scribes beneath the anonymity of secretary hand, but the dating clauses, lists of witnesses and other formulae may provide

---

[19] Listed in J S Hartley and Alan Rogers, *Religious Foundations of Medieval Stamford*, University of Nottingham 1974.

clues to this. But however it is done, it has become clear that a date within a period of approximately twenty years can be assigned to most deeds in the collection.

We do however need to be very clear that the dating clause contained in any title deed relates to the date of the document, but it is not necessarily the date of the transaction. This can be demonstrated from those dated deeds which contain within the list of witnesses an official whose dates of office are known – in particular, the Alderman (i.e. mayor) of the town. These witnesses are often (but not always) listed as '*then* Alderman of Staunford'; and in the fifteenth century when our annual list of Alderman is complete and a full comparison can be made, the gap between the dates when these witnesses held that office and the date given on the title deed can be as large as six years[20]. It is clear then that the date of the document is not the date of the property transfer which could have taken place some years prior to the date given.

The question that then arises is whether listing the rate of survival of these documents will reflect the actual state of the property market in the town. Two different collections may be taken in this respect as some indication of the differing rates of activity in land transactions – the two-hundred-odd deeds formerly belonging to Browne's Hospital, and the 56 deeds now in Magdalen College, Oxford. The former covers some thirty or so different properties in the town, the latter about fifteen. All the Oxford deeds are dated, but apparently nearly half of the Browne's Hospital deeds are undated, although this may reflect Peck's sources and methods of working as much as the nature of the originals[21].

Plotting of these deeds on a time-scale reveals some interesting patterns (Fig.2). Intensive land transactions seem to appear between the years 1370 and 1440 in the deeds of Browne's Hospital, although we cannot be sure that Francis Peck included every document in his listing, and in any case his volume ended in 1461. The Oxford deeds indicate a high rate of activity between 1300 and 1350 and again from 1430 to 1490. Contrasts such as this are possibly explicable on the basis of the small size of the sample; an amalgamation of all categories may in the end lead to an assessment of the differing levels of activity in the land market in this town in different periods.

The frequency with which some properties changed hands can also on occasion be detected. A house in Eastgate which Thomas Phillippe bought in 1500 had changed hands at least seven times in the previous century; another house in St Mary's Street was sold in 1429, 1450 and 1484. A house in St Peter's Street acquired six deeds between 1431 and 1465, while a block of adjacent property in St Mary's Street was subject to no less than 34 transactions between 1300 and 1498. A large body of deeds may throw light on the location and nature of the sites which changed hands frequently.

concessi dedi et hac presente carta mea confirmavi…

---

[20] See Rogers Aldermen 2009

[21] It is not clear if Peck was working from the original deeds and thus was unable to read some of the text or omitted dating clauses when he made his notes, or if he was using notes which had been prepared for him by another antiquarian; see Peck 1979 edn Introduction pages x-xii; Rogers *Archives* 2008.

More detailed analyses of the types of transactions recorded now needs to be undertaken and what follows is something of an impressionistic picture rather than a firm statement of urban history.

During the thirteenth century, one of the clearest features to emerge is the increasing interest of ecclesiastical landlords in property in the town. In part, this impression is a result of the nature of the surviving evidence. Most of the surviving deeds have come from the collections of former religious foundations. Nevertheless, the number of houses within Stamford which became burdened with a rent charge to one or other of the monasteries around the town is perhaps the clearest picture to emerge. From the middle of the thirteenth century, there is a chance to see the growth of lay estates, the investment of merchants in property which slackened off after about 1340 and revived again from about 1440, although in the second phase fewer merchants were involved than in the earlier one. Whether it will be possible to assess the size or the value of any one man's holdings except in particular cases is not yet clear.

The parties were most frequently men. The role of women in the property market in a place like Stamford is intriguing, and much can be seen from these deeds. But women were never used as feoffees, very rarely as executors except for their husbands, never as witnesses; but they bought and sold and especially they quitclaimed their interests to others. But it would seem that they never accumulated a substantial property portfolio in their own right as did a number of men.

Terricus of Cologne (fl.1230s) provides us with one such case. Dr Natalie Fryde has been examining the activities of this alien merchant in some detail. What is clear from the records cited here is that out of a roll containing 58 deeds or bonds, 39 of them relate to land or property in Stamford or the neighbouring Burley. In some of these cases, Terricus appears to have been acting as mortgagor and does not enter into the property; in other cases, he bought houses and apparently leased them. A block of four properties in St Peter's Street came piecemeal into his hands, but his other interests were scattered throughout Stamford in most of the parishes of the town. It is not easy to determine precisely how many different properties are involved, but they were numerous — a block in Castle Dyke and 'the king's free cellar' next door; a garden in Scotgate; a house in St George's parish as mortgagor for the Countess Warenne; a house in St Mary's parish; a shop (newly built), house and rent in All Saints in the Market; a rent in St John's parish; a house in Cleymont (St Michael's parish), some indeterminate rents, twenty acres of arable, three bovates of land, two meadow closes, and so on; and property in Casterton, Wittering and East Deeping as well.

A similar picture can be drawn from deeds relating to the property acquired by William Browne and bequeathed by him to his hospital. The site of the hospital is said to have consisted of three tenements next to Browne's own house; but elsewhere in the town it was the apparently haphazard accumulation of property. We shall never know all the houses Browne sold, for he passed on with each property the deeds relating to that property; for instance, in 1479 he sold the 'Moon and Stars' on the corner of Star Lane to Richard Gregory of Peterborough and William Reeste, and with it went deeds back to the early fourteenth century[22] (he himself kept the deeds of his own house back to at least 1259). We therefore cannot say how much he rationalised his estate by selling

---

[22] PG records

outliers and purchasing properties adjoining those he already possessed. But blocks of property occur - in Behindebak (a row of buildings once in Red Lion Square and now demolished[23]) and in Mallory Lane for example. At least 16 properties in Stamford and a great deal outside the town (Luffenham, South Witham and so on) came in the end to the hospital.

The fortunes of Thomas Philippe, baker, whose property came to Magdalen College, Oxford, may serve as another example. In 1465, his father handed over to him a house in St Peter's Street; in 1472 he bought ten acres of land. In 1483, a house in St Mary's Hill was acquired, and then in 1497-8, he bought up two houses in the prime area of the town, St Mary's Street, one of them being 'le Cressant'. In 1500, he bought a property in St Paul's Street. When he died, he left all this to his son, another Thomas, a cleric and former fellow of Magdalen College, who left it entire to the college, along with the deeds accumulated by his father, reaching back to at least 1300.

pro quatuor marcis argenti quas mihi dedit…

It is collections of deeds like this which yield the greatest fruit. The prices and values of properties are recorded. Terricus laid out at least £156 13s 5d in Stamford alone on his properties. Some were bargains: he paid £6 8s 5d for a house in St Mary's parish which had previously changed hands for £10. A house in St Martin's parish, burdened with a rent of one penny, was sold for 26s in the middle of the thirteenth century[24]. Whether enough references are listed here to enable an assessment of the changing values of property in the town to be made is not clear.

Mortgages, prices and values, rent charges, tolls and dues all appear in the deeds. John Stede raised a mortgage from William Browne in 1486 to rebuild his property in St Mary's Street, but in 1489 he released the property to Browne's executors, although he clearly continued in residence there; he extinguished his debt in 1497 but sold the property in the same year to Thomas Philippe[25]. Rent charges, often to the nuns of St Michael's monastery, Stamford, are frequently reserved - 5s 2d per annum, for instance, from one house in St Peter's Street which Terricus acquired; he extinguished a right of dowry in the same property. This was one of a valuable set of houses - he paid £40 for them. From another house which he bought for £8 13s 4d, rent charges amounted to 3s 7½d per annum, 12d of this to St Peter's church. A 'landgavel' of 13d was admitted as due to the nuns by a tenant in St Martin's[26]. Such rent charges are not so obvious later in the middle ages; presumably some had been commuted or otherwise extinguished, but tolls and some other charges still appear.

[23] See E.C. Till, 'Behindebak', *Stamford Historian*, 2 (1978), pp.44-5.

[24] PRO, E328/16; E326/4804.

[25] This is one of the clearest examples of a mortgage: the deed provides for the repayment of a sum of £32 in eight annual instalments of £4; MCO Stamford deeds 37, 39. In most other cases, a mortgage or some other form of security against loans is the most likely explanation of the transaction.

[26] PRO, E326/4754. The 'landgavel' occurs in other records.

The nature of the transactions involved, whether gift, purchase, quitclaim, mortgage or bond, is not always clear, but it would seem that increasingly feoffees came to be used in these transactions.

concessi Terrico de Colonia burgensi de Stanfordia...

Analysis of the parties involved reveals significant information concerning the social structure of the town. Jews, for instance, played a large part in the town's economy in the thirteenth century, lending money and buying or mortgaging property. David the Jew bought a house in Stamford market place[27]; Absolon, Henry son of Isaac, Isaac Rufus, Abraham and others all occur in deeds up to the reign of Edward I. If the deeds of Terricus are any guide, it was with the help of alien merchants that the stranglehold was broken; many of his customers pleaded their indebtedness to the Jews as the reason for selling him their property, as well as their 'crusading intentions', perhaps a medieval way of expressing bankruptcy.

Other aliens appear at other times, as parties or witnesses – the Normans early, the Flemings rather later. William le Fleming, John Flamenc, Walter Flandrens and their sons, John Franceis and William de Franconia replace Reginald and William le Norman. Later there are Germans like Terricus Teutonicus, and later still a number of Welsh - Ewann Machell, Philip Morgan, Robert Vaughan and of course David Cecyll himself, the ancestor of William Cecil Lord Burghley[28].

Clearer perhaps are occupational groupings, with two main industries predominant, the textile and the leather industries. Drapers, dyers, flaxmen, fullers, spinners, tailors, textors and weavers all appear in force; so too do glovers, saddlers, shoemakers and tanners. Again some correlation with the dates of these deeds, when established, may throw light on the economy of the borough.

Industrial sites are of course themselves the subject of a number of these transactions — and here we are on well-worn ground. Mills, both watermills and windmills, occur; there was a line of mills along the river Welland and its cut above the bridge, but so far below the bridge the deeds have revealed only one such mill, Hudd's Mill; the bridge marked the limit of navigation on the Welland. Whether they were used for fulling is not clear. They were mostly in the hands of monastic foundations, Croxden, Newstead, Pipewell, Peterborough, Thorney and so on. Windmills stood above Scotgate and in Wothorpe. 'Ovens' *(furna)* occur frequently - or perhaps it may be that a small number are the subject of repeated transactions. They may represent kilns or bread ovens or furnaces for iron or tanning. The town 'bakehouse' found its way eventually to the nuns of St Michael by Stamford[29]. Quarries too were sold or leased, although their precise location is more difficult to fix.

Some light is thrown on agriculture in the town's large open fields to the north and west, the meadows to the south and the open fields of Stamford Baron. Strips were

---

[27] PRO, E315/38/59.

[28] PG records etc. See S. Reynolds, *An Introduction to the History of English Medieval Towns* (1977), p 72.

[29] PRO E326/4762.

consolidated at times of sale[30]; and husbandmen and others with names like Adam le Plouman occur among the parties and witnesses. But most of the deeds relate to urban properties; and the parties and witnesses more often include Aldermen, burgesses, bailiffs, *praepositi* and receivers, along with mercers, merchants and a sprinkling of 'esquires', than they do the tillers of the soil. Agriculture, although present in the town (granges, barns, orchards, dove-cotes and gardens, along with muckhills and carriage entrances, bear witness of this) was a sub-culture to a commercial world revealed by the deeds.

quod ego Radulfus de Normanville dominum de Empyingham vendidi…

The commercial world is revealed to us in two main aspects. First there are those members of the urban community engaged in the buying and selling of property within the town. Until the late fifteenth century, it would seem that there were no professional 'estate agents'. On the whole transactions were directly between party and party, without commercial or legal intermediary. This is of course not easy to prove, for a good deal of obscurity surrounds some of the parties. Nevertheless most of them are townsmen well known from other sources, substantial residents if not officially designated as 'burgesses of Stamford'. How many of the town's merchant community are involved in the transactions is not yet clear, but we are dealing with a town with a maximum population of between four and five thousand, so that the number of leading traders and craftsmen would probably not exceed forty or fifty at any one time.

ad itinerem meum in terram Ierosolimitanam per agendum…

The purpose that motivated this group - or at least the vendors - is at times indicated in the deeds or bonds. Debt appears most frequently, perhaps a sign of limited cash flow; pilgrimage is almost equally prominent. Other forms of piety lie behind the alienation of a rent on some property to a religious foundation in the town or outside it; and the range of such bequests throws light on the regional networks of the town's merchants. On the other hand, the frequent quitclaims would have been made at the instance of the grantee, even if they were secured by the grantor. Behind these transactions can dimly be seen the desire for some form of gain (often financial but sometimes spiritual) for the vendor and security in the new title for the purchaser. The increasing demand for security of title also lies behind the growing use and widening scope of warranty clauses.

Huic scripto sigillum meum apposui…

Further light on this commercial sector of the community of Stamford is thrown by a large number of seals still preserved on these deeds. The study of merchant seals is still being developed, and their iconography is obscure, composed as it is of religious symbols, rune-like monographs or other merchant marks. It is not clear how far such symbols were passed on to successive members of the business, with or without difference. Analysis of the seals of succeeding members of the same family may reveal much.

Hiis testibus Henrico filio Alexandri…

---

[30] PRO, E326/4686, 4692, 4862 etc.

Secondly there is the supporting group to the parties, the witnesses to the deeds. It is not necessary here to enter into the discussion on the precise nature of these witness lists; suffice it to say that there is now general agreement that the witnesses were real persons and cognisant to the transaction, whether they were physically present at the drafting of the written record or not. They were the people to be cited to guarantee the transaction, probably as witnesses (in outright sales or gifts) of the act of seisin, wherever that took place. The grouping of witnesses in relation to these deeds does not seem to be haphazard but to have some significance behind it. Many of them appear regularly, some in association with a wide range of parties, others with a more limited connection. Several were themselves parties to other transactions; all seem to have been of much the same social and economic level as the parties. Clerks and chaplains occur frequently in the thirteenth century; and indeed some of these (like 'William the chaplain' whose name occurs at the end of several witness lists in the late thirteenth century) may have been the scribe of the written deed.

The exact role of these witnesses is not clear, for they could have been invoked to secure the interests of either the vendor or the purchaser. Members of the family of the vendor and neighbours of adjoining tenements must have been included in many cases at the instance of the purchaser to make his new title the more secure; but in other cases where the real liability does not appear behind the formal face of the deed, their involvement is more problematical. Certainly an impression is that they are in most cases more closely related to the grantor than the grantee. On occasion the borough itself, in the person of the Alderman or other official, is called upon to ensure the permanence and effectiveness of the transfer.

The evidence of personal names is, however, at best tenuous and may indeed be even misleading on occasion. The analysis of the properties mentioned in the deeds presents a different set of problems and yields its own fruit. The patterns are not yet clear but something may be discerned from the expressions used in relation to the properties subject to the particular transactions recorded. For the language employed in these deeds is not without purpose, and an analysis of the words and phrases relating to both persons and properties as they are used in certain contexts may reveal much of the world view of those who wrote them. The phrase 'of Stamford' to describe some of the parties or witnesses but omitted in other instances; the use or omission of the title 'burgess'; the inclusion of the words *cum pertinenciis* or some other such phrase in describing a particular property — these and other phrases were not chosen without care, and their significance may be uncovered in some circumstances.

totum curthlagium meum ... in quartera extra portam...

The property description thus may throw light on the state of the town's fabric, and with it the economy of the borough. Vacant plots, either the subject of the transaction or on adjacent properties, are recorded in many years[31]. Early in the fourteenth century a rent from houses in the parish of St Michael the Great, adjacent to a 'void place', was granted away, and other void places are noted: two empty places (1382) in St Mary Bynwerk parish; another in the parish of St Michael the Great (1384); a void place in Behyndebak,

---

[31] Descriptions of adjacent plots are likely to refer to earlier periods than the date of the deed, but this point has not yet been proved.

formerly two shops and solars' adjacent to 'a vacant place' belonging to the nuns of St Michael (1410); and 'a vacant plot' in St Mary's parish in which the lessee was to 'rebuild a shop and solar' (1434)[32].

Clearer evidence of decay, stretching from the 1320s to the 1430s, is provided by such phrases as the 'tenement now fallen down' in Scotgate (1323/4); two 'curtilages formerly built on' (c.1350) in St Mary's parish; or messuages 'valued at x and no more because in ruins' (St Michael Cornstall, and in Butcher Street in the parish of St Michael the Great before 1362)[33]. Further evidence may be culled from the processes of 'engrossing': separate tenements of c.1330, the property of St Mary's gild, have been amalgamated into larger units before 1362; and in All Saints in the Market parish, a house sold to the nuns in the early fourteenth century seems to have been subdivided in earlier years[34]. Several cases occur of a man acquiring the adjacent property to enlarge his own house (St Mary's parish and St Martin's)[35], mainly in the fifteenth century. On the other hand, subdivision of the tenements is also shown[36]. Whether from this evidence, together with the signs of new building (e.g. 'newly built' in the 1230s)[37], it will be possible to locate periods of relative prosperity is not yet clear.

Descriptions of urban properties however abound - tenements, messuages, cellars, solars, shops and chambers. 'Tenement walls' are mentioned on several occasions, and gable ends and chimneys on adjacent properties could provide the subject of legal transactions[38]. Cellars (clearly 'undercrofts' such as still survive in the town) are known: a 'cellar under a cellar in the lane leading to le Fysshelepes' in 1362 may also be the earlier 'half a cellar' to the north of the other half rather than a two-tier undercroft[39]. 'Steps into the street' may also indicate an undercroft. A little shop 'eleven feet wide and twenty two feet long, which I retain to my use' when the house was sold[40] reminds us of the emergence of the 'lock-up' from the mid fourteenth century. Often features were combined - a messuage, shop and cellar in St Mary's parish; a shop with a solar built over it in All Saints parish. Rows of shops appear in All Saints[41].

The diversity of urban property may be seen in the names used for them: cottages, tenements, messuages and capital messuages, inns, shops, and so on. A 'manse' within a house paid 1d rent per annum[42]. Courtyards are mentioned in several deeds: thus Robert de Barnardeshill bought the house next door to William de Coventre's 'capital messuage'

---

[32] PRO E326/4736, 4775, 4777; E315/31 /3; MCO deeds, St Mary's parish 1486; Peck, XII.6.

[33] PRO E326/4681; Burleigh House, Exeter MSS 95/28; *Cal Pat Rolls 1361-64*, p 229

[34] Exeter MSS 95/28; *Cal.Pat.R. 1361-4*, p.229; PRO E326/4748.

[35] E.g. PRO E315/44 /69; E326/4766.

[36] PRO E326/4769.

[37] PRO E328/16; E326/4798-4800.

[38] PRO E306/4754, 4766; E328/16, deed 20.

[39] *Cal Pat Rolls* 1361-4 p 228; Exeter MSS 95/28.

[40] PRO E326/4733

[41] BL Harl.MS.3658; PRO E326/4778; E315/38 f.30; E326/4713.

[42] BL Harl.MS.3657.

and with it part of the courtyard and the use of the entry (St Clement's parish)[43]. Gardens and 'places' (presumably yards) were sold to the next-door neighbour[44].

Something of the complexity of medieval urban property may be seen from the deeds relating to a group of houses on the north side of St Mary's Street, later to belong to Magdalen College, Oxford. The deeds here start in 1310. Alverton sold one tenement to Wisbeche (a baker). Wisbeche divided it into three and sold the eastern and northern parts to Nunnes, who had already bought the next-door property. This property had been sold by Maymund to Averey who similarly split it; half went to Apethorpe and thence to Nunnes. Nunnes then bought the garden from Averey's retained half. It seems that Apethorpe did not reside there but Nunnes held it for life from him. Thus by 1330 Nunnes had consolidated his hold on a block of property which remained as one building (though in divided ownership) until both halves passed to the Chestre family (1377), thence to the Longes and thence to feoffees, finally being rebuilt in the 1480s[45].

Such an example reveals that only in exceptional cases can we hope to recover much about individual properties in the town. Even where the number and the details provided in the deeds are good, it is not possible to trace the complexities of ownership and occupation; urban land tenure is too complicated for anything approaching a tenemental history to be feasible. Studies in London on sub-divided tenements, based on the lease-books of some of the liveried companies, reflect the complicated nature of urban holdings. These are, it is true, leasehold, but in freehold areas (like Stamford), town houses were frequently subdivided, both vertically and horizontally, and it is impossible to reinstate such properties from deeds alone, although the permanence of tenemental boundaries is not in question[46]. Nor is it surprising that measured tenemental boundaries are given only in rare cases, like the sale of 'parcel of a curtilage in my tenement' in St Paul's parish, '168 feet long from my tenement north to the tenement of Eustace Malherbe south and 15 feet wide' between two other tenements (1324/5), with licence to pull down and make profits from all buildings there and to build a house within the 'claustral walls' of the messuage there, or the 'one courtyard' *(placea curie)* 20 feet long and 16 feet wide, between two other 'courts' (1295/6). A 'little house' *(parva casa)* retained 'for my own use' in the parish of St George measured 19 feet wide and 17½ feet long; another 'place' in All Saints beyond the bridge was 20 feet long and 13 feet wide, while a messuage in St Peter's parish in 1480 was 30 feet long and 19½ feet wide[47].

quandam domum ... in parochia omnium sanctorum ... iuxta ripam Welandie...

---

[43] PRO E326/4731. Medieval courtyard houses were known in the town and fragments of one or two remain: 14-15 St George's Square, described in Alan Rogers, *Medieval Buildings of Stamford* (1970), p. 33, and in *The Town of Stamford* (RCHM(E), 1976), pp.118-9. Fragments of another one perhaps survive at 5-6 Barn Hill *(Town of Stamford,* pp.61-2), I suspect that the Georgian house at the back of 26 St Mary's Street may represent the fossilised remains of a third; but these cases are doubtful. The George Hotel is a different case altogether, but it clearly had a courtyard, if not two.

[44] PRO E326/5555.

[45] MCO deeds

[46] See John Schofield, 'Some sixteenth and early seventeenth century houses in London' based on the records belonging to the Clothrnongers relating to tenements in London.

[47] PRO E326/4798-4800; E326/16, deed 9.

Such details, when accumulated in bulk and compared with tenements which appear to have survived from the medieval period, may tell us much about Stamford in the middle ages. So too can the topographical references with which these deeds abound. Encroachment on the roads for cellar steps is matched by the erection of chimneys; and other references such as 'half a shop in the market place before and behind'[48] suggest the erection of semi-permanent stalls. Other topographical material of a more traditional nature can be drawn from this material: the location of bridges, water-courses, industrial premises (such as the tanneries at the junction of the Mallory stream and the Welland), common cisterns and the like. It may even be possible to locate areas of relatively large and prosperous housing as against the meaner dwellings at different periods. And this is particularly important in a place like Stamford which has an exceptionally large collection of surviving medieval domestic buildings.

Such in brief are some of the potential uses to which a body of deeds surviving from a medieval town may be put. A study of this nature requires several factors to be successful: a large enough collection of deeds, preferably surviving in identifiable archival groupings; adequate information to secure an approximate date for those deeds which do not contain a dating clause; and the time to process the information contained in them. This 'interim report' suggests that the process will however be rewarding in many circumstances, filling out the barebones of medieval urban life obtained from the more prosaic sources of administrative processes.

Publication
We submitted a completed manuscript of this volume to the Lincoln Record Society in 2009, and it was agreed that it would appear as the volume for 2012-13. But, upon enquiry in 2012, we were informed that their plans had changed and they now intended to publish only a part of the volume in 2015, with no indication if or when they would publish the rest; this decision was made without consultation with us or any reason given. In view of the difficulties of this process, especially for the Introduction and indexes, and in view of the three years already spent waiting, we decided to print 100 copies of this volume with funding provided by one member of Stamford Survey Group. We have been keen to have a full volume on Stamford, the county's second town, in that series for the first time in over 100 years of publishing and regret it has not been possible this time.

Such a large and complex work as this, with so many people involved over such a long time, means that inevitably some errors will remain undetected; in addition, further title deeds are likely to be discovered. We will be grateful for any errors to be pointed out to us, and we will, when necessary, issue a list of amendments and supplements on the Stamford Survey Group website: **www.stamfordhistory.org.uk**

---

[48] PRO E326/4722

REFERENCES

Fryde Natalie, *Ein Mittelalterlicher Deutscher Grossunternehmer: Terricus Teutonicus De Colonia in England, 1217-1247*, Stuttgart: Steiner, 1997.

Hartley and Rogers – J S Hartley and Alan Rogers *Religious Foundations of Medieval Stamford*, University of Nottingham and Stamford Survey Group 1974

Peck: Francis Peck, *Academia Tertia Anglicana, or Antiquarian Annals of Stamford* 1727 [EP Publishers, Wakefield, reprint edition 1979 with introduction by Alan Rogers and John Hartley and index]

RCHM 1977: *The Town of Stamford: a survey by the Royal Commission on Historical Monuments*, London: HMSO 1977

Roffe David, *Stamford in the Thirteenth Century: two inquisitions from the reign of Edward I*, Stamford Paul Watkins 1994

Rogers 1965: Alan Rogers, *The Making of Stamford* Leicester University Press 1965

Rogers 1973: Alan Rogers, Late Medieval Stamford: a study of the town council 1465-1492, in Alan Everett (ed) *Perspectives in English Urban History* Macmillan, 1973

Rogers 2005: Alan Rogers *William Browne's Town: the Hall Book 1465-1492* Stamford Survey Group

ABBREVIATIONS used in the calendar and in the Indexes

And - parish of St Andrew;
ASM – parish of All Saints in the Market;
BH - Browne's Hospital
Bin – St Mary Binwerk parish
BL – British Library Mss
cp - with appurtenances
Exeter MSS – records in Burghley House (provisional listings)
Geo – St George's parish
JB – parish of St John Baptist
LAO - Lincolnshire Archives Office
Mary – parish of St Mary at the Bridge
MCO – deeds in Magdalen College, Oxford
MG – parish of St Michael the Greater
NRA – National Register of Archives lists of Burghley House archives
Peter – St Peter's parish
PG – records of the parish of St George, Stamford (now deposited in LAO; reference numbers here are to the original parish chest)
SB – Stamford Baron (St Martin's, fee of abbot of Peterborough)
vs - versus
Wo – Wothorpe

PART I: THE PUBLIC RECORD OFFICE/THE NATIONAL ARCHIVES

All records are listed by archival groups in alphabetical and numerical order

C47: CHANCERY MISCELLANEA

1. C47/41/172
Ordinances of the gild or fraternity of Corpus Christi of Staunford.

In honour of God and Corpus Christi from ancient time a gild or fraternity in the church of St Mary *ad pontem* of Staunford found (*inveniret*) one chaplain to celebrate daily in honour of Corpus Christi in that church in the morning; the brothers and sisters each year in the feast of Corpus Christi follow the procession with the Body of Christ with lights and great reverence and honour. And to sustain and support the chaplain and other burdens, the fraternity with the licence of the king granted 20 April 24 Edward III [1350] acquired certain lands in Staunford as in the charters which follow. And they have a certain Alderman and certain officers to collect rents and farms.

1.1 C47/41/172(i) (a)   25 March 1352

Grant indented: Joan la Warre and sir Roger la Warre knight for themselves and the heirs of Roger gave licence to John de Chestre of Stanford to grant the remission in one messuage in Staunford which William de Steandeby and Agnes his wife hold for the life of Agnes from John, and after the death of Agnes it shall revert to John and his heirs; so that after the death of Agnes it shall revert to the chaplain at the altar of Corpus Christi in the church of St Mary at the bridge of Staunford, for the salvation of Joan and Roger, for sir John la Warre his brother and Elizabeth wife of Roger, for the salvation of Thomas de Wyke clerk and for the brothers and sisters of the gild of Corpus Christi while they live and for their souls when they die and the souls of sir John la Warre formerly husband of Joan and sir John her son and Margaret wife of this John, and for the souls of all faithful deceased celebrated each day; and also to establish and sustain other works of charity according to the ordinances made therein; the chaplain may enter the messuage after the death of Agnes. Warranty; the seals of Joan and Roger and John de Chestre are appended.

Dated: Swynesheved, Sunday the feast of Annunciation of the Blessed Virgin Mary 26 Edward III.

1.2 C47/41/172(i) (b)   8 October 1349

Grant with warranty by John Knot' of Staunford chaplain to sir Roger de Assewell' rector of the church of Assewell', Henry de Tydeswell' of Staunford, William de Apethorp', John de Cestre, Robert de Wyke, Thomas de Promtefrect [*sic*], Roger de Mundeham, William de Dyngelee and John Nodel of Staunford of a messuage with appurtenances in Staunford in the parish of St Mary at the bridge situated between the tenement of the prior of Durham on the north and the tenement of the aforesaid Robert de Wyke on the south, which messuage was of Richard de Pappele. To have and to hold in perpetuity of the capital lords of that fee for the services owed and accustomed. Warranty by John Knot and his heirs against all people (*gentes*) in perpetuity.

Witnesses: William de Apethorp', William de Shelyngton', Eustace de Assewell', John Bate, Richard de Wirthorp', Robert Fort, William Sadelere of Staunford and others

Given at Staunford, Thursday next after the feast of St Faith the Virgin 23 Edward III.

1.3 C47/41/172(ii)   13 September 1350

Grant with warranty by Henry de Tyddeswell' of Staunford to John de Chestre, William de Apethorp', Thomas de Pontefracto, William de Dyngelee and Roger de Mundham of Staunford of three messuages with appurtenances in Staunford of which one is situated in Bakers' Street (*in vico pistorum*) between the tenement of Robert de Wyke on the west and the tenement formerly of Joan Corszoun on the east, one between the tolbooth of Staunford on the south and the tenement of the nuns of St Michael on the north, and one between the tenement of the aforesaid nuns on the south and the tenement of the prior of Newstead on the north. To have and to hold in perpetuity of the capital lords of that fee for the services owed and accustomed. Warranty by Henry against all people in perpetuity. My seal appended.

Witnesses: Walter de Apethorp', Robert his son, Richard de Ardern', Reginald de Saltby, Henry Shepherd, Robert Fort of Staunford and others.

Given at Staunford, Monday next after the feast of the Nativity of St Mary the Virgin 24 Edward III.

The fraternity has licence to appropriate certain tenements of William de Bohun earl of Northampton formerly (*nuper*) lord of Staunford as appears by letters patent.

2. C47/41/173

Ordinances of the gild of St Martin in the parish of St Martin

In honour of God and St Martin, the ordinances from ancient time in such form are that the brethren and sisters have a certain chaplain celebrating in the church in honour of St Martin for the brethren and sisters and all benefactors and they have found a certain light in that church in honour of St Martin. And it is and was the custom of the fraternity from time immemorial that on the feast of St Martin the brethren have a certain bull which is baited and sold to the profit of the fraternity; and on the same feast the brethren and sisters shall meet to eat and drink. To sustain and support the said chaplain and other works, certain devout men of the town a long time before the statute gave to the gild or fraternity certain rents to the value of 30s per annum; and each brother and sister will give at Michaelmas to support the said burdens one bushel of barley; and the brothers and sisters have a certain Alderman and other officers to collect the rents and enforce the ordinances for the said works. They have no goods and chattels except such as support the said burdens.

3. C47/41/174

These deeds relate to the gild of St Mary – this gild and the gild of Corpus Christi joined together in the late fourteenth century.

<u>Ordinances</u> of the fraternity or gild of St Mary 1212 in the town and parish of St Mary by the bridge of Staunford. There was established in honour of Jesus Christ and the glory of the Blessed Virgin Mary and the congregation of all the saints by many burgesses of Staunford a long time ago (*longi voluntate et memoria*) a gild of the Assumption of the Blessed Virgin Mary; and they ordained between them one chaplain to celebrate daily at the hour of six at the high altar of the church the mass of the Blessed Virgin in perpetuity. To sustain the mass, some of them gave certain tenements and annual rents as in the charters which follow. Later (*Postea*) they chose among themselves an Alderman to govern the gild and they made constitutions concerning the election that the Alderman shall be a faithful discreet man, upright, reliable and honest (*homo fidelis discretis rectis stabilis et honestus*) and that he shall not excuse himself from the office of Alderman except for reasonable cause or need. And they ordained and granted that the major part of the brethren of the gild shall consent to the said election, and that all brethren and sisters shall obey all reasonable precepts and mandates of the Alderman. The mass and the gild shall never go beyond the limits of the parish. An oath to keep the ordinances shall be sworn on the holy Gospels by the Alderman, brethren and sisters of the gild. All the deeds and charters written below were amortised as appears by a charter of the King dated 36 Edward the grandfather of the King that now is.

This heading was written during the reign of Richard II; the date of 1212 would agree with Westlake's view of the origin of the gild; 36 Edward III is 1362; see Calendar of Patent Rolls 1361-64/227-229 for this licence to amortise.

4.1 C47/41/174 (b) i

<u>Grant</u> in free alms with warranty by John Abselon of Staunford for the health of his soul and of the soul of Alice his wife etc to God and St Mary for the maintenance of the mass of St Mary to be celebrated daily in the church of the same St Mary the Virgin situated and constructed at the bridge of Staunford of a cellar with appurtenances situated under the solar of Peter de Wysebech' in the lane near the gate which goes to Fisslepes between the house of the said Peter on each side. Rendering to the lord of the fee the services owed and accustomed.

Witnesses: etc [*sic*]

Given etc [*sic*]

4.2 C47/41/174 (b) ii   26 June 1331

<u>Grant</u> in free alms with warranty by Gilbert at the bridge burgess of Staunford to God and to the maintenance of a daily mass of St Mary in the church of St Mary at the bridge of Staunford for so long as it be celebrated of a shop with solar which is situated in Fishers Street (*in vico piscator'*) between the shop which William Swayn received in free marriage with Juliana his wife towards the north and Gilbert's shop towards the south.

And if at any time the said mass fails, the said shop with solar shall revert to Gilbert and his heirs or assignees, except that celebration be impeded by any interdict.

Witnesses: etc [*sic*]

Given etc [*sic*]

4.3 C47/41/174 (b) iii

Grant and quitclaim in free alms with warranty by Cecily de Almerton' daughter and heir of the late William de Tykincote to God and St Mary and to the maintenance of the mass of the same virgin to be celebrated in the church of St Mary near the bridge of Staunford of a certain house with all appurtenances and liberties pertaining to the said house situated in the parish of St Peter Staunford, namely between the house of Alexander de Tykyncote towards the east and Cecily's houses towards the west. To hold etc to God and St Mary and to the maintenance of the aforesaid mass and the proctor* of the same of the donor, her heirs and assignees etc. Neither Cecily nor her heirs or assignees shall in future exact any right or claim, namely ward(s), relief(s), suit(s) of court, ale and brewing tolls (*aletolles' et braciatric'*), amercement(s) or any other custom, and without any secular service or exaction except [*ms damaged here*]

Witnesses: etc [*sic*]

Given etc [*sic*]
**procurator – i.e. steward*

4.4 C47/41/174 (b) iv

Grant in free alms by Robert de Burton' baker to the maintenance of the mass of St Mary to be celebrated in the church of St Mary at the bridge of Staunford of 12d annually to be received from a certain cellar situated between the house of Ralph le White on the one side and the cellar of Ralph Pekke on the other. If the said mass fails to be celebrated, the said 12d shall revert to Robert his heirs or assignees.

Witnesses: etc [*sic*]

Given etc [*sic*]

4.5 C47/41/174 (b) v

Grant with warranty by William Flemyng' fishmonger of Staunford to Henry de Tydeswell' and William Sadeler', William de Apethorp', Henry de Gretham chaplain and Richard de Spalding' of a messuage with its appurtenances in the parish of St George, Staunford, between the tenement of the prioress of St Michael towards the east and the tenement of Thomas Lincoln' skinner towards the west and the king's highway towards the south up to the tenement of John Bartholomeu towards the north. To have and to hold etc in perpetuity of the capital lords of the fee for the service owed and accustomed.

Witnesses: etc [*sic*]

Given etc [*sic*]

4.6 C47/41/174 (b) vi

<u>*Grant*</u> in free alms with warranty by Cecily widow of John Hastynel in her pure widowhood for the health of her soul and of the soul of John formerly her husband etc to God and St Mary and to the maintenance of the mass of the same virgin to be celebrated in the church of St Mary at the bridge of 2s annual quit rent from those houses which William Wodefoul formerly held in fee farm of Robert at the bridge, which are situated in the parish of St Mary at the bridge of Staunford between Cecily's capital messuage towards the east and her houses towards the west; warranty (clause mentions Alice, not Cecily).

Witnesses: etc [*sic*]

Given, etc [*sic*]

4.7 C47/41/174 (b) vii

<u>*Grant*</u> with warranty by Geoffrey Sayree of Brunne [Bourne] to the Alderman and brothers of the gild of St Mary - for celebrating the mass of the same virgin in the church of St Mary at the bridge of Staunford in perpetuity - for two marks of silver, of the north moiety of a cellar situated in the aforesaid parish of the church of St Mary, namely between the house formerly of Thomas Crik' towards the north and the house of Michael Fauvel towards the south, together with the appurtenances and courtyard adjacent. To hold etc free of all secular service etc saving service to the lord of the fee.

Witnesses: etc [*sic*]

Given etc [*sic*]

4.8 C47/41/174 (b) viii

<u>*Grant*</u> in free alms with warranty by Geoffrey Clyde of 2s of silver to be received annually from his house which is situated between the house of Geoffrey the mercer on the one side and the house of the lady Anabel de Brunne on the other for the maintenance of the service of the mass of St Mary in the church of St Mary at the bridge of Staunford

Witnesses: etc

Given: etc

4.9 C47/41/174 (b) ix

Grant in free alms with warranty by William Bilkes son of Geoffrey the clerk burgess of Staunford to God and St Mary for the maintenance of the mass of the same virgin to be celebrated in the church of St Mary at the bridge of Staunford of 4s annual quit rent from a certain solar which is above a certain shop of William situated in the parish of St Mary aforenoted, between the rent [*sic*] pertaining to the mass of St Mary in the church of All Saints in the Market of Staunford on the south side and the shop of Walter Goion' on the north. To hold etc the said rent to the maintenance of the said mass and to the warden or proctor of the same etc in free alms.

Witnesses: etc [*sic*]

Given etc [*sic*]

4.10 C47/41/174 (b) x

Grant in free alms with warranty by Thomas Bloundes burgess of Staunford' for the maintenance of the mass of St Mary to be celebrated in the church of the same virgin at the bridge of 12d annual rent from a certain house of his which is situated in the parish of St Mary the Virgin aforesaid, namely between the house of William Bilkes son of the late Geoffrey the clerk towards the east and the house of Cecily Palmere towards the west. If the tenants of the aforesaid tenement [*sic*] default in payment of the said rent, the parishioners overseeing the said mass may distrain the said tenants and the movable and immovable goods found in the said tenement etc.

Witnesses: etc [*sic*]

Given: etc [*sic*]

4.11 C47/41/174 (b) xi

Grant in free alms with warranty by Beatrice Page of Staunford to God and St Mary for the maintenance of the mass of the same virgin to be celebrated in the church [of St Mary at the bridge] of Staunford of 2s annual quit rent from a certain cellar and a solar [built above it in the parish of St] Mary at the bridge of Staunford between the lane which is called Cornwansty towards the east and the house of Hugh son of [*ms damaged here*] towards the west. To hold etc to the maintenance of the aforesaid mass and the proctor of the same etc in free alms.

Witnesses: etc [*sic*]

Given etc [*sic*]

Note: *manuscript damaged*

4.12 C47/41/174 (c) i

Grant in free alms with warranty by Richard Page of Staunford and Hawisia his wife to the maintenance of the mass of St Mary to be celebrated solemnly day by day in the church of St Mary at the bridge of Staunford of a certain annual quit rent of 12d from their shop with appurtenances situated in the parish of the aforesaid church between the tenement of Hugh son of Walter de Tykincote towards the west and the lane which is called Cornwansty towards the east.

Witnesses: etc [*sic*]

Given etc [*sic*]

4.13 C47/41/174 (c) ii

Grant in free alms with warranty by Roger Briselance burgess of Staunford to God and St Mary and to the Alderman and brothers of the gild of St Mary for celebrating the mass of the same virgin in the church of St Mary at the bridge of Staunford in perpetuity and for maintaining the alms of the aforesaid gild 12d annual quit rent from the moiety of a cellar situated in the parish of St Mary together with its appurtenances and the court adjacent, namely between the house formerly of Thomas Crik' towards the north and the houses of Michael Fawvel towards the south.

Witnesses: etc [*sic*]

Given etc [*sic*]

4.14 C47/41/174 (c) iii

Grant in free alms with warranty by John Plowman burgess of Staunford for the maintenance of the mass of St Mary the Virgin to be celebrated daily in the church of the same virgin at the bridge of Staunford of 12d annual quit rent with appurtenances from those houses with appurtenances situated in the parish of the same virgin at the bridge between John's houses towards the west and the houses of John Cook' of Lydyngton' towards the east. If celebration of the aforesaid mass ceases, the aforesaid 12d annual quit rent shall revert to John and his heirs or assignees, etc. Warranty to proctor of the mass.

Witnesses: etc [*sic*]

Given etc [*sic*]

4.15 C47/41/174 (c) iv

Grant by Hugh de Tekencote burgess of Staunford to God and St Mary and all his saints and to the brothers of the gild of St Mary at the bridge of Staunford for the maintenance of the mass of the same virgin of 3s annual rent to be received in perpetuity from his house with appurtenances situated in Staunford upon Cleymond in the parish of St Michael in Cornstall'. No warranty.

Witnesses: etc [*sic*]

Given etc [*sic*]

Note: it is likely that the reference to St Michael in Cornstall is an error, since that parish (which vanished by about 1300) does not seem to have extended into Cleymond (Broad Street) while the parish of St Michael the Greater did; see Hartley and Rogers 1974.

4.16 C47/41/174 (c) v

Grant in free alms with warranty by Nicholas son of William de Bernak' formerly ?servant [*serv*] of Richard Brokendissh' to God and to the maintenance of the mass of the Blessed Virgin Mary to be celebrated in the church of St Mary at the bridge of Staunford in perpetuity of 2s 6d annual quit rent from the aforesaid [*sic*] house in the parish of St Martin on the south side of the bridge of Staunford which Ralph de Bedeford' holds situated between the house of William Paplee towards the north and the house of Robert Bole towards the south. To hold etc free of all secular service saving 1d to the lord of the fee at Michaelmas. Warranty mentions the proctor general of the mass

Witnesses: etc [*sic*]

Given etc [*sic*]

4.17 C47/41/174 (c) vi

Grant in free alms with warranty by Hugh de Burlee to the brothers of the gild of St Mary and to the maintenance of the aforesaid mass in the church of St Mary near the bridge of Staunford of a certain annual rent of 2s from a certain shop situated in the parish of St Mary near the bridge of Staunford between the house which was of Geoffrey son of Git towards the west and the house which was of Simon Bray towards the east

Witnesses: etc [*sic*]

Given etc [*sic*]

4.18 C 47/41/174 (c) vii

Grant in free alms with warranty by Stephen de Glatton' chaplain to God and to the mass of St Mary near the bridge of Staunford and to the Alderman and brothers of the gild of the same of a certain annual quit rent of 3s of silver to be received at the four terms from Stephen's tenement with appurtenances which is situated in the parish of St Clement in the street which is called Skoftgate between the tenement of Clement de Molton' towards the east and the tenement of William de Baldeswell' towards the west. If the farm is in arrears by any term, the Alderman and brothers and their successors may enter the said tenement and distrain the goods found there etc.

Witnesses: etc [*sic*]

Given etc [*sic*]

4.19 C47/41/174 (c) viii

Grant with warranty by Hugh de Nassyngton' burgess of Staunford to the fraternity of the gild and to the mass of St Mary the Virgin to be celebrated solemnly each day in the church of the same virgin near the bridge of Staunford of 12d annual quit rent from a certain house with appurtenances situated in the parish of St Clement Staunford' beyond the gate of Scoftgate between the house of Peter Newesel[n' or v'] towards the east and the house formerly of Hugh de Casterton' towards the west

Witnesses: etc [*sic*]

Given etc [*sic*]

4.20 C47/41/174 (c) ix

Grant in free alms by Richard Milisent' of Staunford to God at St Mary and to the Alderman and brothers of the gild of St Mary for celebrating the mass of the same virgin daily in the church of St Mary at the bridge of Staunford in perpetuity and for maintaining the alms of the aforesaid gild of an annual rent of 12d from a house which Thomas le Coupere holds in fee farm of the aforesaid Thomas [*sic*] and his heirs or assignees situated [*word missing*] Scoftgate namely between the house of Hugh de Casterton' towards the west and the house which was of Robert Petit towards the east. If the mass fails to be celebrated in the church of St Mary aforesaid, the 12d rent shall revert to Richard's heirs or assignees.

Witnesses: etc [*sic*]

Given etc [*sic*]

4.21 C47/41/174 (c) x

Grant with warranty by William de Luffenham tanner of Staunford to God and St Mary and to the brothers of the gild of the same virgin and for celebrating a mass of the aforesaid virgin in perpetuity and for maintaining the alms of the aforesaid gild of 12d annual rent from his houses which are situated in the parish of St Mary Bynnewerk' Staunford between the houses of Hugh the mason (*cementarii*) towards the west and the house of Beatrice de Tychemerssh' towards the east.

Witnesses: etc [*sic*]

Given etc [*sic*]

5. C47/41/175   30 January 1389

Note: although not a title deed to property, this document seems too important to leave out.

<u>*Certificate*</u> of Thomas Cok of Staunford Alderman, keeper or master (*custodis sive magistr'*) of the gild or fraternity in the church of Holy Trinity of Staunford registered in the chancery of the king with his seal on Saturday before the feast of the Purification of BVM 12 Richard II: About 24 years ago, certain poor parishioners of the said church, considering the poverty of the rector of the church because of the debts then existing so that there will not be enough to sustain the rector, since only six parishioners live in the parish, established a charitable fraternity in honour of the Holy Trinity in augmentation of the costs and expenses of the divine services (*in augmentacionem cultus divini eorum sumptibus et expensis*); each of them as far as each wishes shall give to God from their own goods in aid of the sustenance of the rector celebrating divine services there and of a light of sixteen candles there before the altar of Holy Trinity. And each year on the feast of Holy Trinity at the church in honour of Holy Trinity they shall meet in one suit of livery and make their offerings as is fitting; and each year on the Sunday after Corpus Christi they shall meet in the Rectory there and they shall have account of the costs and the stock that remains in their hand, and they shall pay and contribute to the rector there as it pleases them to maintain his status; and from the residue if there is any they shall dispose to support the light and the divine services; despite the fact that they do not possess any land, tenements, rents, or other goods or chattels to the use of the gild at present or that they have made or support any other confederation etc. And thus the fraternity has continued from the time aforesaid in honour of the Holy Trinity.

CHANCERY INQUISITIONS AD QUOD DAMPNUM

6. C143/421/4   1392-3

Grant by Robert Prat and William de Maxsey of cottages in the parish of Holy Trinity without Stamford to a chaplain in the church there, retaining land in Stamford

Dated: 16 Richard II

CHANCERY: ANCIENT DEEDS SERIES C

7. C146/3235   26 June 1331

<u>*Grant*</u> by Reymond le Spycer of Staunford to sir Robert de Strauley knight of his curtilage lying on the north side of the cemetery of the church of St Mary de Bynewerk' between the tenement of the prior of St Leonard towards the east and the wall of the town of Staunford towards the west and it extends from the aforesaid cemetery towards the south up to the aforesaid wall of the town of Staunford towards the north.

Witnesses: William de Apethorp', Walter de Apethorp', William Beaufiz, William de Schrobesbiri of Staunford, Robert Broun clerk and others.

Given at Staunford

Seal missing; fragment of tag

Endorsed (i) Carta de Stannford' (? contemporary) (ii) Stanford' (not contemporary) (iii) Stanforthe (not contemporary)

8. Cl46/3891   4 September 1328

Grant by William Bere of Stannford' and Walter de Hameldon' of Staunford to Raymond le Spicer of Stannford' and Edda his wife of their garden in Stannford in the parish of St Mary of Bynewerk' lying on the north side of the church of St Mary aforesaid between the cemetery of the said church on the south side and the wall of the town of Stannford on the north side: it extends from the wall of the town towards the west to the garden of the prior of St Leonard near Staunford towards the east.

Witnesses: William de Apethorp', Roger Scauelere, Walter de Apethorp', William Beaufiz, Henry le Leche burgesses of Stanford and others.

Given at Stannford

Seals (2) missing: tags

Endorsed: (i) Stanford' (not contemporary) (ii) Stanforthe (not contemporary)

CP25 FEET OF FINES/ FINAL CONCORDS
Most of the following entries have been taken from the notes of Feet of Fines which Canon Foster and his team of researchers compiled and which are now in the Lincolnshire Archives Office, FL Transcripts R1-11. Two volumes of Final Concords for Lincolnshire were published – Abstracts of Final Concords temp Richard I, John and Henry III *volume I, privately printed 1896 (edited by W O Massingberd and R Boyd; this is sometimes referred to erroneously as Lincoln Record Society volume 1, for it is entitled* Lincolnshire Records *on the titlepage); and* Final Concords of the County of Lincoln *volume II edited by Canon Foster, 1920. I have not included the Stamford Final Concords from these two volumes in this collection, nor the title deeds which are enrolled on the Pipe Rolls as published by the Pipe Roll Society - only unpublished Feet of Fines. Some items missing from the Foster transcripts have been taken from the originals in the PRO.*

9. CP25/1/132/51/2

Joan who was wife of Reginald de Wyggesle plaintiff by Stephen son of Reginald de Staunford put in her place vs Ralph le Rus and Cecily his wife defendant of 1 messuage in Staunford. Plea of warranty of charter: Ralph and Cecily have acknowledged the messuage to be the right of Joan as that which Joan has of the gift of Ralph and Cecily to have and to hold for Joan and her heirs of Ralph and Cecily for ever; rendering yearly one rose at the Nativity of St John the Baptist for all service, custom and exaction to Ralph and Cecily and the heirs of Cecily belonging; doing therefore to the chief lords of that fee for Ralph and Cecily and heirs of Cecily all the other services which to that

messuage belong. Warranty – and for this Joan has given to Ralph and Cecily 7 marks of silver.
Westminster Quindene of St John Baptist 1 Edward I [September 1273]

10. CP25/1/132/51/12

Benedict le Vylur plaintiff vs Ralph de Stokes and Christiana his wife defendant of 1 messuage in Staunford. Plea of warranty of charter: Ralph and Christiana have acknowledged the messuage to be the right of Benedict as that which Benedict has of the gift of Ralph and Christiana. To have and to hold to Benedict and his heirs of Ralph and Christiana and the heirs of Christiana for ever, rendering therefore yearly 1d at Easter for all service custom and exaction. Warranty. For this Benedict has given to Ralph and Christiana 60 marks of silver.
Westminster Quindene of Easter 2 Edward I [April 1274]

11. CP25/1/132/51/14

Elizabeth prioress of St Michael without Staunford plaintiff by Robert Musgrave put in her place vs Thomas de Hanuill defendant of 16 quarters of wheat which were in arrear to the prioress in respect of the yearly rent of 2 quarters of wheat which he owes to her in respect of his manor of Hacuneby.
Plea: Thomas has acknowledged and granted for himself and his heirs that they henceforth shall render every year to the aforesaid prioress and the other prioresses who shall succeed her and her church of St Michael without Staunford 2 quarters of good wheat at the foresaid manor within the quindene of St Michael. And for this the prioress has granted for herself and the other prioresses who shall succeed her and her church that they henceforth shall keep every year in their church an anniversary for the ancestors of Thomas for ever. And moreover the prioress has remised and quitclaimed from herself to Thomas all the damages which she said she had in respect of the corn unto the day in which this concord was made. And be it known that if Thomas or his heirs or they who shall hold the manor shall have failed in the payment of the corn at any time, it shall be lawful for the prioress and the other prioresses who shall succeed her and her church to distrain them by their chattels found in the said manor and retain them until the full payment of the corn arrears .....and the prioress has received Thomas and his heirs in all the benefits and prayers which henceforth shall be made in her church for ever.
Westminster Quindene of St John Baptist 2 Edward I [September 1274]

12. CP25/1/132/52/6

William Reyner plaintiff vs William de Quenton and Graciana his wife defendant of 1 messuage in Staunford. Plea of warranty of charter: William de Quenton and Graciana have acknowledged the messuage to be the right of William Reyner as that which William Reyner has of the gift of William de Quenton and Graciana. To have and to hold to William Reyner and his heirs of William de Quenton and Graciana and the heirs of Graciana for ever, doing therefore to the chief lords of that fee for William de Quenton and Graciana and the heirs of Graciana all the other services which belong to that messuage. Warranty. For this, William Reyner has given William de Quenton and Graciana 40 shillings sterling.

Westminster Quindene of St John Baptist 5 Edward I [September 1277]

13. CP25/1/133/54/41

Peter de Nortfolk of Staunford plaintiff vs Reginald de Cesterton tannur of Staunford and Ivetta his wife defendant of 4 acres of land in Staunford. Plea of warranty of charter: Reginald and Ivetta have acknowledged the land to be the right of Peter as that which Peter has of the gift of Reginald and Ivetta. To have and to hold to Peter and his heirs of Reginald and Ivetta and the heirs of Ivetta for ever. rendering therefore yearly 1 clove gilly-flower [*clavu gariofi*] at Easter for all services, suit of court, custom and exaction to ... Warranty. For this, Peter has given Reginald and Ivetta 11 marks of silver.

Lincoln Morrow of the close of Easter 10 Edward I [April 1282]

14. CP25/1/133/58/78

John son of William le Fleming plaintiff vs Reginald son of Gilbert de Wodecroft and Isabel his wife defendant of 1 messuage in Staunford. Plea of warranty of charter: To hold to John and his heirs of Reginald and Isabel and the heirs of Isabel, rendering yearly three half pennies at Easter for all service. Warranty. For this, John gave 40s.

Lincoln Month after Easter day 12 Edward I [May 1284]

15. CP25/1/133/58/80

Robert Brucelaunce of Staunforde plaintiff vs Walter Kysk' and Agnes his wife defendant of 2 messuages in Staunford. Plea of warranty of charter to hold to Robert and his heirs of Walter and Agnes and the heirs of Agnes, rendering yearly 1 half penny at Easter for all service to them and all services due to the chief lords. Warranty. For this, Robert gave 10 marks.

Lincoln Quindene of Easter 12 Edward I [April 1284]

16. CP25/1/133/59/33

master John de Lacy plaintiff vs John le Flemyng of Stanford and Cecily his wife defendant of the mediety of 1 messuage in Stanford. Plea of warranty of charter: John and Cecily have acknowledged the mediety of the messuage to be the right of master John as that which he has of their gift. To have and to hold to him and his heirs of them and the heirs of Cecily for ever, rendering therefore yearly 1 half penny at Easter for all services, custom and exaction to them and the heirs of Cecily belonging. And doing therefore to the chief lords of that fee for them and the heirs of Cecily all the other services which belong to that mediety of the said messuage. Warranty. For this, master John has given John and Cecily 60 marks of silver.

Westminster Quindene of St Michael 14 Edward 1 [October 1286]

17. CP25/1/133/60/6

Peter de Wysbech and Sarra his wife plaintiff vs Henry de Langham and Emma his wife defendant of 1 messuage in Staunford. Plea of warranty of charter: Henry and Emma have acknowledged the messuage to be the right of Peter as those which Peter and Sarra have of their gift. To have and to hold to Peter and Sarra and the heirs of Sarra and of Henry and Emma and the heirs of Emma for ever, rendering therefore yearly 1 rose at the feast of the Nativity of St John Baptist for all services, custom and exaction belonging to Henry and Emma and the heirs of Emma. And doing therefore to the chief lords of that fee for Henry and Emma and the heirs of Emma all the other services which belong to that messuage. Warranty. For this Peter and Sarra have given Henry and Emma 1 sore sparrowhawk.
Westminster Morrow of the Ascension 15 Edward I [May 1287]

18. CP25/1/133/60/9

John le Cunte plaintiff vs John son of Peter de Staunford and Maude his wife defendant of 1 acre of land in Staunford. Plea of warranty of charter: John son of Peter and Matilda [*sic*] have acknowledged the land to be the right of John le Cunte as that which he has of their gift. To have and to hold to him and his heirs of the chief lords of that fee by the services which belong to that land for ever. For this, John le Cunte has given John and Matilda 1 sore sparrowhawk.
Westminster 3 weeks from Easter day 15 Edward I [April 1287]

19. CP25/1/133/60/10

Walter Norman plaintiff vs John son of Peter le Clerk of Staunford and Maude his wife defendant of 10s of rent in Staunford. Plea of warranty of charter: John and Matilda [*sic*] have acknowledged the rent to be the right of Walter as that which he has of their gift. To have and to hold to him and his heirs of the chief lords of that fee by the services which belong to that rent for ever. For this Walter has given John and Matilda 1 sore sparrowhawk
Westminster 3 weeks from Easter day 15 Edward I [April 1287]

20. CP25/1/133/60/18

Alured le Mercir and Margery his wife plaintiff vs Isaac Lucas and Juliana his wife defendant of 1 messuage in Staunford. Plea of warranty of charter: Isaac and Juliana have acknowledged the messuage to be the right of Alured as that which Alured and Margery have of the gift of Isaac and Juliana. To have and to hold to Alured and Margery and the heirs of Alured of the chief lords of that fee by the services which belong to that messuage for ever. And Isaac and Juliana have granted for themselves and the heirs of Juliana that they will warrant to Alured and Margery and the heirs of Alured the aforesaid messuage against all men for ever.
Westminster Quindene of St Martin 15 Edward I [November 1287]

21. CP25/1/133/61/23

Thomas de Boudon and Agnes his wife plaintiff vs Gilbert de Burton and Ellen his wife defendant of 1 messuage in Staunford. Plea of warranty of charter: Gilbert and Ellen have acknowledged the messuage to be the right of Thomas as that which Thomas and Agnes have of the gift of Gilbert and Ellen. To have and to hold to Thomas and Agnes and the heirs of Thomas of the chief lords of that fee by the services which belong to those tenements *[sic]* for ever. And for this Thomas and Agnes have given Gilbert and Ellen 1 sore sparrowhawk.
Westminster Month of Easter 17 Edward I [May 1289]

22. CP25/1/133/61/28

William Galbegoky and Maude his wife plaintiff vs John son of Peter le Cordewanyr and Maude his wife defendant of 3 acres of land in Staunford. Plea of warranty of charter: John and Matilda *[sic]* have acknowledged the land to be the right of William as that which William and Matilda have of the gift of John and Matilda. To have and to hold to William and Matilda and the heirs of William of John and Matilda and the heirs of John for ever, rendering therefore yearly 1 chaplet of roses at the feast of the Nativity of St John Baptist for all the service, custom and exaction. Warranty. For this, William and Matilda have given John and Matilda 1 sore sparrowhawk.
Westminster Octave of the Holy Trinity 17 Edward I [June 1289]

23. CP25/1/133/62/5

Alexander de Tykenecote plaintiff vs William son of Geoffrey le vineter of Stamford defendant of 1 messuage in Staunford. Plea of covenant: William has acknowledged the messuage to be the right of Alexander and has rendered it to him in the same court. To have and to hold to Alexander and his heirs of William and his heirs for ever, rendering therefore yearly 1d at the feast of the Nativity of St John Baptist for all service, custom and exaction to William and his heirs belonging. And doing therefore to the chief lords of that fee for William and his heirs all the other services which belong to that messuage. Warranty. For this, Alexander has given William 10 marks of silver.
Westminster 3 weeks from Easter 18 Edward I [April 1290]
 [Endorsed] Roger de Ofyngton puts in his claim etc

24. CP25/1/133/63/32

Andrew Negh of Staunford plaintiff vs William Balle of Staunford and Christiana his wife defendant by John de Brundissh put in the place of William and Christiana of 1 messuage in Stamford. Plea of warranty of charter: William and Christiana have acknowledged the messuage to be the right of Andrew as that which he has of their gift. To have and to hold to him and his heirs of the chief lords of that fee by the services which belong to that messuage for ever. Moreover William and Christiana have granted for themselves and for the heirs of Christiana that they will warrant to Andrew and his heirs the messuage against all men for ever. For this Andrew has given William and Christiana 1 sore sparrowhawk.

Westminster Quindene of St Martin 20 Edward I [November 1292]

25. CP25/1/133/63/56

Annoricus Pikard plaintiff vs Simon de Braunston and Wymarca his wife defendant by Hugh de Offynton put in the place of Simon of 1 messuage in Staunford. Plea of warranty of charter: Simon and Wymarca have acknowledged the messuage to be the right of Annoricus as that which he has of their gift. To have and to hold to him and his heirs of the chief lords of that fee by the services which belong to that messuage for ever. Moreover Simon and Wymarca have granted for themselves and for the heirs of Wymarca that they will warrant to Annoricus and his heirs the messuage against all men for ever. For this, Annoricus has given Simon and Wymarca 10 marks of silver.
Westminster Morrow of All Souls 21 Edward I [November 1293]

26. CP25/1/134/65/52

Peter le Cunneur of Staunford plaintiff vs William de Castro Bernardi of Staunford and Cecily his wife defendant of 1 messuage in Staunford. Plea of covenant: William and Cecily have acknowledged the messuage to be the right of Peter as that which he has of their gift. To have and to hold to him and his heirs of the chief lords of that fee by the services which belong to that messuage for ever. Moreover William and Cecily have granted for themselves and for the heirs of Cecily that they will warrant to Peter and his heirs the messuage against all men for ever. For this, Peter has given William and Cecily 7 marks of silver.
York 3 weeks from St Michael's day 26 Edward I [October 1298]

27. CP25/1/134/66/8

William de Deping of Staunford plaintiff vs Gilbert de Gotesmore [*sic*] and Joan his wife defendant of 1 messuage in Staunford. Plea of warranty of charter: Gilbert and Joan have acknowledged the messuage to be the right of William as that which he has of their gift. To have and to hold to him and his heirs of the chief lords of that fee by the services which belong to that messuage for ever. Moreover Gilbert and Joan have granted for themselves and for the heirs of Joan that they will warrant to William and his heirs the messuage against all men for ever. For this, William has given Gilbert and Joan 5 marks of silver.
York Morrow of St John Baptist 27 Edward I [August 1299]

28. CP25/1/134/69/41

Robert de Potton and Idonea his wife plaintiff vs Geoffrey son of Gilbert de Obbethorp and Mary his wife defendant of 1 messuage in Staunford. Plea of warranty of charter: Gilbert and Mary have acknowledged the messuage to be the right of Robert as that which Robert and Idoneaugh have of the gift of Gilbert and Mary. To have and to hold to Robert and Idonea and the heirs of Robert of the chief lords of that fee by the services which belong to that messuage for ever. Moreover Gilbert and Mary have granted for themselves and for the heirs of Mary that they will warrant to Robert and Idonea and the heirs of Robert the messuage against all men for ever. For this, Robert and Idonea have given Gilbert and Mary 20 marks of silver.

York Morrow of St Martin 31 Edward I [November 1303]

29. CP25/1/134/70/32

Hugh de Hotot plaintiff vs Roger de Uffynton defendant by John de Werymle put in his place of 1 messuage, 2 carucates of land and 10 marks of rent in Uffynton and Staunford. Plea of covenant: Roger has acknowledged the tenements to be the right of Hugh and has rendered them to him in the same court. To have and to hold to Hugh and his heirs of the chief lords of that fee by the services which belong to those tenements for ever. Warranty. For this, Hugh has given Roger 100 marks of silver.

York Morrow of St Martin 32 Edward I [November 1304]

Endorsed: Hugh de Aluerton of Staunford puts in his claim etc

Robert son of Nicholas de Merentishale and Sarra his wife daughter and heir of Roger de Uffington put in their claim

30. CP25/1/135/72/1

Roger de Uffynton plaintiff vs Hugh de Hotot defendant of 1 messuage, 2 carucates of land and 12 marks of rent in Uffyngtone and Staunford. Plea of covenant: Roger has acknowledged the tenements *[sic]* to be the right of Hugh as those which Hugh has of the gift of Roger; and for this Hugh has granted them to Roger; and has rendered them to him in the same court. To have and to hold to Roger of the chief lords of that fee by the services which belong to those tenements for the whole life of Roger. And after the death of Roger, they shall remain wholly to Simon son of the same Roger and Juliana his wife and the heirs of Simon, to hold of the chief lords of that fee by the services which belong to those tenements for ever.

Westminster Octave of the Purification of the BVM 34 Edward I [February 1306]

31. CP25/1/132/75/14

Andrew de Staunford plaintiff vs Alexander le Tayllur of Staunford defendant of one messuage in Staunford. Alexander has recognised the messuage to be the right of Andrew as that which Andrew has of the gift of Alexander. For this, Andrew has granted to Alexander the messuage and has rendered it to him in the same court. To have and to hold to Alexander of Andrew and his heirs for the whole life of Alexander, rendering yearly 1 rose at the feast of the Nativity of St John the Baptist for all service custom and exaction to Andrew and his heirs belonging, doing therefore to the chief lords of that fee for Andrew and his heirs all other services which belong to that messuage. After the death of Alexander, the messuage to revert wholly to Andrew and his heirs. To hold of the chief lords of that fee by the services which belong to that messuage for ever.

Westminster Octave of the Holy Trinity 1 Edward II [June 1308]

32. CP25/1/132/76/22

Roger Staneland de Staunford plaintiff vs Gilbert de Cotesmere and Joan his wife defendant of one messuage in Staunford. Plea of warranty of charter. Gilbert and Joan have acknowledged the messuage to be the right of Roger as that which Roger has of their gift to have and to hold to Roger and his heirs of the chief lords of that fee by the services which belong to that messuage for ever. And moreover Gilbert and Joan have granted for themselves and the heirs of Joan that they will warrant to Roger and his heirs the messuage against all men for ever. For this Roger has given Gilbert and Joan 40s of silver.
Westminster Quindene of St Hilary 2 Edward II [January 1309]

33. CP25/1/135/76/41

Richard Pite and Beatrice his wife plaintiff by Henry de Hale put in the place of Beatrice by writ of the king vs John de Wakerle and Joan his wife defendant by William de Suthorp put in the place of John by writ of the king, of 4 acres of land in Staunford. Plea of covenant: John and Joan have acknowledged the land to be the right of Richard and Beatrice which they have of the gift of John and Joan to have and to hold to Richard and Beatrice and the heirs of Richard of the chief lords of that fee by the services which belong to that land for ever. And moreover John and Joan have granted for themselves and the heirs of Joan that they will warrant to Richard and Beatrice and the heirs of Richard the land against all men for ever And for this Richard and Beatrice have given John and Joan 100s of silver.
Westminster Quindene of Trinity 2 Edward II [June 1309]

34. CP25/1/135/77/22

John de Cnotteshale and Agatha his wife and Geoffrey son of the same John plaintiff vs Cecily who was the wife of Godfrey de Reynham defendant of 1 messuage in Staunford. Plea of covenant: Cecily has acknowledged the messuage to be the right of Agatha and has rendered it to John and Agatha in the same court. To have and to hold to John and Agatha and the heirs of Agatha begotten of her body of the chief lords of that fee by the services which belong to that messuage for ever. And if it happen that Agatha die without an heir begotten of her body, then after the death of John and Agatha the messuage shall remain wholly to Geoffrey and the heirs begotten of his body. To hold of the chief lords of that fee by the services which belong to that messuage for ever. And if it happen that Geoffrey die without an heir begotten of his body, then after the death of Geoffrey the messuage shall remain wholly to the rightful heirs of Agatha. To hold of the chief lords of that fee by the services which belong to that messuage for ever.
Westminster Octave of St Hilary 3 Edward II [January 1310]

35. CP25/1/135/79/8

Geoffrey de Wodeslade and Joan his sister plaintiffs vs William Faderman of Stanford and Alice his wife defendant of 1 messuage in Staunford. Plea of covenant: William and Alice have acknowledged the messuage to be the right of Geoffrey and have rendered it

to Geoffrey and Joan in the same court. To have and to hold to Geoffrey and Joan and the heirs of Geoffrey of the chief lords of that fee by the services which belong to that messuage for ever. And moreover William and Alice have granted for themselves and the heirs of Alice that they will warrant to Geoffrey and Joan and the heirs of Geoffrey the messuage against all men for ever. And for this Geoffrey and Joan have given William and Alice £10 sterling.
Westminster Octave of St Martin 5 Edward II [January 1312]

36. CP25/1/135/79/10

John de Asshewell plaintiff vs William Faderman of Stanford and Alice his wife defendant of 4 acres of land in Stanford. Plea of covenant: William and Alice have acknowledged the land to be the right of John and have rendered it to him in the same court. To have and to hold to John and his heirs of the chief lords of that fee by the services which belong to that land for ever. And moreover William and Alice have granted for themselves and the heirs of Alice that they will warrant to John and his heirs the land against all men for ever. And for this, John has given William and Alice 10 marks of silver.
Westminster Octave of St Martin 5 Edward II [November 1311]

37. CP25/1/135/79/20

Richard Sampson plaintiff vs William Faderman of Stanford and Alice his wife defendant of 2 acres of land and 9s of rent in Stanford. Plea of covenant: William and Alice have acknowledged the aforesaid tenements [*sic*] to be the right of Richard and have rendered them to him in the same court. To have and to hold to Richard and his heirs of the chief lords of that fee by the services which belong to those tenements for ever. And moreover William and Alice have granted for themselves and the heirs of Alice that they will warrant to Richard and his heirs the tenements against all men for ever And for this, Richard has given William and Alice £10 sterling.
Westminster Octave of St Martin 5 Edward II [November 1311]

38. CP25/1/135/79/50

Walter de Scotelthorp and Margaret his wife plaintiff vs Geoffrey Bernard and Alice his wife defendant of 2 messuages in Staunford. Plea of covenant: Geoffrey and Alice have acknowledged the aforesaid messuages to be the right of Walter as those which Walter and Margaret have of the gift of Geoffrey and Alice. To have and to hold to Walter and Margaret and his heirs of Walter of the chief lords of that fee by the services which belong to those messuages for ever. And moreover Geoffrey and Alice have granted for themselves and the heirs of Alice that they will warrant to Walter and Margaret and the heirs of Walter the messuages against all men for ever. And for this, Walter and Margaret have given Geoffrey and Alice 100s of silver.
Westminster Octave of St John Baptist 5 Edward II [September 1311]

39. CP25/1/135/81/27

Eustace Malherbe and Lora his wife plaintiff vs William son of Isolda de Billingburgh and Cristiana his wife defendant of 1 ½ acres of land and 2 ½ acres meadow in Staunford. Plea of warranty of charter: William and Cristiana have acknowledged the aforesaid tenements to be the right of Eustace as those which Eustace and Lora have of the gift of William and Cristiana. To have and to hold to Eustace and Lora and the heirs of Eustace of the chief lords of that fee by the services which belong to those tenements for ever. And moreover William and Cristiana have granted for themselves and the heirs of Cristiana that they will warrant to Eustace and Lora and the heirs of Eustace the messuages against all men for ever. And for this, Eustace and Lora have given William and Cristiana 1 sore sparrowhawk.
Westminster Octave of St Michael 7 Edward II [October 1313]

40. CP25/1/135/81/31

William son of William de Welleby and Margaret his wife plaintiff by Thomas de Salso Marisco put in the place of Margaret by writ of the king vs Elnardus de Salso Marisco defendant, of 7 messuages, 10 tofts, 70 acres of land and 30 acres meadow in Grantham, Anecastre, Willesford, Dembelby, Scot Wilughby, Welleby, Swynestede and Staunford. Plea of covenant: William has acknowledged the aforesaid tenements to be the right of Elnard as those which Elnard has of the gift of William. And for this, Elnard has granted to William and Margaret the said tenements and has rendered them to them in the same court. To have and to hold to them and to the heirs which William shall have begotten of the body of Margaret of the chief lords of that fee by the services which belong to those tenements for ever. And if it happen that William dies without an heir begotten of the body of Margaret, then after the death of William and Margaret the tenements shall remain wholly to the rightful heirs of William to hold of the chief lords of that fee by the services which belong to those tenements for ever.
Westminster Octave of St Michael 7 Edward II [September 1313]
Endorsed Adam son of Robert de Welleby put in his claim. John son of Geoffrey de Swynestede put in his claim etc; the prior of Farleye Monacorum put in his claim etc; William de Colewyk' and Emma his wife put in their claim etc.

41. CP25/1/135/81/36

William del Cley plaintiff vs Robert Broun of Great Casterton and Alice his wife defendant of 1 messuage in Staunford. Plea of covenant: Robert and Alice have acknowledged the aforesaid messuage to be the right of William as that which he had of their gift. To have and to hold to William and his heirs of the chief lords of that fee by the services which belong to that messuage for ever. And moreover Robert and Alice have granted for themselves and the heirs of Alice that they will warrant to William and his heirs the messuage against all men for ever. And for this, William has given Robert and Alice one sore sparrowhawk.
Westminster Octave of St Michael 7 Edward II [September 1313]

42. CP25/1/136/82/29

Henry de Ashhwell and Isabel his wife plaintiff by Hugh de Thorleby put in their place by writ of the king vs John de Knotteshale and Agatha his wife defendant of 1 messuage in Staunford. Plea of warranty of charter: John and Agatha have acknowledged the aforesaid messuage to be the right of Henry as that which Henry and Isabel have of the gift of John and Agatha. To have and to hold to Henry and Isabel and his heirs of Henry of the chief lords of that fee by the services which belong to the messuage for ever. And moreover John and Agatha have granted for themselves and the heirs of Agatha that they will warrant to Henry and Isabel and the heirs of Henry the messuage against all men for ever. And for this, Henry and Isabel have given John and Agatha 40s of silver.
Westminster Quindene of Trinity 8 Edward II [June 1315]

43. CP25/1/136/82/43

Robert de Lymbergh and Mabilla his wife plaintiff by Hugh de Thurleby put in their place by writ of the king vs William de Neweton de Bilyngburgh and Cristian his wife defendant of 1 messuage in Stanford. Plea of warranty of charter: William and Cristian have acknowledged the aforesaid messuage to be the right of Robert as that which Robert and Mabilla have of the gift of William and Cristian, and have remised and quitclaimed it from William and Cristian, the heirs of Cristian to Robert and Mabilla and the heirs of Robert for ever. Warranty. And for this, Robert and Mabilla have given William and Cristian 40s of silver.
Westminster Quindene of Trinity 8 Edward II [June 1315]

44. CP25/1/136/83/24

John Bertelmeu of Staunford plaintiff vs Robert de Aston of Gretford and Alianora his wife defendant of 2 messuages in Staunford. Plea of covenant: Robert and Alianora have acknowledged the aforesaid messuages to be the right of John as those which he has of their gift. To have and to hold to John and his heirs of the chief lords of that fee by the services which belong to those messuages for ever. And moreover Robert and Alianora have granted for themselves and the heirs of Alianore that they will warrant to John and his heirs the messuages against all men for ever. And for this, John has given Robert and Alianora 10 marks of silver.
Westminster Quindene of St Hilary 9 Edward II [January 1316]

45. CP25/1/136/84/8

Richard Pyte of Staunford plaintiff vs John Gabgoky of Staunford defendant of 2 acres of land in Staunford. Plea of covenant: John has acknowledged the aforesaid land to be the right of Richard and has rendered it to him in the same court. To have and to hold to Richard and his heirs of the chief lords of that fee by the services which belong to that land for ever. Warranty. And for this Richard has given John 100s of silver.
Westminster Octave of St Michael 10 Edward II [October 1316]
Endorsed And Robert de Pontefracto puts in his claim

46. CP25/1/136/84/36

John de Ellerker the elder plaintiff vs Robert de Neuwerk' and Matilda his wife defendant of 1 messuage, 2 "shopis", 56 acres of land and 13 acres of meadow in Staunford. Plea of covenant: Robert and Matilda have acknowledged the aforesaid tenements to be the right of John as those which he has of their gift. And for this John has granted to Robert and Matilda the said tenements and has rendered them to them in the same court. To have and to hold to Robert and Matilda of the king and his heirs by the services which belong to that land for the whole life of Robert and Matilda and after the death of Robert and Matilda, the tenements shall revert wholly to John and his heirs quit from the heirs of Robert and Matilda. To hold of the king and his heirs by the services which belong to the tenements for ever. And this concord was made by order of the king.
Westminster Easter day in 3 weeks 10 Edward II [April 1317]

47. CP25/1/136/86/2

Thomas William of Croxton plaintiff by Henry de Morcote put in his place vs Gilbert de Cottesmor and Joan his wife defendant of 2 messuages and 19 acres of land in Staunford. Plea of warranty of charter: Gilbert and Joan have acknowledged the aforesaid tenements to be the right of Thomas as those which he has of their gift. To have and to hold to Thomas and his heirs of the chief lords of that fee by the services which belong to the tenements for ever. Gilbert and Joan have granted for themselves and the heirs of Joan that they will warrant to Thomas and his heirs the said tenements against all men for ever. And for this, Thomas has given to Gilbert and Joan 20 marks of silver
Westminster Octave of St Michael 11 Edward II [October 1317]

48. CP25/1/136/88/17

Richard Bertelmeu plaintiff vs Roger de Lunderthorp of Welleby and Isabel his wife and Thomas de Skuns and [*sic*] Welleby and Matilda his wife defendant of 1 messuage in Staunford. Plea of warranty of charter: Roger and Isabel and Thomas and Matilda have acknowledged the messuage to be the right of Richard as that which he has of their gift. To have and to hold to Richard and his heirs of the chief lords of that fee by the services which belong to the messuage for ever. And moreover Roger and Isabel and Thomas and Matilda have granted for themselves and the heirs of Isabel and Matilda that they will warrant to Richard and his heirs the said messuage against all men for ever. And for this Richard has given to Roger and Isabel and Thomas and Matilda £20 sterling.
Westminster Morrow of Purification of BVM 12 Edward II [February 1319]

49. CP25/1/136/90/7

William de Carleton plaintiff vs Alan de Maydenston and Alice his wife defendant of 1 messuage, 2 acres of land in Staunford. Plea of covenant: Alan and Alice have acknowledged the aforesaid tenements to be the right of William as that which he has of their gift. To have and to hold, to wit, the aforesaid land to William and his heirs of the chief lords of that fee by the services which belong to that land for ever. And for this

William has granted to Alan and Alice the messuage and has rendered it to them in the same court. To have and to hold to Alan and Alice and the heirs of Alan of the chief lords of that fee by the services which belong to that messuage for ever.
Westminster Morrow of All Souls 14 Edward II [November 1320]

50. CP25/1/137/92/8

John Cloket de Staunford plaintiff by Hugh de Thurleby put in his place by writ of the king vs William de Bru[n'ha]m of Staunford and Cecily his wife defendant of a mediety of 1 messuage in Staunford. Plea of warranty of charter. William and Cecily have acknowledged the mediety to be the right of John as those which he has of their gift to have and to hold to John and his heirs of the chief lords of that fee by the services which belong to that mediety for ever. And moreover William and Cecily have granted for themselves and the heirs of Cecily that they will warrant to John and his heirs the mediety against all men for ever. For this, John has given William and Cecily 100s of silver.
York Quindene of St Michael 16 Edward II [October 1322]

51. CP25/1/137/92/27

Andrew Godefelaghe plaintiff by Hugh de Thurleby put in his place vs Thomas de Ardenne and Sarra his wife defendant of 1 messuage in Staunford. Plea of warranty of charter. Thomas and Sarra have acknowledged the messuage to be the right of Andrew as that which he has of their gift to have and to hold to Andrew and his heirs of the chief lords of that fee by the services which belong to that messuage for ever. And moreover Thomas and Sarra have granted for themselves and the heirs of Sarra that they will warrant to Andrew and his heirs the messuage against all men for ever. For this, John has given Thomas and Sarra 100s of silver.
York Quindene of Easter 16 Edward II [April 1323]

52. CP25/1/137/93/39

Henry de Tyddeswell plaintiff vs William de Sutton "harper" and Joan his wife defendant of 1 messuage, 2 "shopis" in Staunford. Plea of covenant: William and Joan have acknowledged the aforesaid tenements to be the right of Henry as that which he has of their gift. To have and to hold to Henry and his heirs of the chief lords of that fee by the services which belong to the tenements for ever. And moreover William and Joan have granted for themselves and the heirs of Joan that they will warrant to Henry and his heirs the tenements against all men for ever. For this, Henry has given William and Joan 100s of silver.
Westminster Octave of Trinity 17 Edward II [June 1324]

53. CP25/1/137/94/2

Nicholas de Staunford clerk plaintiff vs Robert de Bitham of Staunford and Sarra his wife defendant

2 messuages in Staunford. Plea of covenant: Robert and Sarra have acknowledged the aforesaid messuages to be the right of Nicholas and have rendered them to him in the same court. To have and to hold to Nicholas and his heirs of the chief lords of that fee by the services which belong to the messuages for ever. And moreover Robert and Sarra have granted for themselves and the heirs of Sarra that they will warrant to Nicholas and his heirs the messuages against all men for ever. For this, Nicholas has given Robert and Sarra 100s of silver.
Westminster Octave of St Martin 18 Edward II [November 1324]

54. CP25/1/137/94/20

Robert de Pakynton and John de Pontefracto plaintiff by Hugh de Thurleby put in their place by writ of the king vs Thomas de Herbrok' and Emma his wife defendant of 1 messuage in Staunford.
Plea of warranty of charter: Thomas and Emma have acknowledged the aforesaid messuage to be the right of Robert as that which Robert and John have of the gift of Thomas and Emma. To have and to hold to Robert and John and the heirs of Robert of the chief lords of that fee by the services which belong to the messuage for ever. And moreover Thomas has granted for himself and his heirs that they will warrant to Robert and John and the heirs of Robert the messuage against all men for ever. For this, Robert and John have given Thomas and Emma 100s of silver.
Westminster Octave of Purification of BVM 18 Edward II [February 1325]

55. CP25/1/137/95/24

Roesia who was the wife of John de Burford plaintiff by Sampson de Heneseye put in her place vs Henry de Tiddeswell of Staunford and Emma his wife defendant of 1 messuage in Staunford. Plea of covenant: Henry and Emma have acknowledged the aforesaid messuage to be the right of Roesia as that which she has of their gift. To have and to hold to Roesia and her heirs of the chief lords of that fee by the services which belong to the messuage for ever. And moreover Henry has granted for himself and his heirs that they will warrant to Roesia and her heirs the messuage against all men for ever. For this Roesia has given Henry and Emma £100 sterling.
Westminster Octave of St Hilary 19 Edward II [January 1326]

56. CP25/1/137/95/28

Henry de Assewell plaintiff by Hugh de Thurleby put in his place by writ of the king vs John de Walcote of Bedeford and Agnes his wife defendant of 1 messuage in Staunford.
Plea of covenant: John and Agnes have acknowledged the aforesaid messuage to be the right of Henry as that which he has of their gift. To have and to hold to Henry and his heirs of the chief lords of that fee by the services which belong to the messuage for ever. And moreover John and Agnes have granted for themselves and the heirs of Agnes that they will warrant to Henry and his heirs the messuage against all men for ever. For this Henry has given John and Agnes 40s of silver.
Westminster Octave of St Hilary 19 Edward II [January 1326]

57. CP25/1/137/98/29

Mention of fine dated York Quindene of Hilary 3 Edward III. Richard Sampson of Staunford clerk plaintiff vs John Gabbegoky of Staunford defendant of 1 messuage and 1 ½ acres of land in Staunford which William Poucyn and Alice his wife hold in the dower of the said Alice. Plea of covenant; John has acknowledged the tenement to be the right of Richard and to remain to him after the death of Alice. Warranty by John for himself and his heirs. He gave 100s.
Westminster Quindene of Michaelmas 10 Edward III [October 1336]

58. CP25/1/138/100/46

John son of Alexander de Hipetoft and Mabilla his wife plaintiff vs Roger son of John de Thwayt and Christiana his wife defendant of the third part of 6 tofts and 8 "boratarum"* of land and of the fourth part of 12 messuages, 3 mills, 12 saltpits (*sallinarum*), 229 acres of land, 24 acres of meadow, 373 acres of pasture and 38s (*solidara*) of rent in Threkyngham, Holbeche, Flete, Quappelad, Algakirk, Staunford, Repingale and Kirketon in Holand. Plea of covenant: Roger and Christine have acknowledged the third part and the fourth part to be the right of Mabilla. To hold to John and Mabilla and the heirs of Mabilla, subject to the life interest of Amy who was the wife of Laurence de Hollebeche who holds 1 messuage, 2 saltpits, 29 ½ acres 1 rood of land, 11 acres of meadow, 55 acres of pasture, 5s of rent and the fourth part of 1 mill in Hollebeche, Flete, Quappelade, Algerkirk and Kirketon in dower; and of the same Amy in 1 messuage, 2 ½ acres of land in Hollebeche; and of master Ralph de Hollebeche and William de Castre in 1 messuage and 4 acres of land in Quappelade; and of the same master Ralph in 1 saltpit in Hollebeche; and also of Joce Alcas in 2 acres of land and 3 acres 1 rood of pasture in Hollebeche. John and Mabel gave £20. Amy, master Ralph and Joce were present and consenting and they did fealty to John and Mabilla.
Westminster Morrow of the Ascension 3 Edward III / Quindene Trinity 5 Edward III [June 1329; June 1331]
* *?bovates?*

59. CP25/1/138/104/11

Henry de Tiddeswell of Staunford plaintiff by William de Bytham put in his place vs John Arnale and Matilda his wife defendant of 1 shop (*shopa*) in Staunford. Plea of covenant. To hold to Henry and his heirs; he gave 100s. Warranty by John and Matilda for themselves and the heirs of Matilda.
York Quindene of Trinity 9 Edward III/Quindene of Michaelmas 9 Edward III [June 1333; October 1333]

60. CP25/1/138/104/45

Geoffrey de Dalby of Staunford plaintiff vs Reymund le Milner of Gretham and Matilda his wife defendant of the moiety of 1 messuage in Staunford. To hold to Geoffrey and his heirs; he gave 100s. Warranty by Reymund and Matilda for themselves and heirs of Matilda.

YorkIn 3 weeks of Easter 9 Edward III/Quindene of Trinity 9 Edward III [May, June 1335]

61. CP25/1/138/104/49

Nicholas de Eston of Staunford clerk, plaintiff vs Robert le Moyne and Juliana his wife defendant of 4 messuages and 1 toft in the suburb of Staunford. To hold to Nicholas and his heirs; he gave 40 marks. Warranty by Robert and Juliana for themselves and the heirs of Juliana.
York Morrow of John Baptist 9 Edward III [August 1335]

62. CP25/1/138/106/7

Geoffrey de Badyngton parson of the church of Wardeboys plaintiff vs John Templer of Badyngton and Matilda his wife defendant of 4 messuages and 6s of rent in Staunford. To hold to Geoff and his heirs; he gave 20 marks. Witnessed? Warranty by John and Matilda for themselves and for the heirs of Matilda. Giles de Edyngton puts in his claim.
York Octave of John Baptist 11 Edward III/Morrow of Mart [*sic*] 11 Edward III [September, November 1337]

63. CP25/1/138/106/13

Nicholas de Eston of Staunford clerk plaintiff vs Peter de Knotteshale of Staunford defendant of 2 messuages, 1 shop , 3 tofts, 20 acres land, 11s of rent and rent of 3 cocks and 6 hens in Staunford. To hold to Nicholas and his heirs; he gave 20 marks. Quitclaim and witnessed by Peter for himself and his heirs.
York Octave of Michaelmas 11 Edward III [October 1337]

64. CP25/1/138/107/14

Robert de Rondes chaplain plaintiff vs Simon de Wyrthorp and Alice his wife defendant of 1½ acres of land in Staunford. To hold to Robert and his heirs; he gave 40s. Witnessed by Simon and Alice for themselves and the heirs of Alice.
York Quindene of Easter 12 Edward III/ Quindene of Trinity 12 Edward III [April, June 1338]

65. CP25/1/139/108/7

Henry Tyddeswell of Staunford plaintiff vs Richard de Wyrthorp of Staunford and Albreda his wife defendant of 1 messuage in Staunford. Quitclaim and warranty by Richard and Albreda for themselves and the heirs of Richard. Henry gave 100s.
Westminster Quindene of Michaelmas 14 Edward III [October 1340]

66. CP25/1/139/108/26

John de Deen and Margaret his wife plaintiffs vs William de Deen and Agnes his wife defendant of 1 messuage, 32 acres land, 4 acres meadow, 8s of rent and the moiety of 1 lb of pepper in Staunford.
To hold to John and Margaret and the heirs of their bodies of William and Agnes and the heirs of Agnes rendering yearly one rose at the feast of the Nativity of St John Baptist for all service to them and doing all services due to the chief lords. Remainder to Emma, John's sister, for her life, reversion to William and Agnes and the heirs of Agnes. Warranty by William and Agnes for themselves and the heirs of Agnes.
Westminster Quindene of Hilary 14 Edward III/ Quindene of Trinity 14 Edward III [January, June 1340]

67. CP25/1/139/109/4

John le Mazoun chaplain plaintiff vs Geoffrey de Wodeslade and Margery his wife defendant of 4 messuages, 80 acres land and 3 acres meadow in Staunford. To hold to John and his heirs; he gave 100 marks. Warranty by Geoffrey and Margery for themselves and the heirs of Margery.
Westminster Quindene of Easter 15 Edward III [April 1341]

68. CP25/1/139/110/14

Walter de Jernemuth plaintiff by William de Bytham put in his place vs William Barentyn and Cecily his wife defendant of 1 messuage in Staunford. To hold to Walter and his heirs; he gave 100s. Warranty by William and Cecily for themselves and the heirs of Cecily.
Westminster Octave of Trinity 16 Edward III [June 1342]

69. CP25/1/139/110/15

Thomas de Berford parson of the church of St Paul of Staunford plaintiff by William de Bytham put in his place vs John de Aldeburgh and Agatha his wife defendant of 1 messuage and 9 ½ acres land in Staunford. To hold to Thomas and his heirs; he gave 10 marks. Warranty by John and Agatha for themselves and the heirs of Agatha.
Westminster Octave of Trinity 16 Edward III [June 1342]

70. CP25/1/139/110/26

John Masoun chaplain plaintiff vs Robert de Wyke of Staunford and Agnes his wife defendant of 3 messuage, 16 acres land in Staunford. To hold to John and his heirs; he gave 20 marks. Warranty by Robert and Agnes for themselves and the heirs of Agnes.
Westminster Quindene of Easter 16 Edward III [April 1342]

71. CP25/1/139/111/21

Roger de Makeseye of Staunford baker plaintiff vs Walter ate Nonnes of Staunford and Joan his wife defendant of 1 messuage in Staunford. To hold to Walter and Joan for life; remainder to John de Chestre and Lora his wife and the heirs of their bodies; remainder to the right heirs of Joan.
Westminster Quindene of Michaelmas 17 Edward III [October 1343]

72. CP25/1/139/111/31

William de Shilvington of Newcastle upon Tyne plaintiff vs Henry de Carlton of Staunford and Lora his wife defendant of 3 messuages in Staunford. Quitclaim and warranty by Henry and Lora for themselves and the heirs of Lora. William gave £20.
Westminster Octave of Purification 17 Edward III [February 1343]

73. CP25/1/139/112/29

Thomas de Pontefracto of Staunford plaintiff vs Henry de Carleton of Staunford and Lora his wife defendant of 1 messuage in Staunford. Quitclaim and warranty by Henry and Lora for themselves and the heirs of Lora. Thomas gave 10 marks.
Westminster Quindene of Easter 18 Edward III [April 1344]

74. CP25/1/139/112/34

Hugh Tredflour of Staunford plaintiff vs John Templer of Badyngton and Maude his wife defendant of 2 messuages in Staunford. To hold to Hugh and his heirs. He has granted for himself and his heirs that they will render every year to John and Maude for their lives 13s 4d. If Hugh or his heirs fail in the payment of the money at any term, it shall be lawful for John and Maude for their whole lives to distrain Hugh and his heirs or those who hereafter shall hold the messuage by all goods and chattels found in the same and to retain them until the full payment of the money which was in arrears of any term. And after the death of John and Maude, Hugh and his heirs shall be quit of the payment of the money yearly for ever.
Westminster Morrow of the Ascension 18 Edward III/ Quindene of Trinity 18 Edward III [May, June 1344]

75. CP25/1/139/112/43

Walter Chapman of Staunford plaintiff vs John de Weston of Staunford cordewaner and Margaret his wife defendant of 1 messuage and 2 acres land in Staunford. To hold to Walter and his heirs; he gave 10 marks. Warranty by John and Margaret for themselves and the heirs of Margaret.
Westminster Octave of the Trinity 18 Edward III [June 1344]

76. CP25/1/139/114/7
John Cokerel of Staunford plaintiff vs James de Assheby of Staunford and Joan his wife defendant
3 messuages in Staunford. To hold to John and his heirs; he gave 100 marks. Warranty by James and Joan for themselves and the heirs of Joan.
Westminster Quindene of Easter 20 Edward III [April 1346]

77. CP25/1/139/115/6

Nicholas de Eston of Staunford clerk plaintiff vs John Sampson of Staunford and Emma his wife defendant of 1 messuage in Staunford. To hold to John and Emma for life of Nicholas and his heirs rendering yearly one rose at the feast of the Nativity of St John Baptist for all service to them and doing all services due to the chief lords; reversion to Nicholas and his heirs.
Westminster Quindene of Michaelmas 21 Edward III [October 1347]

78. CP25/1/139/116/24

John son of Walter de Tame of Siberton and Margaret his [John's] daughter plaintiffs vs Oliver Wynd of Staunford and Emma his wife defendant of 1 messuage in Staunford. Quitclaim and warranty by Oliver and Emma for themselves and the heirs of Emma. John and Margaret gave 100s.
Westminster Quindene of Hilary 22 Edward III/ Octave of Trinity 22 Edward III [January, June 1348]

79. CP25/1/140/118/19

Richard de Ardern of Staunford plaintiff vs William de Wakefeld of Leycestre and Emma his wife defendant of 3 messuages and 2 shops in Staunford. To hold to Richard and his heirs; he gave 10 marks. Warranty by William and Emma for themselves and the heirs of Emma.
Westminster Morrow of Martinmas 26 Edward III [November 1352]

80. CP25/1/140/118/40

John Bate of Staunford and John his son plaintiff by Alan de Wyrthorp put in their place vs Robert le Wayte and Alice his wife defendant of 1 messuage in Staunford. Quitclaim and warranty by Robert and Alice for themselves and the heirs of Alice. John and John gave 10 marks.
Westminster 3 weeks of Easter 28 Edward III [May 1354]

81. CP25/1/140/118/43

Roger Mundham of Staunford plaintiff by Alan de Wyrthorp put in his place vs Robert le Whayte and Alice his wife defendant of 3 messuages and 7 acres of land in Staunford. Quitclaim and warranty by Robert and Alice for themselves and the heirs of Alice. Roger gave 10 marks.
Westminster 3 weeks of Easter 28 Edward III [May 1354]

82. CP25/1/140/120/4

Thomas de Shordich and Isolda his wife plaintiff by John de Eston put in Isolda's place vs Robert le Smyth and Alice defendant of 1 messuage and 16 acres land in Staunford. Quitclaim and warranty by Robert and Alice for themselves and the heirs of Alice. To hold to Thomas and Isolda and the heirs of Thomas. Thomas and Isolda gave 20 marks.
Westminster Octave of the Purification 30 Edward III [February 1356]

83. CP25/1/140/120/14

John de Merssh of Staunford and Edusa his wife plaintiff vs Thomas de Shordych of Badyncton defendant of 1 messuage and 16 ½ acres land in Staunford. To hold to John and Edusa and the heirs of John. Warranty by Thomas for himself and his heirs.
Westminster 3 weeks of Easter 30 Edward III [May 1356]

84. CP25/1/140/120/27

William Harcourt of St Botulph plaintiff vs Richard de Brynkhill of Staunford and Agnes his wife defendant of 1 messuage and 47 ½ acres of land and 3 acres of meadow in Staumford Quitclaim and warranty by Richard and Agnes for themselves and the heirs of Agnes. William gave 100 marks.
Westminster Morrow of St John Baptist 30 Edward III/Quindene of Michaelmas 30 Edward III [September, October 1356]

85. CP25/1/140/121/4

John de Wyberton and Alice his wife plaintiff vs William de Hamerton and Joan his wife defendant of 1 messuage and 3 ½ acres land in Staumford. Quitclaim and warranty by William and Joan for themselves and the heirs of Joan. John and Alice gave 20 marks.
Westminster 3 weeks of Easter 31 Edward III [May 1357]

86. CP25/1/140/121/10

William de Steandeby of Staunford plaintiff by John de Uffyngton put in his place vs John Kirkeman of Uffyngton and Margaret his wife defendant of 2 messuages and 5acres 1 rood of land in Staunford. To hold to William and his heirs; he gave 20 marks. Warranty by John and Margaret for themselves and heirs of Margaret.

Westminster Octave of Trinity 31 Edward III [June 1357]

87. CP25/1/140/125/16

Nicholas de Eston of Staunford clerk plaintiff vs Hugh Ster of Makeseye taillour and Alice his wife defendant of 1 messuage and 5 acres of land in Staunford. Quitclaim and warranty by Hugh and Alice for themselves and the heirs of Alice. Nicholas gave 50 marks.
Westminster 3 Weeks of Easter 35 Edward III [April 1361]

88. CP25/1/141/128/3

William de Styandeby of Staunford plaintiff vs John Taverner of Staunford and Sarra his wife defendant of 22 acres of land in Staunford. Plea of covenant; quitclaim and warranty by John and Sarra for themselves and heirs of John. William gave 20 marks.
Westminster Quindene of Michaelmas 38 Edward III [October 1364]

89a. CP25/1/141/129/20

Henry Baynbrigge masoun plaintiff vs John Baillif of Casewyk and Cecily his wife defendant of 1 messuage in Staunford. Plea of covenant; quitclaim and warranty by John and Cecily for themselves and heirs of John. Henry gave 10 marks.
Westminster Quindene of Easter 40 Edward III [April 1366]

89b. CP 25/1/141/130/16.

John de Langham parson of St Michael [the Greater], Staunford', Robert de Caumpeden chaplain, and John de Weldon of Staunford plaintiff vs John Spicer of Staunford and Alice his wife defendants of 1 messuage and 2 shops in Staunford. John Spicer and Alice acknowledge the tenements to be the right of John de Weldon; quitclaim from themselves and the heirs of Alice to John de Langham, Robert and John de Weldon and the heirs of John de Weldon. John de Langham, Robert and John de Weldon have given them 20 marks of silver.
Westminster Quindene of Michaelmas 41 Edward III [October 1367].

90. CP25/1/141/130/38

William de Melton parson of the church of the Holy Trinity of Staunford plaintiff vs Robert Josep of Staunford and Lora his wife defendant of 1 messuage in Staunford. Plea of covenant; to hold to William and his heirs. He gave 10 marks. Quitclaim and warranty by Robert and Lora for themselves and heirs of Lora.
Westminster Quindene of Easter 41 Edward III [May 1367]

91. CP25/1/142/135/5

William Abbot of Castelbytham plaintiff vs Robert Cagge of Skyllyngton and Alice his wife defendant of 4 messuages and 64 acres of land in Staunford and Castelbytham. Plea of covenant. To hold to William Abbot and his heirs; he gave 40 marks, subject as to 2 messuages and 4 acres of land to the life interest of William Cormoraunt which he holds by the law of England; and as to 2 messuages and 60 acres of land to the life interest of Alice who was the wife of William Abbot. Warranty by Robert and Alice for themselves and the heirs of Alice.
Westminster Quindene of Hilary 46 Edward III / Westminster Quindene of Easter 46 Edward III [January, April 1372]

92. CP25/1/142/138/34

John Bonet plaintiff vs Hugh Swafeld and Margaret his wife defendant of 1 messuage in Staunford.
Plea of covenant. To hold to John and his heirs; he gave 20 marks. Quitclaim and warranty by Hugh and Margaret for themselves and the heirs of Margaret.
Westminster Octave of Trinity 49 Edward III [June 1375]

93. CP25/1/142/139/9

Thomas Cok of Gretham plaintiff vs John de Wakerle of Staunford and Juliana his wife defendant of 5 messuages, 8 acres 1 rood of land in Staunford. Plea of covenant: to hold to Thomas and his heirs; he gave 100 marks. Quitclaim by John and Juliana for themselves and the heirs of John
Westminster 50 Edward III Octave of the Purification [February 1376]

94. CP25/1/142/139/15

Nicholas Harwode of St Botulph plaintiff vs William de Skirbek of Staunford and Margaret his wife defendant of 1 messuage in Staunford. Plea of covenant to hold to Nicholas and his heirs; he gave 10 marks. Quitclaim and warranty by William and Margaret for themselves and the heirs of Margaret.
Westminster Quindene of Hilary 50 Edward III [January 1376]

95. CP25/1/142/139/18

John Chestre of Staunford sadeler' and Alice his wife plaintiff vs Richard Smyth of Wodeston and Ivetta his wife defendant of 1 messuage and 2 acres of land in Staunford. Plea of covenant to hold to John and Alice and the heirs of John; they gave 20 marks. Quitclaim and warranty by Richard and Ivetta for themselves and the heirs of Ivetta
Westminster 3 weeks of Easter 50 Edward III [May 1376]

96. CP25/1/142/139/40

William Makeseye plaintiff vs William Sawesthorp of Staunford carpenter and Alice his wife defendant of 1 messuage in Staunford. Plea of covenant to hold to William Makeseye and his heirs; he gave 20 marks. Quitclaim and warranty by William and Alice for themselves and the heirs of Alice.
Westminster Octave of Trinity 50 Edward III [June 1376]

97. CP25/1/143/145/38

William Danby plaintiff vs Simon Masone of Staunford and Maude his wife defendant
2 messuages and 1 acre of land in Staunford to hold to William and his heirs; he gave 100 marks; quitclaim by Simon and Maude for themselves and heirs of Maude.
Quindene of Hilary 8 Richard II [January 1384/5]

98. CP25/1/143/146/36

John Geffron, John de Weldon and Richard Chamberlayn vicar of the church of St Martin of Staunford plaintiff vs Richard Jouy of Morcote and Avicia his wife defendant
1 messuage and 4 acres 1 rood of land in Staunford to hold to John, John and Richard and the heirs of Richard. They gave 10 marks; quitclaim by Richard and Avicia and the heirs of Richard; warranty by Richard for himself and his heirs.
Morrow of the Ascension/Octave of the Trinity 10 Richard II [June, June 1386]

99. CP25/1/143/147/43

Robert Stolham, William Stacy and William Everard chaplain plaintiff vs Robert Josep and Lora his wife defendant
1 messuage and 2 shops in Staunford to hold to Robert, William and William and the heirs of Robert; they gave 20 marks. Quitclaim and warranty by Robert and Lora for themselves and the heirs of Lora
Octave of Michaelmas /Octave of Hilary 14 Richard II [October 1390, January 1391]

100. CP25/1/144/149/16

John de Heton parson of the church of Benyfeld and John de Naunby chaplain plaintiffs vs Richard de Leyne of Bulkyngton and Margery his wife defendant of 6 messuage, 3 tofts, and 200 acres of land in Castelbytham, Estbytham and Staumford. To hold to John and John and the heirs of John de Heton; they gave £100. Quitclaim and warranty by Richard and Margery for themselves and the heirs of Margery.
Westminster Quindene of Easter 17 Richard II [May 1394]

101. CP25/1/144/150/27

Stephen Makesey of Staunford and Nicholas Greneham clerk plaintiff vs John Herlyngton of Yakesley defendant of 8 messuages, 45 ½ acres land, 18s of rent, and rent of 1 cock and 2 hens in Staunford and of the advowson of the chantry to the altar of St Nicholas in the church of St Clement of Staunford. To hold to Stephen and Nicholas and the heirs of Stephen; they gave 100 marks.
Quitclaim and warranty by John for himself and his heirs.
Westminster Quindene of Martinmas 20 Richard II [November 1396]

102. CP25/1/144/151/12

Richard Stake of Staunford and Amie his wife plaintiff vs Walter Smyth of Exton and Agnes his wife defendant of 1 messuage in Staunford. To hold to Richard and Amie and the heirs of Richard; they gave 20 marks. Quitclaim and warranty by Walter and Agnes for themselves and the heirs of Agnes.
Westminster Month of Easter 2 Henry IV [May 1401]

103. CP25/1/144/151/13

John Smyth of Staunford plaintiff vs Richard Stake of Staunford and Amy his wife defendant of 1 messuage in Staunford. To hold to John and his heirs; he gave 100s. Quitclaim and warranty by Richard and Amy for themselves and the heirs of Richard.
Westminster Morrow of Ascension 2 Henry IV [May 1401]

104. CP25/1/144/151/17

Andrew Cotyngham of North Luffenham plaintiff vs Richard Stake of Staunford and Amy his wife defendant of 1 messuage in Staunford. To hold to Andrew and his heirs; he gave 10 marks. Quitclaim and warranty by Richard and Amy for themselves and the heirs of Richard.
Westminster Quindene of Trinity 2 Henry IV [June 1401]

105. CP25/1/144/151/31

Henry Cok of Staunford, Gervase Wykes of Staunford and John Fraunceys chaplain plaintiff vs Thomas Soureby of Staunford and Margaret his wife defendant of 1 messuage, 30 acres land in Staunford and Wyrthorp. To hold to Henry, Gervase and John and the heirs of Henry. They gave 20 marks. Quitclaim and warranty by Thomas and Margaret for themselves and the heirs of Margaret
Westminster Morrow of St John Baptist 3 Henry IV [November 1402]

106. CP25/1/144/151/50

John Rawele and John son of Robert Masthorp of Staunford plaintiff vs John Wellowe of Cathorp and Alice his wife defendant of 2 shops in Staunford. To hold to John and

John and the heirs of John son of Robert. They gave 100s. Quitclaim and warranty by John and Alice for themselves and the heirs of Alice.
Westminster Quindene of Easter 5 Henry IV [April 1404]

107. CP25/1/145/156/8

Thomas Harleston of Berughby and John Cobbets of Ryall plaintiff vs Richard Thorneff and Katherine his wife defendant
6 messuages, 5 tofts, 160 acres of land, 6 acres of meadow in Carleby, Witham, Ouneby, Stowe by Depyng, Bourthorp and Staunford to hold to Thomas and John and the heirs of Thomas; they gave 100 marks. Quitclaim and warranty by Richard and Katherine for themselves and the heirs of Katherine.
Morrow of Martinmas 2 Henry VI [November 1423]

108. CP25/1/145/156/30

Thomas Chaworth, knight, John Horspole clerk, Thomas Nevyll esquire, Norman Babyngton esquire and John Taillour chaplain plaintiff vs Michael Cranwell and Katherine his wife defendant
Manor of Grantham called 'le Garette' and of 13 messuages, 6 shops *[etc etc including rents in Grantham and six other named places]* and Staunford, to hold to Thomas and John, Thomas *etc*; they gave 200 marks. Quitclaim and warranty by Michael and Katherine and the heirs of Katherine
Morrow of the Purification 5 Henry VI [February 1427]

107 CP25/1/145/157/17

Thomas Basset of Staumford, Robert Adekyn clerk, John Adekyn and John Chevercourt and Margaret his wife plaintiff vs John Yowe of Whitwell defendant of 1 messuage in the parish of St George in Staumford. To hold to Thomas, Robert, John, John and Margaret and the heirs of John Chevercourt ; they gave 20 marks. Quitclaim and warranty by John Yowe for himself and his heirs.
Westminster Octave of the Purification 8 Henry VI [February 1430]

110. CP25/1/145/157/30

Thomas Basset of Staumford, Robert Adekyn clerk, John Adekyn and John Chevercourt and Margaret his wife plaintiff vs John Yowe of Whitwell defendant
1 messuage in the parish of St George of Staumford to hold to Thomas *[et al, as above]* and the heirs of John Chevercourt; they gave 20 marks. Warranty by John Yowe for himself and his heirs
Octave of the Purification 8 Henry VI [February 1430]

111. CP25/1/145/159/25

Robert Orewyn of Staunford and Thomas Barker plaintiff vs William Reynald of Hameldon son and heir of John Reynald junior and Joan his wife defendant
1 messuage in Staunford to hold to Robert and Thomas the heirs of Robert; they gave £20. Warranty by William and Joan for themselves and the heir of Joan
Octave of the Purification 22 Henry VI [February 1444]

112a. CP25/1/145/160/33

John Scherman, John Chevercourt and John Frebarne plaintiff vs William Scherman and Agnes his wife defendant
1 messuage in Staunford to hold to John, John and John and the heirs of John Scherman; they gave 20 marks. Warranty by William and Agnes for themselves and the heirs of Agnes
Fortnight of Martinmas 30 Henry VI [November 1451]; Octave of Hilary [January 1452]

112b. CP25/1/145/161/9

William Hekham plaintiff vs John Apethorp late of Staunford and Joan his wife defendant
2 messuages and one garden in Staunford to hold to William and his heirs; he gave 40l. Warranty by John and Joan for themselves and the heirs of John.
Fortnight of Easter 32 Henry VI [May 1454]

113a CP25/1/192/3/36
Peter de Monte Forti plaintiff vs Gunfrey (*Gunfridus*) de Legh and Alice his wife defendants, of a quarter part of one messuage, one toft, one hide, and nine and a half bovates and eight acres of land, with the appurtenances in Staunford, Breiles, Northluffenham and Wenge, gift and quitclaim by Gunfrey and Alice and heirs of Alice to Peter and his heirs. He paid ten marks.
Oakham Morrow of St. Peter ad Vincula 31 Henry III [August 1247]

113b CP25/1/192/4/18
Nicholas de Burton and Cecily his wife plaintiff vs Roger de Offinton and Joan his wife defendants, of forty-one acres of land, four acres of meadow, and a third part of one messuage with appurtenances in Tekencote and Staunford: plea of covenant; Roger and Joan recognized the holding to be the right of Cecily and rendered it to her in the same court, and remitted and quitclaimed for themselves and the heirs of Joan to Nicholas and Cecily and the heirs of Cecily. They paid one sore sparrowhawk. [
Westminster One week from Hilary 16 Edward I [January 1288]

113c CP25/1/192/6/20
Thomas son of Walter de Casterton (by John de Caldon) plaintiff vs Clement de Casterton and Margery his wife defendants, of one messuage and seventeen and a half

acres of land with appurtenances in Staunford and Casterton; plea of covenant; Clement and Margery recognized the holding to be the right of Thomas as that which he had by their gift to have and to hold to Thomas and his heirs of the chief lord of the fee for the customary services; warranty by Clement and his heirs to Thomas and his heirs. He paid £20.

York Morrow of St. John the Baptist 8 Edward III, and one week from St. Martin in the same year [June/November 1334]

114. CP25/1/285/26/330

John prior of church of Blessed Mary at Sempringham plaintiff by William de Horbling put in his place vs master Robert Luterel defendant of 4 messuages, 2 carucates of land and 12 marks of rent in Keten and Cotesmore in co. Rutland and of 1 messuage, 1 carucate of land and 10 marks of rent in Staunfford and Casterton in co. Lincoln. Plea of covenant: Robert has acknowledged the tenements to be the right of the prior and his church of St Mary as those which the prior has of the gift of Robert. To have and to hold to the prior and his successors and his church of St Mary of the chief lords of that fee by the services which belong to those tenements for ever. And for this, the prior has granted for himself and his successors that they henceforth shall find every year 3 chaplains celebrating divine service for the soul of Robert and his ancestors, that is to say one secular chaplain for celebrating divine service in the church of St Andrew of Irnham at the altar of St Andrew, another secular chaplain for celebrating divine service in the chapel of the blessed Mary situated in his* manor of Staunford, and a third regular chaplain for celebrating the mass of St Mary daily in the conventual church of Sempringham for ever. Moreover the prior has granted for himself and his successors that they will render every year to Robert for the whole life of Robert 20 marks at 4 terms etc. And after the death of Robert the prior and his successors shall be quit of the payment of the money yearly for ever. And this concord was made by precept of the king.

York Quindene of St Hilary 32 Edward I; afterwards at Westminster in octave of St Martin 34 Edward I [January 1304; November 1306]

* *It would seem this refers to the Luterel manor in Stamford rather than the Sempringham manor in Stamford*

115. CP25/1/285/26/336

Hugh de Aluerton of Staunford plaintiff vs Roger son of Simon de Uffinton and Joan his wife defendant of 3 messuages, 1 ½ acres of meadow, 39s 5d of rent and rent of 1 lb of pepper, the fourth part of 1 lb of cummin and the fourth part of 1 mill in Staunford and Crouland in co. Lincoln. And of 2s 8d of rent and rent of 2 capons [*caponum*] in Eton, Thornhawe, Wetring and Bourghle in co. Northamptonshire and of 12 acres of land in Little Casterton and Bradecroft in co. Rutland. Plea of covenant: Roger and Joan have acknowledged the tenements to be the right of Hugh and have rendered them to him in the same court. And have remised and quitclaimed from themselves and the heirs of Joan to Hugh and his heirs for ever. And for this, Hugh has given to Roger and Joan £20 sterling.

Westminster Octave of Purification of BVM 35 Edward I [February 1307]

116. CP25/1/286/31/194

Eustace Malherbe and Lora his wife plaintiff by the aforesaid Eustace put in the place of Lora vs Geoffrey de Wytteslad defendant of 3 messuage, 40 acres of land and 4 acres meadow in Staunford in co. Lincoln and of 6 acres of land in Burgle in co. Northampton. Plea of covenant: Eustace has acknowledged the aforesaid tenements to be the right of Geoffrey as that which he has of Eustace's gift. For this Geoffrey has granted to Eustace and Lora the aforesaid tenements and has rendered them to them in the same court. To have and to hold to Eustace and Lora of Geoffrey and his heirs for the whole life of Eustace and Lora, rendering therefore yearly 1 rose at the feast of the nativity of St John Baptist for all service custom and exaction to Geoffrey and his heirs belonging. And doing therefore to the chief lords of that fee for Geoffrey and his heirs all the other services which belong to the tenements for the whole life of Eustace and Lora. After the death of Eustace and Lora the tenements shall revert wholly to Geoffrey and his heirs quit of the heirs of Eustace and Lora. To hold of the chief lords of that fee by the services which belong to the tenements for ever.
Westminster 3 weeks from St Michael's Day 14 Edward II [October 1320]

117. CP25/1/286/31/198

John de Ellerker the elder plaintiff vs Robert de Neuwerk and Matilda his wife defendant of 4 messuages, 2 "shopis", 1 garden, 53 acres of land, 6 acres meadow, 4 acres of pasture in Staunford in co. Lincoln and of 10 acres of land and 7 acres of meadow in Staunford and Bradecroft in co. Rutland. Robert and Matilda have acknowledged the foresaid tenements to be the right of John and have rendered them to him in the same court. To have and to hold to John and his heirs, to wit, three messuages and the foresaid garden of the chief lords of that fee. All the residue of the foresaid tenements of the king and his heirs by the services which to the aforesaid tenements belong for ever.
For this, John has given to Robert and Matilda £100 sterling. And this concord as to all the aforesaid tenements except the three messuages and the aforesaid garden was made by order of the king.
Westminster Octave of St Martin 14 Edward II [November 1320]

118. CP25/1/286/32/234

Thomas de Chesterton and Margery daughter of Stephen de Abyndon plaintiffs vs Thomas parson of the church of Depyngge defendant of 1 messuage, 1 mill, 11 acres land, 25 acres meadow, 42s of rent and the mediety of 1 carucate of land in Staunford and Depyngge in co. Lincoln; and of 2 messuages, 1 ½ carucates of land, 24 ½ acres of meadow in Suthorp, Eston, …le, Pillesgate, Bernak, Upton and Makeseye in co. Northampton. Thomas de Chesterton has acknowledged the aforesaid tenements to be the right of Thomas the parson. Of which the same Thomas has 2 parts of the aforesaid tenements of the gift of Thomas de Chesterton. For this Thomas the parson has granted to Thomas de Chesterton and Margery the same two parts and has rendered them in the same court. To have and to hold to Thomas de Chesterton and Margery and their heirs begotten of their bodies, of the chief lords of that fee by the services which to that part belong. If Thomas de Chesterton and Margery die without heir of their bodies, after their deaths the two parts to remain wholly to Stephen de Abyndon and Matilda his wife and the heirs begotten of their bodies to hold to the chief lords of that fee. After the deaths of Stephen and Matilda, if there are no lawful heirs, then the two parts are to remain to the rightful heirs of Thomas de Chesterton to hold to the chief lords of that fee by the services which to those parts belong.

Moreover Thomas the parson has granted for himself and his heirs that the third part of the aforesaid tenements which the aforesaid Stephen and Matilda held in dower of the inheritance of Thomas the parson in the aforesaid vills on the day in which this concord was made and which after the death of Matilda ought to revert to Thomas the parson and his heirs, after the death of Matilda shall remain wholly to Thomas de Chesterton and Margery and their heirs aforesaid.

To hold, together with the aforesaid 2 parts which remain to them by this fine, to the chief lords of that fee. If it happen that Thomas de Chesterton and Margery die without an heir begotten of their bodies, then after their deaths the same third part shall remain wholly to the rightful heirs of Thomas de Chesterton to hold of the chief lords of that fee by the services which to that same third part shall belong for ever.

And this concord was made, Stephen and Matilda being present and acknowledging it – and they did fealty to Thomas de Chesterton and Margery in the same court.

Westminster Octave of St Michael 18 Edward II [October 1324]

119. CP25/1/286/33/255

Simon de Sutton clerk plaintiff vs William de Sutton and Beatrice his wife defendant of 30 acres land, 4 acres of meadow, 2 acres of pasture and the mediety of 6 messuages and 1 toft in Blatherwyk, Wakerle, Laxton and Bolewik in co. Northampton; and of 1 messuage in Staunford in co. Lincoln. William and Beatrice have acknowledged the aforesaid tenements to be the right of Simon as those which he has of their gift. And for this he has granted to them the aforesaid tenements and has rendered them to them in the same court to have and to hold to William and Beatrice and the heirs of Beatrice begotten of her body of the chief lords of that fee by the services which to the aforesaid tenements belong for ever. If Beatrice dies without heirs, then after the death of William and Beatrice the aforesaid tenements to remain wholly to Simon son of Thomas de Sutton and the heirs of his body to hold of the chief lords of that fee by the services which to the aforesaid tenements belong for ever. If Simon son of Thomas dies without heirs, then they shall remain wholly to William brother of the same Simon, clerk and his heirs to hold of the chief lords of that fee by the services which to the aforesaid tenements belong for ever.

Westminster Octave of Holy Trinity 18 Edward II [June 1325]

120. CP25/1/286/39/218

Thomas son of Gilbert de Chesterton of Grantham plaintiff vs Henry Darcy of London and Margery his wife defendant of [*considerable property in Northamptonshire, Lincoln and Lincolnshire including*] some (no details) in Stamford. Thomas gave 200 marks.

York Month of Michaelmas 11 Edward III [October 1337]

121. CP25/1/287/40/289

Roger le Scauelar and Robert Beaufitz plaintiffs vs William Beaufitz and Margaret his wife defendants of 2 messuages and 2 acres of land in Staunford in co. Lincoln; and of 13 ½ acres land in Staunford and Little Casterton in co. Rutland. Plea of covenant. To hold to Roger and Robert and the heirs of Roger; they gave 40 marks. Warranty by William and Margaret for themselves and the heirs of Margaret
Westminster Quindene of Easter 15 Edward III [April 1341]

122. CP25/1/288/46/591

Robert de Wyk of Staunford plaintiff vs Alueredus de Cornwayle and Christiana his wife defendant of 2 messuages and 8 acres of land in Staunford in co. Lincoln. And of 12 acres land in Little Casterton and Bradecroft in co. Rutland. Plea of covenant. To hold to Robert and his heirs; he gave 20 marks. Warranty by Alured and Christiana for themselves and the heirs of Christiana.
Westminster Octave of Michaelmas 35 Edward III [October 1361]

123. CP25/1/288/48/679

John Knyvet and Alianora his wife and Robert his son plaintiff vs John Spycer of Staunford and Alice his wife defendant of 8 messuages, 24 ½ acres land, 8s of rent and rent of 1 cock and 2 hens in Staunford; and of the advowson of the chantry at the altar of St Nicholas in the church of St Clement of Staunford in co. Lincoln and of 17 ½ acres land and the moiety of 1 acre of meadow in Casterton and Keton in Rutland. Quitclaim from John and Alice and the heirs of Alice to John and Alianora and Robert and the heirs of John. John, Alianora and Robert gave 100 marks.
Westminster Quindene of Michaelmas 41 Edward III [October 1367]

124. CP25/1/289/53/51

Ralph de Crophill parson of the church of Cotyngham, Richard de Bytham parson of two parts of the church of Repinghale, John Lopere parson of the third part of the church of Repinghale, Alan de Kirkeby chaplain plaintiffs vs John Goderiche and Alianora his wife defendant. Manors of Ryngesdon and Lesyngham; 3 messuages and 8 acres land and 100s of rent in Kyllyngholme, Staumford and Walcote in co. Lincoln. And of the manor of Fletewyk in co. Bedfordshire, and of 6 marks of rent in Lowesby in co. Leics. And of the manor of Brendeshall in co. Essex and of the manor of Thorn Gobaud in co. Yorkshire.
John and Alianora have acknowledged the aforesaid manors and tenements to be the right of Ralph. And they have rendered the manors of Ryngesdon, Lesyngham, Brendeshall and the tenements to Ralph, Richard, John Lepere [sic] and Alan. To hold to them and the heirs of Ralph. And moreover John and Alianora have granted for themselves and the heirs of Alianora that the manors of Fletwyk and Thorn Gobaud which John de Clinton[?] and Joan his wife hold for the life of Joan of the inheritance of Alianora the day on which this concord was made, and which after the death of Joan ought to revert to John and Alianora and the heirs of Alianora after the death of Joan

shall remain to Ralph, Richard, John Lepere *[sic]* and Alan and the heirs of Ralph. They
gave 400 marks. Warranty by John and Alianora and the heirs of Alianora.
Westminster Octave of Trinity 46 Edward III/Quindene of Easter 4 Richard II [June
1372/ April 1381]
Note: some Lincoln[shire] property not mentioned in the second half of the document.

125. CP25/1/289/54/137

John de Weldon of Staunford and William de Makeseye of Staunford plaintiff vs John
Willy of Kyngesclyve and Joan his wife defendant of 2 messuages, 24 ½ acres land and 1
rood of pasture in Staunford in co. Lincoln and of 1 ½ acres land and 1 acre of meadow
in Pillesgate and Walcote by Bernake in co. Northampton. To hold to John and William
and the heirs of John; they gave £20.
Quitclaim and warranty by John and Joan for themselves and the heirs of Joan.
Westminster Octave of Hilary 9 Richard II [January 1386]

126. CP25/1/293/70/270

William bishop of Lincoln, Ralph Cromwell knight, Nicholas Dixon clerk, William
Tresham, John Taylboys, William Heton, Thomas Palmer and William Stanlowe plaintiff
vs William earl of Suffolk and Alice his wife defendant Manor of Little Burley; 129 acres
of land and 8 ½ acres of meadow in Burley and Pillesgate in co. Northampton; and 9
messuages, 4 tofts, 129 acres of land, 24 acres of meadow and 20s of rent in Staunford,
of which messuages one is called "le Taberd" in co. Lincoln, to hold to the bishop,
Ralph, Nicholas etc *[as above]* and the heirs of Ralph. They gave £200. Quitclaim and
warranty by the earl and Alice for themselves and the heirs of Alice against the prior of
Eye and his successors.
Octave of Hilary 21 Henry VI [January 1443]

127. CP25/1/293/70/283

Ralph Cromwell knight, Richard Moresby clerk, William Gresham, Thomas Palmer and
William Weldon plaintiff vs Elizabeth who was the wife of Richard Grey knight and
Elizabeth who was the wife of Richard Vernon esquire defendant Various manors and
extensive property in South Wytham and Metryngham and property in various places
including *[unspecified]* in Staunford to hold to Ralph etc *[as above]* and the heirs of Ralph.
They gave £1000. Quitclaim and warranty by Elizabeth and Elizabeth and heirs of
Elizabeth who was wife of Richard Grey for herself and her heirs.
Octave of Hilary 22 Henry VI [January 1444]

128 CP25/1/293/72/361

John Browen, William Browen and William Hawlle clerk plaintiff vs John Apethorpe and
Joan his wife and Robert Loryng defendant. Three messuages and 10 acres of land in
Staunford in co. Lincoln, 3 acres of meadow in Staunford in co. Northants, and 12 acres
of land and 2 acres of meadow in Staunford, Bradcroft and Little Casterton in co.

Rutland to hold to John, William and William and the heirs of John; they gave 100 marks. Warranty by John and Joan and Robert for themselves and the heirs of Joan. Octave of St John Baptist 29 Henry VI [September 1450]

129 CP25/1/293/72/364

John Browen, William Browen and William Hawlle clerk plaintiff vs John Apethorpe and Joan his wife and Robert Loryng. Three messuages, 10 acres of land cp in Stamford and 3 acres meadow cp in Stamford, Northants, and 12 acres land and 2 acres meadow in Stamford, Bradcroft and Little Casterton, Rutland; John Apethorpe, Joan and Robert Loryng recognise the property to John Browen; release and quitclaim to John Browne, William Browne and William Hawlle and heirs of John Browne; warranty; payment of 100 marks
Octaves of St John the Baptist 29 Henry VI [Sep 1450]

129a CP25/1/294/79/37

Elizabeth Elmes widow and William Elmes plaintiffs vs Henry Wykes clerk defendant Manor of Swynested, 16 messuages, 200 acres of land, 40 acres of meadow and 40 acres of pasture in Witham and Staunford, Lincs; the manors of Papley and Lilford, Northants; and other property in Northants and Rutland. Quitclaim and warranty by this fine to Elizabeth and William and the heirs of William.
  Morrow of St John the Baptist 10 Henry VII [30 August 1494]

130. CP25/2/25/155/7

Christopher Broun and Richard Beverage clerk plaintiff vs Thomas Laurence and Joan his wife defendants 3 messuages, 1 toft, 1 dovecote and lands in Staunford to hold of the defendants for themselves and the heirs of Joan to the plaintiffs and the heirs of Christopher.
2 Henry VIII [1510-11]

131. CP25/2/25/158/9

Francis Browne esquire, Godfrey Folyambe knight, John Mathewe, James Waren and William Hygdon chaplain plaintiffs vs Robert Browne and Edmund Browne defendants. One messuage, 1 dovecote etc in Stamford to hold of the defendants for themselves and their heirs to the plaintiffs and the heirs of Francis.
19 Henry VIII [1527-8]

132. CP25/2/25/159/22

Edward Broun plaintiff vs Francis Broun esquire defendant One messuage, one dovecote and other prop[erty in Staunford to hold to Edward Broun.
21 Henry VIII [1529-30]

133. CP25/2/25/163/39

Thomas Watson plaintiff vs Richard Morecrofte and Agnes his wife defendant One messuage in Staumfford in the parish of St John the Baptist in le Castell Dyke; warranty from the defendants for themselves and the heirs of Agnes.
26 Henry VIII [1534-35]

134. CP25/2/25/165/29

John Haryngton and ?Thomas Moigne esquire plaintiff vs John Lytell gent defendant Seven messuages and other property in Staunford to hold to the plaintiffs and heirs of Thomas
28 Henry VIII [1536-7]

135. CP25/2/25/167/42

William Berage plaintiff vs Richard Potter and Joan his wife late the wife of John Tyard, Richard Morecrofte and Agnes his wife daughter and heir of John Tyard and Joan defendant Two messuages etc in the parish of St Michael at Arches in Staunford; warranty from defendants for themselves and the heirs of Joan and Agnes
Hilary 30 Henry VIII [January 1539]

136. CP25/2/26/170/46

Henry Lacy and Robert Lacy plaintiff vs Richard Smyth son and heir of William Smyth and Elizabeth his wife defendant Seven messuages, 6 cottages and lands in Staunford to hold to the plaintiffs and heirs of Henry; warranty against the aforesaid Richard and his heirs.
33 Henry VIII [1541-2]

137. CP25/2/26/174/15

John Shepe plaintiff vs Thomas Gedney defendant One messuage and land in Staunford Thomas acknowledges the premises to belong to John.
36 Henry VIII [1544-5]

138. CP25/2/51/365/9

William Compton knight, Robert Norwiche serjeant-at-law to the king, Humphrey Broun serjeant-at-law, Richard Clerk and David Cecille gent plaintiff vs Thomas Willyam senior. and William Willyam defendant Manor of Staumford, 10 messuages, 3 tofts, lands and 40s rent in Staumford. Thomas Willyam and William Willyam have granted for themselves and their heirs that the aforesaid premises which Henry Chambers and Margaret his wife hold for the term of the life of Margaret are to remain thereafter to the heirs of the body of Margaret lawfully begotten of the inheritance of Thomas Willyam

and William Willyam on the day in which this concord was made etc. To hold of the defendants for themselves and their heirs to the plaintiffs and the heirs of William Compton against John abbot of the monastery of St Peter, Westminster* and his successors.
18 Henry VIII
This is probably an error for Peterborough. This manor was in Stamford Baron.

139. CP25/2/51/366/18

David Cecill senior and George Guarles plaintiff vs Henry Hamport *alias* Chambers and Margaret his wife defendant Manor of Staumford, 10 messuages, 3 tofts, lands and 40s rent in Staumford; warranty from defendants for themselves and the heirs of Margaret to the plaintiffs and the heirs of David.
Easter 20 Henry VIII [April 1528]
[*See 138*]

140. CP25/2/51/367/5

Robert Mousedale plaintiff vs Robert Walbyeff and Anne his wife defendant Ten messuages, 6 cottages, lands and 20s rent in Staunford, Depyn, Tallington, Shylyngthorpe, Manthorpe, Barholme and Stowe. Warranty from defendants for themselves and the heirs of Anne. And if it happen that Robert Walbyeff and Anne die without an heir of their bodies lawfully begotten between them, after the death of Robert and Anne the premises shall remain to James Walbyeff and his heirs.
Trinity 21 Henry VIII [May 1529]

141. CP25/2/51/368/15

Thomas Brudenell senior esquire, Walter Hendle, John Bosse, John Colson senior, Griffin Colier and Richard Ball plaintiff vs John Elmys esquire and Edith his wife defendant Manor of Swynested, 16 messuages and lands in Swynsted, Witham and Staunford.Warranty from defendants for themselves and the heirs of Edith to the plaintiffs and the heirs of Thomas.
Michaelmas 23 Henry VIII [September 1531]

142. CP25/2/51/368/24

Thomas Clement, Humphrey Gulson, Thomas Dansey, William Gulson and John Clement plaintiff vs John Houre gent and Joan his wife defendant The mediety of the manor of Carleby, 7 messuages, lands, 6s of rent, rent of 1lb of pepper, 1lb of cummin and common of pasture for 20 beasts and 300 sheep in Carleby, Stanford and Talyngton; also the advowson of the church of Carleby, the alternate turn when it shall happen [*alterna vice cum acciderit*]. Warranty from defendants for themselves and the heirs of Joan to the plaintiffs and the heirs of Humphrey against John Houre and Joan and their heirs.
Hilary 23 Henry VIII [January 1532]

143. CP25/2/52/373/2

Robert Browne plaintiff vs Robert Walbeeff gent defendant Seven messuages, 6 cottages and lands in Barham *alias* Barholme, Stowe and Staunford
30 Henry VIII [1538-9]

144. CP25/2/52/375/15

Thomas Dygname and Robert Stokyll plaintiffs vs Thomas Philyppys clerk defendant Manor of Ufford, 20 messuages, 20 cottages, 12 tofts, 3 dovecotes, 3 watermills, lands and 40s of rent in Ufford and Staunford; the advowson of the church of Ufford, to hold to the plaintiffs and the heirs of Thomas Dygname. Warranty by Thomas Philyppys to Thomas Dygname and Robert and heirs of Thomas Dygname. After the death of Thomas Phylyppys the aforesaid premises shall remain wholly to the president and scholars [*sic*] and their successors to hold of the chief lords of that fee etc.
Hilary 32 Henry VIII [January 1541]

EXCHEQUER ANCIENT DEEDS SERIES A

145. E40/1436

Grant in free alms by Amicia daughter of Geoffrey son of Outhild' widow to the church of St Michael outside Stanford' and the nuns there, for the health of the soul of William de Ketene her husband etc, of her houses which she bought from William Pynkyl of Stanford' and Roger his son, which houses are situated in the parish of Holy Trinity Stanford' between the houses of Henry Pykard towards the west and the houses which she bought from the aforesaid William Pynkyl towards the east. The grant is made to give a pittance to the same nuns twice yearly.

Witnesses: Richard Pecke, Hugh son of Reymer, Walter le Flemeng', Henry de Sybecey, Walter de Brunne, William de Notingham, Andrew Arketel, Isaac Lucas, Alexander Lucas, Robert de Welledon', Ralph de Stokes, William son of David, Norman de Grecton', William Reyner and others.

Seals: slits for tag

Not dated: ? mid 13th century

146. E40/5093   8 September 1352

Quitclaim by John son of Thomas Taillour of Staunford clerk to Walter de Nerford of Staunford and to his heirs or assignees of all his right and claim in those tenements in Staunford outside the east gates which lie between the tenement formerly of Richard Melemakere on the east and the tenement formerly of John Brab[..] rector of the church of Edmerthorp' on the west.

Witnesses: William de Sheluynton', Eustace de Assewell', Hugh Tredeflour, John de Wakirlee of Staunford and others.

Given at Staunford

Seal: oval; ⅞"x ¾"; device and legend indecipherable; green wax; tag

Endorsed: pro terr' in Staunford (seventeenth century)

147. E40/14365   **11 June 1306**

Lease for life by John earl of Warenne to Thomas de la Paneterie his 'vallet' for his service of the whole place where the friars of the sack used to dwell in the suburb of Staunford outside the west gate, with the walls and buildings.

Witnesses: sir [*Monsieur*] William Paynel, sir John de Nevill, sir Thomas de Ponyngg', Eustace Malherbe, Clement de Meltone, Hugh de Aluerton', John Braban, Richard de Thurston', William de Saunford [*sic*] and others.

Given at Estaunford

Seal: missing: traces of red wax; tag

Endorsed: Earl of Warrens grant of tenement in Stamford (not contemporary, nineteenth century hand).
FRENCH

148. E40/15872   **1353-54**

Final concord William son of William Semer deforciant to Robert de Craunford plaintiff in a tenement in Stanford, Northants, valued at 100s Easter term 27 Edward III

EXCHEQUER: DEEDS AND CHARTERS, TRANSCRIPTS

149. E132/3/54 (i)
A small cartulary of the gild of St Mary, Stamford

149.1 E132/3/54 (i)
Grant in free alms by Adam Plowham burgess of Staunford to God and St Mary and to the Alderman and brothers of the gild of St Mary for celebrating the mass of the same virgin in the church of St Mary [at the bridge?] in perpetuity and for maintaining the alms of the aforesaid gild, of 12d annual rent from a shop in Butchers' Street towards [?

the north? which] Henry Moryng' holds of Adam in fee farm in the parish of St John Staunford between the lane which goes towards [illegible] and the shop of the aforesaid Henry on the west.

In witness etc [*sic*]

Given etc [*sic*]

149.2 E132/3/54 (ii)

Bequest in free alms with warranty by (?) sir Alexander son of Reyner burgess of Staunford to God and St Mary and to the Alderman and brothers of the gild of St Mary and for celebrating the mass of the same virgin in the church of [St Mary …] of Staunford in perpetuity, of 12d annual quit rent to be received at Christmas from a shop in the Drapery which […] holds of the aforesaid Alexander in fee farm.

149.3 E132/3/54 (iii)

Grant by William de Sudbury' burgess of Staunford for the health of his soul and of the souls of his predecessors and successors and of the soul of Richard the serjeant of Brunne for the maintenance of the mass of St Mary at the bridge of Staunford in the said church, of 3s annual quit rent to be received quarterly, namely 2s from those two shops which are situated in the market of Staunford 'behinde the bak' by the shop of Alexander Potesmouth' towards the south and 12d from the aforesaid [*sic*] house which is situated in the parish of St Michael the Greater Staunford between the houses of Nicholas de Asseby towards the south and the houses of Hastolf the weaver towards the north.

149.4 El32/3/54 (iv)

Bond by Robert de Rykeman burgess of Staunford to pay the 12d annual quit rent which Alexander son of Reyner de Staunford granted in free alms to God and St Mary and for the maintenance of the mass of St Mary in the church of St Mary by the bridge, Staunford, from that shop which is situated in the parish of All Saints in the Market of Staunff', namely in the Drapery between the shop formerly of Geoffrey de Reynham towards the east and a certain shop of William de Ryppes towards the west: the rent was in arrears to the peril of the soul of the said Alexander and of the soul of Robert. [*See 149.2*]

149.5 E132/3/54 (v)

Grant in free alms by Abselon son of Simon at the bridge of Stannford' for the maintenance of the mass of St Mary to be celebrated in the church of St Mary by the bridge of Staunford' of half an acre of land lying in the field(s) of Staunford' towards the ditch against Aldawe, that namely which lies between the land of Henry rector of the church of St John Staunford towards the east and the land of Michael de Wirthorp towards the west.

149.6 E132/3/54 (vi)

Sale by Henry son of Henry de Tykyncote sometime burgess of Staunford to the brethren of the gild of St Mary at the bridge of Staunford for four marks of silver, of two shops situated in Butchers' Street Staunford between the shops formerly of Richard de Luffenham towards the west on one side and the shop of Reyner de Blatherwyk' towards the east on the other. To hold to the said brothers of the same gild and their successors free of all secular service, saving service to the lord of the fee.

149.7 E132/3/54 (vii)

Quitclaim by Richard de Bukmynstr' weaver to the proctor maintaining the mass of St Mary the virgin to be celebrated solemnly day by day in the church of the same virgin near the bridge of Staunford for 10s sterling of all his right and claim in the name of fee or any manner whatsoever in those houses which he built and erected on an empty plot which he held in fee farm or otherwise of the Alderman and brethren of the gild of St Mary in Staunford, which houses are situated in the parish of St Michael of Cornstall' between the house of William de Bulkyngham towards the east and the house of Peter de Aslekston' towards the west.

149.8 E132/3/54 (viii)

Grant in free alms by Reginald the dyer of Staunford to God and St Mary for maintaining the mass of the same virgin of [*sic*] the church of St Mary at the bridge of Staunford, of half an acre of arable land lying in the field(s) of Staunford between the land of the nuns of St Michael towards the east and the land of Matthew de Wirthorp' towards the west, provided that on the feast of the purification of St Mary, the proctor of the said mass shall pay to the poor [*pauperibus digentibus*] 1½d in the house near the bridge of Staunford.

EXCHEQUER: INQUISITIONS AD QUOD DAMPNUM

150. E151/1/16   9 February 1351

Inquisition: a) writ dated Westminster 28 January 24 Edward III
b)   inquisition at Stamford 9 February 24 Edward III before the escheator of Lincolnshire: jurors include Walter de Apethorpe, William de Apethorpe, John de Ouneby of Staunford barber.

John de Chestre granted to the chaplain at the altar of Corpus Christi in the church of St Mary at the bridge for the gild (i) three messuages with appurtenances held by burgage tenure of William de Bohun earl of Northampton for a rent of 7s p.a. and (ii) reversion of one messuage with appurtenances held of lady Joan de la Warre by burgage tenure at 5d p.a. rent, which Willam de Styandeby and Agnes hold for the life of Agnes, with two suits of court, namely to the great courts at Easter and Michaelmas; total value of the four messuages is 42s.

Dated the feast and year above

Seals: five seals

EXCHEQUER ANCIENT DEEDS SERIES D

151. E210/148   **24 February 1250/1**

Quitclaim by Juliana daughter of John Bottay to Robert son of Aug[nes?] for half a mark of silver of all her claim in three acres of land with appurtenances [...] lying outside of the [...] gate of Stanford', concerning which she had impleaded Robert by a writ of the lord [king in the court of the lord?] abbot of Peterborough.

Witnesses: William son of David then reeve, [...] Roger Betrefare, Samson son of Godric, Walter de Brunne, Gilbert son of [...] his brother, William son of Reiner, Roger Gaugy and others.

Seal missing: slit for tag.

Endorsed: Stamford [not contemporary]
Note: part of charter on right side missing. For Robert son of Agnes, see 182; for this land, see 'arable land' of John Bottay in 413.

152. E210/174   **[1242]**

Lease for twelve years from Michaelmas 1242 by Walter de Bradecrof' to William de Pappelle chaplain for 20s of silver which William paid to Walter of an acre of arable land in the territory of Bradecrof' lying on Sundersoken between the land of St Peter of Stanf' towards the north and the land of William de Hingetorp towards the south: the acre abuts on the land of Walter Ketell' towards the west and on the long headland of the said Walter de Bradecrof' which lies near the great ditch towards the east namely, that acre which is called Pitacre.

Witnesses: Terricus de Collonia, Henry son of Alexander, Henry Sybeti, Herbert the serjeant, Simon the clerk, William de Freyne, Geoffrey Pilloc, Geoffrey at the water, Richard de Bradecrof' cook, Peter son of Richard son of Selove and others.

Seal round; c1⅜; corn; legend imperfect; natural wax; tag; imperfect.

Not dated.

Endorsed Primo anno huius convencionis erit terra warectata et secundo anno erit seminata. Cyrographum Walteri de Willelmo de Pappelle capellano [contemporary]

153. E210/195   1257

Indented agreement between Amicia prioress and the convent of nuns of St Michael outside Stanford' with the assent of sir John de Ketene then their prior, and Isabel prioress and the convent of Wirthorp with the assent and will of sir Walter rector of the church of Nettilham then their warden [*custodis*] for ten shillings of silver regarding all their [the nuns of St Michael] right and claim in a house in Wirthorp which is situated near the cemetery of the same vill towards the south with the toft adjacent. Annual rent to be paid in the church of St Michael outside Stanford [i.e. nunnery] of 12d.

Witnesses: sir Geoffrey de Sancto Medardo, sir Hugh Fauwel, sir Simon de Lindon', Nicholas de Weston', sir William dean of Helpeston', Geoffrey Russel then steward of Peterborough [*senescallo Burgi*], Thomas son of John de Wirthorp and others.

Dated: no dating clause, but opening words are *Anno gre m° cc° l° septimo*

Seal missing: tag.

154. E210/219   1275

Lease for twelve years from Michaelmas 1275 by Hugh son of William de Notingham to Simon de Baston' brother in the house of St Michael near Stanford' for fifty shillings, of ten shillings annual quit rent from those houses in the parish of St Clement Stanford' namely in Schoftegate between the house formerly of Reginald Belleweyer towards the east and that house of Henry Cherl towards the west

Witnesses: William le Mercer, Alan Wirfo, Peter de Dallinge, John 'aquario', Robert called Smith (*dicto fabro*), Thomas the barber and others.

Seal missing: traces of green wax; tag.

155. E210/229

Lease by Matilda de Lenn' prioress of the house of St Michael near Staunford and the nuns there with the will and assent of William de Stokys then their prior to Richard de Buckeby dwelling in the town of Staunford of those houses with all appurtenances situated the parish of St Mary of Bynewerk' Staunford between the tenement which Walter de Glynton' gave to Richard de Croylaund in free dowry with Emma his daughter towards the east and the tenement of Richard de Morkote towards the west. Annual rent to the prioress and nuns and their assignees and successors of four shillings.

Not dated mid/late 13th century
Note: some of charter is missing.

156. E210/427   **11 November 1505**

<u>*Quitclaim*</u> by John Thystilthon' of Staunford husbandman son and heir of John Thistillthon' late of the same to John Taylyor' clerk, Thomas Bewscher', Thomas Bosswel and John Corbye for a certain sum of money paid to Thystilthon' by Thomas Wylliams of all his right and claim in a messuage with appurtenances situated in the parish of St Martin late (*nuper*) All Saints beyond the bridge of Staunford within the liberty of the abbot of Peterborough. The tenement is situated at the east end of the town by the river which is called Wylland' by the land of the chapel of St Thomas the martyr on the east side, and it abuts on the king's highway towards the north and the land late of John Milthon' now of Thomas Cowper towards the south. The tenement is to be held to the use of the said Thomas Wylliarns and of his heirs and executors and for the fulfilment of his last will.

Given at Staunford

Seal: round; 9/16"; a Tudor rose within a roundel; no legend; red wax; tag

157. 1 E210/471(a)

<u>*Grant*</u> by William de Humeth to William son of Wymund of Keton of a house (*domum*) in the town of Stanford' which I have in my hand and which is [situated] between the house of the parson of Pycworth' and the house of William son of John. Annual rent of a pound of cumin or 1½d.

Witnesses: Ralph earl of Chester, Robert de Laay, William Bachun, William de Ryvers, Richard his brother, Hedo the butler, Ralph de Agnis, William de Colevil, William de Weston, Robert de Delenil, Ralph son of Achard, David son of Simon, Alexander his brother, Stephen Basset, Richard of the chamber (*de camera*). William Durbet and many others.

Not dated

157.2 E210/471b)

<u>*Grant*</u> in free alms by Ralph the chamberlain of Houton' dwelling in Wytewell' to the prior and convent of Fynneshed' of a house in the town of Stanford' in the parish of All Saints in the Market which he had by grant of his sometime lord master John de Houton' formerly archdeacon of Northampton. The house is situated between the house which was of the parson of Pycworth' and the house which was of William son of John. Annual rent to the capital lord of the fee of a pound of cumin or 1½d.

Witnesses: William de Notyngham, Andrew Arketel, Alexander Luca(s), William of the exchequer, Ralph de Wytevell' chaplain, Peter de Wakerley, John de Bourle, Richard Aldous and others.

<u>*Not dated*</u> mid-thirteenth century
Note: John de Houton archdeacon of Northampton 1231x1246.

158. E210/482   **13 November 1477**

Grant by William Lancastre and Agnes his wife to Robert Folkelyn, Geoffrey Hampton', Thomas Knott, Henry Grymston' of three cottages with gardens adjacent and their appurtenances situated together in Staunford in the parish of St Martin within the liberty of the abbot of Peterborough in the street called Hyegate at the south end of the aforesaid town near the street to Pyllesyate. The three cottages with gardens William and Agnes lately had by grant and feoffment of Robert Joynour of Staunford and Alice his wife together with John Lancastre and Thomas Folkelyn of the same now deceased.

Witnesses: Henry Cok Alderman of Staunford, John Milton', Henry Barton', Thomas Godfrey, John Grymston and others.

Given at Staunford

Seals: Two seals: (i) rectangular; ⅝" x ½"; device indecipherable; no legend; red wax; tag; defaced.
(ii) ? rectangular; ⅝ x ?; device indecipherable; no legend; red wax; tag; imperfect.

Endorsed (i) Ista carta irro[tulatur] coram senescalo tenenti Cur' ibidem die mercurii in festo sancti Botulphi anno regni regis Edwardi quarti decimo octavo [17th June 1478] (contemporary).
(ii) 9 (not contemporary).
[see 164]

159. E210/644   **13 May 1359**

Grant by Roger de Mundham of Staunford clerk notary public to Richard Taillour of Wirthorp and to Margaret and Katherine daughters of Richard Taillour for their several lives of one messuage with appurtenances in Wirthorp situated between the tenement of William Hayward north and the toft called le Gildhous south; it abuts on the course of the water east; to have and to hold to Richard, Margaret and Katherine of me and my heirs. Rent of one rose at the Nativity of St John the Baptist. Service to the chief lord of the fee. Sealing clause.

Witnesses: Alan? de Wirthorp, William Spirgournell of Wothorp, William Gentill of Staunford ...

Dated Wirthorp Sunday after Ascension 33 [Edward III]

Seal tag only

160. E210/687   **8 July 1406**

Release by Margaret Redynges prioress of the house of St Michael outside Staunford and the convent there with the assent and consent of their whole chapter to John in the Pytte of Staunford of all manner of actions on account of an annual quit rent from an empty plot which is situated in the street of Scoftegate in the town of Staunford, namely between the tenement formerly of Geoffrey Smyth on the east side and the tenement of the duke of York on the west side and it abuts on the king's highway towards the south and on the land of the aforesaid duke towards the north.

Further, lease for eighty years from Michaelmas next following by the same to the same of the said empty plot. Annual rent of 4d.

Given at Staunford in the chapter house of the nuns.

No seal: slits for tag.

Endorsed Johannes in the pytte de Staunford (? contemporary)

161. E 210/791   **4 July 1497**

Grant by John Thistillton' junior of Stanford' Lincs, husbandman to John Taylior clerk, William Radcliff and Thomas Bewscher' of a cottage with garden and other appurtenances situated in the parish of St Martin the bishop beyond the bridge at the east end of the town and which abuts on the king's highway towards the north and the land of the abbot of Peterborough on the west side, to hold to the use of William Willyames and his heirs with remainder to David Willyams, George Willyames, Henry Willyames and finally to Agnes Willyames wife of the aforesaid [*sic*] Thomas Willyames in perpetuity and their several heirs successively. Donees to pay an annual rent to the churchwardens of the parish church of St Martin aforesaid of 3s.4d.

Witnesses: John Corbye, Henry Tounley, Robert Parsons and many others.

Given at Staunford

Seal: round; ⅝"; letter I (? for Iohannes) within a roundel; no legend; red wax; tag.

Endorsed: (i) Staunfurthe (? contemporary) (ii) 13 (not contemporary)

162. E210/799   **28 November 1497**

Assignment by Nicholas Edwarde of Staunford Lincs, pewterer to Robert Grymston' clerk and Henry Grymston' of Staunford 'barker' of a lease of a small empty plot now built upon in the town of Staunford on this side of the bridge of the same town in the street called Estebythewater situated between the tenement of Richard Sapcote on the west side and the tenement of the gild of Corpus Christi and St Mary formerly of John Couper on the east side: the plot extends from the king's highway there towards the south up to the bank of the Welland towards the north. Likewise he assigns all his right etc in an acre and a half of arable land lying in the fields of Staunford Baron'. The plot and acre and a half of land, Nicholas had recently received by indentures dated at Peterborough, Michaelmas 1495 from the abbey and convent of Peterborough. Robert and Henry will hold the properties of the said Nicholas for the term specified in the aforesaid indentures.

Witnesses: Richard Cannell' then Alderman of Staunford, Christopher Broun' merchant of the Staple of Calais, Thomas Philipp', William Radclyff', John Stede with many others.

Given at Staunford

Seal fragment; red wax; tag.

163. E210/807   **4 July 1497**

Grant by Robert Grene of Stamford', Lincs, to Thomas William of Stamford' of a cottage with a garden and other appurtenances situated in Stamford' Baron' at the end of the town on the east side; the cottage abuts on the king's highway towards the north and the land of the abbot of Peterborough on the west side.

Witnesses: John Corby, Henry Grymston and Thomas Vpex? and many others.

Given at Stamford

Seals missing: traces of wax; tag.

164. E210/823   **14 February 1504**

Quitclaim by Geoffrey Hampton' and Henry Grymston' of Staunford at the instance of Robert Folkelyn of Staunford to Thomas Williams of Staunford of all their right and claim in three cottages with gardens adjacent and appurtenances situated in the parish of St Martin within the liberty of the abbot of Peterborough in the street called Hiegate at the south end of the town aforesaid; they abut on the king's highway towards the west and on the street to Pillesyate towards the south and on the croft of St Martin towards the east and on the croft pertaining to the hospital of St Thomas the martyr on the bridge towards the north: the cottages with gardens, Geoffrey and Henry had by grant of William Lancastr' and Agnes his wife.

Dated Stamford 14 February 19 Henry VII

Seals: (i) fragment; 5/8" x ?; ? initial; no legend; red wax; tag.
(ii) missing: traces of red wax; tag

Endorsed
(i) Staunford duobus cotagiis ad finem australi [*sic*] ville (? contemporary)
(ii) 10 (not contemporary)
[see 158]

165. E210/824   **13 February 1505**

Grant by Robert Folkelin' of Stamford' to JohnTayloir clerk, William Radcliff and Thomas Bewscher' of three cottages with gardens adjacent and with their appurtenances situated together in the parish of St Martin within the liberty of the abbot of

Peterborough in the street called Hyegate at the south end of the aforesaid town and abutting on the king's highway towards the west and on the road to Pyllesiate towards the south and on the croft of St Martin towards the east and on the croft pertaining to the hospital of St Thomas the martyr on the bridge towards the north. The cottages with gardens Robert had by grant of William Lancastr' and Agnes his wife. The cottages with gardens are to be held to the use of William Williames and his heirs with remainder successively to David Willyames, George Williames, Henry Willyames and [finally] to Agnes Williames wife of Thomas Williames in perpetuity.

Witnesses: David Willyames, John Corbye, Robert Parsons, Henry Tounley and others named on the dorse of this charter [*there are no names*]

Given at Stamford'

Seal missing: traces of red wax; tag

Endorsed: (i) De tribus tenementis in Hygate in parochia sancti Martini Staunford (? contemporary)
(ii) 12 (not contemporary)

166. E210/1137

Sale by Outhilda widow of William son of Dodus with the assent and counsel of her heirs etc and in order to pay her creditors to Matilda widow of Alexander son of Stanf' [*sic*] for ten marks of silver of two and a half acres of arable land in the territory of Stanf' which abut on the ditch as it goes towards (*super fossam sicut itur versus*) Empingham at Adthelardesford and which land Outhilda bought from Roger son of Geoffrey Iol'.

Witnesses: The dean and chapter of Stanford', Geoffrey son of Herlew' and Richard son of Seluve then reeves of Stanford', Alexander the chaplain, Ralph son of Achard', Alexander son of David, Henry his son, master Henry, Thomas the clerk, Isaac the clerk, Peter the knight, Samson the knight, Gilbert the knight, Robert Gurlewald, Geoffrey de Billesfeld, Peter and Thomas sons of Geoffrey at the gate.

Not dated ? early 13th century

Seal missing: tag

Endorsed: de ii acris terre dat' aliis hominibus (contemporary)

167. E210/1275

Grant in free alms by Robert son and heir of Lewen Sperneton with the counsel and assent of Simon his nephew to the church of St Michael of Stanford' and the nuns there of all the land both pledged and free which his father and ancestors held.

Witnesses: Bernard the priest, Robert the priest, …, Geoffrey the priest, Reiner the priest, Wimund, Geoffrey …, Reiner the smith, Geoffrey Parent, Roger the reeve, Stanwine,

Jocelin the smith, Hacard son of ?Ivva, Lenthen Grugon, Almer the smith, Richard, Peter, Robin nephew of the monk, Thomas the priest, Maurice and many others worthy men

Not dated? late 12th/early 13th century

.

Seal: slits for tag

Endorsed: (i) Carta Roberti filii L...Sperneton de tota terra que fuit dicti Lewinis (contemporary)
(ii) Staunford (not contemporary)

168. E210/1431

Grant by John de Houton' archdeacon of Northampton to Ralph de Houton' his nephew of 28s annual rent which Robert le Burser used to pay him for certain houses with appurtenances in Stanford situated in the parish of All Saints in the Market of Stanford between the house of the parson of All Saints and the house which was William son of Jocelin's. Ralph shall render ... annually to the lord of the fee whatever pertains to the same houses just as the charter made to John by Alexander serjeant of Stanford concerning the said houses attests. Ralph shall hold the said houses as freely as the charter of William Humet concerning the same attests.

Witnesses: John Taleboth of Fincham, Andrew Luvel, John de Empingham, Richard son of the knight of Empingham, William de Grendon', John his brother, William at the cross of Empigham, Ralph Chamberlain of Empigham and others.

Not dated c 1231-46;

Seal: missing: slits for tag

Endorsed (i) Carta Johannis archidiaconi Norhampt' facta Radulfo de Honton' nepoti suo (contemporary)
(ii) Nova carta de domo in parochia omniurn sanctorum (? contemporary)

169. E210/1529   24 June 1483

Receipt by John Broune of Staunford Lincs glasyer for 13s 4d paid to him by Isabel prioress and the convent of St Michael by Staunford.

170. E210/l633   15 April 1335

Surrender by Emma widow (*relicta*) of Walter de Tynewelle of Bradecroft to Isabel prioress of the monastery of St Mary of Wirthorp' near Staunford and the convent there of a messuage with garden adjacent with its appurtenances which the nuns claim to have of her as their right: the messuage with garden is situated between the tenement of the rector of the church of St Peter in Staunford on the west side and Emma's own tenement on the east side and it extends from the king's highway towards the north up to the meadow of Bradecroft towards the south.

Witnesses: Walter atte Nonnes of Staunford, Henry Knolkere of the same, William de Apethorp' junior, Ralph Bek of Bradecroft, Simon le Cartere of the same, Robert Gollok of the same, John Joseph clerk and others.

Given at Bradecroft Easter Eve 1335

Seal missing: traces of natural wax; tag

Endorsed Carta Eme de Bradcroft (? contemporary)

171. E210/1685   **26 September 1341**

Grant with warranty by John Frend of Staunford tanner to John Frend of Estdeping his father of his messuage with appurtenances in Staunford on the fee of the lord abbot of Peterborough, which is situated between the tenement of William de Birthorp' on the west side and the tenement formerly of William Walle on the east side and extends from the king's highway towards the north up to the croft which is called 'Seint Martin Croft'.

Witnesses: William de Birthorp', Ralph Lymbrennere, Thomas Lymbrennere, Peter de Talyngton', Robert Rowe, John Bonde, William de Belmesthorp, Henry Rowe, Simon de Talyngton', William Cloket, Ralph de Neukirke of Staunford and others.

Given at Staunford Monday after the feast of St Mathew the apostle 15 Edward III

Seal missing: traces of wax; tag

Endorsed 7 (not contemporary)

172. E210/1865   **18 February 1359**

Lease with warranty for twelve years by the prioress of the house of St Michael outside Stanford' and the convent there to William Spygurnel of Wyrthorpt and Margaret his wife of five acres of arable land in the fields of Wyrthorpt of which two acres lie in Westcroft between the land of Alan de Wyrthort on the south side and the land of Richard de Wacrile? on the north side (*ins* half an acre at Depdale?... near the land of Alan de Wyrthorpt) and one acre in Nethurfeld near the land of William Heyword and the common pasture, half an acre abuts on the causeway between the land of William Heywort on one side and the land of Robert Depe on the other side, and half an acre abuts on Holbrok between the land of Richard Freman on the east side and the land of John Rowe on the west side and half an acre abuts on Nunwall'. Annual rent of 3s.

Given in the nuns' chapter at Stanford first Sunday in Lent 32 Edward III

Seal missing: tag.

Endorsed (i) Wirthorp' de iii s redd' vacat (? contemporary)
(ii) W. Spigurnel de v. acr' terr' (? contemporary)

173. E210/1868   28 May 1349

Grant with warranty by William de Shylvyngton' of Staunford to Nicholas de Eston' of
Staunford clerk, Thomas de Bernak' vicar of the church of Soterton', William de Sancto
Marco of Osgodeby, William de Corby chaplain and William de Bernak' chaplain, of a
messuage with appurtenances in Staunford which lies opposite the messuage of the
aforesaid William de Shylvyngton' near the gate of Estgate and which formerly belonged
to Roger de Farendon'.

Witnesses: Eustace de Assewell' then Alderman of Staunford, William de Apethorp', John
de Empyngham, Hugh Noble, Walter Noble and others.

Given at Staunford

No seal: slits for tag

Endorsed: Staunford (contemporary)

174. E210/1908   16 February 1345

Quitclaim by William Fadirman of Staunford rector of the church of Redemershill to the
prioress and convent of St Michael's without Staunford of 1d rent p.a. from the house
formerly belonging to Letitia atte Stile.

Witnesses: Robert Russel, Peter Malherbe, Ralph Lymbrennere William de Grantham,
William Gentilo (?)

Given at Staunford

Seal: tag

175. E210/1914

Grant by Reiner son of Robert de Parteneye burgess of Staunford to Robert de [...] in
the vill of Staunford, of [? those houses with appurtenances] which are situated in the
parish of St Mary at the bridge of Staunford between the tenement of William de
Depinge towards the east and the [ ] which was John le Plouman's towards the west.

Witnesses: Hugh de Tykencote, Matthew de Eston', Richard de Graham, Richard at
Cotismor, [...] de Wyssebech', David de Berwedon' and others.

Seal missing: traces of wax; tag

Endorsed: Stanford' sancte ? Marie ... dat' aliis hominibus (contemporary)

Not dated ? late 13th century - early 14th century

176. E210/1935

Sale with warranty by Walter de Sancto Eadmundo burgess of Stanford' to Thomas son of John de Bernardeshil for four marks of silver of those houses with all appurtenances which are situated in the parish of St Mary of Binnewerk in Stanford' between the house of Richard Trouwe [of] Stanford' towards the east and the houses which were of Simon the clerk towards the west. Annual rent to Walter and his heirs or assignees of ½d. or a pair of white gloves and to the nuns of St Michael outside Stanford' and their successors of 6s of silver.

Witnesses: William de Francton', John the spicer then bailiff, Hugh Bunting, Richard Trouwe, Nicholas de Colestewrthe, Hugh de Welledon', Richard de Sancto Eadmundo, William son of Thurstan, William le Wayte of Stanford' and others.

Seal: missing: tag

Endorsed: domus de Benewerk de vi s in parochia Marie de Bynwerk' (?not contemporary)

Not dated

177. E210/1950

Grant by Alice de Wakerle with the assent and will of Reyner son of Hugh son of Reyner to the church of St Michael outside Stanford' and the nuns there of an acre of arable land which Hugh son of Reyner burgess of Stanford' granted her for her service for life. The acre lies in the territory of Stanford' beyond 'Sevenwellesty' between the land of the said nuns of St Michael towards the south and the land of William Faderman towards the north and abuts on the land of the aforesaid nuns towards the east. The grant is made in exchange for an acre of arable land in the fields of Stanford on the other side of the river, of which acre one half acre lies between the land of the monks of St Leonard on the east side and abuts on the manor of Wffington on the north side and on the meadow of the lord earl of Warenne on the south side, and the other half acre lies near the land of Achard the tailor on the south side and abuts on the land of the said monks of St Leonard on the west side and on the land of the aforesaid earl on the east side.

Witnesses: sir Andrew Arketel, Alexander Lucas, Walter [le] Flemeng, Richard de Tynewelle, William Reyner and others.

Seal missing: tag

Endorsed: 1 acr' terra apud sevenwellesti (not contemporary)

Not dated ? mid 13th century

178. E210/1969

Grant by Hugh son of Richard de Wdecroft to the church of St Michael Stanford' and the nuns there of Mary daughter of Ralph son of Firmin of Wdecroft with all her issue (*cum tota sequela sua*) and with all her chattels.

Witnesses: Hugh parson of Bernak then dean of Peterborough, Robert de Sancto Medardo parson of Norton', Geoffrey his brother, William de Sumercotes, Adam de Ufford', John Bottay, William de Pappele clerk, Geoffrey de Turlebi clerk, Serlo de Lindeseya, Hugh the porter of the aforesaid nuns.

Seal: missing: tag

Not dated: ?early 13th century

179. E210/1995

Grant in free alms by Agnes, Beatrice and Matilda to the church of St Michael the Archangel and the nuns there of an acre of land in 'Middlelandis' which lies near the acre which Hugh son of Githa granted to the chapel and brothers of St Thomas the martyr.

Witnesses: Halstan, Matthew, Galerus, Hugh, Robert, priests, Gervase lord [of Agnes et al], Galerus de Lamare, Galerus de Norhburg, Wymund, Angelus, William, Bottay, Parent and others.

Seals: (i) missing: tag fragment; natural wax; (ii) tag missing: (iii) tag
Note: it is not clear that this relates to Stamford

180. E210/2034

Sale with warranty by Richard the Scot shoemaker (*scoticus sutor*) to Agnes daughter of John Stikeling [of] Stanford' for eight shillings of silver of his house with appurtenances which he held at fee farm of the prior and convent of Finnesheved, namely which is situated in the parish of All Saints in the Market of Stanford' between the house of William de Castertune towards the west and the house of John Stikeling towards the east. Annual rent to the prior and convent of Finnesheved of 3s 2d.

Witnesses: William de Fraunctun', Hugh de Welledun', John Franciscus, Alexander Lucas, John le Flemeng and others.

Seal missing: traces of natural wax; tag

Endorsed (i) Stanford' (? contemporary)
(ii) decima carta de domibus in parochia omnium sanctorum staunf (not contemporary)

Not dated ? mid 13th century

181. E210/2049

Sale with warranty by Simon de Clyue dwelling in Staunford to Richard son of Roger Briselaunce of Staunford for 30s of silver of his houses with appurtenances which are situated in the parish of Holy Trinity Staunford between the houses of John son of Walter le Flemeng towards the east and the houses formerly of Richard de Cottesmor towards the west.

Witnesses: sir Elyas rector of the church of Holy Trinity, John son of Walter le Flemeng', John de Burtone, Henry de Eche, Ralph de Stokes, Robert Briselaunce, Robert de Farendon', Richard de Croxtone, William Gabbegoky, William de Picworthe, Hugh de Bondone, Henry de Irnethorp, Richard Lymbrennere and others.

Seal missing: slits for tag

Not dated mid/later 13th century

182. E210/2070

Grant with warranty by Richard Fadirman burgess of Stanford' with the assent and good will of Edusa his wife to the church of St Michael outside Stanford' and the nuns there, William de Hoyland' being then prior, of an acre of arable land with appurtenances in the field of Stanford' which lies between the land of the hospital of St Thomas the martyr at the bridge of Stanford towards the west and the land of Hugh son of Walter de Tykencote towards the east and which abuts on the land of the said nuns towards the north.

Witnesses: Andrew Arketel, William de Notingham, Robert son of Agnes, William le Normand, Norman de Gretton', Alan the clerk and others.

Seal missing: traces of green wax; tag

Endorsed (i) sacri'
(ii) de una acra terre in campo de Stamford' (not contemporary)

Not dated ? mid 13th century
[*see 186*]

183. E210/2087   1235-6

Grant with warranty by Richard son of William de Berc to Terricus de Colonia burgess of Stanford, for four marks, of a plot of land in the parish of St Peter of Stanford' lying between the court of Terricus to the west and the plot which Henry son of Alexander of Stanford had of Richard to the east and butting on the barn of the parson of St Peter's church south and on the town wall north; sealing clause.

Witnesses: Henry son of Alexander, Nicholas his brother, William de Scheldingtorp, Henry Scibeci, Roger the palmer, Walter son of Ketil, Walter Fleming, John son of Sampson, Simon son of Matilda and others.

Dated 20th year of King Henry son of King John

Seal: missing: tag

Endorsed (i) in parochia sancti petri
(ii) Carta Richardi de Berk' qui dedit alteri homini extra castrum (? contemporary)

184. E210/2103   20 January 1330

Grant by Andrew Godfelaugh' of Staunford to William de Depyng' fisher of Staunford and Matilda his wife of a curtilage in the parish of St Michael of Cornestal in Staunford outside the gate of Cornestal lying between the tenement of Thomas de Chesterton' on the east side and the tenement of Thomas de Bedeford' on the west side; it extends from the king's highway towards the south up to the wall of the town of Staunford towards the north. Warranty.

Witnesses: Henry de Assewell', Richard Sampson, Thomas de Bedeford', Nicholas de Toucestr', Robert Sampson, William de Thurleby, William Parmenter clerk and others.

Given at Staunford

Seal missing: tag

185. E210/2218

Quitclaim by Gilbert de Bolewyck' and Cecily his wife to the church of St Michael outside Staunford and Matilda then prioress of the said house and all the nuns there of all their right and claim in those houses with appurtenances which are situated on the fee of the said nuns in the parish of St Martin Staunford between the tenement of William Sampson towards the west and the tenement of Richard Brond' towards the east, extending from the field called Martynescroft towards the south to the river Welland towards the north.

Witnesses: William Puncyn, Reginald Norman, Walter de Wyteryng", William Sampson, Hugh Wyther and others.

Seals: two seals missing: tags

Endorsed (i) sancti martini (? contemporary)
(ii) sacrist' (? contemporary)

Not dated ? late 13th century

186. E210/2247

Sale by Henry de Wakyrl' and Alice his wife to Richard Fadirman burgess of Stanford for 40s of silver of an acre of arable land with appurtenances in the field[s] of Stanford' which lies between the land of the hospital of St Thomas the martyr at the bridge of Stanford' towards the west and the land of Hugh son of Walter de Tykencote towards the east: it abuts on the land of the nuns of St Michael towards the north.

Witnesses: William son of David then bailiff, Robert de Corby, Peter the dyer, Norman de Gretton', William Fadirman, Philip Gaugy, William Reyner and others.

Seals: two seals missing: tags

Endorsed: Carta Ricardi Fadirman de una acra terre empta de Henrico de Wakirle (? contemporary)

Not dated? late 13th century/early 14ᵗʰ century
[*see 182*]

187. E210/2282

Sale with warranty by Geoffrey son of William son of Reginald de Wirtorpt to Henry Hare for 22s which Henry gave to Geoffrey to enable him to accomplish his journey to the Holy Land of a certain toft in the town of Wothorpe, namely that toft which Robert his brother bought from James son of Roger and granted to Geoffrey in exchange for the inheritance which he had in the town of Stanford'. Annual rent of 1d.

Witnesses: Bonhomine capellanus, Roger son of Richard de Elton' priest, Robert son of Accard de Casterton', Robert de Kasewic, Robert Goilard, John son of Peter, Matthew Musca and many others.

Seals missing: slits for tags

Endorsed (i) De Wirtorp (not contemporary)
(ii) Carta Gaufridi filii Willelmi dicti filii Reginaldi de Wirtorp de tofto qua [*sic*] emit de Jacobo (contemporary)

Not dated ? early 13th century

188. E210/2289   15 May 1333

Grant by Richard de Lincoln apothecary [of] Staunford to Henry de Tiddiswell merchant of Staunford of a messuage which is built upon, between the tenement of the nuns of St Michael without Staunford on the west and the tenement of the chantry of St Mary in the church of All Saints in the Market, Staunford on the east

Witnesses: William de Apethorp junior of Staunford, Roger Scavelere, Thomas Ravele, Walter atte Nunys, all of the same, and others.

Given at Staunford Saturday after the feast of the Ascension 7 Edward III

Endorsed (1) une chartre de [Ri]ch de Nicholle
(ii) pro ij me' (?) in le Wollerow

189. E210/2470   **5 September 1414**

Grant with warranty by Sybil Hawe formerly wife of John Hawe of Staunford to William Hawnell' clerk and Simon Uffyngton' chaplain of a cottage with a garden situated in the parish of St Martin Staunford within the liberty of the abbot of Peterborough between the tenement of Robert Burle on the north side and the cottage of the aforesaid Sybil on the south side: it abuts on St Martin's croft towards the east and on the king's highway towards the west. The cottage with garden used to belong to William Stacy of Staunford and John Palfrey senior of Staunford.

Witnesses: Robert Staleham then Alderman of Staunford, Ralph Bonde, William Palfrey, John Corby, Robert Lystere of the same and others.

Given at Staunford 5 September 2 Henry V

Seal: fragment; red wax; tag

190. E210/2506   **29 June 1384**

Grant by Michael de la Pole senior knight to sir Richard Lescrop and sir Edmundo de la Pole knights, Robert de Bolton clerk, John Janne parson of the church of Glemesford, John Leef master chanter of Wygnefeld, Philip de Catesby parson of the church of Grafton and John Soyles parson of the church of Elvyngham, of the reversion of the manor of Messyngham, Lincs, the manors and advowsons of Langham and Peldon, Essex, the manor of Little Burle, Northants, and of property in Staunford, Lincs, and in the city of London, all now held by Alice widow of John de Nevill of Essex knight

Witnesses: sir William Skyppewyth, sir Richard Soalgrave and sir John Plays knights, William Bushy and others.

Given at London the feast of St Peter and Paul? 8 Richard II

Endorsed (i) [copy or draft of] *Grant* of the above to Alice widow of John Nevill of Essex knight.
Witnesses: John Phillippot and William Soalworth, knights
Dated at London, 29 September 1383. *Cancelled*
(ii) [draft or copy] appointment of attorneys by Alice widow of John de Nevill, to give seisin of the above lands
Given at Stamford. No date.
FRENCH.

191. E210/2676   **20 June 1478**

Lease [*draft*] for twenty nine years by the prioress of the nuns of Staunford and her sisters to Robert Heyn' and Kate (?) his wife of a place standing in the parish of the Holy Trinity in the said town of Staunford between the tenement of the gild of Corpus Christi on the east side and the tenement of William Hykham on the west side,. Where it is faulty and ruinous, Robert shall rebuild the place. Annual rent of four shillings. Warranty.

Written at Staunford 18 Edward IV

No *seal*
ENGLISH

192. E210/2727   **29 May 1478**

Lease for thirty one years by Margery Croyland prioress of the house of St Michael near Stamford' and the convent there to John Olier of Depyngate of a shop with a solar built above in the parish of St John Stamford' between the tenements of the gild of Corpus Christi on both sides and abutting on the tenement of the said gild towards the east and on the king's highway towards the west. Annual rent of 3s.

Given in the chapter house of the said prioress and convent.

Seal: fragment; red wax; tag

Endorsed: John Olyer of Depyng (? contemporary)

193. E210/2732   **16 May 1478**

Grant by John Billesby of Wothorp to Henry Cok of Staunford, Robert Hans and Richard Foster of the same and Nicholas Vicary of Colyweston and John Billesby of the same of lands unspecified in the villages and fields of Wothorpe and Eston which he inherited on the death of his father William Billesby.

Witnesses: John Cordale, Robert Reve, William Hamelton, Thomas Cordale and many others.

Given at Wothorpe 16 May 18 Edward IV

Endorsed i. My dede of fevement of byllysby of Worthorp with other mo
ii. Deddes of the convent house in Wyrthorpe.

194. E210/2783   **13 August 1345**

Bond from John son of Andrew de Eston of Staunford to the prioress and convent of St Michael's for payment of one hundred shillings and profits arising therefrom at Staunford the next Easter.

Given at Staunford

195. E210/2828   **9 January 1452/3**

Bond from Simon Hareby esquire for payment of £20 to Elizabeth Weldon prioress and the convent of St Michael's without Staunford.

196. E210/2877

Quitclaim in free alms by Henry de Eston' to the church of St Michael outside Stanford' and the nuns there of a certain messuage in Bradecroft which was Alfric de Kasewick's which is situated between the messuage of the aforesaid Alfric towards the west and the meadow of the lord John de Warrenn' earl of Surrey towards the east.

Witnesses: William de Notingham, Andrew Arketel, Isaac Lucas, Alexander his brother, Hugh Buntyng', John the spicer, Alexander the tailor, Richard de Tynewell', Richard son of Richard Aldus, William Reyner, Geoffrey Gaugy, Nicholas Perte of Bradecroft, Geoffrey son of Sarah of the same and others.

Seal: round; 1 ⅛"; within a roundel, a cross of palm leaves with barbs; [. .]S' HENRICI DE (?) [...]EP; natural wax; tag

Endorsed: Bradcrofte (? contemporary)

Not dated: ? mid/later 13th century

197. E210/2939

Sale by Geoffrey son of Henry Gaugy to Henry Prat for 40s of silver of one and a half acres of arable land in the fields of Stanford' which lie between the land of the nuns of St Michael towards the east and the land of the aforesaid Henry Prat towards the west and abut on the land of the nuns of St Michael towards the south.

Witnesses: William son of David, Henry de Wakerl', Norman de Gretton', Richard son of Richard, Matthew de Virsorp, William Reyner, William Fadirman, Richard son of Aldus, Hugh the smith, Roger Briselaunce and others.

No seal: slits for tag

Endorsed: terra aliis hominibus (not contemporary)

Not dated ?mid/later 13th century

198. E210/2951

Lease by Matilda de Len prioress of the house of St Michael near Stanford and the nuns there with the will and assent of William de Stoke then prior there to John de Glentworthe dwelling in the vill of Stanford and Osanna his wife for their joint and several lives and that of John's next heir and no further, of those houses which are situated in the parish of St Martin Stanford' between the house of Roger de Makeseye towards the north and the house of Simon the marshal towards the south. Annual rent of 6s stirling. Warranty for the term of the lease.

Witnesses: Richard de Stanford', William Burnel, Henry Faderman, Peter de Norfolk', Walter son of Norman, William Poucyn, John le Counte, Theobald de Clari, Adam de Lenn' and others.

No seal: slits for tag

Not dated ? late thirteenth early fourteenth century

199. E210/2973

Quitclaim by Alexander Lucas burgess of Stanford' to the prioress and nuns of the house of St Michael near Stanford' of all his right and claim in those houses situated in the parish of St Mary at the bridge of Stanford' between the house of Agnes Tredegold' towards the east and the house which Roger the carpenter then held of the aforesaid prioress and nuns towards the west.

Witnesses: John son of Walter le Flemang', John Sampson', James Arketel, Andrew Nye, Matthew de Eston', Ailred de Haddestok', Peter de Castirton' and others.

Seal: missing: tag

Endorsed in more than one contemporary hand: Alexander Lucas quiet' clamacio Stamford' beate Marie *ad pontem*

Not dated ? later thirteenth century.

200. E210/2994

Sale by Ralph (? or Richard) Tastard/ton of Bradecroft, shepherd to Henry [blank] ?baker of houses in Bradecroft between his tenement and the meadow belonging to earl Warenne and of a court and croft situated between Thomas de [Wir]thorp's croft on the west and earl Warenne's meadow on the [east] and extending from the houses aforesaid on the north to Bradecroftmill on the south. Rent of 6s to nuns of St Michael.

Witnesses names lost except - de Apethorp

Undated (or date lost) ? late thirteenth century
[Much of the writing is lost]

201. E210/3063

Grant in free alms by William de Tykencot' burgess of Stanford' to the church of St Michael outside Stanford' and the nuns there of a certain empty plot in Barnegate Stanford' lying between the tenement of Peter de Chlive towards the north and the tenement formerly (*quondam*) belonging to Reginald Bretun towards the south for the support of an annual mass for the souls of William and all the faithful departed in the priory church. Warranty for the said place with appurtenances and with all buildings built there or to be built there.

Witnesses: William de Notingham, Andrew Arketel, Hugh son of Henry de Tykencot', Isaac Lucas, Alexander his brother, Richard de Casterton, John de Casterton' clerk and others.

No seal; slits for tag

Endorsed:
(i) Stamford (not contemporary)
(ii) Barnegate (not contemporary)

Not dated ?mid/later thirteenth century

202. E210/3079

Quitclaim by Emma widow of Roger de Wdecroft to the church of St Michael and the nuns there of all her dower rights in three acres of meadow in Wdecroft which her late husband Roger granted to the nuns.

Witnesses: Gilbert then dean of Barnack, Richard vicar of Ecton, John Bottay, John Calabre, Pain de Wdecroft and many others.

Undated: ?early thirteenth century.

203. E210/3245

Grant, quitclaim and confirmation in free alms by Gilbert son and heir of Richard Aldus to Matilda de Len prioress of St Michael outside Stanford' and the nuns there of all his right and claim in 5s annual rent which he used to receive from Walter Godchep of Wyteringg' and Alice his wife for those houses in the town of Stanford' which the said Walter and Alice have by the grant and feoffment of the said Richard Aldus his father and which houses are situated in the parish of St Martin between the houses of Alice Doget towards the east and the houses of Stephen son of Roger de Wiggel' towards the west, to hold of the fee of the said nuns. Warranty.

Witnesses: Alexander Lucas, Andrew Nye, Henry Faderman, Hugh Wyther burgess of Stanf', William Poucyn, Henry Puttok', John de Neull' and others.

Seal: missing: tag.

Endorsed: (i) sacrist' (? not contemporary)
(ii) sancti martini (? not contemporary)

Not dated: ?mid/later thirteenth century.

204. E210/3265

Quitclaim by Gilbert son of William Godric of Stanford' with the assent and will of Margaret his wife and his heirs etc to master Peter ward or pupil of Reiner son of Hereward and to Robert son of Peter the tailor of Stanford' for twenty shillings of all his right and claim in those houses formerly belonging to Sparrus which are situated in the parish of St John of Stanford' by the castle of Stanford' on the east side from the castle.

Witnesses: Walter de Tikencot, Henry son of Al[exander], Richard de Westun', Alexander le Seriant, William de Schedingthorp, Peter son of ?Geoffrey, Adam the porter (*portero*), David the clerk and others.

Seal: missing: tag

Endorsed: Stamford' (not contemporary)

Not dated ?early thirteenth century

205. E210/3290

Quitclaim by Walter son of Walter de Tykencot' to Henry (*Hendrico*) his brother of all his right in the lands and rents beyond the bridge of Staneford in the fee of the abbot of Peterborough bequeathed to Henry by his father.

Witnesses: Richard Pecke, John Sampson, Andrew Arketil, Geoffrey de Wime, master Nicholas de Stanford, Walter de Brun, William of the Exchequer (*de scacario*), Thomas son of Alexander de Quappelad' and others.

Seal: missing: tag

Endorsed:
(i) de domibus in parochia sancti martini
(ii) Stanford' ? not contemporary

Not dated: ?early thirteenth century

206. E210/3334

Confirmation with warranty by Walter son of Robert Goilard of Wretorp to the church of St Michael and the nuns there of the whole tenement of Robert Goilard his father in the town of Wretorp and without, with feedings and pastures and with all other appurtenances without any reservation in free alms saving 'forinsec' service of the lord king and saving a mark of silver annually to the lord of the fee and saving to himself a pound of cumin or 2d [annually].

Witnesses: Henry de Ha[..]villa, Peter his brother, [Brian de] la Mare, Robert son of Geoffrey, Richard de Bernech, Roger de Estona, Walter de Tichencot, Richard Peck, [William le Flamming], Henry son of Isaac, Adam de Ufford, Henry Gaugi, John son of Peter de Wretorp and many others.

Seal missing: tag

*Endorsed:*Confirm' Walteri filii Goliard quam fecit monialibus sancti Michaelis (contemporary).

Not dated ?early thirteenth century
Note: *damaged at edge. E210/3335 is a duplicate of E210/3334. Witness list is more legible. Endorsed: Carta Walteri filii Roberti (contemporary).*

207. E210/3340

Quitclaim by William son of Ralph de Weston' to Robert de Ywarebi of all his right and claim in the house which the same Robert bought from William *home* [himself?] which is situated in the parish of St Mary at the bridge of Stanford', concerning which house William had brought an action by a writ of the lord king in the court of earl William of Warenn'. For this quitclaim, Robert gave William three marks of silver.

Witnesses: Thomas de Horbire then steward of Stanf', Gilbert de Tolethorp, master Sampson, Ralph son of Acard, Geoffrey son of Herlewin and Richard son of Seluve then reeves of Stanford', Clement the vintner, Geoffrey de Billesfeld, Robert Gralewald, Peter the knight, Sampson the knight, Gilbert the knight, Hugh Blundus, Geoffrey 'norrensi' [the Norseman?], Geoffrey the skinner and many others.

Seal: missing: traces of green wax; tag.

Endorsed quiet' clam' de domo in parochia Marie ad pontem aliis hominibus (? not contemporary).

Not dated ?thirteenth century.

208. E210/3354

Sale with warranty by Walter de Gretham with the counsel and will of Agnes his wife to Walter de Tikencote for two marks of silver which Tikencote gave to Gretham and for a cloak and a tunic which Tikencote gave to Agnes Gretham's wife of a certain house in

Stanford' near the bank of the Welond in the parish of St Martin in the fee of the abbot of Peterborough, namely that which is situated between the house of Sampson son of Godric towards the west and the house of Frebern' the weaver (*tixtoris*) towards the east.

Witnesses: Adam de Wfford', Ralph son of Achard, Richard Pecke, Hugh son of Reiner, Alexander Seriant, Clement the vintner, Henry Gaugi, Gilbert Parent, Hugh de Uffinton', William the clerk of Pappele and others.

Seal: round; 1⅛"; fleur de lys; + SIGIL' WALTERI D [?'GR]ETAMI; green wax; tag

Endorsed: Stanford' de domo in parochia sancti martini (not contemporary)

Not dated ?early thirteenth century

209. E210/3372

Bond by Henry de Ketene son of Godfrey de Gistun' to the nuns of St Michael of Stanford' for the annual payment of 12s of silver from his houses in the parish of St Mary of Binewerk', namely from those which formerly belonged to Geoffrey de Maydeford' which are situated in the lane which leads towards Fullers' Street (*vicum fullonum*) on the west side and the house of Eudo the tanner towards the east and which abut on the tenement of Reginald de Adlaxton towards the south, saving service to the lord of the fee, namely a rent of 1d on Palm Sunday. For this bond the aforesaid nuns gave Henry eight marks of stirling in his great necessity. Should Henry or his heirs etc default in payment of the aforesaid rent, the nuns may take into their possession the aforesaid houses and the chattels found within together with all the goods of Henry and his heirs etc within the town and without.

Witnesses: Hugh son of Reyner, Richard Peck', Alexander son of Reyner, William de Framton', Andrew Arketel, Simon son of Matilda, William de Freyne and others.

Seal: missing: tag

Endorsed: Carta Henrici de Ketene de domo una in parochia beate Marie in binwerk - xij so[l] ad iiij terminos anni (contemporary) *[hand changes]* Pitancer Marie benwerk.

Not dated ?early thirteenth century

210. E210/3379

Grant and quitclaim by Andrew son of Stanwi Taillur heir of Achard son of Igmund to the house of St Michael of Stanford' and the nuns there of an acre and a half of arable land in the field of Stanford' which lies between the land of the same nuns and the land of William Fleming at Stumpestan. For this grant the said nuns have granted to Andrew the house which Achard his uncle assigned to the said house [i.e. convent] and nuns for the health of his soul etc. namely the house which is situated between the house of Hugh Capp' and the house of Geoffrey the priest

Witnesses: Robert rector of the church of All Saints Stanford', Reiner, Pain priests, Walter de Tikencot, Henry his brother, Richard Pek, William Fleming, Ralph son of Achard, Henry son of Isaac, Hugh son of Reiner, John Bottai and many others.

Seal: missing: tag

Endorsed: (i) Carta Andree filii Stanwi de acra et dimidia terre. [hand changes] apud Stumpedeston' (contemporary).
(ii) Carta Andree filii Igmundi (contemporary)

Not dated ?early thirteenth century

211. E210/3389

Grant in free alms with warranty by Henry son of Alexander of Stanf' to the church of St Andrew of Osolveston and the canons there of an annual rent of ten shillings which Michael his brother and his heirs etc are held to render to Henry from two shops in the town of Stanf' in the parish of St Michael the Greater beneath the solar which belonged to William son of Dod and which are situated on the east of the houses which belonged to John Norens'.

Witnesses: Hugh de Rippel' then steward, Richard Peck', Walter de Tikencot, Ralph son of Acard, Hugh son of Reiner, William son of David, Henry Sibeci, Walter de Repinghal' and others.

Seal: round; c1⅛"; ? cinque foil; legend illegible; green wax; tag; imperfect.

Endorsed: Carta Henrici Holdierd' de redditu decem solidorum apud Stanford' (? contemporary)

Not dated ?mid thirteenth century

212. E210/3414

Grant with warranty by John Bottay of Stanford' with the counsel and will of his wife and heirs etc to William de Wirthorp' and Inga his wife and to his heirs and assigns - but not to be assigned to a religious house - of that house which is situated in the parish of St Martin Stanford' on his fee near the forge which belonged to William the smith towards the south, which house Hawise *hatertera?* granted to the said Inga. Annual rent of 6d payable at Michaelmas. For this grant William and Inga gave John 2s of silver.

Witnesses: Henry...., William son of David, Sampson son of Godric, Adam de Ufford, Gilbert Parent, Roger de Eston', William Faderman, Ingold de Buedona and others.

Seal: missing: tag

Not dated ? early thirteenth century

213. E210/3464

Grant by Hugh de Vffinton and Matilda his wife (with the assent of his heirs) to the nuns of St Michael's of Stanf' of an acre and a half of land in the croft which belonged to Godric near the land of the same nuns. For this the nuns gave Hugh and Matilda five marks.

Witnesses: Hugh priest, Geoffrey priest, Henry son of Isaac, Sampson son of Godric then reeve, Gilbert Parent, William son of Roger son of Hardekin, Geoffrey son of Roger son of Leta (?), David his brother, John Bottay and many others.

No seal: slit for tag

Dorse
(i) carta Hugonis de Vffinton et Matilde sponse sue de una acra et dimidia terre in crofto quod fuit godrici (contemporary)
(ii) ignorat (later)

214. E210/3486

Quitclaim by Walter son of William de Notingham sometime burgess of Stanford' to the prioress of the church of St Michael near Stanford' and the convent there of all his right and claim in those houses which Hugh son of William de Notingham his brother sold to the said prioress and convent, which houses are situated in the parish of All Saints in the Market of Stanford' between the houses which were Richard de Pincebek's towards the west and the houses of master Richard le Ferun towards the east. For this quitclaim, the aforesaid prioress and convent granted Walter a mark of silver.

Witnesses: Hugh Bunting', William Bilkes clerk, John Sampson, Andrew Neye, Robert le Burser, Alexander the tailor, Geoffrey Rome and many others.

Seal: missing: traces of natural wax; tag.

Endorsed: In parochia omnium sanctorum in foro (contemporary).

Not dated ? later 13th century.

215. E210/3499

Grant with warranty by Reyner son of Hugh son of Reyner of Stamford' to Elizabeth prioress of the nuns of St Michael outside Stamford and the convent there of an acre of arable land in the fields of Stanford on the other side of the river, which lies beyond Sevenewellesty between the land of the said nuns towards the south and the land of William Faderman towards the north and abuts on the land of the said nuns towards the east. The grant is made in exchange for an acre of arable land in the fields of Stamford on the other side of the river which the aforesaid nuns granted to Reyner and his heirs. One half acre lies next to the land of the monks of St Leonard on the east side and abuts on the road to Wffynton' on the north side and on the meadow of the lord earl of

Warennye on the south side. The other half acre lies near the land of Achard the tailor on the south side and abuts on the land of the said monks of St Leonard on the west side and on the land of the said earl on the east side.

Witnesses: William de Notingham, Andrew Arketel, Alexander Luc[as], Walter le Flemmeng, Richard de Tynewell', William Reyner and others.

Seal: missing: slits for tag

Endorsed de i acra Sevewellesti (? contemporary).

Not dated ? later 13th century.

216. E210/ 3538

Bond by Andrew Fauvel to Walter son of Henry de Tykencot' for the payment of 20s annual rent for two houses in the parish of St Mary at the bridge, Stanford', which the same Walter held of Andrew: one house formerly belonged to Reginald Preditas and the other to Hugh le Wyte.

Quitclaim by Andrew of all service which pertained to him and his heirs from the aforesaid houses to the said Walter and his heirs, and pledge by Andrew of his oven which is situated next to the same houses together with the fee aforesaid, as security for payments.

Witnesses: Terricus Teutonicus, Hugh son of Reiner, Geoffrey de Wyme, John son of Sampson, Peter son of Geoffrey, Robert de Nortune, Henry son of of Alexander, Simon son of Alexander, Henry Sybesi, William le Petit, Gilbert at the bridge, Hugh de Bernak, Absolon, Geoffrey Baunduney, Robert son of Mage and others

Seal: missing: tag

Endorsed: Carta Andree Fauveli (contemporary)

Not dated: ?early thirteenth century

217. E210/3596

Bond by Thericus de Colonia burgess of Stanford' and his heirs to the church of St Michael of Stanford and the nuns there for the payment of a rent of 16d to be received annually from 20s, namely from 10s which Nicholas son of Alexander and Auicia his mother owe to Thericus and his heirs for the tenement which they used to hold from Philip de Colevilla and from 10s which Henry le Seriant of Stanford owes to Thericus and his heirs for the tenement which he used to hold of the said Philip in Stanford'.

Witnesses: sir Reiner then dean of Stanford', master Pain rector of the church of St Clement, Stephen parson of the church of St Peter, Richard Peck', Henry son of

Alexander, Alexander le Seriant, Henry Scibecy, Simon son of Matilda, Ralph de Fosse, William de Pappele clerk, Geoffrey de Turleby clerk and others.

No seal: slit for tag

Endorsed: .xxv. carta Terici de Colonia de redditu .xvi. denariis pro Philippo de Colevilla de terra de Bradecroft (contemporary)

Not dated ?early thirteenth century

218. E210/3597

Grant with warranty by Philip de Colevilla to the church of St Michael of Stanford' and the nuns there of an annual rent of 16d to be received from 20s, namely from 10s which Alexander son of David of Stanford' and Auicia his wife used to render to Philip from a tenement which they held of him and from 10s which Herbert le Seriant of Stanford used to render to Philip from a tenement which he held of him in Stanford'. This grant was made for the rent of 16d which Philip's ancestors used to pay to the same nuns from land of Bradecroft.

Witnesses: sir Reiner then dean of Stanford', master Pain parson of the church of St Clement, Stephen parson of the church of St Peter, Henry son of Alexander, Herbert le Seriant, Henry Scibecy, Simon son of Matilda, Ralph de Fosse, William de Pappele clerk, Geoffrey de Turlebi clerk and others

Seal: missing: tag

Endorsed: XXIIII Carta philippi de colevill de redditu XVI d. pro terra de Bradecroft.

Not dated ?early thirteenth century
Note: In same hand as 217

219. E210/3621

Grant in free alms by Auicia daughter of Geoffrey son of Outhilda widow in her free widowhood for the health of the soul of William de Ketene her husband and of her own soul etc to the church of St Michael outside Stanford' and the nuns there of an annual rent of half a mark of silver from the house which Auicia bought from William Pinkil of Stanford and Roger his son before she was married. The house is situated in the parish of Holy Trinity between this house of Henry Pykard on the west and the house which Auicia bought from William Pynkil on the east. The grant is made for a pittance for the nuns for keeping the anniversary of Auicia's husband and payable twice yearly namely 3s 4d on Palm Sunday and 3s 4d on the feast of St Francis the Confessor during the period of her life time and thereafter the whole half mark of annual rent is payable on her anniversary to keep it on the above written terms in perpetuity.

Witnesses: Richard Pecke, Hugh son of Reyner, Walter le Flemeng', Henry de Sybecey, Walter de Brunne, William son of David, Robert de Corbye, Norman de Gretton, Robert de Cottesmor, Andrew the clerk and others

Seal: missing: slits for tag

Endorsed: de vjs' viijd' in parochia sancte Trinitatis.

Not dated ?early/mid 13th century.

220. E210/3656

Grant by Eustace de Kirkeby to Robert de Scaccario of land formerly held by William Brun and two acres called Pittes. Annual rent of a pair of white [gloves?] and ½d.

Witnesses: sir Ivo de Dene, Richard de Dans, Hugh de Dingele, John de Torp, Peter his brother, Ingald de Kirkeby, Adam the clerk of Gretton, Robert Doget of Rokingham, William son of Herbert, Richard Burdun, John de Colevill, Hugh Talun, William de Estun and many others.

Not dated ?early thirteenth century

221. E210/3741

Grant in free alms by Robert de Tichemers with the assent and will of Leticia his wife to the church of St Michael of Stanford' and the nuns there of his house which is between the house of Robert Tinturer and the house which was of Walter the priest.

Witnesses: Robert de Bretevile, Geoffrey Herlewin, Walter de Thichincote and Henry his brother, Reiner Maisent', Richard son of Seloue, Richard de Wittorp, Samson son of Godric, Clement the vintner, Reiner then dean, William chaplain of the church of St Peter, Robert rector of the church of All Saints, Hugh the priest, Henry Pium priest, Andrew the palmer, William Torpel and many others.

Seal: missing: traces of natural wax; tag

Not dated ?early 13th century.

222. E210/3770

Grant indented by Matilda prioress of St Michael outside Stanford' and the convent there with the counsel and assent of sir William de Stokes their then prior to William de Stanford' for the sum of 5s of silver of those houses with appurtenances which the same William bought from Stephen de Novo Loco just as it is contained more fully in the charter of enfeoffment which the same Stephen made to the same William. The houses are situated in the parish of St Martin of Stanford upon the Welond between the houses of Richard son of Hugh Ruffi towards the east and the houses of William Sampson towards the west. Annual rent of 6s 11d. Warranty.

Witnesses: William Burnel, Walter Norman, Richard de Stanford', William Poucyn, William Sampson, Richard son of Hugh Ruffus, Peter de Northfolch', Stephen de Wygele, Ralph de Northborw and others.

Seal: missing: tag

Endorsed sancti martini (?contemporary)

Not dated ?late thirteenth early fourteenth century

223. E210/3800

Grant in free alms by Gilbert de Cesterton' to the church of St Michael outside Stanford' and the nuns there of an annual rent of 6s from Alfric the baker of Bradecroft and his heirs for a toft with messuages which formerly he held of Gilbert in the same village near the cross towards the east. The grant is made for the keeping of the anniversary of Stangrim de Gedeneye and Iveta his wife in perpetuity. Warranty.

Witnesses: master Robert de Schefeld then steward of Peterborough, Andrew Arketel then burgess of Stanford', Robert son of Agnes of the same, Hugh de Tykencote, William de Notingham, William le Normand, Richard de Tynewell', Richard Fadirman and others.

Seal: missing: tag.

Endorsed: Carta de vi s' annui redditus de Bradecroft et quiete clamancia unius oboli de dono Gilberti de Cesterton' (contemporary).

Not dated ? later 13th century.

224. E210/3817

Grant in free alms by Matilda widow of Alexander son of Stanf' to the church of St Michael Stanf' and the nuns there of those two and a half acres of arable land in the field of Stanford which she bought from Outhilda wife of William son of Dodi de Stanf' which abut on the dyke which goes towards (or at) Empingham and which land the same Outhilda bought from Roger Y[.....]

Witnesses: Robert parson of the church of All Saints in the Market, Hugh priest, Thomas the clerk, Geoffrey son of Herlew', Walter de Tikenc', Henry his brother, Andrew the palmer, Kotel son of Ralph.

Seal: pointed oval; c 1½ " (orig.) x 11/16"; fleur de lys; SIGILL' MATI[LDE UXOR]IS ALECAN; green wax; tag; imperfect.

Not dated ?early thirteenth century.

225. E210/3826

Grant with warranty by William son of Pain of Stanford' with the counsel and will of his wife and heirs etc to Peter de Quappelod' of a plot of land for building upon from William's curtilage in the parish of St Martin Stanford', lying between the plot of Geoffrey de Leicestre towards the west and the plot of Reginald Troue towards the east. The plot is eighteen feet in length near the road which goes towards St Michael and thirteen feet in breadth within the walls towards William's curtilage. To be held in fee farm: annual rent of 12d.

Witnesses: Adam de Vfford', William de Sumercotes, Henry Gaugi, Sampson son of Godric, John Bottay, Gilbert Parent, William Faderman and several others.

Seal missing: tag

Not dated ?early thirteenth century

226. E210/3837

Bond with warranty by Robert de Cliue and Isabel his wife and his heirs etc to the church of St Michael outside Stanford' and the nuns there for the payment of an annual rent of 3s, namely those three shillings which sir Reyner rector of the church of Holy Trinity granted in free alms to the aforesaid nuns for a pittance for the nuns on his anniversary. And also the three shillings to be rendered from the house which Reyner granted to Robert and Isabel which he bought from John Casche and which is situated in the parish of St Peter in Fullers Street (*via fullonum*), namely between the house of Walter Suttoc on the west and the house which Matilda formerly wife of Alexander granted to the nuns on the east.

Witnesses: Henry de Sybecey, Richard de Wymundham, Geoffrey at water, Richard Milisaund, Hugh Drie, John Punchelard, Laurence Thanore and many others.

Seal: missing: tag

Endorsed: Joh' Tyler' (not contemporary)

Not dated ?mid thirteenth century.

227. E210/3852

Grant with warranty by Emma Gaugy widow to Philip Gaugy her son of six acres of arable land in the field(s) of Wothorpe' of which three acres lie near the land of Thomas freeman towards the west and three acres lie near the land of the same Thomas towards the east. Annual rent to the nuns of St Michael of 12d at Michaelmas.

Witnesses: sir Roger de Buril', Sampson de Burl', Adam? de Pilisgate, Thomas Freman of Writhorp', William son of David de Stanford', Robert de Corby, William Reyner,

Norman de Gretton', Geoffrey de Haketeya, Henry de Wakyrl', William Fadirman, Geoffrey Gaugy and others.

Seal: missing: slits for tag

Endorsed: Wirthorp (not contemporary)

Not dated ?mid thirteenth century

228. E210/3917

Grant by Nicholas de Colltewrthe with the consent and assent of Agnes his wife and of his heirs etc to the nuns of St Mary of Writhorp of a house in Stanford' which is situated in the parish of St Mary of Binnewerc in Gledegate between the house of Richard de Wymundham towards the east and the house formerly belonging to Henry Pot towards the west. Annual rent to the lord of the fee of 1d payable at Easter ¾d and the feast of St Peter in Chains [1 August] ¼d. Warranty.

Witnesses: master Henry Sampsun, sir Simon de Lindon', Nicholas de Weston', Thomas le Frankelein of Writhorpe, Hugh son of Reiner, Geoffrey Nobil, Robert the tailor, Osbert le Porter, Hugh the butcher and others.

Seal: missing: tag

Endorsed: Staunf' [... Gle]degate (not contemporary)

Not dated ?early/mid thirteenth century

229. E210/3923   5 November 1357

Grant with warranty by John Wynd' of Staunford senior to Richard Taillour of Wyrthorp' of a messuage and a rood and a half of arable land in Wyrthorp, which messuage is situated between the tenement of William Hayward' on the north side and the toft formerly called 'le Gildhous' on the south and abuts on the water course towards the east. The rood and a half of land lie together on 'le Dale' between the land formerly belonging to Richard Freman on the north side and the land formerly belonging to Robert Brotherhous on the south side and abut on 'le Spitelhendland' towards the east.

Witnesses: sir William de Lyndon of Eston', John le Younge of the same, Alan Brotherhous of Wyrthorp', John de Belme of the same, William Spigurnel of the same and others.

Given at Wyrthorp Sunday next before St Martin 'in yeme' 31 Edward III

Seal: missing: tag

230. E210/3945   **5 October 1329**

<u>*Confirmation*</u> by Amabil le Venur prioress of St Michael outside Staunford and the
convent there with the consent of sir William de Oxenford their prior of the charter
which Roger de Cloperton' of Tynewelle and Agnes his wife have of Hugh Alriche of
Bradecroft' concerning his houses situated in the vill of Bradecroft with the curtilage
adjacent to the same between the tenement of William Edelyn of Bradecroft towards the
west and the tenement of Philip de Gretham miller of Bradecroft' towards the east.
Roger and Agnes to hold for the term of their joint and several lives of the prioress and
convent as capital lords of that fee as is contained more fully in the feoffment. Annual
rent to the prioress and convent of 4s.

Witnesses: William de Apethorp' burgess of Staunford, William Edelyn of Bradecroft',
William Scott' of the same, Walter de Tynewelle of the same, Simon Carter of the same
and others.

Given in the house of St Michael outside Staunford, Thursday after Michaelmas 3 Edward
III

Seal: two seals missing: tags

231. E210/4011

<u>*Sale*</u> by Thomas son of John *ad portam* of Bernardeshil to sir Philip the chaplain of
Leicester for two marks of silver of those houses which Thomas bought from Walter St
Edmund burgess of Stanford' and which are situated in the parish of St Mary of
Bynnewerk in Stanford' between the house of Richard Trowe [of] Stanford' towards the
east and the houses which belonged to Simon the clerk towards the west. Annual rent to
the nuns of St Michael outside Stanford' of 6s of silver.

Witnesses: sir Gilbert then dean of Stanford', sir William de Framtona, sir William de
Notingham, John the spicer', Henry at water, Henry Tannar', William le Wayte, Hugh
Beubras, Abraham the butcher, Alan the scribe (*scriptor*), Geoffrey at water, Richard
Trowe and others.

Seal: missing: traces of green wax; tag

<u>*Endorsed:*</u> Stamford' (not contemporary)

<u>*Not dated*</u> ?early thirteenth century

232. E210/4190   **25 January 1418**

<u>*Lease*</u> for forty years with warranty by Agnes Leyke prioress of the house of St Michael
near Staunford and the convent there to Simon Estkyrke parker of Eston' of a tenement
with garden adjacent in Worthorp' situated between the tenement of William Beldesby
on the south side and the cemetery of the same town on the north side and abutting on

the king's highway towards the west. Annual rent of 12d. And the aforesaid Simon shall build new houses on the said tenement and maintain them at his own expense.

Given at Worthorp' Tuesday on the feast of St Paul the Apostle 5 Henry V.

Seal: missing: traces of red wax; tag

Endorsed: Simone Parker of Wyrthorp and William Byllesby in tenur' Roberti Reve (not contemporary).

233. E210/4200   **29 March 1405**

Lease indented for twenty years by Margaret Redynges prioress of the house of St Michael near Staunford and the convent there to William Flete parson of the church of St Peter of the same vill of a messuage with a garden adjacent situated in the parish of St Peter at the corner of Gledgate next to the tenement of the aforesaid church on the west side and the road which leads to 'le Watergate' on the east side, which messuage is 22 feet in length outside the walls and 12½ feet in breadth within the walls. Annual rent of 12d.

Given in the chapter house, Mid-Lent Sunday 6 Henry IV

Seal: missing: tag

234. E210/4212   **1 November 1405**

Lease for twenty years with warranty by Margaret Redynges prioress of the house of St Michael near Staunford and the convent there to William Palfrey of Staunford of ten acres of arable land lying separately in the field(s) of Staunford within the liberty of the abbot of Peterborough. Two acres lie together between the land formerly belonging to Henry Buckeden' on the east side and abut on the land formerly of William Stenby towards the south: one acre lies between the two 'balkes' between the land of Robert Staleham on the north side and abuts on the land of the prior of St Leonard towards the west: one acre lies in the same strip between the land of the aforesaid Robert on the south side and abuts on the land of the said prior towards the west: two acres lie together between the land of the prior of St Leonard on the south side and abut on Burleeseke towards the west: one acre lies near Burleeseke between the land formerly belonging to John Gilder on the west side and abuts on the meadow of the abbot of Peterborough towards the north; two acres lie together between the land of Ralph Bonde on the north side and abut on Burleeseke towards the east: and one acre lies there between the land pertaining to the gild of St Mary at the bridge of Staunford on the north side and the king's highway on the south side. Annual rent of 5s stirling.

Given at Staunford in the chapter house of the said prioress and convent, All Saints' Day, 7 Henry IV

Seal: missing: tag

235. E210/4439   **8 August 1504**

Grant by Robert Jameson' and Alice his wife of Staunford to Thomas Wylyams of Staunford of a curtilage lying outside the west gates of the town of Staunford, namely between the curtilage formerly belonging to John Anable on the east side and the curtilage formerly belonging to John Joseph on the west side and abutting on the field of Staunford towards the north and on the king's highway towards the south. Warranty.

Witnesses: William Rauclyff' then Alderman of Staunford, John Wynter, Thomas Buschyr' with others.

Given at Staunford 8 August 19 Henry VII

Seal: missing: slits for tag

Endorsed: 14 (not contemporary)

236. E210/4523   **14 April 1440**

Lease for twenty years by William Boston' prior of the priory of Fynneshead and the convent there to Edmund Barbour of Stampford' of a plot there in the parish of St Michael in the fish market next to the rectory of St Michael on one side. Annual rent of 10s.

Witnesses: Robert Orwyn of Stampford', John Ward' draper of the same and William Cutt baker of the same and others.

Given at Fynneshed, Feast of Saints Tiburtius and Valerianus, 18 Henry VI

Seal missing: traces of red wax; tag

237. E210/4627   **7 July 1278**

Grant in free alms and quitclaim by Alexander son of Simon burgess of Stanford' to the church of St Michael outside Stanford' and the nuns there of all his right and claim in an annual rent of 2½d which rent William son of William de Notingham burgess of Stanford' was formerly bound to pay to Alexander for certain houses which are situated in the parish of All Saints in the Market namely between the houses of William Bilkes clerk on the east side and the houses of Daykun the Jew on the west side.

Witnesses: Alexander Lucas, Isaac his brother, Hugh de Tikincote 'the old' (*vetere*), Walter de Tilton', Hugh Bunting, Richard de Tynewell', Walter Norman and others.

Given on the feast of the translation of St Thomas 1278

Seal: missing: tag

Endorsed: In parochia omnium sanctorum in foro (not contemporary)

238. E210/4923

Copy of grant by William* abbot and the convent of Peterborough abbey to the nuns of Stamford of the church of St Michael with its appurtenances: The ordering of all the internal and external affairs of the priory to be subject to, and by the counsel of, the abbot and convent. The prelate** who should provide for the goods of the monastery is to be appointed or removed by the abbot and convent; similarly the appointment of the prioress is to be in the abbot and chapter's disposition, as are the reception of nuns and the ordering of the nuns and their possessions. In recognition of subjection, the monastery pays a pension of ½ mark p.a. to the abbey for the improvement of the books in the library.

Undated ? early 15th century copy of original of 1155 x 1175
* *William de Waterville, abbot 1155-1175*
** *i.e. the warden, sometimes known as prior*

239. E210/4927   18 September 1422

Quitclaim indented by Agnes Leyke prioress of the house of St Michael near Staunford' and the convent there to Robert Broun glover of Staunford of all arrears of rent due to them from a certain plot in which Roger Flore of Okeharn esquire feoffed the said Robert, which plot is situated in the parish of St John the Baptist Staunford between the tenement of Thomas Spycer on the south side and the tenement of the prior of Sempyngham on the north side and abuts on the king's highway towards the east. This plot the aforesaid Roger Flore had by grant and feoffment of John Stenby of Staunford, from a parcel of which plot the said prioress and convent sometime had an annual rent but for many years past had received nothing because the said plot was ruinous and not built. Proviso that henceforth the said Robert Broun and his heirs or assignees shall pay to the prioress and convent and their successors 2s.6d annually.

Given at Staunford Friday next after the feast of the Exaltation of the Holy Cross 1422.

Seal: oval; ½ " x ⅜"; letter R; no legend; red wax; tag

Endorsed Staunford' (contemporary)

240. E210/5056   30 September 1418

Lease for twenty years with warranty by Agnes Leyke prioress of the house of St Michael outside Staunford and the convent there to Alan Pedyngton' and Joan his wife of a garden in Worthorpe' which is situated between the tenement of the nuns of St Michael on the north side and the cemetery of the church of the same town on the south side and abuts on the king's highway towards the west. Annual rent of 12d.

Given in the chapter house of the priory Michaelmas 6 Henry V

Seals: (i) round; c⁵/₈"; device indecipherable; no legend; red wax; tag; imperfect.
(ii) ?round; ¾"; within a roundel, a head in profile; legend illegible; red wax; tag; imperfect.

Endorsed: Worthorp

241. E210/5288   4 April 1259

Grant with warranty by Amicia prioress of St Michael outside Stanford' with the assent of the whole chapter and of John de Ketene prior of the same place to Hugh le Bigod of a certain piece of his land with appurtenances around the well which is called Seuewell' namely 24 feet in length and 20 feet in breadth; the plot to be held of the prioress and her successors etc without any service and with free entrance and exit in coming to and going from that well. The grant is made so that the aforesaid Hugh and his heirs or assignees may construct a certain house on the aforesaid plot for covering [...? at] the aforesaid well. The aforesaid prioress also agreed for herself and her successors that the said Hugh and his heirs or assignees may divert the aforesaid course [?of water] through their land by an aqueduct to the house of the Friars Preacher in Stanford'. Hugh is to have free right of entry to repair the aqueduct whenever this should be necessary.

Witnesses: Thomas son of Robert, Hugh Fauvel, Geoffrey de Sancto Medardo, William le Wasteney[a?], John de Wyham, Nicholas de Ellyas, Henry de Suleny, knights, Geoffrey Cra[...], John de Cur[...], Joce[lyn ?] de Brunne, Andrew Arketel, Richard Pekke, Walter le Flemmeng, Walter de Brunne, Robert de Corby and others.

Dated: the feast of St Ambrose 43 Henry III

No *seal:* slits for tag

Endorsed: [...] affirm vacat (not contemporary).
The ms is illegible in parts

242. E210/5303

Grant in free alms by Roger Yol son of Geoffrey Yol of Stanf' with the consent of Christine his wife to the convent of nuns of St Michael of Stanf' of his meadow which is called Brictrimeholm which lies in the north part beyond the king's mill near the meadow of Robert son of Albinus. For this the prioress and convent gave him 10 marks. Warranty.

Witnesses: Geoffrey de Sancto Andrea then dean of Stanf', Matthew priest of St Martin, master Sampson, Robert priest of Scoftegate, Gilbert de Toletorp, William son of Roger de Uffint[on], Geoffrey son of Herlew', Richard son of Seluve, Ralph son of Acard, Clement vinitour, Thomas the clerk, Alexander son of David, Robert son of Albinus, Hugh Blundus and many others.

Seal: missing: tag

Endorsed (i) de prato iuxta molendinum regis (contemporary)
(ii) deberet scribi in quater[nis] (? contemporary)
(iii) praturn iuxta molendinum regis (not contemporary)

Not dated early thirteenth century.

243. E210/ 5456

Sale by Acard son of Ingemund to Richard Pecke of Stanford' for three marks of silver of two acres of land in the territory outside the bridge of Stanford, namely one acre of land of the fee of the abbot of [Peterborough] and the other acre of land of the fee of ... de Bernak' which lie between the land of the son-in-law of Hugh son of Cecily and [? the land] of Richard de Wothorpe' and abut on the land of the nuns of St Michael towards the east and on the road which leads towards [...]ford' towards the west. Warranty.

Witnesses: Ralph son of A[card?], [...] son of Isaac, Gilbert Parent, John Bottay, Robert de Casewic, [...], [...] [...] de Uffint' and many others.

No *seal*, slits for tag

Endorsed: (i) In scripta (contemporary)
  (ii) Sigillum Ac' filii Igemund' factum Ric' Peck' [...] (contemporary)

Not dated ?early thirteenth century
The ms is extensively damaged

244. E210/5459   10 April 1330

Lease for nine years by the prioress of St Michael outside Staunford and the convent there with the consent of sir William de Oxon' then prior of the same place to Ralph Lymbrenner' tanner of Staunford of an acre of arable land lying at Ruskhill' in the fields of Wirthorpe between the land of Richard son of Emma de Wirthorpe towards the north and the land of John Chapeleyn of the same towards the south. Annual rent of 12d. of silver payable at Michaelmas. Warranty.

Given in the chapter house of the prioress and convent Tuesday in Easter week 4 Edward III

Seal: missing: tag

Endorsed: de 1 acra terre in campis de Wirthor' firmat' (? contemporary)

245. E210/5497

Sale with warranty by Richard Peck' of Stanford with the counsel and will of Alice his wife and of his heirs etc to master Alexander son of Richard son of Seluf of Stanford' for twenty four marks of silver of six acres of arable land in the territory of Stanford' on the fee of the lord abbot of Peterborough which are called Angelondes which Richard bought from John Bottay and Hugh de Uffingtona. The six acres lie next to the land of the nuns of St Michael towards the east and near the great ditch towards the west and abut on the land of the said nuns towards the north and on the lands of master Richard and of the aforesaid nuns towards the south.

Witnesses: Walter de Tikenk', Terricus de Colonia, Hugh son of Reiner, Alexander ..., Alexander the serjeant, Richard de Westona, Henry son of Alexander, Nicholas his brother, Henry Sibecy, Clement the vintner, Walter de Brunna, Robert son of Agnes, Andrew son of Arketel, John Bottay, Henry Gaugy, Isaac his brother, Sampson son of Godric, Philip the dyer, Isaac son of Isaac the clerk, Hugh de Bernak', Adam de Ufford, Peter the clerk and others.

No _seal:_ slits for tag

Not dated: ? early thirteenth century

246. E210/5666   **18 July 1341?**

Quitclaim by Richard de Bernardeshill of Wyrthorp to the prioress and convent of Wyrthorp' of all his right and claim in two messuages of three granted to him by Ralph de Wakerle of Wyrthorp which three messuages were charged yearly to the prioress and convent at 6s, i.e. each messuage 2s: the three messuages are situated between the tenement of the said prioress on the west and the tenement of the said Richard on the east. These two messuages are parcels [?of] the third messuage aforesaid [*sic*] and are situated as above. Also grant by Richard of the annual rent of 2s issuing from the third messuage.

Witnesses: Richard Freman of Wyrthorp', Richard son of Ralph ...

Given at Wyrthorp' Wednesday next before the feast of St Margaret 15th regnal year [Edward III?]

Not _sealed._
FRENCH

247. E210/5703

Lease for life by Hugh son of Reyner of Stanford to Alice de Wakerl' of an acre of arable land in the territory of Staunford lying beyond Seveneuell'sti between the land of the nuns of St Michael towards the south and the land of William Faderman towards the north and abutting on the land of the aforesaid nuns towards the east. Annual rent of

1½d at Michaelmas. Upon Alice's death, the land will revert to Hugh or his heirs or assignees. Warranty.

Witnesses: sir Andrew Archetel, John le Fleming', Simon son of Geoffrey, Henry le Ruys, William le Noreys and others.

Seal: missing: tag.

Endorsed: seue[n]welsti (? contemporary)

Not dated ? mid/late 13th century

248. E210/5734 May 1317?

Quitclaim by Bernard son of John de Wakerle in Staunf' to ... [of] Staunford, Agnes his wife and John his son etc for a certain sum of money of all his right and claim in an acre of arable land with its appurtenances lying [?in the parish of St] Martin Staunf' next to the king's highway leading to Pillisgate towards [? the south and the land of the nuns] of St Michael towards the north.

Witnesses: Bernard Bonde, William Bonde, Thomas Faderman, Henry Faderman, ... de Helpston', Boniface the clerk and others.

Given at Staunford the feast of Holy Trinity 10 Edward [II?]

No *seal*, slits for tag

Endorsed: quiet' clam' Bernard' de Wakerle (contemporary)
Note: Ms. is damaged

249. E210/5735

Grant in free alms with warranty by Alice Ruffa widow of Geoffrey son of William de Wirthorp to the church of St Mary and to the prioress and nuns of Wirthorp of a house in the town of Wirthorp with the whole plot which is situated between the house of Reginald ... on the north side and the common oven of Wirthorp on the south side.

Witnesses: sir William dean of Peterborough, sir Thomas priest of Westone, sir Simon de Lendone, sir Geoffrey de Sancto Medardo, Thomas le Freman de Wirthorp, Robert de Wakirle and many others.

Seal; oval; c1" x ¾"; the Annunciation; legend illegible; green wax; tag.

Endorsed: Wyrthorp' (not contemporary)

Not dated ? early thirteenth century

250. E210/5740

Grant with warranty by Clement the vintner son of Michael the vintner with the assent and counsel of Aldusa his wife and of all his heirs etc [to the church of St Michael] the Archangel of Stanford and the nuns there of a house which Geoffrey Geseling of [...situated on the fee of the] abbot of Peterborough in the parish of St Martin by the water and a shop in Butchers' Street which is between [the ? of ? and the ? of ...]coc' the Jew which Geoffrey Duve held of Clement with a chamber 27 feet in length from the toft [of ? and ? feet] in breadth, and another chamber of Clement's same fee, namely 21 feet in length and 13 feet in breadth [which ...]chocus held of him. For this grant and warranty the nuns gave Clement fifteen marks of silver

Witnesses: master Samson, Matthew, Robert, Alexander chaplains, Roger de Thorpel, Gervase de Bernach ..., Ralph son of Achard, Geoffrey son of Herlewin, Ralph Cibici at that time reeve, Roger son of Lece, Geoffrey ... and many others.

No *seal*: slits for tag

Endorsed: Carta Clement me fuit Galfridi (not contemporary)

Not dated: ? early 13th century
Ms damaged

251. E210/6131

Sale by Agnes de Depinge widow of William de Depinge with the counsel and assent of her heirs etc for 2 marks to Walter de Tikencote of a house in Stanford by the bank of the Welland in the parish of St Martin or the fee of the abbot of Peterborough situated between the house of Sampson son of Godric on the west and the house of Frebern the weaver on the east.

Witnesses: Ralph son of Achard, Richard Pecke, Hugh son of Reiner, Alexander Seriant, Herbert the Serjeant, Henry Hodiern, Adam de Vfford, Henry Gaugi, Gilbert Parent, William the clerk of Pappele, Hugh de Vffinton and others.

Seal: round c1" diameter, a bunch of vegetation; SIGILL. AGNETIS DE DEPING.

Endorsed (i) .. Stanford (ii) de domo in parochia sancti martini staunf'. (iii) extrauagant

Not dated

252. E210/6325   7 January 1344

Grant by William de Botillisford' chaplain and Nicholas le Rede of Caldecote chaplain to the prioress and nuns of St Michael near Staunford of an acre and a half of arable land 5 x 5 furlongs in the fields of Staunford in the place called le Nonne Croft', namely between the land of the said nuns on each side and abutting on one headland towards the south on the path which goes from the monastery of the said nuns up to Staunford

Style and on the other headland abutting on the bounds of the meadow of the said nuns towards the north. Warranty.

Witnesses: Henry de Tideswell' of Staunford, Thomas de Ravele of the same, Walter de Apethorp', William de Apethorp', Peter son of Peter Malerb', William Cloket, John de Grofham and others.

Given at Staunford Wednesday next after Epiphany 17 Edward III (his 4th as King of France)

Seals: (i) round; ¾"; animal; legend … VNJ…; green wax; tag
(ii) round; ⅞"; a figure of St Margaret and the dragon; XX SANCTA MARGARETA; green wax; tag

253. E210/6477   11 April 1353

Lease for lives by Agnes Bowes prioress of Wyrthorp and the convent there by the consent of sir John rector of the church of Martinesthorp' warden of the same priory to Geoffrey le Wrythe of Wyrthorp' and William his son of a tenement together with the whole garden adjacent in Wyrthorp' which tenement is situated next to the tenement of William Spigurnel on the south side and the cemetery of Wyrthorp' on the north side. Annual rent of 2s of silver; term to commence at Christmas next. And the aforesaid Geoffrey and William shall make anew a house there near the tenement of William Spigurnel and they shall maintain and repair the whole tenement at their own expense.

Witnesses: Alan de Wyrthorp', Thomas Dorlot of the same, William Hayward of the same and others

Given at Wyrthorp' Thursday after the feast of St Ambrose 27 Edward III

Seal: missing: tag

254. E210/6508   28 December 1343

Appointment by Nicholas le Rede of Caldecote chaplain of William Bolle chaplain as his attorney for livery to the prioress and nuns of St Michael outside Staunford of seisin of an acre and a half of land with appurtenances lying in Staunford in the place which is called le Nonne Croft', which Nicholas together with William de Botillesford' chaplain acquired from Atheline of Kent'.

Given at Staunford Sunday after Christmas 17 Edward III

Seal: missing: tongue.

255. E210/6691

Assignment by master Alexander de Stanf son of Richard son of Selowe to the prioress and convent of St Michael outside Stanf of a lease of those houses which he had in the parish of St Martin with the tenteryard which he hired (*conduxi*) from Alexander son of Gilbert Parent which are situated between the house of Henry de Wakerle towards the north and the house which formerly belonged to Richard the smith towards the south. The said nuns to hold for the term and in the form contained in the cyrograph made between master Alexander and the aforesaid Alexander Parent. Warranty.

Witnesses: master Henry dean of Stanf, Luke son of Gilbert le Scaueler, Isaac and Gilbert his sons, Absalon son of Simon, Gilbert his brother, Henry son of Richard, Robert son of Agnes, Andrew Arketel, John Bottay, Henry Gaugi, William son of David, Adam de Ufford', Hugh de Bernak, Philip the dyer, Sampson son of Godric, Walter Burnild and others.

Seal: missing: tag

Not dated ? mid thirteenth century

256. E210/6837   **24 June 1303**

Grant with warranty by Nicholas Hood butcher of Staunf to the church of St Michael outside Staunf and the nuns there of 3s annual rent in the town of Staunf from a messuage situated on the fee of the abbot of Peterborough beyond the bridge of Staunf between the tenement of John de Wermington' towards the north on one side and the lane which is called Schepisgate Lane towards the south, the other messuage is held in chief from the same ladies at an annual rent of 6d to have and to hold and to receive from Nicholas and his heirs the aforesaid 3s annual rent and the aforesaid 6d. ancient rent.
The grant is made in exchange for a certain annual rent of 4s 4d which the same ladies used to receive from a shop 'in Le Wollerowe' formerly Richard ?Pekke's.
As greater security for the payment to the nuns of the aforesaid rent of 3s etc, Nicholas obliges for himself and his heirs three and a half acres of arable land lying at [ ]oldebolepyt on the fee of the aforesaid abbot.

Witnesses: Bernard de Castr', John Asplon, Bernard Bonde, William Pouncyn, Hugh Chaffare and others.

Given at Staunf Monday on the feast of St John the Baptist 31 Edward I

Seal: missing: tag.

Endorsed: Stanford (? not contemporary).

257. E210/6986   **13 May 1291**

Quitclaim by Geoffrey Gaugy burgess of Staunford' to the prioress and nuns of St
Michael by Stanford' for a certain sum of money of a certain annual rent of ½d which
the said prioress and nuns owed and used to pay each year to Geoffrey from those
houses which are situated in the parish of St Martin Staunford' between the tenement
formerly belonging to Norman de Gretton' towards the south and the tenement of
Agnes Russel towards the north.

Witnesses: William Burnel, Henry Faderman, Richard de Walcote, John le Counte,
William Puncyn, Stephen de Wyggesle and others.

Given in the house of St Michael by Staunford Sunday next before the feast of St
Dunstan the Archbishop 19 Edward I when the lady Matilda de Len was prioress there.

Seal: missing: slit for tag

Endorsed: Mart' (?contemporary)

258. E210/6987   **1282**

Lease indented by Philip Gaugy to Elizabeth the prioress and the nuns of St Michael
outside Staunford of his two cellars under his solar which are situated in the parish of St
Martin Staunford between the house of William de Badington' towards the south and the
capital house of the said Philip towards the north. The aforesaid prioress and nuns to
hold until such times as they [will] have fully received 10s which were in arrears to them
from a certain annual rent of 2s, the term to begin at Easter 1282 and in which term the
prioress and nuns will [have] received the aforesaid rent, which 2s annual rent they
ought to receive from the south cellar nearer to the [house] of William de Badington'.
When the 10s have been fully received, the said cellars ought to revert to the said Philip
and his heirs saving to the aforesaid prioress and nuns and their successors the aforesaid
2s to be received annually from the aforesaid cellar nearer to the house of the said
William de Badington'.

Witnesses: William Reyn', Sampson Reyn', Richard Aldus, William Normand, Richard de
Corby, Richard de Wallecot', William de Badington', William Bryselance and others.

Seal: missing: tag.

Endorsed: ii sol' in parochia Martin (? contemporary)

259. E210/ 6994   **1 June 1306**

Remission by Matilda de Lenna prioress of the house of St Michael by Stanf' and the nuns
there by the consent of brother Stephen of Peterborough then prior of the said house to
Thomas de Stanhowe burgess of Stanf' of 12d annual rent from 7s annual rent which the
prioress and nuns used to receive from the cellar and solar which are situated in the
parish of All Saints in the Market of Stanf' between the tenement of the said Thomas

which he holds from the said nuns on both sides. Annual rent now to be 6s of silver. Thomas and his heirs to have the aforesaid cellar and solar in perpetuity.

Given publicly in the chapter house of the said nuns Wednesday after Trinity 34 Edward I.

Seal: missing: tag.

Endorsed: carta de vii s redditus de uno messuagio in parochia omnium sanctorum (not contemporary).

260. E210/6995   1306-7

Grant indented with warranty by John le Parcer of the house of St Michael near Stanf' and William Belte to Walter de Skylington' tailor of Stanf' for a certain sum of money of their houses situated in the parish of St Mary by the bridge of Stanford in Baker Street between the tenement of William de Deping towards the west and the tenement of Robert le Blund towards the east.

Witnesses: John Asplon, William [? Wy]sebeche, John his brother, Robert Lomb, Gilbert Pettismoch, William the clerk and others.

Given ....35 Edward I*

Seal: missing: tag

Endorsed: de tenemento in parochia sancte Marie *ad pontem* (? not contemporary)
* *Ms is partly illegible; the 35th year of Edward I ran from 20th November 1306 to 7th July 1307.*

261. E210/7099   21 July 1291

Grant by Matilda de Len prioress of St Michael outside Stanford' and the convent there with the assent and will of William de Stokes their prior to Walter Godchep of Wyteringg' and Alice his wife and their heirs and assignees of those houses which they have by grant and feoffment of Richard Aldus which are situated in the parish of St Martin Stanford' between the houses of William Poucyn towards the east and the houses of Stephen son of Reginald towards the west. Annual rent of 5s of silver.

Given in their chapter house Saturday on the morrow of the feast of St Margaret the Virgin 19 Edward I

Seal: missing: tag

262. E210/7307

Grant in free alms by Colicia daughter of Fredegist to the church of St Michael of Stanford' and the nuns there of those houses which she bought from Outhilda and

Emma daughters of Sparrus in the parish of St John near the castle, saving the rent of the lords of that fee. Free possession of the houses for life reserved to Colicia.

Witnesses: Geoffrey son of Herlewin, Ralph son of Acard, Alexander son of David, Henry his son, Henry son of David, Thomas the clerk, Richard Pec, Clement the vintner, Richard son of Seluue, Reiner son of Maisent, Henry son of Isaac, Gilbert Parent, Peter the stonecutter and many others.

Seal: missing: tag

Endorsed:
(i) Carta Colicie de domibus juxta castrum nobis datis (contemporary)
(ii) [Preceding the above] Staunford' [and following the same in the same hand] datat' monialibus (not contemporary)
(iii) Stamford' (not contemporary)

Not dated ? early thirteenth century

263. E210/7337   c 1193

Inspeximus and confirmation by Hugh [of Avalon] bishop of Lincoln of a charter of the prior and convent of St Fromund granting to the nuns of St Michael of Stanford the church of All Saints in the Market reserving to St Fromund a pension of 2 marks p.a. The nuns are to pay the 'episcopalia' and bear all ordinary burdens.

Witnesses to St Fromund charter: William monk, Andrew monk, Geoffrey then dean, Alstan priest', [...] priest, Matthew priest, Alexander priest, Walter priest, Reiner deacon, master Sampson, Geoffrey son of Reiner, and others.

Witnesses: to Hugh's charter; Hamo dean of Lincoln, Benedict abbot of Peterborough, Winer archdeacon of Northampton, Robert archdeacon of Huntingdon, Roger archdeacon of Leicester, master Richard of Swalewecliva, Geoffrey of Lecchelid and Robert de Capella, canons of Lincoln, Walkelin prior of Land', Viyil, master Robert de Glamford, master Damian, Robert de Neouill, Eustace de Wilton and many others.

Seal: missing

Endorsed: confirmacio H. episcopi Linc. super composicione facta monialibus de Stanf' a priore et conventu sancti fromundi de ecclesia omnium sanctorum in foro.

Not dated circa 1193

264. E210/7448

Confirmation by Roger son of Pain de Helpest' to Alexander son of Geoffrey son of [...] and his heirs of a certain toft in the parish of St George in Stanford that toft which William Alexander's brother granted to him (Alexander) which the aforesaid Alexander has. Annual rent to Roger and his heirs of 4d at the feast of St Peter in Chains and at Christmas eight horse shoes with […].

Witness his seal

No *seal*, slits for tag

Endorsed: Stamfor[…] (not contemporary)

Not dated early thirteenth century

265. E210/7612

Bond from Reginald de B… and his heirs to the prioress and nuns of St Michael for faithful counsel and aid in their business. The nuns are to pay his expenses if this takes him outside Rutland.

Witnesses: master Henry then dean of Staunford, master Alexander of Stanford, master Andrew Flemmeng, Hugh son of Reiner, Henry Sibeci […] and others.

Not dated ?early 13th century

266. E210/7617

Grant by Simon son of Alexander burgess of Stanford' to William son of William de Notingham burgess of Stanford' of all that messuage which is situated in the parish of All Saints in the Market of Stanford' between the houses of Henry Fuscedam towards the west and Simon's houses towards the east. Annual rent of 2d.

Witnesses: Walter le Flemeng, William de Francton', Robert de Norton', Hugh.de Welledon', Walter Ketil, Simon Ballard, Gilbert the tailor and others.

Seal: missing: tag

Endorsed: (i) In parochia omnium sanctorum in foro (not contemporary)
(ii) pri (not contemporary; same hand)

Not dated ? early thirteenth century -

267. E210/7621

Grant by Henry Foscedame to William de Notingham burgess of Stanford of all that plot which lies in the parish of All Saints in the Market between Henry's house towards the west and the house of William the skinner towards the east. Annual rent of a grain of cloves.

Witnesses: Simon son of Alexander, William de Tikencote, William de Franton', Hugh de Welledon', Hugh de Tikecote, Gilbert the tailor, Hugh Bonting and many others.

Seal: ? pointed oval; c1⅛" x c¾"; a bird on a branch; S' HENRIC[I F]VS[...]; green wax; tag; imperfect

<u>*Endorsed*</u>: In parochia omnium sanctorum in foro pri (? contemporary)

<u>*Not dated*</u> mid/late 13th century.

268. E210/7669

<u>*Grant*</u> by Walter le Leche of Stamf' to the prioress of the church of St Michael near Stanford' and the nuns there of a house with appurtenances situated in the parish of St Martin Stanford' namely in Webesterisgate between the tenement of the same prioress and nuns towards the north and the tenement of Henry Faderman towards the south and a half acre of [? arable land] with appurtenances of the fee of the lord abbot of Peterborough lying between the land of [...] towards the west and the land of R[...] de Pontefract towards the east and abutting on ? Kilne[...] etc. Warranty.

Witnesses: [...] Faderman, John Sampson, Nicholas de [...], [...], [...], [...], [...], Reginald Noreman and others.

Seal: missing: tag

<u>*Endorsed*</u>: (i) [...] in parochia sancti martini et di' acr[...] iuxta terram Leonardi et terram [...] (contemporary)
(ii) parochia sancti Martini (not contemporary)

<u>*Not dated*</u> ? later thirteenth century
Ms largely illegible.

269. E210/7847   2 August 1301

<u>*Grant*</u> with warranty by William le Carpenter of Bressebor' (Braceborough) to Thomas de Faryndon' then serjeant of the prior of St Leonard by Stamford' for a certain sum of money of his houses situated in the parish of Holy Trinity Stanford' within the east gate between the houses of Henry de Hacunby towards the east and the houses of William son of Richard de Cottismor towards the west, extending from the king's highway towards the south to the town wall towards the north. Annual rent to the prioress and nuns of St Michael near Stanford' of 5s of silver.

Witnesses: William Gabbegoky, Robert de Faryndon', Henry de Hacunby, Alan Lothtoplon, William de Erlistorp', Waryn le Seint, Roger le Fa[...], Alan Pulte, William de Cesterton' clerk and others.

Given at Stamford on the morrow of the feast of St Peter in Chains 29 Edward I

No *seal*: slits for tag.

270. E210/7970   **25 August 1325**

<u>*Confirmation*</u> by William son of Peter de Wakirlee dwelling in Staunford to Thomas
Lymbrennere of Staunford tanner for a certain sum of money a messuage in the liberty
of the abbot of Peterborough in Staunford situated between the messuage formerly
belonging to William Sampson towards the west and the messuage formerly belonging to
Richard Brond' towards the east and it extends in length from St Martin's croft towards
the south up to the river Weyland towards the north. To hold of the prioress of St
Michael outside Staunford' and the convent there according to the feoffment which
Peter, William's father, formerly acquired from the aforesaid prioress of the house of St
Michael and the convent there.

Witnesses: John Cloket, Simon de Helpeston', Bernard Bond', Ralph Lymbrenner',
William Bond' and others.

Given at Staunford Thursday next after the feast of St Barnabas the Apostle 19 Edward II

Seal: missing: tag

271. E210/8117   **28 September 1376**

<u>*Lease*</u> indented for twelve years by Alice Cupuldik prioress of the house of St Michael by
Staunford and the convent there to Adam Snartford bailiff of nine acres of arable land
lying in Staunford in the liberty of the abbot of Peterborough. Three acres lie together on
'le Midilfurlang' and abut on the land of William Steanby towards the south and on the
land of the chapel of St Thomas the martyr towards the north: and one acre lies on the
land of William Steanby on the south side and on the land of Alice Aissewell' on the
north side: and one acre lies between the land formerly Henry Somerby's and the land
formerly John Dalby's: and one acre lies between the land of John Knyuet knight on the
south side and the land formerly belonging to Henry Somerby on the north side: and one
and a half acres lie together at Milnewesyk and abut on le Grendyk towards the south:
and one acre lies between the land of William Makesey on the east side and the land of
the chapel of St Thomas the martyr on the west side and abutting on le Grendik towards
the north: and one rood lies at the Hoysthuhirne, and the other rood lies near the land of
St Thomas the martyr. To hold etc from Michaelmas 50 Edward III. Annual rent of 5s
2d of silver.

Given at Staunford Sunday next before Michaelmas in the year aforesaid

No *seal*: slits for tag

<u>*Endorsed*</u> Staunford (? contemporary)

272. E210/8224   **4 July 1409**

Agreement subsequent to arbitration in a dispute between Agnes Leke prioress of St
Michael near Staunford and the convent there on the one side and John Longe of
Staunforde on the other concerning demands for a certain annual rent of 6s which the
same prioress exacted from the said John from a certain house called 'le Aleseler' within
the messuage of the aforesaid with a solar built above it, whence an assize of novel
disseisin was pending between the aforesaid parties before the justices of the lord king at
Lincoln. It was determined by the arbitration of John Tendale and Hugh Rydell (chosen
on the part of the prioress and convent) and Richard Boresworth and John Steneby
(chosen on the part of John Longe) that in future John Longe should pay only 40d rent
per annum for the aforesaid tenement instead of the 6s per annum claimed by the
prioress; the existing arrears are discharged. The prioress and convent to have liberty to
distrain for arrears, entering by the great gates of the inn or messuage of the aforesaid
John. and by all the doors and openings where he and his servants etc enter in the
aforesaid house called le Aleseler and in the chamber built above it.

Witnesses: John Tendale, Hugh Rydelle , Richard Boresworth and John Steneby, Robert
Lokessmyth' and William Stacy and many others.

Given at Staunforde Thursday next after the feast of St Peter and St Paul 11 Henry IV.

Seal: round 1"; armorial (details are indistinguishable); IOHIS LON[G] DE
[ST]AUNFORD; red wax; tag

273. E210/8225   **1 April 1338**

Bond by Walter atte Nunnes of Staunford to the prioress and nuns of St Michael outside
Staunford for the payment of an annual rent of 6s of silver granted to the same from of
old in free alms to be received from a certain cellar and solar built above together with a
part of a gate annexed to the same cellar situated and enclosed within Walter's capital
messuage towards the east which he holds in the parish of St Mary on (*supra*) the bridge
of Staunford between the tenement of Thomas Pounfrayt on the west side and the
tenement of the said Walter on the east side. If the rent is in arrears at any term, Walter
grants and pledges for himself and his heirs to the prioress etc the right to distrain on his
aforesaid capital messuage.

Witnesses: John de Trihampton', Robert de Pakynton', William de Apethorp', [...], John
Kokerell' and others.

Given at Staunford Wednesday next before Palm Sunday 12 Edward III.

Seal: oval; 1" x 13/16"; within a decorated border, a bust of a nun below a letter W; no
legend; natural wax; tag.

Endorsed in parochia beate marie supra pontem (? contemporary).

274. E210/8365   **20 July 1335**

Lease indented for life by Walter de Hauboys of Staunford clerk and Margaret his wife to Margaret widow of Henry de Leycestre of four acres of arable land lying together in the west field of Staunford at Smethil between the land of the prior of St Leonard on the west side and the land of Henry son and heir of John de Derham on the east side. To hold etc from Michaelmas next at an annual rent of 4d of silver. Warranty.

Witnesses: Eustace Malherbe, Roger Stavelere, William de Apethorp', John de Melton', Henry de Tiddeswell', Thomas de Bedeford', William Josep clerk and others.

Seal: missing: tags

Dated: St Margaret's Day 9 Edward III

275. E210/8462   **23 October 1298**

Quitclaim by Walter son of William de Notingham to the prioress and convent of St Michael outside Staunford and the nuns there of all his right and claim in those houses with their appurtenances which Cecily de Pottesmouth' holds by grant[?]* of the aforesaid nuns in the vill of Stanford'.

Witnesses: Nicholas de Burton', John de Wermynton', John Asplon, William Puncyn, Henry Faderman and others.

Given at Stanford' Thursday next after the feast of St Luke the Evangelist 26 Edward I.

No *seal:* slits for tag

Endorsed in parochia omnium sanctorum in foro (? contemporary)
* *Ms damaged at this point*

276. E210/8536   **5 May 1293**

Grant with warranty by John Asplon burgess of Stamford' to Ranulf de Thurleby dwelling in Stanford' for a certain sum of money of half an acre of arable land with a meadow adjacent with its appurtenances lying in the field of Stanford' on the fee of the lord abbot of Peterborough between the land of the nuns of St Michael on both sides and abutting on the land of Gilbert Martyn towards the south and on the meadow of the lord of Burle towards the north. Annual rent to the almoner of St Michael outside Stanford' namely at the gate of the same house of 20d. of silver.

*Witnesses:*sir Hugh then vicar of the church of St Martin Stamford', John Sampson, Andrew Neye, William Burnel, Henry Faderman, John le Cunte, Bernard Bonde, William Pucyn, Thomas le Rus, William the clerk and others.

Given at Stanford' Tuesday next before Ascension 21 Edward I

Seal: missing: tag

Endorsed:
(i) Staunford (? not contemporary)
(ii) Burle de dimidia acra terre et cum prato adjacente (? not contemporary)

277. E210/8537   **28 February 1297**

Appointment by Geoffrey prior of St Leonard's without Stanford of John Makurneys as attorney to make fine in the king's court for the priory's lay fee in the king's hand.

Dated at St Leonard's Thursday after Ash Wednesday 25 Edward I.

Seal: missing: tongue.

278. E210/8539   **8 October 1301**

Grant with warranty by John de Mortimer of Gretford' clerk to William de Apethorp burgess of Stanford' and William his son for a certain sum of money of two shops with a solar built above situated 'behindebach' in the parish of the church of All Saints in the Market of Stanford' between the tenement of the same William which he holds in the same parish of the prior of Deping towards the north and the tenement which pertains to the maintenance of the mass of St Mary celebrated in the aforesaid church of All Saints towards the south.

Witnesses: Nicholas de Burton', Geoffrey de Cottismor, Eustace Malherbe, Alexander de Tikenkot', Clement de Meuton', John Maturneys, John Braban and others.

Given at Stanford' Sunday next after the feast of the Translation of St Hugh bishop of Lincoln 29 Edward I

Seal: missing: tag

Endorsed: (i) J de Mortimer (? contemporary)
…(ii) de Staunford (not contemporary)

279. E210/8565   **14 April 1347**

Grant by Alice de Farndon' of Stannford' to William de Schiluyngton' burgess of Stannford' of one messuage which tenement is situated in the parish of Holy Trinity within the east gates of the aforesaid town between the tenement formerly John Flemeng's towards the east and the tenement formerly of William son of Richard de Cottesmor' towards the west. Warranty. Sealing clause.

Witnesses: John Cokerel then Alderman of Stanford', Robert de Wike, John de Aldburgh, John de Empyngham, Robert de Berford', Robert Scerr', Hugh Noble, John Martine, John de Twisylton clerk and others.

Given at Stannford' Saturday on the feast of Saints Tiburcius and Valerianus 21 Edward III

Seal: missing: traces of red wax; tag

280. E210/ 8566

Sale by Andrew Arketel burgess of Staunford to the prioress of St Michael outside Staunford and the nuns there for 30s of silver, of 5s 5½d, two hens and a cock annual and quit rent from those houses which Simon de Clyve held of Andrew in the parish of Holy Trinity in Stannford', which houses are situated between the houses of John son of Walter le Flemeng' towards the east and the houses of Hugh de Budone towards the west. To hold etc. by doing accustomed service annually to the lord of the fee, namely to the rector of the church of Holy Trinity and his successors on the feast of St Stephen [26 December] two hens and a cock, and on the Sunday on which is sung *Quasimodo geniti* [Low Sunday] 4d, and on the feast of St Peter in Chains [1 August] 1½d.

Witnesses: Alexander Lucas, Isaac Lucas, John son of Walter le Flemeng, John Burtone, Henry de Ottle, Ralph de Stoukes, Geoffrey le Noble, William de Picworthe, Hugh de Boudone and others.

Seal: missing: tag.

Endorsed: (i) de v s' in parochia sancte trinitatis (? contemporary)
(ii) Stannford' (not contemporary).

Not dated ? mid/late 13th century.

281. E210/8567   28 March 1295

Grant by Richard son of Roger Bryselaunce of Stannford' to William le Carpenter of Bressingburg' and Agnes his wife and William's heirs for a certain sum of money of his houses which are situated in the parish of Holy Trinity Stannford' between the houses of John son of John le Flemmeng' towards the east and the houses of William son of Richard de Cotesmor towards the west.

Witnesses: Nicholas de Burton', Roger de Uffinton', John le Flemeng', Geoffrey de Burton', William Gabegoky, James Arketel and others.

Given at Stannford' Monday next after Palm Sunday 23 Edward I

Seal: missing: tag

282. E210/8576 **14 September 1300**

Lease with warranty for nine crops from Michaelmas 1300 until the said nine crops have been taken by Ralph de Wakerlee of Wyrthorpe and Alice his wife to Thomas de Stanhowe burgess of Stanford for a certain sum of money of two acres of arable land in the fields of Stanford' of which one acre lies in Roberdesdale between the land of the hospital of St Thomas the martyr on the bridge of Stanford on both sides and abuts on the land of the nuns of St Michael towards the east: and the other acre lies at Damesarescros between the land of the hospital of St Giles towards the north and the land of Thomas de Stanhowe which he holds from Marioun widow of Richard de Corby towards the south and abuts on the land of William de Deping towards the east. Should Ralph and Alice default in their warranty within the term of nine years, they grant that they are bound to the same Thomas in reparation in 40s sterling.

Witnesses: William Poucyn of Stanford', Bernard Bonde of the same, William de Lindone of Estone, Ralph his brother of the same, Peter Redberd of the same, Richard Freman of Wrythorpe and others.

Given at Wrythorpe Wednesday on the feast of the Exaltation of the Holy Cross 28 Edward I

283. E210/8601 **29 July 1324**

Grant by William Longman of Stannford' tiler to Andrew Godefalaw burgess of Stannford' and Matilda his wife for a certain sum of money of a curtilage in the parish of St Michael of Cornestal in Stannford' outside the gate of Cornestal between the tenement formerly belonging to Gilbert de Chesterton' on the east side and the tenement formerly belonging to Richard son of Alexander le Taliour on the west side and it extends from the king's highway towards the south up to the town wall of Stannford' towards the north.

Witnesses: Eustace Malerbe, John Absolon', Richard Sampson', Thomas [...]deford, Henry de Assewelle, William de Overton', Robert Broun clerk and others.

Given at Staunford' Sunday next after the feast of St James the Apostle 18 Edward II

Seal: missing: tag

284. E210/8620 **13 April 1308**

Grant by Joan widow of John de Wakerle of Stannford' baker to William Wyma of Staunford' dyer for a certain sum of money of an acre of arable land lying on the fee of the lord abbot of Peterborough in Stannford' in the place which is called Seynt Martinescroft between the land of the nuns of St Michael towards the north and the public way to Pillisgate towards the south: the acre abuts on the land of the aforesaid nuns towards the west.

Witnesses: William Poucyn then bailiff, Henry Faderman, William de Folkingham, Bernard Bonde, William Wyth', Simon de Helpiston', Reginald Norman and others.

Given at Stannford' on the vigil of Easter 1 Edward II

Seal: missing: tag

285. E210/8663   22 July 1319

Lease for life with warranty by Mabel le Venur prioress of St Michael by Staunf' and the convent there with the assent of sir Thomas de Staunf' their prior to Ralph the messenger (*nuncius*) and Joan his wife of a certain tenement in the parish of St Martin Staunf' between the tenement of the lord abbot of Peterborough towards the south and the tenement of Robert de Someredeby towards the north, from the king's highway towards the east to the tenement of Simon de Helpiston' towards the west. Annual rent of 8s: first term beginning Michaelmas 1319. Expulsion for default of payment of rent. Maintenance clause.

Witnesses: John Absalon, Henry Faderman, Simon de Helpiston, Robert de Someredeby, Roger the clerk and others.

Given in their chapter on the feast of St Mary Magdalene in the year noted above

No *seals:* slits for tags

Endorsed: vacat' (not contemporary).

286. E210/8671

Grant in free alms with warranty by Hugh son of William de Notingham sometime burgess of Staunford to the prioress and nuns of St Michael by Staunford of those houses which Hugh had by grant of William his brother, which houses are situated in the parish of All Saints in the Market Staunford between the house formerly belonging to Henry Fuscedame towards the west and the house of William Bilkis clerk towards the east. Annual rent of 2½d of silver.

Witnesses: Alexander Lucas, Hugh son of Henry de Tikencot', Hugh son of Walter de Tikencot', Robert le Taliur of le Colgate, Alexander le Taliur, Henry Brond, Godfrey de Reynham, William Bilkis clerk, Robert le Burser, William le Mercer and others.

Seal: missing: tag

Endorsed In parochia omnium sanctorum in foro (not contemporary)

Not dated: ? later 13th century.

287. E210/8718   **17 November 1308**

Grant by Alice widow of Robert de Harpele of Stannford' to Emma her daughter of her houses situated in Stannford' namely in Baronngate between the tenement of Katherine widow of Augustine de Norfolch' towards the north and the tenement of Walter at the well of Ketene towards the south, and it extends from the king's highway towards the east to Alice's own tenement towards the west. Reversion to the donor and her heirs should Emma die without an heir of her body.

Witnesses: Clement de Melton', Henry de Silton', John de Melton', John Asplon, Henry de Kerbroc', William Sampson, William Joseph clerk and others.

Given at Stanford Sunday next after the feast of St Martin the bishop 2 Edward II.

Seal: missing: tag.

Endorsed de inferiori domo quondam Roberti de Asseburne sol' monialibus sancti Michaelis iis' (not contemporary)

288. E210/8830

Acknowledgement by Nicholas de Wimundham that he has received at fee farm from masters Alexander son of Richard, Peter son of Reiner and Richard son of Richard son of Seleue, executors of the will of Henry son of the same Richard, a toft which used to belong to Sparkoll son of the abbot (*fil' abbatis*), near the porch (*atrium*) of the church of St Michael in Cornstall'. To have and to hold to himself and his heirs or to whomsoever he grants or assigns, except Jews or religious men. Annual rent of 7s namely 4s to the nuns of St Michael outside Stamford which the said Henry bequeathed to the same for the maintenance of the veils of the same nuns, 12d. to the church of St Paul which Henry bequeathed for the maintenance of a lamp […] before the altar of the Blessed Virgin in the same church, and [2s] to be paid to Richard son of Richard and his heirs etc to pray […] for his soul on the day of his anniversary. Nicholas and his heirs will repair the buildings when necessary and pay service of the lord of the fee what pertains to the said toft.

Witnesses: Peter son of Geoffrey and R[ichard] son of Richard Pecke then reeves of Stamford', Terric' de Colon', William de Tykencote, Henry de Sibecei, Henry Gaugi, Alan son of Maurus, Simon son of Matilda, Andrew Cusin, David the clerk and others.

Seal: missing: tag

Not dated ? mid thirteenth century

289. E210/8844

Quitclaim by Isaac the clerk son of Isaac the clerk of Stanford' to Hugh son of Reiner for half a mark of silver of all his right and claim in the house which Isaac his father sold to Hugh as the charter which the same Hugh has of his father attests.

Witnesses: Walter de Tikencote, Ralph son of Achard, Richard son of Seluue, Alexander son of Reiner, Walter de [R]epinghale, Robert son of Isaac, Roger Drie, Ralph son of Fulcon' and several others.

No *seal*: slits for tag -

Not dated ? early/mid thirteenth century

290. E210/8879   20 May 1324

Release and quitclaim indented by Mabel prioress of St Michael's without Stannford and the convent there with the assent of William de Oxon' prior to Thomas de Morton in Stannford, Joan his wife and Walter, Joan's son, of 2s 6d of the five shillings rent payable for a messuage in Stannford leased to Thomas, Joan and Walter for their joint and several lives by John Godwyn who holds it in chief of the prioress and convent. Rent of 2s 6d payable to the prioress and convent; after the death of the lessees on reversion to John Godwyn, the whole 5s payable.

Given in the nuns' chapter 13 Kal June 1324

Seal: missing: tag

291. E210/8897   8 November 1444

Lease indented for thirteen years by Elizabeth Weldon prioress of the nuns and of the house of St Michael near Staunford and the convent there to Robert Cayleflete of Stannford' and Joan his wife and to their assignees of a tavern with two shops situated together in Stannford' in the parish of St Mary at the bridge in the street called Brigstrete between the tenement of the gild of Corpus Christi on the north side and the great gates of the tenement lately Richard Wykys' of Stannford' on the south side. Lease to commence Michaelmas 23 Henry VI. Annual rent of 10s. Distraint and maintenance clauses. For the observing etc of which terms and payments, Robert and Joan bind themselves and their assignees in ten marks to the aforesaid prioress and convent.

Given in the chapter house of the said house 8 November A.D. millo CCCC xliiij and in the regnal year aforesaid.

Seal: missing: traces of red wax; tag.

292. E210/8898

Grant in free alms with warranty by Thomas son of Absalon at the bridge of Stanford' to Amicia prioress of St Michael outside Stanford' and the nuns there of a shop with a solar above in the parish of St Mary at the bridge in Fisher[s] Street between Thomas's shop towards the north and the shop of Roger de Helpiston' towards the south.

Witnesses: William de Notyngham, Andrew Arketel, Alexander Lucas, Isaac Lucas, Walter de Brunne, Hugh son of Henry de Tikencote, Hugh son of Walter de Tikencote, William son of Geoffrey the clerk, Michael Fauuel, Thurstan de Ansex, Thomas Pite, William Wodefoul, Hugh Tatte and others.

Seal: Pointed oval; c1"x c⅝"; device indecipherable; legend imperfect [...G?]NUM[...], green wax; tag; imperfect.

<u>*Endorsed*</u>: (i) Carta Thomas Asplon (? contemporary)
(ii) de una schoppa in parochia sancte Marie *ad pontem* (? contemporary)

<u>*Not dated*</u>? later 13th century/early 14th century.

293. E210/8899

<u>*Grant*</u> in free alms by Absalon son of Simon at the bridge of Stanford for the health of his soul and of the soul of Juliana his wife etc to the nuns of St Michael outside Stanford', together with his body for burial, of an annual rent of 10s from a shop with solar above which is situated in the parish of St Mary at the bridge of Stanford' between the house of Roger de Helpiston' towards the south and Absalon's house towards the north. Absalon made this grant to the said nuns for the making of a pittance annually on the day of his obit and on the day of the obit of Juliana his wife and for keeping their anniversary annually.

Witnesses: master Nicholas Absalon's son, sir Roger then chaplain of the church of St Mary at the bridge of Stanford, Walter de Brunn', William son of David, William son of Geoffrey, Walter de Byri, William Wdeful and many others.

Seal: within a small (1" x 13/16") modern bag of red/purple woven material; tag.

<u>*Endorsed*</u>
(i) Carta Absolon' filii Simonis (? contemporary)
(ii) de una schoppa de redditu x s' in parochia sancte Marie *ad pontem* (? contemporary)

<u>*Not dated*</u> ? mid/later 13th century..

294. E210/8983

<u>*Quitclaim*</u> by Richard formerly son of Walter de Sancto Eadmundo of Staunford clerk to Henry de Dep[in]g [of] Wford' for his service and for half a mark of silver of all Richard's right and claim in those houses with all appurtenances which are situated in the parish of St Mary of Binnewerk' Staunf' between the capital house of the same Henry towards the west and the house of Walter de Glinton' towards the east.

Witnesses: Robert Bunting', Walter de Glinton', Alan de Berham, Henry de Sybton', Roger the dyer, Hugh Fusse and others.

Seal: missing: slits for tag.

Endorsed: benewerc (? contemporary)

Not dated ?

295. E210/8994   14 October 1320

Quitclaim by Bernard Bonde of Staunford' to the prioress of St Michael outside Staunford and the convent there of all his right and claim in one and a half acres of arable land with all their appurtenances lying in the croft of St Michael between the land of the said prioress and convent towards the east and […] land towards the west, that land namely which the nuns had in exchange for the land formerly of Hugh Wych' and Sarah his wife.

Witnesses: Richard Bertilmew then bailiff, Henry Faderman, John Absalon, John Cloket, Simon de Helpiston', Reginald Norman, William Bonde, Thomas Faderman, William his brother and others.

Given at Staunf' Tuesday next after the feast of St Denis 14 Edward II

Seal: missing: traces of ? natural wax; tag

Endorsed: Staunford (? contermporary)

296. E210/9078   24 June 1324

Lease for lives in survivorship with warranty by Mabel prioress of the house of the monastery of St Michael near Staunford of the Cistercian order of St Bernard and the convent there with the consent of sir William de Oxon' prior of the same place to Hugh Buntie of Staunford tanner and Agnes his wife of their houses with garden adjacent in the parish of St Martin in the liberty of the abbot of Peterborough in Stannford [? between the tenement] formerly belonging to Robert de Somerby towards the north and the tenement of the aforesaid abbot towards the south. To hold etc. from the feast of the Nativity of St John the Baptist 17 Edward II. Annual rent of 4s of silver. Maintenance and distraint clauses.

Witnesses: John Clokett', Bernard Bonde, Richard Bertelmewe, William de Birthorp', Robert Broun clerk and others.

Given on the feast of the Nativity of St John the Baptist in the year abovesaid.

Two *seals*; missing: tags

Endorsed: de iiij s' pro i domo in parochia sancti martini (? contemporary)

297. E210/9133   **29 September 1345**

Lease for twelve years from Michaelmas 1345 by the prioress and convent of the house of St Michael outside Stannford' to Robert Russell' of Stannford' of twenty-seven and a half acres of arable land in the fields of Stannford' and Wirthorp' between Saltergate and Rogford in both fields. Eight acres lie together abutting on Salteregate in the fields of Staunford'; one acre which is called Wintes lies next to the land of William de Wirthorp, one and a half acres lie next to the land of the said William on the west side, two acres lie next to the land of the aforesaid William on the south side, four acres abut on the east and west lying together and one acre lies by itself in the same manner in the abovesaid fields.

In the field(s) of Wirthorp' two acres lie in 'le Middelfeld' near the land of Richard Freman, two acres lie near the common headland, one acre lies between the land of William Alsy and the land of Richard Freman, one and a half acres lie in 'le Southfeld' near Eston' Mere, half an acre lies between the land of Richard de Wirthorp' and the land of John Chaplein, one acre lies between the land of the said John and the land of Eve Colbe, one acre lies next to the land of Hugh Alsy on the east side, half an acre lies next to the land of John Chaplein on both sides and half an acre lies between the land of Alice Underbrok' and the land of William Alsy. Annual rent of 11s 6d at two terms. If the rent is in arrears at any term by one month, the prioress and convent may lawfully take possession of the whole land aforesaid with all goods, etc.

Given in the chapter of the aforesaid religious in the feast and year abovesaid.

Seal: missing: tag

298. E210/9434   **29 November 1510**

Grant with warranty by Thomas Phelip of Staunford' Lincs, burgess to Thomas Williams Alderman of the gild of St Martin of the town of Stannford aforesaid of a house situated within the parish of St Martin between the land of the said Thomas Williams on the west side and the land which formerly belonged to Robert Strakar' on the east side: the house abuts on St Martin's croft towards the south and on the river Weland towards the north. Also appointment by Thomas Phelip of Robert Martindale burgess of the vill of Staunford' for livery of seisin of the above houses to the abovesaid Thomas Williams.

Witnesses: Richard Wasclan Alderman of the vill' of Staunford', William ?Ba[loff] bailiff, Robert Martyndale mercer, dame Willyams, Henry Tonley and many others.

Given at Staunford on the vigil of St Andrew the Apostle 2 Henry VIII

Seal: round; 9/16"; ? an elaborate magiscule T; no legend; red wax; tag

Endorsed: Stannford' 6 (not contemporary)

299. E210/9699

Appointment by Margaret Godechepe prioress of the monastery of St Michael of the Cistercian order of St Bernard by Stannford and the convent of the same of Richard Lucas, master Thomas Barker and Peter Wyot as their attorneys in all causes.

Seal missing: tongue

Dating clause omitted: c.1486

300. E210/11069   **25 January 1334**

Bond by Matilda widow of Andrew de Eston in Stannford to the prioress and nuns of the monastery of St Michael's by Stanford in the sum of 30s for the payment of arrears of rent of tenements in Stannford situated in Bradecroft' which she held of them, to be paid should any loss arise to the nuns by reason of a quitclaim made to them by Matilda.

Dated at Stannford Conversion of St Paul 8 Edward III

301. E210/11230   **6 November 1232**

Letters of protection from Henry III for the prioress and nuns of St Michael of Stanford.

Dated at Lambeth 6 November 17 Henry III

Seal missing: tongue.

302. E212/3   **7 September 1422**

Lease with warranty for ten years from Michaelmas next by Agnes Leyke prioress of the house of St Michael near Stannford' and the convent there to William Morwode of Stannford' of four acres of arable land lying severally in St Martin's croft within the liberty of the abbot of Peterborough, of which three acres lie between the land of the gild of Corpus Christi of Staunford on the west and the land formerly of Cristiana Wykes on the east and abutting on the land of the said gild towards the south. And one acre lies between the land formerly of John Stenby on the west and the land lately held by Thomas Corby now held by John Boge on the east and abutting on the land of the said gild towards the south. Annual rent of 4s at four terms; if at any term the aforesaid rent is in arrears by fifteen days, the prioress and convent may lawfully re-enter the four acres and expel the said William. Warranty. Sealing clause.

Given at Stannford on the vigil of the Nativity of the Blessed Virgin Mary 10 Henry V*

Seal: oval; ⅝; central figure; lOHES DUMM[?OR]; red wax; tag

Endorsed: Saint Martyn croft (not contemporary)
* Note that Henry V had died a week previously, 31st August 1422.

PRO EXCHEQUER: AUGMENTATIONS

303. E315/Vol. 31 No. 8   5 May 1434

Lease for a hundred years by Elizabeth Weldon prioress of the nuns of the house of St Michael near Staunford and the convent there to John Englyssh of Staunford locksmith (*lokyer*) of a vacant plot in the parish of St Mary at the bridge at Staunford between the messuage of the gild of Corpus Christi on the east and the messuage of Nicholas Rydel on the west, abutting on the king's highway towards the south and on the tenement of John Pratte towards the north. Annual rent to the prioress and convent and their successors of 3s.4d. John is to build a shop upon the plot with a solar above it at his own expense within the first two years of the above mentioned term. Distraint for arrears.

Dated in the chapter house of the above mentioned house 5 May 12 Henry VI.

Seal: missing: slits for tag,
[*See 348*]

304. E315/Vol. 31 No. 33

Grant with warranty by Henry de Thornhawe of Staunford and Sybil his wife to John son of the late William de Camera of Welledon' and Amabilia his wife, for his service, of their houses with all appurtenances situated near the cemetery of the church of St Michael the Greater , Stanford between the house of Osbert le Megucer towards the west and the tenement of Alfred (*Aluredi*) de Hadestok' towards the east. To hold to the said John and Amabilia and their heirs and assignees freely etc and by inheritance. Annual rent to Alexander Lucas of Staunford and his heirs or assignees of 5s payable quarterly, doing also to the chief lord of the fee all the services which pertain to the same houses.

Witnesses: Richard de Casterton', William de Freyney, Simon le Heyrer, Adam Westrense, Osbert le Megucer, John de Casterton and others.

Seal: missing: slits for tag

Endorsed Stamford

Not dated

305 E315/Vol. 31 No. 150   26 February 1314/5

Quitclaim by Geoffrey de Barsham to Mabel le Venur prioress of the house of St Michael near Staunford and to the nuns there of all his right and claim in a shop with a solar above with all appurtenances situated in the parish of St John, Staunford, between the tenement of Roger Greywerck' towards the north and the tenement formerly of Agnes le

Hervy towards the south, which shop with appurtenances Geoffrey held by […] of the said prioress and nuns for life.

Witnesses: Hugh de Alverton', William de Apeth[orpe], Roger le Schavelere, John Absalon, John le Lung skinner (*pellipario*), Richard de Baldiswell', Roger Greywerck' and others.

Given at Staunford Tuesday after Ash Wednesday 1314.

Seal: missing: slits for tag.

<u>*Endorsed*</u>: quiet' clamacio de i schoppa in parochia Sancti Johannis [contemporary]

306. E315/Vol. 31 No. 198   1 April 1375

<u>*Grant*</u> with warranty by John son of Adam Kupper' of Staunford to sir Simon de Langeton' parson of the church of St George, Stanford, and Henry de Bukeden' of the same vill of his whole messuage situated in the parish of St Mary Bynwerk, namely between the tenement of sir William de Burton' knight on the east and the tenement of William de Apethorp' on the west, the tenement extends from the king's highway towards the north up to the lane which is called 'le Gannok' towards the south. To hold the whole messuage aforesaid with all its appurtenances and with all John's movable and immovable goods wheresoever they will be found, to the aforesaid sir Simon and Henry and to the heirs and assignees of the same freely etc and in perpetuity of the chief lords of the fee by the annual services etc.

Witnesses: John Broun then Alderman of Staunford, John Bonde, Reginald Honyman, Alexander de Morcote, Ralph Cook and others.

Given at Staunford Sunday after the Annunciation of the Blessed Virgin Mary 49 Edward III.

Seal: missing: slits for tags.

307. E315/Vol. 31 No. 229

<u>*Grant*</u> with warranty by Henry Prat burgess of Stamford to Henry Faderman burgess of the same for his service of three acres of arable land with appurtenances in the fields of Staunford, Pillisgate and Burle, of which one acre lies in the fields of Staunford on the fee of the abbot of Peterborough between the land of the nuns of St Michael towards the south and the land formerly of Norman de Grecton' towards the north and which acre is called 'Chekeracre'. One acre lies in the fields of Pillisgate between the land formerly of Peter the dyer (*tinctoris*) towards the east and the land formerly of William Pake towards the west and it abuts on the land formerly of Andrew Arketel towards the south. And two half acres lie in the fields of Burle: one lies between the land formerly of the lord of Burle towards the east and the land formerly of William de Ryhale towards the west and it abuts on the land of the sacrist of Peterborough towards the north in the field which is called 'Blolondis': the other half acre lies between the land formerly of Roger Briselaunce

towards the east and the land of the hospital of St Thomas the martyr at the bridge of Stanford towards the west and it abuts on the road leading towards Pillisgate' towards the north. To hold to the aforesaid Henry Faderman and his heirs or assignees or to the assignees of his heirs freely and by inheritance in perpetuity, saving the service owed and accustomed to the lords of the fee, namely to Gilbert de Bernake and his heirs or assignees 1d at Easter for the acre of land in the fields of Pillisgate, and to the lord of Burle and his heirs or assignees ¼lb of pepper at Easter for the two half acres in the fields of Burle for all services, etc.

Witnesses: William Reyner, Gilbert de Cesterton', Richard Aldus, Walter son of Norman, Peter de Burle.

Seal: missing: slits for tag

Endorsed: Carta Henrici Prat

Not dated

308. E315/Vol. 32 No. 25

Arbitration award by William Kirkestede, William de Irby, William de Burton and Robert de Tynton, rectors of Bernak, Medbourne, Eston by Stannford, and Uffyngton in a tithe dispute between Margaret Redynges prioress of the priory of nuns by Stannford and master William Flete rector of the church of St Paul, Staunford. The prioress has proved the nuns' right to all tithes from All Saints in the Market, St Andrew's and St Clement's. The rector of St Paul is to have all tithes of that church, paying £3 3s 4d per annum to the priory.

Not dated early fifteenth century.

309. E315/Vol. 32 No. 59

Lease indented for lives in survivorship with warranty by Matilda de Len prioress of the house of St Michael near Stanford' and the nuns there with the assent of sir William de Stouk' then their prior to William de Empingham butcher (*carnificem*) dwelling in the town of Staunford and to Alcusa his wife of a certain cellar with a solar built above and with all appurtenances situated in the parish of St Michael the Greater, Stannford, namely at the east end of the meat market (*in orientali capite macelli*) between the tenement of the same prioress and nuns towards the north and the tenements of Richard Wilys and John the apothecary (*apotecarii*) towards the south. Annual rent of 5s payable quarterly, for all secular service, exaction and demand. And the said William and Alcusa, during the whole of their life, will repair and maintain in good condition the aforesaid cellar and solar with appurtenances at their own expense. And if they default in such maintenance or in the payment of the aforesaid rent by one month following the lapse of any term, the aforesaid prioress and nuns or their attornies as owners (*tanquam possessoribus*) may enter their fee and enjoy possession until full satisfaction be made to them for the rent owed.

Witnesses: Alexander Lucas, John de Wermington', Alfred le Mercer, Geoffrey de Cottismor, Henry Faderman, William Burnel, John le Cunte and others.

Not dated

310. E315/Vol. 32 No. 100

<u>*Grant*</u> in free alms with warranty by Hugh the chaplain son of Robert de Norhampton' to the church of St Michael of Staunford and the nuns there of one part of the land of his croft in the parish of St Martin of Staunford on the south side near the land of Peter son of William son of Roger, namely that part which extends in length from the road as far as the toft which was William Angelin's and which is eighteen feet in breadth.

Witnesses: sir Reyner then dean of Stamford, master Pain rector of the church of St Clement, sir Turbert the chaplain, William de Sumerkotis, Henry Gaugi, William son of David, John Bottay, Adam de Offord', William de Pappele clerk and others.

Seal: missing: slits for tag

<u>*Not dated*</u>

311. E315/Vol. 33 No. 5   **9 December 1316**

<u>*Quitclaim*</u> with warranty by John Abselon burgess of Stamford to the prioress of the house of St Michael outside Staunford and the convent there and to their successors of all his right and claim in six acres of arable land in the fields of Staunford, of which three acres lie on the fee of the earl of Warenne between the land of John de Wermington' towards the west and the land formerly of Thok' le Laver towards the east and they abut on the land of the said earl of Warenne towards the north and the ditch of the vill of Staunford (*et super fossatum ville de Staunford*) towards the south: the other three acres lie on the fee of the abbot of Peterborough in 'Hulinstrisdale' between the land of John Norman towards the north and the land of the said John Abselon towards the south and they abut on the land of the said nuns of St Michael towards the east and the land of John Norman and the hospital of St Thomas towards the west.

Witnesses: Eustace Malerbe, William de Apethorp', Roger le Schavelere, William Puncyn, John Cloket', William de Folkyngham burgesses of Stamford and others.

Given at Stamford Thursday after the Conception of St Mary the Virgin 10 Edward II.

Seal: missing: slits for tag

312. E315/Vol. 33 No. 174   **20 February 1306**

<u>*Grant*</u> with warranty by Roger de Ringestede burgess of Stanford to Hugh son of Roger de Birton' burgess of Staunford of one acre of arable land with appurtenances lying in the field(s) of Staunford on the fee of the lord abbot of Peterborough at 'Kilmerisheng'

between the lands of the nuns of St Michael on each side and abutting on the meadow of Peter lord of Burle towards the north and the land of Hugh towards the south. To hold to Hugh and his heirs or assignees freely etc and by inheritance in perpetuity, doing to the chief lord of the fee the annual services etc.

Witnesses: William Poucyn, sir William Burnel chaplain, Bernard Bonde, William Wiyer, William de Folkingham, Henry Fadirman, Reginald Norman, William Joseph clerk and others.

Dated: Quadragesima 34 Edward I.

313. E315/Vol. 34 No. 22   12 December 1372

Grant by Alan de Wirthorp' clerk to Isabel de Maltby prioress of St Michael outside Staunford and the convent there of an annual quit rent of 12d to be received at two terms, namely Michaelmas and Easter by equal portions in perpetuity from his messuage in Wirthorp' which is situated near the toft and garden of the same prioress on the north and the tenement formerly of Robert Brotherhouse on the south: the messuage abuts on the field of 'Wescrofte'. And if the rent is in arrears at any term, the same prioress and convent etc may enter the messuage with its appurtenances and levy a distress etc.

Given at Wirthorp' Sunday after the Conception of St Mary the Virgin 46 Edward III.

Seal: missing: slits for tag

Endorsed: (i) Carta de xii denariis redditus de 1 cotagio in quo Johannes Walton habitat [added in a different hand] jam Robertus Hill' habitat.
(ii) Wyrthorp'

314. E315/Vol. 34 No. 85   6 March 1350

Grant with warranty by Thomas son of Ralph de Hanneby brother and heir of Ralph de Hanneby formerly vicar of the church of All Saints near the bridge, Staunford to William Gentyl of Staunford and Margery his wife and to the heirs and assignees of the same William of an acre of arable land with its appurtenances just as it lies in the field(s) of Staunford between the land of the prioress of St Michael outside Staunford on the north and the land pertaining to the church of All Saints near the bridge of Staunford on the south: the acre abuts on the land of John Wortyn. To hold the aforesaid acre of land with its appurtenances to William and Margery and the heirs and assignees of the same William freely etc in fee, and in perpetuity of the chief lords of that fee for all the services owed and accustomed by right.

Witnesses: John Wortyn, Simon Bonde, Ralph Lymbrennere, William Peykirke, John Bonde senior and others.

Dated at Staunford Saturday after St Chad the bishop 24 Edward III.

Seal: missing: slit for tag.

315. E315/Vol. 34 No. 93

Grant in free alms with warranty by John Bottay of Stanford' to the church of St Michael of Stanford' and the nuns there of an annual rent of 17d in the parish of St Martin of Stanford' to be received at Michaelmas with homages, reliefs and all other appurtenances, namely 7d from the house which was of William the smith (*fabri*) with the curtilage adjacent, which house is situated near the house which was Hugh Cut's towards the north; 6d from the house which was Henry de Wakerle's which is situated near the house which was of Richard de Eston' towards the south; and 4d from the said house which was of Richard de Eston'. To hold to the said nuns and their successors freely and quit of all service and secular exaction.

Witnesses: Hugh vicar of the church of St Martin, William de Pappele chaplain, William de Sumercotes, Adam de Ufford', William de Rihale, Henry Gaugi, Gilbert Parent, Geoffrey de Turlebi clerk, Serlo de Lindeseia, Hugh the janitor (*janitore*) and others.

Seal: missing: slits for tag.

Not dated

316. E315/Vol. 34 No. 114   25 January 1278/9

Grant by Alexander son and heir of Gilbert the tailor (*cissoris*) in the town of Stanford' to the nuns of St Michael outside Stanford' of an annual rent of 10s to be received quarterly from a certain house which is situated in the parish of All Saints in the Market, namely in the corner house towards the corn market (*in domo angulari versus forum bladi*) which house is situated between the houses which formerly were of Matilda Wlneth as much on the west as on the north and which Martin the apothecary (*ipotecarius*) now holds at fee farm from the said nuns. To hold the said rent of 10s of Alexander and his heirs or assignees to the said nuns and their successors freely, peacefully and without any secular service, custom, exaction or demand, in exchange for a certain annual rent of 10s which Alexander had been accustomed to pay to the said nuns for a house which formerly was of Herbert le Seriaunt and upon which Alexander has now built his solar and cellar. And if the said 10s are not paid at the terms abovesaid, the said nuns or their attorney may levy a distress in the said corner house etc. And if for any reason Alexander or his assignees are unable to warrant the said rent of 10s, he grants for himself and his heirs or assignees that the said nuns or their attorney may enter the gates of his hall (*portas aule mee ingredi*) and levy a distress equal to the 10s which the said nuns had been accustomed to receive from the house which formerly was of Herbert le Seriaunt.

Witnesses: Philip de Staneburne, Alexander Lucas, Isaac Lucas, John le Fleming, Richard de Tynewelle, Walter Norman, William Norman and others.

Dated: the Conversion of St Paul 1278.

Seal: missing: slits for tag

Endorsed (i) Carta Alexandri Taylur

(ii) parochia omnium sanctorum in foro de x solidis de domibus angular' super cornerum juxta forum bladi.

317. E315/Vol. 34 No. 138   **25 September 1366**

Quitclaim with warranty by Joan daughter of Robert Josep of Staunford' to William de Melton' parson of the church of Holy Trinity, Staunford and to his heirs of all her right and claim in a messuage with appurtenances in Staunford in the parish of St Paul which is situated between the tenement of the lord earl of Cambridge on the east and the tenement of Raymond le Spicier of Staunford on the west and which messuage with appurtenances the aforesaid William had by grant and feoffment of the aforesaid Robert Josep, Joan's father, and of Laura (*Lore*) his wife, her mother.

Witnesses: John de Chestr' then Alderman of Staunford, Richard de Ardern', John Broun, John Spycer, Robert Pratt', John de Wakirle, Walter de Makesey, Simon Cokerel, John Chaloner of Staunford and others.

Given at Staunford Friday after St Matthew the Apostle and Evangelist 40 Edward III.

Seal: missing: slits for tag.

318. E315/Vol. 34 No. 201

Grant in free alms with warranty by Henry Prat of Stanford' to the church of St Michael, Staunford and the nuns there of two acres of arable land in the territory of Stanford' lying on 'Kelmeresheng' between the land of the said nuns on each side. For this grant the said nuns have received him in the outpouring of their prayers and alms as it were for their brother (*receperunt me in oracionibus et elemosinis suis tamquam pro fratre suo effundendis*).

Witnesses: sir Hugh then dean of Stamford, Richard de Tynewell', Richard Aldus, William Reyner, Gilbert de Cestreton', Richard de Coreby, Geoffrey Gaugy and others.

Seal: missing: slits for tag.

Endorsed (i) Carta Henrici Pratte
(ii) ii acre in Ker'mer'hegg'

Not dated

319. E315/Vol. 35 No. 1

Grant by Sybil prioress of St Michael outside Stanford' and the convent there by the common wish of their chapter and the assent and counsel of sir Roger de Keten' then their prior to William de Sumercote of two houses with their appurtenances in the parish of St Martin, namely those which are situated between the grange of the said William towards the east and the house of Andrew son of Stanwic towards the west; to hold to William and his heirs or assignees freely and by inheritance of the prioress and convent and their successors. Annual rent of 2s 8d payable quarterly for all service and secular demand pertaining to the prioress and convent. However, neither the said William nor his heirs or assignees may alienate the said houses from the said nuns, nor pledge, sell or grant them to Jews or men of religion or to any other to the disinheritance of the house of St Michael (*ad exheredationem domus nostre*).

No seal

<u>*Not dated*</u> early thirteenth century

320. E315/Vol. 35 No. 13   7 March 1302/3

<u>*Lease*</u> indented for life with warranty by Matilda de Lenna prioress of the house of St Michael near Staunford and the nuns there, by the wish and assent of brother Stephen Gocelyn then prior of the said house, to Geoffrey de Barsham mercer (*mercenario*) of Staunford of that shop with the solar built above with appurtenances which is situated in the parish of St John, Staunford between the tenement of Roger Greywerk towards the north and the tenement formerly of Agnes Hervy towards the south. Annual rent of 10s payable quarterly for all secular service and demand whatsoever. And the said Geoffrey will maintain the said shop with appurtenances in good condition at his own expense for the whole term aforesaid. And Geoffrey may not do damage there, neither block up the door or windows, nor alienate the said house in any manner, nor retain the farm during one full term; and if he does, the said nuns and their successors may take the said shop with appurtenances into their possession etc and expel the same Geoffrey.

Witnesses: John Asplon, Peter le Parmenter, William de Saham, William de Deping', Roger Greywerk and others.

Given in the chapter house of the said nuns Wednesday before St Gregory in the year of grace 1302.

Seal: missing: slits for tag

<u>*Endorsed*</u> una schoppa in parochia sancti Johannis et in redditu x solidorum.

321. E315/Vol. 35 No. 19   21 September 1416

<u>*Lease*</u> indented for forty years with warranty by Agnes Leyk prioress of the house of St Michael near Staunford and the convent there to Richard Halom *alias* Milner of Okeham in the county of Rutland of their water-mill situated in the nuns' several pasture called 'le Nunneszerde' in the town of Wyrthorp' together with the pond and all other appurtenances, with free entrance and exit on the east. To hold the aforesaid mill with the stream and all other appurtenances to the aforesaid Richard, his heirs or assignees from Michaelmas next etc. Annual rent of 40d at two terms, namely at Easter and Michaelmas by equal portions. And if the rent is in arrears by one month, the prioress and convent and their successors may levy a distress in the aforesaid mill with its appurtenances etc. And if the rent is in arrears by half a year and sufficient distress cannot be found in the mill, the prioress and convent and their successors may re-enter

the mill etc and hold it in its former state and expel Richard and his heirs and assignees etc. And Richard, his heirs and assignees, during the term aforesaid will repair and maintain the water-mill etc. at their own expense.

Witnesses: John Broun draper, John Steneby, Thomas Spicer, Thomas Basset, John Longe junior and others.

Given in their chapter house Monday after the Exaltation of the Holy Cross 4 Henry V.

Seal: missing: slit for tag.

322. E315/Vol. 35 No. 50   29 September 1388

Lease for lives in survivorship by Alice Coupeldyk prioress of the house of St Michael near Staunford and the convent there to John Spaldyng of Wirthorp' tailor, Asselina his wife and Robert their son, of a messuage with a garden adjacent and with its appurtenances situated in the town of Wirthorp' between the tenement which Emma de Wirthorp' recently held on the east and the common croft of the town of Wirthorp' on the west and abutting on the king's highway towards the cross (*contra crucem*) towards the south and on the field(s) of Wirthorp' towards the north. Annual rent to the prioress and convent or their successors of 12d of silver.

Witnesses: John Weldon', John Hawe, William Sybeston' of Staunford, Robert Smith, John Bury, Simon Heyward of Wirthorp' and others.

seal: missing: slits for tag.

323. E315/Vol. 35 No. 98

Quitclaim by Walter called 'Leche' dwelling in Staunford to the prioress of St Michael outside Staunford and to all her successors of all his right and claim in those houses which are situated in the parish of St Martin, Stanford, between the grange which formerly was of John de Rippez on the east and the tenement of the aforesaid prioress on the south.

Witnesses: William Puncyn, Henry Faderman, John de Wakerl', Bernard Bonde, Roger de Makeseye, John the smith (*fabro*), William Faderman clerk and others.

Seal: missing: slit for tag.

Endorsed: (i) Carta Walteri Leche de Stanford'
(ii) quieta clamacio de domibus in parochia sancti Martini

Not dated

324. E315/Vol. 35 No. 235   **12 March 1342**

Grant with warranty by Thomas de Huntingdon' of Staunford furbisher (*furbour*) to Atthelina de Kent' of Cotherstoke and her heirs and assignees for a certain sum of money of a messuage with a curtilage adjacent with appurtenances in Staunford in the parish of St Paul, which messuage is situated between the tenement in part of Geoffrey Briselaunce and in part of Walter le Noble on the east and the tenement pertaining to the rectory of the church of St Mary of 'Bynnewerk' on the west: the messuage etc extends from the king's highway towards the north up to the tenement formerly of Eustace Malherbe towards the south. To hold the aforesaid messuage etc to the aforesaid Atthelena and her heirs and assignees of the chief lord of that fee for the services owed and accustomed, well, freely and by inheritance in perpetuity.

Witnesses: Henry de Tiddiswell, William de Schelington', Geoffrey de Wodeschlade, Hugh de Walington', Thomas de Schirlond, John de Empingham, John de Uffington', Geoffrey Brislaunce, Reginald de Salteby, William Gentil, John de Aldborugh, Robert Schalonner of Staunford and others.

Given at Staunford Tuesday on the feast of St Gregory the Pope 16 Edward III.

Seal: missing: slits for tag.

325. E315/Vol. 36 No. 110   **15/17 April 1298**

Confirmation by the official of the bishop of Lincoln sitting in St Michael's church, Cornstall, Stannford of a composition between Matilda prioress of St Michael's near Stannford and the convent there, and William de Preston vicar of All Saints near the bridge [*sic*], Staunford; William promises on oath to pay an annual pension of 20s to the nuns if he is able to pay. In case of dispute, an inquisition is to be made by the men of the parish into his ability to pay. Remission of all arrears.

Witnesses: William Poucyn then bailiff, Henry de Luffenham, Henry Faderman, Bernard Bond, Reginald Normane, Benedict de Brampton, John de Novo Loco and others.

Dated at St Michaels 15 April 1298; the Official's confirmation 17 April.

326. E315/Vol. 37 No. 20

Lease with warranty by Stephen de Novo Loco of Staunford to William Bonne of Staunford for seven marks of silver of his houses with all their appurtenances which are situated on the Welland (*super _Welond*) in the parish of St Martin between the houses of William Sampson towards the west and the houses which Stephen granted to Geoffrey his son towards the east with the whole curtilage adjacent just as it extends in breadth between the curtilage which Stephen sold to Richard son of Hugh Ruffus towards the east and his wall towards the west and in length in a straight line from the corner of the great solar up to the east jamb of the gate towards the croft of St Martin with the whole gate and with free entrance and exit through the gate. And in like manner with an annual quit rent of 3s 5½d with reliefs, escheats etc to be received quarterly, namely 10d at

Christmas, 10d at Easter, 10d at the Nativity of St John the Baptist [24 June] and 11½d at Easter from that house with appurtenances which Stephen granted to the said Geoffrey his son, which house is situated between the houses of the said Richard son of Hugh Ruffus towards the east and the houses which he sold to William Bonne towards the west. To hold to William Bonne and his heirs or assignees freely and by inheritance in perpetuity. Annual rent to the nuns of St Michael and their successors of 6s 11d and payable quarterly, namely 20d at Christmas, 20d at Easter, 20d at the Nativity of St John the Baptist and 23d at Michaelmas, and to Stephen and his heirs or assignees of a clove (*unum clavuin gariophili*) at Easter for all services, customs, exactions and for all other secular demands pertaining to anyone.

Witnesses: William Reyn', Richard Aldus, Sampson Reyner, Philip Gaugy, Peter de Norff', Thomas de Wissynden', William Pucyn, William Samps', Stephen de Wiggele, Ralph Rowe and others.

Seal: missing: slit for tag

Not dated ? late thirteenth century.

327. E315/Vol. 37 No. 26

Grant in free alms with warranty by Gilbert Parent of Stanford' to the church of St Michael of Stanford' and the nuns there of ten acres of arable land in the fields of Stanford' of the fee of the lord abbot of Peterborough: namely one acre lying near the land of William son of David outside the courtyard of the said nuns, one acre near 'Sevenwellis', six acres at 'Lingcroft', and two acres in 'Midilfurlang'. And over and above these ten acres, confirmation by Gilbert to the same nuns of three acres at 'Kirnersheng' with the meadow adjacent. To hold freely and quit of all secular exaction in perpetuity. Further, quitclaim by Gilbert of all his right and claim in the aforesaid lands and in all rents, lands and possessions which he or Geoffrey his father or any of his predecessors granted or sold to the aforesaid nuns. For this grant and quitclaim, the nuns give Gilbert two and a half marks of silver.

Witnesses: Alexander dean of Stanford', Walter de Tikencote, Richard Pecke, Hugh son of Reiner, Hugh de Stiandebi, Adam de Ufford then reeve (*tunc preposito*), Sampson son of Godric, Henry Gaugi, Hugh de Uffinton' and others.

Seal: missing: slits for tag

Endorsed: (i) Carta Gilberti Parent de Decim acris terre cum prato adiacente.
(ii) Stamford'

Not dated

328. E315/Vol. 37 No. 37

Quitclaim by Thomas March' son of Peter March' to Amice prioress of St Michael Stamford and the convent there of all his right and claim in a certain messuage which

Reginald the tanner holds in Writthorp' with its appurtenances. Further Thomas declares that he and his heirs or assignees are bound [*ms missing*] the said prioress and her successors in 4s annual rent to be received from him and his heirs or assigns from a certain messuage and half a virgate of land with its appurtenances which he holds of the said prioress in Writthorp': the rent to be paid 2s at Michaelmas and 2s at Easter. And if Thomas, his heirs or assignees do not pay the said rent at the terms written above, the said prioress and convent and her successors may distrain Thomas etc in the said messuage and land.

Witnesses: sir Geoffrey Russel then steward of Peterborough (*tunc senescallo Burgi*), [...], master Henry Sampson rector of the church of Eston', Thomas son of John le Freman, Roger de Merle, Walter de Hybern clerk and others.

Seal: missing: slit for *Seal*

Endorsed: (i) Carta Thome March' de uno mesuagio et iiii solidis annui redditus (? contemporary)
(ii) Wirthorp (? contemporary)

Not dated ? mid/later thirteenth century

329. E315/Vol. 37 No. 76   22 December 1331

Lease indented for life and three years thereafter with warranty by the prioress and convent of the nuns of the house of St Mary of Wyrthorp' to William de Byrthorp' of Staunford of all the arable land with appurtenances which they had in the fields of Staunford' in divers tillages above Rogeford' (*in diversis culturis supra Rogeford'*). Annual rent of half a pound of pepper at Michaelmas and performance annually on behalf of the prioress and convent and their successors of all services owed and accustomed to the chief lords of that fee.

Witnesses: Richard Bertelmew of Staunford, John Cloket of the same, Bernard Bonde of the same, Richard Lymbrenner' of the same, Richard Freman of Wyrthorp', Richard de Wakerlee of the same, Alan de Wyrthorp' clerk and others.

Given at Wyrthorp' Sunday next before Christmas 5 Edward III.

Seal: missing: slit for tag.

330. E315/Vol. 37 No. 142

Grant in free alms with warranty by Alice daughter of Walkelin de Stanford' to the church of St Michael of Stanford' and the nuns there of her houses with all appurtenances in the parish of St Michael the Greater of Stanford' which are situated at the head of Butchers' Street (*ad caput vici carnificum*) near the lane which goes towards Colgate, very close (*propinquiores*) to the house of Henry Gaugi towards the south. To hold to the said nuns in free alms, doing the annual service owed to the lord of the fees.

Witnesses: master Henry dean of Stanford, master Pain rector of the church of St Clement, William de Pappele rector of the church of St Mary of Binnewerc, sir Michael vicar of the church of St Martin, Thomas vicar of the church of St Andrew, Hugh son of Reiner, Henry son of Alexander, Henry Gaugi, John Bottay, William son of David, William de Scheldingtorp', Peter de Casterton', Adam de Ufford', Hugh the janitor and others.

Seal: missing: slit for tag.

Not dated

331. E315/Vol. 37 No. 207   13 May 1364

Foundation by Katherine Russell prioress of St Michael without Stannford and the convent there of the anniversary of John de Spoford late vicar of the church of St Andrew Staunford and confessor of all the members of our convent, for money given by his executors. *Placebo, dirige* and mass with note are to be said on his anniversary and his name is to be entered in the martyrology of the house and read in chapter among the benefactors.

Dated in the chapter at St Michael's in Pentecost 1364 (*en semoigne de Pentecost mil trescentz lx et quart*) and 38 Edward III
FRENCH

332. E315/Vol. 38 No. 34   27 October 1451

Inspeximus by Alexander Prowet inceptor in canon law, precentor of Lincoln and official and keeper of the spiritualities of the Bishopric of Lincoln *sede vacante* of admission of Michael priest to the vicarage of St Martin's, Stanford with all vicarial burdens at the presentation of the prioress of St Michael's Staunford and the convent of the same: the vicarage consists in all small tithes of the said church and the chapel of Burlee and the corn tithes and tithes from crofts and curtilages in the parish, saving a pension of 2 marks per annum to the nuns; and also of the admission of Hugh de Stanford priest to the said vicarage at the presentation of the nuns: the vicarage to consist of the offerings (*altaragia*) but the nuns are to support the chapel of Burlee, if necessary, and the vicar is to pay only synodals, the nuns providing hospitality for the archdeacon and bearing all burdens.

Dated at Lincoln 27 October 1451

333. E315/Vol. 38 No. 44   29 December 1359

Lease indented for twelve years with warranty by Agnes de Brakenbregh' prioress of St Michael outside Staunford and the convent there to John de Belue of Wyrthorp' and Emma his wife of two acres and a rood of arable land with appurtenances in the fields of Wyrthorp' of which one and a half acres lie together in 'le Middelfeld' near the land of William Hayward' on the east and abut in one headland (*in uno capite*) on the land of Alan

147

Aylcy towards the south and in the other headland (*in alio capite*) on the land of Alan Brotherhous towards the north. One half acre lies in 'le Netherfeld' near the land formerly of Richard Freman towards the east and the land formerly of Hugh Aylcy towards the west. One rood lies at Holbrok between the land of William Hayward' towards the south and the land of Robert Rowe towards the north and it abuts on the land of William Wenge towards the west. To hold the aforesaid land with appurtenances to the aforesaid John and Emma from Christmas 33 Edward III etc. Annual rent of 12d of silver at Easter for all other services and demands. And if the aforesaid rent is in arrears at the aforesaid term, the same prioress and convent etc may levy a distress etc.

Given in the aforesaid priory at Staunford Sunday after Christmas in the year aforesaid.

No seal

334. E315/Vol. 38 No. 87

<u>*Quitclaim*</u> by Robert son and heir of Walter le Flemeng formerly burgess of Stamford to Elizabeth prioress of St Michael outside Staunford and the nuns there of all his right and claim in that shop with solar above and with all its other appurtenances in Staunford which is situated between the house formerly of Henry le Specer towards the north and the house formerly of John le Schavelere towards the south, which shop with the aforementioned solar etc Walter his father granted to the aforesaid nuns and their successors in free alms, according to what is contained in the charter of feoffment of the aforesaid Walter which remains in the hands of the aforesaid nuns.

Witnesses: Hugh Buntyng', John le Flemeng son of Walter, John le Flemeng de Cornestal', William Bilkesle vyneter, Hugh de Tykencote, Sampson Reyner, William Reyner, Walter son of Norman, Henry Faderman, Geoffrey le Mercer, Philip Gaugy and others.

Seal: missing: slit for tag.

<u>*Not dated*</u>

335. E315/Vol. 38 No. 143   20 July 1331

<u>*Lease*</u> for five years by the prioress and convent of St Michael outside Staunford to sir Hugh de Northburg' rector of the church of Bernak' near Staunford of all manner of corn tithes (*omniamodo decimas garbarum*) which the said nuns were accustomed to receive from time immemorial within the limits of the field of Pilisgate and of the field of Bernak' from the lands which are held of the fee of the manor of Burle near Staunford. Annual rent to the prioress and convent of 13s 4d.

Given in the house of the said nuns on the feast of St Margaret the virgin 1331.

Seal: missing: slit for tag

<u>*Endorsed:*</u> Bernak' Pylysgate et Burley (? not contemporary)

Note: these tithes were regularly leased by the nunnery to the rector of Barnack – Nicholas de Appultre in 1310 and Simon de Northburg in 133, E315/41/145; E315/33/64.

336. E315/Vol. 38 No. 190

Grant with warranty by Ralph son of Henry son of Ascelin of Staunford by the assent and wish of Luneday his mother to the church of St Michael outside Staunford and the nuns there for 22s 8d of silver which the nuns paid to Ralph in his great necessity (*in mea magna necessitate*) of an annual rent of 3s 6½d of silver and all his right and claim with all escheats and appurtenances which his father and predecessors had and which Ralph and his heirs or assignees can have in future (*habere poterimus*) from those houses which his father Henry son of Ascelin of Staunford formerly granted at fee farm to Randolph le Messager and Matilda his wife, which houses Peter de Ingethorp and Matilda his wife held. The houses are situated in the parish of All Saints in the Market of Staunford between the houses which David the Jew held at fee farm from Geoffrey the scribe (*scriptore*) towards the east and the houses of Simon Ballart and Reyner de Stiandbi towards the west. The rent is to be received quarterly namely 10½d at the Nativity of St John the Baptist [4 June] for the altar of the Holy Trinity, 10½d at Michaelmas for the altar of St Mary Magdalene, 10½d at Christmas for the altar of Holy Trinity and 11d at Easter for the altar of St Mary Magdalene, and is to be used for providing a light before the aforesaid altars (*ad luminare inveniendum coram predictis altaribus*) in the church of St Michael outside Staunford. To hold the said rent of Ralph and his heirs or assignees to the nuns and their successors freely etc without any service and secular exaction and demand pertaining to the lord of the fee and to Ralph etc. And if Ralph and his heirs or assignees do not pay the said rent to the nuns or their successors at the said terms or within the octaves, they will double the said rent as a penalty (*dictum redditum nomine pene dupplicabimur*). Furthermore, the nuns and their assignees may distrain those dwelling in the said houses by their chattels until they make full satisfaction to the nuns.

Witnesses: Hugh son of Reyner, Alexander his brother, Richard Pecce, Walter le Fleming, William de Francton', William son of David, Peter Cokkesnol and others.

No seal

<u>Endorsed</u>: (i) Carta Marie Peke Peck' [*sic*]
(ii) omnium sanctorum in foro

Not dated

337. E315/Vol. 38 No. 239

Grant with warranty by Juliana daughter of John Bottay of Stanford' to the church of St Michael of Stanford' and the nuns there of an annual rent of 22d to be received at Michaelmas with homages, reliefs and all other appurtenances in the parish of St Martin of Stanford, namely 6d from the house situated at the exit of the town towards Writhorp' (*ad exitum ville versus Writhorp'*) near the house of William the smith (*fabri*) towards the north, 9d from the house of Clement the vintner (*vinetarii*) which Ingald de Buwedon' holds at fee farm, 6d from the house which Thomas de Bradecroft holds and 1d from the house of Geoffrey le Daubur. To hold of Juliana and her heirs to the said nuns and their successors freely etc. Annual rent of 6d within the octave of Michaelmas for all service and secular demand. For this grant, the aforesaid nuns gave Juliana 16s of silver which she gave to Sarah (*Sarre*) her sister for her marriage (*ad se maritandum*) whereupon Sarah in the court of the lord abbot of Peterborough quitclaimed to Juliana and her heirs or assignees all her right and claim in the aforesaid rent.

Witnesses: Walter de Tikenk', Hugh son of Reiner, Clement the vintner (*vinetario*), Walter de Brunna, Henry Gaugi, Isaac his brother, Sampson son of Godric, William son of David, William de Sumerkotes, Adam de Ufford', Henry de Wakerle, William de Pappell', Hugh de Bernak', Philip the dyer (*tinctore*), Peter de Stanford' clerk and others.

Seal: missing: slit for tag

Endorsed: (i) concessio monialibus pro pluribus tenementis et xxii denariis.
(ii) parochia sancti Martini

Not dated

338. E315/Vol. 38 No. 240

Grant in free alms with warranty by Alpeisa daughter of Geoffrey son of Reiner of Stanford' to the church of St Michael of Stanford' and the nuns there of those houses with appurtenances in the parish of St John of Stanford' which are situated between the house of Luke the skinner (*pelliparii*) towards the south and the house of Gervase the stonecutter (*incisoris*) towards the north. Annual rent to the lord of the fee or his assignee of 9½d at three terms, namely 2d at Christmas, 6d at Easter and 1½d at the feast of St Peter in Chains [1 August] for all service and secular exaction: so that one moiety of the rents issuing from the said houses be assigned for a pittance of the aforesaid nuns each year and the other moiety be assigned for purchasing the smocks of the same (*ad camisias earumdem comparandas*).

Witnesses: master Henry then dean of Stanford', master Pain rector of the church of St Clement, William de Pappele rector of the church of St Mary de 'Binnewerc', Michael vicar of the church of St Martin, John Bottay, Henry Gaugi, Adam de Ufford', Hugh de Bernak', Henry de Wakerle, Hugh the janitor and others.

Seal: missing: slit for tag.

Not dated

339. E315/Vol. 38 No. 243

Grant with warranty by Alice de Nevilla called prioress of St Michael of Stanford' and the whole convent there, by common assent of the whole chapter and by the counsel of Henry de Fiskerton' then their prior to Nicholas son of Alexander of a certain house in the parish of St Mary 'Binnewerch', namely that which Nicholas le Mariner once held and sold to them. The house is situated between the land of Richard de Eston' towards the north and the land which was of Andrew de Ketene towards the south. To hold of the prioress and convent to Henry* and his heirs freely and quit of all secular service pertaining to them, saving 1d 'de Ware' which the aforesaid Nicholas and his heirs will pay annually to the heirs of Peter Punteis in the octave of Easter. Annual rent of 3s 6d payable quarterly. And neither Nicholas nor any of his heirs may sell or pledge the house to any clerk, layman or Jew without the common assent and licence of their whole chapter.

Witnesses: Alexander then dean of Stanford', Hugh vicar of St Martin, Richard vicar of the church of St Mary 'Binnewerch', Walter de Tikencote, Ralph son of Achard, Richard Pecke, Henry son of Alexander, Michael his brother, Hugh son of Reiner, Alexander his brother, Andrew the palmer (*palmero*), Henry his son and others.

Seal: missing: slit for tag.

Endorsed (i) de domo in Benewerk' affirmat'
(ii) vacat

Not dated
* *probably error for Nicholas*

340. E315/Vol. 39 No. 49

Grant indented with warranty by Matilda de Lenna prioress of St Michael near Stanf' and the nuns there by the consent of brother William de Stok' then prior of the same place to Augustine de Norfolch' woolmerchant (*lanatori*) of Stanf' of a certain courtyard enclosed within walls, together with the walls aforesaid on each side, with free entrance and exit and with other appurtenances: the courtyard lies in the parish of St Mary near the bridge of Staunford and the entrance of the same courtyard lies between the tenement formerly of Henry le Specer towards the east and the tenement of Roger le Carpenter towards the west. And the said courtyard with entrance extends in length from the king's highway towards the south up to the tenement of the said Augustine towards the north. To hold to Augustine and his heirs and assignees freely and by inheritance in perpetuity. Annual rent of 3s payable quarterly for all secular service and demand. And if the farm is in arrears by three terms, the prioress and nuns and their successors may take possession of the said courtyard with appurtenances, etc.

Witnesses: Andrew Nye, Alfred (*Alfredo*) le Grat', Peter de Wysebeche, John Asplon, John Bonet, Robert de Greton' and others.

Seal: missing: slit for tag.

Endorsed: (i) devenerit ad firmam
(ii) vacat

Not dated

341. E315/Vol. 39 No. 239

Grant in free alms with warranty by master Nicholas son of Absolon of Staunford to the church of St Michael outside Staunford and the nuns there of 25s annual rent with appurtenances to be received from two houses with appurtenances in the town of Staunford namely 16s of silver payable quarterly from one house which Richard de Sancto Edmundo held of master Peter the pupil (*alumpno*) of Reyner formerly dean of Staunford, in the parish of St Mary at the bridge situated between the house which was of Robert *ad arcam* towards the east and the house of the said Richard towards the west: and 9s of silver payable quarterly from one other house which Adam de Staunford dyer (*tinctor*) formerly held of the said master Peter in the parish of St John, situated between the ditch of the castle of Staunford' towards the west and the houses which were of Ralph Halvere towards the east, saving to the said nuns a rent of 3s received from of old from the said house. To hold to the said nuns and their successors freely and quit of all exaction and secular demand in perpetuity, saving the service of the lord of the fee.

Witnesses: sir Gilbert de Biham then dean of Stamford, Hugh son of Reyner, Richard Peck', Walter le Flemeng', Walter de Brunne, William son of David, Robert de Corby, William son of William son of David and others.

No Seal

Endorsed: in parochial Sancte Marie *ad pontem* de ix solidis [de] domibus iuxta castrum datis monialibus.

Not dated

342. E315/Vol. 39 No. 241

Grant with warranty by Stephen de Novo Loco to Geoffrey his son for his service of his houses with all appurtenances situated in the parish of St Martin Staunford between the houses formerly of Richard Selleware towards the east and Stephen's houses towards the west with each gable and with the gable of his solar in his courtyard as they extend from the west gable of the aforesaid houses in a straight line up to the gable of Stephen's solar aforesaid along the boundaries fixed between them there and thus from the gable of that solar in a straight line up to the east corner of Stephen's postern gate; which for himself and his parties and for Geoffrey and his parties he makes common (*quam michi et meis sibi et suis constituo communem*) in perpetuity; together with 32d annual quit rent with appurtenances to be received quarterly from the houses of Richard son of Hugh Russel. To hold of Stephen and his heirs or assignees to the aforesaid Geoffrey and his heirs or assignees or the assignees of his heirs freely etc.and by inheritance. Annual rent of 3s 5½d of silver payable quarterly, namely 10d at Easter, 10d at the feast of St John the Baptist [24 June] 10d at Michaelmas and 1½d as 'langovele' and 10d at Christmas for all services, customs, exactions and for all other secular demands pertaining to anyone.

Witnesses: William Reyner, Philip Gaugy, Geoffrey Gaugy, Peter the dyer (*tinctore*), Gilbert de Wodecroft, Richard Faderman, Walter Burnild, Thomas de Luffenham, Richard Aldus, Reg[inald] de Wiggele, William Sampson, Thomas de Wissynden', John de

Wissynden', Walter de Luffenham, Richard Russel, Robert Wodefoul, Saul (*Sawale*) Saddyng', Richard Calve, Thomas de Burgo and others.

Seal: missing: slit for tag.

Endorsed (i) sacrist' (? contemporary)
(ii) sancti martini (? contemporary)

Not dated late thirteenth/early fourteenth century.

343. E315/Vol. 40 No.187

Sale with warranty by Peter Damisel of Stanford' to Alexander de Pilesiate tanner (*tannatori*) for three marks of silver which Alexander gave to Peter to quit him from indebtedness to the Jews (*ad me de iudaismo aquietandum*) and for a tunic of burrel of a certain house with appurtenances in the parish of All Saints beyond the bridge of Stanford' near the bank of the Welland (*iuxta ripam Welondie*) namely that house which is situated between the house which was of Roger Gurram towards the east and Peter's house towards the west. To hold to the said Alexander and his heirs or assignees freely and quit of all service and secular exaction pertaining to Peter or his heirs. Annual rent to the lord of the fee of ½d at Michaelmas for all service.

Witnesses: John Bottay, Henry Gaugi, Sampson son of Godric, Hugh de Bernak', Alexander Burnild', Reiner his sons, Geoffrey Doget, Richard Aldus, William de Pappele clerk and others.

Seal: missing: slit for tag.

344. E315/Vol. 40 No. 215   3 May 1357

Lease for lives in survivorship with warranty by the prioress and nuns of the house of St Michael outside Staunford to William Bride miller (*molendinario*) of Staunford and Marieria his wife of two messuages in Staunford with their appurtenances. One messuage is situated in the parish of St Mary 'de Beynwerk' between the tenement formerly of Geoffrey de Ryngusdon' towards the east and the lane which is called 'Westwellelane' towards the west. The other messuage is situated in the same parish between the tenement of sir William de Burton knight towards the north and the tenement formerly of Adam Garlemonger' towards the south. Annual rent of 5s of silver payable quarterly; if the rent is in arrears at any term by one month, the prioress and nuns may distrain all the goods in the two messuages etc. And William and Marieria during the whole of their lives will maintain at their own expense all the houses constructed in the aforesaid two messuages etc.

Given at Staunford the Invention of the Holy Cross 31 Edward III.

No seal: slits for tags.

Endorsed: dimissio de v solidis de ii messuagiis in parochia beate Marie Bynwerk.

345. E315/Vol. 40 No. 219

Sale with warranty by Warner son of Ailrich de Kasewik to Richard the chaplain his brother for four marks of silver of a house with appurtenances which he bought from Herbrand situated in the parish of St Michael of Stanford' between the house of Geoffrey de Tornaham to the east and the house of Robert Godemor to the west; to hold to Richard and his heirs or assignees well, peacefully and by inheritance and free of all secular service pertaining to Warner or his heirs.

Witnesses: Walter de Tikencot', Ralph son of Achard, Richard Pek, William Fleming, Henry de Tikencot', Clement the vintner, Henry son of Alexander, Hugh son of Reiner, Walter Stude, Geoffrey the clerk and others.

Seal: missing: slit for tag.

Endorsed: (i) Stanford' de domibus in parochia sancti Michaelis
(ii) tercia de domibus in parochia suprascripta.

Not dated

346. E315/Vol. 40 No. 227

Bond by Simon son of Geoffrey de Stanford to pay to the nuns of St Michael's without Stanford 14s per annum for a messuage in the parish of St John Stanford situated between the house formerly Richard Fuscedame's to the south and the house of Gervase the tailor to the north. This messuage was given to the nuns by Alpeisa, Simon's sister.

Witnesses: Terricus de Colonia, Hugh son of Reiner, Henry Scibeci, Walter le Fleming, John son of Sampson, Walter son of Ketil, John Botay, Henry Gaugy, Isaac son of Henry, William son of David, Walter de Brunna, Apsolon at the bridge, Gilbert his brother, Peter de Casterton, Peter son of Geoffrey, Alan son of Mor and others.

Not dated ? early thirteenth century.

347. E315/Vol. 40 No. 271   **21 February 1333**

Agreement between the prioress and convent of St Michael without Staunford and John le Bellegetere of Staunford that whereas Geoffrey de Fardon of Staunford has let to John for the term of eight years a messuage by the east gate of Staunford from which 5s annual rent is due to the prioress and convent, which rent is 25s in arrears; the prioress and convent shall not distrain for the arrears during John's tenancy provided that he pays the rent as due.

Witnesses: William de Birthorp, Ralph le Lymbrennere, Thomas le Lymbrennere, William de Belmisthorp, Ralph de Neukyrk, John de Folkyngham, Richard Bertilman of Staunford and others.

Dated at Stannford Sunday before St Peter in cathedra 7 Edward III

348. E315/Vol. 41 No. 38   **5 May 1430**

Lease for fourscore years from Elizabeth Weldon prioress of the nunnery of St Michael
near Stannford and the convent of the same to John Englyssh of Staunford locksmith
(*lockyer*) of a vacant plot in the parish of St Mary at the bridge, Stannford between the
messuage of the gild of Corpus Christi on the east and the messuage of Nicholas Rydel
on the west, abutting on the king's highway to the south and on the tenement of John
Pratte to the north. Annual rent to the prioress and convent and their successor of 3s 4d.
John Englyssh to build a shop and solar over on the plot at his own expense within the
first two years, and to keep it in repair.

Dated in the nun's chapter house 5 May 8 Henry VI
[See 303]

349. E315/Vol. 41 No. 46

Grant in free alms with warranty by William son of William the smith (*fabri*) of Staunford
to the church of St Michael outside Staunford and the nuns there of 6d annual quit rent
with appurtenances to be received at the feast of the Invention of the Holy Cross [3
May] from his houses which are situated in 'Webesteregate' in the parish of St Martin,
Stanford, between the houses of Henry Prat towards the south and the houses formerly
of Ingald de Budone towards the north. The grant is made for keeping William's obit. To
hold the rent to the nuns and their successors freely etc and by hereditary right in
perpetuity.

Witnesses: William Reyner, Richard Aldus, Gilbert de Cestertone, Henry Faderman,
Walter son of Norman, Henry Prat, Richard de Corbye, William de Stapilford', William
son of Hugh the smith (*fabri*), Philip Gaugy and others.

Seal: missing: slit for tag

Endorsed: (i) sacri
(ii) sancti Martini in ye Webistirg'

Not dated

350. E315/Vol. 41 No. 117   **29 September 1428**

Grant with warranty by William Byllesby of Worthorp' to Richard Byllesby of Eston' his
son and to Margaret his [Richard's] wife of five acres of arable land lying in the town and
fields of Eston' and Worthorp', of which one acre of land lies in 'Braudeswro' between
the land of the rector of Eston' on the north west and the land of John Freberne on the
south west, abutting on the land of the lord of Eston' on the north west and on the land
of the nuns of St Michael on the south west: annual rent to the chapel of St Thomas on
the bridge of Stanford of 1d. And one acre lies in 'Braudeswro' between the land of the
said nuns on the north west and the land of John Pechell' on the [southwest and one
headland abuts on the land of the lord of Eston' on the northwest and the other on the
land of the said nuns on the southwest. And half an acre lies on 'le sponge' between the

land of John Pechell' on the south] side and the land of the prioress and convent of Coventre on the north side and one headland abuts on 'le Sponbrok" towards the west and the other on 'le Melnebalke' toward the east. And one rood of land lies near Parkwall' between the land of the lord of Eston' on the south side and the land of John Pechell' on the north side and one headland abuts on 'le Sponboork' [*sic* for 'Sponbrook'] towards the west and the other on 'le Mylnebalke' towards the east. And one rood lies in 'le Calowcrofte' between the land of the lord of Eston' on each side and one headland abuts on the land of the said nuns on the north and the other on the land of the said nuns on the south. And one rood lies on 'le Vatyrgalle' between the land of the abbot and convent of Crowland towards the north, and one acre and three roods of land lie between [the land] of the said nuns on the south side and by the road leading to the town of Northampton aforesaid on the north side and one headland [abuts] on the town of Worthorp' towards the east and the other on 'le Graves' towards the west. To hold the aforesaid five acres of land with all their appurtenances to the aforesaid Richard and Margaret his wife and to their heirs and assignees of the chief lords of that fee for the services owed and accustomed by right in perpetuity.

Witnesses: John Bussches, John Lowthorp', Robert Schepey, John Andrewe of Worthorp' and many others.

Given at Worthorp' Michaelmas 7 Henry VI
[*See 449*]

351. E315/Vol. 41 No. 133

Grant and quitclaim with warranty by Matilda formerly wife of Hugh de Uffintona in her widow right to the church of St Michael outside Stanford' and the nuns there of all the land with appurtenances in the croft which lies between the town of Stanford' and the house of St Michael aforesaid and which abuts on the road which goes to Wirthorp' towards the south. To hold freely and quit of all service and secular exaction pertaining to Matilda or her heirs, saving the service of the lord of the fee.

Witnesses: Hugh then vicar of the church of St Martin of Stanford', Turbert chaplain of the church of All Saints, William de Sumercotes, John Bottay, Henry Gaugi, Adam de Ufford', Sampson son of Godric and others.

Not sealed

Endorsed (i) xxxi Quieta clamancia Matildis quondam uxoris Hugonis de Uffinton' de crofto iacente inter villam et domum Sancti Michaelis.
(ii) omnino ignorat
(iii) Stamford'

Not dated

352. E315/Vol. 41 No. 135

Lease from Elizabeth prioress of St Michael without Stanford and the convent of the same with the assent and will of Henry de Ouerton then prior to Richard Testard of Bradecroft of a toft and messuage in the village of Bradecroft situated between the messuage of Alric de Casewyke and the meadow of earl John de Waren. Rent of 6s per annum.

Witnesses: William de Notingham, Andrew Arketel, Alexander Lucas, Walter le Flemmeng, William Wilkes, Nicholas Pert, Alric de Casewike, Thomas clerk and many others.

Not dated ? late thirteenth century
Note: Overton was prior in 1271

353. E315/Vol. 41 No. 138

Chirograph lease indented for life by Petronilla prioress of the church of St Michael of Stanford' and the convent there by the assent and will of sir William their prior to Simon de Sancto Dionisio burgess of Stanford' of seven and a half acres of arable land in the territory of Stanford', namely two and a half acres lying on 'Hennehowe', two and a half acres at the cross of Rihale, one acre lies near the road which goes to Lincoln and two acres lie between the church of St Leonard and the town of Stanford'. To hold to the said Simon freely etc, so that Simon will plough, manure, sow, harrow, hoe and reap the aforesaid lands and gather, bind and stack the sheaves; and he will meet from his own resources all expenses of the aforesaid lands: all this he will do in order to receive a moiety of the profit of the same lands. And if any fault is found in the aforesaid land on account of the manuring etc, the prioress and convent or their warden may take possession of the lands with the whole crop and hold them until Simon has made amends. And also be it known that when Simon dies, his part of the crop of the said lands - with all the aforesaid lands - will be appropriated to the said nuns (*in usus proprios dictarum monialium deveniet*) for the health of his soul and the souls of his predecessors and successors.

Witnesses: Michael vicar of the church of St Martin, William de Pappelea parson of the church of St Mary of 'Binnewerc', Henry Gaugi, John Bottay, Philip the dyer, Geoffrey de Turlebi clerk, Hugh the janitor, Adam de Ufford, Geoffrey de Turlebi serjeant and others.

Seal: missing: slit for tag.

Endorsed: (i) Symonis de sancto Dionisio
(ii) vacant

Not dated

354. E315/Vol. 41 No. 140

Grant by Elyas de Hampton with the assent of Cicely de [...] his wife to Agnes de Suthluffenham daughter of Isaac le [...] of a messuage situated in the parish of St Michael Cornestall outside Cornestall gate between the house of Richard de Athelokston to the west and the house formerly belonging to ... de Wywell to the east. Annual rent of 2s to the prior and convent of Fineshade. For this grant, Agnes gave to Elyas four marks and to Cicely four ells of burnet and a supertunic.

Witnesses: Hugh son of Reiner, [...] Fleming, Andrew de Cornestall, William palmer, Robert dyer, Gilbert de Clive, Brond [... Ath]lokston and many others.

Not dated ? mid thirteenth century.

355. E315/Vol. 41 No. 242

Sale by William de Couentre to Robert de Bernardeshil for three marks ... of one house in the town of Stanford, namely that house which William de Wimundeham held of him and which is situated by the church of St Clement, and for 30s of another house in the town of Stanford, namely that which Thurstan son of Robert held of him and which is situated between his capital house and the house which he [i.e. Robert] bought from him first. Annual rent to William and his heirs of 1d.

Witnesses: Geoffrey the priest, Richard the priest, Ralph son of Achard, John Franceis, John his son, John Flammenc, Samson beyond the bridge, Geoffrey de Glint', Michael de Glint', Geoffrey son of Richard de Glinton', Herbert, Geoffrey de Exton'.

Seal: missing: slit for tag.

Endorsed: (i) be Willelmo de Coventre (contemporary)
De terra in Stanford
(ii) Quinta de domo iuxta ecclesiam Sancti Clementis (not contemporary)

Not dated ? early thirteenth century

356. E315/Vol. 41 No. 252

Grant with warranty and acquittance by Henry Prat of Staunford to the prioress of St Michael outside Staunford and the convent there of his houses situated on the fee of the same prioress and convent in the parish of St Martin, Staunford by the forge which was formerly of William the smith (*fabri*) at the exit of the town opposite the road which leads to Wyrthorp' towards the south. For this grant the said prioress and convent have granted Henry for the whole of his life, should his own provisions be lacking (*si defectus victus mei de rebus meis mobilibus et inmobilibus michi totaliter inveniat*) bread and ale to be received from their cellar and rations (*liberacionem coquine*), the same as the daily rations of a nun of the house of St Michael. And also the prioress and nuns have received Henry and Matilda as a brother and sister in their prayers and in all the benefits in the said house of St Michael from this hour forever.

Witnesses: Hugh Bunting', William Bilkis vintner, Andrew Nye, John le Flemang' junior, Robert le Flemang', John Saunsom, Walter Norman, William Pouncin, Richard the clerk and others.

Not sealed

Endorsed Staumford' (not contemporary)

Not dated ? late thirteenth/early fourteenth century.

357. E315/Vol. 41 No. 261   29 September 1323

Lease by Mabel prioress of St Michael outside Staunford and the nuns there with the consent and will of brother William de Weston' then their prior to Cecilia Portesmouth widow of William de Foderingeye of Staunford of their houses which are situated in Staunford in the parish of All Saints in the Market between the tenement of Henry de Pirebrok' on the west and the tenement of the aforesaid Cecilia which formerly was master Richard le Ferrenn's on the east and they extend from the king's highway towards the north to the tenement of the same Cecilia which formerly was Alured le Mercer's towards the south; to hold in perpetuity [*sic*]. Annual rent to the prioress and convent and their successors of 16s of silver. Cecilia is to maintain the houses and not to alienate them without the prioress' and nuns' consent.

Given in the chapter house of the said religious, Michaelmas 17 Edward II

Seal: missing: slit for tag.

Endorsed: Indentura xvi s' de domibus in parochia omnium sanctorum in foro (not contemporary).

358. E315/Vol. 41 No. 267   24 June 1413

Lease for a hundred years from Agnes Leyke prioress of the house of St Michael by Staunford and the convent of the same to John Bonde *alias* Marchaunt of Staunford and Agnes his wife of a shop with solar over in the parish of St John the Baptist Staunford between the tenement of the gild of Corpus Christi on both sides and abutting on the king's highway to the south. Lease from the Nativity of John the Baptist 1 Henry V. Annual rent of 4s to the prioress and convent. John and Agnes are to repair and keep up the shop and solar.

Dated at Staunford the feast and year above written

359. E315/Vol. 42 No. 66   3 February 1335

Quitclaim by Matilda widow of Andrew de Eston in Stannford to the church of St Michael without Stannford and the nuns there for her soul's health and that of her mother Cicely of all right in a croft of meadow in Bradecroft which Hugh Alrych held sometime of the said nuns. Sealing clause: sealed with Matilda's seal and that of the deanery of Stannford.

Witnesses: Bernard Bonde of Stannford, William de Birthorp of the same, Thomas de Ravel of the same, William in ye Walles of the same, Robert Flemyng of the same and others.

Dated at Stannford Saturday after the Purification of the BVM 9 Edward III

Seal: missing

360. E315/Vol. 42 No. 74   20 May 1492

Lease for nine years from Margaret Gudchepe prioress of the priory of St Michael beside Stannford and the convent of the same house to William Morcote late of Peykyrke and Alice his wife and John Lambard of all arable lands, meadows, pastures, and commodities belonging to the prioress and convent occupied in the name of their husbandry in the fields of Staunford, Worthorp, Eston, Colyweston, Burley, and Badyngton, together with the priory's tithes in the said fields; also all houses without the 'Syster yate' of the priory; three closes, namely 'the Warden yarde', 'the Cloose at Worthorp', and 'the Cloose besyde the Spitell in Staunford'; the house which Agnes Hede dwelleth in; the little Granery, the little stable, half the profits of the dovehouse, the house which the said prioress and convent's shepherd of late dwelled in, except the brewhouse and the bakehouse when the prioress and convent use it, and except the tithes in the field of Worthorp which the priest there has for his salary, also lease of chattlels and 'stuffe of husbandrye' as specified in an inventory, and pasture for 12 kine and a bull in Wenton by Cottesmore. The farmers to pay to the prioress and convent yearly 28 quarters and 1 bushell of wheat, 6 quarters of rye, 80 quarters of malt, 5 quarters of barley, 4 cartloads of hay, 6 hogs (price 2s 8d each), 1 ox (price 13s 4d), 1 boar (price 5s), 1 porkett (price 20d), 2 fat wethers, 2 fat lambs, as much straw as the prioress and convent need for baking and brewing; and they are to carry or cause to be carried 60 cartloads of wood per annum from the forest of Clyve to the priory, and as much stone and mortar as the priory needs for repairs; the farmers to bear the cost of keeping 8 kine and 12 capons; the farmers to have 'drosse and dregges' from the priory; at the end of the term to give seedcorn to the priory and to sow the land; the farmers to give 1 pig of every litter to the priory, a quarter of draffe to keep an ox for Christmas. Any dispute is to be referred to Thomas Sapcote, Robert Hans of Staunford and William Spencer of the same. The prioress and convent to pay the farmers 26s 8d per annum for better performing of covenants.

Dated in the chapter house of the priory.
[*see* 653]

361. E315/Vol. 42 No 75

Grant in free alms by Abraham Godriche burgess of Stanford to the proctors of the fabric of the church of St Mary of Bynnewerch' Staunford of his shop situated in the parish of All Saints in the Market, Staunford, namely in Butchers street between the shop formerly of John Pudelprest towards the west and the shop formerly of Richard de Luffenham towards the east. Annual rent to the nuns of St Michael by Staunford of 4s and to the capital lord of the fee 2s.

Witnesses: William de Notingham, Robert son of Isaac, Walter de Tilton', Hugh Chyld, William Douve, Walter de Brigestok', Robert de Makeseye, David Galun, William Hod, Robert Bunting, Laurence the tanner, William de Stretton' tanner, Alan de Berham clerk, Hugh Fusse, William de Empingham and others.

Seal: missing: slit for tag

Not dated ? late thirteenth century

362. E315/Vol. 42 No. 78

Grant by William de Covintre to Fineshade Priory and the brethren there of the houses which Robert de Bernardeshil held of him in the town of Staunford and quitclaim of 1d rent which Robert used to pay him.

Witnesses: Robert parson, Ralph son of Achart, John Francus, John Flemang, Randulf Mercer, Baldewin Faber, Geoffrey de Extun and others.

Seal: missing: slits for tag

Endorsed: De William de Couentre de Stanford [another hand] de domibus quas Robertus de Bernardishil tenuit prima carta de dom. iuxta ecclesia sancti clementis.

Not dated ? early thirteenth century.

363. E315/Vol. 42 No. 103

Sale by Philip de Leycestria priest to Henry de Deping burgess of Stanford for two marks of sterling of those houses which he bought from Thomas son of John at the gate of Bernardishil which are situated in the parish of St Mary of Binewerc in Stanford between the houses formerly of Richard Trowe towards the east and the houses of Henry de Deping towards the west. Annual rent to the nuns of St Michael outside Stanford of 6s of silver.

Witnesses: sir William de Notingham', William Colin, Robert Bunting', Alan de Berwham' clerk, Roger de Binewerc clerk, Roger the dyer, Thomas le Ferur, Thomas Lomb, Michael the tanner and others.

Seal: missing: slits for tag

Endorsed: de domibus de Benewek' reddend' monialibus vi s' per annum (? contemporary).

Not dated ? late thirteenth century.

364. E315/Vol. 42 No. 118   11 March 1294

Grant by William Bunne of Makeseye tanner of Stanford to Gilbert de Bolewyk wool merchant of Stanford and Cecilia his wife of his houses which are situated in the parish of St Martin Stamford between the house of William Sampson towards the west and the houses of Richard Brond towards the east, extending from the field towards the south to the river Welond towards the north. Annual rent to the prioress and nuns of St Michael outside Stamford and their successors of 6s 11d.

Witnesses: William Burnel, Henry Faderman, Bernard Bonde, William Poncyn, William Sampson, Simon de Helpiston', William Bonde, Walter de Wyterryngg', Hugh Wycher, William Subbyri, William the clerk and others.

Dated: Thursday before the feast of St Gregory 22 Edward I

Seal: missing: slit for tag

Endorsed: sancti Martini (? contemporary) sacrist' (? contemporary)

365. E315/Vol. 42 No. 146

Grant by Marioria prioress of the church of St Mary Wyrthorp and the convent there to Thomas son of Walter *in solio de Wyrthorp'* of all their right and all their part of a house in the town of Stanford which Robert the white sold to them and which is situated 'en le Westgate' between the house of Rose daughter of Gilbert Sturri and the said Thomas' part of that house on the west. Annual rent to the prioress and convent of 3s.

Witnesses: Thomas le Freman of Wirthorp, William de Notygham burgess of Stanford, William de Tykingcote and many others.

Seal: missing: slit for tag

Not dated ? early thirteenth century

366. E315/Vol. 42 No. 148   27 November 1443

Lease for thirty years by Elizabeth Weldon prioress of the house of St Michael by Staunford and the convent of the same to John More of Okeham, Rutland, miller of his watermill situated in the nuns' pasture called 'le Nunnesyerde' in the town of Wyrthorp, together with the pool and right of entry and egress. Annual rent to the prioress and convent of 40d for the first 13 years and 4s thereafter; repairing and distraint clauses.

Witnesses: Thomas Buttle then Alderman of Staunford, William Broun draper, Richard Wright, John Page, Laurence Taylour and others.

Dated in the chapter house of St Michael's Wednesday after the feast of St Katherine 22 Henry VI

367. E315/Vol. 42 No. 158

Bond by Robert son of John Flandrens' of Stanford to the nuns of St Michael of Stanford for the annual payment to the said nuns of 12d for all service pertaining to them for four acres of arable land in the fields of Stanford which abut on the land of Richard Peck' of Stanford towards the south and on the land of Peter son of Geoffrey towards the north, which four acres Robert holds of the aforesaid nuns and which once Robert son of Albin (*Albini*) held of them.

Witnesses: Hugh de Rippele then steward of Stanford', Ralph son of Acard', Richard Peck', Walter de Ticenc', Hugh son of Reiner, Hugh de Stiandebi, John Franceis, Henry son of Alexander, Herbert the serjeant, William son of David, Henry Sibeci, Nicholas son of Alexander, Adam Porter, Alan son of Mor, Robert Futsadame and others.

Seal: missing: slit for tag.

Endorsed: (i) Carta Roberti filii Johannis Flandrens' de xii d' pro quatuor acris terre quas Robertus filius Albini tenuit (? contemporary)
(ii) Inquirend' (? not contemporary)

Not dated ? early thirteenth century

368. E315/Vol. 42 No. 159

Exchange between the prioress and convent of St Michael's with the will of William de Stokes prior and Hugh de Tikencote burgess of Stannford of an acre of arable land given by Hugh to the prioress and convent situated between the land of Walter Norman to the east and the land of the prioress and convent to the west and abutting on 'le Spiteldic' at one end and on the highway to Northampton at the other; for an acre of arable land given by the priory to Hugh situated between the land of the hospital of St Giles to the east and Hugh's land to the west, one end abutting on the way to Pillesgate and the other on the way to Burle.

Witnesses: William Burnel, Henry Faderman, Richard de Staunford, Richard de Corby, Richard Aldus, John le Cunte, William Poucyn and others.

Seal: missing: slit for tag

Endorsed: j acra in escambium

Not dated late thirteenth century.

369. E315/Vol. 42 No. 172   **15 July 1338**

Grant by Walter atte Nonnes to Simon Bolle of Staunford and William son of Eustace Bolle of the same of a messuage with curtilage adjacent in Staunford and which is situated in the parish of St Paul between the tenement of Geoffrey Briselaunce and the tenement of Thomas de Bedeford on the east and the tenement pertaining to the rectory of the church of St Mary of Bynnewerk on the west; the messuage extends from the king's highway towards the north to the tenement formerly of Eustace Malherbe towards the south.

Witnesses: Henry de Tyddiswell', John Bertilmeu, John de Empingham, Geoffrey de Wodeslade, Thomas de Bedeford, John de Uffyngton', William de Thorleby of Staunford, John Josep clerk and others.

Given at Staunford

Seal: missing: slit for tag

370. E315/Vol. 42 No. 186   **1 August 1320**

Lease by Mabel Venur prioress of St Michael outside Staunford and the convent there with the assent and will of sir Thomas de Staunford then prior to Thomas Lymebrenner of Staunford tanner of a messuage situated in the parish of St Martin Staunford between the messuage formerly of William Sampson towards the west and the messuage formerly of Richard Brond' towards the east: it extends in length from St Martin's croft towards the south to the river Weland towards the north. Annual rent to the prioress and convent and their successors of 7s 3d of silver, of which sum 3d is paid for 'landgabule'.

Witnesses: John Cloket', Simon de Helpeston', Bernard Bonde, William Bonde, Ralph Lymebrenner, Peter the dyer, Richard Bertelmew then bailiff of the abbot of Peterborough and others.

Seal: missing: slit for tag

Endorsed: In parochia sancti Martini (? contemporary)

371. E315/Vol. 42 No. 226   **4 May 1508**

Indenture of appraisement dated 4 May 23 Henry VII between the prioress of the convent of the house and priory of St Michael beside Staunford to Roger Sawnder and Elizabeth his wife late of Kirkeby beside Dene, Northants, farmers to the prioress and convent. Goods appraised by Harry Townley of Staunford, Robert Parsons of the same town, William Lye of Careby and William Smyth of Staunford and delivered to the farmers: animals and equipment and twenty five ryggs of wheat in the fields lying in a place by the nuns called 'longlands' and two headlands of wheat which the said twenty five ryggs abut on, and twenty four ryggs of wheat called 'shortlands' abutting on the said two headlands, and two acres of rye lying by the said shortlands abutting east and west upon the land of the said prioress and convent, and three acres of rye in 'medulfurlong' abutting on longlands on the north and the land of the said prioress on the south, and two acres of rye above the said medulfurlong abutting on the 'Spitulcrosse' against the south, and an acre of wheat called the convent's acre on the east of longlands aforesaid, abutting on shortlands on the north, and three acres of rye in the Netherfeld abutting on master Sapcote on the south and two acres of rye in the same field abutting on master Sapcote on the east and on master Hartgrave on the west, and two acres of wheat abutting on master Hartgrave on the west and on master Sapcote on the east, and two acres of rye in the same field abutting onto Harry Townley on the west and Thomas Dicons on the east, and a four acre piece lying in 'hye feld' abutting on a place called Derebowyth, and two ryggs of peas called goryd acre abutting on Sawces' acre on the south.

No dating clause
ENGLISH

372. E315/Vol. 42 No. 258

Grant by Alexander son of Luke le Scaveler of Stanford to Agnes widow of Henry son of Gilbert the tailor of Stanford that her kitchen raised under his eaves should remain there (*coquinam suam levatam subter severundam meam in pace residentem*); the said kitchen is fourteen feet long. Likewise, a certain pentice twenty feet in length raised in the courtyard of the said Agnes under his wall. Provided that the said Agnes and her heirs or assignees will keep the walls of his houses free from damage. Annual rent to Alexander, his heirs or assignees of a rose.

Witnesses: Henry de Ocle, Isaac Lucas, John Noble, Ralph de Stokes, John son of Walter le Flemang', Geoffrey son of Geoffrey Noble, Peter son of Richard Selive of Stanford and others.

No seal

<u>*Endorsed*</u>: Alysaundre le fil Luce de Stannford (not contemporary).

<u>*Not dated*</u> ? later thirteenth century.

373. E315/Vol. 42 No. 261   8 November 1444

Lease for thirteen years by Elizabeth Weldon prioress of the nuns and house of St Michael outside Staunford and the convent to Robert Cayleflete of Staunford and Joan his wife of a tavern with two shops situated together in Staunford in the parish of St Mary at the bridge in the street called Brigstrete between the tenement of the gild of Corpus Christi on the north and the great gates of the tenement lately of Richard Wykys of Staunford on the south. Annual rent to the prioress and convent of 10s.

Given in the chapter house of the said house 8 November 1444.

374. E315/Vol. 42 No. 276

Confirmation by William de Tykyncot' to the prioress and nuns of St Michael outside Staunford and their successors of an annual capital rent of 5s of silver as capital lords of the fee from his capital messuage in Staunford in the parish of St Peter. For payment of which annual rent he binds his aforesaid capital messuage and his tenement annexed to it held in chief from the lord earl of Warenne, to whosesoever hands they shall come.

Witnesses: Hugh de Stiandeby, Peter son of Geoffrey, Richard [?Guero], Ralph son of Acard', Richard Pec, William Flemming, Henry son of Alexander serjeant, Thomas the clerk.

Seal: missing: slit for tag

Not dated ? early thirteenth century.

375. E315/Vol. 43 No. 49

Sale by Alice daughter of Achard de Stanford with the assent and will of Robert her son to John Ruffus son of Hugh Dulle of Stanford for five marks of silver of a moiety of that house in the parish of St Mary at the bridge of Stanford which used to belong to Achard her father and which she inherited: the house is situated between the house of Thedricus de Colon' towards the west and the house of Richard the baker towards the east on the fee of St Cuthbert of Durham. Annual rent to the church of St Leonard outside Stanford of 2d at Easter and a cock and a hen at Christmas.

Witnesses: Walter de Tikencot, Henry his brother, Hugh son of Reiner, Alexander his brother, Clement the vintner, Walter his son-in-law, John son of Sampson', Adrian son of Ralph, Geoffrey Noreis, Gilbert Mariscall, Isaac Ruffus, Thomas the clerk, Absolon at the bridge, Gilbert his brother, William son of David, Thomas de Marra', David the clerk, Geoffrey Lorem', and others.

Seal: missing: slit for tag.

Endorsed: (i) Stanford
(ii) paroch' Marie dom' aliis dat' hominibus
(iii) nunc in manibus Magistri Thome Phelipp

Not dated ? early thirteenth century.

376. E315/Vol. 43 No. 61   **1 November 1317**

Remission by Mabel le Venour prioress of St Michael outside Staunford and the convent there with the assent and will of brother Thomas de Staunford prior to Richard in the Wylngures of Staunford and Matilda his wife for the term of their life of 4s of silver from an annual rent of 16s of silver from certain houses in the parish of All Saints in the Market, Staunford lately acquired by Richard and Matilda from Thomas de Stanhough', and those houses namely which are situated between the tenement of William de le Clay towards the west and the priory's corner houses (*et domus nostras corniculares*) towards the east, and which extend from the king's highway towards the south to the houses of the said Thomas de Stanhough towards the north: and those houses which are situated in the same parish between the said corner houses towards the south and the houses formerly of Henry Brond towards the north, and which extend onto the king's highway towards the east

Given in their chapter house the feast of All Saints 11 Edward II

Seal: missing: slits for tags

377. E315/Vol. 43 No. 68

Grant by William Reyner to Walter son of Robert Tokes of Northluffenham and Agnes William's daughter in free dowry with the aforesaid Agnes of an annual quit rent of 10s from two tenements namely. 3s and a cock and two hens at Christmas from the houses which Richard le Lymbrenner held of William in fee opposite the plot formerly of William de Eston' which is situated on the Welond and 7s from a solar which is situated on the Welond opposite the house formerly of Gilbert de Wodecroft which Hugh de Exton' dyer formerly held of William [Reyner]: together with two acres of arable land in the fields of Stanford' of which one acre lies in St Martin's croft and is called 'Chardieacre' and the other lies between the land of Roger Briselaunce towards the east and the land of the hospital of St Thomas the martyr at the bridge of Stanford towards the west. Annual rent to William and his heirs or assignees of 6d.

Witnesses: Richard Faderman, Richard de Tinnewelle then bailiff, William le Normaund, Richard son of Richard, Walter son of Norman, Thomas de Luffenham, Sampson Reyner, Philip Gaugy and others

No seal

Endorsed Redditus monial' de domo Estbyewatre (? contemporary)

Not dated ? late thirteenth century

378. E315/Vol. 43 No. 69

Quitclaim by William Stoyle miller and Agnes his wife to the church of St Michael outside Staunford and the nuns there of all their right and claim in a solar which they held at farm of the said nuns at their will. The solar is situated in the parish of St Peter of Staunford above a cellar which pertains to the capital house of the same nuns which formerly Gere the miller of the said nuns used to hold at farm: the solar overhangs towards the king's highway on the east end (*quod quidem solarium pendet versus viam regiam in capite orientali*).

Witnesses: Hugh Buntyng', Hugh de Aluerton, Robert Buntying, William 'in ye Walles', William Reyner, Richard Aldus, Walter son of Norman de Grecton', Philip Gaugy and others.

Seal: missing: slits for tag

Endorsed quiet' clainac' de uno solario paroch' sancti petri (? contemporary)

Not dated ? late thirteenth/early fourteenth century

379. E315/Vol. 43 No. 73

Bond by Gilbert Prudum son of Robert Prudum of Empingham to pay to the church of St Michael without Stanford and the nuns there 4s per annum for a bovate of land in Bradecroft which William son of Thomas de Yngetorp held sometime, except for 3 acres, of which one is called Tunkeacre and lies on Nomanneslond, one acre lies on the east side of Linghau between the land of Henry de Tikencote and the land of Osbert de Brunn, half an acre extends beyond the road by the six acres of the castle, and half an acre lies between the land of Henry de Tikencote and the land of David the scribe and abuts on the furlong of William de Perch.

Witnesses: Reiner then dean of Stanford, Richard and Pain priests, William de Pappele clerk, William de Sumercotes, Adam de Vfford, Hugh the porter, Serlo de Lindeseia and others.

Seal: missing: slit for tag

Endorsed Carta Gilberti prudum de Redditu iiii^or solidorum pro una bouata terre in territorio de Bradecroft preter tres acras (? thirteenth century)

Not dated early thirteenth century.

380. E315/Vol. 43 No. 80

Grant by John the tailor formerly the 'ward' of sir Henry Engayne (*Johannes Cissor alumpnus quondam domini Henrici Engayne*) for thirty marks of silver of his houses which are situated in the parish of St John, Stanford, namely in Colgate between the house of William son of Geoffrey vintner towards the east and the house formerly of John le Scawelere towards the west. Annual rent to the heirs of William de Tikinkote of 11s stirling and to the prioress and nuns of St Michael by Stanford of 5s stirling and to John and his heirs of a chaplet of roses.

Witnesses: William son of Geoffrey vintner, Hugh Bunting, John de Burton', Nicholas de Eston', William Reyneri, Richard Aldus, John de Wermington', Robert Rikeman, Peter the skinner, Simon Chyld, Nicholas Pot, John de Kastirton' clerk and others.

Seal: missing: slit for tag

Endorsed: de v s' in parochia sancti Johannis

Not dated ? late thirteenth/early fourteenth century

381. E315/Vol. 43 No. 95   **?10 November 1301**

Quitclaim by Cecilia daughter of Matilda de Stanford to the prioress and nuns of St Michael by Stanford of all her right and claim in that tenement which she claimed before the justices of the lord king by a writ of novel disseisin: the tenement is situated in the parish of St Mary by the bridge Stanford between the tenement of Agnes Hervy towards the east and the tenement of Roger le Carpenter towards the west.

Witnesses: Andrew Neye, John Asplon, Alfred le Grater, Peter de Wysebeche, Roger le Carpenter, Augustine de Norfolch', John Franceis, John le Cunte, Robert de Creton' and others.

Given at Stamford feast of St [Martin?] 1301.

Endorsed: quiet' clam' de tenemento in parochia sancte Marie iuxta pontem

382. E315/Vol. 43 No. 100   **29 September 1327**

Lease for twenty years by Mabel prioress of St Michael outside Staunford and the convent there with the consent of sir William de Oxford then their prior to Thomas le Lymbrenner' of Stanford tanner of one selion of arable land lying in St Martin's croft in the fee of the abbot of Peterborough in Staunford between the land of the aforesaid Thomas on the west side and the land of Ralph Lymbrenner on the east side: the selion abuts on the land of William de Apethorp' towards the south. Annual rent to the prioress and convent of 21d.

Witnesses: John Cloket', Bernard Bonde, Ralph Lymbrenner, William de Birthorp', William de Belmesthorp' and others.

Endorsed:
(i) limbren'
(ii) 1 selio iac' in martynescrofte (not contemporary)

383. E315/Vol. 43 No. 101

Grant in free alms by Gilbert Parent to the house of St Michael of Stanford and the nuns there of an acre of arable land in the territory of Stanford lying below the town at the west by the forges near to the land of William son of Roger Ardekin and abutting on the croft of Hugh the priest at the north.

Witnesses: Robert rector of the church of All Saints, Pain the priest, Walter' de Tikencot', Henry his brother, Richard Pek, Ralph son of Achard', Henry son of Isaac, Sampson, Hugh de Huffinct', Isaac son of Roger, John Bottai and others.

Endorsed: Carta Gilberti Parent de una acra terre subtus villam iuxta fabricas (contemporary).

Not dated ? early thirteenth century.

384. E315/Vol. 43 No. 140

Quitclaim by John son of Peter Seliue de Staunford to Margery de Wakerle in Writhorp' widow of Richard de Wakerle for the sum of 6d of silver which Margery gave to John of an annual quit rent of a ½d which she used to pay him each year for an acre of arable land lying in the field of Writhorp which is called 'douveacre'.

Witnesses: Hugh Bunting, Gilbert de Cesterton', Roger Reve burgesses of Stanford, Thomas the freeman of Writhorp, Henry Redberd of Eston' and others.

Seal: missing: slit for tag

Endorsed: Staunf' pro 1 acra (? probably not contemporary)

Not dated mid/late thirteenth century.

385. E315/Vol. 43 No. 158   **4 October 1338**

Quitclaim by Adam le Taillour of Raundes to Athelina de Kent her heirs or assignees of all his right and claim in a messuage and an acre and a half of land in the town of Staunford which messuage is situated in the parish of St Mary beyond the bridge of Staunford in the street which is called le Bakestergate between the tenement of Alfred de Depyng' on the west side and the tenement of William de Apethorp' junior on the east side: the acre and a half of land lie in 'le Nunnecroft' between the land of the nuns of the house of St Michael outside Staunford on each side. The messuage and land aforesaid the aforesaid Athelina had by grant and feoffment of sir Robert de Raundes priest, Adam's brother.

Witnesses: Thomas de Rauele, William Norman of Staunford, Alan de Wyrthorp', Geoffrey Dorlot, William de Grantham and others.

Given at Staunford Sunday after Michaelmas 12 Edward III

Seal: missing: slit for tag

386. E315/Vol. 43 No. 204   **16 November 1482**

Lease for ninety years by Simon prior of the priory of Fynneshed and the convent there to John Killyngworth' of Stamford 'fremason', Joan his wife and to John, Thomas and William Killyngworth their sons of a tenement with a garden situated in Stamford in the parish of St Mary between the tenement of Christopher Broun merchant on the east and the tenement of John Frebarne on the west: the garden lies in the parish of St George in Staunford between the garden of John Walcot on the east and the garden of John Page on the west, and the head of the said garden abuts on the highway on the south and the garden of Robert Crane on the north. Annual rent to the prior and his successors of 8s.

Given at Fynneshed 16 November 22 Edward IV

Seal: missing: slit for tag

<u>*Endorsed*</u> Killyngworth'
ENGLISH

387. E315/Vol. 43 No. 223   **26 March 1334**

<u>*Lease*</u> for six years from Easter 8 Edward III by the prioress and convent of St Michael outside Staunford to Richard de Brigestok' of Staunford butcher of a messuage situated in the parish of St Michael the Greater, Staunford between their tenement towards the east and the tenement which Stephen de Sleford holds of them towards the south. Annual rent to the prioress and convent and their sucessors of 6s 6d of silver.

Witnesses: William de Dalby, William Wynd, John de Folkyngham, Robert Stontandgay, William Faderman, Richard Bertilmeu, William le Listere of Staunford and others.

Given at Stannford Saturday the vigil of Easter in the above year

Seal: missing: slit for tag

<u>*Endorsed*</u> Indentura i mesuagium in parochia sancti Michaelis maioris (? contemporary) micaelis (? contemporary)

388. E315/Vol. 43 No. 229   **9 September 1338**

<u>*Grant*</u> by Robert de Raundes priest to Atheline de Kyent widow of John de Brampton of a messuage situated in the parish of St Mary at the bridge Stannford between the messuage of Alfred de Deping of Stannford to the west and the messuage of William de Apethorp of Stannford junior to the east.

Witnesses: William de Apethorp junior, Thomas Ranle, William in the Wallis, Hugh Jakis (?),
Bernard Bonde, William de Brunham, John Bertilmeu' of Staunford, Hugh Jakis and others.

Dated at Stannford 9 September 12 Edward III

389. E315/Vol. 43 No. 249

<u>*Grant*</u> in free alms by Sibyl daughter of Ingoldus de Kirkeby to the church of St Michael outside Stanford and the nuns there of an annual rent of 6s from those houses which Thomas Maymunt held at fee farm from John Ruffus which are situated in the parish of St Mary at the bridge Stanford between the house formerly of Ralph Rick' towards the east and the house of William de Tykincot' towards the west; and Sibyl gave to Beatrice de Tikincot' seven marks of silver for the aforesaid rent.

Witnesses: Hugh son of Reyner, Richard Peck, Andrew Arketel, John Spicer, William son of David, Walter Flemang', Hugh son of Walter de Tikincot' and others.

No seal

*Endorsed:*Carta de vi s' redd' in parochia beate Marie *ad pontem* iiii^a carta (? not contemporary).

Not dated ? early thirteenth century.

390. E315/Vol. 43 No. 252   9 August 1307

Quitclaim by Thomas de Bedeford tawyer of Stanford to Henry de Leycestre and Margaret his wife of all his right and claim in a house with a curtilage adjacent which house he had of Gilbert Bolwyk. The aforesaid house and curtilage are situated in the parish of St Paul Stanford by the house of the aforesaid Henry de Leycestre on the east and the house of the abbot and convent of Crowland on the west.

Witnesses: Eustace Malerbe, master William de Borw vicar of the church of Moltoun, John Wolwyndere, Henry Empyngham, Geoffrey Noble, Robert de Faryndon' and others.

Given at Stanford Wednesday the vigil of St Laurence 1 Edward II

Seal: missing: slit for tag

Endorsed: parochia Pauli de una domo et curtilagio

391. E315/Vol. 43 No. 263   30 April 1329

Quitclaim by Margaret widow of Walter de Hauboys Parva sometime burgess of Staunford to Agatha de Leycestre her sister of her right in all her tenements and property in the town and fields of Staunford by hereditary right.

Witnesses: Eustace Malherbe, William de Apethorp, Roger le Scauelere,   Robert Bryselaunce, Hugh le Noble, Robert de Lymborgh and others.

Dated at Staunford, Sunday feast of St Mark the Evangelist 3 Edward III
Note: 'die dominica in feste sancti march evangel': The feast of St Mark (25 April) in 1329 fell on a Tuesday.

392. E315/Vol. 43 No. 290

Grant by Henry de Toft citizen of Stanford and Amfalisia his wife for the health of their souls and the son of Richard formerly rector of the church of St Mary at the bridge of Stanford to the church of St Mary of Finnish' and the canons there of that house with appurtenances which Richard priest formerly rector of the church of St Mary at the bridge Stanford once held, the house namely which is situated in the parish of St Michael the Greater, Stanford between the house of Geoffrey de Thornhawe at the east and the house of Robert Godeman towards the west. For this grant, the canons gave Henry and his wife eleven marks of silver.

Witnesses: Richard Pecke, Henry Sibecei, Walter de Brunna, Andrew Arketil, Michael at the lane (*ad_venelam*), Peter de Castertona, William de Frantona, William Ferrario and many others
.

No seal

Endorsed   (i) de domo iuxta Corwensti in parochia sancti michaelis (? contemporary)
(ii) prima de domo in parochia sancti Michaelis maioris (? not contemporary).

Not dated? early thirteenth century.

393. E315 Vol. 43 No. 295

Grant by Nicholas Hod of Stanford to Eustace le Forester burgess of the same vill of an acre of arable land lying in the field of Stanford on the fee of the abbot of Peterborough between the land of Reginald Norman towards the east and the land of the nuns of St Michael towards the west: the acre abuts on the land of the hospital of St Giles towards the south and on a certain green ditch (*et super quamdam viridem fossam*) towards north. For this grant Eustace gave Nicholas four marks of silver.

Witnesses: Alexander Lucas, John de Wermynton', Reginald Norman, William Burnel, Henry Faderman, Alfred le Mercer, Robert de Farnedon', Thomas le Rous, Elias the clerk and many others.

Seal: missing: slit for tag

Endorsed: Stanford (? not contemporary)

Not dated? late thirteenth century

394. E315/Vol. 44 No. 14   **4 March 1290/91**

Lease for lives in survivorship by Matilda de Len prioress of the church of St Michael outside Stamford and the convent there with the counsel and assent of William de Stokes then their prior to John de Effinton' smith and Matilda his wife of that house with curtilage which Richard de Corby once held of them situated in the parish of St Martin Stamford between the tenement of the said Richard de Corby and the tenement of Alice widow of Gilbert de Cesterton'. Annual rent to the prioress and convent of 8s of silver.

Given in the nuns' chapter 4 March 1290

No seal

Endorsed: vac' (? not contemporary)

395. E315/Vol. 44 No. 34   **10 February 1520**

Lease for forty nine years by Dame Alice Andrew prioress of the monastery of St Michael the Archangel beside Staunford and the convent there to Thomas Williams of Staunford gentleman of their tenement with the garden belonging to it in the parish of St Martin Staunford which was lately held by sir John [O?]bys priest and which is situated between the tenement of Edward Sapcott' gentleman on the north side and a tenement of the abbot of Peterborough on the south side and abutting on the king's highway against the west. Annual rent to the prioress and convent and their successors of 4s.

Dated: 10 February 11 Henry VIII

No seal
ENGLISH

396. E315/Vol. 44 No. 54

Grant in free alms by Hugh son of Reyner of Stamford to the prioress of St Michael outside Stamford and the nuns there for his soul's health and that of his wife Juliana of 4s annual rent for a pittance for the convent to be made annually in the refectory upon his anniversary: the rent is from the houses of Warin 'longi' which are situated in the parish of St Martin between the houses of Geoffrey le Normaunt' towards the south and the houses of William son of Walter de Thorp' towards the north.

Witnesses: Andrew Archetel, Walter le Fleming, John le Fleming, Hugh de Tikenchot', Geoffrey le Noble, Robert son of Isaac, William Reyner and others.

Seal: missing: slit for tag

Endorsed: de iiii s' ad pitanciar' in parochia Sancti Martini (? not contemporary)

Not dated ? early thirteenth century

397. E315/Vol. 44 No. 59

Sale by Margery prioress of Writhorp and the nuns there to Alice widow of Nicholas de Writhorp for 16s sterling of a certain house situated in the parish of St Mary of Bynnewerk' in Staunford, namely in Gledegate between the house of Walter de Notingham towards the east and the house of Adam de Spalding towards the west, which house the prioress and convent bought from Nicholas de Colstewrth'. Annual rent to the lord of the fee of 1d of silver.

Witnesses: Thomas the freeman of Writhorp, Robert de Wakerle of the same, Robert Bunting, Walter de Glynton', Laurence the tanner, Michael de Empingham, Henry de Deping, John de Casterton burgesses of Staunford and others.

No seal

Endorsed: domus de Gleteqate

Not dated ? late thirteenth century

398. E315/Vol. 44 No. 142

Sale for 8s by Damisona widow of Roger Bonus of Stanford to Hugh at corner (*ad corneram*) mercer of half an acre of arable land in the field of Sundersokne lying between Hugh's land to the north and the land of William Pert of Bradecroft to the south and abutting on the land formerly belonging to Thierry de Colonia to the west and on the land formerly belonging to Henry de Tykencot' to the east. Rent to Damisona of ½d per annum.

Witnesses: Hugh Bunting senior, William Perte of Bradecroft, Nicholas his son, Richard Thron, Robert son of Brond, Richard de Wyterhing, Roger brother of Wlmer 'ferroner' and others.

Seal: missing: slit for tag

Endorsed: 'de j acra terre' (later)

Not dated ? early/mid thirteenth century

399. E315/Vol. 44 No. 150

Grant in free alms by Ralph de Stok' burgess of Staunford to the prioress and nuns of St Michael by Staunford of the whole meadow which he had in 'Brodheng' namely a broad acre (*unam acram large mensure*) lying between the meadow of the abbot of Peterborough towards the west and the meadow formerly of William de Tykencot' towards the east: the land abuts on the bank of the Welland (*super ripari torrentis de Weland*) towards the north and on the meadow of the castle of Staunford towards the south. Half the broad acre Ralph bought from Henry son of Henry de Tykencot' and the other half from Hugh Fusse.

Witnesses: Hugh son of Henry de Tykencot', Hugh son of Hugh Bunting, Alexander le Taliur, Henry Brond, Walter de Glynton', Simon son of Hugh Child, Walter Kec, Henry Euerard, John de Casterton clerk and others.

Seal: missing: slits for tag

Endorsed: Carta Radulfi de Stokes de una acra prati large mensure (contemporary)

Not dated: ? late thirteenth century

400. E315/Vol. 44 No. 161

Grant in free alms by Robert son of Walter Seled and William son of David of Stanford to the church of St Michael of Stanford and the nuns there for the bedclothes of the same nuns (*ad vestura lectorum earumdem monialium*), of an annual rent of 9s 6d to be received from Richard Birun and his heirs or assigns for a shop situated between the house of Roger Bettrefare towards the south and the house of the aforesaid William son of David towards the north, with a moiety of a solar as it was, [...] and with a cellar over (*desuper*), the shop 12½ feet in breadth and 15 feet in length and with a courtyard between the house of Roger Bettrefare towards the south and the wall of Hugh de Hirnham towards the north as much as pertains [*? sc. to the shop*] up to the wall of the aforesaid William son of David and with the latrine, the gutter of the houses of Bartholomew son of William excepted.

Witnesses: sir Andrew rector of the church of St Clement, sir William de Pappele rector of the church of St Mary of Binnewerc', sir Richard vicar of the church of St Martin, master Robert vicar of the church of St Andrew, John Bottay, William de Sumercotes, Sampson son of Goderic, Adam de Vfford, Henry de Wakirle, John de Pappele, William Faderman, Hugh the smith, Henry the carpenter and others.

No seal

Endorsed: (i) Istum Redditum Habemus per Dominum Aungerum de Risinges. Cuius Anime deus Propicietur, Amen. (contemporary)
(ii) Staunford (not contemporary)

Not dated ? early thirteenth century

401. E315/Vol. 44 No. 166   **8 October 1404**

Writ of King Henry IV appointing William Thirnyng and Robert Tyrwhyt as justices to hear the assize of novel disseisin between Margaret Redynges prioress of St Michael's by Stannford and John Longe of Staunford and Elizabeth his wife and others concerning a tenement in Staunford.

Dated: Teste me ipso at Coventry 8 October 6 Henry IV

402. E315/Vol. 44 No. 168   **5 June 1359**

Quitclaim by Roger de Mundham of Staunford clerk notary public to Richard Taillour of Wirthorp' and to Margaret and Katherine his daughters and to their heirs or assigns of all his right and claim in a messuage in Wirthrop' which is situated between the tenement of William Hayward on the north and the toft which is called 'Gildhous' on the south and which abuts on the watercourse towards the east.

Witnesses: John le Yonge of Eston', Alan de Wirthorp', William Spigournell of the same, William Gentill of Staunford, John Josep clerk and others

Given at Wirthorp Wednesday after the feast of the Ascension 33 Edward III

Seal: missing: slits for tag

403. E315/Vol. 44 No. 202

Grant in free alms by master Alexander son of Richard son of Seloue of Stanford to the church of St Michael outside Stanford and the nuns there for the keeping of his anniversary each year in perpetuity of an annual rent of 8s from those houses which he bought from Gilbert son of Baldwin situated in the parish of St Paul, Stanford between the houses which belonged to Richard son of Seloue his father in the same parish towards the east and the houses which were of Wace the tanner towards the west.

Witnesses: sir Hugh son of Reiner, sir Richard Pece, sir Walter Flandrense, sir Henry Sibeci, sir Robert son of Agnes, sir William de Frantun, sir William de Frenei and others.

No seal

Endorsed: de viii solid' in parochia Sancti Pauli (? not contemporary)

Not dated ? early 13th century

404. E315/Vol. 44 No. 243

Grant by Beatrice de Tikinkot' widow to Sibyl daughter of Ingoldus de Kirkebi of an annual rent of 6s from those houses which John Maymunt held at fee farm of John Ruffus which are situated in the parish of St Mary at the bridge Stanford between the house formerly of Ralph Rick' towards the east and the house of William de Tikincot' towards the west.

Witnesses: Hugh son of Reyner, Richard Peck', William son of David, Walter Flemang', Hugh son of Walter de Tikincot', John de Sudbiri, Walter de Biri, Stephen the clerk and others.

Seal: missing: slit for tag

Endorsed: Redd' vi s' in parochia beate Marie *ad pontem* (not contemporary) iij[a] carta.

Not dated ? early thirteenth century.

405. E315/Vol. 44 No. 246

Quitclaim by Juliana daughter of John Bottai to St Michael's Stanford and the nuns there, for 2s paid by the nuns, of all right in lands, possessions, etc. which sometime belonged to John Bottai her father or Emma her mother within or without the town held from the nuns.

Witnesses: William son of David then reeve, Henry de Wakerle, William Faderman, Norman de Grettune, Matthew de Wirthorp, John de Papele, William de Wakerle and others.

Seal: missing: slit for tag

Endorsed 'quieta clamacio monialibus de Fer' et ferementa'

Not dated mid/late thirteenth century.

406. 315/Vol. 44 No. 257   25 September 1327

Quitclaim by Margaret widow of Henry de Leycestre sometime burgess of Staunford to Agatha her daughter of all right in all tenements etc. in the town and fields of Staunford.

Witnesses: Eustace Malherbe, William de Apethorp, Roger le Shauelere, Walter le Haluere, Thomas de Bedford, Robert Briselaunce, Robert de Normantoun and many others.

Dated at Staunford

Seal: missing: slit for tag

407. E315/Vol. 44 No. 260

Grant in free alms by Ralph son of Achard of Stanford to the house of St Michael of Stanford and the nuns there of a rent of 2d in the town of Stanford, namely the rent of that house situated between the house of John Cassus and the house of William Beubraz, from which house the aforesaid nuns receive annually 5s rent, which rent Matilda wife of Alexander bought and assigned to the aforesaid house and nuns.

Witnesses: Robert rector of the church of All Saints Stanford, Azelinus the priest, Reiner the priest, Pain the priest, Walter de Tikencot', Henry his brother, William Fleming, Richard Pek, Henry son of Isaac, Peter son of Geoffrey, Hugh son of Reiner and others.

No Seal: slit for tag

Endorsed: Carta Radulfi filii Acardi de redditu ij den' domus site inter domum Johannis Cassi et domum Willelmi Beubraz (contemporary).

Not dated ? early thirteenth century.

408. E315/Vol. 44 No. 269

Grant in free alms by Norman de Grettona burgess of Stanford to the church of St Michael without Stanford and the prioress and nuns there for the observance of his anniversary on the day of his death in perpetuity of an annual rent of 4s from the house which is situated in the parish of St Martin between the house of Richard Scot on the north and the house of the aforesaid Norman on the south.

Witnesses: sir Richard Gerveth' vicar of St Martin's, Andrew Arketyl, Isaac Lucas, Alexander his brother, Peter the dyer, William le Normand, William Reyner, Walter son of Norman de Grettona, William son of William son of David, Thomas de Luffinham, Walter his brother and many others.

Seal: missing: slit for tag

Not dated mid thirteenth century

409. E315/Vol. 44 No. 279

Grant by Benedict of Peterborough (*de Burg*) clerk to the church of St Michael Stanford and the nuns there of 4s rent per annum which he bought from William at lane of Stanford.

Witnesses: Geoffrey Russel steward of 'burg', Robert Peverel of 'burg', William spicer of 'burg', Thomas at hall of 'burg', Hugh son of Reyner of Stanford and many others.

Seal: missing: slit for tag

Endorsed: de iiijs in Staunford prout in carta michaelis filius wilielmi monialibus facta testatur.

Not dated early/mid thirteenth century

410. E315/Vol. 45 No. 62   11 June 1342

Quitclaim by Joan daughter and heir of Robert Flemmyng of Staunford to the prioress of the house of St Michael outside Staunford and the convent there of all her right and claim in a certain tenement with south and north gables in the town of Staunford in the parish of St Mary of Bynewerk' in the street which goes to the wells which are called 'Westewelles' between the house formerly of Andrew son of Henry de Tykencote towards the north and the houses which formerly Walter called 'frere' held towards the south: and which tenement William Motte of Ocham plumber formerly held of the said nuns.

Witnesses: Walter de Apethorp' of Staunford, William de Apethorp' of the same, Thomas de Rauele of the same, Robert de Haringworth' of the same, John de Grosham of the same, Reginald de Salteby of the same and others.

Given at Staunford Tuesday the feast of St Barnabus apostle 16 Edward III

Seal: missing: slits for tag

411. E315/Vol. 45 No. 91   **18 November 1311**

<u>*Quitclaim*</u> by Letitia widow of William Dod' of Wyrthorp to Nicholas de Goseberdkirke fuller of Stanford of all her right and claim in those houses situated in Wyrthorp between the tenement of Ingerammus the sawyer towards the north and the tenement of Thomas at the well (*ad fontem*) towards the south, saving to herself for the whole of her life her lodging in the same houses.

Witnesses: Henry Faderman, William de Folkingham, William Wyrthir of Stanford, Ralph de Wakirle, Ingerammus the sawyer of Wyrthorp and others.

Given at Wyrthorp Thursday before the feast of St Edmund the king 5 Edward II

Seal: missing: slit for tag

412. E315/Vol. 45 No. 269

<u>*Quitclaim*</u> by Margaret widow of Adam son of Acard son of Luue to the nuns of St Michael outside Stanford for two marks of silver of all her right and claim in three acres of arable land which lie towards the house of the said nuns of St Michael by the land of Isaac son of Henry towards the east.

Witnesses: John Bottay then reeve, Henry Gaugy, Sampson son of Goderic, Philip the dyer, Reiner son of Alexander, Richard Grom, Richard son of Aldus, Adam de Ufford, Robert Sauvage and others.

Seal: missing: slits for tag

<u>*Endorsed*</u>: quiet' clam' de iii acris terre iuxta terram sancti monialium (? probably not contemporary)

<u>*Not dated*</u> ? early thirteenth century.

413. E315/Vol. 46 No. 61

<u>*Grant*</u> in free alms by John Bottay with the assent of Emma his wife and of his heirs to the nuns of St Michael of Stanford of his whole croft, namely all the arable land which he had near the land which the same nuns have of Hugh de Uffinton', saving and excepting his rents and men. For this grant the aforesaid nuns gave John 60s of silver.

Witnesses: Hugh the priest, Geoffrey the priest, Henry son of Isaac, Samson son of Goderic then reeve, Gilbert Parent, William son of Roger son of Hardekin, Geoffrey and David sons of Roger son of Lece, Hugh de Uffinton', Roger son of Sparcolf, Robert de Casewic and many others.

Seal: missing: slit for tag

Endorsed: Carte Johannis Bottay de crofto et terra arabile iuxta croftum Hugonis de Huffinton' et croftis monialium.

Not dated ? early thirteenth century

414. E315/Vol. 46 No. 190

Grant by Richard priest son of Alric de Casewik rector of the church of St Mary at the bridge Stanford to Amfelisia his ward (*alumpne*) of that house which Richard bought from Warner his brother, namely that which is situated in the parish of St Michael the Greater of Stanford between the house of Geoffrey de Tornah' at the east and the house of Robert Godeman towards the west.

Witnesses: Richard Pek, Ralph son of Achard, Walter de Tikencot', William Fleming', Hugh son of Reiner, Henry de Tikencot', Henry son of Alexander, Clement the vintner, Walter de Reppinchall', Robert Fuscedam, Alan son of More, William Scheldincthorp', David the clerk, Adam Porter' and many others.

No seal

Endorsed (i) Stanford (not contemporary)
(ii) de domo in parochia sancti Michaelis maioris (not contemporary)
(iii) secunda de domo in parochia suprascripta (not contemporary)

Not dated ? early thirteenth century

415. E315/Vol. 46 No. 256   **2 October 1356**

Lease for fourteen years from Michaelmas 30 Edward III by Margaret atte See prioress of St Michael outside Staunford and the convent there to sir Robert de Apethorp priest of an acre of arable land lying in the fields of Staunford on the fee of the abbot of Peterborough in a place called 'Martynescroft' between the land of the same sir Robert on the east and the land of William de Styandeby on the west: the acre abuts on the land of the same sir Robert on the south. Annual rent to the aforesaid prioress and convent 6d of silver.

Given in the priory of the aforesaid house Sunday after the feast of St Michael in the above written year.

 Seal: missing: slits for tag

Endorsed R' Apethorp' (contemporary)

416. E315/Vol. 46 No. 282

Grant by Nicholas de Colstewrthe with the consent and assent of Agnes his wife and of his heirs to the nuns of St Mary of Writhorp of 7s annual rent in the town of Stanford in the parish of St Michael the Greater from those houses which Alexander Godriz sold to him, namely a solar with a cellar situated between the house formerly of Geoffrey Ofnemaiden towards the south and the oven which is called 'feldhofne' towards the north. Service to the lords of the fee of 12d at Easter and 12d at Michaelmas.

Witnesses: master Henry Sampsun, sir Simon de Lindon', Nicholas de Weston', Thomas le Frankelein of Writhorp, Hugh son of Reiner, Geoffrey the noble, Robert the tailor, Osbert le Porter, Hugh the butcher and others.

Seal: missing: slit for tag

Endorsed (i) Staunford parochia sancti Michaelis vii solid' annui reddit' (not contemporary)
(ii) Wyrthorp (not contemporary; post-medieval hand)

Not dated ? early thirteenth century

417. E315/Vol. 46 No. 284   26 May 1293

Quitclaim by Phelicia and Auota sisters and heirs of Isaac Lucas and Juliana his wife for the health of the souls of the aforesaid Isaac their father and Juliana their mother etc to the prioress and convent of St Michael outside Stanford of all their right and claim in two shops and a solar built above situated in the parish of All Saints in the Market of Stamford between the tenement of Alfred le Mercer towards the east and the tenement of Simon Child' towards the west.

Witnesses: John de Worminton', Geoffrey de Cotesmor', Alfred le Mercer, Simon Child', William Bunting and others.

Given at Stanford the feast of St Augustine of England bishop 21 Edward I

Seal: missing: slits for tags

Endorsed Stamford (? contemporary)

418. E315/Vol. 46 No. 285

Grant by master Alexander son of Richard son of Seloue of Stanford to the church of St Michael of Stanford and the nuns there for the celebration of his anniversary of a rent of ½ mark per annum from the shops which he bought of Gilbert son of Baldwin situated in the parish of St Paul Stanford, between the houses which used to belong to Richard son of Selove his father in the same parish to the east and the houses which used to belong to Wace tanner to the west.

Witnesses: Reiner then dean of Stanford, master Pain rector of the church of St Clement, Hugh vicar of the church of St Martin, Turbert priest of the church of All Saints beyond the bridge, William de Pappele priest, William de Sumercotes, John Bottay, Adam de

Vfford, Peter ward (*alumpnus*) of Turbert the priest, Geoffrey de Turlebi clerk, Serlo de Lindeseia, Hugh the porter and others.

Seal: missing: slit for tag

Endorsed: Carta magistri Alexandri ii' in parochia sancti pauli de dim marc

Not dated early thirteenth century

419. E315/Vol. 47 No. 4

Lease by Sybil called prioress of St Michael of Staunford and the convent there [by the assent] of sir William de Saint Albans their prior to Philip the dyer of Staunford and to his heirs or assigns, religious men or Jews excepted, of their house which was of William Quichors situated by the cemetery of St Martin with a curtilage and a certain plot from the courtyard of Samson son of Godric up to the corner of the courtyard of Adam de Ufford, seven feet in breadth towards the south and ten feet towards the north. Annual rent to the prioress and convent of 40d sterling.

Witnesses: sir Michael vicar of the church of St Martin, John Bottay, Henry Gaugy, William son of David, Isaac son of Henry, Samson son of Godric, Peter the dyer, Richard Grom, Richard son of Aldus, Reiner son of Alexander, William de Burgo, Adam de Ufford and many others.

Seal: missing: slits for tag

Not dated ? early thirteenth century

420. E315/Vol. 47 No. 40   14 September 1418

Lease for life and one year by Agnes Leyke prioress of the house of St Michael by Staunford and the convent there to John Derby vicar of the church of All Saints in the Market Staunford, of three acres of arable land lying separately in the field(s) of Staunford, of which three acres two lie together on either side of 'Empyngate' between the land of John Stenby on either side and they abut on 'le Grenedyke' towards the west and on the land pertaining to the chantry of St Nicholas in the church of St Clement towards the east; and one acre lies by 'Kyngesrys' between the land of John Thomasson' on the south and the land of Thomas Spycer on the north and it abuts on the land of the same Thomas towards the east and on the headland of Margery Makesey towards the west. Annual rent to the prioress and convent of a rose, if requested.

Given in the chapter house of the said prioress and convent 14 September 6 Henry V

Seal: missing: slit for tag

421. E315/Vol. 47 No. 93

Lease for life by N [*sic*] prior and the convent of St Fromund to (Richard Peck clerk son of Richard Peck *del*) [*substituted on dorse* John de Diston our clerk and a secular clerk his assign successively for life] of their corn tithes of the castle demesne of Stanford, together with the tithes of cheese, butter, wool, and lambs, except the tithe of Sundersok. Annual rent to the priory of 3 marks.

Witnesses: Alexander then dean of Stanford, master Henry son of master Samson, Robert Rusca monk, Thomas de Gerun clerk, master Richard son of Henry, Isaac son of Isaac, Reiner priest, and the whole chapter of Stamford and others.

Seal: missing: slits for tag

Endorsed: (i) Litera pro ecclesia sancti petri stafrod
(ii) Dimissio ad firmam de decimis castri de staunford viii.

Not dated early thirteenth century

422. E315/Vol. 47 No. 113

Sale by Henry son of Alexander de Stanford with the counsel and will of Hodierna his wife and of his heirs and friends to John Bottay for one mark of silver of an annual rent of 12d which Henry bought from Matilda widow of Hugh de Vffintuna, namely 6d from the house of William the smith in the parish of St Martin which is situated by the house which was of Hugh Chitt [*or* Chut] towards the north and 6d from the house of Henry de Wakerle in the same parish which is situated by the house which was of Richard de Estona towards the south.

Witnesses: Richard Peck', Walter de Tikenk', Clement the vintner, Sampson son of Godric, William son of David, Henry Gaugy, Isaac his brother, Hugh de Bernak', Adam de Ufford, Peter the clerk and others.

Seal: missing: slits for tags

Endorsed: de domo Willelmi fabri et de domo Henrici de Waker' (? contemporary)

Not dated ? early/mid thirteenth century

423. E315/Vol. 47 No. 200

Grant in free alms by Hugh son of Wimund to the nuns of St Michael of Stanford of the houses which his father granted to Clemencia Wimund's wife with two acres of land, of which one lies across the road to 'Burle broc' near the land of Bride Agnes and the other acre lies between the land of Henry son of Isaac and the land of William son of Sarah at 'Charedic'.

Witnesses: Alexander then dean, Reiner the priest, Henry son of Isaac, Gibert Parent, Samson son of Godric, Adam de Vfford', John Botai, William son of Roger, Robert de Casewic, Henry Gaugi, Hugh Cornil, William Papele, Alexander son of Bu[...]lt and many others.

Seal: missing: slits for tags

Endorsed: (i) bis scripta Carta Hugonis filii Wimundi de domibus Clementie uxoris sue et duabus acris terre (? contemporary)
(ii) ii acr' in Burlebrok (? contemporary)
(iii) Inquirend' (not contemporary)

Not dated ? early thirteenth century

424. E315/Vol. 48 No. 55

Quitclaim by Henry son of Roger son of Lece of Stanford to the nuns of St Michael of Stanford of all right in three roods of arable land in the fields of Stanford in the fee of the lord abbot of Peterborough, namely those which lie between the croft which was of Leuina and the land of Henry son of Isaac and abut on the town towards the north and on the headland of the aforesaid Henry son of Isaac towards the south, which three roods Geoffrey, Henry's brother, granted to the aforesaid nuns in free alms.

Witnesses: Walter de Tikencot', Richard Pek, Ralph son of Achard, William Fleming, Henry son of Isaac, John Bottay, Sampson son of Godric, Adam de Hufford', Hugh de Huffinct', Gilbert Parent and many others.

No seal

Endorsed: (i) Confirmacio Henrici filii Rogeri de tribus rodis terre iuxta croftum Leuine quas Galfridus frater eius nobis dedit (contemporary)
(ii) de iii rodis terre citra pontem (not contemporary)

Not dated ? early thirteenth century

425. E315/Vol. 48 No. 94   18 July 1320

Sale by William son of Peter de Wakerle of Staunford to Mabel prioress of St Michael outside Staunford and the convent there of a messuage in the liberty of the abbot of Peterborough in Staunford situated between the messuage formerly of William Sampson towards the west and the messuage formerly of Richard Brond' towards the east: the messuage extends in length from St Martin's croft towards the south up to the river Weland towards the north, which messuage Peter de Wakerle William's father formerly had of the feoffment of Matilda de Len formerly prioress of the said St Michael and convent. William surrenders the messuage on account of his poverty and inability to pay to the nuns of St Michael the annual rent of 7s 3d with which the messuage is charged.

Witnesses: John Clokett', Bernard Bonde, William Bonde and others.

Given at Staunford Friday before the feast of St Margaret virgin 14 Edward II

Not sealed

Endorsed: sancti Martini (? contemporary)

426. E315/Vol. 48 No. 168   4 October 1503

Receipt from Robert abbot of Peterborough for 10s pension from the church of St Martin on this side of the bridge Stannford from the prioress of St Michael's without Stanford.

Dated 4 October 19 Henry VII [1503]

427. E315/Vol. 48 No. 253   1291

Lease from Matilda de Len prioress of St Michael without Stanford and the convent there with the will and assent of William de Stokis then prior to Thomas de Bradecroft and Alice his wife for their joint and several lives of houses in Bradecroft between the tenement of Roger called Micheloune to the west and the tenement of Richard Tastard which he holds from the prioress and convent to the east; together with a meadow lying in the croft of Bradecroft which Alan de Bradecroft priest son and heir of Alric Fisher (*pistoris*) granted to the prioress and convent between the Alric's meadow to the west and Richard Tastard's to the east, abutting on the mill of John earl Warenn' to the south.

Witnesses: John de Werminton', Andrew Neye, Walter de Glinton, Walter de Tunnewell, Walter Kek, Hugh Perce, Henry clerk, and many others.

Seal: missing: slits for tag-

Endorsed: de viij s' annui redditus de Bradecroft'.

428. E315/Vol. 48 No. 269

Sale by Richard Poth of Stanford to Henry son of Gilbert tailor of Stanford, together with his houses and all rents which are situated in the parish of St Paul Stanford, of an annual quit rent of 2s which Hugh son of Walter de Tykencot' is bound to pay annually to Richard his heirs and assigns, namely for a plot of a curtilage which Richard demised to the said Hugh which lies by Henry's wall towards the north and the houses of Simon son of Geoffrey in Cornestall' towards the south and extends to the courtyard of the said Henry towards the east and to the courtyard of master Hugh towards the west. For this [present] sale and for the sale of his houses, Henry gave Richard fourteen marks of silver.

Witnesses: Andrew Arket', William de Notingham, Isaac Lucas, Alexander his brother, Richard de Cottesmor, Gilbert le Taillur, Ralph de Stokes, Geoffrey the noble, Hugh son of Walter de Tykencot' of Stanford and others.

No seal

Endorsed: Rekard Pod de Staunford (not contemporary)

Not dated ? mid thirteenth century

429. E315/Vol. 49 No. 176   **9 September 1338**

Appointment by Robert de Raundes chaplain of Geoffrey Dorlot as his attorney to grant to Athelyna de Kyent widow of John de Brampton' full seisin of an acre and a half of arable land lying in the fields of Staunford, namely in 'le Nonnecroft'.

Witnesses: Thomas Raule, William Norman, Thomas Lymbrenner', Ralph Lymbrenner', William de Grantham, Geoffrey Dorlot and others.

Given at Staunford the day after the Nativity of the BVM 12 Edward III

No seal

430. E315/Vol. 50 No. 15   **21 March 1314**

Quitclaim by Hugh de Aluerton in Stanford to the prior and canons of Finesheued of all suit of court and other services which might be exacted from them by reason of some tenements they hold in the parish of St Clement in Stanford.

Witnesses: Stacy Malherbe, Clement de Melton, William de Apethorp, Hugh Auuery, Thomas de Morton, Henry de Silton and many others in the said town of Stanford.

Dated at Stanford the feast of St Benedict abbot 7 Edward II

Seal: missing: slits for tag

Endorsed: (i) 'Remissio Hugonis de Aluerton de sectis curie pro domibus iuxta ecclesiam sancti clementis in staunf'
(ii) Quarta de domibus iuxta ecclesia sanct clementis

431. E315/Vol. 50 No. 57   **7 November 1444**

Quitclaim by William Byllesby of Worthorp' to John Billesby de Worthorp his son of all right in all lands and tenements which he had in the village and fields of Worthorp.

Dated at Worthorpe Monday after St Andrew apostle 23 Henry VI

432. E315/Vol. 51 No. 23

Grant in free alms by Ralph the chamberlain of Houtone' dwelling in Wytewell' to the prior and convent of Fynnisheued of a house in the town of Staunford in the parish of All Saints in the Market which he had by grant of his lord the late master John de Houton' sometime archdeacon of Northampton, namely that house which is situated between the house which was the parson of Pycwrthe's and the house which was of William son of Iolanus. Annual rent to the lord of the fee of a pound of thyme or 1½d.

Witnesses: William de Notingham, Andrew Arketel, Alexander Luca, William de Scaccario, Ralph de Wytenell' priest, Peter de Wakerle, John de Bourle, Richard Aldous and others.

Seal: missing: slits for tag

Endorsed: (i) de tenemento in parochia omnium sanctorum in foro Stanford' (? contemporary)
(ii) prima carta Staunford de domo in parochia omnium sanctorum (? contemporary)

Not dated? mid thirteenth century
[See 157.2]

433. E315/Vol. 52 No. 61

Confirmation by Stanwi Taillur of Stanford to the house of St Michael of Stanford and the nuns there of the grant of an acre and a half of arable land in the field of Stanford which lie at Stumpeston' between the land of the same nuns and the land of William Fleming, which grant Andrew, Stanwi's son, made to the aforesaid house and nuns for delivery and quitclaim of the house which Achard son of Igmund assigned to the aforesaid house and nuns.

Witnesses: Robert rector of the church of All Saints, Reiner and Pain priests, Walter de Tikencot', Henry his brother, Richard Pek, William Fleming, Ralph son of Achard, Henry son of Isaac, John Bottai and many others.

Endorsed (i) carta Stanewi Taillur de concessione unius acre terre ad Stumpedeston (?contemporary)
(ii) Carta Stanwi Taillur

Not dated? early thirteenth century

434. E315/Vol. 53 No. 32

Grant by Alexander son and heir of Gilbert the tailor in the town of Stanford to the nuns of St Michael outside Stanford of an annual rent of 2s from the houses which formerly belonged to Jose in the parish of All Saints, namely in the street which is called 'bihindebak' which houses are situated between the houses which used to belong to the said Gilbert the tailor on the north and the houses of the prior of Depinge on the south in exchange for a certain annual rent of 12d which Alexander used to pay to the said nuns for the east part of his hall and for a rood and a half of land lying in the territory of Stanford, namely between his land on the north as on the south and abutting on the lands of the earl Warenne belonging to the castle on the west as on the east.

Witnesses: sir Alexander Lucas, Andrew Arketil, John le Fleming of Cornstal, Walter de Tylton', Isaac Lucas, Richard de Tynewelle, Walter Norman, William Norman.

Seal: missing: slit for tag

Endorsed: parochia omnium sanctorum in foro de ii s' behyndeyebak' in excambium (two hands, ? contemporary)

Not dated: ? later thirteenth century

435. E315/Vol. 54 No. 12

Pardon by sisters Richild and Mathilda sisters of Geoffrey the villein […] to the nuns of St Michael of Stanford of one pound of cumin which Richild and Matilda ought to receive from the land of Geoffrey their brother the villein.

Witnesses: (*et teste priore nostro datur ei tunc*)

Seal: missing: slit for ? tag

Endorsed: Carta Richold' et Mathildis (contemporary)

Not dated ? twelfth century

436. E315/Vol. 54 No. 38   28 April 1300

Writ of King Edward I appointing William Juge and Nicholas Fernband justices to take the assize of novel disseisin between Cecily daughter of Matilda and the prioress of St Michaels by Staunford concerning a tenement in Staunford.

Dated: Teste me ipso apud Rokingham 28 April 28 Edward I

PRO EXCHEQUER E326-9: ANCIENT DEEDS SERIES B

437. E326/200

Sale by Matthew vicar of the church of St Martin to the church of St Michael of Stanford' and the nuns there for three marks of silver which Matilda de Bereham nun of the aforesaid church gave him of a moiety of a toft and house which he bought from Walter Wnwyne.

Witnesses: Alstan, Robert, Hugh, Waleran priests (*sacerdotibus*), Roger (*Rogerio*) son of Lece, Clement the vintner reeves (*prepositis*), Gilbert the clerk, Gilbert Parent, Robert son of Wym', Hugh his brother, Robert the Count (*comite*), William son of Ang'lo and others.

Furthermore, grant by the aforesaid Matilda (*Matildis*) to the convent of St Michael of the rent of the same house for a pittance each year on the feast of St Mary Magdalene [22 July] by the consent of Peter the prior, the prioress and the whole convent. [Added in a different hand] This sale and house he [i.e. Matthew] warrants against all men.

Seal: missing: tag

Endorsed: (i) Carta Mathei vicari ecclesie Sancti Martini de medietate tofti et domus q' fuerunt Wnwine (? contemporary)
(ii) Inquirend' (not contemporary)

Not dated? early 13th century

438. E326/434

Grant (*tradiderunt et concesserunt*) indented with warranty by Matilda de Len prioress of the Church of St Michael outside Stanford' and the convent there by the wish of William de Stokes then prior of the said house to Hugh called Wither dyer (*Wither tingtorem*) of Stanford and his heirs and assignees of half an acre of arable land lying on the fee of the lord abbot of Peterborough on the north side of the wood of Bornle and the land abuts on Bornle Sik' between the land of Margery formerly wife of Geoffrey le Mercer towards the south and the land of Geoffrey Norman towards the north in exchange for half an acre of arable land lying on the fee of the lord abbot of Burg' in Kilmersingge between the land of the said prioress and convent towards the west and the land of Robert Footh towards the east. To hold to the said Hugh his heirs and assignees freely etc. saving service owed and accustomed to the lord of the fee without any secular service exaction and demand in perpetuity. And if the said prioress, convent and their successors, for the exchange thus made, are impleaded by the statute of the lord King or are oppressed in any way (*Et si contigat dictam priorissam conventum et earum successores pro excambio sic facto per domini regis statutum inplacitari seu in aliquo pergravari*) they may enter and recover their land thus exchanged and likewise may Hugh, his heirs and assignees enter and recover their land.

Witnesses: William Burnild', Richard de Stanford', Bernard Bonde, John de Wakerle, John called 'le counte' and others.

Seal: fragment; natural wax; tag

Not dated late 13th/early 14th century

439. E326/639

Sale with warranty by Aylric (*Ayilricus*) de Bradecroft to Henry formerly (*quondam*) son of Hugh de Eston' tailor (*cissoris*) and Alice his wife for 24s sterling of a certain house with the whole curtilage situated in the vill of Bradecroft, namely in the east headland (*capite*) of Bradecroft near the cross between the meadow which is of the demesne of the castle of Stanford towards the east and his own tenement towards the west. To hold to the said Henry and Alice and to their heirs or assignees freely etc. and by inheritance. Annual rent of 3s sterling payable quarterly for all secular service, exaction and demand.

Witnesses: Nicholas de Perte, William Palmer, Nicholas Keck', Geoffrey son of John the palmer, Ketel, Michael de Caldecote, Hugh de Oselstone, Walter son of Nicholas Keck' and others.

Seal: round; 26; fleur de lys; + S'AILRICI D' BRADECROFT; green wax; tag

Endorsed: Carta de iii solidis annui redditus de Bradecroft (contemporary)

Not dated mid/late 13th century

440. E326/640   **18 June 1333**

Grant with warranty by Agnes daughter of Henry Trille of Bradecroft near Staunford in her maiden right (*in mea pura virginitate et legitima potestate*) to sir Hugh de Upton' chaplain for a certain sum of money of a messuage with appurtenances in Bradecroft which formerly was of Richard Testard' of Bradecroft and is situated between the messuage of Simon Gollock' towards the west and the meadow of the lord earl of Warenne towards the east. To hold the said messuage with appurtenances to the aforesaid Hugh, his heirs and assignees freely etc. and by inheritance of the prioress and convent of St Michael outside Staunford, capital lords of that fee, for the services which pertain to the said messuage in perpetuity.

Witnesses: William Edelyn, Ralph Beck' of Bradecroft, Bernard Bonde, William de Belmisthorp', William de Byrthorp', Richard Bertilmeu, Robert de Sempingham of Staunford and others.

Given at Bradecroft Friday after St Barnabas the Apostle 7 Edward III

Seal: round; 15; two hands crossed; legend unintelligible; green wax; tag

Endorsed: de i messuagio in bradecrof' (contemporary?)

441. E326/641   **7 November 1315**

Grant with warranty by Hugh Alryth' of Bradecroft to John Maturneys and Cecily his wife for a certain sum of money of a certain croft of meadow with all its appurtenances in Bradecroft lying between the meadow of Henry de Schilton' on one side and the meadow of William Edelin on the other and it abuts on the pond (*stagnum*) of the earl of

Warenne towards the south and Hugh's courtyard (*curiam*) towards the north. To hold the said croft of meadow with all its appurtenances to the aforesaid John and Cecily and to the heirs of the same Cecily of the capital lords of that fee for the services owed and accustomed.

Witnesses: Robert de Castr' of Keten', William Edelin of Bradecroft, William Schot of the same, Walter son of Clement de Magna Casterton', William de Apeth' of Stamford and others.

Given at Staunford Friday the day after St Leonard 9 Edward II

Seal: missing: tag

Endorsed: Carta Hugonis Alryth' de Bradecroft (contemporary)

442. E326/643

Grant in free alms with warranty by Alfric the baker (*pistor*) of Bradecroft to the church of St Michael outside Stanford' and the nuns there of an annual rent of 3s to be received quarterly from Henry Messore and his heirs or assignees from a messuage with appurtenances in the vill of Bradecroft near the cross. To hold of Alfric and his heirs freely etc by hereditary right etc with all liberties, easements, wards, reliefs and escheats pertaining to the aforesaid tenement. He wishes and assigns 12d of that rent to be distributed to the poor at the gate of the said house, 12d for providing linen cloth in the guest house and 12d for covering the table in the house of the lay sisters (*duodecim denarios de isto redditu ad distribuend' pauperibus ad portam dicte domus. Et duodecim denarios ad inveniendam lineam telam in hostilria. Et duodecim denarios ad cooperiendam mensam in domo conversarum*).

Witnesses: William de Notingh', Andrew Arketel, Roger de Burlee, Robert son of Agnes, Richard de Tynewelle clerk, Nicholas le Pert of Bradecroft, Thomas le Freman of Writhorp and others.

Seal: as in 439

Not dated later 13th century?

443. E326/652

Grant by Roger de Torpel to the nuns of St Michael of Staunford of a rent of 7d and ½d p.a. which Robert Fauvel owed to me from land which he held of me in Bradicroft, saving the sale which he made to my wife Marie of 3 acres and 1 rood of this land, of which Symon *clericus* will respond to her for 3d from three half acres which he holds of the same tenement to the profit of the said rent, and also 2s and ½d annually from one toft, 6 roods of land which Symon *clericus* holds in the said Bradecroft and 12d annually from a certain *tirodis* of meadow in Blakemilde which Robert son of Geoffrey holds, in pure alms for the souls of Mary my wife; to have one pittance on her anniversary, that is 2 June. I and my heirs will have no part on the said alms. Warranty. Sealing clause.

Witnesses: Gervase de Bernake, Pag' de Helpeston, Geoffrey de Norburc, Symon Borehard, Roger de Bonevile, John Sarazin, Walter Clerk and many others.

Seal: tag only

Dorse: Scripta cum cartis de bradecroft iuxta Stanford.
Cart' Rogeri de Torpel de Redditu terre que fuit Roberti fauvel in Bradicroft apud Ufford?

Stanford [19th century]

Summa iijs viijd
Summa total' de Feodo Rob Fauvel vjs iiijd

Not dated: 13th century

444. E326/2479

Grant in free alms by Waleran son of Ralph de Helpest' by the counsel and concession of Helen his wife and of his heirs to the church of St Michael the Archangel of Stanford' and the nuns there of the holm which is at the west of his mill as far as the old ditch from which water flowed into the high bank which is now worn down (*hulman que est aput occidentem molendine mee usque ad veterem fossam unde aqua cucurrit in altam ripam que modo obtusa est*) and of two acres of land in Mitglemedue, namely one which is commonly called Lauemannes Acer and the other which is called L'uentifote. He made this grant on that day on which he assigned his daughter Maxiena to God and to religion.

Witnesses: Matthew the chaplain, Roger son of Pain, Ralph de Huff', Robert clerk of Haxstun', Ralph Fauvel, Geoffrey son of Waleran.

Seal: missing: slits for tag

Endorsed: Carta Waleranni filii Rad' de Helpiston' de hulma que est apud occidentem molendine sue et de ii acris prati in Mikilmedue. (not contemporary)

Not dated ? late 12th/early 13th century

445. E326/2903   **23 April 1402**

Lease indented for fifty years with warranty by Margaret Redynges prioress of the house and convent of St Michael near Staunford to Thomas Sadeler of Staunford and Agnes his wife of a tenement and an acre of arable land with appurtenances lying within the liberty of the abbot of Peterborough which tenement is situated in the parish of St Martin, Staunford, in the street (*vico*) called 'Webstergate', namely between the vicarage of St Martin on the south side and the tenement of Alice Dunkotley on the north side and it abuts on the king's highway towards the west. And this acre of land lies on this side of (*citra*) Lawmanesforthe between the land of John Wryght' on the east and the land of John Gilderr' on the west and abuts on the meadow of the lord abbot of Peterborough aforesaid. To hold to the aforesaid Thomas and Agnes his wife and their heirs from Pentecost [14 May] A.D. 1402 etc. Annual rent of 12d at Pentecost. Doing for the aforesaid tenement and land the service owed and accustomed to the capital lords of the fee. If the said rent of 12d is in arrears at any term or by fifteen days, the prioress her successors or assignees may levy a distress in the aforesaid tenement and acre of arable land etc. And the aforesaid Thomas and Agnes and their heirs shall maintain and repair the said tenement with its appurtenances by their own resources (*sumptibus sue proprie*).

Given in the chapter house of the same prioress and convent St George's Day 3 Henry IV.

Seal (i) round; 20; a shield of arms, namely a fess nebuly between three (?) rooks; * S - IOHN (?) VE....; red wax; tag
(ii) round; 10.5; capital P; no legend; red wax; tag

Endorsed: (i) Indentura Thome Sadeler et Agnetis uxoris eius
(ii) Indentura Priorisse et conventus monial' sancti Michaelis iuxta Staunford (contemporary)

446. E326/3201

Confirmation by Richard son of William de Berch to the church of St Mary of Finnesheved and the canons there of the grant and charter which master Alexander de Stanford' made to them of a certain croft outside the gate of Scoftegate and of the whole of Richard's right and claim in a rent of 12d which he was accustomed to receive from the said croft from Richard Pecke senior, just as the charter attests which the same Richard has of William de Berch his [i.e. the donor's] father. Also confirmation of the grant and charter which William de Coventre made in free alms to the aforesaid church and canons of three messuages with all their appurtenances in the vill of Stanford'.

Witnesses: Henry Hodiern', Henry Sybici, Richard de Weston', William Petit, Hugh de Tikencot', John le Franceis and others.

Seal pointed oval; c40 x c26; vessel, jug; S' RIC... FIL' WILEL'I D'. B....; green wax; tag; imperfect

Endorsed (i) confirmacio Ricardi de Berc de crofto de Stanford (? contemporary)
(ii) de crofto extra portam Staunford (not contemporary) (iii) de domibus iuxta ecclesiam sancti ... (not contemporary) (iv) secunda carta de crofto extra portam (not contemporary)
(v) illegible

Not dated ? early 13th century

447. E326/3361

Sale with warranty by Richard Pek' of Stanford' by the counsel and wish of Alice his wife and of his heirs and friends to master Alexander son of Richard son of Seluf of

Stanford' for thirty seven marks of silver which Alexander gave to Richard in his great necessity (*in mea magna necessitate*) of his croft below (*de sub*) Smithill' which he bought from William de Berk' son of William son of Achard with the appurtenances belonging to the same croft as it extends in length and breadth with the toft which he bought from Thomas the smith (*fabro*) of Stanford' which lies outside the gate of Scoftegate as it extends in length and breadth from the house of Robert Coifer as far as Smethell'. To hold of Richard and his heirs to the aforesaid Alexander and his heirs or assignees etc freely and by inheritance, doing annually the service owed to the lords of the fees.

Witnesses: Walter de Tikote, Terricus de Colonia, Hugh son of Reiner, Alexander his brother, Henry son of Alexander, Nicholas his brother, William Petit, William de Scheldingtorp', Alexander the serjeant (*serviente*), Richard de Weston', Henry Sibecy, Simon son of Matilda, Simon the clerk, Peter son of Lece, David the clerk, John Franceis, John his son, Alexander son of Baldwin, Gilbert his brother, Hugh the Lame (*claudo*), Henry son of Richard, Richard his brother, Robert son of Agnes, Thomas Lambesheved', Clement the vintner, William son of David, Henry Gaugy, John Bottay, Sampson son of Godric, Peter the clerk and others.

Seal: missing: tag

Endorsed: (i) Carta Ricardi Pekke de Stanford' (? contemporary)
(ii) tertia de Crofto (not contemporary)

Not dated ? early 13th century

448. E326/3581

Grant with warranty by Nicholas son of Thomas the clerk of Stanford' by the counsel and assent of Amabil' his mother to Walter de Sancto Edmundo of his houses in the parish of St Mary Binnewerc which are situated between the house of Richard Trou towards the east and the house which Simon the clerk holds from David the clerk towards the west. To hold freely and by inheritance to Walter his heirs or assignees, doing annual service to the nuns of St Michael and to the lord of the vill of Stanf'. Annual rent to Nicholas and his heirs of a pair of white gloves or a ½d at Pentecost for all service pertaining to him or his heirs.

Witnesses: John son of Samson, Walter Flemeng, Richard Peck', Robert de Norton', Apsat' son of Simon, Gilbert his brother, Walter de Brunne and others.

Seals:(i) round; 35; fleur de lys; + S' NICHOLAI . FIL' TOME . CLERICI; green wax; tag
(ii) round; 33; fleur de lys; + S' AMABLE   UXORIS … CLERICI; green wax; tag

Endorsed: (i) de domibus in benewerk' (? contemporary)
(ii) de annuo servicio fac' monial' (? contemporary)

Not dated early 13th century

449. E326/3763   **8 March 1440**

Lease with warranty by William Belesby of Worthorp' to Agnes recently wife of William Langham of Staunford and John Clerke of the same for the term of Agnes's life of a messuage and two acres of arable land lying separately in the fields of Eston' and Worthorp'. The messuage is situated in Worthorp' between the tenement of the house of St Michael on the north side and on Belesby's tenement towards the south and abuts on the croft of the house of St Michael towards the east and on the king's highway towards the west. And of the said two acres with their appurtenances, one acre lies in the field of Eston' between the land of John Pechel on the west side and the road (*viam*) called Bulgate on the east side and it abuts on the road called Saltergate on the south side and on the vill of Worthorp' on the north side. One rood lies in the field of Worthorp' in the place called Watergalle between the land of the abbot of Croyland on each side and abuts on the road which goes to Northampton' towards the south and on the land of the abbot of Croyland towards the north. And three roods lie together in le Westcrofte between the land of the house of St Michael on the south side and the road which goes to Northampton towards the north and abuts on 'le graves' towards the west and on the land of the house of St Michael towards the east. To hold the aforesaid messuage and the said two acres of land with their appurtenances to the aforesaid Agnes and John etc of the capital lords of the fee for the services owed and by right accustomed. And after Agnes's death the messuage and said two acres of land with their appurtenances are to remain to Richard Belesby's son, his heirs and assignees in perpetuity to hold of the capital lords of the fee for the services owed and by right accustomed.

Witnesses: John Pechel of Eston', John Frebarne of the same, Thomas Fale recently of Worthorp', John Andrew and John Busshe of the same and others.

Given at Worthorp' 8th March 18 Henry VI

Seal: shield-shaped; 13 x 8; merchant's mark; no legend; red wax; tag
[See 350]

450. E326/4293

Grant in free alms by Matilda formerly wife of Alexander Stanford' to the church of St Michael of Stanford' and the nuns there of 5s annual rent which she bought from William son of Godric from a house which is between the house of John Cas and the house of William Belbraz, saving service to the lord of the fee.

Witnesses: Robert rector of All Saints, Henry Pium priest (*sacerdote*), Alexander son of David, Walter de Tichincote, Henry his brother, Thomas the clerk, Andrew the palmer (*palmario*), Simon the clerk, Abraham.

Seal: pointed oval; c40 x c27; fleur de lys; +.. . .ATILDIS UXORIS ALECA; green wax; tag; imperfect

Endorsed: Carta Matild' uxoris Alex' Stanf' de redditu v solidorum de domo sita inter domum Johannis Cas et domum Willelmi Beubraz (later hand)

Not dated ? early 13th century

451. E326/4541

Sale and quitclaim with warranty by Robert son of Peter the tailor of Stanford' to master Peter pupil (*alumpno*) of Reiner formerly dean of Stanford' for six marks of silver of his whole part of an annual rent of 16s with appurtenances to be received quarterly, in which Richard de Sancto Eadmundo and his heirs or assignees were bound to Robert and his heirs for those houses with appurtenances in the parish of St Mary at the bridge of Stanford' which are situated between the house of Richard de Sancto Eadmundo towards the west and the house which was of Robert ad Archam towards the east. To hold to the said master Peter and his heirs or assignees and to the heirs of his assignees freely and quit of all service and secular exaction, saving service to the lord of the fee.

Witnesses: Richard Peck', Henry Scybeci, William de Francton, Reyner son of Matilda, Henry his son, Peter son of Geoffrey, Reginald son of Peter, Hugh son of William de Torpel', David the clerk, William de Freynei, William de Pappele chaplain and others.

Seal: round; 37; fleur de lys; + SIGILL' ROBERTI FIL' PETRI TAILVR; green wax; tag

Endorsed: parochia Marie *ad pontem* domibus aliis hominibus dat' (? contemporary)

Not dated ? early 13th century

452. E326/4542

Grant with warranty by Ingusa widow of John the Red (*ruffi*) of Stanford' in my pure widowhood and free right to Beatrice de Tykencot' of an annual rent of 6s from those houses which are situated in the parish of St Mary at the bridge of Stanford between the house formerly of Ralph Ricke towards the east and the house of William de Tykencot' towards the west. To hold of Ingusa and her heirs to Beatrice and her heirs or assignees freely and by inheritance: the rent to be received quarterly.

Witnesses: Walter le Flemenk, Hugh son of Walter de Tykencot', John de Sudbiri, Walter de Biri, Ralph de Stokis, Flurkin, Matthew the clerk, Hugh son of Ivo the clerk and many others.

Seal: round; c34; fleur de lys; legend illegible; natural wax; tag; defaced; imperfect

Endorsed: (i) ii carta (not contemporary) (ii) Stamford (not contemporary)

Not dated ? early 13th century

453. E326/4544

Grant and quitclaim in free alms by Alexander de Tykencot' burgess of Staunford to the church of St Andrew the Apostle of Osolveston' and the canons there of two houses in the parish of St Mary at the bridge of Stamford with their appurtenances situated near the houses of Robert de Makeseye towards the north and the oven of Fauvel (*et furnum Fauvel*) towards the west; of which houses one was of Reginald Predicas and the other was of Hugh le Whyte. To hold to the said canons and their successors in free alms saving to Alexander and his heirs one custom which is called 'aletol'. Neither Alexander nor his heirs will be able to exact any right or claim in the said houses or in the services or customs deriving from the same excepting 'Aletol' and this without doing fealty (*et hoc sine fidelitate facienda*)

Witnesses: Nicholas de Burton', Geoffrey de Cottesmor', Hugh de Swafend, Clement de Melton' of Stanford and Robert de Stocton' at that time seneschal of the same and others.

Seal: round; 16; a shield (no trace of any armorial device); legend illegible; natural (very dark brown) wax; tag

Not dated ? late 13th/early 14th century

454. E326/4547   **26 September 1334**

Appointment by John called le Taylour of Staunford clerk of Peter Bertilmeu of Staunford chaplain as his attorney to deliver to sir Robert de Raundes chaplain full seisin of a messuage with appurtenances situated in the parish of St Mary at the bridge of Staunford between the messuage of Alfred (*Alueredi*) de Deping' of Staunford towards the west and the messuage of William de Apethorp' of Staunford the younger (*minoris*) towards the east. To hold to the same Robert and his heirs or assignees in fee simple according to the tenor of the charter of feoffment made to the same Robert by John.

Given at Staunford Monday after St Matthew the Apostle 8 Edward III

Seal as in 462; imperfect
[*See 456*]

455. E326/4548

Grant with warranty by Reiner the chaplain son of Hereward (Herward') de Stanford' to Peter Taillur and his heirs of those houses with all appurtenances in the parish of St Mary at the bridge of Stanford which formerly (*quondam*) were of the aforesaid Hereward his father; namely the houses situated between the house which was of Robert Trive towards the east and the house which was of Roger de Ioholm' towards the west. To hold of Reiner his heirs or assignees freely and by inheritance. Annual rent of 8s of silver, 4s at Michaelmas and 4s at Easter for all secular service and exaction saving service to the lord of the fee.

Witnesses: Alexander dean of Stanford, Hugh the chaplain, Walter de Tikencot', Richard Pek, Ralph son of Achard, Robert the cordwainer (*Cordvan*), Peter son of Geoffrey, Robert Franceis, William Torpell', Robert de Larche, ?Waleran (*Wall*) the baker, Roger Blund and many others.

Seal: missing: slits for tag

Endorsed: in parochia sancte Marie *ad pontem* de domibus datis aliis hominibus (not contemporary)

Not dated early 13th century

456. E326/4549   26 September 1334

Grant with warranty by John called le Taylour of Staunford clerk to sir Robert de Raundes chaplain for a certain sum of money of a messuage with appurtenances situated in the parish of St Mary at the bridge of Staunford between the messuage of Alfred (*Alueredi*) de Deping' of Staunford towards the west and the messuage of William de Apethorp' of Staunford the younger (*minoris*) towards the east; to hold the said messuage with appurtenances to the aforesaid Robert and his heirs or assignees freely and by inheritance of the capital lord of that fee by the services owed and accustomed from the said messuage in perpetuity.

Witnesses: William Apethorp' the younger, Thomas de Rauele, William in the Wallis, Hugh Jakis, Bernard Bonde, William de Brunham, Richard Bertilmeu of Staunford and others.

Given at Staunford Monday after St Matthew the Apostle 8 Edward III

Seal: fragment; as in 454 and 462

457. E326/4550

Grant with warranty by William son of Geoffrey the clerk of Staunford to William de Bereford of two houses in the parish of St Mary at the bridge of Staunford with appurtenances situated near the houses of Robert de Makeseya towards the north and the oven of Fauvel (*furnum Fauvel*) towards the west, of which houses one was of Reginald Predicas and the other was of Hugh le Wyte. To hold of the donor and his heirs to Bereford his heirs or assignees freely and by inheritance in perpetuity. Annual rent to the church of St Andrew of Osolveston' and the canons there of 30s of silver, 15s at Michaelmas and 15s at Easter for all secular service, exaction, suit of court and all other things pertaining to the donor or his heirs.

Witnesses: master Robert de Redmild', Richard de Castreton', John le Flemmyng, Robert le Flemmyng, Elias the clerk, Richard the clerk and others.

Seal: pointed oval; c32 x 21; stag's or horse's head couped at the neck, facing right: … WILLELMI FIL GALFRIDI; natural wax; tag; defaced; imperfect

Endorsed de Staunford (contemporary)

Not dated late 13th/early 14th century

458. E326/4551

Grant in free alms with warranty by Alexander de Quappelade for the soul of himself, of Constance his wife and of Henry formerly his son who is interred in the church of Fynnesheved etc to the church of St Mary of Fynnesheved and the canons there of half a mark of annual rent from his houses situated in the parish of St Mary beyond the bridge of Stanford which Gervase the tailor (_cissor_) and Aldusa formerly his wife used to hold of him. The rent to be paid by Alexander or his heirs at Martinmas at the said place and term, namely for making a certain pittance for the soul of the said Henry at the term aforenamed in the monastery of Fynnesheved in perpetuity. If Alexander or his heirs at the aforenamed term do not fully pay the said money to the canons, the canons may enter the said houses and levy a distress etc.

Witnesses: Richard Peck', Walter the Fleming (_flamidrensi_), John his brother, Richard de Cottesmor, William de Notingham, William de Scaccario, William de Sutbyris and many others.

Seal missing: tag

Endorsed: (i) Alexandri de Quappelade [hand changes] de tenemento contra ecclesiam sancte Marie (not contemporary)
(ii) de dimidia marca de domo in parochia beate Marie (not contemporary)
(iii) prima carta de predicta dimidia marca in parochia beate Marie (not contemporary)

Not dated ? early 13th century

459. E326/4553

Sale with warranty by Thomas de Marham and Avice daughter of Denise daughter of Acard Parmenter of Stanford' (_Avicia filia Dionisie filie Acardi parmenter de Stanford'_) his wife by the assent and wish of their friends and heirs to John the Red (_ruffo_) son of Hugh Dulle of Stanf and Yngusa his wife and their heirs for five marks of silver of a moiety of that house with its appurtenances in the parish of St Mary at the bridge of Stanford' which was formerly of Acard Parmenter grandfather of the aforesaid Avice and which is situated between the house of Terricus the German (_teonici_) towards the west and the house of Richard the baker towards the east; to hold to the said John and Ingusa his wife and to their heirs or to whomsoever they shall assign, except to a house of religion, freely and by inheritance. Annual rent to the church of St Leonard outside Stanford' of 1d on the Sunday after Easter and a cock and a hen at Christmas for all secular service and exaction.

Witnesses: Walter de Tikenc', Richard Peck', Henry de Tikenc', Hugh son of Reiner, Alexander his brother, Clement the vintner (_vinit_), William son of David, Henry son of

Alexander, Nicholas his brother, Henry Sibeci, John Samson, Adrian son of Ralph, Geoffrey Norens', Gilbert the marshal (*marescallo*), Isaac the Red (*ruffo*), Thomas the clerk, John de Brunne, Apsal' *ad pontem*, Gilbert his brother, Walter de Brunne, Geoffrey Lorimer, Geoffrey Banduney and others.

Seals: (i) round; c27; fleur de lys; legend mostly wanting; + SIC .... ; natural wax; tag; defaced; imperfect
(ii) missing: tag

Not dated

460. E326/4622   10 October 1308

Grant with warranty by Henry de Oseberneby dwelling in Essenden' to master Geoffrey de Makeseye for a certain sum of money of his houses in the parish of St Paul Stanford situated with all their appurtenances between the tenement of the rector of St Mary of Bynewerk' Stanford towards the west and the tenement of Walter le Halver towards the east, just as they extend from the king's highway towards the north as far as the garden of Eustace Malherbe towards the south. To hold to the said master Geoffrey and his heirs or assignees freely and by inheritance in perpetuity of the capital lord of the fee for the service owed and accustomed.

Witnesses: Eustace Malherbe of Stanford', Henry de Empingham of the same, Clement de Melton' of the same, Henry de Leycestr' of the same, Hugh Alfred (*Aluredo*), Robert de Farendon', John Blanchard', Stephen Funne then receiver (*tunc resceptore*) and William the clerk and others.

Given at Stanford Thursday the day after St Denis 2 Edward II

Seal: pointed oval; c32 x 19; fleur de lys;...INRICI D' OSB...; natural wax, tag; imperfect

461. E326/4623

Grant with warranty by Richard Peck' of Stanford' to Peter the pupil (*alumpno*) of Reiner the chaplain, son of Hereward (*Herwardi*) de Stanford' for his service of an annual rent of 8s from that house in the parish of St Mary at the bridge of Stanford' which is situated between the house of Richard de Sancto Eadrnundo towards the west and the house which was of Robert ad Archam towards the east: the rent to be received at two terms namely 4s at Easter and 4s at Michaelmas. To hold to the said Peter and his heirs or assignees freely etc. of Richard and his heirs without any service and secular exaction.

Witnesses: Walter de Tikencote, Peter son of Geoffrey, John son of Sampson, Adrian son of Ralph son of Achard, Walter son of Ketil, Richard de Weston', Henry Scibeci, Herbert the serjeant (*serviente*), John Franceis, Adam Porter, William de Pappele clerk and others.

Seal: missing: traces of green wax; tag

Endorsed: Redditus viii solidorum in parochia beate Marie *ad pontem* (not contemporary)

Not dated ? early 13th century

462. E326/4624   **23 September 1334**

Quitclaim with warranty by John called le Taylour of Staunford clerk to Robert de Raundes chaplain for a certain sum of money of all his right and claim in a messuage with its appurtenances [situated as described in 456].

Witnesses: William Apethorp' the younger, Thomas de Rauele senior, William in the Wallis, Hugh Jakis, Bernard Bonde, William de Brunham, Richard Bertilmeu of Staunford and other.

Given at Staunford Friday after St Matthew the Apostle 8 Edward III.

Seal: sexfoil with alternate lobes and points; 20 x 14; within a circle, a flower; legend barely legible, ? SIG O NIS FIL', natural wax; tag.

463. E326/4681   **7 May 1324**

Grant with warranty by John de Bedeford' clerk to Thomas de Morton' of Staunford and Joan his wife and to Walter son of the same Joan for a certain sum of money of his tenement with its appurtenances formerly built, now in ruins but to be built again (*nuper edificatum modo obrutum set tamen edificandum*) which tenement is situated in Scoftegate Street (*in vico de Scoftegate*) between the tenement formerly of Godwin de Exton' on the east side and the tenement of Roger de Scotelthorp' on the west side. To hold the aforesaid tenement with all its appurtenances to the aforesaid Thomas and Joan his wife and Walter and to the heirs or assignees of the same Walter of the capital lord of that fee for the services owed and accustomed, well, peacefully and by inheritance in perpetuity. Annual rent in perpetuity to the prioress and convent of St Michael outside Staunford of 4s of silver payable quarterly for all other services and secular demands.

Witnesses: William de Apethorp', Roger le Scaveler', Henry de Pirebrok', Roger de Scotelthorp', William del Cley, John de Friseby, Simon Broun, William Joseph clerk and others.

Given at Staunford Monday after St John before the Latin gate 17 Edward III

Seal: oval; 18 x 15; standing figure, possibly bishop with pastoral staff; S' IOH ...DEFOR ...; natural wax, tag; defaced

Endorsed: Redditus monial' in parochia omnium sanctorum (? contemporary)

464. E326/4682   **14 April 1360**

Lease indented for eighty years with warranty by Thomas de Bernak' parson of the church of Braytoft' and William Corby vicar of the church of Corby to the prioress of St

Michael outside Staunford and the convent there and to their successors of seven acres of arable land with their appurtenances just as they lie in the field(s) of Stamford within the liberty of the lord abbot of Peterborough, of which land six acres lie together between the land of the nuns of the same priory on each side and abut on Burlesyk towards the east and one acre lies in le Martynescroft' near the king's highway on the south side and the land of the same prioress and convent on the north side. To hold the aforesaid seven acres of arable land with their appurtenances to the prioress and convent and their successors from Easter 34 Edward III etc. Annual rent of a white rose at the feast of the Nativity of St John the Baptist [24 June], and during the term aforesaid the prioress and convent and their successors will do the other services which pertain to the aforesaid land to the lord of the fee.

Witnesses: William Gentyl of Staunford, John Wortyng of the same, Robert Rowe, Simon Bonde, John de Pykworth of the same and others.

Given at Staunford Tuesday after the octave of Easter 34 Edward III

Seal: (i) oval; c25 x 22; on the left, standing, St John the Baptist holding a roundel with the Agnus Dei: on the right a figure (presumably the owner of the seal) kneeling in prayer before the Lamb:
above the roundel to the right the letter T and on the lower left side the letter B: the background diapered; legend illegible; natural wax; tag; slightly imperfect

(ii) round; 20; on the left standing beside a tree, St Katherine holding her wheel: on the left a figure (presumably the owner of the seal) kneeling before the saint; S' WILLELMI WICHARD; natural wax; tag

465. E326/4683   **25 November 1342**

Grant with warranty by Athelina de Kent formerly wife of John de Bramton' to William de Botilleford' chaplain and Nicholas le Rede of Caldecote chaplain and to their heirs or assignees of all that tenement with its appurtenances which is situated in the vill of Staunford in the parish of St Mary the Virgin at the bridge, namely in Bakers' Street (*in vico pistorum*) between the tenement of Alfred (*Alueredi*) de Depyng' on the west side and the tenement of William de Egilton' on the east side. To hold the whole tenement aforesaid with its appurtenances to the aforesaid William and Nicholas and their heirs and assignees freely etc in fee and in perpetuity of the capital lords of that fee for the services owed and by right accustomed.

Witnesses: Henry de Tiddeswell' of Staunford', Walter de Apethorp' of the same, Thomas de Rauele of the same, John Kokerell' of the same, John Bate of the same and others.

Given at Staunford Monday on the feast of St Katherine the Virgin 16 Edward III

Seal: oval; 22 x 18; the coronation of the Virgin: the virgin on the left and Christ on the right, both seated; legend illegible; green wax; tag

466. E326/4684   **13 November 1350**

Pardon indented by Margaret del See prioress of St Michael outside Staunford and the convent there to Robert de Billesfeld' guardian (*custos*) of Alice daughter and heir of John de Eston' son of Andrew de Eston' of 4s 8d of silver of an annual quit rent of 11s 8d of silver from a messuage with appurtenances in Staunford in the parish of St John which formerly was of Andrew de Eston' and which Robert holds until Alice's coming of age; the rent of 7s of silver payable quarterly. And immediately on Alice's coming of age, the aforesaid messuage with its appurtenances will be charged in perpetuity of the aforesaid rent of 11s 8d of silver as existed previously to the prioress and convent and their successors.

Given at Staunford Saturday after Martinmas (*festum sancti Martini in yeme*) 24 Edward III

Seal: oval; 19 x c16; a lion curled up, facing towards the right, beneath a stylised tree; legend illegible; red wax; tag; imperfect

Endorsed: carta quondam Andr' de Eston' de Redditu xi solidorum (contemporary)

467. E326/4685

Quitclaim by Alice widow of Geoffrey de Keten' in her widow right to the church of St Michael outside Stanford' and the nuns there of all her right and claim in a certain tenement which Robert le Burser holds of the said nuns in the parish of All Saints in the Market of Stanford. Thus that neither Alice nor her heirs nor anyone on account of her shall be able to exact anything by reason or name of widow's dower or by any other way appurtaining to her. For this remission and quitclaim, the nuns gave her 5s 6d in her great necessity.

Witnesses: William de Notingham, Hugh Bunting, John Plouman, Richard de Tinewelle then master of the chapel at the bridge, Reginald the dyer (*tinctore*), Thomas Sauvage and others.

Seal: pointed oval; 37 x 23; a stylised flower; S CT… GALFR … D' K…; green wax; tag; partially defaced

Not dated ? later 13th century

468. E326/4686   **1348/9**

Exchange indented made 22 Edward III between the prioress of St Michael near Staunford on the one part and Henry de Tyddeswell' on the other, namely confirmation (*concessit et per hanc indénturam confirmavit*) by the said Henry to the said prioress and convent of St Michael and their successors of a piece (*peciam*) of arable land which is called Morelaker and lies on Brakenhyl between the land of the said prioress on each side: one headland (*capud*) of which piece abuts on Burlesike towards the north. To hold the said Morelaker to the said prioress of St Michael, the convent of the same and their successors in exchange for an acre of arable land lying on Portesgate between the land of the said Henry on each side: one headland of which acre abuts on the king's highway which leads to Pyllesgate (*que ducit apud Pyllesgate*) and which acre the prioress and convent of St Michael confirm (*concesserunt et per hanc indenturam confirmaverunt*) to Henry his heirs or assignees. Proviso that the arrangement made does not incur the prejudice of the lord king nor of either party by the constitution of the religious (*dummodo non incurrat in preiudicium domini regis nec neutri partis per constitucionem religiosorum editam*).

Given at Staunford

Seal: ? round; c22; within a decorated border, a shield (no trace of any armorial device); legend illegible; natural wax; tag

469. E326/4687   **4 October 1349**

Lease indented for twelve years with warranty by the prioress and convent of St Michael outside Staunford to John Bate of Staunford and his executors of twelve acres of land with their appurtenances in the fields of Staunford just as they lie in divers parcels, of which three acres lie at Holgate near the land of lady le Despenser on the north side, one acre lies there between the land of Nicholas de Eston' and the land of the abbot of Swynesheved, three acres lie beyond the ditch of the vill between the land pertaining to the chapel of St Thomas the martyr and the land of Eustace de Assewell', two acres lie at Tolthorpsty between the land of the earl of Northampton (*North'e*) and the land formerly of William de Bolewyk', half an acre lies in Kyngesrys between the land formerly of Waleran (*Walranni*) de Baston' on each side, one rood lies there near the land of the rector of the church of Holy Trinity on the east side, one acre lies there between the land of Robert de Brigestok' and the land formerly of Henry de Silton', a half acre lies there between the land formerly of Margaret de Greywerk' and the land of the prior of St Leonard, a half acre lies between the land formerly of John le Wollewynder and the land of the rector of the church of St John, and a rood lies there which is called le Honyhevedlond. To hold the aforesaid twelve acres of land with their appurtenances to the aforesaid John and his executors from Michaelmas 23 Edward III etc. Annual rent of 8s of silver payable quarterly. And if the rent is in arrears at any term, then the aforesaid prioress and convent or their successors may levy a distress in the aforesaid twelve acres or in the parcels of the same etc.

Given at Staunford Sunday after Michaelmas in the year abovesaid

Seal: oval; c25 x 21; possibly a spray of flowers upon a bank; no legend; red wax; tag; imperfect

470. E326/4688   **31 August 1388**

Quitclaim with warranty by Simon Bolle of Staunford'senior to his brother Eustace Bolle's son William and to his heirs and assignees of all his right and claim in a messuage with a garden adjacent with its appurtenances in Staunford in the street which is called le Estgate (*in vico qui vocatur le Estgate*): the messuage is situated between the tenement of Geoffrey Briselaunce on the east side and the tenement pertaining to the rector of the church of St Mary Bynnewerk', Staunford on the west side, which messuage with garden adjacent the aforesaid Simon and William recently acquired jointly in fee (*nuper coniunctim in feodo adquisivimus*) from Walter atte Nonnes of Staunford.

Witnesses: John Bertilmeu, Richard de Pappele, John de Empingham, Thomas de Bedeford', Geoffrey Briselaunce of Staunford and others.

Given at Staunford' Monday after the Decollation of St John the Baptist 12 Edward III

Seal: oval; c18 x c14; bust of a man in profile, looking to the left; legend mostly wanting; natural wax; tag; imperfect

471. E326/4689   16 August 1345

<u>Obligation</u> by John son of Andrew de Eston' of Staunford to pay the prioress and convent of St Michael outside Staunford' 100s of silver at a certain term, and grant by the prioress and convent that if John pay them a rent of 11s 8d from a tenement formerly of Adam le Lyster in Estaunford' which is situated in the parish of St John which is to say all the waters and the hall just as it is very near to the castle towards the west in length and breadth as far as the water of the Welland and which Adam granted to Nicholas de Eston' lyster in exchange for other tenements which Nicholas granted Adam in the parish of All Saints in Estaunford', and from which rent a certain Nicholas Absolon of Staunford granted to the said prioress and convent 9s, and the residue was due to them from ancient time, the said obligation shall be null and void. An assize of novel disseisin having been brought by the prioress against John before sir William de Thorp' and his fellows because the rent was in arrears for a long time whereupon the aforesaid agreement was made.

Given at Estaunford' Tuesday after the Assumption of Our Lady 19 Edward III.

Seal: round; 11/16"; stag running towards the left; + ALAS BOWLES: red wax; tag FRENCH

472. E326/4690   12 August 1339

<u>Lease</u> indented for thirty years with warranty by Athelina de Kent to John de Wyththam of Staunford barber (*barbitonsor*) and Isabel his wife of her tenement with appurtenances in Staunford' namely in Bakers' Street (*in vico Pistorum*) which is situated between the tenement of Alfred (*Aluredi*) de Deping' on the west side and the tenement of William de Egilton' on the east side. To hold the aforesaid tenement with appurtenances to the aforesaid John and Isabel and their heirs and assignees from Michaelmas next etc. Annual rents on behalf of Athelina and her heirs (i) to the prioress and convent of St Michael outside Staunford' and their successors of 10s of silver payable quarterly; (ii) to the proctor of the mass of St Mary celebrated in the church of All Saints in the Market Staunford 12d of silver payable at the same terms; and (iii) to the lord John de Warenne (*Warrenn*) earl of Surrey and his heirs 6d of silver at Easter for all other services and demands. If the aforesaid rent of 10s to the aforesaid prioress and convent and their successors is in arrears by one month after the lapse of any terms, Athelina and her heirs may levy a distress in the same tenement etc. And they may expel the aforesaid John and

Isabel, their heirs and assignees from the said tenement and put other tenants in the same at their will. And John and Isabel and their heirs shall maintain, repair and rebuild the houses of the aforesaid tenement by their own expenses. And because the houses of the aforesaid tenement had been in ruins (*fuerant ruinose*) at the time of making this indenture, Athethina remitted to John and Isabel 40s of silver of the rent of the four years next following for the repair and rebuilding of the aforesaid houses, which money Athelina paid to the prioress and convent.

Witnesses: Henry de Tyddiswell', William de Apethorp', Richard de Lincoln', John Bate, Alfred (*Aluredo*) de Deping' of Staunford and others.

Dated at Staunford Thursday after St Laurence the martyr 13 Edward III

Seal: round; 19; illegible; natural wax; tag; imperfect
[See 473]

473. E326/4691   22 August 1339

Indenture by the prioress and convent of St Michael outside Staunford. Recently Athelina de Kent by her indenture dated at Staunford Thursday 12 August 1339 leased to John de Wyththam of Staunford barber (*barbitonsori*) and Isabel his wife her tenement with appurtenances in Staunford which is situated in Bakers' Street to hold for a term of thirty years, just as the said indenture attests the more fully, which messuage [*sic*] with its appurtenances whosoever possessed it is charged to the prioress and convent of St Michael and their successors in perpetuity of an annual quit rent of 16s; the same prioress and convent for themselves and their successors remit to the aforesaid John and Isabel and to their heirs or assignees 6s of the aforesaid 16s annual quit rent up to the end of the aforesaid thirty years. The 10s of silver to be paid quarterly. After the term of thirty years, the aforesaid tenement with appurtenances is to be charged of the rent of 16s as previously. The prioress and convent have received from the aforesaid John and Isabel by the hands of the said Athelina 60s of silver as rent for the first six years of the said thirty years.

Given in the chapter house of the said prioress and convent Sunday after the Assumption of the Blessed Virgin Mary 13 Edward III

Seal as in 472; imperfect

Endorsed: tenementum in vico pistoris in manu Thome de Thistilton' (not contemporary)

474. E326/4692   30 November 1337

Grant with warranty by Simon de Worthorp son of Alan de Ringesdon' and Alice his wife daughter of Bernard Bonde of Staunforde to sir Robert de Raundes chaplain his heirs and assignees for a certain sum of money of a certain plot (*placeam*) of land of five selions lying in the fields of Staunford, namely 'en le Nounnecroft' between the land of the nuns of the house of St Michael outside Staunford on each side. To hold the aforesaid plot of land of five selions with all its appurtenances just as it lies in length from the path (*semita*) which leads from the gates of the nuns up to Staunford and the meadow of the said nuns, to the aforesaid sir Robert his heirs or assignees freely etc of the capital lords of that fee for the services owed and accustomed to the said capital lords in perpetuity.

Witnesses: John de Harwedon', Thomas de Raule, Roger Mindham, William Fadirman, William Norman, William de Grantham and others.

Given at Staunford the feast of St Andrew the Apostle 11 Edward III

Seals: (i) missing: tag
(ii) pointed oval; c32 x 18; stylised flower; natural wax; tag; defaced, imperfect

475. E326/4693   16 April 1337

Quitclaim with warranty by Geoffrey formerly son of Geoffrey de Makeseye for himself and his heirs to Walter atte Nonnes of Staunford and his heirs of all his right and claim in a messuage with curtilage adjacent and with all its other appurtenances in Staunford which is situated in the parish of St Paul between the tenement of Geoffrey Briselaunce in part and the tenement of Thomas de Bedeford' on the east and the tenement pertaining to the rectory of the church of St Mary of Bynwerk' on the west, and it extends from the king's highway towards the north as far as the tenement formerly of Eustace Malherbe towards the south, which messuage with curtilage etc the aforesaid Walter recently had by lease from Geoffrey for the term of his life.

Witnesses: Geoffrey de Wodeslade, Richard de Linc', John Cokerel, John Bate, John de Empingham, Thomas Noble, William Joseph clerk and others.

Given at Staunford Wednesday after St Tiburtius and St Valerian 11 Edward III

Seal: round; 19; a stylised four-leaved flower; legend partly wanting, unintelligible; red wax; tag; imperfect

476. E326/4713

Confirmation in free alms with warranty by Margaret formerly wife of Reiner son of Maisent' to the house of St Michael of Stanford' and the nuns there of 4s annual rent in the market of Stanford' from the shop which was of her father and which is situated between the shop of Henry son of Alexander and the shop of Simon de Hoklei which rent Reiner formerly Margaret's husband granted to the said house and nuns. To hold to the aforesaid house and nuns freely etc of Margaret and her heirs in perpetuity.

Witnesses: Robert rector of the church of All Saints of Stanford', Reiner the priest (*presbitero*), Pain the priest, Walter de Tikencot', Henry his brother, Richard Pek, William Fleming, Hugh son of Reiner, Henry son of Alexander, John the Frenchman (*Gallico*), Gilbert the Noble (*nobili*), Henry son of Isaac, Sampson and many others.

Seal: round; c44; fleur de lys; ...E UXORIS REI... ; natural wax; tag; imperfect

Endorsed (i) Inquirend' (not contemporary)
(ii) Carta Margarete quondam uxoris Reineri filii Maisent de redditu quattuor solidis in foro (later hand)

Not dated ? early 13th century

477. E326/4714

Sale with warranty by Stephen de Riston' rector of the church of St Paul Stanford to Robert de Makeseye burgess of Stanford and Agnes his wife for four marks of silver of his houses with all appurtenances which he purchased from William de Morlond situated in the parish of the aforesaid church of St Paul between the house of the abbot of Vaudey (*vallis dei*) towards the east and the house formerly of Richard Buncheklot towards the west. To hold to the same Robert and Agnes and their heirs or assignees freely and by inheritance in perpetuity. Annual rent to the nuns of St Michael near Stanford' of 8s sterling, payable quarterly for all secular service, exaction, custom and demand, saving the service owed to the lord of the fee.

Witnesses: Isaac Lucas, Henry de Okele, Robert de Welledon', John son of Walter le Flemeng, Ralph de Stok', Andrew son of Peter and others.

Seal: pointed oval; 33 x 22; upon a nest resting on the branches of a tree, a pelican in her piety feeding three young: + MORS PELICANI PASSI…; natural wax; tag

Endorsed: de viii solidis in parochia Sancti Pauli (? contemporary)

Not dated ? late 13th/early 14th century

478. E326/4715

Grant in free alms with warranty by Avice daughter of Geoffrey son of Outhild' in her widow right for the soul of her husband William de Ketene and for her own soul etc to the church of St Michael outside Stanford and the nuns there of an annual rent of one mark of silver from a house with appurtenances which she bought before her marriage (*quam emi antequam desponsata fuissem*) from William Pinkil of Stanford' and Roger his son. The house is situated in the parish of Holy Trinity between the house of Henry Pichard on one side towards the west and the house which she bought from William Pinkil on the other side towards the east. The grant is made for a pittance of the nuns twice yearly, namely half a mark on Palm Sunday and the other half mark on the feast of St Francis the Confessor [4th October] for keeping the anniversary of Avice's husband during her life time, and after her death the whole mark aforesaid of annual rent shall revert for keeping her anniversary at the aforesaid terms in perpetuity. To hold to the aforesaid nuns and their successors of Avice and her heirs or assignees in perpetuity. And if Avice or her heirs or assignees default in payment at the appointed terms, the nuns or their warden (*vel earum custodi*) may seize the aforesaid house with appurtenances and levy a distress etc.

Witnesses: Richard Pecke, Hugh son of Reyner, Walter Flemeng, Henry de Sybecey, Walter de Brunne, William son of David, Norman de Grettone, Robert de Cottesmor, Andrew the clerk and others.

Seal: pointed oval; c29 x c19; stylised flower; ...AVICIE ...; natural wax; tag; defaced, imperfect

Not dated ? early 13th century

479. E326/4717

Sale and quitclaim with warranty by Hugh de Uffinton' by the counsel and assent of Matilda his wife and of his heirs and friends especially for acquitting his lands and houses within the vill and without which when he received them from his aforesaid wife Matilda were pledged in Jewry, to Richard Peck' of Stanford' for 100s of silver of his whole part of the tillage (*culture*) which is called 'langelondes' in the fields of Stanford' towards the west, next to the land which he bought from John Bottai towards the east and next to the great dike (*magnam foveam*) which divides the field of Stanford' and the field of Writhorp towards the west with the meadow and all things pertaining to the said tillage in length and breadth. To hold to the said Richard and his heirs or assignees freely and by inheritance and free of all service and secular demand pertaining to Hugh or his heirs, saving the service of the lord of the fee. And if any of his heirs should wish to oppose or contradict in any way the said sale and quitclaim, Hugh de Uffinton' grants (*volo concedo et hac presenti carta mea confirmo*) to the said Richard Peck' and his assignees his houses in the parish of St Martin with all appurtenances and with his rents within the vill and without, namely those houses which he bought from Hugh Cappe and which are situated near the road (*iter*) which goes towards St Michael.

Witnesses: Walter de Tikencot', Henry son of Isaac, Adam de Ufford, William de Burgo, Samson son of Godric, Gilbert Parent, John Bottay, Henry Gaugi, Adam the dyer (*tinctore*) and others.

Seal: ? round; c27; no identifiable device; SIGILL HVGON[I]S NOR... ; green wax; tag; imperfect

Endorsed: Carta Hugonis de Ufinton' de longelond' (not contemporary)

Not dated? mid 13th century

480. E326/4718

Quitclaim by Outhilda daughter of Sparrus in her widow right by the counsel of her friends and the assent of her heirs to Robert son of Hereward of Stanf' of all her right and claim in the houses with appurtenances situated near the castle which were of Sparrus her father. To hold to the aforesaid Robert and his heirs or assignees freely and by inheritance etc of Outhilda and her heirs in perpetuity, saving service to the lord of the fee annually. For this quitclaim the aforesaid Robert gave Outhilda 8s of silver. And confirmation (*concessimus et sigillis nostris confirmavimus*) by Margaret and Richilda daughters of the aforenamed Outhilda to the aforesaid Robert and his heirs or assignees of the aforesaid quitclaim which Outhilda their mother made to him and quitclaim to him of all their right. And for this quitclaim the aforesaid Robert gave them 2s.

Witnesses: William son of David and Herbert the serjeant (*serviente*) then reeves (*tunc prepositis*), Ralph son of Acard, Walter de Tikenc', Richard Pec, William Flameng, Hugh son of Reiner, Henry son of Alexander, Reiner Midedo, Thomas the clerk, Ivo the watchman (*excubia*), Alexander the serjeant (*serviente*), William Coife.

Seal: missing: one tag surviving, on each side of which slits for tag

Endorsed: de domibus iuxta castrum (? contemporary)

Not dated ? early 13th century

481. E326/4719

Grant in free alms by Gilbert de Kyrkeby roofer (*coopertor*) of Stanford' to the church of St Michael outside Stanford' and the nuns there of his messuage with appurtenances which is situated in the parish of St Martin Stamford between the messuage of William Faderman towards the east and the road which goes towards the said nuns. Annual rent to the lord of the fee of 1d. at Michaelmas for all services and secular exactions.

Witnesses: sir John Rolond then prior of the same place, Hugh vicar of St Martin then dean, Richard de Tynewell' clerk, William Faderman, Henry Faderman, Philip Gaugy and William Reyn', and others.

Seal: pointed oval; c32 x 19; stylised flower; … GILBERT … KIRKE …; green wax; tag; imperfect

Not dated ? late 13th/early 14th century

482. E326/4720

Sale with warranty by Andrew son of Stanewi of Stanford' by the counsel of Emma his wife and of his heirs and friends to Walter de Tikecote for 46s of silver of one acre of profit yielding land (*unam acram terre lucrabilis*) in the territory of Stanford' which is called Pitacre in the fee of the lord abbot of Peterborough, lying between the tillages (*culturas*) of the nuns of St Michael; the acre abuts on the great ditch (*magnam fossam*) which goes towards Aldehaue. To hold of Andrew and his heirs to Walter and his heirs or assignees freely and quit of all service and all exaction, rendering annually to the lord of the fee the accustomed service.

Witnesses: Henry son of Isaac, Richard Pecke, William Fleming', Adam de Wfford', John Bottay, Gilbert Parent, Henry Gaugi, Alexander Burnild', Reiner his son, Hugh de Wffinton', Adam the dyer (*tinctore*) and others.

Seal: oval; c32 x c25; device unidentifiable; ?? SIG AND... ; natural wax; tag; imperfect, defaced

Endorsed: de Pitaker versus Aldawe (? contemporary)

Not dated ? early 13th century

483. E326/4721

Grant in free alms with warranty by Geoffrey son of Roger son of Lece by the assent and counsel of Christine his wife and of his heirs to the church of St Michael of Stanford' and the nuns there of three roods of arable land which he bought from Acharde son of Hingemund lying between the croft which was of Levina and the land of Henry son of Isaac: the three roods abut on the vill towards the north and on the headland (*forarium*) of the aforesaid Henry son of Isaac towards the south. The nuns will possess the land freely etc. and without any earthly service or secular exaction etc in perpetuity, saving the service of the lord of the fee.

Witnesses: Henry son of Isaac, Sampson son of Godric, Adam de Wfford, Henry de Gaugi, William son of Roger, Gilbert Parent, John Bottay, William the clerk of Pappelea, Alexander son of Burnild, Reiner his brother and many others.

Seal: missing: tag

Endorsed: Carta Galfridi filii Rogeri de tribus rodis terre iuxta croftum Levive (? contemporary)

Not dated ? early 13th century

484. E326/4722

Confirmation by Reiner the priest (*presbiter*) son of Hereward (*Herwardi*) de Stanford' to Peter the clerk his pupil (*alumpno*) and to Robert son of Peter the tailor his nephew (*nepoti*) and to their heirs or assignees of the houses with appurtenances situated near the castle of Stanford on the east side and the moiety of a shop in the market before and behind near the shop which was of Arketil Cordewaner on the south side, which houses Robert, Reiner's brother, bequeathed to Peter and Robert in his will. To hold to the said Peter and Robert and their heirs and assignees freely and quit of all service and secular exaction, saving the service of the lord of the fee.

Witnesses: Walter de Tikencote, Richard Peck', Ralph son of Acard, Hugh son of Reiner, Henry son of Alexander, Herbert Seriant, Henry Cibeci, Peter son of Geoffrey, John son of Sampson, William the clerk and others.

Seal: round; 33; fleur de lys; + SIGIL' ... HERE ... ; natural wax; tag; imperfect

Endorsed: de domibus iuxta castrum di' shopp' (? contemporary)

Not dated? early 13th century

485. E326/4723

Grant indented (*concessisse dimisisse et hac presenti scripto nostro cyrograffato confirmasse*) with warranty in perpetuity by Amice de Stokes prioress of St Michael outside Stanford' and the convent there by the assent and wish of Hugh de Leycestre then their prior to Sampson Chyld of Stanford' of a certain plot (*placiam*) with appurtenances in the parish of St Michael the Greater of Stanford on Cleymunt which is situated between the house of William Haukyshey towards the east and their houses towards the west which plot is 20 feet in length and 16 feet in breadth. To hold the said plot with appurtenances to the said Sampson Chyld and his heirs or assignees freely and by inheritance. Annual rent of 12d of silver at two terms namely 6d at Michaelmas and 6d at Easter and half a stone of tallow (*dimidiam petram sepe*) at Christmas for all service, secular exaction and demand.

Witnesses: Andrew Arketil, William de Notingham, Walter Flemmaung, Robert son of Agnes, Alexander Lucas, Hugh Chyld, William Duve and others.

Seal: round; 25; a stag running towards the right; + SANSON' CHILD: CARNI(F)ICIS; green wax; tag

Endorsed: (i) Stanford' in parochia sancti Michaelis (not contemporary)
(ii) de xii denariis annui redditus (not contemporary)

Not dated? early 13th century

486. E326/4724

Grant in free alms by Odo the clerk of Empingeham to God and St Mary and to St Michael the Archangel and to the nuns there of Stanford of his house at the north of the church of All Saints in the Market of Stamford, namely that which he bought from Robert son of Hugh son of Dodus (*Dodi*) with all its appurtenances for the health of his soul and for the health of Ivette daughter of sir Robert de Tolzorp etc. To hold freely etc. Annual rent to sir Ralph de Bruenchurt for all custom of 12d. Odo made this grant to the nuns to relieve the scarcity of their refectory (*ad relevandam inopiam refectorii earum*).

Witnesses: sir Richard then seneschal of Stanford, master Sampson, master Henry, Matthew and Robert and Alexander chaplains, Ralph son of Achard, Geoffrey son of Herlewin, Walter de Thicincothe, Richard son of Selif, Reiner son of Meissentus (*Meissenti*), Ralph Sibici.

Seal: round; 41; a bird with wings closed looking to the left; +SIGILL . . . ONIS DE ENPINGHAM; natural wax; tag

Endorsed: (i) Carta Odonis de domo in parochia omnium sanctorurn [hand changes] in foro Stanford' (contemporary)
(ii) Carta Odonis clerici de Empingham de quadam domo in parochia omnium Sanctorum in foro Stanford' (? contemporary)

(iii) Alanus filius Mor (not contemporary)
(iv) Inquirend' (not contemporary)

Not dated ? late 12th/early 13th century

487. E326/4725   5 July 1344

Indenture by the prioress and convent of the house of St Michael outside Staunford.
Recently sir William de Corby chaplain and sir Nicholas de Walcote chaplain by their
indenture dated at Staunford Wednesday on the vigil of the Nativity of St John the
Baptist 18 Edward III [i.e. 23 June 1344] leased to John de Wytham of Staunford barber
(*barbitonsori*) and to Isabel his wife their tenement in Staunford which is situated in
Bakers' Street to hold for a term of thirty years, just as the said indenture attests more
fully, which messuage with appurtenances whosoever possessed it is charged to the
prioress and convent of the house of St Michael and their successors in perpetuity of an
annual quit rent of 16s. The same prioress and convent for themselves and their
successors remit to the aforesaid John and Isabel and to their heirs or assignees 6s of the
aforesaid 16s annual quit rent up to the end of the thirty years. The 10s of silver to be
paid quarterly. After the term of thirty years the tenement is to be charged of the rent of
16s as previously. The prioress and convent have received from the aforesaid John and
Isabel by the hands of the aforesaid sir William and sir John 40s [*sic*] of silver as rent for
the first six years of the aforesaid thirty years.

Given in their chapter house Monday after the feast of the Apostles Peter and Paul in the
year abovesaid.

Seal: round; 19; a pelican in her piety feeding three nestlings; legend partly wanting,
unintelligible; natural wax; tag; imperfect

Endorsed: domus in vico pistorum in manu Thome de Thistilton' (not contemporary)

488. E326/4726

Quitclaim by John Bottay to the nuns of St Michael's Stanford of all right in rents, lands
and possessions which his father, predecessors, or he granted or sold to the nuns. For
this quitclaim the nuns gave 2s towards John's journey.

Witnesses: Hugh priest of St Martin's, Walter de Tinginchote, Richard Pec, Adam de
Wford, Samson son of Godric, William de Burg and others.

Seal: fragments ; ? a fleur-de-1ys ...[IOH]ANNIS BO[TTAY].

Endorsed: (i) Carta Johannis bottay de concessione et confirmacione se ipsius et suorum
predecessorum.
(ii) Parochia sancti martini.

Not dated

489. E326/4727

Sale with warranty by Andrew son of Stanwin of Stanford' to Walter the doctor (*Waltero medico*) for 20s of those houses with appurtenances in the parish of St Martin which are situated between the houses formerly of William de Somercote towards the east and the house formerly of William de Pappele towards the south. To hold freely etc and by inheritance to the aforesaid Walter and his heirs or assignees. Annual rent to the nuns of St Michael outside Stanford' of 4s 4d payable quarterly for all secular service, exaction and demand.

Witnesses: Richard Gernet then vicar, William Reyner, William de Bradecroft, Roger Briselaunce, Philip Gaugy, Geoffrey Gaugy, William Normaund, Geoffrey le Mercer and others.

Seal: round; 30; fleur de lys; legend mostly wanting; + S' AND...; green wax; tag; imperfect

Endorsed: (i) Carta vetera Walteri Leche (not contemporary)
(ii) de iiii solidis de domibus in parochia sancti Martini (not contemporary)

Not dated later 13th/early 14th century

490. E326/4728

Confirmation and quitclaim (*concessisse ac totaliter de me et heredibus meis et assignatis.. . . quietumclamasse*) by Hugh de Tykencote burgess of Stamford of the grant of that acre of arable land which Walter son of Walter de Tykencote made to the said [*sic*] prioress and convent and their successors in free alms, which land is situated between Hugh's land towards the east and the land of the said prioress and convent towards the west and abuts on the highway which leads towards Northampton.

Witnesses: Hugh Buntins, Andrew Neye, Alfred le Grat', Richard son of Wolm', Henry Faderman, William Poucyn, Bartholomew de Norh't' and many others.

Seal: missing: fragment of tag

Endorsed: Stamford' (not contemporary)

Not dated late 13th/early 14th century

491. E326/4729

Grant by Michael son of William *ad venellam* of Staunford by the assent and counsel of Emma his wife to Benedict de Burg' clerk for a certain sum of money, of 4s of silver annual rent to be received quarterly from a messuage situated near le Colegat of Staunford between 'le houensty' in the parish of St Michael in the cemetery of the two churches on the west side and the houses of John son of Maurice on the east side. The grant is made for celebrating the donor's anniversary. To hold etc in perpetuity.

Witnesses: Hugh son of Reyner, Henry Sibecy, Walter de Bronne, Walter Ketel and Robert son of Agnes de Staunford and many others.

Seal: round; c29; fleur de lys; … D' LA VE…; natural wax; tag; imperfect

Not dated ? mid 13th century

492. E326/4730

Sale with warranty by Damysona formerly wife of Roger Bony to Alice de Wirthorp formerly wife of Nicholas […'] for 4s of silver of 6d annual rent with appurtenances which she was accustomed to receive from the houses which the said Nicholas husband of the said Alice formerly held of her, which houses are situated in the parish of St Peter Stanford, between the tenement formerly of Roger Beuubraz towards the south and the tenement of the prior of Huntingdon' towards the north. To hold the said 6d annual rent with appurtenances to the said Alice and her heirs or assignees freely and by inheritance. Annual rent of ¼d at Easter for all services, customs, exactions, reliefs, wards, suits of court and for all other manner of secular demands pertaining to anyone.

Witnesses: William de Frannton', Hugh de Weldon', Alexander Lucas, William de Tykencote, Simon de Makezeya, Richard Trow, William Reyner and others.

Seal: pointed oval; 36 x 24; fleur de lys; DAMISOVN FIL'E ALEXANDR; natural wax; tag

Not dated ? mid/late 13th century
* *name erased*

493. E326/4731

Sale with warranty by William de Coventre to Robert de Bernardeshil or his assignee for three marks of a house with its appurtenances in the vill of Stanford', namely that house which William de Wimundeham held of Coventre and which is situated near the church of St Clement. And for 30s, another house with its appurtenances in the vill of Stanford', namely that house which Thurlstan son of Robert held of Coventre and which is situated between his capital house and the house which Bernardeshil first bought from him. And for 30s a third house with its appurtenances in the vill of Stanford', namely that which is situated between his capital house and the second house which the aforesaid Bernardeshil bought from him, with a certain part of Coventre's courtyard as it was provided between them. Also grant to the same Robert de Bernardeshil his heirs or assignees of access and entrance to Coventre's private chamber (*communionem et introitum camere mee private*) thus that Robert may have an open door in the aforesaid chamber towards his courtyard. To hold of Coventre and his heirs to Bernardeshil and his heirs or assignee freely and by inheritance. Annual rent of 1d at Michaelmas for all services and customs pertaining to the aforesaid houses.

Witnesses: Geoffrey the chaplain, Richard the chaplain, Ralph son of Achard, John le Franceis, John his son, John le Flamenc, Samson ultra pontem, Geoffrey de Glint', Michael de Glinton', Geoffrey son of Richard de Glinton', Herbert, Geoffrey de Extone and others.

Sseal: missing: tag

Endorsed: (i) De Willelmo De Coventre De Stanford' (? contemporary)
(ii) de domibus iuxta ecclesiam sancti Clementis (not contemporary)
(iii) sexta de domibus juxta ecclesiam sancti Clementis (not contemporary)

Not dated
[see 505]

494. E326/4732

Notification by Peter the clerk pupil (*alumnus*) of Reiner the chaplain of Stanford' and Robert son of Peter the tailor that they their heirs or assignees are bound to the prioress and convent of St Michael of Stanford' for the annual payment of 3s which they ought to render from the houses situated near the castle of Stanford on the east side which Colicia daughter of Fredegill' bought from Outhilda and Emma daughters of Sparrus and granted to the aforesaid prioress and convent. The aforesaid Outhilda, notwithstanding the first sale made to the aforesaid Colicia, after the latter's death instituted an inquiry with Robert son of Hereward, Colicia's husband, concerning the same houses and the same Robert by the assent and counsel of his friends granted to the aforesaid Outhilda 8s of silver and to her daughters Margaret and Richilda 2s for quitclaim and for all their right in the aforesaid houses just as it is contained in their charter. These houses with their appurtenances Peter and Robert hold of the same prioress and convent by grant of the nuns made to them following the death of the aforesaid Robert son of Hereward by service of paying the aforesaid 3s annually at the four terms. And Peter and Robert, their heirs or assignees shall do service to the lord of the fee. Sealed in the full court of Stamford

Witnesses: Alexander dean of Stanford', John de Colemere, Henry rector of the church of St John, Walter de Tikencot', Richard Pecke, Ralph son of Acard (*Achardi*), William Fleming', Hugh son of Reiner and others.

Seal: (i) as in 496; natural wax; tag; imperfect, defaced
(ii) missing: tag

Endorsed: Carta Petri clerici alupni [*sic*] Reineri Decani de Stanf' et Roberti filii Petri cissoris de Redditu trium solidorum de domibus que fuerunt Colicie iuxta castrum Stanf'. (? contemporary)

Not dated early/mid 13th century

495. E326/4733

<u>*Grant*</u> with warranty by Peter son of Reginald de Stanford' to Juliana his sister for her service and for two and a half marks of silver which she gave to him in his necessity of the whole of that messuage with appurtenances (except one small shop 11 feet in breadth and 22 feet in length which he retains for his own use) which was his father's in the parish of St John of Stanford' and of the fee of the same church. To hold to the aforesaid Juliana and her heirs or assignees etc. Annual rent of 4s of silver payable quarterly and two hens on the feast of St John the Evangelist [27 December] at Christmastide and 5d [namely] 4d on the Sunday after Easter and 1d on the feast of St Peter in Chains [1 August] for all secular service. And Reginald may not sell nor alienate by any other manner the said rent of 4s nor the said shop which he holds without the assent and counsel of the said Juliana.

Witnesses: master Henry then rector of the church of St John, William de Sutbyris and Hugh Torpel then reeves (*tunc prepositis*), Adam le Plouman, Hugh son of Reginald, Henry the dyer, Bartholomew the goldsmith (*aurifabro*), Ralph the goldsmith and many others.

Seal: missing: slits for tag

<u>*Not dated*</u>? mid 13th century

496. E326/4734

<u>*Sale*</u> with warranty and acquittance by master Peter the pupil (*alumpnus*) of Reiner formerly dean of Stanford' to master Nicholas son of Absalon de Stanf' for twenty marks of silver of an annual rent of 28s with appurtenances from two houses with appurtenances in the vill of Stanford' namely 16s of silver to be received quarterly from one house which Richard de Sancto Eadmundo once held of him in the parish of St Mary at the bridge which is situated between the house which was of Robert ad Archam towards the east and the house of the said Richard towards the west, and 12s of silver to be received quarterly from another house which Adam de Stanford' dyer formerly held of him in the parish of St John and which is situated between the ditch of the castle of Stanf' towards the west and the houses which were of Ralph Halvere towards the east. To hold to the said master Nicholas and his heirs or assignees and to the heirs of his assignees freely etc. Annual rent for the said house with appurtenances near the ditch of the castle of 3s of silver payable quarterly to the nuns of St Michael outside Stanford' for all service and secular exaction saving the service of the lord of the fee.

Witnesses: sir Richard vicar of St Martin then dean of Stanford, Richard Pecke, Hugh son of Reyner, Walter le Flemeng, Andrew Arketel, Walter de Brunne, Robert de Coreby, William son of David, Robert son of Agnes, Hugh son of Henry de Wakerl' chaplain and others.

Seal: round, 34; estoile with crescent moon below, between two lilies; + SIGIL' PETRI ALVNI REINERI CAPELLANI; green wax; tag

Endorsed: parochia Sancte Marie *ad pontem* de iii solidis de domibus iuxta castrum (not contemporary)

Not dated ? early 13th century
[*See 494*]

497. E326/4735

Lease indented for nine years with warranty by Robert son of Ascelin de Aistona to the nuns of St Michael of Stanford' of half an acre of meadow in Mikilmedue which lies between the meadow of Hugh Kokil towards the west and the meadow of Matilda mother of the aforesaid Robert towards the east and abuts on the field which is called Stonefeld' towards the south. For this lease (*pro hac dimissione et concessione*) the aforesaid nuns gave the aforesaid Robert 5s of silver in his great necessity. This agreement was made the Easter after the election of sir Martin the monk in the abbey of Peterborough at the twelfth lunar cycle (*ciclo lunari currente per duodecim*). At the end of nine years and when nine crops of the aforesaid half acre have been received by the nuns (*et novem vesturis predicte dimidie acre a prefatis monialibus pleue et integre perceptis*) the aforementioned half acre of meadow will revert to the aforementioned Robert or his heirs. [Added in a different hand on the fold at the foot of the charter] And three crops for 30d at farm (*Et tres vesturas pro xxx denariis super firmam*).

Witnesses: sir Hugh dean of Bernake, sir Richard vicar of Etton', Peter the chaplain of Badinton', Ralph de Mortuo Mari, Geoffrey de Lehaum', Roger de Bernevill', Richard Lanceleve, Pain his brother, Walter the clerk of Ufford', Warin the clerk and others.

Seal: round; 32; fleur de lys; … ROBERTI FIL…; green wax; tag; imperfect.

Endorsed: Staunford (not contemporary)

Not dated c1226/7

498. E326/4736

Grant with warranty by Orabilia wife of William de Camera of Welledon' in her widow right to Sibyl (*Sibilie*) her daughter for her service of her houses with all their appurtenances which are situated in the parish of St Michael the Greater Stanford, in the two cemeteries between the houses of Alexander le Megucer towards the west and an empty plot (*vacuam placeam*) towards the east. To hold to the said Sibyl and to her heirs or assignees freely and by inheritance. Annual rent to Alexander Lucas his heirs and assignees of 5s of silver payable quarterly for all secular service, exaction and demand.

Witnesses: John the spicer (*speciario*), Osbert the janitor (*Janitore*), William de Freine, Alexander le Megucer, Osbert his son, John *carbonario*, Peter son of Richard Stanford' and others.

Seal: pointed oval; c33 x 20; fleur de lys; * S'ORABILI. . .E CAMERA: green wax; tag

Endorsed: de domibus in parochia sancti Michaelis maioris (? not contemporary)

Not dated mid/late 13th century

499. E326/4737

Quitclaim by Margaret and Richilda daughters of Outhilda daughter of Sparrus de Stanford' to master Peter the pupil (*alumpno*) of Reiner son of Hereward and to Robert son of Peter the tailor (*cissoris*) of Stanford' and to their heirs or assignees of all their right and claim in those houses with appurtenances which were of Sparrus which are situated in the parish of St John near the castle of Stamford on the east side of the castle (*iuxta castrum Stanford' ex parte orientali a castro*) concerning which houses Margaret and Richilda impleaded the said Peter and Robert by a writ of the lord king in the court of the lord earl of Warenne (*Warennie*) at Stanford' and to the same Peter and Robert delivered the said writ in the full court of the said earl. To hold to the said Peter and Robert and their heirs or assignees freely etc in perpetuity without any service and secular exaction saving the service of the lord of the fee. For this quitclaim Peter and Robert gave Margaret and Richilda 20s of silver. And if by process of time Margaret and Richilda presume to contravene this their deed, they will give to the aforesaid Peter and Robert and their heirs or assignees 40s sterling as a penalty, their pledge notwithstanding any royal prohibition or privilege of court.

Witnesses: Walter de Tikencot, Henry son of Alexander, Richard de Weston', Alexander le Seriant, William de Scheldingtorp, Peter son of Geoffrey, Adam the porter (*portero*), David the scribe (*scriptore*) and others.

Seal: (i) missing: tag*
(ii) round; c36; fleur de lys; S RIC... ; natural wax; defaced, imperfect

Endorsed: Stamford (not contemporary)

Not dated ? early 13th century
* *tag made from part of a title deed as follows:* ... I Richard de Crauden gave to Robert Alumpno for his service and for ten ...

500. E326/4738

Notification by Adam the dyer of Stanford' that he and his heirs or assignees (a religious house or Jews excepted) are held to pay annually to master Peter the clerk pupil (*alumpno*) of Reyner formerly dean of Stanford and to Robert son of Peter the tailor of Stanford and to their heirs or assignees 12s of silver at the four terms for those houses situated in the parish of St John of Stanford' between the ditch of the castle of Stanford towards the west and the houses of Ralph towards the east, which houses Adam holds at fee farm of the aforesaid Peter and Robert as the charter of the same attests. And if Adam or his heirs or assignees etc wish to sell or lease (*dimittere*) to anyone the said houses, the said Peter and Robert and their heirs or assignees will have preference (*propinquiores erunt*) over any other provided that they will be willing to give as much as any other to Adam and his heirs or assignees for the said houses. And if Adam or his heirs or assignees default in paying the said farm fully at the said terms, the said Peter and Robert or their heirs or assignees may distrain that fee in all things etc.

Witnesses: master Henry de Stanford', Terricus the German (*teutonico*), Hugh son of Reyner, Richard de Westun', Reyner son of Matilda, Henry his son, Peter de Castertona, Andrew de Cornestal, Ralph le Halver, Simon de Sancto Dionisio and Adam called 'plouman' then reeves (*tunc prepositis*) and others.

Seal: missing: traces of green wax; tag

Endorsed: de domibus iuxta castrum unus homo dedit alteri homini (not contemporary)

Not dated ? early/mid 13th century

501. E326/4739

Grant in free alms with warranty by Walter le Flemang' burgess of Stanford to the church of St Michael outside Stanf' and the nuns there of annual quit rent of one mark to be received at two terms, namely 6s 8d at Michaelmas and 6s 8d at Easter from his shop which is situated between the house of Henry the spicer (*speciarii*) which he holds of Walter in fee farm towards the north and the house formerly of John le Scaveler towards the south. To hold to the said nuns and their successors freely etc without any secular service [or] exaction. If Walter or his heirs or assignees default in payment of the aforesaid mark of annual quit rent at the terms fixed, the aforesaid prioress and convent of St Michael and their successors may distrain the aforesaid shop with all its appurtenances as much within the hundred of Stamford as without by the chattels found in the said shop etc. For Walter and his heirs and assignees, the nuns renounce all remedy of the canon and civil law, all writs sued and to be sued and especially the writ of prohibition concerning chattels and the privilege of crusaders (*renunciant in hac parte pro me et heredibus meis et assignatis omni juris remedio canonici et civilis omnibus literis impetratis et impetrandis et maxime prohibicioni Regio de catallis et privilegio crucesignatorum*) etc.

Witnesses: Walter de Brunnia, William de Notingham, William de Francton', Alexander son of Luke, William de Sudbir', John his brother, William son of Geoffrey the vintner, William de Freiney, Richard son of Richard son of Aldusa (*Alduse*) and others.

Seal: round; 24; sleeved arm, the hand clasping a sword; WAI...; green wax; tag; imperfect

Endorsed: Carta Walteri Flemmig (? contemporary)

Not dated mid/late 13th century

502. E326/4740

Confirmation with warranty by Alice (*Aliz*) de Nevill' called prioress of St Michael of Stanf' and of the whole convent there by common assent of their whole chapter and by counsel of Henry de Fiskirton' then their prior to Robert son of John the Fleming (*Flandrensis*) of

Stanf of four acres of profit-yielding land (*quatuor acras lucrabiles*) in the fields of Stanf which abut on the land of Richard Peck' of Stanf towards the south and on the land of Peter son of Geoffrey towards the north. To hold freely etc to himself and to his heirs or assignees, save any religious house except the house of St Michael of Stanf according to the tenor of the charter which Robert son of Albinus de Stanf had of them. Annual rent of 12d payable at two terms, namely 6d on Palm Sunday and 6d at Michaelmas for all service. For this confirmation, Robert gave the prioress and convent one mark of silver.

Witnesses: Hugh de Rippel' then seneschal of Stanf, Ralph son of Acard, Richard Peck', Walter de Tikenc', Hugh son of Reiner, Hugh de Stiandebi, John Franceis, Henry son of Alexander, Herbert the serjeant (*serviente*), William son of David, Henry Sibeci, Nicholas son of Alexander, Adam Porter, Alan son of Mor, Robert Futsadame and others.

Seal: missing: slits for tag

Not dated early/mid 13th century

503. E326/4741

Quitclaim by Matilda formerly wife of Gilbert Parent of Stanford' to the church of St Michael of Stanford' and the nuns there of all her right and claim as widow's dower in the arable lands in the fields of Stanford' which Gilbert Parent formerly her husband granted to the nuns in free alms.

Witnesses: sir Hugh vicar of St Martin, Turbert chaplain of All Saints, William de Pappell' chaplain, Hugh the janitor, Peter and Geoffrey clerks and others.

Seal: oval; small; fleur de lys; no trace of legend; natural wax; tag; defaced, imperfect

Endorsed: (i) Gilberti Parent (contemporary)
(ii) quiet' clam' de terris in Staunf (not contemporary)

Not dated ? early 13th century

504. E326/4742

Grant in free alms with warranty by Gilbert son of Baldwin de Staunforde to the convent of the house of St Mary of Wyrthorp for his soul and for the soul of Alexander his brother etc, namely for the clothing of the whole convent of the aforesaid house of Wyrthorp (*ad vesturam totius conventus predicte domus de Wyrthorp*) of a certain rent of 10s of a messuage with appurtenances in the vill of Staunforde which is situated in the parish of St Clement outside the gate of Scofthegathe between the houses of Robert son of Robert the carter (*caretarii*) towards the east and the houses of Henry son of Gunnild towards the west. And be it known that the aforesaid rent of 10s will be received quarterly namely in payments of 31½d [*sic*]. To hold to the said convent freely etc, annual rent to the lord of the fee of 5½d at Easter.

Witnesses: William de Nothynham, Hugh de Thykyncothe, Gilbert de Chastrethone and many others.

Seal: round; 31; fleur de lys; • S GILBERTI FIL' BALDEWINI; green wax; tag

Not dated ? early/mid 13th century

505. E326/4743

Sale with warranty by William de Coventre by the assent of his heirs to Robert de Bernardeshil' or his assignee for three marks of a house with its appurtenances in the vill of Stanford, namely that house which William de Wimundham held of him and which is situated near the church of St Clement. To hold of William and his heirs to Robert and his heirs or assignee freely and by inheritance; annual rent for all services and customs pertaining to the aforesaid house of 1d at Michaelmas.

Witnesses: Geoffrey the chaplain, Ralph son of Achard, John Franceis, John his brother, John Flamenc', Samson ultra pontem, Geoffrey de Glint', Michael de Glinton', Geoffrey son of Richard de Glint', Herbert, Geoffrey de Exton'.

Seal: round; 35; fleur de lys; + SIGIL' WILLEL' DE ...; red wax; tag; defaced, imperfect

Endorsed: (i) De Willelmo De Coventre De Stanford' (? contemporary)
(ii) tercia de domibus iuxta ecclesiam sancti Clementis (not contemporary)

Not dated ? early/mid 13th century
[See 493]

506. E326/4744

Sale with warranty by Nicholas Mariun of Stanford' to Geoffrey de Ketene 'le mercer' for three and a half marks of silver of his house with appurtenances in the parish of All Saints in the Market of Stanford' situated between the houses formerly of Balcock' (*quondam Balcock*) towards the west on the one side and the houses of the aforesaid Geoffrey towards the east on the other. To hold to the said Geoffrey de Ketene and to his heirs or assignees of Nicholas and his heirs or assignees freely etc saving the service of the lord of the fee, namely a cock and a hen at Christmas for all service and secular exaction and demand. And if the aforesaid Nicholas and his heirs or assignees are unable to warrant the aforesaid houses [*sic*] with appurtenances to the said Geoffrey and his heirs or assignees, Nicholas etc will give to Geoffrey etc in exchange the value thereof from his houses in Clippessil.

Witnesses: Richard Peck', Andrew Arketell', Henry Sibecy, Richard de Westona, John the Frenchman (*Gallico*), Simon son of Alexander, Robert de Northona, Adam Plouman, William de Franctona then reeve (*tunc prepositio*), William son of Thurstan, John the spicer, Ulmer (*Wlmero*) Ferrun, Herbert Ferrun and others

Seal: round; 27; fleur de lys; + SIGILL' NICHOLAI MARIVN; green wax; tag

Endorsed: Inquirend'

Not dated ? early/mid 13th century

507. E326/4745

Grant at fee farm (*dimiserunt et ad feodi firmam tradiderunt*) indented with warranty by the prioress and convent of the house of St Michael outside Staunford to Andrew son of Matilda 'in le Hirne' of Staunford of their houses in the parish of St John Staunford which Alpoysa daughter of Geoffrey granted to them between the houses of Gervase the tailor towards the north and the houses of Luke son of Richard towards the south. To hold to Andrew and his heirs of the said prioress and convent and their successors. Annual rent of 14s of silver payable quarterly in perpetuity. And if the aforesaid Andrew or his heirs default in payment of the said farm, the said prioress and convent and their attornies may enter the said houses and distrain the goods found therein etc.

Witnesses: Henry Sibici, Walter Ketil, Gilbert *ad pontem*, William son of Adam, Henry le Furner and others.

Seal: round; 23; stylised flower; S' ANDR' FIL' MATILD; green wax; tag

Endorsed: dimissio domorum in parochia Sancti Johannis (not contemporary)

Not dated ? later 13th century

508. E326/4746

Grant with warranty by William Burnild to the prioress of St Michael outside Stanford' and the convent there and to their successors of a plot (*unam placeam*) situated in the parish of All Saints, Stanford, 20 feet in length and 13 feet in breadth between the tenement of Peter de Northfolk' towards the east and the tenement of Walter de Wymundham towards the west; the plot abuts on Quichorsberne towards the south. To hold that plot with appurtenances of William and his heirs and assignees to the aforesaid prioress and convent and their successors freely etc in perpetuity.

Witnesses: sir William vicar of the church of All Saints, William Poucyn, Bernard Bonde, Reginald Norman, Simon de Helpestone and many others.

Seal: pointed oval; 35 x 20; stylised flower; S' WILL' BVR.. .LD; green wax; tag; imperfect

Endorsed: Stamford (not contemporary)

Not dated: ? later 13th century

509. E326/4747

Grant with warranty by Geoffrey the tanner (*tannator*) of Wlberdstoke to the prior and canons of the church of Finnesheved for half a mark of silver of the easement in the west gable of his house which is situated in the parish of St Michael the Greater in Stanford', thus that the canons may set in, set above or join a beam (*itaquod possint tignum inponere vel supraponere seu iniungere*) and use the gable for their easement. And the said prior and canons shall keep the said gable free from damage from the descending gutters to their gutter (*et dicti prior et canonici a stillicidiis decendentibus ab eorum stillicidio dictam gablam servabunt indempnem*),

Witnesses: Richard Peck, Hugh son of Reiner, Henry Sibecy, Andrew Arketel, Walter the Fleming (*Flamidrensi*), Walter Ketel, Alan Mor and many others.

Seal: round; c32; fleur de lys; . . .GALFRIDI D' WILBARSTVK...; natural wax; tag; imperfect

Endorsed: (i) Carta Galfridi tannatoris Stanford. [hand changes] de domo iuxta corwensti in parochia sancti Michaelis (? contemporary)
(ii) Carta de domo in parochia supra scripta (not contemporary)

Not dated ? early/mid 13th century

510. E326/4748

Grant in free alms by Geoffrey the mercer (*mercenarius*) son of Walkelin de Keten' to the church of St Michael outside Stanford and the nuns there of his houses with appurtenances in the parish of All Saints Stanford, situated between the houses which were formerly of Balcok' towards the west on one side and his houses which he holds of the said nuns at fee farm towards the east on the other side. And if the said Geoffrey and his heirs or assignees are unable to warrant the aforesaid houses with appurtenances to the said nuns, he etc will give to them in exchange the value thereof from the houses which he holds of them. Warrants from all suits, services and secular demands as much 'forinsec' as 'extrinsec'.

Witnesses: sir Gilbert then dean of Stamford, Hugh son of Reiner (Reneri), William de Francton', William son of David, John le Specer, Hugh de Tykencot', Richard the smith (*fabro*), Ulmer the farrier (*ferrario*) and others.

Seal: round; 33; fleur de lys; + S IDI... green wax; tag; imperfect

Not dated ? mid/early 13th Century

511. E326/4749

Grant in free alms with warranty by John Bottay of Stanford' to the church of St Michael outside Stanford' and to the nuns there of all his right and rent in a messuage in the parish of St Martin of Stanford' which Mauger the weaver (*tixtor*) held of him for 12d annual rent at Michaelmas.

Witnesses: Reiner dean of Stanford', Hugh vicar of St Martin, master Pain, Walter de Tikencote, Hugh son of Reiner, Adam de Ufford, Henry Gaugi, William de Pappele clerk and others.

Seal: round; 27; fleur de lys; + SI HANNIS BOTAI; green wax; tag; imperfect

Endorsed: (i) Carta Johannis Botay de domo Maugeri in parochia sancti Martini [hand changes] iuxta domum Willelmi de Pappele (contemporary)
(ii) donacio monialibus parochia sancti Martini (not contemporary)

Not dated ? early 13th century

512. E326/4750

Grant in free alms by Hugh son of Wimund by the assent of Levina his wife and of his heirs to the nuns of St Michael of Stanford of the houses which his father granted to Clementia his wife in the parish of St Martin with two acres of land of which one lies beyond the road to Burlebroc (*trans viam ad Burlebroc*) near the land of Agnes Bude and the other acre lies between the land of Henry son of Isaac and William son of Sarah (*Sarè*) at Charedic.

Witnesses: Alexander the dean, Reiner the priest (*sacerdote*), Henry son of Isaac, Samson son of Godric, Adam de Ufford, John Bottai, William son of Roger, Robert de Casewic, Henry Gaugi, Hugh Cornil, Alexander son of Burnild.

Seal: missing: traces of green wax; tag

Endorsed: (i) parochia Sancti Martini (not contemporary)
(ii)… bis scripta (not contemporary)
(iii) una acra trans viam ad Burleb' et alia acra apud Kar'dik (not contemporary)
(iv) Carta Hugonis filii Wimundi de domibus Clemencie uxoris sue et duabus acris terre (? contemporary)

Not dated? early 13th century

513. E326/4752

Sale with warranty by Nicholas messenger (*nuncius*) of the lord Richard illustrious earl of Cornwall to the prior and canons of the church of St Mary of Fynnesheved for twenty marks of silver of all that house with appurtenances in Stanford which he had by grant of the lord King Henry III, namely that house which formerly was of Cok the Jew of Stanford situated in Colgate between the houses formerly of Michael '*de la venele*' on the west side and the houses formerly of Cok and Avegaya (*Avegaye*) the Jews on the east side. To hold to the same prior and canons freely etc. Annual rent to sir Gilbert de Preston' and his heirs of 1d at Michaelmas for all service, custom and action and secular demand pertaining to the aforesaid house. And if Nicholas predeceases his wife, he wishes that his heirs satisfy her regarding her widow's dower from his tenement in the vill of Berkhamstede.

Witnesses: sir Richard Pecke, sir Hugh son of Reyner, sir Walter le Flemming, sir John his brother, sir Walter Ketel, sir Henry Sibecey, sir William de Tikencote, sir Hugh his brother, sir William de Fraunton', sir Hugh de Weled' and many others.

Seal: pointed oval; 33 x 19; estoile above a crescent moon; + S' : NICHOLAI : NUNCII; red wax; tag

Endorsed: (i) Stanford' Colgate (not contemporary)
(ii) de domibus in Colgate Staunf' (not contemporary)
(iii) septiam in parochia Sancti Michaelis (not contemporary)

Not dated ? mid 13th century

514. E326/4753

Sale (*concessimus vendidimus et hac presente carta nostra confirmavimus*) with warranty by Roger de Sowe and Margery his wife to William de Scaccario his heirs or assignees of the whole of their tenement with appurtenances which they had in the parish of Holy Trinity outside the east gate of Stanford. To hold freely and by inheritance to the aforesaid William and his heirs or assignees, by doing the annual service pertaining to the aforesaid tenement to the lord of the fee.

Witnesses: Richard Peck', Hugh son of Reiner, Walter de Brunn', Andrew Arketel, William de Fraunton', Hugh de Tykencote, Henry de Ockel', Richard de Cotismor, William de Picwrze, William Reyner, Alan son of Mor and others.

Seal: (i) missing: traces of green wax; tag
(ii) pointed oval; c35 x 25; a bird, possibly a peacock, with an antler above and below it; .
. .ARGARI ROGER....; green wax; tag; imperfect

Endorsed: (i) secunda carta de domo in Cornestal (not contemporary)
(ii) Carta extranee (not contemporary)

Not dated ? mid 13th century

515. E326/4754

Notification by Geoffrey Atwater (*ad aquam*) fuller (*fullo*) son of Reginald de Stanford' priest (*sacerdotis*) that he, his heirs or assignees are bound to pay annually to the nuns of the church of St Michael outside Staunford and their successors half a mark of silver at the four terms and 3d as 'landgovel' at Michaelmas for those houses in the parish of St Martin of Stanford' situated between the house of Roger Gaugi towards the west and the house which was of Richard Selleware towards the east, and for the curtilages pertaining to the said houses together with the plot (*placea*) outside the said curtilages towards the south, as it extends in a straight line (*linealiter*) from the corner of the wall of the said Richard Gaugi as far as the wall which formerly was of Richard Selleware. And if Geoffrey and his heirs etc. default in payment of the said money, the said nuns and their successors may distrain the said fee etc.

Witnesses: Hugh son of Reiner, Richard Pecke, Henry Scibeci, William son of David, Henry de Wakerle, Peter the dyer, Richard son of Alduse, John de Pappele, William de Pappele chaplain and others.

Seal: pointed oval; an eagle regardant between two lilies; + S' GALFRID ... QUAM; green wax; tag

Endorsed: (i) carta Galfridi ad aquam de dimidia marca et iii denariis pro landegavel (? not contemporary)
(ii) Sancti Martini (not contemporary)
(iii) sacri' [prohably sacrista or sacriste] (not contemporary)

Not dated ? early 13th century

516. E326/4755

Sale with warranty by Henry son of Roger son of Lece to Walter de Tikencot' for four and a half marks of silver of an acre of land beyond the bridge of Stanford on the fee of the abbot of Peterborough which lies between the land formerly of Hugh Cornel and the road which leads towards Peterborough near Scardic. To hold to Walter and his heirs or assignees freely and by inheritance, saving the service of the lord abbot of Peterborough.

Witnesses: Ralph son of Acard, Richard Peck', William son of David, John Bottay, Samson son of Godric (*Godriz*), Adam de Ufford', William de Burgo, Gilbert Parent, Hugh de Uffinton' and others.

Seal: ? round; small; fleur de lys; legend mostly wanting, illegible; natural wax; tag; imperfect

Endorsed: de una acra terre ultra pontem Staunf' (not contemporary)

Not dated early/mid 13th century

517. E326/4756

Quitclaim by Henry de Corby and Sarah (*Sarra*) daughter of Peter son of Lecia (*Leciè*) his wife to the prioress of the church of St Michael near Stanford' and the convent there and to their successors of all their right and claim in their houses in the parish of St Martin Stanford which they held of the same prioress and convent for 4s annually. The quitclaim is made for detention of arrears of the said houses, namely 46s, and because Henry and Sarah have been unable to make satisfaction on account of their very great necessity and poverty. The houses are situated between the tenement of Roger de

Makiseye tanner (*tannatoris*) towards the north and the tenement of the lord abbot of Peterborough towards the south.

Witnesses: Alexander Lucas, Andrew Nye, John Sampson, Gilmin called 'Norman', Simon the marshal (*marescallo*), John de Rippis, Richard de Stanford', Henry Fadirman, William Puncyn, Walter the doctor (*medico*) and Thomas called 'Poth' clerk, and others.

Seals: (i) fragment; a cinquefoil; legend mostly wanting; S' HEN....; natural wax; tag (ii) no *Seal:* slits for tag

Endorsed: quiet' clam' de domibus in parochia Sancti Martini (not contemporary)

Not dated late 13th century

518. E326/4757

Grant in free alms with warranty by Henry lord of the fee of Plateni to the prioress and nuns of Wyrthorp' and to their successors of thirty acres of arable land with appurtenances lying in the field of Staunford in divers tillages on Rogeford' (*in diversis culturis supra Rogeford'*).

Witnesses: Matthew *ad pontem*, Andrew *in venella*, Hugh Goldstone, William Hardekin, Robert Damisoun, William Arnald, Michael Touke of Staunford and others.

Seal: missing:slits for tag

Endorsed: Carta de xxx acris terre in Staunford (? contemporary)

Not dated ? later 13th century

519. E326/4758

Lease indented for life with warranty by Amice prioress of the church of St Michael outside Staunford and the convent there by common assent and by the consent and wish of John their prior to William de Pappele chaplain of three acres of arable land with appurtenances in the fields of Staunford, of which one acre lies between the land of William de Frauncton' towards the north and the land of John le Fleming towards the south and it abuts on the road (*viam*) which is called Holegate which goes to Little Casterton towards the east. And two acres abut on the links (*super lingis*) towards the north and on the road which goes to Great Casterton towards the south and lie near the land of the castle of Staunford towards the east. Annual rent of 1d for all service and secular exaction. After William's death the said three acres with appurtenances will revert to the prioress and convent in the state in which they are on the day on which William dies, whether the land is sown or not (*sive terra fuerit seminata sive non*).

Witnesses: John le Fleming, Robert Brond, William Faderman, Matthew de Wirthorp, Adam de Pappele, Geoffrey Kydenoth, Hugh de Hempingh' clerk and others.

Seal: missing: slits for tag

Endorsed: (i) de iii acris in Holgat' (? not contemporary)   (ii) Staunford   (?not contemporary)

Not dated ? later 13th century

520. E326/4759

Sale with warranty by John Russel and Agnes his wife to Henry de Wirtorp for 17s of silver of half an acre of arable land with appurtenances lying in the fields of Stanford on Brakenhil between the land of the nuns of St Michael towards the west and the land formerly of Henry Gaugi towards the east: the half acre abuts on the land of Gilbert de Norburg' towards the south. To hold to the said Henry and his heirs or assignees freely and by inheritance saving the service of the lord of the fee for all secular service, exaction and demand.

Witnesses: William son of David, Norman de Grettun', Henry de Wakerley, Matthew de Wiryorp, Hugh the smith, William Faderman, William the Norman (*Normanno*), Gilbert de Norburg', Roger Briselaunce and others.

Seals: (i) no *Seal:* slits for tag; (ii) missing: tag; (iii) no *Seal:* slits for tag

Not dated ? late 13th century

521. E326/4760

Grant in free alms with warranty by Reginald le Bretun son of Simon de Ketene to the church of St Mary of Esseby and the canons there of an annual rent of 2s in the vill of Stanford from his burgage (*burgagio*) which he had by grant of sir Richard de Atteneston': the rent to be received at Michaelmas.

Witnesses: sir Terri le Tieis, Hugh son of Reiner, Walter le Flamenc, John son of Samson (*Sansonis*), Richard son of Richard Pecke, Gilbert the Noble (*nobili*) and many others.

Seal: fragment; natural wax; tag

Endorsed: Carta de Staunford (not contemporary)

Not dated ? early 13th century

522. E326/4761

Sale with warranty by Peter son of Geoffrey son of Herlewin burgess of Stanf' to Henry son of Walter de Tikencot' for £10 of silver of a moiety of a meadow outside the west gate which is called 'leffeynescroft' which he bought from William de Berkec. To hold to the said Henry de Tikencot and his heirs or assignees freely etc. of Peter and his heirs. Annual rent at Easter of 6d for all service and demand and for all secular exaction etc.

Witnesses: sir Hugh son of Reiner de Stanf', Richard Pecke, Andrew Arketell', Henry Sibecy, sir Alexander clerk of Quappellode, John Sampson, Walter Flemang', Thurstan de Bisex, Roger Drie, Peter son of Richard and others.

Seal: missing: fragment of a tag

Endorsed: (i) De medietate unius prati extra portam occidentalem Staunford (not contemporary)
(ii) Carta de quoddam prato extra portam (not contemporary)

Not dated early/mid 13th century

523. E326/4762

Grant in free alms with warranty by William de Colevill' by the assent and counsel of his heirs and friends to the church of St Michael of Stanford' and the nuns there of 5s sterling in his oven of Stanford', which of old used to be the oven of Asciria sister of Acard (*quinque solidos sterlingorum in furno meo de Stanford' qui antiquitus solebat esse furnus Ascirie sororis Acardi*) and which William de Humeto granted to him for his service: the money to be received at two terms, namely 2s 6d at Easter and 2s 6d at Michaelmas from whosover holds the aforementioned oven whether William or his heirs or another. The surplus (*superplusagium*) of the oven will remain to William and his heirs.

Witnesses: Geoffrey chaplain of St Andrew, Gilbert chaplain of St Mary, Matthew of St Martin, Thomas the clerk, Robert de Colevill', Geoffrey son of Herlewin, Herbert de Lundr', Hugh Stute and William his son, Ralph de Wion, Clement the vintner (*vinitore*), William de Torpel, Luice the clerk son of Geoffrey, Robert son of Matthew and others.

Seal: missing: tag

Endorsed: Staunford (not contemporary)

Not dated early/mid 13th century

524. E326/4763

Grant with warranty and acquittance by Robert Sturri to the nuns of St Mary of Writhorp and their successors of a moiety of a messuage with all appurtenances in the vill of Stamford, namely in the parish of St Mary of Binnewerc, which messuage is situated between the house of Emma de Writhorp towards the west and the house of Rose Sturri towards the east. To hold of Robert and his heirs to the said nuns and their successors freely etc. Annual rent to the lord of the fee of ¾d namely ½d at Palm Sunday and ¼d at the feast of St Peter in Chains [1 August] for all secular service and demand.

Witnesses: master Henry Sampson (*Sampsun*) and sir Simon de Lindon', Nicholas de Weston', Thomas le Frankelein of Writhorp, Hugh son of Reiner, Geoffrey the Noble (*nobili*), Robert the tailor (*cissore*), Osbert le Porter, Hugh the butcher (*carnifice*) and others.

Seal: pointed oval; c29 x c19; fleur de lys; * S' R ...VRRI; green wax; tag; imperfect

<u>Endorsed</u>: Carta pro mesuagio parochie de Bynwerc (not contemporary)

<u>Not dated</u> early/mid 13th century

525. E326/4764   **17 November 1328**

<u>Grant</u> with warranty by Alice widow of William Faderman of Staunford tanner (*tannatoris*) in her widow right to Simon the smith (*fabro*) in the house of St Michael outside Staunford of a house in the parish of St Martin Staunford, near the street (*iuxta vicum*) which is called Webestergate situated lengthwise between the tenement of Geoffrey de Wodeschlade towards the north and Alice's tenement towards the south, and it extends as far as the door of her barn (*et extendit se usque ad hostium grangii mei*) towards the east. To hold the aforesaid house with another house adjoining and with all appurtenances to the aforesaid Simon and his heirs or assignees of the capital lord of that fee for the services owed and accustomed freely etc in perpetuity.

Witnesses: Geoffrey de Wodeschlade, Bernard Bonde, Richard Bertelmeu, John Clokett', William de Birthorp' burgesses of Staunford and others.

Given at Staunford Thursday after Martinmas 2 Edward III

Seal: pointed oval; 30 x 18; stylised flower; S' ALISCIE FIL'... THOME NOR..; green wax; tag

<u>Endorsed</u>: de i domo in Webster'gat' (? contemporary)

526. E326/4765   **12 July 1331**

<u>Grant</u> with warranty by Thomas de Rauele of Staunford to Hugh de Thurleby and Margaret his wife and to the legitimate heirs of their bodies of an acre of meadow with appurtenances lying in the meadows of Staunford which is called Brodeeng between the meadow of John de Assewell' on the east and the meadow formerly of William del Cley on the west and it abuts on the meadow of the lord earl of Warenne towards the south and on the bank of the Welland (*Welond*) towards the north. To hold the aforesaid acre of meadow with its appurtenances to the aforesaid Hugh and Margaret and their heirs of the capital lord of that fee for the services owed and accustomed freely and by inheritance in perpetuity. And if Hugh and Margaret die without an heir of their bodies, the aforesaid acre of meadow with its appurtenances will remain to the heirs of the aforesaid Hugh in perpetuity.

Witnesses: Roger le Scavelere, Roger de Scotelthorp', Walter Halvere, John de Friseby, John de Rippis, Robert Hotot', Thomas Lutipati, John Shereman clerk and others.

Given at Staunford Friday after the Translation of St Thomas the martyr 5 Edward III

Seal: fragment; natural wax; tag

<u>*Endorsed*</u>: Carta Hugonis de Thorlleby de prato quod adquisivit de Thoma de Raule (not contemporary)

527. E326/4766   13 September 1332

<u>*Lease*</u> indented for the term written below with warranty by William de Byrthorp' of Staunford to the prioress and convent of St Michael outside Staunford of two acres of arable land with appurtenances lying in the field of Staunford, of which one acre lies between the land of Thomas de Bedeford' towards the north and the land of the said prioress and convent towards the south and the other acre lies between the land of the same prioress and convent towards the north and the land of Alice le Walker' towards the south, and both acres abut on 'burlesike' towards the east, in exchange for two other acres of arable land also lying in the field of Stanford which the same prioress and convent leased to the same William for the same term written below and which two acres lie together in the croft of St Martin between the wall and the enclosure (*oblong*) of the same wall enclosing (*includentem*) the tenements of divers burgesses of the vill of Stamford towards the west and the land of the same nuns, divided from the said two acres by stakes and posts fixed in the land (*per gades et trabes in terra fixos*) towards the east: these two acres extend from the king's highway towards the south up to the wall of the said William towards the north. To hold the said two acres of land thus leased by the aforesaid William to the said prioress and convent in exchange as it is said before, to the same prioress and convent from the Michaelmas following the date of these presents up to the end of William's life and two years thereafter, freely etc for the other two acres aforesaid; after the lapse of which term the land leased by William will revert to him and his heirs.

Witnesses: William de Belmisthorp', William Faderman tanner (*tannatore*), Robert de Haringworth', Peter de Talyngton', Robert de Sempingham, William de Graham, Richard Bertilmeu of Staunford and others.

Given at Staunford Sunday after the Nativity of the Blessed Virgin Mary 6 Edward III

Seal: fragment; natural wax; tag

<u>*Endorsed*</u>: Staunford

528. E326/4767   26 July 1335

<u>*Grant*</u> by Simon Bolle burgess of Stanford' and Alice his wife. Lately Alexander de Quappelode their predecessor by his deed granted in free alms to the prior of Fynneshed' and his successors an annual rent of 6s 8d to be received at Martinmas from his houses in Stanford' in the parish of Our Lady beyond the bridge, which houses one Gervase le Taylour and Aldouse his wife used to hold of the said Alexander. And by the

same deed Alexander granted that if at any time the said rent was in arrears, the said prior and his successors might levy a distress in the said tenements. Simon and Alice grant that they will pay to the said prior and his successors the aforesaid annual rent of 6s 8d at Martinmas, and at any time that the said rent is in arrears the aforesaid prior and his successors may levy a distress as well in all his tenements in the said town as in his houses aforesaid.

Given at Estanford' Wednesday after St James the Apostle 9 Edward III

Seal: (i) missing: green wax; tag (ii) oval; 18 x 14; a grotesque; legend illegible; green wax; tag
FRENCH

529. E326/4768   1 April 1335

Grant with warranty by John Cloket burgess of Stanford' to John de Clyve butcher (*carnifici*) of Stanford' burgess for a certain sum of money of three acres of arable land with appurtenances in the field of Stanford lying together at Kirkestedis on the fee of the lord abbot of Peterborough between the land of the nuns of St Michael outside Stanford' towards the south and the land of the hospital of St Thomas the martyr upon the bridge of Stanford towards the north: and the three acres abut on the headland (*foreram*) of the said nuns towards the east and the land of the aforesaid John de Clyve towards the west. To hold the said land with its appurtenances to the aforesaid John de Clyve and his heirs or assignees freely and by inheritance of the capital lord of the fee for the services owed and accustomed in perpetuity.

Witnesses: William de Morcote then bailiff of the liberty (*tunc ballivo libertatis*), William de Birthorp, Ralph Lymbrennere, John le Bonde, Thomas Lymbrennere, Peter de Talingtone, John de Folkingham and others.

Given at Stanford Saturday before St Ambrose the Bishop 9 Edward III

Seal: hexagonal; c19 x c17; a bell; legend mostly wanting, illegible; red wax; tag imperfect

530. E326/4769   20 January 1332

Appointment by John de Aswelle of Stannford of William son of Peter de Bazule as attorney for livery of seisin of his part of a house and garden in Stannford to the prior and canons of Finnisheued.

Dated at Stanford Monday the feast of St Fabian and St Sebastian 5 Edward III.

Seal: missing: tag

531. E326/4770   **18 April 1379**

Lease indented for fourteen years with warranty by Alice Coupeldyk' prioress of the
house of St Michael near Staunford and the convent there to Walter Oyler' of Staunford
and Isabel his wife of three acres of arable land with their appurtenances lying separately
in the field(s) of Staunford, of which one and a half acres of the aforesaid land lie
between the land of the prior of St Leonard on the south and the land of Walter
Makeseye on the north and abut on the land of the prior of St Leonard towards the east:
the other one and a half acres lie between the land of Alice de Asshewell' on the south
and the land of Walter Makeseye on the north and abut on the land of the prioress and
convent aforesaid towards the east.   To hold the said three acres with their
appurtenances to the aforesaid Walter and Isabel, namely from Easter 2 Richard II etc.
Annual rent of 2s of silver at the feast of St Peter in Chains [1 August] and at Christmas
by equal portions. And if the said annual rent is in arrears at any term by fifteen days, the
aforesaid prioress and convent or their successors may re-enter the aforesaid three acres
with their appurtenances and again hold the land in fee in perpetuity (*et penes se in feodo
inperpetuum retinere*) and expel the said Walter and Isabel.

Witnesses: Robert Prat then Alderman of Staunford (*tunc Aldermanno Staunfordie*),William
de Styandeby, John Spycer, John Weldon' and others.

Given in the chapter house of St Michael aforesaid and on the day and year aforesaid.

Seal: (i) traces of natural wax; tag
(ii) round; c13; legend mostly wanting, * I ...; natural wax; tag; imperfect

Endorsed: Walterus Olyer' de Stanford' (? contemporary)

532. E326/4771   **11 April 1379**

Lease indented for lives in survivorship with warranty by Alice Coupeldyk' prioress of the
house of St Michael near Staunford and the convent there to Simon Mason' of Staunford
and Matilda his wife of five acres of arable land with their appurtenances lying together
in the field of Staunford on le Hyegh'dyk between the land of John de Weldon' on the
west side and the land of William Makeseye on the east side: the five acres abut on the
land of Simon Bonde towards the south and on the land pertaining to the chapel of St
Thomas on the bridge of Staunford towards the north. Annual rent of 2s 6d of silver,
namely at the feast of St Peter in Chains [1 August] and at Christmas by equal portions.
Expulsion for arrears of rent [as in 531].

Witnesses: Robert Prat then Alderman of Stamford, William de Styandeby, John de la
Panetrie, John Spycer, John Weldon, William Makeseye and others.

Given in the chapter house of St Michael aforesaid Monday after Easter 2 Richard II

Seals: (i) round; 22; an animal (possibly a fox) running to the left; legend illegible; red wax;
tag; defaced
(ii) ? round; c22; incorporating on the right a kneeling figure; legend illegible; red wax;
tag; imperfect

533. E326/4772   **27 October 1383**

Lease indented for lives in survivorship with warranty by Alice Coupeldyk' prioress of the house of St Michael near Staunford and the convent there to John Scherwynd' of Staunford and Alice his wife of four acres of arable land lying separately in the field(s) of Staunford in the liberty of the abbot of Peterborough: three acres of the aforesaid land lie together in the croft of St Martin, namely between the land of John Willy on the west and the bookland (*terram hered'*) of sir John Knyvet on the east, and one acre of the aforesaid land lies between the land of William de Styandeby on the west and the land of Thomas Corby on the east, and the said four acres of arable land abut on the land of the said John Willy towards the south. Annual rent of 4s of silver at two terms, namely at Easter and Michaelmas by equal portions. And if the said annual rent is in arrears at any term by fifteen days, the aforesaid prioress and convent or their successors may levy a distress by the goods and chattels found on the aforesaid land etc.

Given at Staunford Tuesday the vigil of the Apostles Simon and Jude 7 Richard II

Seals: (i) round; 18; pelican in her piety feeding three nestlings; legend illegible; red wax; tag
(ii) round; 16; a device (defaced) crowned; no legend; red wax; tag; defaced

Endorsed: (i) Johannes Scherwyhnd (? contemporary)
(ii) Sent Martyn croft (not contemporary)

534. E326/4773   **1 October 1403**

Surrender by William Makesey of Staunford to Margaret Redynges prioress of the nuns of St Michael outside Staunford and the convent there in the presence of William son of Henry de Staunford, John Aldewerk, Thomas de Walyngton' and Henry Bateman of Staunford of all his title and right in a messuage with its appurtenances situated in the parish of St Paul, Staunford, which messuage Roger Mundham of Staunford by his indenture (*per cartam indentatam*) held of the said prioress and convent for his good service for the term of his life.

Given at Staunford Monday after Michaelmas 5 Henry IV

Seal: round; 18.5; a shield of arms namely a chevron between three lions rampant; * S' IOHANNIS DE BES …; red wax; tag.

Endorsed: Staunford (? contemporary)

535. E326/4774   **5 October 1385**

Lease indented for ten years by Alice Cupuldik' prioress of the house of St Michael near Staunford and the convent there to Robert de Burle' of Staunford carpenter of an acre and a half of arable land lying in the liberty of the abbot of Peterborough between the land of Simon de Wikilsey on the west and the road which leads from the lane (*et viam quam* [*sic*] *ducit de venella*) called 'Schepcoteslane' up to Bulpite on the east, and the land abuts on the tenement formerly of Thomas Chestirton' towards the north at one head (*ad unum caput*) and on the land of the master of the hospital at the other head (*ad aliud caput*) towards the south. To hold the aforesaid acre and a half of arable land with appurtenances to the aforesaid Robert and his assignees from Michaelmas 9 Richard II etc. Annual rent of 12d of silver at two terms, namely at Christmas and at the feast of St Peter in Chains [1 August] by equal portions. If the rent is in arrears at any term, the aforesaid prioress and convent may levy a distress on the aforesaid land.

Given in their chapter house at Staunford Thursday after Michaelmas in the year abovementioned

Seal: missing: slits for tag

Endorsed: dimissio Roberto Burle carpentario (? contemporary)

536. E326/4775   **3 August 1384**

Lease indented for lives in survivorship with warranty by Alice Coupeldyk' prioress of the house of St Michael near Staunford and the convent there to John Chestr' of Staunford sadeler and to Alice his wife of an empty plot (*unam vacuam placeam*) with its appurtenances in the parish of St Michael the Greater Stanford, between the tenement of the said John Chestr' on the south and the tenement formerly of Nicholas Sleford' on the north, and it abuts on the tenement of the said John Chestr' towards the west and the land called Clementeslane towards the east. Annual rent of 1d of silver at Easter for the first twenty years of the term of the life of the said John and Alice, and thereafter 12d of silver at the same feast. And if the said annual rent is in arrears at the aforesaid feast by fourteen days, the aforesaid prioress and convent or their successors may levy a distress in the said empty plot with its appurtenances etc.

Witnesses: John Broun then Alderman of Stamford, William de Styandeby, John Spycer, Robert Prat', Richard Forster and others.

Given at Staunford Wednesday after St Peter in Chains 8 Richard II

Seals: (i) round; c1"; green wax; tag; imperfect
(ii) round; ½", a letter, possibly an I or A with a palm branch on each side; no legend; green wax; tag; imperfect

Endorsed: Indentura j chestre sadeler et Alicie uxoris eius (? contemporary)

537. E326/4777   **19 May 1411**

Grant with warranty by John Apethorp' son and heir of William Apethorp' of Staunford to Thomas Bove of Staunford chaundeler and to Alice his wife of an empty plot lying Behyndebak' in the parish of the church of All Saints in the Market of Staunford between the tenement of the prior of Depyng' on the north and the empty plot of the nuns of St Michael on the south and abutting on Behyndebak' towards the east: on this empty plot [i.e. that being granted by William] there were formerly situated two shops with solars built above (*quondam fuerunt scituate due schoppe cum solariis superedificatis*). To hold the aforesaid empty plot with its appurtenances to the aforesaid Thomas and Alice their heirs and assignees in perpetuity of the capital lords of that fee for the services owed and accustomed by right.

Witnesses: Ralph Bonde then Alderman of Stamford, John Stenby, Thomas Spycer, John Broun draper, Alexander Mercer, John Pratt', John Fraunceys of Staunford and others.

Given at Staunford the feast of St Dunstan 12 Henry IV

Seal: round; 22; a rose within a roundel of rich tracery; no legend; red wax; tag

538. E326/4778   **11 June 1423**

Lease indented for ten years with warranty by Agnes Leek prioress of the house of St Michael near Staunford and the convent there to John Schelford' cordewaner of Staunford of a shop with solar built above situated in the parish of All Saints in the Market of Staunford on the corner (*super corneram*) between the tenement formerly of John Steneby on each side, namely the west and north. To hold the said shop with solar built above to the aforesaid John from the feast of St John the Baptist [24 June] next etc. Annual rent of 3s payable quarterly. And the said John will repair and maintain the said premises at his own expense during the aforesaid term etc. And if the said rent of 3s is in arrears at any term by fifteen days or if at any time during the aforesaid term the said shop with solar is not competently repaired, the said prioress and convent and their successors may re-enter the said premises and detain them (*et penes se detinere*).

Given at Staunford feast of St Barnabas the Apostle 1 Henry VI

Seal: round; 13; letter E and a cross; no legend; red wax; tag

539. E326/4779   **6 January 1426**

Lease indented with warranty for fifty years by Agnes Leeks prioress of the house of St Michael near Staunford and the convent there to William Morwode of Staunford and John Sibily of the same chaplain of an empty plot and a garden lying separately in Staunford within the liberty of the abbey of Peterborough. The empty plot lies between the tenement of John Sapcote on the south and the tenement of the same John (formerly of William Gentil) on the north and it abuts on the cemetery of the church of St Martin towards the west and on Martynescroft towards the east. And the garden lies between the garden of Emma Salteby on the west and the tenement of Richard Corby on the east and it abuts on the river Weland towards the north and on Martynescroft towards the south. To hold the aforesaid empty plot and garden with their appurtenances to the aforesaid William and John and their assignees from Epiphany [6 January] 4 Henry VI etc. Annual rent of a red rose at the Nativity of St John the Baptist [24 June] if it be requested.

Furthermore, lease with warranty for the term of the life of the same John Sibily by the said prioress and convent to the aforesaid William Morwode and John Sibily of a tenement with its appurtenances situated within the aforesaid liberty, namely between the tenement of Henry Colson' on the west and the tenement of John Bogy on the east: it abuts on the river Weland towards the north and on Martynescroft towards the south. Annual rent of a peppercorn at Christmas if it be requested. And the said William and John will repair and maintain the said tenement with its appurtenances at their own expense during the aforesaid term. And if during John Sibily's lifetime either William or John leases (*ad firmam dimittere*) the said tenement with its appurtenances for a certain term of years and the same John dies within that term, the prioress and convent for themselves and their successors grant that the farmer will have and enjoy the said tenement for the whole of the term granted to him on condition that each year after the death of the said John Sibili the said farmer pays to the said prioress and convent 2s in quarterly instalments. And further, it was agreed between the aforesaid parties that the said William and John will build anew a house on the aforesaid empty plot from their own expenses, which house, kept in good repair, they will surrender at the end of their term (*et sic illam domum bene et competenter reparatam in finem termini eorum dimittent*).

Given in the chapter house of the prioress and convent on the feast and in the year abovesaid.

Seals (i) round; 15; St John the Baptist holding the Lamb and banner; 'iohe...' ; red wax; tag; partly defaced.
(ii) oval; 11 x 12; monogram; no legend; S' elyzavthi huvvill; red wax; tag.

Endorsed: Sant Martyn croft (not contemporary)

540. E326/4780   4 July 1432

Lease indented for twenty years with warranty by Elizabeth Weldon' prioress of St Michael near Staunford and the convent there to William Morwode of Staunford of five acres of arable land lying separately in the croft of St Martin within the liberty of the abbot of Peterborough, of which three acres lie together between the land of the gild of Corpus Christi of Stamford on the west and the land formerly of Cristiana Wykes on the east and abut on the land of the said gild towards the south. And one acre lies between the land of the said William on the west and the land recently of Joan Boge on the east and abuts on the land of the said gild towards the south. And the other acre lies between the land of the said gild on the north and the road which goes towards Pyllesgate on the south. To hold the aforesaid five acres of land with appurtenances to the aforesaid William and his assignees from Michaelmas next etc. Annual rent of 5s payable quarterly. And if the aforesaid rent is in arrears at any term by one month, the aforesaid prioress and convent and their successors may re-enter the aforesaid land and hold it again in its former state (*et in pristino statu suo rehabere*) and expel William and his assignees etc.

Given at Staunford 4 July 10 Henry VI

Seal: round; 15; no legend; red wax; tag; imperfect.

<u>*Endorsed*</u>: Sant Martyn croft (not conteriporary)
[See 562]

---

541. E326/4781   **10 September 1470**

<u>*Lease*</u> indented for forty years with warranty by Margery Croyland' prioress of the nuns near Staunford and the convent there to John Corby senior of Staunford and Joan his wife of a messuage, a grange and a croft with thirteen acres of arable land and meadow situated and lying in the vill and fields of Staunford and Pyllesyate within the liberty of the abbot of Peterborough. The messuage is situated in 'le Highgate' between the tenement of the said abbot of Peterborough on the south and the tenement of Richard Sapcote on the north and abuts on the king's highway towards the east; the grange is situated near le Nunes Style between the grange of the gild of Corpus Christi on the east and the croft of the nuns on the west; and the croft lies between the tenement of the gild of Holy Trinity on the north side and Shepcotelane on the south side. And ten and a half acres of arable land lie in the field of Staunford and two and a half acres of meadow lie in the field of Pyllesyate. To hold the aforesaid messuage, grange and croft with the thirteen acres of land and meadow to the aforesaid John Corby senior and to Joan his wife and to their assignees from Michaelmas next etc. Annual rent of 8s 6d at two terms, namely at Easter and Michaelmas by equal portions. And during the aforesaid term John and Joan and their assignees will repair and maintain the aforesaid messuage and grange together with the close of the croft by their own expenses. And if the aforesaid rent is in arrears at any feast aforementioned by a month, the aforesaid prioress and convent or their deputies may enter the aforesaid messuage, grange and croft and levy a distress etc. And if the rent is in arrears by a quarter, the aforesaid prioress etc may re-enter the aforesaid messuage, grange and croft with their appurtenances and hold them again in their former state and expel the said John and Joan and their assignees etc.

Given in the chapter house of the prioress and convent 10 September A.D. 1470.

Seals: two, of same design etc. namely square; 10.5; stylised flower; no legend; red wax; tag

<u>*Endorsed*</u>: Indentura Johannis Corby de Staunford (not contemporary)

---

542. E326/4782   **24 September 1438**

<u>*Lease*</u> indented for sixty years by Elizabeth Weldon' prioress of the nuns of the house of St Michael near Staunford and the convent there to William Corby *alias* Chubbok' of Staunford of two granges with the garden adjacent situated together in Staunford in the parish of St Martin in the street called Webstergate between the grange recently of Ralph Bonde (now of William Aldewynkle) on the north and the free tenement of Joan Sappecote on the south. And the said garden is 15⅞ yards in length and in breadth 13½ yards at the west end (*ad caput occidentale*) and 6¾ yards at the east end (*ad caput orientale*).

To hold the aforesaid two granges with the garden adjacent and their appurtenances to the aforesaid William, his heirs and assignees from Michaelmas next etc. Annual rent of 2s of silver at two terms, namely Easter and Michaelmas by equal portions. And during the term aforesaid, William, his heirs and assignees will repair and maintain the aforesaid two granges with the garden adjacent at their own expense. And if the aforesaid rent of 2s is in arrears by a year and a month, the aforesaid prioress and convent and their successors may re-enter the said two granges and their garden etc and occupy them in their former state (*et in pristino statu suo possidere*) and expel the said William his heirs and assignees etc. [No warranty]

Given in the chapter house of St Michael 24 September 17 Henry VI

Seal: round; c16; head of a woman (full face) in a wimple; legend illegible; red wax; tag; imperfect

Endorsed: (i) Indentura Staunford ye Nonys (not contemporary) (ii) Hikham tenet (not contemporary)

543. E326/4783

Sale and quitclaim with warranty by Robert son of Peter the tailor (*cissoris*) of Stanford' to master Peter the pupil of Reiner formerly dean of Stanford' for four marks of silver of his whole part of an annual rent of 12s with appurtenances in which rent Adam de Stanford' dyer and his heirs or assignees were bound to the same master Peter and to himself for those houses situated in the parish of St John of Stanford' between the ditch of the castle towards the west and the houses of Ralph le Halvere towards the east. To hold to the said master Peter and his heirs or assignees and to the heirs of his assignees freely etc without any service and secular exaction etc saving the service of the lord of the fee.

Witnesses: Richard Peck', Henry Scibeci, William de Francton', Reiner son of Matilda, Henry his son, Peter de Casterton, Adam the dyer, Reginald son of Peter, William de Freney, David the clerk, William de Pappele chaplain and others.

Seal: round; c36; fleur de lys; + SIGILL' ROBERTI FIL' PETRI TAILVR; green wax; tag

Endorsed: (i) quiet' clamacio unius hominis alteri homini de domibus iuxta castrum (? not contemporary) (ii) Staunford (not contemporary)

Not dated

544. E326/4784

Sale with warranty by Hugh son of Wimund de Stanford' by the counsel and assent of Leviva his wife and of his heirs to William de Sumercot' and his heirs or assignees for twelve marks of silver which William gave to Hugh for his most pressing business (*in meo maximo negotio*) of that house with appurtenances in the parish of St Martin of Stanford', namely that which formerly was of Wimund his father and which is situated between the house formerly of Achard son of Yncmund at the south and next to the street which goes towards Writthorp' (*et proxima vico quo itur apud Writthorp*) at the north. To hold to William and his heirs or assignees well etc and by inheritance and free of all secular service and exaction pertaining to Hugh or his heirs, saving the service of the lord of the fee.

Witnesses: Hugh the chaplain, Pain the chaplain, Richard Pek, Walter de Tikencot, Ralph son of Achard, Clement the vintner, Henry son of Isaac, John Bottai, Adam de Hufford', Henry son of Roger, William son of Roger, Sampson son of Godric, Gilbert Parent, Robert de Kasewik and many others.

Seal: missing: fragment of tag

Endorsed: Stamford (not contemporary)

Not dated ? early 13th century

545. E326/4785

Sale and quitclaim with warranty by Adam son of Achard son of Luwe de Stanford' to William de Pappell' chaplain the son of William for half a mark of silver of all his right and claim in the north moiety of that house with the moiety of the curtilage appurtaining to the house in the parish of St Martin of Stanford' which is situated between the house of William son of David towards the north and the house of master Isaac son of Roger son of Lece towards the south. To hold to the said William or his assignees freely etc without any secular service and exaction pertaining to Adam or his heirs: rendering the annual service pertaining to the same tenement to the heirs of Walter de Torp or their assignees, just as attests the charter of Jordan de Stanford' tailor which he made to Adam and the said William.

Witnesses: John Bothay, William de Sumercotes, Henry Gaugy, Sampson son of Godric, Gilbert Parent, Henry de Wakerle, Adam de Ufford', Roger de Eston', Geoffrey Doget', Isaac son of Henry, Warin the Long (*Longo*), Henry son of Peter, Hugh de Bernak', Peter son of William, Peter the clerk and others.

Seal: round; 33; fleur de lys; + SIGILL' ADE FIL ACARDI; green wax; tag

Endorsed: (i) quiet' clam'
(ii) Carta Ade filii Achardi facta Willelmo capellano de una domo (? contemporary)

Not dated ? early 13th century

546. E326/4786

Sale with warranty by Richard de Sancto Edmundo to Peter the dyer of Stanford' for three and a half marks of silver of an acre of arable land in the fields of Stanford which he bought from master Alexander son of Richard son of Selofd' of Staniford: the acre lies in the croft of St Martin beyond the bridge of Stanford between the land of the nuns of St Michael outside Stanford' towards the north and the ditch (*fossat*) on the left side of the road which goes towards Burley towards the south and it abuts on the headland of the said nuns (*et abbuttat super terram dictarum monialium que est forera*) towards the west and on the king's great highway at the cross of Burley towards the east. To hold the said acre of arable land to the said Peter and his heirs or assignees freely and by inheritance, saving the service of the lord of the fee for all secular service, exaction and demand pertaining to anyone.

Witnesses: Hugh son of Reyner, Richard Peck', Andrew Arketel, Robert son of Agnes, William son of David, Robert de Corby, Norman de Grettun', William Normann', Henry de Wakerly, William Bond dyer, Richard son of Aldus, Richard son of Richard, William son of Reyner and others.

Seal: round; c32; fleur de lys; •. ...RICARDI DE SANCT...; green wax; tag; imperfect

Endorsed: Carta Ricardi de Sancto Edmundo de una acra (? contemporary)

Not dated mid/late 13th century

547. E326/4787

Sale and quitclaim with warranty by Gilbert son of Ywen (*Yweni*) de Stanford' to Henry son of master Sampson or his assignee for half a mark of silver which the said Henry gave to Gilbert for a tunic worth 2s which the same gave to Alice, Gilbert's mother, of all his right and claim in a croft with all its appurtenances in the parish of St John of Stanford; namely the toft which is situated very close (*propinquius*) to the croft of Quenilda Wimplere towards the south and the church of St John towards the north and which croft Gilbert formerly used to claim as of his hereditary right (*et quod croftum ego Gilbertus vendicabam aliquando mihi tanquam meum ius hereditarium*). To hold to the said Henry or his assignee freely and by inheritance. Annual rent to the church of St John of 8d at Easter for all secular service and exaction.

Witnesses: Alexander dean of Stanford', Sampson Pain [and] Clement chaplains, Reiner Mideto, Peter Taillur, John Stikeling', Richard Fuscedo', Nicholas the goldsmith (*aurifabro*), Ralph Alver, John the Little (*Parvo*), John his son, Peter de Castreton' and others.

Seal: missing: tag.

Not dated ? early 13th century

548. E326/4788

Grant with warranty by Hugh Mercer' burgess of Stanford' to Joan his daughter for her service of four and a half acres of arable land with appurtenances lying in the field of Stamford which is called Sundersokn' of which four acres, one acre and a rood lie between the land of the rector of the church of St Peter of Stanford' towards the north and the land of Damisona widow of Roger Boni towards the south and abut on the land of William de Perte of Bradecroft' towards the west; two half acres cross (*transversant*) the road which goes towards Empingham but lie separately, namely one half acre lies between the land of William de Tykencot' towards the east and the land which lady Beatrice formerly wife of Terricus de Colonia then held as widow's dower towards the west and abuts on the headland (*foreram*) of William de Perte of Bradecroft' towards the north: the other half acre lies between the lands of the aforesaid William and Beatrice and abuts on the aforesaid headland of William de Perte towards the north. Three roods lie on either side between the lands of Hugh Fusce and abut on six acres which are of the demesne of the castle of Stanford towards the road which goes towards Empyngham towards the west and on the land of the rector of the church of St Peter of Stanford' towards the east. Half an acre lies on the north side of the land of William de Perte and abuts on the land formerly of Terricus de Colonia towards the west and on the land formerly of Henry de Tykencot' towards the east. One half acre lies between the land formerly of Henry son of Alexander towards the south and the land which lady Beatrice formerly wife of Terricus de Colonia then held as widow's dower towards the north and abuts on the land formerly of Henry de Tykencot' towards the east. One rood lies on the north side of the land of the rector of the church of St Peter Stanford and abuts on the land which is of the demesne of the castle of Stamford, and another rood lies between the land formerly of Henry son of Alexander towards the south and the headlands of Walter Ketell', William de Perte of Bradecroft' and lady Emma Atwater (*ad aquam*) abut on the aforesaid rood towards the north. To hold to the said Joan and his heirs or assignees freely etc and by inheritance. Annual rent to Hugh and his heirs or assignees or to the assignees of his heirs of 3½d at Easter for all secular service, exaction and demand.

Witnesses: Simon son of Alexander, Robert son of Brond, Simon Ballard, Richard Ferron', Ulmer Ferron', Roger their brother, William the Mercer (*mercero*), William son of Thurstan and others.

Seal: missing: tag

<u>*Endorsed*</u>: Sudirsokin (not contemporary)

<u>*Not dated*</u> mid/late 13th century

549. E326/4794   **9 May 1397**

<u>*Condition of a bond*</u> in £100 from William Flete rector of St Peter's church Stannford to Margaret Redynges prioress of the priory of St Michael without Stannford for the observance of the award of the arbitrators masters William Kyrkestede, William de Burton, Robert Toynton and William Irby rectors of Bernak, Eston by Stannford, Uffington and Medbourne, or the decree of John Burbach official of [the bishop of] Lincoln in a dispute concerning the tithes of corn, hay and autumn fruits in the fields and meadows of Stannford on the northern side of the Weland.

Dated at Stannford 9 May 1397

Seal: fragment, illegible.

Endorsed: Wills Flete persona ecclesie sancti petri

550. E326/4795   **28 March 1297**

Quitclaim by Amice widow of Alexander Lucas of Stanford' to Matilda de Len prioress of St Michael outside Stanford' and the nuns there of all her right and claim as widow's dower or in any other manner whatsoever in three acres of arable land lying on Langelond in the field of Stanford.

Witnesses: Alfred (*Alueredo*) le Mercer, Nicholas de Burton', John de Werminton', Richard le Blund', William Pucyn and others.

Given in the monastery of St Michael outside Stanford' Wednesday after the Annunciation of the Blessed Virgin 25 Edward I and A.D. 1296

Seal: missing: tag

Endorsed : (i) Stamford (ii) Quiet' clam' de iii acris terre in longlonde (not contemporary)

551. E326/4796   **1 April 1296**

Quitclaim by Alice formerly wife of Hugh de Tykyncote formerly burgess of Staunford in her widow right to Matilda de Len prioress of St Michael near Staunford and to the convent there and to all their successors of all her right and claim as widow's dower or in any other manner whatsover in an acre of arable land with appurtenances lying in the field of Staunford between the land of the aforesaid prioress and convent towards the east and the land of Richard de Hersaldoun towards the west; the acre abuts on the land of Gilbert de Cesterton' towards the north. The aforesaid Hugh sold this acre of arable land to William Briselaunce.

Witnesses: William Puncyn, Henry Federman, Richard de Hersaldoun, Bernard Bonde, William the clerk and others.

Given at Staunford Saturday next after the Sunday on which is sung *Quasimodo geniti* [Low Sunday] A.D. 1296.

Seal missing: tag and strands of green thread.

Endorsed: (i) quiet' clamant' Alicie uxoris Hugonis de Tykencote (contemporary)
(ii) Stamford (not contemporary)

552. E326/4797   **22 March 1315**

Quitclaim by Hugh son of Roger de Birton' in Stanford' to the prioress of the house of St Michael outside Stanford' and the convent there for a certain sum of money of all his right and claim etc in a tenement which is situated on the fee of the lord abbot of

Peterborough in the parish of St Martin Stanford, namely between the tenement of the said lord abbot towards the south and the tenement of Roger de Makisseie towards the north; it abuts on the King's highway towards the east.

Witnesses: William Puncyn then bailiff (*tunc ballivo*), William Wyther, Bernard Bond, Henry Fadirman, Thomas Fadirman, Henry de Rippes and others.

Given at Stanford Vigil of Easter 8 Edward II

Seal: oval: 22 x 16; an animal crouching beneath a stylised tree; legend illegible; natural wax; tag

Endorsed: quieta clamacio de tenemento in parochia sancti Martini

553. E326/4798   **29 July 1324**

Grant with warranty by Robert Briselaunce of Staunford tailor to Geoffrey son of the late master Geoffrey de Makesey for a certain sum of money of a certain parcel of his curtilage in Staunford' in the parish of St Paul, which parcel lies 168 feet in length from his own tenement towards the north as far as the tenement of Eustace Malherbe towards the south and 15 feet in breadth between the tenement of the aforesaid Geoffrey towards the west and the tenement formerly of William Ithoun towards the east. To hold the aforesaid parcel of the curtilage aforesaid to the aforesaid Geoffrey and his heirs or assignees of the capital lord of that fee for the services owed and accustomed, well, peacefully and by inheritance in perpetuity.

Witnesses: Eustace Malherbe, William de Apethorp', Roger Scaveler', Hugh de Thurleby, Walter de Hauboys, William Joseph clerk and others.

Given at Staunford Sunday after St James the Apostle 18 Edward II

Seal: round; 18; clasped hands; legend mostly wanting; red wax; tag; imperfect

554.1 E326/4799   **21 January 1325**

Indenture witnessing an agreement that whereas recently Geoffrey son of the late master Geoffrey de Makeseye by a certain indenture made between himself and Walter de Skilington' of Staunford leased for a term of twenty years not yet past his one messuage with its appurtenances in Staunford situated in the parish of St Paul together with a certain parcel of his curtilage annexed to the same messuage on the east side, granting by the same deed to the same Walter licence to pull down all the buildings of the same messuage with the walls of the house, the enclosing walls, the gates, doors and windows etc and to make his profit: and also the same Geoffrey by a certain deed made at a later date remitted in fee and quitclaimed the aforesaid premises to the aforesaid Walter and his heirs; the aforesaid Walter or his heirs at the end of the aforesaid twenty years will surrender to the aforesaid Geoffrey or his heirs the abovesaid messuage with the aforesaid parcel of the curtilage and with a house built in the same messuage near the king's highway according to the tenor of the aforesaid lease, whereupon the said

Geoffrey or his heirs will acquit the aforesaid Walter and his heirs of the pulling down of the said messuage etc. And if at the end of the aforesaid twenty years either party contravenes this agreement, the offending party will pay to the other £10 of silver etc.

Witnesses: Eustace Malherbe, William de Apethorp', Roger Scaveler', Hugh de Thurleby, Henry de Tiddeswell', William Joseph and others.

Given at Staunford Monday after St Fabian and St Sebastian 18 Edward II

Seal round; 16; three flowers in a pot; legend illegible; red wax; tag; imperfect
[see 554.2; printed in T Madox Formulare Anglicanum *pp 138-9]*

554.2. E326/4800   20 August 1324

<u>Lease</u> with warranty for twenty years by Geoffrey son of the late master Geoffrey de Makeseye to Walter de Skilington' of Staunford of his messuage with all its appurtenances which is situated in Staunford in the parish of St Paul between the tenement of Robert Briselaunce on the east side and the tenement pertaining to the rectory of the church of St Mary of Bynewerk' on the west side, together with that parcel of a curtilage on the east side of the aforesaid messuage which Geoffrey recently acquired in fee from the aforesaid Robert Briselaunce. Thus that the aforesaid Walter, his heirs and assignees will hold the aforesaid messuage etc from Michaelmas next etc freely etc. Annual rent of 5s of silver payable quarterly. Furthermore, the aforesaid Geoffrey gave licence to the aforesaid Walter to pull down all houses then built in the said messuage and remove all timber, slate and stones of the walls of the said messuage with the gates, doors and windows and with all the iron found in the same messuage and thence to make his profit whensoever he wished. For which timber, slate, stones, gates, doors, windows and iron and the other buildings aforesaid, the aforesaid Walter within the first year of the aforesaid term will construct and build anew at his own expense a certain house within the aforesaid messuage, 16 feet in breadth from the west end of the same (*a capite occidentali eiusdem*) up to the east end (*usque ad caput orientale*) near the king's highway. And at the end of the aforesaid term Walter and his heirs will surrender to Geoffrey and his heirs the aforesaid newly constructed house and the enclosing walls around the said messuage.

Witnesses: Eustace Malerbe, William de Apethorp', Roger Scaveler', Hugh de Thurleby, Walter de Haubovs, William Joseph clerk and others.

Given at Stanford Sunday after the Assumption of St Mary 18 Edward II.

Seal: oval; 21 x 17.5; within a cusped and traceried circle, above two clasped hands two busts (one of a man and one of a woman) facing each other with a flower between them, all within a roundel of fine arabesque; no legend; red wax; tag.

555. E326/4801   29 September 1326

<u>Lease</u> with warranty for eighty years by Richard son and heir of Richard de Baldeswell' of Staunford to the prioress of St Michael outside Staunford and the convent there of his

messuage with its appurtenances which is situated in the parish of St Mary of Bynewerk' between the tenement which was of the aforesaid Richard de Baldeswell his late father on the north and the tenement of Henry son of Richard Denganye on the south, which messuage with appurtenances is held in chief of the aforesaid prioress and convent by the annual rent of 2s. To hold the aforesaid messuage with appurtenances to the aforesaid prioress and convent and their successors from Michaelmas 20 Edward II etc freely etc. Richard acknowledges that the prioress and convent have paid him for the farm of the aforesaid messuage for the whole term aforesaid.

Witnesses: William de Apethorp', Roger Scaveler', Hugh de Thurleby, Walter de Apethorp', William Beaufiz burgesses of Stamford, William Joseph of the same clerk and others.

Given at Staunford Michaelmas in the year abovesaid

Seal: round; c18; flower; legend illegible; red wax; tag; defaced, imperfect

556. E326/4804

Sale with warranty by William le Paumer burgess of Stanford' to Gilbert de Kirkebi roofer (*copertori*) for 26s of silver of that house with appurtenances which is situated in the parish of St Martin beyond the bridge of Stanford' between the house of William Faderman towards the east and the road which goes towards the nuns of St Michael outside Stanford' towards the west. To hold the said house with appurtenances to the said Gilbert and his heirs or assignees freely etc and by inheritance. Annual rent to the lord of the fee of 1d at Michaelmas for all services, customs, exactions and all other secular demands pertaining to anyone.

Witnesses: William Faderman, Richard son of Richard, William le Normaund, Norman de Grecton', Roger Briselaunce, Philip Gaugy, William Reyner, John Russel, Thomas Savage, Henry Prat, Robert the tailor, William Briselaunce, Hugh the smith (*fabro*), William his brother, William Leggepeny and others.

Seal: oval; 27 **x** 17; to the left a hand clasping a palm branch and to the right an estoile above a crescent moon; C * S' WIL'L'I LE PAUMER ; green wax; tag

Not dated ? early 14th century

557. E326/4862

Sale with warranty by Damisona formerly wife of Roger Boni of Stanford' in her widow right to Hugh the mercer (*mercero*) of Stanford for 12s of silver of a rood of arable land in the field of Sundersokne lying between the land of the aforesaid Hugh towards the north and the land of the rector of the church of St Peter of Stanford' towards the south: the rood abuts on the land of the castle of Stanford towards the west. To hold to the said Hugh and his heirs or assignees freely etc and by inheritance. Annual rent of ¼d at Easter for all service and secular exaction pertaining to the said land.

Witnesses: Simon Ballard, Hugh Chyld, Robert Brond', Richard de Biterhingge, William the mercer, William Pert of Bradecroft, Nicholas his son, Richard Throu and others.

Seal: oval; c35 x 19; fleur de lys; [S'] DAMISOV[N FIL'E A]LEXSAND[RI]; green wax; tag

Not dated mid/late 13th century
[See 558, 560]

558. E326/4867

Sale with warranty by Damisunna formerly wife of Roger Boni of Stanford in her widow right to Hugh de Cisterna mercer and Agnes his wife and to their heirs or assignees for 16s of silver of a rood of arable land with appurtenances in Sundersokene lying between the dower land of lady Cecily formerly the wife of Henry son of Alexander towards the south and the headlands (*forere*) of Walter Ketell', William Pert of Bradecroft and lady Emma Atwater (*ad aquam*) which all abut on the aforesaid rood towards the north. To hold to the said Hugh and Agnes and to their heirs or assignees freely etc. and by inheritance. Annual rent of ¼d at Easter without any secular service, exaction and demand pertaining to the said land.

Witnesses: Walter Ketell', Robert son of Isaac, Hugh son of Henry de Tikencot, William de Rippes, Hugh Bunting, Simon Ballard, William Pert of Bradecrof', William le Mercer, Peter son of Richard Stanford' and others.-

Seal as in 557

Not dated mid/late 13th century

559. E326/4871

Grant in free alms with warranty by master Alexander son of Richard son of Selef de Stanford' to the church of St Mary de castro ymelis?' and the canons there of his whole croft below Smethhil (*de sub_Smethhil*) which he bought from Richard Peck' with the appurtenances belonging to the same croft as it extends in length and breadth just as the charter which Alexander had of the aforesaid Richard attests. Similarly, grant of a certain house with appurtenances in Cornestal which is situated between the house of John Walentru towards the east and Alexander's house towards the west. Paying annually a pair of gloves at Easter to Richard Peck' and his heirs for the aforesaid croft and doing service for the aforesaid house with appurtenances to the lord of the fee as much as pertains to the tenement.

Witnesses: Tericus de Colonia, Hugh son of Reiner, Alexander his brother, Henry son of Alexander, Nicholas his brother, William the Little (*parvo*), Alexander the serjeant (*serviente*), Henry Sibeci, Richard de Weston', William son of David, David the clerk and others.

Seal: missing: slits for tag

Endorsed: (i) Carta Magistri Alexandri filii Ricardi filii Seled de quodam crofto extra Stanford et de uno mesuagio in Cornestal (? contemporary)
(ii) de crofto sub smethil et de domo in Cornstal (not contemporary)
(iii) prima carta de domo in Cornestal et ulteria et de crofto extra portam (not contemporary)

Not dated ? early/mid 13th century
* *the church of St Mary, Castle Ymel, i.e. Fineshade priory, Northamptonshire*

560. E326/4882

Sale with warranty by Damisona formerly wife of Roger Boni son of Alexander son of David de Stanford' in her widow right to Hugh de Cisterna mercer and Agnes his wife for three marks of silver of the moiety of two and a half acres of arable land in the field of Sundersokene of which one acre and one rood lie near the land of the rector of the church of St Peter of Stanford' towards the north and the land of the said Damisona towards the south and abut on the land of William Pert of Bradecroft' towards the west and on the land of Peter de Castertona and on the great green ditch which leads towards Great Casterton (*et super magnam viridam fossam que viam ducit versus magnam castertonam*) towards the east. To hold to the said Hugh and Agnes and to their heirs or assignees freely etc and by inheritance. Annual rent of ½d at Easter for all secular service, exaction and demand pertaining to the said land.

Witnesses: Richard Peck', Andrew Arket', Robert son of Isaac, William de Francton', Hugh de Welledon', Walter Ketell', Hugh de Tikencot, Simon Ballard, Hugh Bunting, William Pert of Bradecroft, Richard the smith (*fabro*), William le Mercer, Hugh Fustedam, Alexander son of Osbert de Brunna, Peter son of Richard son of Selive de Stanford' and others.

Seal: as in 557 etc.; natural wax

Not dated ? mid 13th century

561. E326/5438   29 September 1388

Lease indented for lives in survivorship with warranty by Alice Coupeldyk' prioress of the house of St Michael near Staunford and the convent there to John Spalding' of Wirthorp' taillour, Asselina his wife and Robert their son of a messuage with a garden adjacent and with its appurtenances situated in the vill of Wirthorp' between the tenement which Emma de Wirthorp' recently held on the east and the common croft (*croftum commune*) of the vill of Wirthorp' on the west and it abuts on the king's highway opposite the cross (*contra crucem*) towards the south and on the field of Wirthorp' towards the north. Annual rent of 12d of silver at two terms, namely Easter and Michaelmas by equal portions. And if the said annual rent is in arrears at any feast aforesaid by fifteen days, the aforesaid prioress and convent or their successors may levy a distress in the aforesaid messuage with its appurtenances etc. And the aforesaid John, Asselyna and Robert during the term of their lives will repair and maintain the said messuage by their own expenses.

Witnesses: John Weldon', John Hawe, William Sybeston' of Staunford, Robert Smith, John Bury, Simon Heyward' of Wirthorp' and others.

Given in the house of St Michael aforesaid Tuesday on the feast of Michaelmas 12 Richard II

Seals: (i) round; c17; device defaced; legend illegible; red wax; tag; defaced
(ii) round; c17; no legend; red wax; tag
(iii) missing: traces of red wax; tag

Endorsed: Johannes Spaldyng de Wyrthorp (? not contemporary)

562. E326/5440   3 February 1438

Grant with warranty by William Morwod' of Staunford to William Fletcher of Wyrthorp' and Joan his wife of four and a half acres of arable land lying separately in the field of Wyrthorp' which four and a half acres with their appurtenances Morwod' had recently by grant and feoffment of John Depyng of Staunford 'schomaker'. To hold the aforesaid four and a half acres with their appurtenances to the aforesaid William Fletcher and to Joan and to their heirs or assignees in perpetuity of the capital lord of that fee for the services owed and accustomed by right.

Witnesses: John Bushy, Robert Belesby, Robert Schepey, John Loghthorp', Robert Hill and others.

Given at Wyrthorp' 3 February 16 Henry VI

Seal: as in 540 etc; fragment

563. E326/5552

Grant in free alms with warranty by Roger son of Elis de Helpistun to the church of St Michael the Archangel of Stanford' and the nuns there of five roods of meadow in the meadow which is called 'Mikil medue' which lie between the meadow of sir Roger de Torpel and the meadow of Simon le Hengleis and abut on the field of Stoue towards the south and on the field of Ioholm (?Lo[l]holm) to the north. The nuns to hold freely etc and quit of all earthly service and secular exaction etc. And if Roger and his heirs are unable to give warranty, they will give to the nuns in exchange to the value of the aforesaid meadow.

Witnesses: Pain de Helpistun, Ralph de Mortemer, Geoffrey son of John, Pain Laceleve, John de Bernake, Gilbert son of Ralph, William Clerk of Pappelea and many others.

Seal: pointed oval; 44 x 28; fleur de lys; + SIGILL' ... FIL' . ELISIDI ; natural wax; tag; imperfect

<u>*Endorsed*</u>: Carta Rogeri filii Elye de [Helpist]un de v rodis ... Mikilmedue (? contemporary)

<u>*Not dated*</u> ? early 13th century
Note: it is not clear this is Stamford although there was a Mikilmeadow in Stamford

564. E326/5553   29 September 1448

<u>*Lease*</u> by William Aldwyncle armiger, William Browne of Staunford merchant and John Browne of Staunford merchant, Thomas Catarall clerk, Geoffrey Jerman clerk, John Kirkeby and William Clidlowe to Robert Browe armiger of all manors, lands, tenements, woods, meadows, pastures, rents, goods and chattels etc and advowsons of churches and free chapels and goods and chattels mobile and immobile which they had by feoffment of Roger Munke clerk in Rutland, Lincolnshire, Cheshire, Herefordshire, Shropshire and Warwickshire in England and Wales from Michaelmas 27 Henry VI for ten years at a rent of £200 p.a.

Dated the feast and year abovesaid.

Seals: five seals
(i) the Browne merchant mark very clear 7/8" round red wax; approx 8 mm deep
(ii) large W surmounted by ?crown?; 7/8" red wax round
(iii) merchants'mark 8-sided red wax c7/8"
(iv) red wax fragments
(v) red wax 5/8" 8-sided merchants' mark

None of the other seals is more than 3 mm deep.

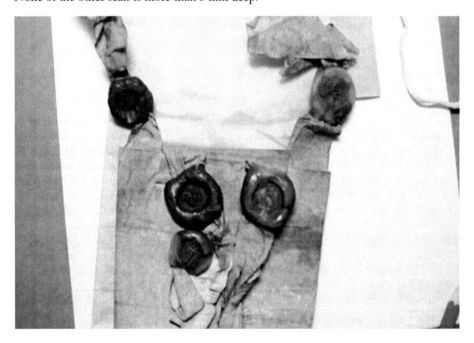

565. E326/5555   **25 July 1296**

Quitclaim by Beatrice who was the wife of William Burneld of Staunford in her widow right to Matilda de Len prioress of St Michael and the convent there of all her right and claim as widow's dower or in any other manner whatsoever in a plot of a courtyard (*in una placea curie*) 20 feet in length and 16 feet in breadth which lies in the parish of All Saints beyond the bridge of Staunford between the courtyard of Walter de Wymundham towards the west and the courtyard of Peter de Norf' towards the west [*sic*]*.

Witnesses: William Puncyn then bailiff (*ballivo*), William Burnel, Henry Faderman, Bernard Bonde, Reginald Norman, Thomas Faderman, Walter de Wyteryng, John de Wakerle, Peter de Norf' and others.

Given at Staunford Wednesday before St Peter in Chains 24 Edward I

Seal: oval; stylised flower; ATRI; natural wax; tag; fragment.

Endorsed: Stamford (not contemporary)
* *scribal error for 'east'*

566. E326/5673   **16 June 1497**

Lease indented for thirty one years with warranty by Margaret prioress of the house of St Michael near Staunford and the convent there to Thomas Depying of Eston' near Staunford of a watermill with its appurtenances situated at Worthorpp' near Staunford. To hold the aforesaid mill with its appurtenances to the aforesaid Thomas and his assignees from the feast of the Nativity of St John the Baptist [24 June] next etc. Annual rent of 6s 8d at two terms, namely at Christmas and at the feast of the Nativity of St John the Baptist by equal portions. And the aforesaid Thomas and his assignees will repair and maintain the said mill with its appurtenances at their own expense during the whole term aforesaid and thus kept in good repair, they will surrender the mill at the end of the said term of thirty one years. And during the whole term aforesaid, neither the aforesaid Thomas nor his assignees will alienate or lease the said watermill without the licence and wish of the aforesaid prioress and convent. And if the aforesaid rent is in arrears at any term by fifteen days the aforesaid prioress and convent and their successors may re-enter the said watermill with all its appurtenances and hold it again in its former state and expel the said Thomas and his assignees etc.

Given at Staunford 16 June 12 Henry VII A.D. 1497

Seal: ? oval; 11 x 7; divided in two parts, in the upper part a crown and in the lower part an unidentified device; no legend; red wax; tag

Endorsed: Tomas Depyng' (not contemporary)

567. E326/6024   **28 June 1385**

Lease indented for lives in survivorship with warranty by Alice Coupeldyk' prioress of the house of St Michael near Staunford and the convent there to Walter Cay of Eston' wright and Avice his wife of a messuage with its appurtenances situated in the vill of Wirthorp' between the tenement of the chapel of St Thomas the martyr Staunford on the north and the tenement formerly of Andrew Vyne on the south and abutting on the king's highway towards the east and on le West croft towards the west. Annual rent of 12d at Easter and Michaelmas by equal portions. And if the said annual rent is in arrears at any feast aforesaid by fifteen days, the aforesaid prioress and convent and their successors may levy a distress in the messuage aforesaid etc. And the aforesaid Walter and Avice for the whole term of their life will repair and maintain the said messuage by their own expenses and at the end of the life of the same they will surrender the aforesaid messuage in a fit state.

Given in the chapter house of St Michael Wednesday after the Nativity of St John the Baptist 9 Richard II

Seals: two of identical design etc.; round; c18; monogram or merchant's mark, crowned; red wax; tag; both damaged

568. E326/6136   **24 April 1363**

Grant with warranty by William de Peykirke junior of Staunford to William Bustard' vicar of the church of St Martin Staunford of a rood of arable land with its appurtenances lying in the field of Wyrthorp', namely in le Middelfeld' near the land formerly of John Rowe on the north and abutting on the headland (_foreram_) of Alan Aylcy on the west. To hold the aforesaid rood of arable land with its appurtenances to the aforesaid William Bustard' and his heirs and assignees freely etc in fee and in perpetuity of the capital lords of that fee for the services owed and accustomed by right.

Witnesses: William Gentil of Saunford' [_sic_], John Wortyng' of the same, Henry Wade of the same, William Hayward of Wyrthorp' and William de Weng' and others.

Given at Staunford Monday after St George the martyr 37 Edward III

Seal: round; 17.5; within a cusped and traceried circle, a quatrefoil; legend illegible; natural wax; tag

Endorsed: Carta Willelmi Peykyrke junior Willelmo Bustard una roda in campo de Wyrthorpe (not contemporary)

569. E326/6281   **12 November 1357**

Quitclaim by Cecily who was the wife of William de Brunham of Staunford to Richard Taillour of Wyrthorp' of all her right and claim in a messuage and a rood and a half of arable land with appurtenances in Wyrthorp' which messuage is situated between the tenement of William Hayward on the north and the toft called le Gildhous on the south and abuts on the watercourse towards the east: and the aforesaid rood and a half of land lie together between the land formerly of Richard Freman on the north and the land formerly of Robert Brotherhous on the south and abut on le Spitelhevedland towards the east.

Witnesses: William Gentyl of Staunford, John Wortyng of the same, John le Younge of Eston', John de Belme of Wyrthorp', Alan Brotherhous of the same and others.

Given at Wyrthorp' Sunday after Martinmas (*festum Sancti Martini in iyme*) 31 Edward III

Seal: round; 19; natural wax; tag

570. E326/6374   25 November 1528

<u>*Lease*</u> indented for twenty one years by dame Margaret Staynbury prioress 'in ye monastory or nunry' of St Michael near Stamford and the convent there to Ralph Peyn recently the miller in Dodyngton and to Margaret his wife 'and to ye longer lyver of them' of a watermill in Worthorp with the house adjoining and a little parcel of ground adjoining the west side of the said mill. Annual rent of 9s sterling at two terms, namely at Michaelmas and at the Annunciation of Our Lady by equal portions. And the said Ralph Peyn will build, uphold and maintain the said mill at his own proper costs and charges etc and thus sufficiently repaired etc he or his deputies will surrender it at the end of the said term of twenty one years. Ralph may let the said mill to any other man for any part of the lease of the said twenty one years provided he has the counsel and consent of the said prioress and convent or their successors.

Given at the said priory 25 November 20 Henry VIII

Seal: round; 22.5; within a circle, a shield of arms namely a lion rampant; : S : SUBSIDV: ...; red wax; tag; imperfect
ENGLISH

571. E326/6861   4 September 1526

<u>*Agreement*</u> between Margaret Stourborn prioress and the convent of the nuns beside Stannford and John Tossewold and Alice his wife: all debts from the priory to John and Alice for money lent to Alice Andrew late prioress are remitted in exchange for a corrody. The prioress and convent also to have of the produce of John and Alice 3 cattle, half the wool, lambs and calves and all the milk except for that of one cow which they are to maintain, and they are to cultivate John and Alice's land and bear wood for them.

<u>*Dated*</u>:   4 September 1526

Seal: 2 tags
ENGLISH

572. E326/8078   **30 May 1329**

Lease for five years from John de Queurecheyo monk and Geoffrey Gervasii called English (*dictus Anglicus*), proctors of the prior and convent of St Fromund, diocese of Coutances, made in the presence and with the will and consent of brother Alexander prior of St Fromond, to sir William de Wygeton rector of Botelesford, diocese of Lincoln, of all lands, rents, churches, pensions and possessions which the priory has in England together with the right of presentation if a vacancy occurs during the lease to the churches of Saxeby, Grafton, St Peter, St John, St George, St Michael and St Paul, Stanford; and the vicarage of Bondeby together with the fruits of Bondeby (the vicar's portion excepted). For this lease Gilbert [*sic*] is to pay 105 marks sterling; lease to begin 6 May 1331.

Dated at Schirbourn in the presence of the prior (who affixed his seal)

Seal (i) ? three saints; legend illegible
(ii) red wax; the virgin and child; S[...] SERTIN[...]

Endorsed: Dimissio per Prioram sancti Fremundi de omnibus possessionibus in anglia pro xlii marcis
  xi.

573. E326/8127   **29 August 1374**

Lease indented for lives in survivorship with warranty by sir John de Empyngham fellow monk of the abbot of Pippwell', warden of the hospital of St Thomas the martyr on the bridge [of Stamford] to Adam Grethed of Worthorp' and to Margery his wife and to their two children of a messuage and two and a half acres and a rood of land with appurtenances as they lie in the vill and field of Worthorp'.
The messuage ... of the aforesaid vill, abutting on the king's highway which goes towards Eston and the tenement of the nuns on the south, And the aforesaid two acres ... and lie between the land formerly of Robert Brotherhous on each headland. And the aforesaid half acre lies on ... strete and abuts on the land formerly of William de Wenge on each headland (*ex utroque capite*). And one rood abuts on le Saltergate and lies between ... Dorlot on one side and the land of Robert Smyth of Worthorp on the other side. Annual rent of 2s 2d payable to sir John quarterly. Distraint and eviction clauses [the precise terms are wanting].

Witnesses: Robert de Belesby, Thomas Spalding, Thomas Wenge of Worthorp [? and others].

Given at Worthorp Decollation of St John the Baptist 48 Edward III

Seal: fragment; natural wax; tag
Note: left hand edge of the deed is missing

574. E326/8268   **26 July 1335**

Grant/undertaking by Simon Bolle of Stamford and Alice his wife to pay to the prior of
Fyneshevid a rent of 6s 8d per annum granted to them by Alexander de Quappelade and
receivable from houses in Estaunf[ord] in the parish of St Mary beyond the bridge, one
of which houses Gervase le Taillour and Aldus his wife.

Dated at Estannford

Seal: an ox; tag for another seal.

Endorsed: Carta [simonis] bolle ... [?de] ...
FRENCH

575. E326/8780   **1 July 1390**

Grant by Andrew prior of the priory of St Fromund, Coutance diocese, and the convent
of the same to John Luscote prior of the London Charterhouse, of the church of
Bondeby, Lincoln diocese, and the advowsons of the churches of SS Peter, Paul, John,
Michael, George and All Saints in Stanford, Saxeby, Grafton and Bondeby, together with
110s per annum rent from Stanford and the tithes of the castle and its property, and
generally all possessions of the priory in England. Rent to the priory of St Fromund of 3
marks per annum on the restoration of peace between England and France.

Dated at St Fromund 1 July 1390

Seals: (i) oval: the virgin and child between two angels (ii) oval, damaged, a standing figure

Endorsed: (i) Indentura quarta Prior et Conventus Sancti Fremundi dederunt Johanni
luscote Priori London et Conventui prioratum de Bondeby cum pertin' xxiiij.
(ii) Co. Lincoln No. 2 E 25 (modern hand)

Note: The St Fromund copy dated at London Charterhouse 15th July.

576. E326/8782   **14 September 1343**

Lease indented for five years from Michaelmas next made by Alexander prior of St
Fromund and the convent of the same to sir Roger de Clonne rector of the church of St
Peter Stanford, of the church of Bondeby diocese of Lincoln, together with all their
other possessions in England, and the advowsons of the churches of Grafton; SS Peter,
John, George, Michael and Paul, Stannford, and Saxeby church, and the vicarage of
Bondeby and all temporalities. Rent of 15 marks to be paid to the prior and one mark
paid to the convent per annum (except when the property is in the king's hands) to be
paid at Shirburn .Warranty and re-entry clauses.

Dated in chapter at St Fromund the feast of the Exaltation of the Holy Cross 1343.

Endorsed: Lease of church of Bondy Lincs No 4 E27 [not contemporary]

577. E326/8783

Grant by master William prior of St Fromund and the whole convent there by common counsel of their convent to the nuns of St Michael of Stanford of the church of All Saints in the Market of the same vill with all things appurtaining to it, paying to the prior and convent the ancient pension (*antiquam pensionem*) namely of two marks of silver each year. And the nuns shall pay 'episcopals' and recognise all 'ordinaries', saving their pension.

Witnesses: Alexander then dean, Reiner chaplain of St Andrew, Alexander Solfa and the whole chapter of Stanford, Roger de Torpel, Geoffrey de Leheum, Clement the vintner and many others.

Seal missing: tag

Endorsed: (i) Stanford. confirmacio Willelmi prioris sancti Fromundi et conventus eiusdem loci de ecclesie omnium sanctorum foro (? not contemporary)
(ii) Co. Lincoln E29 No. 6 (not contemporary; post medieval hand).
(iii) dd xvi (not contemporary)

Not dated early 13th century.

578. E326/8784

Copy of grant by the nuns of St Michael to the hospital of St Sepulchre founded by Brond and subject to them (from which the nuns were to receive one mark per annum only; the head of the hospital was to be chosen by mutual consent of the two houses) of the right to a burial ground.

Witnesses: Gerard priest, Reiner priest, Hilil priest, Geoffrey priest, Asard priest, Alexander, Geoffrey, Reiner, Wimund, Peter clerks, Hugh palmer, Henry, William Combe, William son of Dodi palmer, David his son, Simon of the bridge (*de ponte*), Geoffrey *rol* and many others, clerks and laymen.

No date: late fifteenth century copy of late twelfth century original.
Note: The hospital was founded in 1170

579.1 E326/8785(a)

Grant in free alms with warranty by Philip de Colevilla to the church of St Michael of Stanford' and the nuns there of an annual rent of 18s 8d which Thericus de Colonia burgess of Stanford and his heirs are held to render to Philip and his heirs or assignees from 20s, namely 10s which Alexander son of David de Stanford' and Alice his wife were accustomed to render to Philip on Palm Sunday for the tenement which they held of him and 10s which Herbert le Seriant of Stanford' was accustomed to render to the same Philip for the tenement which he held of him in Stanford at two terms, namely 5s at Easter and 5s at Michaelmas for the tenement which he held of him in Stanford'. And if

Philip and his heirs are unable to give warranty, they will give to the nuns a fair exchange to the value of the aforesaid rent from their other tenement.

Witnesses: Reiner dean of Stanford', master Pain rector of the church of St Clement, Hugh vicar of the church of St Martin, Stephen parson of the church of St Peter, Walter de Tikencot, Hugh son of Reiner, William de Sumercotes, John Bottay, Henry Gaugi, William de Pappele clerk, Geoffrey the clerk and others.

Seal: missing: tag

Endorsed: (i) xxvi Carta Philippi de Colevilla de redditu xviii solidorum et viii denariorum in Stanford' (? contemporary)
(ii) Hoc tenementum tenet Alexander le Taylur de Staunford (not contemporary)
(iii) Redditus decem et octo solidorum et octo denariorum Staunford (not contemporary)
(iv) Co. Lincoln No. 9 E32 (not contemporary)
(v) 285 (not contemporary)

Not dated: 13th century
Note: probably before November 1235 when a dispute between Alice prioress of St Michael of Stamford and Philip de Colevilla concerning the rent of 18s 8d was heard before the King's court at Writele [see indenture attached, 579.2].

579.2 E326/8785(b)   24 November 1235

Final concord in the king's court at Writele the quindene of St Martin in the twentieth year of king Henry son of king John between Alice prioress of St Michael of Stanford plaintiff and Philip de Colevill defendant concerning 18s 8d rent in Stanford; Philip acknowledges that the said rent is the right of the prioress and church as that which he gave the prioress from 20s, namely 10s per annum from Herbert le Seriant for a tenement which he held from Philip in Stanford and 10s from Nicholas son of Alexander for a tenement which he held from Philip in Stanford. Herbert and Nicholas were present and acknowledged the debt. Thericus de Stanford who used to receive the rent was present and quitclaimed the rent to the prioress.

Endorsed: cyrograph. In curia regis de redditu xx solidorum.

580. E326/8835   14 March 1543/4

Grant by Thomas Maners earl of Rotelond, lord of Hamelak Trusbur and of Belver to Henry Dygby Robert Trurton, Roger Forest and John Netlam gentlemen, of all manors, messuages etc in Braunston super le hyll (Northt), Ketton, Lyttell Casterton and Tolthorp (Rutland), Greyngham, Colsterworth and Stannford (Lincs), lately belonging to the late monastery of Newsted by Stannford. Also in Swynfen, Ratby and Groby (Leics) late of the late monastery of Garodon; lyttell Paunton (Lincs), Stapleford, Wymondham, Leicester, Humberston (Leics), lately of the late monastery of Broxton; Sellybrygg, Orliance or Scalton (Yorks) late of the late monastery of Ryvaulx; Elme, Elmyth, Upwell and Owtwell (Norf) late of the late monastery of Nuneyton; Kirby Woodhowse and

Notyngham (Notts) late of the late monastery of Garodon; Water Fulford and York (Yorks), to be held subject to the provisions of an indenture of 31 March 1543 [*see* 581].

Signed: Thomas Rutland

Seal: fragment: coronet, part of garter, helm, mantling

Endorsed with note of livery of seisin; also "nota pro alia seisura in Norf intrand' (this has been done)".

581. E326/8836   31 March 1543

Sale by Thomas Erle of Roteland lord of Hamelak Trusbur and of Belvoyer to Harry Digby, Robert Thurston, Roger Forest and John Netlam gentlemen for £1271 of all his manors, messuages etc. in Braunston on the hyll (Northt), Ketton, Lyttell Casterton and Tolthorp (Rutland), Greiyngham , Colsteworth and Stannford (Lincs) late of the late monastery of Newystede next unto Stannford; Sellybrygg, Orlyance or Scalton crofte (Yorks) late of the late monastery of Ryvaulx; Swynfen, Ratby, Growby' (Leics) late of the late monastery of Garodon; Lyttyll Paunton, Stapleford, Wymondham, Humberston, Leycester (Leics) late of the late monastery of Broxton; Elme, Elmyth, Upwell, Owtwell (Norf) late of the late monastery of Nuneyton; Kyrbyewodhouse (Notts) and Notyngham late of the late monastery of Garydon; Waterfulford (Yorks) and York. No more of the purchase price to be paid than can be raised by sales during the performance of the earl's will, and the money raised to be used for the performance of the will. The residue of the lands to revert to the earl's heirs.

Signed: Thomas Rutland

Seal: (signet) a peacock
ENGLISH

582. E326/9111   18 October 1442

Letters of confraternity from friar John prior of the Carmelite friars at Stannford to Robert Swatbon and Anne (?) his wife.

Dated at Stannford 18 October 1442

583. E326/9920

Sale by Richard Hallof of Stanford impelled by great poverty (*magna pauperitate preventus*) to Walkelin the butcher of Stanford' for eight marks of silver of all the land and plot as much in shops as in houses (*totam terram et placiam tam in sopis quam in domibus*) which he had between the house which was of Hugh Clevebert and the bakehouse (*domum furni*) which was of William son of Acard. To hold the land etc to the same Walkelin and his wife and to their heirs freely etc of Richard and his heirs in perpetuity. Annual rent to the lord of the fee of 5d on Palm Sunday. Richard and his heirs warrant the land aforesaid with the houses and shops situated in it.

Witnesses: Ralph son of Acard, Geoffrey son of Herlewin, Reiner Midedo and Andrew the palmer (*palmigero*) then reeves (*tunc prepositis*), Richard Pecke, William de venella, Andrew de Swafeld, William de Leircestr', Joscelin Franceis, Hugh de Tal[…]t, Gilbert son of William son of Godric, Heine the butcher, Richard de Blarew', Hugh the cook (*coco*), Roger the palmer, Peter son of Gervase, Alexander son of David, Thomas the clerk.

Seal: round; 40; in the form of a fleur de lys; ? tradesman's tools; + SIGILL' RICARDI HALFLOF; green wax; tag

Endorsed: Stanford (not contemporary)
Stamford P 19 (modern)

Not dated ? early 13th century

584. E326/10095

Quitclaim by Hugh de Tychemers by the assent and wish of Bricthva his wife and of his heirs made by him in the full court of Stanford after he had touched the holy gospels of all his right and claim in the houses in the vill of Stanford' which Robert de Tychemers his brother granted in free alms to the church of St Michael of Stanford' and the nuns there. For this his quitclaim the aforesaid nuns granted him 60s sterling in the presence of many worthy men. Sealing clause.

Witnesses: Reiner then dean of Stanford, William chaplain of the church of St Peter, Robert rector of the church of All Saints, John de Colemer' then seneschal of Stanford', Ralph son of Acard, Walter de Thikencot', Richard Pecke, Walter Flandr', Clement the vintner, Henry de Thikencot', Henry de Keten', Reiner son of Maysent, Richard son of Seleve, Henry son of Alexander, Henry son of David, Gilbert the Noble (*nobili*) and many others.

Seal: round; 38; fleur de lvs; + SIGILL' HUGONIS : DE : TIKEMERIS; green wax; tag

Endorsed: (i) ii Stanf' (? contemporary) -
(ii) Carta Hugonis de Tichemers de quieta clamacione de domibus que fuerunt Roberti de Tichemers fratris sui in Stanford' (? contemporary)
(iii) Stanford 284 (not contemporary)
(iv) £20 (*del*) (19 *ins*) (not contemporary)

Not dated

585. E326/10096   c1288

Lease indented for lives with warranty by the prior and convent of Fynnesheved to Robert de Ryhale and Cecily his wife of those houses which the prior and convent had by grant of Ralph the chamberlain (*camerarii*) in the parish of All Saints Stanford between the house which was of the parson of Pikwrthe on one side and the house of William son of Iolan (*Iolani*) on the other with all their appurtenances liberties and free customs within the aforesaid vill of Stamford. To hold of the aforesaid prior and convent to the aforesaid Robert and Cecily from the Nativity of St John the Baptist [24 June] in the year of grace 1288 and 16 Edward I etc. Following the death of the said Robert and Cecily, the aforesaid houses will revert to the said prior and convent. Annual rent of 20s of silver payable quarterly. And be it known that the said houses and all other buildings pertaining to them needed repair (*emendacione indiguerunt*). And Robert and Cecily will repair them at their own expense and maintain them in good condition for so long as they live. And the said prior and convent or their attornies may visit the said houses and buildings as often as they wish during the year. And if the buildings be in need of maintainance or any amendments, they should be repaired at once within fifteen days at Robert's and Cecily's expense, as it was said. And if the said houses fall into decay through the fault or negligence of the aforesaid Robert and Cecily or through any other misfortune or suffer damage in any other manner, at once the houses should be repaired by the aforesaid Robert and Cecily, lest on account of this any of the rent be withdrawn or retained etc. Also it was agreed that if Robert or Cecily cease in payment of the rent at any term by one month, the aforesaid prior and convent may reseize the aforesaid houses and all contents and hold them again free and quit etc. And the aforesaid Robert and Cecily may not alienate, pledge or let at farm the aforesaid houses without the consent and wish of the aforesaid prior and convent or their successors etc. And if the said prior and convent are impleaded by any of the heirs of Roger le Ferrur, formerly tenant, the said Robert and Cecily etc will keep them exempt (*conservabunt... indempnes*). And also they will preserve all liberties pertaining to the said houses against whomsoever, according to the tenor of the charter of sir William de Humeth made to William son of Wymund de Ketene. And to all this the said Robert and Cecily have bound themselves and all their goods etc thus that no executor of theirs shall have any administration of the said goods until full satisfaction has been made to the said prior and convent or their successors by the view of law-worthy men chosen by them.

Witnesses: Hugh Bunting, Godfrey de Reynham, Alfred the mercer (*Aluredo mercennario*), John de London', John de Casterton' clerk and others

Seal: missing: tag

<u>Endorsed</u>: (i) Henricus de Offingtone et Ysabella uxor eius heredes quondam Rogeri le Ferur et quondam tenentes dictorum domorum sunt adhuc in arreragiis pro dictis domibus in lx solidis argenti. Et solebant reddere pro dictis domibus per annum ii marcas. Si velint placitare solvant etc. (contemporary)

(ii) Convencio de Ryhale de domibus nostris in foro Stantford' (contemporary)

(iii) 279 (not contemporary)

(iv) 2 - 20 (not contemporary)

<u>Not dated</u> c1288

586. E326/10097

Grant (*dimisi et concessi et hac presente carta mea confirmavi*) with warranty by Hugh son of Reiner de Stanford' by the assent and wish of Juliana his wife and of his heirs and friends, to Warin Iver of Helmhom' and Emma his wife and to their heirs or assignees - men of religion excepted - of that house with appurtenances which he bought from Henry Gaugi in the parish of St Martin of Stanford', namely that house which is situated between the house of Bartholomew the clerk towards the south and the house of Walter de Torp towards the north. To hold to the aforesaid Warin and Emma and their heirs or assignees etc. in fee-farm (*in feodofirmo*) of Hugh and his heirs or assignees freely etc and by inheritance. Annual rent of 4s of silver payable quarterly for all service and secular exaction. For this grant (*dimissione et concessione*) Warin gave Hugh two marks of silver. Warranty.

Witnesses: William son of David, John Bottay, William de Sumercotes, Alan de Ufford', Henry Gaugi, William de Pappele, Adam son of Achard, William the clerk, Gilbert Sotico and others

Seal: missing: slit for tag

Endorsed: (i) Stanford St Martin (not contemporary); (ii) 182 (not contemporary) 2 – 22 (*del*) (*ins* 21) (not contemporary)

Not dated

587. E326/10098

(a) *Confirmation* by Thomas son of Hugh de Berth to the church of St Michael and the nuns there of all lands etc which his father gave or sold to the monastery.

Witnesses: Mathew, Hugh, Robert and Alexander priests, master Samson, Richard, Roger son of Lize (?)

Seal: oval, a bird (? eagle)

Not dated ? twelfth century

(b) *Protection* for the nuns of St Michael from William de Humet constable for lands granted by him, his wife, ancestors or men.

Not dated ? twelfth century

588. E326/10378   **24 July 1256**

Indulgence from Henry bishop of Whithorn (*Candida Casa*) for those who contribute to the fabric of the church of the nuns of St Michael without Stanford.

Dated at York 24 July 1256

Seal: tag

589. E326/11216   1 April 1529

Lease indented for sixteen years by the prior of Newsted beside Staunford and the convent there to Robert Haver of Staunford of a close called northmylne hollme and a parcel of meadow called
ye Kychyn meydow on the west side of their house. Annual rent of 25s, namely 12s 6d at the feast of St Ambrose [4 April] and 12s 6d at the feast of St Denis [9 October]. If the said annual rent is in arrears at the abovenamed feasts or within fifteen days thereafter, then the said Robert or his executors will forfeit to the said prior or his successors 40s as a penalty. And neither Robert nor his executors shall break any parcel of ground nor shall they cut down any willows within the said northmylln holm or kychyn medow without licence asked and obtained of the said prior or his successors. And Robert promises that he shall not do damage with his cattle or horses to any parcel of ground belonging to the said prior and convent lying near to the said northmyln holme and if he does, he shall make amends under penalty of 20s sterling for each offence.

Dated 1 April 1529 and 19 Henry VIII

Seal: oval; c17 x 8; ? a capital I; no legend: red wax; tongue, tie

Endorsed: (i) Robert Haver' (? contemporary) (ii) Staunford (iii) The Will (not contemporary)
(iv) Newstead Priory near Stamford, Lincs 3 Deeds (*del*) L12-1 (not contemporary)
ENGLISH

590. E326/11853   17/22 August 1472

Citation from Richard Burton LL.Lic, president of Lincoln consistory court, addressed to the dean of Stamford to cite master Roger Bolton rector of St Peter's Stamford to answer for his non payment of £3 3s 4d per annum due to the nuns by composition for tithes from St Peter's according to the composition made between the priory and William Flete then rector of St Peter's together with injunction that Roger Bolton should not receive tithes in the fields of Stamford on the north side of the Weland.

Dated: at Uffyngton 17 August 1472

Seal: missing::tag

Endorsed: with note of the decree in favour of the priory 22 August 1472 in St Michael's parish church Staunford.

591. E326/12238

Grant in free alms by Alan de Lindon' to the church of St Michael of Stanford' and the nuns there of the whole tenement in the territory (*teritorio*) of Wirthorp which they have of the fee of Robert Goliardi with the services, rents, pastures, meadows and all other appurtenances pertaining to the same tenement saving the service of 'forinsec' of the lord king and an annual rent to Alan and his heirs of a mark of silver at two terms, namely half a mark at Easter and half a mark at Michaelmas for all services, demands and suits pertaining to him or his heirs.

Witnesses: Nicholas de Nevilla, Hugh parson of Bernak' then dean of Peterborough, William then chaplain of Weston', Simon then chaplain of Eston', Roger de Nevilla, Peter de Weston', Hugh de Bernak', William Sumercotes, William de Rihale, William de Pappele clerk and others.

Seal: round; c23; possibly equestrian; … ANI D…..ND… green wax; tag; imperfect

Endorsed: Wirthorp confirmatio Alani de Lindun' de tenemento de Writhorp' (? contemporary)

Not dated ? early 13th century

592. E326/12395   31 May 1519

Grant from Alice Andrew prioress of the nuns of St Michael beside Stanford to Thomas Wylliams of the parish of St Martin Stannford, Edward Sapcote, Richard Flower esquiers, John Thornef, John Hardegrave, Robert Walbyff, John Durante, William Wylliams gentlemen, Robert Person, Thomas
Vawsher, William Owen and Thomas Folkelyn freeholders and parishioners of the parish of St Martin of all their lands lying in Brakenell for their cowpasture yearly to be common for the prioress and the parishioners without any rent; and of 20s p.a.; also quitclaim of all right to one acre of land lying in the close of the gild of St Martin. This grant is in exchange for the parishioners' grant that the prioress and convent shall have three closes lately inclosed to their own use, whereof one lies near Holdhaw, one is called Longlandes, and the third lies before the gates of the priory.

Dated 31 May 1519

Seals: (i) a flower or leaf … PRAI (?) (ii) a fleur de lys (iii) a leaf (damaged) (iv) indecipherable (v) fragment (vi) fragment (vii and viii) traces only (ix and x) fragments (xi) traces only
ENGLISH

593. E326/12756   June 1338

Final concord in the king's court held at York between Robert de Rondes priest plaintiff and Simon de Wyrthorp and Alice his wife deforciants concerning an acre and a half in Staunford. Simon and Alice acknowledge that the land is Robert's. For this Robert gave 40s. Trinity term 12 Edward III

594. E326/12961

Grant by Robert de Stokes to the nuns of St Michael at Staunford of one messuage with appurtenances which Robert son of Geoffrey … Warranty clause.

Endorsed … de Stokes dedit …
Largely illegible

595. E326/12964

Grant in free alms by Oger son of Jordan to the church of St Michael by Stamford and the nuns there of four acres lying by the wall (_super murum_) in … in return for prayers for my soul and all my predecessors …. Sealing clause.

Witnesses: …Matthew, Geoffrey, Alexander chaplains, David son of … Symone de Ponte, Geoffrey Noel, Hugh de Pont', William …
Note: Largely illegible: no date can be seen; late 13th or early 14th century.

596. E326/13528   [1402-3]

Lease indented by Margaret Redyngges prioress to Richard … of six acres of land …

Dated in the chapter house of the nuns at Staunford … 4 Henry IV

Seal: tag only
Note: Largely illegible.

597. E327/43

Settlement of dispute concerning church of All Saints in the Market Stanford: grant of the church by the prior and convent of St Fromund to the nuns of St Michael of Stanford, the nuns to pay an annual pension of four marks to the priory of St Fromund, and to pay _episcopalia_ and bear all ordinary burdens.

Witnesses: William monk; Andrew monk; Geoffrey then dean; Halstan priest; Robert priest; Mathew priest; Alexander priest; Reiner deacon; master Samson; Geoffrey son of Reiner and others.

Seal: missing: tag for seal

Endorsed (i) Carta ecclesia omnium sanctorum in foro (early thirteenth century)
(ii) Carta prioris et conventus de Sancto fromundo de ecclesia omnium sanctorum in foro per compositionem amicabilem

Not dated ? early thirteenth century

598. E327/235   **20 August 1324**

Lease for twenty years by Geoffrey son of master Geoffrey de Makeseye to Walter de
Skilington of Stannford of a messuage in the parish of St Paul in Stannford between the
tenement of Robert Briselaunce on the west and the tenement of the rectory of St Mary
de Bynewerk on the east together with part of a curtilage on the east of the said
messuage which Geoffrey lately acquired from Robert Briselaunce at 5s rent p.a. Licence
to Walter to demolish the houses on the messuage and to appropriate the materials for
which he is to build a new house.

Witnesses: Eustace Malherbe, William de Apethorp, Roger Scauelere, Hugh de Thurleby,
Walter de Hauboys, William Joseph clerk, and others.

Dated at Stannford Monday after the Assumption 18 Edward II

Seal: portion of seal, red wax

Endorsed: 'Parochia sancti pauli' (later hand) and (C17) 'Dimissio'.

599. E327/251   **1527-8**

Demise by the nuns of St Michael by Stamford to Isaac Mychell of Blandford of the
profits of papal indulgences.

Dated 19 Henry VIII

600. E327/666

Release and quitclaim by Robert abbot of Peterborough at the instance of Amabilia
prioress of St Michael Stanford of an annual rent from 80 acres of land in the fields of
Stanford – i.e. 3s annuity which our bailiffs have paid to us in the name of landgavel
from the time of abbot Martin. Sealing clause.

Teste in the chapter house of Peterborough.

Seal: green wax; oval 4cms by 6 cms; central figure; SIGILL. ROBER …. SI. PETRI ;
damaged at base
one other tag

Endorsed: Carta de Relaxacione trium solidorum de langavell sci martin de Stanford
[contemporary]
ccxxiiij (deleted).

No date

E328/16/1: *A cartulary of Terricus of Cologne. Items are undated.*

601. E328/16/1/1

Sale by Ralph de Normanvile lord of Empyngham to Therricus de Colonia burgess of Stanford for 60 marks sterling of houses with appurtenances in the parish of St Peter in Stanford without reserve; namely, the houses which belonged to Robert de Tichemers and which Robert bought from Geoffrey son of Godhue and which Ralph holds of the nuns of St Michael of Stanford; situated between the houses which belonged to Robert Tinctor to the west and the houses which belonged to Richard Futsadame to the east; to hold to Terricus, his heirs and assigns rendering annually to the nuns 5s 2d sterling on the feast of St Michael (31d) and at Easter (31d) for all services, dues and customs, saving however service to the lord of the fee. Warranty. Sealing clause.

Witnesses: Peter son of Geoffrey, Hugh de Stiandeby, Richard Grave, Alexander then reeve of Stanford, Ralph son of Acard and many others.

602. E328/16/1/2

Sale by Ralph de Normanvile to Terricus de Colonia burgess of Stanford of houses with appurtenances situated in the parish of St Peter which Ralph bought from Richard Futsadame between the houses which belonged to Robert Tichemers to the west and the house of Matilda de Burgo to the east, for 100s sterling; Terricus made a grant of these houses to Leticia widow of Robert de Tichemers for her dower rights in the houses of Robert Tichemers which are situated between the houses which belonged to Robert the dyer and the aforesaid house which belonged to Richard Futsadame; to hold to Terricus and his heirs and assigns freely, saving the service of the lord of the fee. Warranty. Sealing clause.

Witnesses: Walter de Tikencot, Ralph son of Acard, Richard Pecce and many others.

603. E328/16/1/3

Sale by Henry de Tolthorp in order to acquit himself of debts to Jews to Terricus de Colonia burgess of Stanford for 8 marks of 5 acres of land in Casterton

604. E328/16/1/4

Sale by William de Chirchefeld to Terricus de Colonia for 10s of half an acre of arable land in Little Casterton

605. E328/16/1/5

Quitclaim by John son of Geoffrey Croweheved to Terricus de Collonia and his heirs or assigns of the house in St Peter's parish which Matilda daughter of Gamel de Burgo and Cecilia, John's mother, out of fear of poverty and to support themselves and John sold to Terricus, to hold to Terricus and his heirs and assigns. Sealing clause.

Witnesses: Hugh de Ryppele, Ralph son of Acard, Walter de Ticencote and many others.

606. E328/16/1/6

Grant by Robert de Standeford with the assent of his wife and his associates [*consiliis et assensu uxoris mee et amicorum meorum*] to Terricus de Colonia of one carucate of land in Wittering. [see 607, 625, 628].

607. E328/16/1/7

Grant by Ridell to Robert de Standeford of demesne land as in 606 above.

608. E328/16/1/8

Sale by Henry de Tolthorp son of Gilbert de Tolthorp for 4s of one rood of arable land in Little Casterton

609. E328/16/1/9

Sale by Roger son of Ulfric *ad fontem* [or *pontem*) to Matilda countess of Waranne and Terricus of Cologne [*Colonensis*] burgess of Stanford for 12½ marks of all that toft and appurtenances both within the wall of the town and without situated between the house which belonged to Sampson Stavelere and the house which belonged to Robert Rowland in the parish of St George, except for a little house [*parva casa*] which Roger retained to his own use sited beside [*juxta*] the road on the west, 19 feet wide and 17½ feet long, to hold to Matilda and Terricus or assigns, rendering 2d on Palm Sunday to Roger and his heirs for all services, dues and relief. Warranty. Sealing clause.

Witnesses: John de Bassingburne, Nicholas de Chenet, Richard de Maneriis and many others.

610. E328/16/1/10

Grant by Geoffrey son of Robert de Baston to Terricus of a meadow in Walceteholm to hold of Geoffrey son of Robert and his heirs rendering annually one half penny at Easter. Warranty. Terricus gave Geoffrey 2 marks for this grant.

Witnesses: Robert son of Geoffrey, John Sauvel, Richard Pecce and many others [see 22].

611. E328/16/1/11

Sale by Alice wife of Acard furrier (*pelliparius*) and Alice her daughter and Robert and Sampson sons of Henry Acard in their penury to Terricus de Colonia for 7s of their part of their court which pertains to their house in the parish of St Mary at the bridge to the end of the court as is shown by the wall there; to hold to Terricus, his heirs or assigns. Warranty. Sealing clause.

Witnesses: Walter de Tikencote, Henry de Tikencote, Richard Pek and many others [see 620].

612. E328/16/1/12

Sale by Robert son of Herewad of Stanford to Terricus de Colonia for 3 marks of one acre of arable land in the territory of Stanford lying between the half acre of land belonging to the church of All Saints in the Market and the land of Wido son of Wimund and heading onto the plot of land [*cultura*] which is called Kingespis. Warranty. Sealing clause.

Witnesses: Walter de Tikencote, Henry his brother, Ralph son of Acard and many others [see 630].

613. E328/16/1/13

Sale by Peter Tenche of Stanford to Robert Ruff and Beatrice his wife daughter of Peter's sister for ten marks towards Peter's journey to the Holy Land [*ad itinerem meum in terram Ierosolimitanam*] of his house in the town of Stanford in the parish of St Mary at the bridge, namely the one house [*sic*] situated between the house of Ralph son of Fulco to the west and the house of Alice wife of Acard to the east; to hold to them and the heirs of Beatrice's body saving the service of the lord of the fee. Warranty to Robert and Beatrice and the heirs of Beatrice. Sealing clause.

Witnesses: Walter de Tikencote, Ralph son of Acard, Richard Pek [see 624].

614. E328/16/1/14

Sale Geoffrey de Billesfeld son of Robert to Terricus de Colonia for 30s of his curtilage in the suburb outside the gate of Scotgate [*in quartera extra portam de Scotesgate*] abutting on Geoffrey's land there; rendering to Geoffrey and his heirs 1d at Michaelmas. Warranty. Sealing clause.

Witnesses: Walter de Tikencote, Peter son of Geoffrey, Richard Peke and many others.

615. E328/16/1/15

Grant by Henry son of Gilbert de Tolthorp to Terricus de Collonia of land in Casterton.

616. E328/16/1/16

Sale by Ralph son of Fulco de Stanford to free him from his debt to the Jews to Terricus de Colonia burgess of Stanford for 2½ marks of 5 acres of arable land in the territory of Stanford lying between the land which belonged to Sampson knight on both sides, and one headland to the south lies on the land of the said Sampson, in the headland to the north nine selions of the said five acres lie on the hundred acres of the castle: to hold to Terricus, his heirs or assigns, rendering annually to Ralph and his heirs one halfpenny, or one [half-penny] by Albaric glover [*cirothicarum*] at Easter; and the land shall be free of any relief of 1d. Warranty. Sealing clause.

Witnesses: Ralph son of Acard, Walter Tikencote, Henry his brother and others.

617. E328/16/1/17

Sale by Henry de Ketne to Terricus de Colonia for ten marks of two acres of land in the territory of Stanford which Henry bought from Jordan Dacus son of Oger Dacus, lying between the land of the monks of St Leonard and the land which belonged to Roger son of Margaret and butting on the town ditch (*fosse*) of Stanford. Warranty. Sealing clause.

Witnesses: William son of Odo, Robert son of Albinus, William de Seldingthorp.

618. E328/16/1/18

Sale by Reginald the bursar (*Bursarius*) of Stanford in his necessity to render his dues to his creditors and to facilitate his journey to Jerusalem, with the assent of Richard his son and Quinelda his wife, to Terricus de Colonia burgess of Stanford for 5 marks of his houses in the parish of All Saints in the Market situated between the house of Gerard clerk and the house which belonged to Roger Caretarius and Brihtine his wife. Warranty; sealing clause.

Witnesses: Peter son of Geoffrey, Hugh de Standeby, Richard Grave, Alexander then reeve and many others [see 631, 633].

619. E328/16/1/19

Sale by Adam Dyer son of Robert to Terricus de Colonia with the assent of Clement and Geoffrey, Adam's sons, to repay debts owed by Adam to the Jews, of a house with appurtenances which Adam bought from William Dyer, situated between the house which belongs to the church of St Peter and the house which belonged to Walter the priest (*sacerdos*) for 100s paid to Adam to settle his debts to the Jews (*ad solvenda debita que debui in judaismo*) to hold to Terricus, his heirs or assigns; and Adam and Isabella his wife and their heirs provide warranty; saving service to the lord of the fee. Sealing clause.

Witnesses: Hugh de Rippele then bailiff of Stanford, Ralph son of Acard.

620. E328/16/1/20

Quitclaim by Alice widow of Acard the skinner (*pelliparius*), Alice her daughter. and Robert and Simon sons of Alice to Terricus de Colonia, his heirs and assigns of an action and claim for damages against Terricus concerning the gable of their house in the parish of St Mary at the bridge and the wall against the curb (*versus curvam*). Terricus has half a mark for this release and quitclaim. Warranty; sealing clause.

Witnesses: Ralph son of Acard, Walter de Tikencote, Richard Pek.

621. E328/16/1122

Confirmation by Robert son of Geoffrey de Suthorp of the grant by Geoffrey son of Robert de Bastone to Terricus de Colonia, his heirs and assigns of meadow in Walkoteholm.

Witnesses: John Sauvel, Hugh de Bernak, Geoffrey de Bernak [see 610]

622. E328/16/1/23

Sale by Matilda daughter of Gamel de Burgo and Cecilia her daughter, moved by pressing poverty and with the assent of their heirs to Terricus de Colonia, his heirs and assigns, of their house with appurtenances in the parish of St Peter by the castle which they acquired from Richard Futsadame in exchange for their house in the parish of St John, situated beside the house which once belonged to Roger Dyer (*tinctor*), for 30s paid by Terricus to them for their great business (*grande negocium*). Warranty and sealing clause.

Witnesses: Hugh de Rippele, Ralph son of Acard, Walter de Tikencote.

623. E328/16/1/27

Sale by Geoffrey de Billesfeld son of Robert clerk, revoking certain lands which I have entered, to Gunilda widow of Ketel de Stanford for 5 marks which she has paid to me of 2 acres of arable land lying in the field of Stanford along a footpath (*inde pedale*) between the land formerly of Ketel and the land of Peter son of Geoffrey son of Herlewin, and half an acre on gallows hill (*super collem pendentem*) which stood on the land of Robert son of Albinus; to hold of me and my heirs by Gunilda or her assigns at an annual rent of 2d payable at Easter, free of other dues and 2d relief. Warranty. Sealing clause.

Witnesses: Walter de Tikincote, Ralph son of Acard, Richard Pek.

624. E328/16/1/28

Sale by Robert Ruffus merchant of Stanford to Terricus de Colonia for 9 marks and 8s 8d to acquit me of my debts to Jews of my house in the parish of St Mary at the bridge situated between the house of Ralph son of Fulco Poke and the house which I bought from Peter Tenche, free of all dues. Warranty; sealing clause.

Witnesses: Peter son of Geoffrey, Hugh de Stiandeby, Richard Grave, Alexander then reeve and many others [see 613]

625. E328/16/1/29

Sale by Geoffrey de Billesfeld to Terricus de Colonia for 2½ marks of one acre of arable land in the territory of Stanford lying on gallows hill (*per collem penedentem*) between the land of the heir of Ketle the woolmerchant (*lanarii*) and the land formerly of Nicholas de Luffeham, and abuts on the road leading to Little Casterton; at an annual rent of 1d payable at Easter. Warranty; sealing clause.

Witnesses: Walter de Tikencote, Ralph son of Acard, Richard Pec and others [see 614, 623]

626. E328/16/1/30

Sale by William de Burgle with the assent of his wife and of his heir to Terricus de Colonia for one mark of one acre of arable land in the field of Burgele between the land which Terricus bought from Evermere and the land of the monks of St Leonard. Warranty; sealing clause.

Witnesses: William de Richalde, Evermere.

627. E328/16/1/32

Sale by Thomas Palefrer and Christiana his wife daughter of Peter de Wakerley to Terricus de Colonia for 7 marks which he has handed to us in acquittance of debts to Jews, of an annual rent of 11s 6d in the parish of St John of Stanford which Peter Talmur owed to us for the house which belonged to Peter the knight (*Petri militis*) next to the house which belonged to Gilbert the knight on the east. Warranty, saving 6d which Terricus shall render annually to the abbot of Peterborough for that house. Sealing clause.

Witnesses: Ralph son of Acard, Walter de Tikencote, Richard Pek and others

628. E328/16/1/33

Sale by Walter son of Hugh Scute of Stanford with the assent of Idonea his wife to Terricus de Colonia for 9 marks of a house in Clerimunt situated between the grange of Peter son of Geoffrey son of Herlewin in the parish of St Michael and the house of Adam de Upford husband of Gunnore, which house Hugh Scute, Walter's father, once bought from Geoffrey son of Godhue of Westgate. Sealing clause.

Witnesses: Peter son of Geoffrey, Richard Grave, Alexander servant of Hugh de Stiandeby then reeve.

629. E328/16/1/35

Grant confirmation by William de Burgle to Terricus de Colonia burgess of Stanford and his heirs and assigns of 3 acres of arable land of his fee in the field of Burgele, which Evermer de Burgele sold to him, lying next to Salegate and abutting on the land of William son of Acel de Wautervile and on the land of Mabel de Walmuford. Sealing clause.

Witnesses: Walter de Tykencote, Walter le Fleming, Richard Peke and others [see 626]

630. E328/16/1/36

Sale by Wydo son of Wido de Stanford to Terricus de Colonia for 18s of half an acre of arable land in Stanford next to the acre which Terricus bought from Robert son of Hereward and on the other side next to the land of the nuns of St Michael, abutting on the ploughland of the castle called Kingesric. Warranty; sealing clause.

Witnesses: Ralph son of Acard, Walter de Tykencote, Richard Pek and others [see 612]

631. E328/16/1/38

Grant and confirmation by Roger son of Richard de Eston to Reginald Bursar of Stanford of one shop in the parish of All Saints in the Market Stanford which Reginald built at his own costs between the house of Roger Carter and the house of Gerard the clerk; Reginald to hold it of Roger in fee by hereditary right at an annual rent of 3s payable in equal instalments at Michaelmas and Easter. Warranty; sealing clause.

Witnesses: Richard de Lenford chaplain then steward of Stanford, William de Weston, Thomas de Tolthorpe and others [see 618, 633]

632. E328/16/1/39

Sale by Evermerus de Burgele with the assent of Walter his heir to Terricus de Colonia for 3 marks of 3 acres of arable land in the field of Burgele lying next to Salegate and butting on the land of William de Watervill son of Atel' on one side and on the land of Mabel de Willmeford on the other; rendering an annual rent of 1d at Easter for a light in the chapel of St Mary of Burgele. Warranty; sealing clause.

Witnesses: William de Burgele, Hugh vicar of St Martin's church, William de Watervill' son of Atel and others [see 626, 629]

633. E328/16/1/40

Confirmation by Richard son of Reginald Bursar of Stamford in his legitimate right (*in legitima potestate mea*) to Terricus de Colonia burgess of Stanford and heirs and assigns of houses in the parish of All Saints in the Market situated between the house of Gerard clerk and the house of Roger Carter and Brihtina, which house Reginald father of Richard sold in his necessity and to pay his debts to go on pilgrimage to the Holy Land of Jerusalem. Warranty, saving service to lord of fee; sealing clause.

Witnesses: Hugh de Styaneby, Peter son of Geoffrey, Richard Grave, Alexander then reeve, Walter de Tykencote and others [see 618]

634. E328/16/1/42

Confirmation of sale by Margaret daughter of Ada Carpenter of Stanford formerly wife of Nicholas de Luffenham with the assent of her heirs and kinsmen to Terricus de Colonia for 4 marks and 15s 4d paid to acquit her of Jewry of three acres of arable land in the field of Stanford, namely one acre lying between the land which belonged to Ketel and the land which Ketel's wife bought from Geoffrey de Billefield, abutting on the land of Peter son of Geoffrey; and an acre which lies between the land of the hospital of St Thomas of Stanford and the land of Walter Ketel, abutting on the land of Peter son of Geoffrey; half an acre lying between the land which belonged to Ketel and the land which Terricus bought from Geoffrey de Billefield; and half an acre which is called Gorebrod Halfaker which lies between Smehthil and the land which belonged to Geoffrey de Billefield; to hold at an annual rent of 11d, payable at Easter for all secular dues. Warranty; sealing clause.

Witnesses: Ralph son of Acard, Walter de Tykencote, Richard Pek and others

635. E328/16/1/43

Confirmation of sale by William Feraby(?) of Stanford to Terricus Tyeis burgess of Stanford for 13 marks paid for William's acquittance from Jewry in his great need, of his houses in the parish of St Peter of Stanford situated between the house of Henry Sybecy and the castle dyke; at an annual rent for the lord of the fee 19d at Easter and Michaelmas and to the fabric of the church of St Peter 12d payable at Christmas and Easter; and to Geoffrey Cothanke and his heirs or assigns 12d at Michaelmas and the Nativity of St John the Baptist; and to Dionisius and his heirs ½d. at Palm Sunday. Warranty; sealing clause.

Witnesses: Walter de Tykencote, Henry de Tykencote, Hugh de Rippele and others.

636. E328/16/1/44

Confirmation of sale by Philip de Colevill' son of Robert de Colevill' with the assent of his kinsmen and heirs to Tehodricus [*sic*] de Colonia burgess of Stanford and his heirs and assigns for 10 marks of half of three bovates of land in whole in the fields of Stanford which lie in Sundersokene and which belong to me by hereditary right, and at the same time half of that whole meadow in Bradecroft belonging to that land in Sundersokene in the parish of St Peter, which half Tedricus [*sic*] holds of me at farm; Tederricus and his heirs to hold this land of Philip and his heirs at an annual rent of one white falcon at Easter. Warranty; sealing clause.

Witnesses: Pagan rector of St Clement, master Henry of St John, Walter de Tykencote and others.

637. E328/16/1/48

Sale by Inga sister of Thomas son of Lewin of Stanford on account of her poverty to Terricus de Colonia for 17d of half an acre in the field of Stanford lying next to the land of Ralph son of [ms missing] and butting on Neumenitrone(?) on one side and on the land of Holy Trinity church on the other side. Warranty and sealing clause

Witnesses: Walter de Tykencote, Ralph son of Acard and others.

638. E328/16/1/49

Sale by Christiana daughter of Peter de Wilek in her widowhood to Terricus de Colonia for 7 marks paid to Christiana to free certain lands which were mortgaged to the Jews (*que obligate fuerunt in judaismo*) of an annual rent of 11s 6d in the parish of St John in the town of Stanford, which rent Peter the tallowman (*taliator*) rendered to Christiana for a house which he held at fee farm which once Peter knight held next to the house of Gilbert knight to the east; to hold free of all dues save 6d per annum due to the abbot of Peterborough from that house; quitclaim of all '*dominion*' which Christiana had or could have in that rent. Warranty by Christiana and Henry [*sic*]; sealing clause.

Witnesses: Ralph son of Acard, Richard Pek and others [see 627]

639. E328/16/1/50

Confirmation of sale by Walter son of William son of Martin de Bradecroft to Terricus de Colonia burgess of Stanford for 3½ marks of 3½ acres of meadow in Bradecroft Meadows lying in Broding between the meadow of Henry son of Alexander on the east and the meadow of William le Pert on the west and butting on the banks of the Welland to the north and the Castle meadow to the south; at an annual rent of 1d due at Easter. Warranty by Walter and his heirs; sealing clause.

Witnesses: Henry son of Alexander, William de Tykencote and others.

640. E328/16/1/51

Confirmation of grant by Philip de Coleville to Terricus de Colonia burgess of Stanford for 16 marks and two robes of 1½ bovates of land lying in Sundersokne next to the land which Terricus bought of Philip with its meadow and all other appurtenances; also annual rents of 23s arising from the town of Stanford: namely, a rent of 10s from a tenement which Alexander son of David sometime held as relief of 10s belonging to it; a rent of 10s which Herbert le Sergant of Stamford used to render to Philip for his toft in the parish of St Peter; and a rent of 3s from land which Henry de Tykencote held of Philip in the territory of Stanford; to hold of Philip rendering annually 20s at Palm Sunday (15s) and Michaelmas (5s). Warranty; sealing clause.

Witnesses: Ripemund de Lydle, Richard de Bernak and others.

641. E328/16/1/52

Confirmation of grant by Robert le Here to Terricus de Colonia burgess of Stanford for 20 marks and a premium of one robe to Robert and one robe to Alice Robert's wife and one robe to Ralph, Robert's son, of all his land and houses in the parish of St Peter the Little (*in parochia Sancti Petri Parva*) which Robert had by grant of king John; also the house once called "the King's free cellar" (*liberum celarium domini Regis*) and all rights Robert had in the timber and stones belonging to the lands of the hospice and also in the length and breadth of the hospice itself and in the lands which belonged to the capital messuage; to hold of Robert rendering annually to the king the customary service of one gilded galley (*unam galeam deauratam*) and to Robert and his heirs half a pound of cinnamon or 1d at the octave of Easter. Warranty.

Witnesses: Andrew Bukerel then mayor of London, Ralph Esey, John Normann and others

642. E328/16/1/53

Confirmation of sale by Walter son of William son of Martin de Bradecroft for 3 marks to Terricus de Colonia burgess of Stanford of one acre of meadow in Broding lying between the meadow of William le Pert on the west and the meadow of Walter on the east and butting on the banks of the Weland north and the Castle meadow south; Terrichus [*sic*] and heirs to hold it of Walter by rent of 1d at Easter. Warranty; sealing clause.

Witnesses: William de Tikencote, Henry Sybely and others [see 639]

643. E328/16/1/55

Confirmation of grant by Reginald de Broc to Terricus de Colonia burgess of Stanford for 20s of all Reginald's rent and all appurtenances belonging to it which William de Coventre once held of William son of William de Berc in the parish of All Saints in the Market of Stanford; to hold of Reginald. Warranty, sealing clause.

Witnesses: Richard de Casterton then constable of Stanford and others.

644. E328/16/1/56

Confirmation of sale by Richard de Callewithe to Terricus de Colonia burgess of Stanford for 3 marks of one acre of arable land in Stanford field on Sundersokene, of which a half acre lies between the land of the parish of the blessed Peter to the south and the land of Terricus to the north, and the other half lies between the land of Terricus on both sides and abuts on the land of Gilbert de Ingelthorp to the east, which acre Richard bought from Richard son of Henry. Warranty; sealing clause.

Witnesses: Henry son of Alexander.

645. E328/16//57

Confirmation of sale by Robert son of William son of Yoselin de Stanford with the assent of Matilda Robert's wife, his heirs and kinsmen to Terricus de Colonia Tetonico burgess of Stanford of a house in the parish of All Saints in the Market situated between the house formerly of William Vife and the house formerly of Thurstan Leatherworker (*Alutarii*) for 17 marks and 3s to acquit me of debt and for a robe; to hold to Terricus his heirs and assigns (except religious), reserving 4d at Palm Sunday to the lord of the fee. Warranty to Terricus and his assigns (except any house of religion); sealing clause.

Witnesses: Ralph son of Acard, Walter de Tykencote and others.

646. E329/66   **20 March 1421/2**

Lease for forty years by Agnes Leek prioress of the house of St Michael by Staunford and the convent there to Andrew Draper of Staunford and Isabel his wife of a shop with a solar built above in the parish of St John in Staunford between the tenement of the gild of Corpus Christi on each side and abutting on the tenement of the said gild towards the east and on the king's highway towards the west. Annual rent to the prioress and convent and their successors of 3s 8d. Repairing clause. Further, after the aforesaid term of forty years, the aforesaid prioress and convent and their successors grant the aforesaid shop with solar to one of the sons of Andrew and Isabel for the term of his life, for the rent of 3s 8d as above mentioned.

Dated in the chapter house of the prioress and convent, 20 March 1421/2

Seals: (i) hexagonal; ⅝ x ½"; ? merchant's mark; no legend; red wax; tag.
(ii) oval; ¾ x ⅝"; ? St Margaret and the dragon; S MARGARETA DRAPROME? red wax; tag.

Endorsed: Indentura de Andr[...] Draper

647. E329/90

Grant in alms by Angelinus de Stanford' to the monastery of St Michael of Stanford and the nuns there of four acres of land, namely those which he bought from Geoffrey the cellarer (*Sellario*) which lie by the street near the stone which is commonly called Stumpedestan (*iuxta stratam prope lapidem vulgo vocatur Stumpedestan*). The service pertaining to the land is to be done to the abbot of Peterborough.

Witnesses: Reiner the dean, Gerard, Halstanus, Geoffrey priests, master Roger, master Robert, Geoffrey de Durea (?), Geoffrey Par[ent?], Roger, Geoffrey Fauer?, Reiner, Absalon, Robert.

Seal: round: 1⅜" : a beast's head: + SIGILLUM ANG...IN... : natural wax: tag

Endorsed: (i) Carta Angelin de quattuor acris terre iuxta Stumpedeston (?contemporary) (ii) de iiii acris iuxta Stumpedeston (contemporary)

Not dated ? late 12th century

648. E329/435   **15 April 1361**

Quitclaim: Agnes de Brakynberugh prioress of the nunnery of St Michael outside Staunford and the convent there send greetings to all Christ's faithful. There are two tenements in Staunford pertaining to the daily mass of Saint Mary celebrated in the church of All Saints in the Market Staunford which are totally in ruins and fallen down. The tenements are held in chief of the lord of the castle of Staunford, of which one lies in 'le Wolrowe' between the tenement of John Knyvet on the west and the priory's own tenement on the east, and the other lies on the corner by the lane which leads to the castle of Staunford opposite the tenement of the prior of Sempringham. The tenements are charged to the prioress and convent of a certain annual rent.

Quitclaim by Agnes de Brakynberugh prioress of the nuns of St Michael without Stanford and the convent there with the assent etc of sir William de Bryggesthorp then their warden and at the instance of William Steandeby then Alderman of Staunford, Nicholas Eston literate (*viri literati*), William de Apethorp, Richard Bardern, John de la Merch, Nicholas de Plumbton, Robert de Briggestok, Walter Chapman, Roger de Colton, Richard de Harstan, John Page taverner and Alan Cuppere parishioners of All Saints in the Market and proctors of the daily mass aforesaid, to the same proctors of all arrears from the said two ruinous tenements, also of all annual rent save 20d of silver. The prioress and convent undertake to rebuild the two tenements within two years and to maintain them. Provision for distraint for arrears.

The seals of the nuns and of the proctors are attached; and because these seals are not well known, the seal of the dean of Staunford is also attached.

Dated at Staunford 15 April 1361

Seals: 10 in all, black wax

(i) round; 13/16"; a shield of arms, chevron between three crosses formy; * S' IOHIS DE DENTONE ; natural wax; tag

(ii) as 537; natural wax

(iii) round; ¾" ; two figures (male and female) facing each other; legend imperfect; natural wax; tag

(iv) round; ¾"; shield of arms, chevron (rest defaced); legend illegible; natural wax; tag

(v) round; c¾"; includes a standing figure; legend imperfect; natural wax; tag; fragment

(vi) round; ½"; device and legend indecipherable; natural wax; tag

(vii) round; ⅞"; cross and letter E surmounting a W in a roundel with a diapered ground; * WILLELMUS DE STANDBI; natural wax; tag

(viii) oval; c1" x ⅞"; device and legend indecipherable; natural wax; tag; imperfect and defaced

(ix) round; 11/16"; ?container with three flowers?; legend illegible; natural wax; tag

(x) round; c¾" ; shield of arms, chevron (rest defaced); legend imperfect and illegible; natual wax; tag

(xi) round; ⅝"; device and legend indecipherable; natural wax; tag

(xii) round; ¾" ; legend illegible; natural wax; tag

PRO LR 14-15 LAND REVENUE ANCIENT DEEDS SERIES E

649. LR 14/212   **14 June 1515-16**

Grant Nicholas Byllybe of Stannford to Thomas Templer clerk of St Michael's nunnery by Stamford of two tenements in Wothorpe between the tenement of Thomas Maydnwell on the south side and the tenement of the nuns on the north side, one head abuts on the king's highway west and the other head on a tenement of the nuns on the east, with all appurtenances in the fields of Wirthorpe and Easton, Northants, formerly of the gift and feoffment of John Byllysbye of Stanford. I have attached my seal.

Witnesses: William Smyth of Worthorp, John Lambarde of the same, William Benson of the same and many others.

Dated: at Worthorpe 14 June 7 Henry VIII.

Seal: missing: one tag only

650. LR 14/215

Lease by indenture by Fineshade Priory to Alfred le Regrater of Stanford of a cellar in the parish of St Mary at the bridge, Stanford, Lincs next to (*juxta*) the house of Alfred on the east side at a rent of 5s p.a. payable at the four quarters. Repair clause. Warranty.

Witnesses: Hugh Bunting, Alfred le Mercer, John de Casterton, John de Tikincote, William de Scaccar', William de Lindon, Robert le Tanour and others.

Seal: seal on tag sewn into bag

Endorsed: Priory of Conishead (*del*) Fineshade [19th century]
Quarta de cela in parochi' be Maria [contemporary]

Not dated 13th century

... celariuxs parochia Ste Mari' [contemporary]

651. LR 14/892/5   30 September 1536

Lease by indenture: Robert abbot of Thorney and convent to Maurice Johnson of Staunfford dyar and Jane his wife of all messuages, tenements, shops, houses, buildings, gardens and yards in the parish of Allhallowes between the messuage of William Rankell on the west, the Flax Market on the east, the king's highway against All Hallowes Church against the north part, extending down to the Castell dyke against the south; with all appurtenances etc; from the feast of St Michael the archangel next for 99 years ; rent 13s 4d p.a. in equal portions at the feasts of the Annunciation and St Michael Archangel. Re-entry clause; seals have been attached.

No witnesses

Dated: 30 September 28 Henry VIII

Seals: two tags; fragments.

Endorsed Mauryce Johnson [contemporary, perhaps signature]
ENGLISH

652. LR 14/892/23   **8 February 1528**

Grant by Thomas Forster clerk to Henry Lacy and John Ley feoffees to the use of the abbots of Thorney of a garden in Cornstall Street in St George's parish Stamford, Lincs between the garden of the abbot of Thorney east and the garden of the queen west, abutting on the king's highway north; which garden I had by gift and feoffment of William Radclyffe gent, to the use of the abbot of Thorney and his successors. Warranty. Appointment of attorney to deliver seisin John Ward.

Dated: Staunford 8 February 19 HenryVIII

Seal: fragment red wax

Dorse:
Dom William Hygedon clericus
Dom William Lawson clericus
Dom Richard Hawe clericus
Dom Robert Berege clericus
were present at the sealing of this charter

Pertains to land in Stawmford

Dom Ralph Shepherd clericus
Robert Roose?
Alexander Taverner
Robert ...
John Hesward
were present at the delivery of seisin of the above written premises
[contemporary]

653. LR 14/917   **20 May 1482**

Lease indented by Isabel Savage prioress of St Michael's nunnery Stamford to William Morcote late of Peykirke for 10 years of all lands etc in the fields of Stanford, Worthorp, Eston, Colyweston, Burley and Badyngton (Bainton) and all tithes; also all manner of houses without the sisters' gate of the priory; and three closes, the Warden's Yard, the Close at Worthorp and the close beside the Spitell in Stanford; the house which Agnes Hode lives in, the litill granary, the litill stabell, half the .. dovshous, the house which the priory shepherd lately dwelled in, the brewing and bake house – except reserved to the nuns at such time as they shall occupy it for baking; except also tithes in Worthorp which the priest there is accustomed to receive for his salary. Lease to William and Alice his wife together with all goods and husbandry stuff as listed in an inventory attached to this lease [missing]; with pasturing for 12 kine and a bull in the fields of Wenton by Cottesmore yearly between the feast of SS Philip and James and Lammas; not to alienate it to others without the consent of the prioress and convent. The farmers shall deliver to the nuns each year 28 quarters and one bushel of wheat, 6 quarters of rye of good quality, 28 quarters of malt well made, 9 strykes, 6 quarters of barley from under the riddle, 4 cart loads of hay, 6 hogs between Martinmas and Christmas, one ewe worth 13s 4d, one boar worth 5s, one porker worth 20d, a fatte weder and at Michaelmas even a fatte weder, at Easter even a fatte lambe, at Whitsun even a fatte lamb, as much straw as is necessary for brewing and baking, 60 cart loads of wood from Clyve forest; they shall cart stone, mortar, and sand as necessary; they shall repair the priory and the three closes at their cost; also the cost of summering and wintering of 8 kine; 12 capons each year; the farmers shall have all draffe and dregges; the nuns are not to keep any sow or cattle during the period of the lease; the farmers must keep the arable in good tilth; in the last year they will supply 41 quarters of good barley seed to be sown by the farmers, and return the land in good condition; must keep all produce in the barns and not elsewhere; if any dispute, arbitrators are Robert Hans of Staunford and William Spenser of Staunford; right of re-entry. Pledges are William Morcote, Richard Morcote of Peterborough, Robert Toche? of Peterborough, William Hareby otherwise William Rannes of Glynton in £100. Sealing clause

Dated: in the chapter house on 20 May 22 Edward IV

Seal: one seal slit.
[*see* 360]

654. PRO SC11/426 SPECIAL COLLECTIONS: CARTULARY OF NUNNERY OF ST MICHAEL AND ST MARY, STAMFORD

The following list of deeds is undated; the cartulary is an early thirteenth century compilation, prior to 1238. The cartulary is divided into different locations - only the Stamford property is catalogued here. The numbering is as in the original. The nature of the grant is only given where the original indicates whether it is a grant, release, confirmation, or quitclaim.

654. CARTE DE STAMFORD

1. *Grant* by Robert de Tichemers to the nuns of one house (*domum*) with appurtenances situated between the house of Robert Tinturer and the house once of Walter the chaplain

2. *Quitclaim* by Hugh de Tichemers of the houses which belonged to Robert de Tichemers his brother in Stanford

3. Ralph de Normanville to the nuns of 5s rent from the house which was of Robert de Tichemers

4. Nicholas son of Alexander rent of 3s 6d from a house in Binnewerc

5. Peter the rector of the church of Pickworth of one house in the parish of All Saints in the Market

6. Mathew vicar of the parish church of St Martin of half a toft and the house with it, formerly belonging to Wnwine

7. Margaret formerly wife of Reiner son of Maisent of a rent of 4s in the market

8. Clement vinitor of the house which belonged to Geoffrey Gesling in the parish of St Martin and two shops in Butcher Street (*in vico carnificum*).

9. Richard Albi of a booth (*de botha*) in Butcher Street

10. Ralph son of Achard of a rent of 6½d from the house which John seeks and which John Crouheft held next to the house of Reginald Keling

11. Colice (*Colicie*) of a house next to the castle given to us

12. Mathew vicar of St Martin of a house in which William de Pappele lives

13. A certain house in Butcher Street which Felicia de Stokes bought and assigned to the pittancer, which house Alan de Len holds

14. Simon (*Sym*) son of Alexander of a rent of 5s drawn from the house situated between the house of John Cays and the house which was of William Beubraz

15. Ralph son of Achard of a rent of 2d from the house situated between the house of John Cassi and the house of William Beubraz

16. Matilda the wife of Alexander of Stanford of a rent of 5s from the house situated between the house of John Cas and the house of William Beubraz

17. Peter clerk the pupil of Reiner dean of Stamford and Robert son of Peter Tailor (*cissoris*) of a rent of 3s? from the houses which belonged to Colice beside the castle of Stamford

18. William son of Roger son of Harbin de Stanford of a house and toft which belonged to Levenod? in the parish of St Martin next to the house of John Bottay

19. Robert son of John Flanders (*flandrens'*) of 12d from 4 acres of land which Robert son of Albini held.

20. Henry de Stanford and Matilda his wife of a rent of 12d from a house in the parish of All Saints in the Market Stanford next to the house of Matilda Smalpoke

21. Peter parson of Pikeworde from the houses which belonged to Turgisi in the parish of All Saints in the Market Stanford

22. Odo of a house in the parish of All Saints in the Market Stanford

23. *Grant by indenture* by the Hospital of St Thomas the martyr at the bridge of Stanford to the nuns of an annual rent of one silver mark

655. LANDS

1. Ralph son of Achard of a rent of 2d for part of the tenter land (*cita tentoria*) next to the meadow of the Hospital of St Thomas

2.   John Bottay by grant and gift of himself and his predecessors

3.   John Bottay of a croft and arable land next to the croft of Hugh de Huffinton

4.   Angelina of 4 acres of land next to Stumpedeston

5.   Gilbert Parent of 2 acres of land at St Leonard's

6.   Richard Peck of 2 acres of land given to us

7.   Stanewi taillur by gift of one acre of land at Stumpedeston

8.   William son of Roger of half an acre at Laumanford

9.   Gilbert Parent of one acre of land under (*subtus*) the town next to the forge (*fabricas*)

10. Gilbert Parent of a toft which belonged to Angelina

11. Gilbert Parent of ten acres of land with meadow lying ...

12. Gilbert Parent of 2 acres at the Bulepit and at 'Schord'.

13. Gilbert Parent of 2 acres of land in Chinemeresenge

14. Wimund son of Turstan of four acres of land

15. Andrew son of Stanewi of one and a half acres

16. Confirmation by Henry son of Roger of a grant of three roods of land next to the croft of Leuine which Geoffrey his brother gave to us

17. Robert de Sperveton of all the lands which belonged to the said Lewin.

18. Ralph son of Geoffrey de Pilesyate of half an acre of land at Suelisheved

19. Agnes, Beatrice and Matilda of one acre of land in Middillondes

20. Asceria daughter of Joslan of land with an oven (*furno*) which belonged to Argrim

21. *Quitclaim* by John Bottay of a toft which belonged to Angelina Bulebals

22. Robert son of Albini of 4 acres of land beyond (*ultra*) Depedale

23. William son of Roger of half an acre of land

24. Walter de Torp of half an acre of land

25. Ralph son of Fulco de Stanford of 3 acres of land and of a certain meadow at Kines...

26. Geoffrey son of Roger of 3 roods of land next to the croft of Leuine

27. Leswin son of Segrim of four acres of land of which one acre ... at Lund ... [*MS torn*]

28. *Final concord* of Roger son of Lece of one acre and a half of land

29. Hugh son of Wimund of houses of Clementia his wife and two acres of land

30. Hugh de Uffinton and Matilda his wife (*sponse*) of one and a half acres of land in the croft which belonged to Godric

31. *Quitclaim* by Matilda formerly the wife (*uxori*) of Hugh de Uffinton of the croft lying between the town (*villam*) and the house of St Michael.

656. BRADECROFTE

1. *Final concord* between the convent of Southwick and the nuns of St Michael for half a mark in Bradecroft

2. Lucy de Humet for half a mark in Bradecroft

3. *Confirmation* of William de Humet of the deed of the said canons of Southwick

4. *Confirmation* of the same William of the said half a mark in Bradecroft given to the nuns

Property at Thurlby and Wenton

657. *On the dorse of the roll is the following:*

From the church of All Saints in the Market two marks due to the monastery of St Fromund.
From the church of All Saints at the bridge two marks
From the church of St Martin two marks
From the church of St Andrew six marks
From the church of St Clement one mark
From the chapel of St Thomas at the bridge one mark
...

Rents from houses in the town of Stanford

Terricus de Colonia for a house 5s (at Easter xxxd, at Michaelmas xxxd)
Herbert Le Serjant 10s
Nicholas son of Alexander 10s
Alexander son of Reiner 4s for the house in ... (at each term and at Easter 3d and at the feast of St John the Baptist 3d)

Matilda de Wakerle 6s for the houses which ... to the synagogue (*scolo Judeorum*) and for a certain place which lies next to the cemetery of St Martin (at each of the four terms 8d).

Scolicia 3s for the house (at each term 9d)

Annor 7½d and four capons (at the Nativity ...)

Dungund 7½d for the house in ... (at Michaelmas ...)

Hugh son of Godric 4s (at each term 12d)

.... (at Easter 7d and at Michaelmas 7d)

John Flamang 12d for land (at Easter 6d and at Michaelmas 6d)

Henry de Tikencote 12d for meadow (at Michaelmas...)

The wife of Richard Ruffus 3d for half an acre of land held for her life (at Michaelmas)

John Petit 6½d for two houses (at Easter)

Henry Sabeci 2d for land (at Michaelmas)

Richard Petitprudom 1d for meadow (at Michaelmas)

From the house of Solfa 3s 6d for her life

Clockematin 12d by legacy of Robert Baker (*pistore*)

Ralph son of Achard 2d for meadow next to the tenter (at Michaelmas)

Robert chaplain one mark for houses in the market

Thomas Bosse 3 and 3s for houses [?error for 3s 3d?]

Wlnat 16d for a house and given at farm 10½d 3½d [*sic*]

Wlmar 3s 6d

Gerard clerk 6s for a house

Nicholas son of Alexander 3s 6d

Mathew 4s 8d to the Infirmary

Mr Alexander son of Richard son of Seluve 4d for meadow next to the castle on the south side

Total of the common rents 51s
to the Kitchen ... 6d
To the Vestry 16s 4d

List continued
Philip Gaugi ...

From the other part of the town [i.e. Stamford Baron]:

William 5s to the Infirmary

Mauger two shillings

Clemens 18d

Adam de Ufford 6s 8d for a house

From the toft next to the cemetery with the oven 3s

Clemens for the oven 3s

Item for a house ...

From the house of Wimund 3s and 2s to the kitchen and 12d to the infirmary

From the house of Alrith 2s

Salendin 18d

From the house next to the sheepfold by gift of Gilbert Parent 6d

W Franceis 5s

For three roods of land [given] by the son of Richard de Eston 1d

For the house of Geoffrey Doget

For the house of Sym[on] de Ely 5s (to the sacristy)

Henry le Gaugi for meadow 8d
Hugh Smith (*faber*) 6d for one acre of land
Walter de Burglea 4d for land at Pilesiate

To the commons 26s
To the kitchen 5s 5d

Other places

<u>De Wirtorp</u>
From the nuns for tofts 4s 8d
Peter March 3s 4d or lands with crofts
Agnes de Stanford 12d for 7½ acres
Robert son of Arnewi 3½d
John de Wirtorp for part of his lands 1d
Richard Petitprud[hom] 1d
Robert Miller 1d for a toft
Aelard 3s for a house and lands of Henry Hare
Philip 12d for a house
Richard 18d for a toft

...

<u>From Bradecroft</u>
Robert 3s for lands
Walter 6s 4d

PART II: DEEDS IN OTHER COLLECTIONS

Records are listed by location of archival deposit in alphabetical order

BRITISH LIBRARY (BL)

658. BL Add. Ch. 6092   27 February 1396

Grant of Thomas Draper of Stannford to William Wardale of Stannford and Agnes his wife of a messuage in Cornstall in parish of St George Stannford between the messuage formerly belonging to John Broun on the west and John Risbek's messuage on the east, and abutting on the said John Broun's garden to the north and on the king's highway to the south. This messuage formerly belonged to Richard Weste of Derby.

Witnesses: Robert Stolam Alderman of Staunford, John Longe, John Spycer, John Gylderr, Walter Wace and others.

Given at Staunford Monday after feast of St Mathias 19 Richard II.

Seal: worn; ? a cross.

659. BL Add. Ch. 20242

Confirmation of grant in free alms of William de Hum [Humet] the King's constable to St Michael's, Stanford and the nuns there of ½ mark silver which his wife Lucy gave to the said church from her land of Bradecroft which she bought from Tostenus [?Tostig?] Bodin, with William's assent.

Witnesses: Jordan de Hum, Richard de Hum, William de Sae, Henry his [i.e. William de Sae's] brother, Gilbert de Valle, William de Hasteinvill, Saluagius, David his son

Seal: tag for seal.

Undated

660. BL Add. Ch. 21153

Grant of Matilda de Dyua to St Michael's Stanford and the nuns there for the soul of William de Dyua her husband of the chapel of Uptona insofar as it belongs to her in free alms.

Witnesses: Richard de Burgo, Richart chaplain of Hengiston, .. de Astona, Geoffrey de Uptona, Stephen de Eringtona, Ralph de Tichemers, Henry P... baker, and others.

Seal: slits for seal

Undated mid-thirteenth century/.

Ms damaged, some witnesses' names lost

661. BL Add. Ch. 66631   25 April 1430

Quitclaim of John Browe of Stannford to Richard Lee of Stannford wright, Richard Cokke and William Storeton of the same, and the heirs and assigns of Richard Lee, of all right in a messuage in Stannford in the parish of St Mary at the bridge between the messuage formerly belonging to John Morely on the west and Thomas Basset's tenement on the east, and abutting on the king's highway to the south and on the tenement formerly belonging to John Marcheford to the north. This messuage the said Richard, Richard and William lately had of the grant and feoffment of Robert Bendow, Robert Smyth, John Upton, John Preston clerk, Andrew Draper and Robert Tost of Stannford.

Witnesses: Thomas Basset Alderman of Stannford, John Broun draper, Thomas Spycer, John Whytesyde, Thomas Fox, William Lutte, William Gryndere of Stannford and others,

Dated at Stannford St Mark's day 8 Henry VI

Seal: coat of arms with chevron and chief; inscription

HARLEIAN CHARTERS

662. 50 I127   20 September 1431

Lease by John Golafre armiger, Andrew Sperlyng and Robert Danvers to John Hampden armiger, Thomas Hasley, Richard Restwold armiger, Thomas Walsyngham and William Hervy of the manors of Wyngfeld, Stradbroke, Oldewyngefeldhall, Hurtes, Swannes [and other places] and lands in … Norfolk, Suffolk, Yorkshire (including a chief messuage in Hull called le Courthall) and also all lands and tenements with appurtenances in Staunford Lincs and also the manor of Burley with appurtenances in Northamptonshire. Sealing clause.

Dated 20 September 10 Henry VI

Seals: three red seals, all indistinct.

50H28 is letter of attorney to deliver these properties.

663. 52 A22

Grant Lucia de Hum[et] to the church of St Mary of Sudwic [Southwick, Hants] and the canons there in free alms of half a mark rent in lands in Bradecroft which land is held by Turstan Bocli… by gift of my lord (husband) and the lands which Richard de Humet gave to Turstan saving a rent of 2s 4d in the land which Lewin holds and 3s in the lands which Osward holds and 16d which William Warin holds; in return for annual prayers

290

for the health of my soul and my husband William de Humet's soul and Richard my son and my ancestors.

Witnesses: Jordan de Humet, Richard de Humet, Baudewin Wac, Ralph de Agnis, Hugh de Cardonvilla, Bartholomew de Mortuomari, William le Bigot, William Hasteinville, Gilebert de Valle, William de Sae, Henry de Humet his brother, William clerk de Aupegart'.

Seal: slits for seal tags

Endorsed: Car' Lucie de Humet de Redditu dim' marc' in Bradecrodt

Not dated

664. 54 C7   **21 March 1379**

Lease indented Aleise widow of sir John de Nevylle of Essex of the one party and sir Michiel de la Pole the elder and sir Esmond de la Pole knights of the other party: Aleise grants and leases at farm to Michael and Esmond her manor of Langham, Essex except the advowson of the church there and the manors of Bierlee in Northants and Harpiswell, Lincs with all lands and tenements in Staunford and elsewhere which Aleise had by gift and feoffment of sir Michiel in Northamptonshire and Lincolnshire from the close of Easter next for 40 years; rent to dam Aleise in the abbey of Byleigh, Essex of 100 marks p.a. at Christmas, Easter, the Nativity of John the Baptist, and Michaelmas. Arrears and re-entry clause. Enclosure of park at Langham. Sealing clause. When she dies, all payments cease.

Dated at London 21 March 2 Richard II

Seal: circle 3cms diameter; red shield in device

Endorsed: Irro in dorso Claus Cancellar' et infracsripti mense marcij anno infrascripto FRENCH

665. 54 C9   **4 July 1383**

Agreement by sir Richard le Scrope, sir Esmond de la Pole, Robert de Bolton clerk, John … parson of the church of Glemesford, John Leef master of the almshouse of Wyngefeld, Philip de Gatesby parson of the church of Grafton and John Wele parson of the church of …fingham, to hold the manor of Langham Essex and the other lands listed in 662 including Little Burley, Northants and Staunford, Lincolnshire and the city of London, which Aleise formerly wife of John de Neville of Essex granted to sir Michael de la Pole

Dated in London 4 July 7 Richard II

Seal tag
Text is illegible in places.

666. 54 C10   **21 November 1383**

Grant by Aleise formerly wife of sir John de Neville of Essex to sir Michael de la Pole the elder and sir Esmond de la Pole of the manor of Langham Essex and other lands listed in 662 including the manor of Petit Burley Northants and lands and tenements in Staunford, Lincs from Christmas next for 40 years at an annual rent of 100 marks.

Dated in London 21 November 7 Richard II

Seal: tag only

667. 54 I15   **12 October 1431**

Lease William de la Pole earl of Suffolk, John Shardelowe knight and Thomas Hoo armiger to John Hampden armiger, Thomas Haseley, Richard Rosewale armiger, Thomas Walsyngham and William Hervy of the same properties as in 662. Warranty clause.

Dated 12 October 10 Henry VI

Seals: two red seals and one further tag – obscure.

For British Library Harl 3658 Cartulary of Deeping St James, see Additional Deeds below

BROWNE'S HOSPITAL DEEDS

These are now in the Lincolnshire Archives Office (LAO). There is a list prepared by LAO but item 670 is taken from other notes as the document is now damaged. The spelling of personal and placenames here is as in the list rather than the deeds. The reference is in each case LAO, BHS

668. 7/12/10

Copies of three deeds relating to Stamford on one parchment:

(a) *Grant* by Henry son of Alexander de Stanforde to Joseph chaplain son of Joseph Stanford of an annual rent charge of 5s from a house which Richard son of Henry son of David holds of Henry in fee, which house is situated on Cleymunde in the parish of All Saints in the Market place of Stamford between a house of Richard de Weston on the east and the house of William Cat on the west.

Witnesses: dom William rector of All Saints etc (*no further witnesses given*)

Undated (13th/14thC)

(b) *Grant* by Joseph chaplain of Stamford to the church of St Mary *de novo loco* [Newstead] at the bridge of Uffington and the canons there of the above rent charge for the sake of the soul of Joseph and Henry son of Alexander and his predecessors.

Undated (13th/14thC?)

(c) *Quitclaim* by Richard Pecke son of Richard Pecke of Stamford to the canons of Newstead by the bridge of Uffington of his interest in the above rent charge.

Witnesses: Henry Sabecy etc

Undated (13th/14thC?)

669. 7/12/11   **1 August 1529**

Lease for 41 years by Richard Cecell of Stamford esquire to John Muston warden of the Bedehouse in Stamford of a barn with a garden and yard adjoining in Stamford in the parish of St Andrew situated between the grounds of the prior of Newstead, William Radclyff gent and the tenement of the said warden on the west and the lane called Sterlane in part and the tenement of the abbot of Bourne on the east, abutting the highway south and the way called Cleymont north. Rent p.a. 6s

Dated: 1 Aug 21 Henry VIII (1529)
(with a translation)

670. 7/12/24   **4 July 1488**
Grant by William Broune of Stamford merchant of the Staple of Calais to Thomas Stokk clerk, Henry Wykes, Thomas Hikeham, Robert Grymston and John Taillour clerks, John Coton and William Hawkyns chaplains, David Malpas esquire, Robert Fitzacreley, John Gregory and Thomas Kesteven of Stamford aforesaid, of his manors of Swafield and North Withome Lincs with all the lands, tenements etc and property belonging thereto in Swafield, Counthorpe, North Withome, South Withome, Twyford, Stenby, Gunby, Colsterworth, Woollesthorp, Wyllsthorp and Bargham [Barholm]; also the following tenements in Stamford, namely a tenement in the parish of St Peter late[1] in the tenure of William Buck; one tenement in the parish aforesaid at Malory Brigge with appurtenances late in the tenure of Helena Bellamy; and one my tenement in the same parish and one acre and a half of meadow in the meadows of Bredcroft now in the tenure of Thomas Peryman; and a shop in the parish of All Saints in the same town of Stamford now in the tenure of William Bullok draper; and one shop there next the shop aforesaid still [late] in the tenure of William Bernard patynner; and a tenement in the same parish late in the tenure of Robert Johnson shoemaker; and two tenements together situated in the same parish with a grange in Scotgate late in the tenure of John Sabyn; and another tenement in the same parish now in the tenure of John Beever tailor; and a tenement in the same parish late in the tenure of John Sherman at Mallory Brigge...; and my tenement in the parish of St Michael late in the tenure of Richard Tailour; and a tenement in the parish of St Andrew with one acre of meadow at lez Smale Brigges late in the tenure of John Thistilton; and a tenement or hospice in the parish of (St Mary) at the bridge of the town of Stamford called le Aungell late in the tenure of John Young tailour; and a tenement in the parish of St Martin within the liberty of the abbot of Peterborough, namely Estbythewater late in the tenure of John Barford junior; and a

---

[1] Wright gives in every case 'now in the tenure of' rather than 'late in the tenure of'.

tenement in the same parish late in the tenure of John Gybson; and a tenement in the same parish late in the tenure of Robert Dudley sawer; and a garden in the same parish late in the tenure of Robert Lambe tailour; 3 acres of meadow in the Estmedewe at Smalebrigges and 3 roods in the said meadow which are indivisible in Lincolnshire. Also William Broune grants to the same feoffees 60 acres of arable land in various places in the fields of Stamford, in the counties of Rutland and Lincoln and one close with appurtenances as is enclosed in a stone wall in Bredcroft in the county of Rutland, and another close with a dovecote in the same with appurtenances in Bredcroft in Rutland; and all my lands, tenements, rents etc in North Luffenham, Sculthorpe and Stretton in Rutland. Also William Broune grants to the same feoffees all my lands and tenements etc in Estone (Easton) by Stamford, Wothorp, Barnake, Pillesyate, Wallcote and Warmyngton in Northamptonshire; William Broune appoints Henry Toky as attorney for livery of seisin.

Witnesses: Robert Hans Alderman of Stamford, John Sabyn of the same, John Hunt of Witham, John Mower of the same, John Aleyn of Swynsted, Bartholomew Holme of Swafield, John Haydy of Estone, William Scarburgh of North Luffenham, Henry Okeley of Pillesyate and many others

Dated: Stamford 4 July 1488 (with translation 19c)

Seal: tag cut short

Part of this document faded through damp: the additions come in part from my own notes taken in the 1960s and in part from the transcript made by H P Wright and published in his book, The Story of the Domus Dei of Stamford *1890 pp 19-22.*

CAMBRIDGE UNIVERSITY LIBRARY: *See Additional Deeds (Thorney) below*

DEVON RECORD OFFICE

Simcoe : Catalogue Ref. 1038 M

671. Ref. 1038 M/T/9/1   **1 July 1353**

Grant Robert de Wyk of Staunford to William de Steandeby of Staunford of all his goods and chattels living and dead in a tenement in Staunford in the parish of All Saints in the Market place that is on Cleymont which Steandeby received from Wyk in fee on the same day

Dated at Staunford Monday after SS Peter and Paul 27 Edward III

672. 1038 M/T/13/1   **11 June 1415**

Grant by Henry Bracy of Fodryngey to William Bracy of Fodryngey of all his lands and tenements in Barnewell, Cambridgeshire, in Tansoner (Tansor), Wermyngton (Warmington), Aylyngton, Suth Wyke (Southwick), Nassyngton and Staunford in Northants, and Rutland.

Witnesses: Peter Mavan, John Knight, Robert Browe esqs, Nicholas Morys, John Marchall clerks.

Dated at Fodryngey feast of St Barnabus 3 Henry V

Note: 23 April 1418, the same property except Staunford ("all the lands and tenements … in the towns and fields of Fodryngey, Nassyngton, Wermyngton, Bernewell by Cambridge and the county of Rutland") is settled by William Hale clerk on feoffees, William Bracy, Peter Mavan esq, John Bekyngham, John Ethell of Staunford; witnesses John Broun, William Potton, Thomas Rathewell, …, Robert Boteler 1038 M/T/13/2. John Ethell of Staunford gave to feoffees (including Richard Wryght of Staunford) the same lands ("and tenements … in Northamptonshire, Rutland, Huntingdonshire and Cambridgeshire") 22 January 1429; John Brygge of Staunford chaplain is attorney to deliver seisin. 1038 M/T/13/4 and 5. The Stamford property (unspecified) is probably included in the' lands in Northants' mentioned.

673. 1038 M/T/13/6   **1 October 1499**

Quitclaim by John Verney knight, Guy Wulston knight, Robert Harecourt knight, Robert Brudenell, John Danvers, Christopher Broun, John Burgoyn, William Coke, John Glynton, Thomas Mountegen, Nicholas Fazakyrley and John Colston to John Taillor and Henry Wykes clerks of the manor of Swynsted Lincs, manor of Wolfehouse Rutland, manors of Papley and Lylford Northants, manor of Hogyngton [Oakington] Cambs, manor of Cassyngton Oxon, together with all lands and tenements in Swynsted, Witham, Staunford, Brodyng, Bredcrofte, Great Casterton and Little Casterton, Lincs, Warmyngton, Papley, Ogerston, Pokbroke [Polebrook], Artelyngborough [Irthlingborough], Lylford, Wyxsthorpp [Wigsthorpe], Achirche [Thorpe Achurch], Pylton, Benefeld, Northants, Hogyngton, Cambs, Henley on Thames, Rotherfeld Grey, Baggerygg [(Badgemore], Watlyngton Hill, Cassyngton, Worton (in Cassington), Somerford (in Cassington) and Bladon Oxon, Walyngford Berks, and Hamyldon (Hambleden), Chyr Feld and Skyrmote (Skirmett in Hambleden), Bucks, which Verney et al held with Walter Elmes, John Wylles and others by deed from Elizabeth Elmes widow, daughter and heiress of William Broun of Staunford deceased

Dated: 1 October 15 Henry VIII

674. 1038 M/T/13/7   **20 December 1499**

Deed of gift in tail by John Taillor clerk and Henry Wykes clerk to Elizabeth Elmes widow of John Elmes of Henley on Thames, Oxon., merchant of the 'Stapule calicie' and daughter and heiress of William Broun of Stamford Lincs, merchant of the same staple of the manor of Swynsted, Lincs, manor of Wolfehouse, Rutland, manors of Papley and

Lilford, Northants, manor of Hogyngton, Cambs, also lands and tenements in Swynsted, Wytham, Staunford, Brodyng, Bredcroft, Great and Little Casterton, Lincs., Warmyngton, Papley, Ogerston, Pokbroke, Artelyngborough, Lylford, Wyxsthorpp, Achirche, Pylton and Benefeld, Northants., and Hogyngton, Cambs., which Taillor and Wykes held with John Verney knight, Guy Wolston knight, Robert Harecourt knight, Robert Brudewell and others by deed from Elizabeth Elmes. The premises are to be held by Elizabeth for life and after her death by William Elmes son of Elizabeth and his heirs. If William dies without heirs, the premises are to remain to John brother of William and his heirs. Attornies to grant seisin: John Colston and John Holyngton.

Witnesses: William Warner vicar of Lilford, William Cook of Oundell merchant, Robert Beamond, William Baker of Papley, Henry Elyss, William Aburn of Lylford, Richard Mower of Wytham, Henry Watgott, John Webster, John Maxsey of Swynsted, Robert Stelyngton.

Dated: 20 December 15 Henry VII

Endorsed: (i) The Intail of Brown's Estate upon Wm and John Elmes sons of Elizabeth Elmes daughter of the said Brown dated 20 December 1500 15 Henry VII [not contemporary]
(ii) Thentayle of all Brownes lands.

DURHAM CATHEDRAL ARCHIVES
These notes were provided by Dr Alan Piper

675. D.C.D. Register II, fol. 275r   29 May 1370

Gift in perpetuity by John [Fossor] prior and the convent of Durham to sir William de Botelesford rector of St Mary Bynwerk Stanford and John Broune burgess of Stannford of a plot of land in Staunford lying in the close of the Carmelite friars opposite the gate of the Franciscan friars in the parish of Holy Trinity outside the east gate.

Dated at Durham in the chapter house.

676. D.C.D. Register II, fol 340r   17 May 1366

Gift in perpetuity by John [Fossor] prior and the convent of Durham, to sir William de Botelesford rector of [St Mary] Bynwerk Staunford and Robert de Welton burgess of Stannford of a plot of land in Staunford lying in the close of the Carmelite friars opposite the gate of the Franciscan friars in the parish of Holy Trinity outside the east gate.

Dated at Durham, in the chapter house.

677. D.C.D. Register III, fol.223r-v   **(i) 1 April 1438 (ii) 10 April [1438]**

Indentured Agreement recording lease for forty years with warranty by [John Wessington] prior and the chapter of Durham to William Syngalday of Stamford of a tenement now waste in Stamford in the lane called Cornewelsty or Chynelane between the tenement of William Syngalday and the garden of Alice Bassett to the west and the lane to the east, and between the tenement of Alice Bassett to the south and William's own tenement to the north, being 15 royal rods long, 3¾ rods wide at the north end and 8 rods wide at the south end, for an annual rent to the prior and chapter [of Durham] or to the prior of the cell of St Leonard by Stamford of 12d at Michaelmas and 2 capons at Christmas and the performance of suit of court at the two great leets of St Cuthbert in Stamford; the lease is to begin at Easter next [13 April 1438]. Rights of distraint and re-entry in case of arrears of rent are reserved to the prior and chapter [of Durham] or the prior of the cell. William will, within two years, build and subsequently maintain a stone house on the waste with a door onto the high road by which the lord may effect entry and distraint as necessary.

Dated: one part at Durham in the chapter house 1 April 1438, the other part at Stamford 10 April [1438].

678. D.C.D. Register III, fol. 310 r-v   **1 June 1438**

Indentured Agreement recording lease for eighty years with warranty by [John Wessington] prior and the convent of Durham to William Ledys of Stamford tailor of two adjacent cottages in the parish of St Mary at the Bridge Stamford in the street called Brigstrette super Westrawe between the tenement formerly Thomas Bassett's to the north and the tenement belonging to the Gild of Corpus Christi to the south and between the high road to the east and the wall enclosing the tenement of Thomas Bassett to the west, of which cottages the southern is 25 royal rods long and 6¼ rods wide and the northern is 23 royal rods long and 6⅛ rods wide, for an annual rent to the prior and convent [of Durham] or to the prior of the cell of St Leonard by Stamford of 6s 8d payable by equal portions at Christmas and the Nativity of St John the Baptist for the first twenty years, with an augmentation of 4d [per annum] after each twenty years throughout the whole term for the renewal of these indentures* and the performance of suit of court annually at the two great leets of St Cuthbert and an annual payment of 2½d to Lord de la Ware; the lease is to begin at the Nativity of St John the Baptist next [24 June 1438]. William will within twelve years rebuild and maintain at his own expense the two cottages, namely, on the one next to Thomas's tenement a hall and a chamber with a solar, and on the other a parlour (*parlocutorium*) and a kitchen. Rights of distraint and re-entry in the case of arrears of rent and of re-entry in the case of sale or alienation by the lessee or delay in building are reserved to the prior and chapter [of Durham] or prior of the cell.

Dated at Durham Pentecost 16 Henry VI.
* *wording uncertain*

679.1 D.C.D. Register IV, fol. 127v   **9 November 1461**

Appointment by John [Burnby] prior and the chapter of Durham of master Richard Barton monk of the house professor of theology (*sacre pagine*) and prior of St Leonard's by Stamford and Thomas Barbur of the same town as attorneys to recover from William Ledys the tenant arrears of rent for two cottages in Stamford which he holds of the prior and convent on an eighty year lease, to implead him if necessary before any judge and to enter and hold the two cottages as provided by the terms of the lease.

679.2 D.C.D. Register IV, fol. 135r

Appointment by John [Burnby] prior and the chapter of Durham of master Richard Barton monk of the house professor of theology and prior of St Leonard's by Stamford, sir Thomas Lewyn monk of the house, sir William Rosby and master John Paynell bachelor of laws and notary public, as proctors in the matter of the appropriation of the parish church of St Mary of Bynwarke by the west gate of Stamford in the patronage of the prior and convent to the parish church of St Peter in the same town in the patronage of [blank in MS] with full powers to appear before any judge both on this matter and on that of the exchange of a garden beside the aforesaid church of St Mary [*text ends, incomplete*].

680. D.C.D. Register IV, fol. 191v   8 May 1480

Gift with warranty by William Broune Alderman and the brethren of the gild of Holy Trinity Stamford to Robert [Ebchester] prior and the convent of Durham of ½ acre of land in the fields of Stamford lying between the lands of the prior and convent to the north and the south and between the meadow of the duchess of York to the east and the land of the gild to the west, in exchange for another ½ acre of land given by the prior and convent to the gild as described fully in another charter.

Dated at Stannford 8 May 20 Edward IV

681. D.C.D. Register IV, fol. 216r   17 May 1480

Gift with warranty by Robert [Ebchester] prior and the convent of Durham to William Broune Alderman and the brethren of the gild of Holy Trinity Stamford of ½ acre of land in the fields of Stamford between the land of the gild to the south and the land formerly of William Broune merchant to the north and the east and abutting on the high road to the west in exchange for another ½ acre of land given by the gild to the prior and convent; and appointment of William Yowdale prior of St Leonard's by Stamford to deliver seisin of the land.

Dated at Durham 17 May 20 Edward IV.

DURHAM CATHEDRAL ARCHIVES: EBORACENSIA

682. 1.4. Ebor. 3

Notification by Stephen King of England of his grant in free alms for the souls of King Henry and his other ancestors and himself to God and the church of St Mary of Stamford of 3 acres from his demesne of Stamford.

Witnesses: William Martel, Baldwin son of Gilbert and Richard son of Ursi.

Given at Stamford [perhaps 1139-41]

Seal: missing, strip cut from foot with tie

683. 1.4. Ebor. 4

Quitclaim by William son of Acard to the prior and convent of Durham and the prior and monks of St Leonard of Stamford, over all articles in their charter to Elias his son concerning the three churches of St Mary at the bridge and St Mary in Binewerk in Stamford and Normanton.

Witnesses: Geoffrey dean of Stamford, Peter prior of St Michael of Stamford, Walter chaplain, Reiner chaplain, Alexander chaplain, Ralph son of Acard, Peter knight, Samson knight, Isaac clerk, Clement son of Michael, Robert son of Stenketel, master William Spiritus and many others.

Seal: on doubled strip.

No Date

684. 1. 4. Ebor. 5

Quitclaim by Elias son of William son of Acard before the chapter of Stamford of 3 churches, 2 in Stamford (St Mary at the bridge and St Mary in Binewerk) and the third in Normanton, based on a charter from the monks of Durham.

Witnesses: Geoffrey dean of Stamford, Peter prior of St Michael of Stamford, Walter chaplain, Alexander chaplain, Reiner chaplain, Robert chaplain, Ralph son of Acard, Peter knight, Samson knight, Isaac clerk, Clement son of Michael, Robert son of Stenketel and many others.

Seal on doubled strip

No Date

685. 1.4. Ebor. 7

Notification by Geoffrey dean and the chapter of Stamford and Peter prior of St Michael of Stamford of the sworn quitclaims in the chapter of Stamford by William son of Acard and Elias his son to the prior and convent of Durham and the prior and monks of St Leonard of Stamford concerning all articles in their charter to Elias concerning the churches of St Mary at the bridge and St Mary in Binewerk in Stamford and Normanton for which they have had satisfaction.

Seal: on doubled strips

No Date

686. 1.4. Ebor. 18a

Confirmation sworn on the altar of St Leonard by William son of William son of Acard of the grant made by his father to the monks of St Leonard of Stamford of all the land he held in fee of Acard his own grandfather.

Witnesses: master Samson, Richard de Wakerle, Henry de Casterton, Reginald chaplain of St Paul, Walter chaplain of St Peter, Peter de Martinwast, William son of Roger de Uffington, John deacon, Roger de Uffington, Alexander clerk and many others.

Seal: on doubled strip.

No Date

687. 1.4. Ebor. 18c

File of copies of deeds relating to Ingoldsby, Rippingdale and other places including:
Grant in free alms by Ralph son of Ralph de Normanville for the souls of himself, his ancestors and successors, to God, the church of St Leonard's outside Stamford and the monks of Durham there of a rent of 4s a year from his half of Kingsmill outside Stamford held of him in perpetual farm by the prior and canons of the new place at Uffington bridge [Newstead] to maintain a lamp at the high altar in St Leonard's church.

Deeds relating to Walcot, Swayfield

Grant in free alms by Emma daughter of Ralph son of Acard of Stanford in her free widowhood for 7 marks and for the souls of herself, her ancestors and successors, to God, the house of St Leonard and the monks of Durham there of an annual rent of 10s from a house in the parish of St Mary's at the bridge Stanford between that formerly of Isaac Ruffe to the west and that formerly of John Sampson's son to the east with escheats and reliefs, for 12d a year to Richard Peke.

HARVARD LAW SCHOOL LIBRARY SPECIAL COLLECTIONS

688. Deeds 343: HOLLIS number: AQC4965   23 November 1445

Grant by Thomas Moreton of Steanford to Henry Burley of Staunford chaplain of a messuage in Staunford in the parish of St John between the tenement of William Sutton to the eastern part and the tenement of the aforesaid Thomas Moreton to the western part and abutting on the king's highway to the south and with the tenement of the prior of Novo Loco [Newstead] juxta Staunford to the north.

Witnesses: John Page then Alderman of Staunford, William Broun, Richard Lee, William Storeton, John Warde.

Given at Staunford on the feast of St Clement the pope [23 November] 24 Henry VI [1445].

Seal: 1.9 cm.; red wax, bearing a crucifix with the letters TM (?) and a legend beginning ORA.

LINCOLNSHIRE ARCHIVES OFFICE

689. CRAGG 5/1/231   13 March 1538/9

Gift and grant by King Henry VIII to Richard Manners esquire of all the house and site of the late priory of Newstead by Stamford, all the church, bell, tower and cemetery of the same priory, all messuages, houses, buildings, granges, gardens, dovecotes, orchards, lands and soil within and without the site; the manor of Newstead called the Pryours manor in Lincs, Northants, Leics, and Rutland; arable land (281 acres), meadow (28 acres) and pasture (8 acres) in Uffington formerly belonging to the monastery; all manors, messuages, granges, lands etc in Newstead by Stamford, Uffington, Stamford, Braunston, 'Kneuerthe', Boddington, Ketton, Grayingham, Bottesford, Colsterworth, Casewick and Little Casterton as in the time of John Blakett late prior.

Seal: Great Seal attached by green and cream silk cords, good impression but defective and parts broken.

Endorsed: Irrotulatur per me Johannem Wyseman auditorem Newstead.

690. 2ANC 3/B/16   11 March 1540/41

Grant by King Henry VIII to Charles duke of Suffolk of (1) manor or grange of Hundleby, parcel of Stixwould; (2) manor of Legsby, parcel of Sixhills; (3) rectory and advowson of Billinghay, parcel of Catley; (4) the Greyfriars in Stamford with the belfry, church and cemetery there; (5) the Blackfriars in Boston with the belfry, church and cemetery there.

Seal: Great Seal, black wax suspended on cords.

691. 2 ANC 3/B/25   **20 March 1552/53**

Lease until 20 March 1559/60 from William marquis of Winchester one of the executors of Charles duke of Suffolk, and Richard Bartye esquire and Katherine his wife widow of the duke of Suffolk to John Trye esquire of a third part of a fifth part of the site of Revesby Abbey with the abbey's Lincolnshire possessions, the priory of Thornholm, the granges of Canwick, Coltham, St Thomas, Hanby and Hundleby, lands in Burwell, Calceby and Sausthorpe, the demesnes of Stonely and Erbury priories (Warwicks), the commanderies of Temple Bruer, Maltby and Skirbeck, the east and west granges in Scampton and North Carlton, the granges of Rearsby, Swinthorpe, Snelland, Sturton Sheepwash and Linwood, the parsonage of Billinghay, and the houses of Blackfriars in Boston and Greyfriars in Stamford.

Considerations: Trye is to pay to the Treasurer of Augmentations £203 19s 7d at Michaelmas following as the fifteenth of £3059 13s 6d due to the Crown from the duke's estate and £99 7s 1¼d to Richard Bertie and Katherine as the fifteenth of £1490. 6s 6d remaining from the profits.

692. M.C.D. 263   **5 July 1338**

Grant by Walter de Skylyngton of Stamford to John de Somerdeby chaplain of houses in the parish of St Paul Stamford between a tenement late of Robert de Lymberugh on the east and a lane called Starlane on the west and extending from the king's highway on the south to a tenement of the abbot of Bourne on the north.

Witnesses: Henry de Tyddiswell, Robert de Pakyngton, Richard de Lincoln, Thomas de Berugh, William de Makeseye, John de Empingham, Thomas de Bedeford of Stamford, John Josep clerk and others.

Dated at Stamford Sunday after the feast of SS Peter and Paul 12 Edward III.

Seal

693. HILL 2   **(c.1303)**

Notification of obligation by prior and convent of Sempringham with assent of Philip master of the Order to master Robert Luteril rector of Irnham and his heirs in return for lands and tenements in Ketton, Cottesmore and Casterton, Rutland, and in Stamford, to maintain three chaplains celebrating divine service in the church of St Andrew Irnham, in the chapel of St Mary in the manor of Stamford given to them by master Robert, and in the conventual church of Sempringham; for the souls of Robert, his father and mother, all his related ancestors and successors and all faithful christians; and also to support a scholar studying holy writ and philosophy at Stamford. Any suits arising from this are to be under the jurisdiction of the bishop of Lincoln; the prior and convent are to pay £20 a year to the bishop of Lincoln for any default.

Witnesses: Robert de Fligisthorp, Philip de Paunton, Theobald de Nevyle, John de Folevyle, Roger de Mortayn, Ralph de Sancto Laudo, Geoffrey de Brunna knights,

William Iuvene of Billisend, William de Blaunkneye of Kysby, Geoffrey Carpenter of Corby, Robert super Montem of Lavington, Hugh son of Edda de Irnham.

Seal: two slits for seal tags

Endorsed Convencio inter Priorem et Conventum de Sempigham et dominum si per Cantar' Trium Capellanorum pro defunctis

Not dated
Note: *LAO Misc. Dep. 210 is a copy, though not a counterpart, of this deed.*

694. MISC. DEP. 12   1 June 1509

Quitclaim by John Hussey knight to Robert Brudnell justice of the bench and lately sergeant at law, Christopher Browne esquire and William Radclyffe of all right and title in all lands and tenements in the town and fields of Stamford and in Pilsgate, Northants which the said Robert, Christopher and William lately had together with Roger Urmeston knight and William Elmesse now deceased by feoffment of the said John Hussey knight and Margaret Alwether sister and heir of Gregory Blewyt.

Seal: fragment of red seal on tag.

Endorsed: Xp^cr [Christopher] B. Staunf' et Pilsegat

695. REVESBY ABBEY PAPERS RA1, BOX IV/96   1265

Inventory of hospital of St Thomas on the bridge, Stamford

NORTHAMPTONSHIRE RECORDS OFFICE

696. FITZWILLIAM 498   22 May 1421

The finding of John Waryn and others forming a jury at Castre [Castor, Northants] in an inquisition concerning certain lands etc. in Castre and Stamford, namely: that Thomas Brerle purchased them from John de Pantre lately dwelling in Castre and then died seised of the same, after whose death Thomas Brerle as his son and heir entered into possession and sold and alienated certain portions, and seeing he was on the point of death granted them to Thomas Wykys and John Lay who thereupon entered into possession on condition that Elizabeth wife of the said Thomas Wykes and mother of the said Thomas Brerle should have the same for her life and after her death the same to be sold to the best advantage and the money obtained to go to the support of chaplains in the parish church of Castre to celebrate masses etc. And the said John Lay seeing that the lands and tenements were going to great ruin and dilapidation, with consent of the parishioners and neighbours, went to the said Elizabeth to incite and implore her to put the same in fitting state of repair and thus fulfil the last will and declaration of Thomas Brerle.

Dated at Castre 22 May, 9 Henry V.

Seal of the jury.

697. FITZWILLIAM 499, 500   1 June 1421

Grant and counterpart by John Lay to William Kynwolmerssh clerk senior, master Thomas Whiston clerk, Richard Coventre clerk, John Wakerle esquire, Thomas Brake clerk, William Aldewyncle, John Brake and William Lay of all the lands etc which the said John Lay had jointly with Thomas Wyke by feoffment of Thomas Brerle son of Thomas Brerle in Castre and Stamford.

Witnesses: Richard Wytelbury esquire of Milton, Geoffrey Cordel, Thomas Edows and others.

Dated at Castre 1 June 9 Henry V.

Seal

NORTHUMBERLAND RECORD OFFICE:
Papers of the Middleton Family of Belsay:

698. Ref. ZMI II, C 1. f.35

Confirmation by Osbert son of Nigel de Lambart to the monks of Croyland of his father's gifts to the monks of the churches of Ingolsby, of Sapertonia and St Michael's in Stamford.

Witnesses: John de Threkingham(?), Ralph de Brun, Robert chaplain of Ingoldsby, Peter de Moreton and many others.

Seal: oval: a man on horseback passant holding a sword upright in dexter hand with shield sinister arm

No date

NORTH YORKSHIRE RECORD OFFICE, JERVAULX COLLECTION

699. Ref : ZJX I 4/3   28 December 1377

Lease for life from John Knyvet knight son of Richard Knyvet to Peter Goldsmith of Staunford of a messuage with a grange adjoining situated in the parish of All Saints in the Market of Staunford; namely between the tenement once Alan Cupper's on the east and the tenement belonging to the mass [*misse*] of the blessed Mary in the market place on the west. Rent 6s 8d p.a.

Witnesses: John Broun then Alderman of Staunford, William de Styandeby, John Spycer, Richard de Ardern, John Chestre and Simon Cokerell.

Dated Monday next after the nativity 1 Richard II

OXFORD: MAGDALEN COLLEGE (MCO)
The deeds are given in order of the number attached to them in the collection, not in order of the page number of the catalogue which is in chronological order. I am grateful to the college staff and Dr G L Harriss for help with this part of the collection.

700 MCO Stamford 1   **19 December 1497**

Grant from John Stede burgess of Staunford to Thomas Philipp of Stannford draper and John Bryden' clerk of two tenements in Stannford in the parish of St Mary between the tenement of John Frebarne to the east and that of the gild of Corpus Christi to the west, abutting on the king's highway to the south, which he had by the gift of Henry Wykes clerk.

Witnesses: Richard Cannell Alderman of Stannford, John Frebarne, William Radclyff, Thomas Edwarde, John Claypole.

Given at Staunford 19 December 13 Henry VII.

Seal: small red *Seal*: an animal (? dog) and a tree.

701 MCO Stamford 2   **20 April 1470**

Release and quitclaim from William Broun' of Staunford merchant to Elizabeth Storeton' widow of William Storeton' of all his right in a messuage with a garden in Estgate in the parish of St Paul between the messuage called Goddeshows to the east and the tenement of the gild of the Holy Trinity to the west, abutting on the highway to the north and on the street *(vicum)* called Cornstall to the south.

No witnesses

Given at Staunford 20 April 10 Edward IV.

Seal: small seal; a swan.

702 MCO Stamford 3   **20 December 1497**

Release and quitclaim from John Stede of Stannford Lincs burgess to Thomas Philipp of Stannford draper and John Byrden' clerk of all his right in the two tenements in

Staunford in the parish of St Mary between the tenement of John Frebarne to the east and that of the gild of Corpus Christi to the west

No witnesses

Seal: missing

Dated 20 December 13 Henry VII.

703 MCO Stamford 4   24 November 1483

Grant from John Stede of Staunford and Anabel his wife to Thomas Philip, William Gaywode and Geoffrey Hampton of a tenement in the parish of St Mary by the bridge of the town of Staunford between the tenement of William Broune merchant called Le Belle on the south and the tenement of the prior of Broke on the north, abutting on the highway on the east and on the tenement of John Molle on the west; which they had conjointly with Henry Cok, John Molle and Nicholas Edward by the gift and feoffment of Margery Goldesworth widow, of Henry Hopkyns chaplain, and of Alexander Tyard.

Witnesses: John Dycon Alderman of Staunford, Robert Nevour, John Tovy, John Langton, William Duraunt.

Given at Staunford 24 November 1 Richard III

Seals: two small seals both a female head with inscription 'Iohis Stede'

704 MCO Stamford 5   5 March 1431

Condition (indented) of a grant from John Clerk of Talyngtone chapman on the same day to Robert Broun husbandman and John Palfreyman of Staunford of a messuage in Staunford in the parish of St Mary of Bynwerk and 20 acres of arable land lying separately in the fields of Staunford, namely that they shall pay 40 marks by annual instalments during five years.

No witnesses

Dated: Staunford 5 March 9 Henry VI.

Seal: effaced.

705 MCO Stamford 6   20 February 1477

Grant from Margery Goldesworth widow, Henry Hopkyns chaplain and Alexander Tyarde to John Stede of Staunford and Anabel his wife, Henry Cok, John Molle, and Nicholas Edwarde of a tenement in the parish of St Mary by the bridge of Staunford between that of William Broune merchant called Le Belle on the south and that of the prior of Broke on the north abutting on the highway east and on the tenement of John

Molle in the west; which they, together with William Caunce clerk and Thomas Middelton' both deceased had lately by the gift and feoffment of the said Henry Cok.

Witnesses: John Dycone Alderman of Staunford, William Hikeham, Robert Nevour', Thomas Philip, William Duraunt.

Given at Staunford 20 February 16 Edward IV

Seals: one small seal (a fleur-de-lys); the rest lost

706 MCO Stamford 7   23 June 1425

<u>Release</u> from John Palfreyman of Staunford and Alexander Hyne of the same to John Warner of Staunford, John Smyth clerk, Alexander Mercer and Robert Strykeswold of Staunford of all their right in a messuage with a garden in Estgate in the parish of St Paul Staunford between the messuage called Goddeshous on the east and the tenement of John Corby formerly Thomas Cok's on the west, abutting on the highway north and on the street of Cornstall south; which they together with John Browe lately had by the gift and feoffment of Elizabeth Mercere of Staunford.

Witnesses: Thomas Spycer Alderman of Staunford, John Broun draper, John Longe, Robert Bendow, Thomas Bloston', John Halyday of Staunford.

Given at Staunford Saturday the vigil of the Nativity of St John the Baptist, 3 Henry VI.

Seal: one small seal; second seal tag.

707 MCO Stamford 8   20 May 1330

<u>Release</u> from William de Apethorpe of Staunford to Walter de Skilington called atte Nonnes of Staunford of all his right in a parcel of a curtilage in. Staunford in the parish of St Mary near the bridge lying in breadth from the grantor's tenement which the said Walter and Joan his wife hold for the term of their lives on the east and the tenement of the said Walter on the west and lengthways from the chamber of the grantor in his said tenement called 'la Ivy Chaumbre' north to the tenement of Walter Auerey and Margery his wife south: which parcel of a curtilage the grantor lately acquired from the said Walter Auerey and his wife Margery as attested in their deed which he has delivered to the said Walter de Skilington.

Witnesses: Hugh de Thurleby, Henry de Tiddeswelle, John Bertilmeu, Roger Scavelere, Hamo de Fouldon, William Flemying, William de Makeseye burgesses of Staunford, William Joseph clerk.

Given at Staunford, Sunday after the feast of St Dunstan archbishop 4 Edward III.

Seal: round seal; a star "…. Galfridi"; green wax

708 MCO Stamford 9   **15 June 1425**

Grant from John Browe of Staunford to John Warner of Staunford, John Smyth clerk, Alexander Mercere and Robert Strykeswold of Staunford of a messuage with a garden in Estgate in the parish of St Paul Staunford between the messuage called Goddeshous on the east and the tenement of John Corby formerly Thomas Cok's on the west, abutting on the highway north and on the street of Cornstall south which he together with John Palfreyman and Alexander Hyne lately had by gift and feoffment of Elizabeth Mercere of Staunford.

Witnesses: Thomas Spycer Alderman of Staunford, John Broun' draper, John Longe, John Whiteside, Thomas Bloston' of Staunford.

Given at Staunford, Friday after the feast of St Barnabus apostle 3 Henry VI.

Seal: round seal of arms; a chevron between three twigs or branches; a chief, thereon .... ("Sigillum Johannis Browe"); red wax

709 MCO Stamford 10   **22 May 1470**

Grant from Elizabeth Storeton' widow of William Storeton' to Nicholas Bryghton' and Alice his wife, Robert Parnell clerk, Henry Cok and John Rychardson' of a messuage with a garden in Estgate in the parish of St Paul Staunford, between the messuage called Goddeshous on the east, the tenement of the gild of the Holy Trinity on the west, abutting on the highway north and on the street called Cornstalle south.

Witnesses: Thomas Kesteuene Alderman of Staunford, William Broun', John Broun', Robert Hans, William Hawkys, John Markeby, John Hyxson'.

Given at Staunford 22 May 10 Edward IV

Seal: round seal with letter W; red wax.

710 MCO Stamford 11   **20 August 1478**

Grant from William Hikeham of Staunford Lincs to William Broune marchaunt, John Gregory, George Chapman', Robert Hans and John Gybbes of Staunford of a messuage lately built formerly divided into two houses in the parish of St Mary Staunford, between the highway and the houses lately of Henry Milton on the east and the tenement lately of the earl of Suffolk on the west abutting on the king's highway to the north and on William Hikeham's land on the south; and also three cottages situated together in Cornstall between the garden lately of John Longe on the east and the lane called Erleslane on the west abutting on the highway north and on the garden lately of Thomas Basse on the south.

Witnesses: Henry Cok Alderman of Staunford, Thomas Kesteven', John Nele, John Dycon, William Gaywode.

Given at Staunford 20 August 18 Edward IV

Seals: slits only.

711 MCO Stamford 12   20 July 1436

Grant from John Warner of Brunne to William Storeton' of Staunford baker, William Broune of the same and John Munke of the same clerk of a messuage with a garden adjacent in Estgate in the parish of St Paul Staunford between the messuage called Goddeshous on the east and the tenement of John Corby, formerly Thomas Cok's, on the west, abutting on the highway north and on the street of Cornstall south as described in the deed of 25 June 1414 [722] which he together with John Smyth clerk deceased, Alexander Mercer and Robert Strykyswold had by gift and feoffment of John Browe.

Witnesses: John Page then Alderman of Staunford, John Broune draper, Robert Bendowe, Laurence Taylour, John Clerke, Thomas Pope, William Skryvener of Staunford.

Given at Staunford 20 July 14 Henry VI.

Seal: small seal, with letter R.

712 MCO Stamford 13   26 July 1489

Release from John Stede and John Fraunceys of Staunford to Thomas Stok clerk, Henry Wykes clerk, and Thomas Kesteuen of Staunford of all their right in two tenements, one grange and one garden in Staunford, of which the two tenements are in the parish of St Mary between the tenement of John Frebarn' on the east and that of the gild of Corpus Christi on the west, abutting on the highway on the south; and the grange is situated in Scoftgate Gate in the parish of St Clement between a grange of the rectory of St Clement on the west; and the garden is in the parish of St George the martyr between the garden of John Pounceby barber on the west and a lane on the east [blank for name of lane], and abuts on the king's highway to the south.

No witnesses

Dated 26 July 4 Henry VII.

Seals: two plain seals (one with an animal, the other illegible).

713 MCO Stamford 14   5 June 1310

Grant from Hugh de Alvertone burgess of Stanford to William de Wysebeche fisher of Stanford of his houses in the parish of St Mary at the bridge of Stanford between the tenement of John de Stokes to the west and that lately of John Maymund to the east, reaching from the highway south and to the tenement of John le Longe skinner of Stanford north.

Witnesses: John Sampson of Stanford, Eustace Malherbe, Clement de Meltone, John de Wermigton', Henry de Oyltone, Hugh Auerey, Roger le Skauellere, John Abselon, John le Counte, William de Deping, Robert le Blound, John de Wysebech', John Neue, William de Apethorp', John Mancourneys, Alan de Rothewell, Thomas Hasteuel, Richard Pyte, Geoffrey le Stynour (or Styvour), Richard Messager, John de Melton', William Benet clerk, all of the same.

Given at Stanford Friday before Pentecost 3 Edward son of Edward.

Seal: small round wax *Seal:* merchant's mark; inscription illegible.

714 MCO Stamford 15   17 July 1336

<u>*Grant*</u> from Henry de Tiddeswelle of Staunford to Walter atte Nonnes of the same and Joan his wife in consideration of the receipt of a certain sum of money of a messuage in Staunford which the said Henry lately acquired from Walter Auerey situate in the parish of St Mary at the bridge between the tenement of the said Walter on the west and that which he holds of William de Apethorp for the term of his life on the east.

Witnesses: John Bertilmeu, Robert de Pakington', Richard de Linc', John Cokerel, William Flemyng', William de Makeseye, John Sampson, William Joseph clerk.

Given at Staunford Wednesday before the feast of St Margaret the Virgin 10 Edward III.

Seal: round wax seal; merchant's mark with letter H.

715 MCO Stamford 16   20 July 1436

Another original copy of 711, adding after the words "William Storeton baker", "and Elizabeth his wife". Small seal. Minor spelling variants.

716 MCO Stamford 17   24 August 1480

<u>*Release*</u> from Margery Goldesworth of Staunford Lincs widow to John Stede of Staunford and Anabel his wife of all actions against them.

No witnesses

Given at Staunford 24 August 20 Edward IV.

Seal: small seal (a shield with arms).

717 MCO Stamford 18   **30 December 1454**

Lease in perpetuity from William Rouceby chaplain to Hugh Phelippe (Phelyppe) and Katherine his wife of a messuage in Staunford in the parish of St Peter, late of St Mary of Bynnewerke between the tenement lately of Thomas Warde on the east and that lately of John Wortynge now called the rectory of the said parish of St Mary of Bynnewerke, abutting on the highway to the south; which messuage he lately had conjointly with Nicholas Caldecote esquire, William Rouceby carpenter and Robert Brownn' late of Staunford glover by the gift and feoffment of John Clerke late of Talyngton.

Witnesses: Laurence Mylton' Alderman of Staunford, William Broun', John Broun', Richard Cok, Robert Derley, Simon Canon.

Given at Staunford Monday before the feast of Circumcision 33 Henry VI.

Seal: small seal letter R. and crown.

718 MCO Stamford 19   **24 August 1466**

Grant from William Cawns clerk to Henry Cok of Staunford of a tenement in the parish of St Mary by the bridge of Staunford between the tenement called le Belle on the south and that of the prior of Broke on the north, abutting on the highway on the east and on the tenement of John Molle on the west, which tenement he lately had conjointly with Richard Goldysworth and Katherine his wife, Richard Lee and Walter Stokkys deceased by the gift and feoffment of John Parker late of Staunford vyntener.

Witnesses: Robert Hans Alderman of Staunford, Thomas Gregory, John Gregory, Robert Nevour, Thomas Middleton'.

Given at Staunford 24 August 6 Edward IV.

Seal: small *Seal:* a star of David.

719 MCO Stamford 20   **24 August 1429**

Grant from Richard Walynton of Staunford clerk and Richard Saltby of the same chaplain to Robert Lee smith, Robert Bendowe, John Whytesyde and Richard Lee wright of Staunford of a tenement in the parish of St Mary by the bridge of Staunford between that of the prior of Broke on either side and abutting on the tenement of Thomas Basset on the south and on the highway north; which they had conjointly with Emma Saltby deceased by the gift and feoffment of Roger de Ouresby parson of the church of St George of Staunford.

Witnesses: Thomas Basset, John Palfreyman, Thomas Spicer, John Leche goldsmith, John Englysshe of Staunford.

Given at Staunford 24 August 7 Henry VI.

Seals: two small seals with letters (one W, one illegible).

720 MCO Stamford 21   19 May 1498

Grant from John Stede of Staunford Lincs burgess to Thomas Philipp of the same draper of two tenements in Staunford in the parish of St Mary between the tenement of John Frebarne to the east and that of the gild of Corpus Christi to the west, abutting on the king's highway to the south which the said John had by gift and release of Henry Wykes clerk, Thomas Stok' clerk, and Thomas Kesteuen' late of Staunford.

Witnesses: Richard Canell Alderman of Staunford, William Radclyff, John Claypole, Robert Crane, Geoffrey Hampton'.

Given at Staunford 19 May 13 Henry VII.

Seal: small seal.

721 MCO Stamford 22   30 December 1454

Grant by William Rouceby priest to Hugh Phelyppe and Katherine his wife of the property described in 717 above. Same witnesses except John Broun.

Seal: letter I (?) - not same seal as MCO 18.

722 MCO Stamford 23   25 June 1414

Grant from Elizabeth Mercere sometime daughter of Henry Kyrkeby of Staunford widow to John Browe of Briggecasterton', John Palfreyman of Staunford and Alexander Hyne of the same of a messuage with a garden in Estgate in the parish of St Paul Staunford between the messuage called Goddeshous on the east and the tenement of John Corby formerly Thomas Cok's on the west, abutting on the highway north and on the street of Cornstall south.

Witnesses: Robert Staleham Alderman of Staunford, John Stenby, Thomas Spycer, John Broun' draper, John Northorp', Thomas Walyngton', Henry Bateman of Staunford.

Given at Staunford Monday after the Nativity of St John the Baptist 2 Henry V.

Seal: round seal, a shield with a cock (or eagle? very faint) "Sigillum Thome Spy…[?]; red wax

Endorsed: (early 16th century): domus parochia (Stanforde) sancti pauli proxima goddes house
Philipe

723 MCO Stamford 24   **8 October 1465**

Grant from Hugh Phelyppe of Staunford husbandman and Katherine his wife to Thomas Phelyppe mercer their son, Katherine his wife and William Etegose of Bullewyk of a messuage in Staunford in the parish of St Peter formerly [*dudum*] St Mary of Bynnewerke conveyed to them by William Rouceby in the deed of 30 December 1454 [717].

Witnesses: Robert Hans Alderman of Staunford, William Hekeham, Thomas Holton, Robert Derley, William Trewe, John Barkere, John Wylchare.

Given at Staunford 8 October 5 Edward IV.

Seals: two seals with initial R and crown (not the same).

724 MCO Stamford 25   **20 May 1433**

Grant from John Clerke of Talyngton' to William Rouceby chaplain, Nicholas Caldecote esquire, William Rouceby carpenter and Robert Broune of Staunford glover of a messuage in Staunford in the parish of St Mary of Benewerke between the tenement lately of Thomas Warde on the east and that lately of John Wortyng now called the rectory of that parish on the west, abutting on the highway south; which messuage with other lands and tenements in Staunford he conjointly with William Boneton' clerk lately deceased and Geoffrey Petard still surviving had by gift and feoffment of John Warner and Richard Thorneff.

Witnesses: John Broune 'drapyer', Thomas Basset, Richard o' the Lee wright, William Flaxman, William Tyard of Staunford.

Given at Staunford 20 May 11 Henry VI.

Seal: round seal, a merchant's mark: inscription illegible; red wax.

725 MCO Stamford 26   **14 December 1497**

Grant from Henry Wykes of Staunford Lincs clerk to John Stede of the same of two tenements in Staunford in the parish of St Mary between the tenement of John Frebarne to the east and that of the gild of Corpus Christi to the west, abutting on the king's highway to the south, which he had by the gift of Henry Wykes clerk; which (among other lands and tenements) he conjointly with Thomas Stok clerk and Thomas Kestev' formerly of Staunford both deceased had by the gift and confirmation of the said John Stede and John Frraunceys formerly of Staunford.

Witnesses: Richard Cannell Alderman of Staunford, Christopher Broun' merchant of the staple of Calais, William Radclyff', John Frebarne, Thomas Edward.

Given at Staunford 14 December 13 Henry VII.

Seal: small seal.

726 MCO Stamford 27   **21 April 1432**

Grant from Robert Broun' of Staunford husbandman to John Everard of the same chaplain, William Rouceby of the same wright and William Rouceby of the same chaplain of a messuage with a garden in Staunford in the parish of St Mary of Bynwerk between the toft lately of John Wortyng called the rectory of that parish on the west and the tenement late of Thomas Warde on the east, abutting on the highway south and on the garden of Robert Burton' north; which messuage he conjointly with John Palfreyman had by the gift and feoffment of John Clerke of Talyngton'.

Witnesses: John Palfreyman Alderman of Staunford, Thomas Basset, John Broun' draper, Robert Bendowe, William Gyddyng flaxman of Staunford.

Given at Staunford 21 April 10 Henry VI.

Seal: small seal with initial I.

727 MCO Stamford 28   **18 May 1490**

Grant from Alice Bryghton' of Staunford and Robert Parnell clerk to Roger Richardson and William Richardson' the sons of Nicholas Richardson' *alias* Bryghton' late of Staunford of a messuage with a garden in Estgate in the parish of St Paul Staunford between the messuage called Goddeshous on the east, the tenement of the gild of the Holy Trinity on the west, abutting on the highway north and on the street called Cornstalle south, which they together with the said Nicholas Richardson' *alias* Brighton', Henry Cok and John Richardson', all deceased, had by the gift and feoffment of Elizabeth Storeton' widow.

Witnesses: Thomas Philip Alderman of Staunford, John Gregory, John Dycon', John Yetson', John Fissher.

Given at Staunford 18 May 5 Henry VII.

Seals: two blank seals.

728 MCO Stamford 29   **25 December 1447**

Grant from John Parkere of Staunford vyntener to Richard Goldysworth, Katherine his wife, William Cawns clerk, Richard Lee and Walter Stokkys of a tenement in the parish of St Mary by the bridge Staunford between the tenement called Le Belle on the south and that of the prior of Broke on the north, abutting on the highway east and on the tenement of John Molle west, which he had conjointly by the gift and feoffment of William Caunce clerk and Henry Scherman'.

Witnesses: Laurence Milton' Alderman of Staunford, John Page, Robert Nevyr, John Molle, Thomas Basse of Staunford.

Given at Staunford, the feast of the Nativity of Our Lord 26 Henry VI.

Seal: small seal, with merchant's mark; red

729 MCO Stamford 30   22 July 1350

<u>*Release*</u> from Katherine daughter of Walter de Aylyngton to John de Cestre of Staunford of all her right in a messuage in Staunford in the parish of St Mary at the bridge between the tenement of Thomas de Pontefracto on the west and that of the said John which was William de Apethorp's on the east, extending from the highway south to the churchyard of the church of St Michael the Greater north; which messuage belonged to her grand-father Walter atte Nonnes of Staunford.

Witnesses: Henry de Tyddeswell', William de Apethorp', Roger de Mundham, William de Steandeby, Richard de Wirthorp', Conrad de Weldon', Walter de Baldeswell', John Bate, Richard Barbier of Staunford.

Given at Staunford Thursday the feast of St Mary Magdalene 24 Edward III.

Seal: round seal of arms, effaced; white wax.

730 MCO Stamford 31   20 May 1433

<u>*Release*</u> from Geoffrey Petard of Talyngton' to William Rouceby chaplain, Nicholas Caldecote esquire, William Rouceby carpenter and Richard Broune [*recte* Robert] of Staunford glover of all his right in the messuage in the parish of St Mary de Benewerke as detailed in John Clerke's charter of the same date [724] , between the tenement lately of Thomas Warde on the east and that lately of John Wortyng now called the rectory of that parish on the west, abutting on the highway south.

Dated 20 May 11 Henry VI.

Seal: with letter H. and palm leaf
[see John Clerke's charter of the same date 724]

731 MCO Stamford 32   5 June 1457

<u>*Grant*</u> from John Neel of Staunford barber to John Molle and Alice his wife, William Hekam', Robert Nevere, Richard Lyttestere and Thomas Basse of a messuage in Staunford in the parish of St Mary by the bridge between the tenements of the prior of Broyk on both sides, abutting on that lately of Thomas Bassett on the south and on the highway on the north; together with a garden in the street called Scoftegat between the tenement of the rector of the church of St Clement on the west and that of John Abethorp' on the east

Witnesses: John Page Alderman of the town of Staunford, Thomas Gregory, John Estwyk, Richard Goldesworth'.

Given at Staunford 5 June 35 Henry VI.

Seal: round seal; a merchant's mark? (includes letter W); red wax.

732 MCO Stamford 33   **28 December 1377**

Release from Walter Makesey of Staunford to Richard de Chesterfeld clerk, Henry de Barton'clerk, Robert de Morton' of Bautre, James de Keueton' clerk, Margaret widow of John Chestre of Staumford and John Longe of Staumford and their heirs of all his right in a messuage in Staumford in the parishes of St Mary and St Michael next to the tenement late of Thomas de Pountfret on the west, abutting on the king's highway south, which messuage was formerly John de Chestre's of Staumford.

Witnesses: John Broun of Staumford, William de Steynby of the same, John Spicer of the same, John de Weldon' of the same, Robert de Staumford.

Given at Staunford, Monday before the Circumcision 1 Richard II.

Seal: round seal of arms, too faint to be made out; in the sinister, a quatrefoil "S' Thome L...."; red wax.

733 MCO Stamford 34   **26 August 1466**

Grant from Henry Cok of Staunford to Margery Goldysworth widow, William Caunce clerk, Henry Hopkyns chaplain, Alexander Tyard and Thomas Middleton' of a tenement in the parish of St Mary by the bridge Staunford between the tenement called Le Belle on the south and that of the prior of Broke on the north, abutting on the highway east and on the tenement of John Molle on the west; to hold for the term of the life of Margery and also of Alice daughter of Richard Goldesworth according to the last will and testament of the said Richard.

Witnesses: Robert Hans Alderman of Staunford, William Hykeham, Robert Nevour, John Molle, John Estwyke.

Given at Staunford 26 August 6 Edward IV.

Seal: small seal with letter P; red wax

734 MCO Stamford 35   **10 June 1500**

Grant from Roger Rychardson' otherwise called Roger Bryghton' of Tychemarsh, Northants and William Rychardson' *alias* William Bryghton' of Staunford, Lincs, sons and heirs of Nicholas Bryghton' late of Staunford and Alice his wife to Thomas Phelyp' Alderman of the town of Staunford of a messuage with a garden in Estgate in the parish of St Paul Staunford between the messuage called Goddeshows to the east and the tenement of the gild of the Holy Trinity to the west, abutting on the highway to the north and on the street *(vicum)* called Cornstall to the south which they had by the gift and feoffment of the said Alice Bryghton' their mother and which she together with the said Nicholas her late husband, Robert Parnell clerk, Henry Cok and John Rychardson', all deceased, had by the gift and feoffment of Elizabeth Storeton' widow of William Storeton.

Witnesses: William Spencer, William Ratclyff, John Cleypole, Robert Crane, Andrew Stodard.

Given at Staunford 10 June 15 Henry VII.

Seals: two plain seals, with leaves pressed on the wax.

735 MCO Stamford 36   11 March 1511

Grant from Thomas Phyllyppe of Staunford Lincs draper to Thomas Phyllyppe clerk his son of all his manors, messuages, lands and tenements etc in the towns and fields of Staunford (Lincs), Owndell (Northants) and Nortluffenham (Rutland); appointing William Grenefeld of Staunford his attorney to give seisin.

Witnesses: Richard Wastlen esquire Alderman of Staunford, William Radclyff, Thomas Cowper, Thomas Clopton, William Hynkersell', Robert Sandwath, William Snoo, John Ley burgesses of the said town.

Given at Staunford 11 March 2 Henry VIII.

Seal: round seal; merchant's mark (a woolpack.(?)); red wax.

736 MCO Stamford 37   12 October 1486

Confirmation (indented) of the grant of the same date [738] from John Stede and John Fraunceys of Staunford Lincs to William Broune of the same, in which one tenement is described as being in the parish of St Mary called Le Cressaunt and as being of the annual value of 4 marks, the other adjacent and of the annual value of 13s 4d, the grange in St Clement's parish 10s, and the garden in St George's parish 3s.4d.; namely, that if the said J Stede and J Fraunceys pay the said W. Broune £4 for 8 years until the sum of £32 be fully paid, and also shall fully repair the said tenements and find sufficient tenants to pay the said annual rents for 8 years, then the said premises shall revert to J Stede and J Fraunceys and their heirs and the said grant shall be null and void.

No witnesses

Dated 12 October 2 Henry VII.

Seals: two small seals (one a female head and 'Iohis (or Iohn) Stede', the other an animal).

737 MCO Stamford 38   **12 February 1450**

Grant from Richard Lee of Staunford to John Molle of the same 'sadelere' for the whole
of his life of a tenement in the parish of St Mary the Virgin by the bridge in Staunford
between the tenements of the prior of Broke on both sides and abutting on that lately of
Thomas Bassett on the south and on the highway north; and also a garden in the street
called 'le Scoftegate' (Schofftegate) between the tenement of the rector of the church of
St Clement on the west and that of John Apethorpp' on the east, abutting north on the
highway, with remainder on the death of the said John to his daughter Elizabeth and the
heirs of her body; failing whom, the said tenement and garden are to be sold and the
whole profits to be spent in celebrating for the souls of Robert Lee, the said John and
Elizabeth and all to whom they are bounden and in other almsdeeds.

Witnesses: William Broun' Alderman of Staunford, John Broun', John Page, Richard
Blowghyn', William Hykkam.

Given at Staunford 12 February 28 Henry VI.

Seal: small
[See 751]

738 MCO Stamford 39   **12 October 1486**

Grant from John Stede of Staunford and John Fraunceys of the same to William Broune
of the same merchant of two tenements, a grange and a garden in Staunford of which the
two tenements are in the parish of St Mary between the tenement of John Frebarn' on
the east and that of the gild of Corpus Christi on the west, abutting on the highway on
the south; and the grange is situated in Scoftgate Gate in the parish of St Clement
between a grange of the rectory (of St Clement) on the west and a grange of Christopher
Palfreyman on the east and abuts on the king's highway to the north; and the garden is in
the parish of St George the martyr between the garden of John Pounceby barber on the
west and a lane on the east [blank for name of lane], and abuts on the king's highway to
the south; which they lately had by the gift and feoffment of Richard Wermouth clerk,
Henry Wykes clerk, Robert Hanse and Henry Cok of Staunford.

Witnesses: Thomas Kesteven' Alderman of Staunford, John Gregory, John Gybbes, John
Dycon', Henry Cok.

Given at Staunford 12 October 2 Henry VII.

Seals: two small seals (one a female head and Iohis [Stede]; the other an animal); red wax.

739 MCO Stamford 40   **5 June 1484**

Release from John Molle of Staunford Lincs 'sadelere', Robert Nevoure and Richard
Litstere of the same to William Hikeham (being in his possession) of all their right in a
messuage in the parish of St Mary by the bridge and in a garden in Scoftegate between
the tenements of the prior of Broke on both sides, abutting on the tenement lately of

Thomas Bassett to the south and the highway to the north; and in a garden in a street called Scoftegate between the tenement of the rector of St Clement to the west and the tenement of John Apthorp' to the east.

Dated 5 June 1 Richard III.

Seals: three blank seals.

740 MCO Stamford 41   14 August 1328

Grant from Walter Auerey of Staunford and Marjorie his wife to William de Apethorp of Staunford in consideration of the receipt of a certain sum of money of a garden in Staunford in the parish of St Mary at the bridge extending in length from the building of the messuage in which they dwell to the south to the chamber of the messuage of the said William called le Yvi chambre to the north, and in breadth from the tenement of the said William west to the tenement of Walter atte Nonnes east.

Witnesses: Hugh de Thurleby, Roger Scauelere, Henry de Tiddeswelle, Walter atte Nonnes, William Flemyng, John Bartholomew, Andrew Godfelaugh, William Joseph.

Given at Staunford Sunday vigil of the Assumption of BVM 2 Edward III.

Seals: two round seals; nearly effaced; white wax.

741 MCO Stamford 42   10 March 1442

Release from William Rouceby carpenter and Robert Broune of Staunford glover to William Rouceby chaplain of all their right in a messuage in Staunford in the parish of St Mary of Benewerke between the tenement lately of Thomas Warde on the east and that lately of John Wortyng now called the rectory of the said parish on the west, abutting on the highway south.

Given at Staunford 10 March 20 Henry VI.

Seal: one small seal, with letter I.

742 MCO Stamford 43   22 May 1498

Release from John Stede of Staunford Lincs burgess to Thomas Philipp' of Staunford draper, being in possession, of all right in two tenements in the parish of St Mary Staunford between the tenement lately of John Frebarne to the east and the tenement of the gild of Corpus Christi to the west, abutting on the king's highway to the south which he had by grant of Henry Wykes clerk, Thomas Stoke' clerk and Thomas Kesteuen late of Staunford.

Witnesses: Richard Canell Alderman of Staunford, William Radclyff, John Claypole, Robert Crane, Geoffrey Hampton'.

Dated 22 May 13 Henry VII.

Seal: small seal.

743 MCO Stamford 44   **27 April 1480**

Extract from the Roll of the Court and View of Frankpledge of Cecilia duchess of York held at Staunford, allowing the claim made by the prior of Broke to a piece of land as his freehold, measuring 30 feet in length by 19½ feet in width annexed to his messuage in the parish of St Peter adjacent to the rectory of the church of that parish.

On the dorse, the names of the jurors making the inquisition: John Wykys, William Wod, Christopher Palfreyman, Thomas Howys, Robert Broun, William Darley, Ralph Holand, John Care, John Wurdeler, William Hebbys, John Barbour, Robert Sylton, Robert Bauntre, Thomas Clopton.

Dated Thursday after the feast of St George martyr 20 Edward IV.

744 MCO Stamford 45   **19 March 1347**

Grant from William de Apethorp of Staunford to John de Cestre of Staunford and Lora his wife of a messuage in the parish of St Mary at the bridge between the tenement of the said John and Lora on the west and that of Robert Pyte on the east and extending from highway east to the grantor's tenement which was formerly that of Thomas de Birton on the north.

Witnesses: John Cokerel Alderman of Staunford, Robert de Wyk, Robert de Pakyngton, William Flemyng, Richard de Pappelee, Robert Pyte, Richard de Wirthorp, Geoffrey de Marcheford of Staunford.

Given at Staunford Monday after the feast of St Gregory pope 21 Edward III.

Seal: small round seal; ornamental (unclear); white wax.

745 MCO Stamford 46   **2 March 1432**

Release from John Palfreyman of Staunford to Robert Broun of Staunford husbandman of all his right in the tenement in the parish of St Mary of Bynwerk between the rectory of the said parish to the west and the tenement of Thomas Warde to the east abutting on the highway south and the garden of Robert Burton' north, which they jointly had by gift and feoffment of John Clerk of Talyngton'.

Witnesses: Thomas Basset of Staunford, Thomas Spycer, John Broun draper, William Flaxman, William Rouceby of the same.

Given at Staunford 2 March 10 Henry VI.

Seal: small red seal (a stag under a tree?)

746 MCO Stamford 47   **31 March 1336**

<u>*Grant*</u> from Walter Auerey of Staunford to Henry de Tyddeswell of the same merchant, in consideration of the receipt of a certain sum of money, of a messuage in the parish of St Mary by the bridge in Staunford between the tenement of Walter atte Nunys on the west and that of William de Apethorp' senior on the east, extending to the highway south.

Witnesses: Walter atte Nunys, William Flemmyng', William de Apethorp' junior, William de Thurleby burgesses of Staunford.

Given at Staunford Sunday Easterday 10 Edward III.

Sea1: small seal, effaced; white wax.

747 MCO Stamford 48   **10 October 1479**

<u>*Release*</u> from John Dycon of Staunford to William Hikeham of the same (being in possession) of all his right in a messuage in the parish of St Mary at the bridge at Staunford between the messuage of the gild of Corpus Christi and the Blessed Mary in the tenure of Thomas Stable on the east and the inn [*hospicium*] of the said William Hikeham called Le Antelope on the west, one end abutting on the south partly on the inn of Le Taberd and partly on Le Antelope, and north on the highway; which messuage he together with John Stede had by the gift and feoffment of John Gygoure clerk, John Etton' and Thomas Gunby.

Given 10 October 19 Edward IV

Seals: missing

<u>*Endorsed:*</u> vijs viid

748 MCO Stamford 49   **22 February 1325**

<u>*Grant*</u> from William de Wysebech senior of Staunford to Walter atte Nunnes burgess of Staunford, in consideration of the receipt of a certain sum of money, of his houses in the parish of St Mary at the bridge Staunford between the tenement of Walter Awerey to the east and that of the grantor to the west, extending from the highway south to the courtyard of the said Walter north.

Given at Staunford Friday the feast of St Peter *in cathedra* 18 Edward son of Edward.

Witnesses: Eustace Malherbe, William de Apethorpe', Roger Scauelere, Andrew Godfelaugh', Richard Pite, John Bertelmeu, William Parmenter clerk.

Seal: round seal, broken; a female figure; inscription illegible; green wax.

749 MCO Stamford 50   **4 December 1483**

Release from Henry Cok of Staunford, John Molle and Nicholas Edwarde of the same to Thomas Philip' of Staunford mercer (being in possession) of all their right in a tenement in the parish of St Mary by the bridge Staunford between the tenement of William Broune merchant called Le Belle on the south and that of the prior of Broke on the north, abutting on the highway on the east and on the tenement of John Molle on the west

Dated 4 December 1 Richard III.

Seals: two small seals (one with letter I).

750 MCO Stamford 51   **15 February 1472**

Grant from William Sutton of Staunforde iremonger, Alexander Tyarde of the same bocher and Martin Worthen of the same to Thomas Phillipp of Staunforde mercer, William Hikeham, William Gaywode and Geoffrey Hampton' of ten acres of arable land, of which four lie together in the field of Staunforde between the land of Robert Hans on the south and that of the rectory of St Peter on the north, the east end abutting on the land of John Edenham of Staunforde plasterer; one acre in the same field between the land of John Edenham on the north and that of the church of St John the Baptist on the south, abutting east on the green ditch; three acres together with same field between the land of Peter Sowtere on the west and that of Thomas Bayarde on the east, the north end abutting on the land of Robert Darley; a half acre in same field between the land of John Knott of Tynwell on the south and that of William Broune on the north, the east end abutting on 'Empyngham gate'; and one acre and a half in same field between the land of the rector of St Peter on the south and that of Robert Skynner on the north, abutting west upon 'Empyngham gate'; which he had by gift and feoffment of William Rouceby late of Staunforde chaplain.

Witnesses: John Gregory Alderman of Staunford, Robert Nevoure, John Nele, John Decon', John Molle.

Given at Staunforde 15 February 11 Edward IV

Seals: three small seals

751 MCO Stamford 52   **12 February 1450**

Power of attorney from Richard Lee to William Bressere of Staunford ferrour to give seisin to John Molle of Staunford sadler of the property conveyed in the above deed [737].

Given at Staunford 12 February 28 Henry VI.

Seal: small

752 MCO Stamford 53   21 July 1436

Release from Alexander Mercer late of Staunford and Robert Strikyswold of the same to William Storeton' of Staunford, William Broun draper of the same and John Munke of the same clerk of all their right in the messuage and garden adjacent conveyed in the preceding deeds of John Warner's of 20 July [711, 715].

Given at Staunford 21 July 14 Henry VI.

Seals: one missing; the other, the letter T.

753 MCO Stamford 54 (a)   12 February 1300

Grant from Herbert son of William le Mercer formerly burgess of Stanford and Aldusa his wife to Walter de Wyssenden burgess of the same, in consideration of the receipt of a certain sum of money, of all the houses in the parish of St Mary at the bridge Stanford situated between the house of Roger son of Simon de Vffyngton to the west and that of Alfred le Grater to the east.

Witnesses: Andrew Neye, John Sampson, Clement de Meutone, Peter de Wyssebech, Roger Rove, Alfred le Grater, John Absalon, John le Cunte, John le Seler.

Given at Stanford Friday before St Valentine the martyr 28 Edward son of Henry.

Seals: two round seals; black wax:
(i) a star: "…Herbert le Merc"
(ii) an eagle: S'Alduce ux' Herberti"

Endorsed: Carta Herberti le Mercere (contemporary)

754 MCO Stamford 54 (b)   12 February 1450

Original copy of *grant* as in 737, but substituting in place of the last clause, a clause that if the said Elizabeth die without issue, then the premises shall remain to the said John Molle and his heirs and assignees.

755 MCO Stamford 55   11 February 1473

Release from John Murdok of Staunford executor of the testament of Elizabeth Storeton' to Alice Bryghton' widow of all actions against her.

Given at Staunford 11 February 12 Edward IV

Seal: small seal with merchant's mark and monogram.

756 MCO Stamford 56   18 July 1482

Discharge by John Palady *in decretis baccal'*, commissary general of John bishop of Lincoln in the archdeaconry of Northampton to Thomas Philipp' of Stamford executor of the late William Edgose formerly of Bulwyk of all further account of his administration.

Dated 18 July 1482.

Seal: faint impression of official seal, broken: a canopied figure; beneath, a demi-figure with hands clasped; inscription illegible.

757 MCO Stamford 57   20 May 1433

Bond from John Clerke of Talyngtone to William Rauceby chaplain in 20 marks.

Endorsed with the condition, namely, that the said John shall indemnify the said William against any claim on the part of Avicia Cooke or her kin to a tenement lately acquired from the said John in the parish of St Mary of Benewerke.

Dated 20 May 11 Henry VI.

Seal: small seal (the Lamb and Flag?)

758. PECK, *ANTIQUARIAN ANNALS OF STANFORD*
mostly (but not all) from Browne's Hospital

While compiling his Academia Tertia Anglicana or Antiquarian Annals of Stanford *1727, Francis Peck set out to acquire all he could about the history of Stamford, both original material and notes. In particular, he purchased from the son of the Rev William Forster (formerly rector of St Michael the Greater in Stamford and later of St Clement Danes in London and then warden of Browne's Hospital 1703-8) all the documentation that Forster had collected in anticipation of writing a history of the town. It would seem that these were in note form drawn from the original title deeds relating to the Hospital's property in Stamford but the original title deeds have now disappeared (the title deeds to the properties outside of Stamford remain with the Hospital and are now in the Lincolnshire Archives Office, see above items 668-670. For a fuller discussion and Peck's letter of purchase of these notes, see Alan Rogers,* William Browne's title deeds and late medieval Stamford, *Archives vol xx 2009 pp 1-7).*

Peck published the notes from these deeds in that book up to the year 1460 and marked them with the initials BH to indicate their source. All materials after this date have been lost when Peck's papers were lost (Rogers and Hartley, Introduction to reprint edition of Peck *1979 pp x-xii; and Peck's Preface pp x-xii). He also included one or two other stray deeds which he collected from various sources; these have been included here and noted. I have corrected the text where the correction is obvious, for the palaeography of the note-taker was somewhat lacking; much of most texts are missing.*

Where a date appears in brackets, this indicates that Peck does not know the date of the deed but because of the chronological nature of his book, he puts it under a particular year in his text. Almost certainly the deed was undated or the date was illegible. Because of his determination to adhere strictly to this chronological sequence, it is very likely that when a deed refers to an earlier transaction, Peck has detached that information and inserted it into the year of the earlier transaction as a separate entry. One example of this may be the entries on page 12/6, another may be 14/2 and 14/3; sSee also 13/13. I have left all such deeds undated to be dated from internal evidence. The notes rarely indicate the nature of the deed and at times it is stated to be a sale where it is clearly a release or a quitclaim. I have removed such statements unless there seems good reason to include it (e.g. 12/13). Peck sometimes adds his own comments about these deeds; unless he indicates the source of the information contained in these comments, I have omitted them.

On several occasions Peck includes from these notes an entry reading (for example) "Alderman of Staunford this 8 & 9 R2 John Brown. B.H". Since the only records drawn upon, so far as is known, from Browne's Hospital were deeds, presumably these notes come from deeds in which the Alderman's name appears as a witness. I have inserted these entries as a separate deed so that we may get some rough impression of the number of transactions which are represented in this (now lost) collection.

Peck also cites information from Mr Forster (he includes some letters which Mr Forster wrote to other persons) and on one occasion (11/66) indicates against this information the letters BH which denotes the material came from Browne's Hospital.

Peck's book is divided into chapters with separate pagination; thus 9/18-19 refers to chapter 9 pages 18-19.

758. NOTES OF DEEDS FROM PECK

1. 9/18-9 Thomas son of Peter Marche of Staunford to ... one half acre lying in Wirthorp meadows between the meadow of Walter west and the meadow of William east, heading upon the cross called Maydenes Cross south and on the bank of the Welland north [prob undated, late thirteenth century; Peck, writing of the year 18 Edward I, 1289-90, says "about this time if not earlier"]

2. 9/19 Henry Morin of Stanford to Samson son of Roger Cokla of Stanford one house in Hovensty situated between the house of Nigel Madding north, a house sometime of Robert Lennes of the other part, to have and to hold etc paying therefore yearly to the lord of the fee or his assigns 12d at the two terms of the year [undated, "about this time if not earlier"; under 18 Edward I 1289-90]

3. 9/20 Philip Gangy [Gaugy] of Stanford clerk to Hugh Child burgess of Stanford a yearly rent of 12d with appurtenances, i.e. reliefs, escheats etc, to be received from those houses which Simon son of the said Hugh held of him on the lane called Ovensty [undated: under 18 Edward I 1289-90]

4. 9/22 Emma daughter of Walter de St Eadmundo late burgess of Staunford to Walter de Staunford the physician her house in the parish of St Michael's the Greater , namely in the south head of the lane called Feldovensty between her tenement north and south, a tenement of Roger de Offington west and the aforesaid lane east. ["about this time or some time before" 19 Edward I 1290-91]

5. 9/22 Emma[2] wife of Bartholomew de St Feriolo to Walter the physician of Stanford a house in Colgate etc. Ralph then rector of the church of St Mary at the bridge was appointed surety for this transaction. [Peck says 1291]

6. 9/22 Richard son of Richard le Ferun of Stanford clerk to Walter de Stanford physician one little empty place lying near the lane called Ovenesty in the parish of St Michael the Greater between a place of Symon Child north and a house of Bartholomew the clerk south. ["when I find not"]

7. 9/26 Bartholomew de St Feriolo burgess of Stanford to Walter de Stanford physician a house in the parish of St Michael the Greater being the same which Emma (daughter of Walter de St Eadmundo) wife of Bartholomew gave to the said Walter the physician [in 19 Edward I, 1290-91] before her marriage. Witnesses: Alexander Lucas, Geoffrey de Cottismore etc burgesses of Stanford. [Peck says 1293]

8. 9/28 ... Chyld burgess of Staunford to William de Saham apothecary a tenement in the parish of St Michael the Greater in the lane called Ovenesty between a tenement of Hugh Hod north and a tenement of Walter the physician south. [Peck puts this under 25 Edward I 1296-7]

9. 9/30 W de Saham apothecary of Stanford to Walter the physician one void place situated in the parish of St Michael the Greater in the lane there called Feldovensty between a tenement of Hugh Hod north and a tenement of the said Walter south. [Peck says "in the beginning of 26 Edward I" 1297-98].

10. 9/30-31 Matilda prioress of the church [monastery] of St Michael by Staunford and the nuns there with the assent of their prior sir William de Stob... gave in exchange to Walter the physician of Stanford two pieces of arable land lying in the north field of Stanford, whereof one piece lies between the land of Symon de Morchore east and the land of the prior of St Leonard west, abutting on the land of the lord earl Warenne etc for a certain house situated in St Martin's parish in Webstergate between a tenement of their own north and a tenement of Henry Faderman south, and for one half acre of arable land with the meadow adjoining in the fee of the abbot of Peterborough which lies between their own land west and the land of Robert de Pontefract east abutting on Kilinereshenge north etc. [Peck puts this under 26 Edward I 1297-98]

11. 9/34 Emma wife of Bartholomew de St Feriolo to Walter the physician all her right and claim in those houses standing in the parish of St Michael the Greater Stanford near the lane called Feldovensty east, between a tenement of the said Walter in Colgate and her tenement contiguous to the same tenement south, and a curtilage of the same Walter north. [Peck puts this under 27 Edward I 1298-99]

12. 9/34 Emma [as above] to the same Walter houses in Colgate in the parish of St Michael the Greater between the houses of the said Walter east and north and a tenement of Roger de Offington west and the king's highway south. [27 Edward I 1298-99]

---

[2] Peck says that this Emma is the same as Emma daughter of Walter de St Eadmund; see 7 below.

13. 9/34 Ralph de Casterton bought of John Stykeling his houses in the parish of St Peter Stanford standing between the lane called Puntdelarchsty east and the house of John Puntdelarches west "and that house which is nearer to him Ralph on the forsaid lane" etc for 15 marks of silver paid him in his necessity. [27 Edward I 1298-99]

14. 9/34 John Braban "bought of" Richard Baldeswel merchant his right in a certain rent of 10s due from some houses there. [27 Edward I 1298-99]

15. 9/34 John son of John Gilbert barber of Stanford to "the foresaid John Braban" houses in the parish of St Peter. Witnesses: Robert the bursar etc. [27 Edward I 1298-99]

16. 9/45 Letitia daughter of Hugh Hod late burgess of Stanford gave to Nicholas Hod burgess of Staunford one shop standing in the parish of St Michael the Greater in the lane called Feldovensty. [29 Edward I 1300-01]

17. 9/47 Roger le Porter of Stanford to Richard le Clerc (son of Richard le Ferun late of Stanford[3]) one place in the parish of St Michael the Greater in the street called Ovensty between the other place of the same Richard south and the houses of Simon Child north; also the whole court of the place between his hall in the street called Ovensty in the same parish south and his cellar and the gallery over it in the same street north as far as the gable end of the same gallery. [under 30 Edward I 1301-02, Peck says "about this time or before"]

18. 9/48 Richard son of Roger le Porter to Reginald Smeremen of Staunford his house standing in Colgate in the parish of St Michael the Greater between the lane leading to the market east and the house of Bartholomew the preacher west. ["about this time" 30 Edward I 1301-2]

19. 9/54 Augnes ... of Staunford to Augnes a house standing in the lane called Punchelardsty in St Peters parish Stanford between a tenement of John Braban north and the castle dyke south. [32 Edward I 1303-04]

20. 9/56 Hugh Pert of Bradecroft to Beatrice late the wife of Joseph le Ferrour burgess of Staunford his houses in the village of Bradecroft situated between a house of the nuns of St Michael west and a house of ... east as they extend themselves from the king's highway north and the milldam of Bradcroft south. Witnesses: W Edelyn of Bradcroft, Walter de Tinwell of the same. ["the same year" 33 Edward I 1304-05]

21. 9/56 Hugh son of Matilda late the wife of Aylrich of Bradcroft "sold" his share *in furno* (oven) in Bradcroft to William Scot of Bradcroft. Witnesses: W Edelyn, Walter de Tinwel etc. Dated 33 Edward I [1304-5]

22. 9/58 Beatrice widow of Joseph le Ferrour burgess of Stanford to William de Apethorpe burgess of Staunford her houses with a croft and ... curtilages situated in the village of Bradcroft between a tenement of the nuns of St Michael west etc. Witnesses: Edelyn of Bradcroft, Hugh Pert of the same. Dated at Stanford 34 Edward I [1305-6].

---

[3] Peck puts these words in brackets – it is not clear if they come from the deed

23. 9/58 ... relict of Reginald Smereman of Staunford to Walter the physician one shop standing in the parish of St Michael the Greater between a tenement of the aforesaid Walter west and the lane called Feldovensty east. [34 Edward I 1305-06]

24. 9/58 Nicholas de Flemang son of John de Flemang of the East Gate late burgess of Stanford "now also sold the houses and lands of Clement de Melton burgess of Stanford". [34 Edward I 1305-06]

25. 10/2 John son of Bartholomew de St Feriolo in Staunford to Walter the physician the houses etc standing in Colgate in the parish of St Michael the Greater between a tenement of the said Walter east and a tenement of Walter Wiseman west. [Peck puts this under 2 Edward II 1308-9]

26. 10/8 Agnes late the wife of Peter de Nousle of Bradecroft released to Walter son of Walter de Tinwel of Bradecroft etc one piece of meadow lying in the crofts of Bradecroft between the meadow of John Drayton east and the water running from the fountain [*a fonte*, or spring] west and abutting on the king's highway north and about the water of the Welland south. Dated: Staunford 19 January 1315

27. 10/8 Milicent relict of Gilbert ... late burgess of Staunford to Stephen de Sleford butcher in Staunford two rods of land in Sundersoken in the county of Rutland. Dated Staunford Monday before Hocktide 8 Edward II (1 April 1315)

28. 10/8 Deed relating to the Angel Inn in the parish of St Mary's at the bridge; Nicholas de Burton lord of Tolethorpe was a witness. [8 Edward II 1314-15]

29. 10/8 John de Knotteshale to Henry de Ashwell houses standing in the parish of St Michael Cornstal Staunford between a tenement of the prior of Newsted east and a tenement of Richard de Baldeswell west as they extend from the king's highway north as far as the wall of the town of Staunford south. [8 Edward II 1314-15]

30. 10/9 Geoffry le Parchmener to Walter son of William de Apethorp houses standing in the parish of St Peter between a tenement of the said Walter east and a tenement of Gilbert de Wymondham west, extending from the king's highway north as far as the castle dyke south. [9 Edward II 1315-16]

31. 10/10-11 Agnes relict of Symon Chyld of Staunford to Henry the physician of Staunford a void place of ground lying in the parish of St Michael the Greater in the street called Feldovenesty between a tenement of Richard de Brigestoke north and a tenement of the said Henry the physician south. Witnesses: Roger le Scanclerc, John le Long, Richard le Coupere etc burgesses of Staunford. [Peck puts this under to 10 Edward II 1316-17]

32. 10/13-14 Robert the physician of Staunford to Alice late the wife of W de Folkyngham clothier in the same [town] two cellars with the shop above situated in the parish of St Martin Staunford between a tenement of Stephen de Sleford north and a tenement of John de Folkingham south extending from the king's highway west to a tenement of the said Stephen east, to be held of the capital demesne of that fee etc.

Witnesses: Richard Berthi then bailiff of the lord abbot of Burg etc. [Peck puts this under 12 Edward II 1318-19]

33. 10/15 Agatha de Reynham relict of John de Knotishale burgess of Staunford to John Blackman woolmerchant in Staunford one tenement in the parish of St Clement without Scoftgate between the tenements of Richard Baldeswel on either part, extending from the king's highway north to the croft of W Bunting late burgess of Staunford south. [12 Edward II 1318-19]

34. 10/22 Robert le Flemyng of Staunford to John de Christemnes burgess of Staunford two acres of arable land lying in Staunford fields near the mill that was Eustace Malherbe's abutting on the land of the priory of St Leonard east. [20 Edward II 1326-27]

35. 11/1 Robert the smyth in Staunford to John Christemnes burgess of Staunford all the tenement which is in the parish of St Clement without Scoftgate between a tenement of Richard Pyth east and a tenement of the aforesaid John Christemnes north. [1 Edward III 1327-28]

36. 11/2 Robert son and heir of Simon Peert of Bradecroft to Henry le Knocker of Stanford a messuage with a public oven erected in the same and a curtilage adjoining with appurtenances situated in Bradecroft extending from the king's highway south to the arable land of W Edelyn and Simon de Brassingburg north. Dated at Bradecroft Thursday after Lammas Day 2 Edward III (4 August 1328).

37. 11/3 Alice relict of W Folkynham clothier to Cecily her daughter and John and Peter her sons a house in the parish of St Martin. [2 Edward III 1328-29]

38. 11/3 Simon de Brassingburg of Bradecroft and Alice his wife to Henry le Knocker of Stanford leather-dresser one house with their meadows in Bradecroft, the house extending from the king's highway south to the garden of the said Henry north. Dated at Bradecroft Tuesday St Valentine Day 3 Edward III (14 February 1329)

39. 11/6 Henry de Empyngham chaplain of Staunford to Richard de Pappele fishmonger of Staunford one acre of arable land "above" the fee of the abbot of Burg between the lands of the nuns of St Michael on either side and abutting on the king's highway north and on Burle lound south; also three rods of arable land lying above the fee of the lord abbot of Burg between the land of Thomas de Chesterton south and the land of the hospital of St Giles north and abutting on Burlesyk west and on the lands of the nuns of St Michael east. [Peck says 7 Edward III, 1333-34]

40. 11/12 Thomas son of Robert de Stapelford to Richard de Hawville of Staunford the western moiety of one messuage situated on Cleymont between a tenement of Hugh le Rede west and the other moiety east, together with the reversion of the other moiety. Witnesses: Richard de Tiddiswel, Roger le Skanclerc burgesses of Staunford etc. Dated Staunford ... 8 Edward III (1334-35)

41. 11/34 Emma relict of Richard de Baldeswel of Staunford to W son of Robert de Dyngele of Ingethorp one grange with a garden adjoining without the gates of Scoftegate situated between a tenement belonging to the mass of the Blessed Virgin celebrated in

the church of All Saints in the Market at Staunford east, and extending from the king's highway north to the arable land of sir William de Burton knight south. Witnesses: Thomas de Ravele Alderman of Staunford and Robert le Moigne of Staunford. Dated 24 December 11 Edward III (1337)

42. 11/34-35 Adam de Normantoun rector of St Mary Bynwerk to Richard de Rothwel of Staunford and Agnes his wife a messuage situated in the parish of St Mary Bynwerk between a tenement of Richard Randolf east and the street which leads down to the river Welland west. [Peck puts this under 12 Edward III 1338-39]

43. 11/35 Reymund de Nottingham of Staunford apothecary to Amice his daughter one shop with a loft etc situated byhindebak between a tenement of John lord Warenne south and a tenement of the late Henry Bronds north and annexed to the shop of Nicholas de Eston east. [Peck puts this under 14 Edward III 1340-41]

44. 11/35 Henry de Carelton of Staunford to John Mazoun all his tenements there whereof one is situated in the parish of St Mary ... [at the bridge] between a tenement of Walran de Baston west and the street called Corewensty east; another tenement is situate between a tenement of the lord abbot of Croyland north and the town wall of Staunford south in the same parish; and one tenement standing in the same parish between a tenement of John de Pekebriggs west and a tenement of the late Henry de Silton. [Peck puts this under 14 Edward III 1340-41]

45. 11/35-36 Walter le Halver burgess of Staunford to John his eldest son two messuages jointly situated in St Andrews parish near the way called Claymond, and the one piece of land adjacent with one dovecote standing in the same which were formerly Peter de Wermyngtons; with one spring on the west part of the said messuages; all of which are situated between a messuage of Margaret who was the wife of Hugh de Thurleby east and a messuage of the said Walter west, and abut on the common way called Claymond south and upon the town wall of Staunford north. [Peck puts this under 14 Edward III 1340-41; see 758.55]

46. 11/36 Deed: Witnesses: W le Fleming Alderman of Staunford ... Dated ... November 14 Edward III (1340)

47. 11/36 Deed: Witnesses: W le Flemyng Alderman of Staunford ... Dated Sunday feast of St Botolph 15 Edward III (17 June[4] 1341).

48. 11/36-37 William in the Waulles to Robert de Scotelthorp one messuage situated in the parish of All Saints in the Market between a tenement of the prior of Fineshade of the one part and a tenement of Emma de Baldeswel of the other, and likewise one shop with a loft etc situated between a shop of the late William del Cley (or Clev) of the one part and the king's highway called Wollrowe of the other. [Peck puts this under 15 Edward III 1341-42]

49. 11/37 John Blackman of Staunford the elder to John Cokerel one house built within his messuage which stands without the gates of Scoftegate between the tenements

---

[4] Peck says the feast of St Botolph was celebrated on 23 March but the date in the *Handbook of Dates* is 17 June

of the aforesaid John Cokerell ... and a tenement of W de Skelton north; extending from the king's highway east to the land of sir William de Burton knight west; the which house extends from a certain chamber to the hall of my messuage aforesaid annexed north and to my garden south. [Peck puts this under 15 Edward III 1341-42]

50. 11/38 Deed. Robert de Ashbourn of Staunford merchant [Peck puts this under 17 Edward III 1343-44]

51. 11/38 W Man of Tallington to John son of Nicholas de Okeham goldsmith of Staunford one shop with a loft etc situated in the street called Byhyndeback. [Peck puts this under 17 Edward III 1343-44].

52. 11/38 Robert son and heir of John de Folkyngham of Staunford to sir Thomas de Bernack parson of the church of Stretton upon the Fosse one messuage in Staunford upon the fee of the lord abbot of Burg situated between a tenement of W Wynd south and a tenement of the late Walter de Hallestead north extending from the king's highway west to St Martins croft east. [Peck puts this under 17 Edward III]

53. 11/39 Peter son of Cecily daughter of Alice sometime wife of W de Folkyngham clothier to John Young of Easton two cellars with a loft etc [as in 32]. [Peck puts this under 19 Edward III 1345-46]

54. 11/39 Thomas de Bernack sometime parson of Stretton on the Fosse afterwards vicar of Sutirton in Holland to John le Yonge of Eston a messuage in Staunford in the fee of the abbot of Burg [as 32 above] together with another messuage called Swal... Stede situated between a tenement of W Wynd north and a tenement sometime of W Lystere south extending from the king's highway west to St Martins croft east. [Peck puts this under 19 Edward III]

55. 11/43-4 John son of Walter le Halver to Richard de Hauville burgess of Staunford the messuages etc given to him by his father [as in 45]. [Peck puts this under 21 Edward III 1347-48]

56. 11/46-47 Stray deed relating to land in North Witham

57. 11/47 John de Apethorpe of Staunford to Reymund le Knokker of the same in one place with appurtenances in Bradecroft extending from the king's highway south to the garden of the same Reymund north. Dated at Staunford Sunday after the feast of the Purification [no year: Peck puts it under 23[5] Edward III which gives 8 February 1349]

58. 11/47 W Apethorp burgess of Staunford to John Knot chaplain four messuages, one cottage, 17 acres of arable and one acre of meadow; three messuages are together situated upon Cleymount between a tenement of the abbot of Crowland east and a tenement of Robert de Wykes west; the other messuage is situated in the street called Behyndebak between a tenement of the abbot of Thorney north and a tenement belonging to the mass of St Mary in the Market south. The cottage lies between a

---

[5] The text of Peck gives this year as 29 Edward III but it is clear from the context that this is a misprint for 23 Edward III as it comes between the year 22 Edward III on page 11/46 and 24 Edward III on page 11/48. The sequence of years is firm.

tenement belonging to the mass of St Mary near the bridge east and a tenement of W de Melton west. Two acres of land abut on the land of the nuns of St Michael etc north and the land sometime belonging to the castle of Staunford south; two acres abut on the land belonging to the chapel of St Thomas the martyr north. [Peck puts this under 24[6] Edward III]

59. 11/49 Deed Richard de Waltham parson of Colines-weston [Collyweston] by Stanford. [26 Edward III, 1352-53]

60. 11/49 Deed Witness: W de Steandeby Alderman of Staunford. Dated Staunford Friday in Whitsun week 26 Edward III (1 June 1352)

61. 11/51 W de Steandby burgess of Staunford to Robert de Wylingham one messuage in the liberty of the abbot of Burg in St Martins in the street called le Hyegate between a tenement of John Young of Eston north and a tenement of ... Malherbe south, extending from the king's highway west to the land of sir William de Birthorp east. Witnesses: W de Schyllington Alderman of Staunford etc [Peck puts this under 27 Edward III 1353-4]

62. 11/56-57 Deed [probably not Stamford deed] refers to Henry Engayne now at Eston supra montem by Staunford [under 29 Edward III]

63. 11/57 Indenture[7]: sir Geoffrey de la Mar knight and Dame Joan his wife to John Savage of Stanford, lease of King's Mills at Stanford for ten years at rent of 40s a year . Witnesses: Richard Personric, William Her... Thomas, Geoffrey, Henry Deynes etc Dated at Empingham Monday feast of St Matthew the apostle 29 Edward III (21 September 1355)

64. 11/58 Deed Witnesses: John de Chestre Alderman of Stanford. Dated Monday after feast of Annunciation 32 Edward III (1 April 1358[8])

65. 11/58 W Mous of Stanford to W Everard a garden with appurtenances in Bradecroft. "The same year" [1358-59]

66. 11/58 Deed mentions a wooden cross standing in Staunford fields in the county of Rutland. [32 Edward III 1358-59]

67. 11/58 Deed mentioning Thomas de Bernak rector of St Peter's church Stanford. [32 Edward III 1358-59]

68. 11/58 Nicholas de Eston of Staunford to John Savage baker one messuage situated in the racoun rowe in the parish of St Michael the Greater between a tenement of John Templer south and a tenement of W de Apethorpe north, extending from the king's highway east to a tenement of Richard de Lincoln west [32 Edward III] [see 758.78]

---

[6] see previous footnote
[7] This is probably not a BH deed as Peck says the original is in his hands and he does not give it the BH reference he gives to all the other deeds.
[8] this date is suspect as the feast of the Annunciation in 1358 was also Palm Sunday.

69. 11/63 W son of Thomas Lymmbrenner of Staunford to W de Flete of Staunford one garden beneath the liberty of the abbot of Burg etc between a tenement of W Sadeler of Staunford west and the way which leads to Burle east, abutting on Borough-gate north [40 Edward III] [see 758.70]

70. 11/63 W de Flete to W Rouland of Staunford of the above garden [undated]

71. 11/64 William son of John de Apethorpe to Robert de Aepthorpe [*sic*] one tenement in Westgate in the street called le Gannoks situated between a tenement of the aforesaid Robert east and a tenement of the prior of Sempyngham west, extending from the king's highway north to a tenement of the said prior south. [42 Edward III 1368-69]

72. 11/64 Henry Brond of Staunford to Alan Capper of the same one shop with a loft etc in the street called Behyndebak situated between a schop [*sic*] of Joan who was the wife of Reimund Spycer south and a schop [*sic*] of Robert Gressinghale north, extending from the king's highway west to a tenement of Richard de Ardern east. [42 Edward III 1368-69]

73. 11/64 Deed ... an acre of land at the Thwertdykes between the green fosse west and butting upon the Tunge north. [43 Edward III, 1369-70]

74. 11/65   Robert Grissinhale to Richard Baroun of Willesthorpe two shops in Staunford in the parish of All Saints in the Market between a tenement of Henry Brond south and a tenement of Walter de Baldeswel north, extending from the way called Behindebak west to the king's highway east. [44 Edward III 1370-71]

75. 11/65 Deed Witnesses: W de Styandeby Alderman of Staunford 44 Edward III (1370-71)

76. 11/65 Quitclaim[9] by Alice daughter of Richard Cokerel of Staunford to the executor of the will of John Yonge the elder of Eston by Staunford all actions. Dated Eston Sunday after Epiphany 44 Edward III (12 January 1371)

77. 11/65 Richard Ellington parson of Eston by Staunford, John Tyler and Roger Clerk of the same chaplains to John Young three messuages in Staunford beneath the liberty of the abbot of Burg etc. [45 Edward III 1371-72]

78. 11/65-6 John Savage to W Brid of Staunford his messuage in racoun rowe between a tenement of John Templer etc [as above 68] [45 Edward III 1371-72]

79. 11/66 Gilbert Jakes to Thomas de St Ives one empty place in le Gannok between a tenement of the aforesaid Gilbert east and a tenement of the prior of Sempyngham etc. [46 Edward III 1372-74]

80. 11/66 John Brown was Alderman of Staunford 48 and 49 Edward III [Peck cites this information as coming from BH deeds but it is not clear how unless he acted as a witness to more than one deed]. [1374-76]

---

[9] this is not a BH deed

81. 11/67 Adomar Malherbe of Staunford to sir Richard vicar of the parish church of All Saints beyond Staunford bridge and to sir John Bond chaplain one garden in the liberty of the abbot of Burg between a tenement of Robert de Burlee north and a garden of John Spycer south, abutting on the king's highway west. [Peck says "the same year" i.e. 50 Edward III, 1376-77]

82. 12/2 Thomas de Wadingtoun of Staunford to John Broun of Staunford, W de Melton parson of the parish church of Holy Trinity at Staunford, Robert de Bury parson of the parish church of St Paul at Staunford and to John Bonde of the same chaplain one messuage situated in the parish of St Mary at the bridge with a curtilage adjacent, between the lane called Corwansty east and a messuage of John Taverner west, abutting on the king's highway south and on a tenement of Margery Marchesfeld north etc. Witnesses: John de la Panetrie etc. [1Richard II 1377-78]

83. 12/2 John de Crouland of Staunford to John Bonnde chaplain one messuage with appurtenances situated within Staunford in the liberty of the abbot of Burg, namely Est-by-the-Water, situated between a tenement of the said John de Crouland east and the empty place called the Pynfold late John de Wyteryngs west, extends from the king's highway south to the bank called Welland north. [1 Richard II 1377-78]

84. 12/2 Walter Baldeswel of Staunford to W Hamerton one shop with one loft etc situated in the parish of All Saints in the Market between a tenement of Richard Ardern south and a shop sometime of Richard Brasyers of Willesthorpe north and abutting on the king's highway called Behynde-the-bak west, which was the shop of Alan Capper. [1 Richard II 1377-78]

85. 12/2 Agnes wife of Alan Capper of Staunford to Peter Goldsmith of the same shop with a loft etc [as in 758.84] [1 Richard II 1377-78]

86. 12/2 Peck says that John Broun was Alderman of Stamford 1 Richard II [1377-78] and cites BH deeds

87. 12/3 John son of Agnes Hert of Staunford to John Trenchepayn one messuage situated in the parish of St Michael the Greater ... in Colegate in the lane called racones rowe between a tenement of Richard Forester south and a tenement of W Brid north, abutting on the king's highway east and a tenement of John Hert west. [2 Richard II 1378-79]

88. 12/3 Peck says that Robert Prat was Alderman of Stamford 2 Richard II [1378-79] and cites BH deeds

89. 12/3 John Trenchepayn to W Makesey of Staunford and W Brid of Rihale one messuage [as in 758.87]. [3 Richard II 1379-80]

90. 12/3 W Makesey to W Brid the said messuage [758.87] on condition that W Brid and heirs or assigns shall pay yearly for ever to the warden of the chantry of the church of St Clement in Staunford six shillings silver. [3 Richard II 1379-80]

91. 12/3 Peck says that Henry Bukeden was Alderman of Stamford 3 Richard II (1379-80) and cites BH deeds.

92. 12/5-6 Richard Hawvel to John his son several messuages in Stanford which he bought of Walter le Halver in 21Edward III. [3 Richard II 1379-80]

93. 12/6 Peck says that Henry Bukeden was Alderman of Stamford 4 Richard II (1380-81) and cites BH deeds

94. 12/6 Deed: Witness: John Long Alderman of Staunford. Dated Monday after Assumption of BVM 5 Richard II [19 August 1381]

95. 12/6 Deed ... one empty place situated in the parish of St Mary Bynwerk in Stanford in the street called the Gannoc between the empty place of Robert Grymes east and a tenement of the prior of Sempyngham west, abutting on the king's highway north and a garden of the prior of Sempyngham south. [5 Richard II 1381-82]

96. 12/6 Gilbert Jakes to Thomas de St Ives the above empty place [Peck says "sometime later" than 5 Richard II 1381-82]

97. 12/6 William Everard to W Thomas of Staunford parchemyner one curtilage beneath his close with appurtenances in Bradecroft between the land of lord Thomas le Despenser knight east and a garden of sir Reymund Knokker chaplain west, abutting on the king's highway south and on the land of sir John Hawvell chaplain north. Witnesses: W de Styandeby Alderman of Staunford etc. Dated at Staunford Thursday after the feast of St Mathew apostle [5 Richard II – i.e. 26 September 1381]

98. 12/6 sir Richard perpetual vicar of the parish church of All Saints beyond the bridge of Staunford and sir John Bonde chaplain to John Spycer of Staunford one garden within the liberty of the abbot of Burg between a tenement of Robert de Burlee north and a garden of the said John Spycer south, abutting on the king's highway west. [6 Richard II 1382-3]

99. 12/8 Alderman of Stamford John Spycer 6 Richard II [1382-83]

100. 12/8 W de Bottesford rector of St Mary Bynwerk 6 Richard II [1382-83]

101. 12/10 John Brown Alderman of Stamford 8-9 Richard II [1384-86]

102. 12/13 Joan sometime wife of Simon Cokerel to Walter Mace two acres of arable land lying together in little Burlee fields between the land of the late[10] Gilbert de Chesterton west and the land of the late W Wych east, abutting on the land of the Fir[m][11] of St Peter north and the king's highway south. [9 Richard II 1385-6]

103. 12/13 Joan late the wife of Simon Cokerel of Staunford to W Stacy one shop with loft above and one and a half acres of arable land; which shop is situated behynde-the-back in the parish of All Saints in the Market between a shop of the late Richard Ardern north and a shop of John Long south; the acre and a half of land lie together at Pertes

[10] this may be "late of" rather than "of the late"
[11] thus in Peck.

crosse between the way called Tynwell-gate north and the parson of St Peter's land south. [10 Richard II 1386-87]

104.12/13 Gilbert Jakes of Staunford "quitted" to W Styandeby of the same all claim to two acres of meadow lying together in Brodeing between the meadow of John Long north and the Holm near Eston mill-holme south, abutting on Estholm west. Witnesses: Thomas Cok Alderman of Staunford etc. Dated: Saturday after feast of St Thomas apostle 10 Richard II (22 December 1386)

105.12/18[12] "Several persons" to sir John Machon warden of the chantry of St Clement Staunford one messuage and one empty place with appurtenances in the town of Staunford wherof the messuage is situated in the parish of St Peter Staunford between a tenement of the gild of BVM at Staunford west and St Peter's church east, abutting the king's highway north and a tenement of John Tyler south; and the said empty place lies between a tenement of John Chester west and a street called selverstrete east, abutting the king's highway south and a tenement of John Chester north. Witnesses: John Longe Alderman of Staunford etc. Dated: Staunford Sunday after the feast of St Barnabas 11 Richard II (14 June 1388)

106.12/20 Henry de Herdeby rector of St Michael the Greater [12 Richard II 1388-89]

107.12/21 John de Sowresby Alderman of Stamford 13 Richard II [1389-90]

108.12/21 Walter Baldeswel to Thomas Storm of Staunford chapman one shop with a loft above situated behinde-the-bake in the parish of All Saints in the Market between a shop of the late Richard Ardern north and a shop of John Long south. Witnesses: Richard Forster etc. Dated Thursday after feast of St James apostle 13 Richard II (29 July 1389)

109.12/21 Alderman of Stamford 14 Richard II Henry Bukeden [1390-91]

110.12/21-22 John Fulsham of Staunford to Richard de Depyng one garden in the liberty of the abbot of Burg in the Hyegate between a garden of the nuns of St Michael south and a garden of the late sir W Hastmel chaplain north, as it extends itself to the king's highway east. [14 Richard II 1390-91]

111.12/28 Alderman 16 Richard II John de Apethorpe [1392-93]

112.12/29 Alderman 17 Richard II John Spicer [1393-94]

113.12/29 Will of Sarra Tanner[13] of Stamford etc. I will that John Brown and Maud his wife my daughter have all the rents and tenements etc in the parishes of St Mary at the bridge and St George to them and their heirs etc, with remainder to the brethren and sisters of the gild of St Mary at the bridge and Corpus Christi for ever. I will moreover that the said John, Maud and their heirs have two messuages situated in Spalding with six acres of meadow there, with remainder to the brethren and sisters of the gild of Holy

---

[12] there is no reference B.H. given in Peck; it may be a Town Hall deed .
[13] other sources show that the original read Taverner

Trinity of Spaldyng for ever. Dated Friday feast of SS Simon and Jude (28 October) 1394

114. 12/29-30 Margot relict of John Croyland of Staunford to John Bonde rector of St Mary at the bridge one messuage in the parish of All Saints beyond the bridge in the liberty of the abbot of Burg between his own proper messuage east and a messuage of John Hawe west abutting the king's highway south and the water called Weland north. [18 Richard II 1394-95]

115. 12/30 John Bonde parson of St Mary Bynwerk to Thomas Catworth of Staunford skinner and Roger Palfreyman one messuage etc situated in Staunford the liberty of the abbot of Burg, to wit est-by-the-water between a tenement of John de Croulande east and a tenement of the abbot of Burg west, abutting the king's highway south and the bank called Welond north; which messuage was John de Croulandes. [18 Richard II 1394-95]

*116.*12/30 John Marchefeld to Henry Herdbi one messuage standing in Collegate in the parish of St Michael the Greater Stanford between a tenement of Thomas Barbur east and a tenement of the prior of Fynneshede west abutting the king's highway north and a garden of John Brown taverner of Staunford south. [18 Richard II 1394-95] *[See 125]*

117. 12/30 William Rouland of Staunford to Thomas Barker of Staunford a garden in the liberty of the abbot of Burg between a tenement of Thomas Corby west and a way which leads towards Burlee east abutting towards Burle-gate north and on the land of John Chester sadeler south. [18 Richard II 1394-95]

118. 12/30 Another deed this year mentions a messuage standing in St Mary Bynnewerk between a tenement of late Richard Randolfes [18 Richard II 1394-95]

119. 12/30 Deed mentions sir William rector of St Mary Bynnewerk [18 Richard II 1394-95]

120. 12/30 Deed Witnesses: John Long Alderman of Staunford. Dated the feast of St Michael 18 Richard II (29 September 1394)

121. 12/30 Deed Witnesses: Robert Locksmith Alderman of Staunford. Dated the feast of St Edmund king and martyr 18 Richard II (20 November 1394)

122. 12/30 Deed Witnesses: John Long Alderman of Staunford. Dated the feast of St Clement 18 Richard II (23 November 1394)

123. 12/30 Deed Witnesses: Robert Stolam Alderman of Staunford. Dated Thursday before the purification 18 Richard II (28 January 1395)

124. 12/33[14] Final concord between Stephen Makeseye of Staunford and ... Grenham clerk complainants and John de Herlington of Yakesley defendant touching eight messuages, 54 acres of land, 18 shillings of rent etc in Staunford and the advowson of

---

[14] this is not a BH deed

the chantry at the altar of St Nicholas in the church of St Clement in Staunford [20 Richard II 1396-97]

125. 12/33 H Herbi of Staunford to Richard Bulwike of Staunford messuage in Collegate [as in 116]. [20 Richard II 1396-7]

126. 12/33 Joan late wife of Richard Baron to ... her son two shops situated in All Saints in the Market between a tenement of Reginald Mercer south and tenement of John Longe north extending from the way called behynde-bak west to the king's highway of another part east. Witnesses: William Stacy Alderman of Staunford. Dated 1 May 20 Richard II (1397)

127. 12/40 Walter Smith of Extone to Richard Stake of Stanford a messuage situated in All Saints in the Market between a tenement of the prior of Fyneshed of the one part and a tenement of Robert Stoleham of the other part and one shop with a loft etc in the same parish between a shop of Geoffrey Bemfeld of the one part and the king's highway called Wolrowe of the other; and four acres and three rods of land lying separated in Staunford fields which were John Pursers by demise of the lord of the town. [21 Richard II 1397-98]

128. 12/41 John de Apethorpe Alderman of Stamford 22 Richard II [1398-99]

129. 12/41 Richard Stake to John Smith of Staunford a messuage situated in All Saints in the Market between a tenement of prior of Fyneshed south and a tenement of Robert Stoleham north. [22 Richard II 1398-99] *[See 127]*

130. 12/41 John Spycer of Stanford to Stephen Manlyster ? of Stanford a messuage with four acres of arable land in the town and fields of Stanford and Bernack; which messuage is situated in the liberty of the abbot of Burg between a messuage of W de Sybeston east and a messuage of John Palfreyman the younger west, abutting on Martynscroft south and the king's highway north. [22 Richard II 1398-99]

131. 12/42 Deed: Witnesses: John Spycer Alderman. Dated 28 February 23 Richard II [?][15]

132. 13/4 Laurence Hawvile rector of All Saints beyond the bridge of Staunford to John Everard and William Sybbeston two messuages in the liberty of the abbot of Burg whereof one was situated in est-by-the-water between a tenement of William Sybbeston east and a tenement late Anice Brown west, extending to the king's highway south and the banks of the Welland north; the other in est-by-the-water between a tenement of John Croyland east and a tenement of the abbot of Burg west abutting on the king's highway south and on the bank of the Welland north. [1 Henry IV 1399-1400]

133. 13/4 John Jakes son and heir to Gilbert Jakes of Staunford to Robert Dufhouse of Staunford mercer a messuage with a dovecote in Bradecroft in the parish of St Peter Staunford. Witnesses: John Longe Alderman of Staunford etc. Dated: Staunford Friday after Conception [2 Henry IV – i.e. 10 December 1400]

---

[15] this date is inaccurate; the 23rd year of Richard II was a short one (June to September 1399) as he was deposed.

134.13/5 W Rowland of Staunford to Agnes wife of John Gilder esquire a garden [as 69 and 117]. [under 3 Henry IV]

135.13/6 Deed Witnesses: Stephen Makesey Alderman of Staunford Thursday after the feast of St Michael 4 Henry IV (4 October 1403)

136.13/6 Robert Dufhouse of Staunford mercer to John of the pitt of the same a messuage with a dovecote situated in Bradecroft in St Peter's parish. Witnesses: Stephen Makesay Alderman of Staunford etc. Dated Tuesday next after the feast of Sts Peter and Paul [4 Henry IV – i.e. 3 July 1403]

137.13/6 Deed mentions John Stabley rector of the parish church of St John the Baptist in Staunford. [5 Henry IV 1403-4]

138.13/7 John Palfreyman of Staunford to John Longe of the same a parcel of a garden in Cornstall in St George's parish, containing in length 15 virgates and a half by the king's standard and in breadth 8 virgates, between a garden of John Longe the elder west and his own garden east, abutting on an 'orchat' of the said John Longe the elder south and a garden of the same John north. [8 Henry IV 1406-7]

139.13/7 Lawrence Hawvell chaplain of Staunford to Ralph Taylor of Staunford one messuage situated in the liberty of the abbot of Burg, to wit east-by-the-water between a tenement of Robert Staleham east and a tenement of Richard Staunton of Burg west abutting the king's highway south and on the bank of Welond north, which was Richard Palfreymen's chaplain of Staunford [9 Henry IV 1407-08]

140.13/7 John Everard chaplain of Staunford "confirmed" the above messuage to the same Ralph Taylor which messuage the foresaid John and William Sibston chaplain had by gift of Lawrence Hawvell vicar of All Saints beyond the bridge of Staunford [9 Henry IV 1407-08]

141.13/7 Richard Paynton *alias* Ramsey of Staunford to Godfrey Gedney one messuage situated in the parish of St George between a garden of Thomas Barker east, a messuage of the abbot of Thorney west, abutting on the town wall south and the king's highway north. [10 Henry IV 1408-9]

142.13/7 William Bradecroft of Staunford to John Hawvell vicar of All Saints in the Market a piece of meadow lying in the crofts of Bradecroft between the meadow of John in the pitt east and the meadow of John de Apethorpe west abutting on the mill holme south and the king's highway north. Witnesses: John Palfreman Alderman of Staunford etc. Dated Friday eve of St Thomas apostle 11 Henry IV (20 December 1409)

143.13/7-8 Nicholas Hickson of Withorp to John Brown of Staunford draper two shops with appurtenances situated in the parish of All Saints in the Market between a tenement of late Richard Merceres south and a tenement of John Longe north extending from the way called behynde-bak west to the king's highway of another part east, which shops were Robert Barons of Willesthorp chaplain. [11 Henry IV 1409-10]

144.13/8 Richard Bulwick of Staunford bocher to John in the pitt of Staunford and to Robert Parker of the same two gardens in Bradecroft abutting the king's highway south etc. Witnesses: Ralph Bond Alderman of Staunford. Dated Tuesday after feast of St Matthias 12 Henry IV (3 March 1411)

145.13/8 Deed. Witnesses: John Chandeler Alderman of Staunford etc Dated Wednesday after the feast of St Thomas apostle [13 Henry IV - i.e. 23 December 1411]

146.13/8-9[16] Prior of Beauvale Notts to trustees (John Grene of Grantham, William Asheby esquire, John Lurley and Roger Dalim chaplain and their heirs the perpetual advowson of St Paul's church in Stanford. Witnesses: Alexander Hyne Alderman of Staunford, John Steneby, John Longe, William Lyttyl, John Allcok and others. Dated 3 June 1 Henry V (1413).

147.13/9 Ralph Tailour of Staunford to Richard "Freston *alias* Freston" [*sic*] of Staunford walker and John Corby one messuage with a garden situated in the parish of All Saints beyond the bridge of Staunford est-by-the-water, in the liberty of the abbot of Burg, to wit between a messuage of Robert Stalam east and a messuage of the foresaid abbot west, abutting on the bank of the Weland north and on the way towards Burg south, which messuage was sometime L Hawville's vicar of the said church of All Saints. [1 Henry V 1413-14]

148.13/9 Deed Witnesses: Robert Stalam Alderman of Stanford. Dated: Friday feast of conception of BVM [1 Henry V – i.e. 8 December 1413].

149.13/9 John de Apethorp to John de Apethorp a messuage in the parish of All Saints in the Market between a tenement of John de Apethorp deceased and the lane called Mallory Lane west. [2 Henry V 1414-5]

150.13/13 "In the 6 H 5 John Palfreyman and John Mylton bought a messuage in St George's parish described as Godefry Gedney's" [see 141] . (1418-19)

151.13/13 Ralph Taylour to Roger Cliff of Staunford a messuage [as 139]. [6 Henry V 1418-19]

152.13/13 John Ward of Staunford bocher and Katherine Giffard to William Rawceby of Staunford chaplain and William Rippengale of Staunford their shops with a loft etc together situated between the shops late of John Clive east and a shop late of Stephen de Sleford west, extending from the Butchers street south unto Woolrow north, which shops they had lately by gift and feoffment of Richard Walington clerk and John Lindesey chaplain. [6 Henry V 1418-19]

153.13/13 Deed. Witnesses: John Stenby Alderman of Staunford etc Dated Monday after St John the Baptist [6 Henry V – i.e. 5 September 1418]

---

[16] not a BH deed; original in hands of Rev Samuel Rogers vicar of All Saints in Stanford

154.13/13 Deed. Witnesses: John Stenby Alderman of Staunford etc Dated Thursday before the feast of SS Simon and Jude (6 Henry V 27 October 1418[17])

155.13/13 Margaret relict of Richard Bulwike to Thomas Basset merchaunt a messuage as in "18 Richard II and 7 Henry V[18] above". [*sic* – given under the year 7 Henry V 1419-20]

156.13/13 Deed ... refers to eight acres of arable land lying at Lynghawe between the land of the rector of the parish church of St Peter [north] and the land belonging to the chapel of St Thomas the martyr on the bridge south abutting on Tynwell mere west. [7 Henry V 1419-20]

157.13/13 John Trenchepayn to Thomas Basset of Staunford two cellars with lofts etc in the parish of St Michael the Greater situated together in the street called Covenesty between a tenement of his own which he then inhabited north and a tenement of the prior of Fyneshede south. [8 Henry V 1420-21]

158.14/1 Geoffrey Walsh of Badyngton to John Badburgham of Bulwic six messuages and 12 acres of arable land lying severally in the town and fields of Staunford as well in the liberty of the abbot of Burg as in the demesne of Edward late duke of York. Also two messuages together situated in the parish of St George between Pekkes-hall-yarde north and a grange belonging to the prior of St Leonard south, abutting on a garden late of W Salteby east and the king's highway west. And one messuage situated in Cornstall between a tenement of Rector of the church of St Paul east and a tenement late of Thomas Storme west, abutting on the king's highway south and on a garden of Henry Cokk north. And one messuage in Cornstall situated between a tenement of the abbot of Thorney east and a tenement of lord Edward late duke of York west, abutting on a garden of John Longe south and the king's highway north.[19] [1 Henry VI 1422-23]

159.14/1 John Smith of Staunford to John Brown draper two shops situated in the parish of All Saints in the Market whereof one is situated in the Scobothes between a tenement of the lord Edward late duke of York north and a shop of the said John Brown south, abutting on the king's highway east. And the other shop is situated between a shop of John Alcock north and a shop of the aforesaid John Brown south, abutting on the way called behynde-the-bak west; which shops were of John Longe of Staunford. Also one messuage in the parish of All Saints in the Market between a tenement of the prior of Finneshevede south and a tenement of W Staleham north. Witnesses: Thomas Basset Alderman of Staunford etc. Dated 4 March 1 Henry VI (1423)

160.14/1-2 Deed ... three acres of arable land lying in Deepdale between the land of the prior of St Leonard west and the land of the rector of the church of Holy Trinity east; and two acres lying in the Kings-rise between the land belonging to the chantry in St Clements church west, abutting on Bermergores. [2 Henry VI 1423-24]

---

[17] It would seem that one of the dates of these two deeds is wrong. But the regnal year for neither deed has been recorded.

[18] These dates should read 20 Richard II and 12 Henry IV: see 125 and 144

[19] Peck continues with a different transaction. I cannot agree that this and the next transaction are all part of one deed, so I have separated them despite the fact that there is no date to this deed.

161.14/2   John Whiteside of Staunford to John Brown a garden lying in Cornstall Staunford between the town wall east and a tenement of John Stockton clerk west, abutting on the said wall south and the king's highway north; which garden was of Thomas Barker of Staunford corviser. [3 Henry VI 1424-25]

162.14/2 Deed   ... two acres lying together, abutting on the headland of the rector of Bynnewerk church north. [3 Henry VI 1424-25]

163.14/3 John Brown to Henry Whiteheved of Staunford bocher [as in 161]. [4 Henry VI 1425-26]

164.14/8 John Brygge parson of St Clements to Laurence Cheyne etc six messuages and twelve acres of arable land lying in the town and fields of Staunford both in the liberty of the abbot of Burg and in the demesne of Edward late duke of York. [8 Henry VI 1429-30]

165.14/8[20] "Fines were levied between" Thomas Basset of Staunford, John Chevercourt and Margaret his wife complainant and John Vowe of Whitwel defendant of a messuage and lands in the parish of St George in Staunford, the right of John Chevercourt. Peck says "In 1430".

166.14/9 John Everard of Staunford chaplain to W Morewod a messuage with curtilage situated in Wollrowe between a tenement of John Brown draper east and ... Tynwel west, abutting on the king's highway south. [9 Henry VI 1430-31]

167.14/10 Laurence Cheyne esquire to Richard Cokke, Richard Lee and John Halyday vicar of All Saints in the Market six messuages and 12 acres of arable land in the town and territory of Staunford as well in the liberty of the abbot of Burg as in the demesne of Edward late duke of York in the county of Lincolnshire and Pillesgate in Northamptonshire. [12 Henry VI 1433-34]

168.14/10[21] Robert Browe to Richard Wilcoks of Staunford a messuage in Staunford in the liberty of the abbot of Burg in St Martins parish in a certain street called Est-by-the-water between a messuage late of Thomas Corby west and the king's highway which leads to Burley east, abutting on the king's highway north and upon Martinscroft south; which messuage was of Agnes Melton. [12 Henry VI 1433-34]

169.14/11 W Morwood[22] of Staunford to Thomas Basset a messuage situated in the parish of St Michael the Greater between a messuage of the said Thomas west and the lane called Cheyne Lane east. [13 Henry VI 1434-35]

---

[20] this is not a BH deed; it is a copy of a court record in private hands.
[21] this deed is not marked BH but is clearly one of the Hospital's deeds.
[22] Peck points out that William Morwode was contracted to build the church at Fotheringhay at this time. As mason, Peck says he was Alderman in 1436, Peck 14/11-12. But there may have been more than one W Morwode at this time.

170.14/11[23] Richard Wilcoks to Nicholas Ward of Staunford baker a messuage which he had of Robert Browe (see 168); the same Nicholas Ward to Thomas Semark esquire and Thomas Gassale of Withering wright. [14 Henry VI 1435-36]

171.14/12 John Brown of Staunford draper to William Browne his son his entire shop, lately four shops together situated in the parish of All Saints in the Market between a tenement of the duke of York south and a tenement of Margaret Sutton north, abutting on the king's highway east and the way called behyndbak west. The said John Brown appointed John Halyday[24] his attorney to deliver seisin of the same to his said son. Witnesses: Richard Lee Alderman of Staunford. Dated Tuesday after the feast of St Matthias the apostle 15 Henry VI (26 February 1437)

172.14/13 John Warner of Brune [Bourne] to William Rolstone of Staunford a grange situated in the parish of St Clements in the place called Skoftgate without the north gate between a grange of the rector of St Clements east and the end of the town west, abutting on the king's highway north and a croft of Robert Burton south. [16 Henry VI 1437-38]

173.14/13[25] John Chenecourt [Chevercourt] to William Gydding, Richard Lee and John Briggs clerk a messuage with appurtenances lying in the parish of St Peter between a house of the gild of the BVM east, another of Simon Sclater west, the king's highway north and another house of the said gild south; to hold to them and their heirs for ever to the use of his will. Dated 17 June 17 Henry VI (1439)

174.14/13 William Rollestone of Staunford to William Brown marchant the grange which he had of John Warner in 16 Henry VI [172]. [17 Henry VI 1438-39]

175.14/13 Richard Barker *alias* Tyler of Burley constituted W Ledys of Staunford taylor his attorney to deliver to John Smith of Burley *literatus* full seisin of and in a tenement in Hyegate in St Martins parish. [17 Henry VI 1438-39]

176.14/13 Deed ... an acre of arable land having the land of the holy nuns east and forty perches of land called litle-dale west, abutting on Empyngham way north and Tynwel heath south; which acre lies at Tynwel gallows. 17 Henry VI (1438-39)

177.14/13 Deed ... a place called Kings-rise in Staunford field. 17 Henry VI (1438-39)

178.14/14 John Smyth chaplain to William Brown a messuage situated in the street called Hyegate etc. Witnesses: Richard Lee Alderman etc. Dated 29 March 18 Henry VI (1440)

179.14/14 John Burley [26] vicar of Wotton by Wodestoke in Oxfordshire to Robert Browe etc a tenement in Heygate between a tenement of the nuns of St Michael by

---

[23] It is not clear if this is one deed or more than one; or if this refers to sub-clauses in some previous deed. But the transactions are clear. The date is also uncertain.
[24] Vicar of the church of All Saints in the Market
[25] Peck says this deed comes from the parish records of the church of All Saints in the Market, not from BH
[26] Peck asserts that John Burley and John Smyth are one and the same.

Staunford south and a tenement of John Young north, abutting on the king's highway west and on Martinscroft east. Witnesses: John Bolde mayor of Wodestoke, John Bryd valet of the crown etc. [17 Henry VI 1438-39]

180.14/14 Deed in English: mention of Syr John Smyth preest of Burley; John Brid parker or yeoman of the crown. Dated 7 April 18 Henry VI (1440)

181.14/14 Richard Cokke of Staunford dimised to farm to Richard Blogwyn a tenement with two shops annexed situated in the parish of St Mary by the bridge called the Aungel of the hope and a grange with garden in Cornstall for the yearly rent of viij marks. [1440]

182.14/15 William Brown to John Brown the elder a messuage situated in the parish of All Saints in the Market between a tenement of the said William Brown late John Smith,s south and the vicarage of the same church north, abutting on the town wall east and the king's highway west; which messuage was of W Welden and W Kelby. [19 Henry VI 1440-41]

183.14/15 John Lyndesey clerk to Robert Clerc and Isabell his wife a certain croft with dovecote situated in Bradecroft in the parish of St Peter with a certain piece of meadow beneath the toft aforesaid lying between the way wherin you go from Staunford to Broding and a certain mill of Richard duke of York commonly called Bradecroft mills etc which toft etc were of John Jakes. Witnesses: Robert Brown Alderman of Staunford etc. Dated at Staunford Monday after the Nativity 20 Henry VI (1 January 1442)

184.14/15-16 Robert Clerk and Isabell his wife to John Chevercourt, John Bryg, Henry Burlee, Richard Lee and Richard Cokk "the premises last mentioned". Witnesses: Robert Brown Alderman etc. Dated at Staunford Saturday the morrow of the Purification 20 Henry VI (3 February 1442). Enrolled in the castle of Staunford on Tuesday after the feast of St Valentine 21 Henry VI "and there was paid viijd in the court for so doing" (20 February 1442)

185.14/16-17[27] Court roll in which sir John Smyth chaplain vicar of Wodestoke [*sic* – see 179] confesses that he unjustly sold to William Lewys of Okeham a messuage with appurtenances situated in the liberty of the abbot of Burg in Stanford; but William Ledys of Staunford "occupier" sued as the rightful owner; letters testimonial dated at Oxford 15 March 1442.

186.14/17 John Geffron and John Herby to Richard Blogwin of Staunford one messuage that was of W Knight situated in the parish of St Michael the Greater in the street called Colgate between a tenement of Henry Sharp husbandman west and the land called Silverstreet east, abutting on the king's highway south and on a tenement of the said Henry north. Also one shop with loft etc situated in the parish of All Saints between a shop of John Brown south and the king's highway north, abutting on a shop of lord Richard duke of York east and the way called by-hind-bak west. Dated 20 March 21 Henry VI (1443)

187.14/17 Richard Blogwin to Ralph lord Cromwell, Thomas Palmer and W Armstone all the above premises. Dated 1 May 21 Henry VI (1443)

---

[27] this document was in the hands of Peck and was probably not a BH deed.

188.14/20 John Folklyn of Cantbrig and John Sybely of Staunford clerks to W Hanford chaplain a tenement and one acre of arable land situated in the town and field of Staunford in the liberty of the abbot of Burg between a tenement of the said abbot west and a tenement of John Sapcote (late of W Staleham) east, abutting on the king's highway south and on the water of the Wyland north; which was of Henry Warde of Staunford sadyler. [24 Henry VI 1445-46]

189.14/20-21 Margery relict of ... Drayton, daughter of William de Bradecroft, to her youngest son John Drayton a meadow "there"[28], 25 Henry VI (1446-47)

190.14/21 Henry Burlee etc to master William Brown a toft, dovecote and piece of meadow in Bradecroft. Witnesses: Richard Lee wright Alderman of Stanford etc. Dated at Staunford 12 June 25 Henry VI (1447)

191.14/21 John Apethorp of Staunford to W Storeton a tenement situated in the parish of St Michael the Greater in the street called Racon-rowe between a tenement of the said William Storeton south and a tenement of the said John Apethorp north, abutting on the common way called racon-rowe east and a garden of John Byllings west. [26 Henry VI 1447-48]

192.14/21-22 Richard Cokke of Staunford to W Armestone of the same tyler one shop with loft etc and one void place situated in the parish of All Saints in the Market between a tenement of late of John Brown draper south and a shop late of the same John [Brown] north, abutting on the way called behyndbak west and on the shop which John Sutton late of Staunford took and held of the lord of Staunford east. And the said void place is situated in the same street called behyndbak between a tenement of late of the aforesaid John Brown north and a void place of Peter Girdler south, abutting on a shop late of Elizabeth Mercer east and on the street aforesaid called behyndbak west; which were of John Palfreyman. [26 Henry VI 1447-48]

193.14/22 ... a tenement in the parish of St Mary Bynnewerk between a tenement of the chapter of Staunford sometime of John Apethorp east and a garden of Robert Sherman sometime the aforesaid John Apethorp west. [26 Henry VI 1447-48]

194.14/38 W Hanford chaplain to Richard Goldesworth a messuage [as in 188]. Witnesses: Thomas Gregory Alderman. Dated 9 October 31 Henry VI (1452)

195.14/38 Richard Goldesworth to W Storeton of Staunford baxter a messuage [as in 194]. Dated 16 December 31 Henry VI (1452)

196.14/43 Richard Cokk of Staunford and John Halyday vicar of All Saints in the town aforesaid to William Brown a messuage situated in the parish of St Mary at the bridge between a tenement of late of Richard Lee east and a tenement belonging to the gild of Corpus Christi and the blessed Virgin of the one part, and a tenement sometime of W Stacy of the other part west, abutting on the king's highway south and a tenement of John Vowes north. Also a messuage situated in the parish of St George in the place

---

[28] probably in Bradecroft

called Cornstall between a tenement of John Capron of either part, abutting on the king's highway south and a garden of Henry Cokk north. [33 Henry VI 1454-55]

197.14/44 Richard Witham of Grantham clerk to W Dykeman of Staunford one messuage between the workhouse late of Thomas Wyng south and the king's highway which leads towards the high cross north, abutting on the common road west and a workhouse late of W Bocher east; which messuage was of John Mott of Grantham who had it of Robert Lowick of Staunford. Witnesses: John Gregory Alderman etc. Dated 3 March? 34 Henry VI (1456)

198.14/45 Richard Cokk of Staunford merchaunt to W Gydding two acres of arable land lying together in Staunford fields in Sundersoken, whereof one and a half acres are called the headlandys and lie in the fields aforesaid and divide the field of Staunford and the field of Tynwell towards the north and south. [36 Henry VI 1457-58]

199.14/45[29] W Dykeman of Staunford mercer to W Brown marchaunt one messuage in the parish of All Saints in the Market between a shop late of Thomas Weng south and the street called Wolle-rowe north, abutting on the common road west and a shop and workhouse of Robert Skynner bocher east; which was of Richard Witham of Grantham clerk. Witnesses: William Hikeham Alderman etc. Dated 26 October 36 Henry VI (1457)

200.14/47 John son of Richard Cokk to William Brown merchaunt one messuage in Staunford situated in the parish of St Mary at the bridge called the Aungel and one grange with a garden adjacent on Cornstal. [37 Henry VI 1458-59]

201.14/47 Robert Young of Staunford to W Tundur and W Ole one garden lying in the liberty of the abbot of Burg in the street called Webster-gate between a garden of W Pope south and a tenement of the said abbot in part and a garden of Corpus Christi gild in part north, abutting on Webster-gate aforesaid east and the lands of the nuns of St Michael west. [37 Henry VI 1458-59]

202.14/66 W Storeton of Stanford to William Brown of the same merchant a tenement etc which he had from Richard Goldesworth [see 194 and 195 above]. [1459-61]

759. PRIVATE HANDS   20 January 1458
A photocopy of the following deed is in private hands in Stamford – the location of the original has not been provided.

Grant by William Armeston of Staunford sclatter to John Barewe of Staunford labourer of one messuage with cartilage adjacent situated beyond the northern gate of the town in the street commonly called Scottegate between the tenement of the late John Apethorpe on the west and the tenement of the warden of the chantry of St Nicholas in the parish of St Clement on the east, the king's highway on the south and land of the late Robert Burton towards the north. To hold of the chief lord of the fee by due service and accustomed law. Warranty clause. Sealing clause.

---

[29] Peck does not divide this transaction from the previous one, but it is clear it is a separate deed.

Witnesses: William Hekham then Alderman of Staunford, Richard Knotte, Robert Skynner bocher, John Grene, John Barr and many others.

Dated at Staunford 20 January 36 Henry VI .

760. REGESTA REGUM ANGLO-NORMANNORUM
vol. iii no 87

Grant by Henry II to the church of Holy Trinity Stamford and monks of Belvoir who own it of ten acres of royal demesne at Stamford in increase of the holding of the church

Not dated (1154-1189)

SELDEN SOCIETY

761. vol. 15 pp14-5   29 September 1316

Mabel prioress of St Michael's versus Eustace Malherbe for 8s of rent of which Eustace Malherbe disseized Matilda de Leune [Len] former prioress.   Original gift was by Alexander son of Richard son of Selona de Stamford.

Dated Michaelmas 10 Edward III
See Selden Society volume 45 pp 6-15.

762. vol. 53 No 660 pp319-20   1219

Prior of St Fromund versus Roger de St John concerning advowson of St Peter's.

763. vol. 53 No 699 pp338-40   1219

Prior of St Fromund versus James le Sauvage about the same

Prior of St Fromund versus abbot of Westminster: as above – St Fromund's right confirmed

764. vol. 53 No 700 pp340   1219

Pleas at Nottingham 1219: case 489 and case 700, Alice widow of Robert de Stanford complains that whereas by judgment of the court of the lord king she has recovered seisin of the third part of two messuages with appurtenances in Stamford (*Stanford*) which she claims as her dower ... against Henry son of Samson and Peter son of Geoffrey which she recovered from them by default so that the sheriff was commanded to give her seisin thereof, and since those messuages are in the town of Stanford wherein the sheriff does not set his hand, by the sheriff's command the bailiffs of Stanford were ordered to give her seisin thereof, and the bailiffs wished to assign her her third part in bare land and the buildings to the tenants, and she seeks that this may be emended. Her sureties for the prosecution against the bailiffs, her faith and Richard de Glendon of the county of Northamptonshire.

Note: it is not clear if the sheriff mentioned is the sheriff of Lincolnshire or Northamptonshire. The fact that her surety was of Northamptonshire suggests that the property lay in Stamford Baron (Northants) where the writ of the sheriff of Lincolnshire did not run.

SPALDING GENTLEMEN'S SOCIETY: *See Additional deeds, Wrest Park Cartulary of Crowland Abbey below.*

STAMFORD: PARISH AND TOWN HALL RECORDS

PARISH RECORDS, STAMFORD

At the time of taking these notes, the records were in the parish chest; they have, I believe, now been transferred to the Lincolnshire Archives Office and will have different call numbers.

ST GEORGE'S PARISH

765.1 PG1/1   **1324-5**

Release by Almedus Deppines to Walter Skillington of houses in the parish of St Paul situated between the tenement of Robert de Lynberew east, Star Lane west

Dated 18 Edward II.

765.2 PG1/2   **5 July 1338**

Grant Walter de Skylyngton of Staunford to dom John de Somerdeby chaplain for a certain sum of money (*pecunia*) paid to Walter of his houses situated in the parish of St Paul between the tenement formerly (*quondam*) of Robert de Lymberugh east and the lane called 'Starlane' west, extending from the king's highway south to the tenement of the abbot of 'Bruna' north; to hold of chief lord by due service. Warranty.

Witnesses: Henry de Tyddiswell, Robert de Pakyngton, Richard de Lincoln, Thomas de Berugh, William de Makeseye, John de Empingham, Thomas de Bedeford of Staunford, John Josep clerk and others.

Given at Staunford Sunday after the feast of SS Peter and Paul 12 Edward III.

Seal: tag

Endorsed: (i) Walter skellington's ffeofment to John Somerdby of a messuage att Starr Lane — 12 Edri tertii. No. 2. (17th C hand)
(ii) 12 Edward 3 (contemporary).

765.3 PG1/3   **6 July 1340**

Grant John de Somerdeby chaplain to John Nodel of Staunford, his heirs and assigns for a sum of money of one messuage with garden adjacent in Staunford situated in the parish of St Paul between the tenement of Hugh le Noble east and the lane called 'le Star Lane' west, extending from the highway south to the tenement of the abbot de Brune north, to be held of the chief lord by due service. Warranty.

Witnesses: Geoffrey de Wodeslade, John de Empingham, John de Uffington, Thomas' de Bedeford, Geoffrey Briselaunce, Thomas le Noble of Staunford and others.

Given at Staunford Thursday after the translation of St Thomas the martyr 14 Edward III and of France 1 Edward.

Seal tag

Endorsed: Feofment from John Somerdby to John Nodell 14 Edri. 3 [17th C] . No. 3.

765.4 PG1/4   **1340-41**

Grant by John Nodel to Remund Notingham and Joan his wife and Thomas their son: one messuage as in 765.3.

Dated: 14 Edward III.

765.5 PG1/5   **18 March 1370**

Lease indented from John son of Reymund Spycer of Staunford and Joan who was the wife of Reymund to Emma Waryn of Staunford for life, one messuage in Staunford situated between the tenement of William de Melton parson of the church of Holy Trinity east and the lane called 'le Star Lane' east, extending from the highway south to the tenement of the abbot de Bronne north, to hold of John and Joan and their heirs, rendering 13s 4d per annum in silver at the four quarterly feasts. Re-entry clause if rent is 15 days unpaid. John and Joan will maintain and repair the messuage at their own costs. Warranty.

Witnesses: John Broun, John de Wakirle, John Chalonier, Henry Plomer, Robert Towyn of Staunford and others.

Given at Staunford Monday after St Gregory 44 Edward III.

Seal: tag and fragment

Endorsed: Lease from John son of Remund and Frances [*sic*] his wife to Emme Waring [*sic*] 44 Edri 3tii [17th C] No. 5. 44 Ed. 3.

765.6 PG1/6   7 February 1441

Grant William Roversby of Staunford chaplain and John Marcham to Jeffrey Reest of Staunford, Agnes his wife and William Brown, messuage and garden in the parish of St Paul.

Dated: 7 February 19 Henry VI.

765.7 PG1/7   1480-81

Grant William Browne of Staunford merchant to William Reest of Peterborough and Richard Gregory of the same, messuage and garden in the parish of St Paul.

Dated: 20 Edward IV.

765.8 PG1/8   28 April 1494

Release and quitclaim from Isabella late (*nuper*) wife of William Reeste of Peterburgh Northants for myself and my heirs to Richard Gregory of Peterborough his heirs and assigns of all my right (*ius*) and claim in one messuage in Staunford with garden adjacent in the parish of St Paul between the lane called 'Starelane' west and the tenement late of Henry Cokke east, abutting on the highway south.

Given at Peterborough 28 April 9 Henry VII.

Seal: tag

Endorsed: Release from Isabell Reest to Richard Gregory 28 April 9° Henr. 7. No. 8 [17th C] 9 H 7

765.9 PG1/9   1 May 1494

Grant by Richard Gregory of Peterburgh Northants to William Spenser of Staunford, Thomas Goodloke clerk and John Byrde clerk of one messuage in Staunford with garden adjacent situated in the parish of St Paul between the lane called 'Starelane' west and the tenement of Beatrice Cock east, abutting on the highway south, which messuage I had jointly (*simul*) with William Reeste now deceased by gift and feoffment of William Browne formerly (*quondam*) of Staunford 'marchant', to hold of the chief lord by due service. Appointment of attorneys, Geoffrey Hampton of Staunford and Robert Vaghhan of Marham Northants to give seisin.

Witnesses: John Dycons Alderman of Staunford, John Frebarne, Thomas Philipp, William Radclyff and many others.

Given at Staunford 1 May 9 Henry VII.

Seal: tag

<u>*Endorsed*</u> 1ᵐᵒ Maii 9ᵒ Hen. 7ᵐⁱ   Richard Gregorye. Release to William Spencer of a Messuage &c att Starr Lane end. No. 9 [17ᵗʰ C] 9 H 7.

766.1 PG2/1   **31 May 1419**

<u>*Grant*</u> by Margery Makesey of Stauntord in tree widowhood to Emma Salteby of Staunford of parcel of my garden in the parish of St George which lies between the garden of John Longe east, the garden of Emma Salteby west, abutting on my garden north and the garden of Emma Salteby south; 9 yards (*virg*) long and 7 yards wide by standard measures, to hold of chief lord by due service. Warranty.

Witnesses: John Palfreyman then (*tunc*) Alderman of Staunford, John Stenby, Thomas Basset, John Broun draper, Robert Toft, Richard Chaundeler, Roger Wythum of Staunford and others.

Given at Staunford Wednesday the feast of St Petronilla 7 Henry V.

Seal: tag

<u>*Endorsed*</u>: Margery Makesey to Emma Salteby Wednesday the feast of St Petronilla 7 Hen. 5 [19th C]. Makesey enfeoffs Emma Saltby of parcell of a garden in St Georges parish 7° H. 7 [*sic*] [17th C].

766.2 PG2/2   **15 June 1419**

 <u>*Release*</u> Nicholas Grenham clerk to Emma Salteby of Staunford, heirs and assigns of all his right and claim in one parcel of garden in St George's parish Staunford [as 766.1].

Given at Seyton Thursday after St Barnabus the Apostle 7 Henry V.

Seal: tag

<u>*Endorsed:*</u> (i) Nicholas Grenham clerk to Emma Salteby Thursday after the feast of St Barnabus 7ᵗʰ Hen. 5 [19th C]
(ii) Grenham Released to Saltby 7ᵒ H. 5° [17th C].
(iii) A garden in St Geor parishe [16th C]

767.1 PG3/1   **23 May 1458**

<u>*Grant*</u> by Richard Goldesworth of Staunford and Katherine his wife to John Nele of Staunford and Agnes his wife of one messuage in the parish of St George between 'Pekesallyard' north and the messuage of John Nele south, abutting on the highway west

and 'Pekesall yard' east, which messuage I lately (*nuper*) held jointly with John Lyndesay clerk by gift and feoffment of Juliana Whithed in her widowhood; to hold to John Nele and Agnes and their heirs and assigns of the chief lord by due service. Warranty.

Witnesses: William Hykham then (*tunc*) Alderman of Staunford, Richard Blogwyn, Thomas Gregory, John Capron, Robert Nevour and many others.

Given at Staunford, 23 May 36 Henry VI.

Seal: two tags with fragments

Endorsed: (i) St George's Parish Staunford 23 May 36 Hen. 6. Goldesworth and wife to Nele and wife. Feoffment of a Mess, now (1813) three houses occupied by Andrews, Dixon and Hambleton. Old Church Estate No. 1.
(ii) Grant from Goldesmith [*sic*] to Jo. Nele 36 H6 [17th C].

767.2 PG3/2   **1491-2**

Grant John Nele to Alice Basham his daughter and William Radclyffe of Staunford gent of a messuage in the parish of St George, the house of John Nele south, Pecksall yard north, highway west, Pekesall yard east

Dated 7 Henry VII.

767.3 PG3/3   **1 May 1498**

Grant Alicia Basham of Staunford and William Radclyff of Staunford Lincs gentilman to Nicholas Trygge of Staunford notary public of one messuage in the parish of St George between the messuage late (*nuper*) of John Nele senior south and Pekesall yarde north, abutting on highway west and on Pekesall yard east; which messuage we had by gift and feoffment of John Nele late of Staunford senior as is contained in his charter to us to hold to Nicholas Trygge, his heirs and assigns of the chief lord by due service. Warranty.

Witnesses: Richard Canell then (*tunc*) Alderman of Staunford, Thomas Philipp, John Cleypole, Barnard Richeman, Thomas Couper, Thomas Langar and many others.

Given at Staunford 1 May 13 Henry VII.

Seal: 2 tags

Endorsed: (i) St George's Parish Staunford 1 May 13 H 7. Alice Basham and William Radclyffe to Nich. Trygge, Feoffment of a Messuage now (1813) three Messuages in the occupations of Andrews Dixon and Hambleton. Old Church Estate No. 3
(ii) Grant from Alice Basham and William Radclyffe to Tho. [*sic*] Trigg 1mo Maii 13° H 7. 4 [17th C]
(iii) Basham etc. enfeffd Nic. Trigg [16th c].

767.4 PG 3/4   **2 May 1498**

Grant Nicholas Trygge of Staunford Lincs notary public to Alice Basham of Staunford, William Radclyff of the same gent, Thomas Hikham, Richard Wermouth, Henry Wykys and Robert Grymston of the same clerks, my messuage in the parish of St George between the messuage late (*nuper*) of John Nele senior south and Pekesall yarde north, abutting on the highway west and Pekesall yard east, which messuage I had from Alice Basham and William Radclyff as in his charter [767.3] is more fully explained, to hold of chief lord by due service. Warranty.

Witnesses: Richard Canell then Alderman of Staunford, Thomas Phelipp, John Cleypole, Barnard Richeman, Thomas Cowper, Thomas Langar and many others.

Given at Staunford 2 May 13 Henry VII.

Seal: tag

Endorsed: (i) St George's Parish Staunford 2 May 13 Hen. 7. Nicholas Trygge to Alice Basham, Thomas Hikham, Richard Wermouth, Henry Wykes, William Radclyffe, Robert Grymston. Feoffment of a Messuage now (1813) three Houses in the occupation of Andrews Dixon & Harnbleton, Old Church Estate, No. 4.
(ii) Feoffment from Nicholas Trigg to Alice Barsham and others 2nd May 13 H 7 [17th C].
(iii) A messuage in St gor parishe conveyed by Trig to Basham etc. 13 H 7 [16th C].

767.5 PG3/5   **1 October 1509**

Grant Philip Morgan late of Staunford Lincs gent and Elena his wife, David Cecell of Staunford gent, Thomas Williams of the same and Nicholas Trygge of the same gent to Thomas Hobson of London gent, John Heron of the same mercator, John Foster of Staunford clerk and Elizabeth Wastlen of Staunford of one of our tenements situated in the parish of St George between the tenement late of John Nele south, Peksal yard north, abutting on street west and Peksall east; which tenement we held with William Elmes late (*nuper*) deceased by gift and feoffment of William Radclyff of Staunford gent, to hold to them, their heirs and assigns to the use of Elizabeth Wastlen, her heirs and assigns of the chief lord by due service. Warranty.

Witnesses: Thomas Lacy of Staunford, John Dalton, Thomas Langard, Richard Witham and many others.

Given at Staunford 1 October 1 Henry VIII.

Seal: 4 tags

Endorsed (i) St George's Parish Staunford 1 Oct. 1 Hen. 8. Philip Morgan, Elene his wife and others to Thomas Hobson Gent and others Feoffment of a Messuage now (1813) three Houses. Old Church Estate, No. 5.
(ii) Irro[tulatur] ad Cur[iam] tent[am] in castro Staunford xiii die Septembris anno Regni Regis Henr. octam Quinto [contemporary].

(iii) David Cecill and other enfeoff Hobson and others 1 Hen. 8 [17th C].

(iv) A tenement in paroch Sti Georgii [17th]

767.6 PG3/6   **18 December 1542**

Sale indented by John Richemond of Stamford Lincs chandeler and Reginald Cobbe of the same barber to Richard Sysyll armiger, John Hardgrave armiger and Henry Lacy gent for £10 of:

(i) one messuage and a garden contiguous adjacent in the parish of St George, common street west, close of John Hardegrave east, one head abuts on land (*terra*) of John Hardegrave south and the other on a cottage belonging to the almshouse of Staunford (*domum elemosinarii*)

(ii) one garden in the parish of St George near (*prope*) to Watergate lane between the tenement late (*nuper*) of John Lyttler now in the tenure of John Aleyn south and the land of Robert Walleff north, one head abuts on the land of John Richemond east and the other on the common lane called Watergate lane west;

(iii) a second garden lies near (*prope*) Watergate lane between the land of Richard Sysyll south and the land of John Alyn late (*nuper*) of John Lyttler north, heads on the land of John Richemond east and on Watergate lane west;

(iv) a third garden in the parish of St George directly against (*directe versus*) le Watergate between a certain common lane west and the common lane called le Watergate lane east, heads on another lane beside (*prope*) le Watergate south and on a close of John Hardegrave north; to have and to hold to the use of Richard Sysyll, John Hardegrave and Henry Lacy, their heirs and assigns. Warranty. Appointment of attorneys to deliver seisin, William Watts and John Rede.

Dated 18 December 34 Henry VIII.

Seals tags

Endorsed (i) St Georges Parish Stamford 18 Dec. 38 [*sic*] Hen. 8. John Richmond and Reginald Cobbe to Richard Sysyll Esq. and others, Feoffment of a Messuage and Garden and three other Gardens being All the Old Church Estate. No. 6 [1813 hand].

(ii) Richmond et al enfeoff Rich Sysyll Hen Lacy et al 34 H 8 [17th C].

STAMFORD TOWN HALL DEEDS
These records remain in Stamford Town Hall[30]

768. TH 8A/1/1   **23 June 1381**

Release and quitclaim from John Geffron to Henry Bugden of Staunford and dom Simon de Langeton parson of the church of St George Staunford of my right (*ius*) and claim in a tenement in the parish of St John the Baptist in the street called le Baxteregate between the tenement of the nuns of St Michae1 by Staunford on the east and the lane called le Ouenesty on the west, abutting on the king's road on the south and on a house (*domum*) called seint Johannis Ovene on the north.

Witnesses: William de Styandeby then Aldernaman [*sic*] of Staunford, John Spycer, John Brun, John Longe, Reginald Styward, Robert Loksmith, William Stacy and others.

Dated at Staunford Friday after the feast of Corpus Christi 5 Richard II.

Seals: round; 1½"; arms (chevron, two stars in chief one star beneath) and inscription around; red wax

769. TH 8A/1/2   **24 November 1393**

Grant Hugh Bukedon of Staunford to William Lyncoln of Staunford osteler, John Stuklee parson of the church of St John the Baptist Staunford and Edmund Knokker of the same chaplain of a messuage in Baxstergate in the parish of St John aforesaid between the messuage of the nuns of St Michael by Staunford on the east and the common lane on the west, abutting on the bakery (*pistrin'*) called Seynt Johns Bakhous on the north and on the king's road south, which messuage he had by gift and feoffment of John Spycer of Staunford and Robert Pratt' of the same, to hold of the chief lord of the fee by due service. Warranty.

Witnesses: John Longe then Alderman of Stanford, Gervase Wyke, Robert Stolam, William Stacy, William Raas barbour of the same and others.

Dated at Staunford Monday after the feast of St Clement the pope 17 Richard II.

Seal: oval, 1"; damaged; small scutcheon surrounded by decorative border; red wax

770. TH 8A/1/3   **1 February 1410**

Grant by William Lyncoln of Staunford osteler and John Stuklee parson of the church of St John the Baptist Staunford to Nicholas Rydell of Wyteryng and Ivette his wife of a messuage in Baxtergate in the parish of St John between the messuage of the nuns of St Michael by Staunford east and the common lane west, abutting on the house called Seint John Bakhous on the north and the king's road south, which messuage William and John together with Edmund Knokker chaplain lately (*nuper*) had by gift and feoffment from

---

[30] I am grateful to John Hopson for help with these deeds.

Hugh Bukkedon of Staunford, to hold of the chief lord of the fee by due service. Warranty.

Witnesses: John Palfreyman then Alderman of Staunford, John Longe, Robert Staleham, William Stacy, Thomas Spycer, John Fraunceys of Staunford and others.

Dated at Staunford Saturday after the feast of St Agatha the virgin 11 Henry IV.

Seals tags (two).

771. TH 8A/1/4   7 August 1452

Grant by Richard Knot of Staunford to Joan late (*nuper*) wife of Robert Broun of Staunforde glover of one tenement on a corner (*sit super corneram*) in the parish of St John Staunford between the tenement late (*nuper*) of Thomas Spycer on the north and west and abutting on the king's road on the east; which tenement Robert Knot held conjointly with Robert Broun of Staunford glover and Elena his wife by gift and feoffment of John Hochon late citizen and 'wolman' of London and Margaret his wife, to hold of the chief lord of the fee by due service. Warranty.

Witnesses: Richard Blogwyn then Alderman of Staunford, William Broun, John Broun, William Sutton, John Toon and many others.

Dated at Staunford Saturday after the feast of St Peter ad vincula (*post festum sancti Petri quod dicitur advincula*) 30 Henry VI.

Seal: round; 1 ½ "; shield (but damaged); red wax.

772. TH 8A/1/5   20 January 1458

Grant William Armeston of Staunford sclatter to John Barowe of Staunford laborer of one messuage with adjacent curtilage situated outside the north gates of the town of Staunford in the street (*vico*) commonly known as Scoffegate, between the tenement late (*nuper*) of John Apethorp on the west and the tenant of the warden (*custos*) of the chantry of St Nicholas in the parish of St Clement Staunford on the east, abutting on the king's road on the south and on the land late (*nuper*) of Robert Burton on the north, to hold of the chief lord of the fee by due service. Warranty. Sealing clause.

Witnesses: William Hekham then Alderman of Staunford, Richard Knotte, Robert Skynner bocher, John Grene, John Barr and many others.

Dated at Staunford 20 January 36 Henry VI.

No tag or seal

773. TH 8A/1/6   **29 March 1472**

Indenture (chirograph) of lease dated by Thomas Holton and John Gybes chamberlains of the town or borough of Staunford with the assent and consent of John Gregory Alderman of Staunford and all the community to Thomas Gregory of Staunford of one garden lying in Staunford between the tenement of the prioress of the nuns of Staunford on the east and the tenement of the abbot and convent of Vaudey (*Valle dei*) on the west, abutting on the king's road north and on the garden called 'Lytyll Paradys' on the south, to hold from Easter 12 Edward IV for 80 years, rendering 12d per annum to the chamberlains at the two terms of Michaelmas and Easter. Arrears clause; sealing clause (seals of the office of the chamberlains and of Thomas [Gregory]).

Dated at Staunford as above [*sic*] 1472.

Seals: red wax, a bird or animal in a plain circle, ½".

774. TH 8A/1/7   **20 July 1486**

Indenture of lease by John Stede Alderman of the town or borough of Staunford, the comburgesses and all the community of that town or borough by unanimous assent and will to William Bewshire of Staunford of one parcel of meadow and pasture which lies on each side of the water of the Weyland, commonly known as 'seynt leonadesford', between the land of the abbot of Peterborough on the south and the land of the prior of St Leonard in part and the land of Robert Hans in part on the north; the western head abuts on the monastery of St Leonard and the eastern head abuts on the land of the master of the hospital or chapel of St Thomas the martyr on the bridge of the town of Staunford; to hold the meadow and pasture with the water belonging to it from Michaelmas last for 99 years, rendering annually to the chamberlains of the town or borough of Staunford for the first 40 years 16s sterling at the usual four terms in the year; after the first 40 years 20s. And William Bewshire or his heirs or assigns shall build anew on the meadow, pasture and water there one house with two water mills and all other necessary appurtenances belonging to the mill, and they shall maintain this new mill during the whole term. And the said farmers, their heirs and assigns shall have all crops (*blada*) grown on the land there. Arrears clause; warranty clause by the Alderman, comburgesses and the whole community of the town or borough. Sealing clause.

Dated in the common hall at Staunford 20 July 1486 1 Henry VII.

Seal: tag.

775. TH 8A/1/8   **1 December 1524**

Indenture of lease made the first day of December 17 Henry VIII (1524 *inserted*) Robert Sandwath and John Fenton chamberlains of the borough and town of Staunford to Thomas Halame prior of Newsted 'besid' Staunford and the convent: a parcel of ground lying without the town walls of Staunford without the postern gate next to St John Wells on the west part of the lane called 'bowdyslane', containing in length 5 score and 8 feet and in breadth 40 feet, butting on the water of Weland against the south and the town walls on the north, late in the tenure of William Rankell, to hold the said void ground from Michaelmas last for 80 years, at a rent of 12d per annum at Michaelmas. Arrears clause; sealing clause.

Date as above.

Seal: red wax, fragment.
ENGLISH

776. TH 8A/1/9   26 December 1544

Sale by Richard Morecroft of Okham Rutland and Agnes his wife for a sum of money to Richard Potter of Stamford, Lincs, all one garden lying in the parish of St Peter the apostle in Stamford between the garden of Anthony Broun armiger on the west and the tenement late (*nuper*) of John Palfreman on the east, abutting on the wall (*murum sive clausuram*) of the town of Stamford called 'the town wall' on the north and on the lane called 'Spycers Lane' on the south; which garden contains by estimation in length from the south to the wall on the north 83 yards (*virgas terre voc' yeardes*) and in length at the north end (*finem*) of the garden 23 yards and at the south end 28 yards, to hold of the chief lord of the fee by due service. Warranty clause; power of attorney by Richard Morecroft and Agnes to Roger Beyll of Stamford and John Alen of the same to deliver seisin.

Dated 26 December 36 Henry VIII.

Seals: two tags

777. TH 8A/1/10   19 January 1547

Arbitration award by sir John Harryngton of Exton, Rutland to settle a dispute between the Alderman and comburgesses of Staunford and John Morysby of Staunford Lincs smith and Margaret his wife daughter and heir of William Burton late of Staunford deceased concerning the title to two messuages, the one called the 'Antylop' and the other 'at the brygge ende' where one Agnes Hall widow now dwells. The town claims William Burton left these two messuages to the town by will, but John Morysby and Margaret claim them as of her inheritance. John Morysby and Margaret get the bridge end property in freehold and they get the Antelope for their two lives.

Dated 19 January 38 Henry VIII.

Seals: (i) oval; 1"; animal or bird in circle; red wax
(ii) fragment; same symbol
(iii) fragment; same symbol
ENGLISH

BURGHLEY HOUSE

The private records of the Exeter family held at Burghley House contain much material relating to medieval Stamford and its suburbs, including title deeds to properties in the town. Parts of these records were listed by Patrick King, Archivist for Northamptonshire County Council, in the 1960s for the National Register of Archives (NRA). Currently, more work on housing and cataloguing the archives is being undertaken.

The following notes have been taken from two sources. The first part comes from the NRA lists (in the Northamptonshire Records Office); the second part comes from material provided by the house itself. It is not certain that this will complete the material in the collection relating to the town and its suburbs before 1547. But this summary does indicate some of the riches of this collection of archives and it makes this information immediately available to local historians.

The two lists are presented here with minor amendments. The originals are not yet accessible to researchers. This must be regarded as an interim list until a full catalogue of the originals can be prepared. I have not been able to view the originals to check dates and names where the readings are doubtful.

778. Ex 17/1   c 1275
Bond of Ysaac 'burgensis' to the nuns of St Michael to pay a rent charge

779. Ex 18/64   1516
Lease to the abbot of Crowland of a barn in Stamford in the parish of All Saints

780. Ex 22/1   1337
Grant Henry de Tyddiswell to sir John le Mazoun chaplain of a house in Little Burley near Stamford, 125 ½ acres arable, 6 ½ acres of meadow in Burley, 30 acres in Stamford and 2 ½ acres in Pilsgate.

781. Ex 22/2   1445-1463
Restoration: John Taillour *alias* Milton was outlawed in 1445; Ralph lord Cromwell acquired his house in Little Burley; Taillour was pardoned 1462 and property restored in 1463

782. Ex 31/56   1354
Copy of deed uniting the convent of Wothorpe to the nuns of St Michael Stamford

783. Ex 33/3   1479
Grant Thomas Sapcote to feoffees of lands in Stamford St Martins (fee of abbot of Peterborough) , Stamford Lincs (the fee of the duke of York) and in Barnack, Pilsgate, Tinwell, Ketton and South Luffenham

784. Ex 33/4   1482
Grant by John Kylham to William abbot of Peterborough of the hospital on Stamford bridge and the house of lepers of St Giles belonging to it

785. Ex 47/9   1527
Conveyance of the manor of Little Burley and lands in Pilsgate and Stamford to Richard Cecil

786. Ex 52/22   **1514**

Ratification of lease to Thomas Williams of a house in St Martins and land in Pilsgate

787. Ex 53/1   **1458**

Letter from William Hykeham Alderman and the comburgesses of Stamford to the duke of York certifying that John Wykes is the rightful owner of a 'place' in Stamford and that he did not enter it forcibly.

788. Ex 53/2   **1508**

Lease by feoffees of Mr William Spenser to the parsons of St Martin, St Mary, St Michael, St George and St John and to the bailiff of Stamford of a messuage in St Martins Stamford in trust for an annual requiem.

789. Ex 53/4   **1484**

Lease by Thomas Kilham master and warden of the hospital of John the Baptist and St Thomas and of St Giles leper hospital to John and Margaret Ryley of two tenements between the chapel (south) and a common *vinarium* (north) abutting on king's highway east, from Michaelmas 2 Richard III; lease for sixty years at a rent of 8s p.a. – they are to rebuild it with a hall, shop and two chambers in wood with a stone chimney in the hall and with a kitchen in the rear next to the garden in the next four years; together with the adjacent garden at the rear of the said tenements[31]

790. Ex 53/10   **1541**

Bargain and sale by John Durante of Barrowden to Robert Hayter of one acre of land in St Martins Stamford.

791. Ex 53/11   **1541**

Lease by Edward Sapcott to Thomas Grensyde of a messuage opposite the George in St Martins, Stamford.

792. Ex 53/12   **1547**

Lease by sir Edward Sapcott to John and E Myllner of Burgons house next to St Martin's churchyard.

793. Ex 54/4   **1540**

Royal grant to Richard Cecil of the house of St Michael's [nunnery], Stamford and lands in Wothorpe, Collyweston, Easton, the rectories of St Martin's church and Wothorp church and two manors in Wothorp.

794. Ex 80/3   **1539**

Grant by abbot of Peterborough to Richard Cecyll of the office of bailiff of Tinwell and Stamford St Martins.

795. Ex 80/5   **1544**

Grant by Henry VIII to David Vyncent of the reversion of the manor of Pilsgate with advowsons and lands in Barnack, Bainton, Walcote, Southorpe and Stamford St Martins.

---

[31] For text, see Hartley and Rogers 1974 p 52.

796. Ex 89/1   **14 Dec 1527**
Sale: sir William Compton knight to Richard Cissyll: Recites that Thomas Wyllyams the
elder of Stamford Lincs, executor of the testament of master John Taylor, executor of
the testament of Henry Wykes clarke and survivor of all the executors of the same Henry
and Wyllyam Wyllyams son and heir apparent of the said Thomas Wyllyams, by
indenture dated 20 June 18 HVIII, for a certain sum of money sold to the said William
and his heirs the manor of Lyttel Burley next Staumford with all lands, tenements etc in
Litell Burley, Olde Burley, Pillesyate and Staumford which sometime were Henry Wykes,
which sir William Compton now sells to Richard Cissyll. 19 Henry VIII

797. Ex 90/1   **1499**
Charter of Margaret Frebarne to sir Thomas Lovell and five others of all the lands in
Stamford she inherited from William Morewode and Margaret her parents and from
William Wode and John Frebarne her husbands.

798. Ex 90/7   **1500**
Quitclaim from sir Thomas Lovell to sir John Huse and others of all his rights in the lands
of Margaret Frebarn.

799. Ex 90/8   **1500**
Charter of sir Thomas Lovell, sir John Huse and others to John Herdegrave and others of
the same lands. Witnesses include David Syssill.

800. Ex 90/9   **1513**
Charter of David Cecell to the trustees of his will of all his lands in Stamford and a
meadow in Yarwell.

801. Ex 91/1   **1535**
Letter of Walter James Moryce to Robert Wyngfeld concerning the letting of land in
Stamford now let to David Cicell to … Dycons of Peterborough and other property in
Maxey, Torpell, mills etc.

802. Misc References: Ex 31/59; 33/4; 53/3-9; 76/72   **1482 - c1540**
Deeds, collation of master, lease, accounts of rent collectors and rental of the hospital of
St Thomas on the bridge

**803. Misc References: Ex 33/3; 34B/1, 6; 52/39; 53/3; 74/1-10; 80/2-3; 98/5-7, 23-
4**   **1227- 1531**
Charters and other deeds, agreement with the abbot of Crowland, homage roll (1299-
1478), manorial records, lease – Peterborough abbey

ADDITIONAL DEEDS RECENTLY IDENTIFIED AND LISTED

804. MB 2/71   **6 Nov 1486**
Richard Sapcote esquire son and heir of Katherine to Anne Sapcote his wife, John Thorp
clerk, Thomas Halle merchant, Thomas Hanworth chaplain, Thomas Monke chaplain
and William Hoddesson, grant of his manor in Grantham called The Garet and also all

his lands,tenements, meadows, feedings, pastures, rents and services in Staumford Lincs and in Worthorp and Burley, N'hants; also appointing Miles Broke and John Faukes as his attorneys

805. MB 4/24   Undated, pre 1290

Hildana, widow of William de Berke to William son of Henry of Tykencote and Juliana his wife, grant of all her dowry in Stamford, namely 4s per annum from a messuage called Inga' hall, 9½d from the messuage which was William Palmer's, and 7½d from the messuage of Emma Lekisheuit contingent upon her inheritance from her late husband.

806. MB 4/25   Undated, pre 1290

Alexander son of Rener' Maisent of Stanford to Philip parson of the church of Carleby, son of Dom Richard de Cotes, grant and quitclaim of houses in St Paul's parish, Stamford, namely the houses which were once of Reginald Lambethest', with abuttals, for a payment of one mark.

807. MB 4/27   24 Jan 1294

Gilbert son of Henry de Redyngges burgess of Stamford to Robert son of Adam of Spalding, quitclaim of the rights he has through the death of Hugh of Tykynchote of Stamford senior in a tenement with appurtenances in the parish of St Mary at the bridge of Stamford with abuttals

808. MB 4/28   12 June 1303

Agreement [*Norman French*] between Eustace Malerb' merchant of Stamford and Hugh of Alverton burgess of Stamford concerning merchandise for five years, for which Hugh will pay four marks, with part of Kinggesmilne.
Dated: Wednesday after the feast of St Barnabus 1303

809. MB 4/29   Undated

John son of the late Walter plumbar of Ocham to John le Plouman burgess of Stamford, grant for half a mark of silver of a tenement plot in the parish of St John's Stamford with abuttals and measurements; rent a clove of garlic
[tied to MB 4/30, 31 and 32]

810. MB 4/30   6 April 1308

Gilbert de Cotesmor of Stamford and Joan his wife to Roger le Skaveler of Stamford, grant of a house with adjacent curtilage in the parish of St John's Stamford with abuttals
[tied to MB 4/29, 31 and 32]

811. MB 4/31   3 March 1311

John de Warenne earl of Surrey to Roger le Skaveler burgess of Stamford, grant of a vacant plot in the parish of St John's Stamford with abuttals and measurements; rent 2s
[tied to MB 4/29, 30 and 32]

812. MB 4/32   3 Sept 1321

John de Warenne earl of Surrey to John Sprigg' steward of Stamford, appointment as his attorney to deliver seisin to Robert de Newerk and Matilda his wife of a vacant plot in Stamford and also to Roger de Skavaler, grant of a vacant plot
[tied to MB 4/29, 30 and 31]

813. MB 4/33   **5 Feb 1317**
Walter Halver of Staunford to Henry of Pirbrok burgess of Stamford, grant of 2 acres of arable in Sundersoken in Stamford field with abuttals, in consideration of a certain sum of money paid by Henry.

814. MB 4/34   **20 May 1322**
Marjory widow of Walter Wyseman of Stamford to Henry de Pyribrok burgess of Stamford, grant and quitclaim of all rights she had in three acres of arable in the field of Stamford called Sundersoken beyond the road to Empingham between the land of Richard de Baldeswelle to the west and the land of Cecilia de Pottesmuth to the east and abutting upon Tinwell Field towards the south, for a certain sum of money paid by him.

815. MB 4/35   **27 May 1326**
Walter atte Nunnes of Stamford to Ranulf Drynckedregges of Stamford quitclaim of all actions he had.

816. MB 4/36   **15 Nov 1328**
Beatrix daughter of William del Cley of Stamford to William her father and Emma her mother lease of two cellars with solars built upon them in Stamford in the parish of All Saints in the Market with abuttals, rent 1d

817. MB 4/37   **21 May 1329**
Walter atte Nunnes burgess of Stamford to Ranulf Drinkedregges burgess of Stamford, grant of a curtilage in the parish of All Saints in the Market lying upon Cleymund with abuttals

818. MB 4/38   **9 July 1339**
Hugh le Rede of Stamford skinner to Hugh de Thurleby of Stamford and Margerie his wife quitclaim in respect of a building plot in Stamford in the street of Cleymount with abuttals

819. MB 4/39   **11 July 1331**
Robert Wayte of Seusterne to Heny Botterwyk of Stamford spicer, quitclaim to the right to a messuage in the parish of St Clements in Stamford with abuttals

820. MB 4/40   **28 Jan 1335**
Ranulf Drinkedregges of Stamford to Agnes widow of Hugh Averey late burgess of Stamford, grant of a curtilage in the parish of All Saints in the Market lying upon Cleymund with abuttals

821. MB 4/41   **6 July 1337**
Walter atte Nonnes of Stamford to Ranulf Drinkesdregges quitclaim of all actions

822. MB 4/42   **25 Nov 1338**
Roger le Skaveler of Staunford senior to Margaret de Thorleby of Staunford, grant of a messuage in St John's parish, Stamford, situated between a tenement of the abbot of Crokeden on the south side and a tenement of the prior of Sempringham in part and a tenement formerly of Nicholas de Dodyngton in part on the north side, and it extends to the king's highway towards the east [and] to Castle lane towards the west, together with 30 acres of arable in the field of Little Casterton (with abuttals and field names)

823. MB 4/43   **17 July 1346**
Gilbert Basset of North Luffenham and Emma his wife the widow of Andrew Godfelaugh of Stamford to Thomas son of Andrew, quitclaim of right to a messuage in Stamford upon Cleymont with abuttals
[tied to MB 4/44]

824. MB 4/44   **18 July 1346**
Thomas son of Andrew Godfelaugh Stamford to Robert de Wyk of Stamford and Walter de Baldeswell of Stamford, grant of a messuage in Stamford upon Cleymont with abuttals
[tied to MB 4/43]

825. MB 4/45   **26 July 1348**
John bishop of Lincoln to Robert de Wyk of Stamford, licence for permission to have a private oratory in his house restricted to the use of him and his household so as not to detract from oblations due to the church of the parish in which it is situated

826. MB 4/46   **31 May 1349**
Dameta de Pyribrok daughter of Henry de Piribrok, appointment of Walter de Rameseye to be her attorney for the delivery of seisin to Thomas Pontefracte of Stamford, Robert de Wyk, Roger de Mundham, and Roger le Lecha of all her lands and tenements in Bradcroft, Tynwelle and Little Casterton

827. MB 4/47   **13 May 1355**
John de Bosesworthe of Staunford to Robert de Wyk and Eustace de Assewell burgesses of Staunford, demise of all the lands and tenements which he has in the town of Stamford by enfeoffment of Margaret late wife of Henry de Kyrkeby of Staunford, for the term of the life of Margaret, for an annual rent 30s.

828. MB 4/48   **8 Aug 1358**
William Enot of Tallington chaplain to Robert Wyke, grant of three messuages with appurtenances in Stamford, one on Cleymound, one with a dovehouse in Star Lane and one in Estgate with abuttals and 6s annual rent from houses in the parish of St Michael the Greater in Stamford

829. MB 4/49   **either 4 Feb or 12 Aug 1361**
Robert de Wyk of Staunford, appointment of Nicholas de Sclefford of Staunford as his attorney for delivery of seisin to Thomas Spicer of Staunford of all the lands and tenements which formerly were of John Russel of Helewell chaplain in Helewell, Bytham and elsewhere in Lincolnshire. Dated: Thursday after the feast of St Laurence 1361

830. MB 4/50   **21 Aug 1361**
John de Spofford perpetual vicar of St Andrews Stamford to Katherine widow of Robert de Wyk of Stamford, grant for her whole life of the manor of Little Burghley with appurtenances; also a messuage with two shops belonging to it in the parish of St Mary at the Bridge Stamford with abuttals. On her death the property goes to Edmund son of Robert.

831. MB 4/51   **19 June 1373**
William son of Reginald de Salteby of Staunford to Laurence de Grofham of Staunford and Simon Lyster of Staunford, grant of two tenements upon Cleymound in Staunford just as they are situated together between the tenement of the lord of the castle of Stamford on the west side and his own tenement on the east side, extending from the king's highway towards the north to the tenement of John Knot of Gretham towards the south.

832. MB 4/52   **28 Oct 1376**
Thomas Brereste of Castor near Peterborough: appointment of Walter Wase of Stamford, John de Belton, and John Spandeford of the same place as his joint and several attorneys for the delivery of seisin of all his lands and tenements, rents, meadows and pastures in Stamford and Uffington to Phillip Gernon' of St Botholf [Boston]

833. MB 4/53   **4 Dec 1404**
Thomas Wyles of Stamford to Robert Grene parson of the church of Alwalton, John Noppe parson of the church of Marham, John Stubley parson of the church of St John Stamford and Thomas Corby of the same place, grant of all the lands he holds in Lincs and Northants

834. MB 4/54   **21 Feb 1420**
William Flete clerk of Stamford to Henry Barker of Stamford and Richard West of Stamford tailors, quitclaim of rights of one acre of arable in Stamford with field names and abuttals, which land he held jointly with sir John Trussell knight and Thomas Mortymer esquire by the grant of Henry Cok of Stamford

835. MB 4/55   **3 May 1421**
John Stenby son of William Stenby of Stamford, appointment of Simon Uffyngton of Stamford chaplain as his attorney for the delivery to Lord Thomas Langley bishop of Durham, Lord Thomas la Warr lord la Warr, John Wodehous, Roger Flore esqs, John Palfreyman, John Alcok, Thomas Spycer, William Staleham, Thomas Basset, Ralph Bonde, Ralph Herward, John Everard, John Smyth, Richard Walyngton clerks, John Leche and John Ethell of Stamford of seisin in one messuage, one cottage, three shops, three barns and one vacant plot in Stamford.

836. MB 4/56   **4 April 1428**
Elizabeth Wykes of Stamford widow of John Palfreyman of Stamford, Thomas Bassett and Richard Wykes of the same place, grant of all her lands and tenements, meadows, feedings and pastures, rents and services with all their appurtenances which she has in Stamford and Castor

837. MB 4/57   **24 June 1464**
Robert Browe esquire to Thomas Greneham esquire, Richard Knotte of Tynwell and Robert Strykyswold of Stamford, grant of two acres, one rood of meadow in Stamford with field names which he had by grant of Gervase Wykes of Castor near Peterborough

838. MB 4/58   **24 March 1435**
Thomas Chapelleyn to Richard Wykes and Elizabeth Wykes, bond for £10 endorsed with a condition relating to the building and repair of an inn called le Sarsynneshed [Saracen's Head] in the parish of St Mary at the Bridge Stamford

839. MB 4/59   **7 June 1451**

Indenture: John May and Margaret his wife and John Wykes to Alexander Tyard of Stamford, lease of four acres of arable in Stamford with field names; term of six years, rent 2s 8d

840. MB 4/60   **4 Jan 1458**

Juliana Whithed of Stamford widow to Richard Goldesworth of Stamford and Katherine his wife and John Lyndesay of the same chaplain, grant of a messuage with appurtenances in the parish of St George with abuttals which they held jointly with John Clerke and Ralph Bryan by the grant of Richard Cokke of Stamford

841. MB 4/61   **25 Nov 1464**

William Escher rector of the church of St Clements in Stamford to John Wykes and Alice his wife, quitclaim of all his rights in the lands and tenements and services with all other appurtenances which he had by the grant of the said John Wykes

842. MB 4/62   **17 Feb 1469**

John Wylchar of South Luffenham formerly of Stamford to Robert de Woston of Stamford barker, quitclaim of his rights in a tenement with appurtenances in the parish of St Mary de Benewarke in Stamford with abuttals

843. MB 4/63   **10 Jan 1470**

Indenture: John Gybbes and Thomas Holton chamberlains of the town or borough of Stamford with the consent of Thomas Kesten then Alderman of Stamford and the whole company to Robert Clerke furbyscher, lease of a garden in the Pynnefold with abuttals; term of 40 years, rent 8d

844. MB 4/64   **3 April 1493**

John Wykes gent to David Philipp esquire, Nicholas Billesdon, Robert Hans, John Dykons, John Frebarne, Henry App', John Clerke, Henry Mordyt clerk, Richard Fletcher and David Cicill, grant of five messuages with appurtenances in Stamford, one in the parish of All Saints upon Clyppeshull, another in the parish of St John the Baptist, another in the parish of St Michael, another in the parish of St Mary at the Bridge called the Inn de le Beere, and another in the parish of St Mary on the lane descending to the river, with abuttals

845. MB 4/65   **16 Aug 1508**

Robert Beymond formerly of Stamford gent to Ralph Bowman, William Grenefeld and Robert at Damlys, grant of a messuage in the parish of St Peter the Apostle in Stamford with abuttals which he had by the grant of John Cleypole formerly of Stamford and his wife in a charter dated 27 Nov 1503

It is not clear that the next two deeds relate to Stamford, although the persons do.

846. MB 7/34   **undated**

Henry son of Reiner Nee of Stamford with the consent of Ingusa his mother and Clement his brother to Henry son of William son of Godric for 2½ marks for a plot of land which was Geoffrey Walg' next to the land which leads to the mill of Etrowe

847. MB 7/35   **undated**
Henry son of Roger de Westby to John[?] son of Geoffrey de Staunford, sale for 2s 6d of two selions at Lundgate with the meadow belonging to it, with abuttals and also four selions, which the said John[?] holds from him

848. MB 9/47   **undated**
Henry Faderman to Walter son of Norman, grant of three roods of arable in the fields of Stamford that lie above the dyke between the land of the said Walter on the east and west, in exchange for one acre of land in the fields of Burghley which lies between the land of Toke Lannator towards the west and the land of Henry Prat towards the east and abutting on the land of the lord of Burle on the south

849. MB 9/48   **undated**
William de Tykencot burgess of Stamford to the nuns of St Michael outside Stamford, indented grant in perpetual alms of 2s 6d annual rent and the tithe of a moiety of Kingesmilne and one acre of arable lying in the field of Burgle near Salegate saving to me three acres on the west side

850. MB 9/49   **23 June 1304**
The prioress of St Michael outside Stanford and convent to Peter de Burlee, indenture concerning the ecclesiastical court case and settlement about the tithes of wood of the said Peter within the parish of Stamford St Martin's and his chantry in the chapel of Burghley

851. MB 9/50   **19 May 1314**
Roger Kelmingworthe chaplain to Henry Faderman burgess of Stamford and Sybil his wife and Dom William their son chaplain, grant of all his goods and chattels in his messuage and rents in Stamford together with all his merchandise and beasts and all the crops on his land in Stamford Burghley and Pilsgate.

852. MB 9/54   **28 Aug 1385**
John Scherewynd of Staunford to William Stacy, Robert Loksmith and John Bugh of the same, indented grant of all the lands tenements and appurtenances which he had in Stamford in the liberty of the abbot of Peterborough and also all his goods and chattels during their lives according to a certain charter and in the event of their death it reverts to Alice, John Scherewynd's wife.

853. MB 9/55   **7 Oct 1465**
Thomas Gregory of Staunford to John Myllton of Staunford, Richard Foster and Thomas Knote of the same place, grant of one acre of arable with appurtenances beyond Stamford bridge within the liberty of the abbot of Peterborough which he formerly had by the grant of Alard Boysse of Brun'.

854. MB 9/56   **10 Feb 1473**
Henry Hopkyns of Staunford chaplain to Dom William Hall' of Staunford, Dom Henry Wykes, Dom William Canon of the same chaplain, John Gybbes and Henry Cokke, lease of all those lands and tenements, meadows feedings and pastures with appurtenances in Stamford and in the meadow of Worthorpe which belong to the dean and chapter of Staunford which he formerly held jointly with Dom Henry Burley late of the same place

chaplain by the grant of John Lindesay and John Brygge clerks, John Chevercourte and other trustees.

855. MB 9/57 1493-4

Rent roll for Stamford St Martin's with memorandum of exchange between the abbot of Peterborough and the prioress of St Michael's nunnery granting the abbot one acre brede [*sic;* perhaps 'broad acre] on the back side of the George from the water side to the highway and granting the prioress four half acres of land at the south end of Quarell Close next to the lands of the prioress and convent.

856. MB 9/58 10 Feb 1500

Francis Sapcote son of Thomas Sapcote esquire and Thomas Williams of Staunford innholder, indented demise of a tenement and yard adjoining late in the tenure of Robert Wright in St Martin's Stamford with abuttals, for 20 years from Lady Day next, rent 10s.

857. MB 9/59 undated

Robert son of Reginald de Writhorp with the assent of his wife and heirs to God, St Guthlac and the abbot and convent of Crowland, quitclaim of the meadow called Millesti in Wothorpe, which his ancestors and he held unjustly, lying next to two acres on the west side, of which he sold 1½ acres to Richard de Easton and in remission of their sins he will pay 1d rent annually.

858. MB 9/60 undated

A terrier of land formerly belonging to William Fauvel in Wothorp and Easton, viz Netherfield, Middlefield, Southfield, Eastfield and meadow

859. MB 9/61 5 June 1322

William de Gretton of Staunford to Emma Bertelmew of Staunford for a certain sum of money, grant of three half acres of meadow with appurtenances in Wothorpe with abuttals.

860. MB 9/62 6 Oct 1341

John son of John de Castirton of Staunford barber and Emma his wife to Richard de Pappele of Staunford, quitclaim of their rights in 1½ acres meadow with appurtenances in Wothorpe which Richard formerly acquired from them.

861. MB 9/63 30 Sept 1377

Alan de Wyrthorp to Katherine his younger daughter, grant of a messuage and adjoining curtilage with appurtenances in Wothorpe with abuttals.

862. MB 9/64 7 April 1399

Robert Kokke of Weston to Henry Percy, John Russell, and John Trussell knights, John Tyndale and John Bret esquires, John Burley, John Horspate, William Fischer, Thomas Derebogh't and Thomas de Collum, grant of a messuage and adjoining curtilage in Wothorp with abuttals which he had by the grant of Thomas Boltham of Staunford and Katherine his wife.

863. MB 9/65   **27 May 1399**
Robert Taylour of Wyrthorp living in Bykelesworthe, Northants, to Robert Spenser of
Wyrthorp, grant of one messuage two acres and half a rood of arable in Wothorpe with
abuttals and field names.

864. MB 9/66   **14 Jan 1376**
John Fawvel of Walcote to John Weldon of Staunford, grant of all his lands, tenements,
meadows, feedings, pastures and other appurtenances in Wothorpe and Easton which
were formerly of Richard Freman of Wirthorp
[tied to MB9/67 and 68]

865. MB 9/67   **1 May 1387**
Emma de Wirthorp of Staunford widow to Emma daughter of Henrison her former
servant, grant of one acre of arable with appurtenances in the south field of Wothorp
with abuttals and after her death the remainder is to go to Richard Bulwyk of Staunford
butcher and after his death to be distributed for celebration of mass and other alms
[tied to MB9/66 and 68]

866. MB 9/68   **22 June 1410**
Richard Bullewyk of Staunford to John Dyester of Collyweston, Nicholas Morys and
Robert Morys of the same place, grant of all the lands and tenements which he had in
Wothorpe formerly of Robert Spencer
[tied to MB9/66 and 67]

867. MB 9/69   **11 May 1403**
Robert Spenser of Wirthorp to Richard Bullewyk of Staunford, grant of a messuage, two
acres and half a rood of arable in Wothorpe with abuttals and field names

868. MB 9/70   **7 April 1403**
Robert Spenser of Wyrthorp to Richard Bullewyk of Staunford, grant of a messuage with
adjoining garden in Wothorpe with abuttals which he had by the grant of John Jolyvet of
Wothorpe
[tied to MB 9/71]

869. MB 9/71   **4 March 1468**
William Smyth of Yakesle to Dom Thomas Fyssher rector of Collyweston, John
Whitewell of the same place, John Frebarn and William Gent of Easton, grant of a
messuage in Wothorpe with all the lands, tenements, meadows, feedings and pastures
belonging to it
[tied to MB 9/70]

870. MB 10/1   **24 Sept 1405**
Robert Levot/Lenot of Staunford to Richard Bullewyke of Staunford, grant of a
messuage with appurtenances in Wyrthorp with abuttals and a field name

871. MB 10/2   **7 April 1426**
William Grene of Gumby to Robert Othe hille of Wyrthorp, grant of a messuage, one
acre and one rood land in Wothorpe with abuttals

872. MB 10/3   **4 Nov 1469**
Thomas Herryes also known as Saddyngton of Worthithorppe to John Cordale, John
Waters, William Hamilton and John Serle, grant of lands and tenements, meadows,
feedings and pastures with appurtenances in Wothorpe

873. MB 10/4   **20 Aug 1471**
John Pomerey abbot of the monastery of St Mary *de pratis* of Leicester appointing John
Cordall and Robert Ball of Worthorp as his attorneys to take seisin in the lands and
tenements, meadows, feedings and pasture with appurtenances in Wothorpe which he
formerly held jointly with Ralph Beaufo formerly of Saddington senior, Richard Smarte
rector of the church of Chepyng Wardon, Richard Power rector of the church of
Wakerley, Robert Curtas chaplain now deceased amongst other lands and tenements
from the gift of John Sadyngton and Amicia his wife formerly of Leicester and for the
delivery to Thomas Sadyington son of Agnes Sadyngton daughter of John and Amicia.

874. MB 10/5   **21 Aug 1471**
John Pomeroy abbot of the monastery of St Mary *de pratis* of Leicester to Thomas
Sadyington son of Agnes Sadyngton daughter of John and Amicia, demise of all the
lands and tenements, meadows, feedings and pasture with appurtenances in Wothorpe
which he forrmerly held jointly with Ralph Beaufo formerly of Saddington senior,
Richard Smarte rector of the church of Chepyng Wardon, Richard Power rector of the
church of Wakerley, Robert Curtes chaplain now deceased amongst other lands and
tenements from the gift of John Sadyngton and Amicia his wife formerly of Leicester.

875. MB 10/6   **20 Feb 1479**
William Gaywode of Staunford, John Whitley canons of St Mary *de pratis* Leycestr', John
Frebarne and John Watir with the consent of Thomas Herreys *alias* Thomas Sadyngton
to John Bussh, lease of one piece of land on Wothorpe with abuttals and measurements
which they had by the gift of the aforesaid Thomas Herreys; also appointment of John
Fr3unceys and Robert Reve as their attorneys for delivery of seisin

876. MB 10/7   **6 Oct 1486**
Thomas Sadyngton *alias* Harreys son of Agnes Sadyngton daughter of John Sadyngton
and Amicia his wife formerly of Leycestr' to William Gaywode of Staunford, quitclaim of
his rights in all those lands, tenements, meadows, feedings and pastures in Wothorpe
formerly of John Sadygton and Amicia his wife which he had by the gift of Dom John
Pomerey abbot of the monastery of St Mary *de pratis*, Leicester.

877. MB 10/8   **26 April 1508**
Richard Lychefeld of Worthorp near Stamford and Agnes his wife to Edward Mylner of
Howgton in the parish of Lamport, Northants, quitclaim of his rights in all those lands,
tenements, meadows, feedings and pastures in Wothorpe which the said Agnes formerly
held by the gift of Thomas Harres *alias* Sadyngton as dowry

878. MB 10/11   **27 Sept 1438**
John Saddyngton of Leicestr' to Richard Johnson *alias* Harryson of Buckton and Agnes
his wife, John's daughter, grant of all the lands and tenements, meadows, feedings and
pastures, rents, reversions and services in Wothorpe and Easton

879. MB 10/12   **28 Nov 1410**
Roland Gyldale to John Jurdon of Worthorp near Stamford, grant of 2½ acres of arable
with appurtenances in Wothorpe with parcels abuttals and one field name
[tied to MB 10/13-16]

880. MB 10/13   **3 April 1445**
John Judon of Wirthorp to William Fletcher tyler of the same place, grant of 2½ acres
of arable in Wothorp with field and road names and abuttals
[tied to MB 10/12, 14-16]

881. MB 10/14   **28 Jan 1445**
John Brygge of Staunford clerk to William Fletcher of Worthorp and Robert Bealsby of
the same place, grant of 1½ acres of arable in Wothorp with field name, road name and
abuttals
[tied to MB 10/12-13, 15-16]

882. MB 10/15   **28 July 1480**
William Fletcher of Worthorp tyler to John Corby of Stamford and Katerine his wife and
Dom John Obys [Ovys?], grant of three acres of arable in Wothorpe with abuttals field
and road name
[tied to MB 10/12-14, 16]

883. MB 10/16   **4 Oct 1523**
Katerina Corby late wife of John Corby to Thomas Gallow *alias* Welles, grant of three
acres of arable in Wothorp with abuttal, field and road name, formerly held jointly with
her late husband and Dom John Ovys chaplain
[tied to MB 10/12-15]

884. MB 10/17   **20 April 1477**
Thomas Herreys *alias* Sadyngton son of Agnes daughter of John Sadyngton and Amicia
his wife formerly of Leycestr' to William Gaywode of Staunforde, John Whitley canon
of the monastery of St Mary *de pratis* of Leycestr', John Frebarne and John Watir, grant
of all his lands and tenements, rents, reversions and services, meadows, feedings and
pastures with appurtenances in Worthorp and Eston

885. MB 10/18   **8 August 1480**
William Fletcher of Worthorp to Robert Reve and William Hamilton guardians of the
parochial church of Wothorp, Thomas Cordale, John Waturs, Richard Cordale, Robert
Schepey, William Serle, Robert Hamulton and William Waturs, grant of one acre three
roods of land in Wothorpe and Easton with abuttals

886. MB 10/19   **16 July 1492**
John Frebarn of Staunford and John Watir to John Bussh, quitclaim of their rights in the
lands and tenements, rents, reversions and services, meadows, feedings and pastures
with appurtenances in Worthorp and Eston formerly of Thomas Harreys *alias* Sadyngton

887. MB 10/21   **26 April 1500**
Richard Lychefeld and Agnes his wife formerly the wife of Thomas Herrays *alias*
Sadyngton deceased, to John Bussh, quitclaim of their rights in a piece of land in

Wothorpe with abuttals and also their rights in two messuages with other lands meadows and pastures in Wothorpe and Easton

888. MB 10/22   **6 Dec 1505**
Will of John Busshe of Easton on the Hill near Stamford providing for his burial in the chapel of St Mary in the church of All Saints Easton, leaving animals to the rector and property in Easton, money to Lincoln Cathedral and to a gild founded there for burial lights and the repair of the bells, to another gild property in Easton, to John Churchgate a messuage in Wothorpe after his wife's death, etc

889. MB 10/23   **7 Jan 1506**
Richard Lichefelde of Staunford and Agnes his wife widow of Thomas Harris formerly of Bughton Northants, to Edward Miller of Hangynghoughton Northants and Alice his wife, daughter of Elizabeth Luk deceased, next heir of Thomas Harris, grant of their lands and tenements, meadows, feedings and pastures with their appurtenances in Wothorpe and Easton, formerly of John Saddyngton of Leicestr', and appointment of William Miller of Laungeport and William of Hangynghoughton as their attorneys

890. MB 10/24   **25 April 1506**
Margaret Bussh of Easton widow and John Chyrchegate executors of the will of John Bussh formerly of Easton to Edward Mylner and Alice his wife, quitclaim of all rights in lands and tenements, rents, reversions and services, meadows, feedings and pastures with their appurtenances in Wothorpe and Easton which were formerly of John Frebarne of Staunford and John Wat'

891. MB 10/25   **32[sic] Sept 1506**
Margaret Busshe widow of John Busshe formerly of Easton on the Hill, John Chirchegate and Thomas Well' of the same place and William Rattcliff of Staunford gent to Thomas Madewell of Stamford, Edward Mylner of Hougton and John Luk of Marston Trussell, receipt for 40s paid

892. MB 10/44   **undated**
Henry de Braibruc from Hugh de Broy, indented demise of 20s 9d worth of rent which Alvas de Wardon owes for a tenement which he holds in Stanford and 2d which John de Bueles owes for the tenement which he holds from the same in Stacheden and 5s 3d which Roger Coc' owes for a tenement in the same place and 12d which Robert Goldston owes for a tenement in the same place and 6d which William Percesvil owes for a tenement which he holds in Dilwik and 6d which Miles de Stamford owes for a tenement in Stamford.
[tied to MB 10/40-43]

893. MB 10/46   **3 Feb 1361**
Robert de Wyk of Staunford to John Knyvet son of Richard Knyvet of Suthwyk junior, Dom William de Melton parson of the church of Holy Trinity Stamford, Dom John Spofforde perpetual vicar of St Andrew's church Stamford and Dom Philip of Deepyng chaplain, grant of all lands tenements etc in the counties of Lincs, Northants and Rutland.

894. TUD 1/22   **1 Dec 1528**
John Thomas of Staunford' dyer to Peter Symon, Robert Salett, Thomas Sutton, William Rankell junior and Richard Clerk of Staunford, grant of a messuage with appurtenances in the parish of St Peter the apostle in Stamford with abuttals, which he had by the grant of William Grenefeld and Robert Tales de Staunford
[small intact seal attached]

895. TUD 1/23   **1 June 1540**
Thomas Tanner de Staunford yeoman, to William Lee clerk, Joan Watson widow and John Watson, at the special request of John Whitton of Staunford clerk: confirmation and delivery of a messuage with adjoining garden and appurtenances in Stamford in the parish of St Mary de Bynwark (with abuttals) abutting south on the royal road called Westgate, which he formerly held with Thomas Walker deceased to the use of the said John Whytton by the grant of William Radclyff and David Cecell, together with appointment of Symon de Staunford as his attorney to enter and deliver seisin on his behalf.
[Endorsed with confirmation of delivery]

896. TUD 1/24   **12 Nov 1531**
Francis Browne esquire to Edmund Browne gentleman, indented grant of two acres of arable called Belmangoret' with abuttals, including the land of Wykes now Cicell on the east and of the rector of St Clement's on the west, in exchange for a yard called Swyneyard and an adjoining garden with abuttals including Clypshyll waye on the east.
[Endorsed with confirmation of the taking of possession on the same day]

897. TUD 1/25   **30 June 1545**
Constance Jones of Coly Weston, Northants widow, Jasper Jones her son in the county of Essex yeoman, and William Jones her son citizen of London to Robert Haver of Staunford innkeeper and Agnes Haver his wife, indented bargain and sale of two tenements in the parish of St Paul's, Stamford with abuttals, including St Paul's parsonage west and the town walls north.

898. TUD 1/51   **18 Sept 1527**
sir Henry Willobye knight, William Mering, John Markam knights and Richard Sapcote esquire to Thomas Williams of Stamford gentleman, reciting that Henry, William, John and Richard are feoffees to the use of Agnes wife of William Wake of Herwell', Northants gentleman, and late wife of Francis Sapcote deceased, for her life, of lands and tenements, meadows and pastures, rents, reversions and services with appurtenances in Stamford, Pilsgate, Barnack, Tinwell and other towns, of which Agnes had been enfeoffed by Thomas Sapcote of Burley: indented demise at farm for 40 years, at the request of Agnes and William, of all such messuages, lands and tenements, lessues [*sic*], lees, meadow, pastures and common of pasture with appurtenances in Stamford, Pilsgate, Wothorpe and Easton [note that this does not agree with the list of places subject to the trust], subject to rents of 15s 10d and 2s respectively due to the abbot of Peterborough and the prioress of the nuns of Stamford
ENGLISH

899. TUD 1/52   **1 Dec 1542**
Edward Sapcott of Burley, Rutland esquire to Noel Floode, in consideration of good service etc, grant of an annuity or annual rent of 40s arising from the messuages, lands,

tenements and other hereditaments with their appurtenances in Stamford St Martin within the liberty of Burg in both the counties of Northants and Lincolnshire.
Endorsed in English with memorandum of surrender of the annuity by Noel Floode to sir William Cycyll knight for £8.

900. TUD 1/53   **24 Feb 1544**
Richard Cycell' of Burley, Northants esquire to Robert Walbeef of Barholme, Lincs gentleman, indented demise for life of a garden with a gallery built upon the garden, adjoining a house in Stamford St Martin's with an associated right of way; rent 4s

901. TUD 2/05   **Undated, pre 1539**
Terrier of the lands and pasture belonging to Thomas Gedney of Stamford lying in the fields of Worthorpp'.
[English; refers to the abbot of Crowland]

902. TUD 2/06   **7 May 1512**
William Radcliff and Thomas Wells to John Churchgate chaplain, grant of all the land and tenements, meadows, feedings and pastures with appurtenances in Worthorppe which he had by the grant of John Busshe

903. TUD 2/07   **1 Oct 1513**
William Ratclyff formerly of Stamford gentleman, Thomas Wellys and Margaret Busche widow of John Busche of Eston' to John Churgayt chaplain, grant of a cottage with adjoining garden in Worthorp' with abuttals

904. TUD 2/08   **9 Nov 1513**
John Churchegate clerk to Thomas Wells of Eston', grant of two messuages or tenements with all the lands, arable, meadows, feedings, pastures, woods, underwoods, commons and other appurtenances in Worthorppe which he had by the grant of William Radcliff and Thomas Wells, feoffees of John Busshe deceased, according to the will of the said John Busshe

905. TUD 2/09   **3 Jan 1514**
John Churchegate clerk to Thomas Welles of Eston', quitclaim of all his right in two messuages or tenements with all the lands, arable, meadows, feedings, pastures, woods, underwoods, commons and other appurtenances in Worthorppe

906. TUD 2/10   **18 Jan 1528**
Thomas Myller of Buckton' husbandman to Thomas Maydwell', Thomas Wyllyams, John Fynton' and Thomas Watson, grant of land, tenements, meadows, feedings and pastures, rents, reversions and services, hereditaments and appurtenances in Worthorpe and Eston' to the use of the said Thomas Maydwell'; appointment also of Thomas Crystoffer and John Cordall' as his attorneys to take possession and deliver seisin

907. TUD 2/11   **24 Feb 1543**
Robert Hall of Stamford gentleman to Richard Sycyll' esquire and John Abram clerk, grant of two acres of meadow with appurtenances in the meadow of Worthorp' lying divided, with description of parcels and their abuttals [N.B. Stump' Crosse] known as Chapter land, which he had by the grant of William Harrison of Stamford clerk by a

charter dated 17 Feb 1533; appointment of William Wattes and Thomas Tydde to be his attorneys for the taking of possession and delivery of seisin

ADDITIONAL ITEMS

BRITISH LIBRARY

908. BL Add. Ch. 24912   Easter ... Henry IV

Final concord between Richard Stake of Staunford and Anna his wife and Walter Smyth of Exton and Agnes his wife of one messuage with appurtenances in Staunford; Walter and Agnes recognise the messuage as that which Richard and Anna have by gift of William and Agnes; Walter and Agnes remise and quitclaim the property to Richard and Anna and the heirs of Anna. Warranty to Richard and Anna; for 20 marks of silver paid by Richard and Anna to Walter and Agnes.

Dated: Lincoln, the month of Easter ... Henry IV

909. BL Add. Ch. 54368   27 November 1324

Sale by Alvredus de Depping dwelling (*manens*) in Staunford to Walter de Skelyngton also dwelling in Staunford for a sum of money which he gave to me, of my houses with appurtenances situated in the parish of St Paul Staunford between the tenement of Robert de Lymeborwe [*sic*] east and the lane called Star lane west; extending from the king's highway south to the tenement of the abbot of Bourne north; to hold to Walter Skelyngton and his heirs free of all charges save to the chief lord of the fee. Warranty. Sealing clause.

Witnesses: Eustace Malherbe, John Willowyndere, John de Empyngham, Walter de Haubois, Robert de Normanton and others.

Dated: Staunford, Tuesday before the feast of St Andrew, 18 Edward son of Edward.

Seal: two tags

Stowe 937 Cartulary of Pipewell

(All charters are undated).

910.1 Stowe 937, fol. 103

Grant by Margaret formerly the wife of Robert serjeant of Staunford grant in perpetual free alms to the convent of Pipewell with the assent of Nicholas my son of my houses in Estegate Staunford which were of my husband Robert free of all charges save rent of 1d at the time of the Salutation [Annunciation] and 1d at the time of harvest (*messioni*); also a rent of 4d, of which 3d shall be taken from the two properties adjacent to these houses to the south (*propinquoribus vicinis ex parte australis*).

910.2 Stowe 937, fol. 103d

Grant by Beatrice late the wife of Walter de Tikencot of Staunford to the convent of Pipewell of a rent of 5s silver per annum at the Nativity from my houses in the parish of St George between the house of Achard de Styendbi east and the house of Henry Goldsmith (*Aurifabri*) south on the corner (*angulo*); Pipewell shall freely take the rent of 5s p.a. from the said houses without contradiction. Sealing clause.

910.3 Stowe 937, fol 151 (i)

Grant by Beatrice formerly the wife of Walter de Tikencote to the convent of Pipewell of our lands and houses in Staunford which were of Robert le Serjant and Margaret his wife; Warranty clause

Witnesses: Ralph son of Achard and others

910.4 Stowe 937, fol 151 (ii)

Sale by William de Weston [?Welton?] son of Ralph de Weston to Simon de Pacewell for 21 marks of silver of all my solar in the parish of St John Staunford, with two shops which lie under the solar to the west which William Talliator is holding of me, and my oven (*furnum*) and all issues from the solar and shops and oven, rendering per annum 1 lb of pepper or 7d at Easter for all services. Warranty clause. Sealing clause.

910.5 Stowe 937, fol 151d (i)

Grant by Dom de Pateshull to the convent of Pipewell for my soul of all my house and lands which were of Dieulesacre Judeo son of Samuel de Stanford between the houses of William son of Roger de Offinton and the house of Clemens Vintner (*venetarii*) in the parish of St Michael of Staunford which were held of Reiner son of Hugh de Berne/Bourne, free of all service save 8d per annum at Ascension to the lord and 1d at ... [torn].

910.6 Stowe 937, fol 151d (ii)

Indenture of lease between Pipewell abbey and Dieulacres son of Samuel the Jew (*Judeum*) of Staunford of his houses in Staunford in the parish of St Michael by the cemetery at fee farm, which Dom William de Pateshull gave to Pipewell in free alms, rendering 20s p.a., 10s at the feast of St Thomas the Apostle and 10s at the Nativity of St John the Baptist.

910.7 Stowe 937, fol. 152

Grant by Walter de Pateshull son of Simon de Pateshull to Pipewell convent of all my solar in the parish of St John Staunford and the two shops under the solar (east) and the service of two shops under the solar (west) which William le Talur holds of me and my oven which I have in that parish to the north of that church and all my tenement in which that solar, shops and oven stand, together with all issues from that property. Warranty clause. Sealing clause. Free of service save paying to me and my heirs one silver mark per annum, half a mark at Easter and half a mark at Michaelmas.

CAMBRIDGE UNIVERSITY LIBRARY (CUL)
Red Book of Thorney vol ii
(Most charters are undated).

911.1 Add Mss 3021, fol. 253 (i)
Sale by John son of Geoffrey de Thornhawe heir of Henry my brother to Andrew son of Henry de Tikencot, one house (*domum*) in the parish of St Michael in Cornstal between the house of Ernald de Casterton weaver (*textoris*) east and the house of Walter Gosenol west, for six silver marks which he gave me by his hands; to hold to Andrew, his heirs and assigns free (except religious houses) of all service saving service to the lord of the fee. Warranty. Sealing clause.

Witnesses: Richard Peck, Peter son of Geoffrey and others

911.2 Add Mss 3021, fol. 253 (ii)
Grant by Andrew son of Henry de Tikencote to Clement rector of the parish church of St Michael in Cornstal in Stanford of the said house in the parish of St Michael in Stanford between the house of Ernald de Casterton east, and the house of Gilbert de Cliva west; in exchange for the houses and appurtenances which Clement bought of Geoffrey Bulhernes and of Henry chaplain, to hold to Clement and his heirs or assigns excepting religious houses free of all services and exactions saving service to the lord of the fee. Warranty; sealing clause; witness clause (no names).

911.3 Add Mss 3021, fol. 253 (iii)
Sale by Clement rector of the parish church of St Michael in Cornstal son of Reiner Heie of Stanford to Hugh de Bledelawe vicar of Makeseya for 20 silver marks which he gave me, of that same house with appurtenances in the parish of St Michael in Cornstal in Stanford between the house of Ernald de Casterton east and the house of Gilbert de Cliva west, which house Andrew son of Henry de Tikencote gave in exchange for those houses with appurtenances which I bought from Geoffrey Bulehernis and from Henry chaplain situated in the parish of St Michael, to hold to Hugh, his heirs and assigns except religious houses, free of all service save service to the lord of the fee. I Clement give warranty. Sealing clause; witness clause.

911.4 Add Mss 3021, fol. 253d (i)
Grant by Hugh de Bladelawe vicar of Makeseya to abbot and convent of Thorney those houses which I bought in Stanford from Clement rector of St Michael in Cornstal to hold to the abbot and successors paying the services due. Sealing clause; witness clause.

Memo: whoever is abbot of Thorney shall take annually from those houses 10s rent at Michaelmas and Easter; the houses are let to Geoffrey son of Richard de Deping clerk and his heirs by the abbot and convent of Thorney for 10s rent p.a., as follows:

911.5 Add MSS 3021, fol. 253d (ii)
Indenture: Geoffrey son of Richard de Deping clerk is held to the abbot and convent of Thorney and their successors for 10s p.a. for the houses in the parish of St Michael in

Cornstal of Stanford which they had by gift of Hugh vicar of Makeseya; payable in full, 5s at Michaelmas and 5s at Easter. Warranty clause; distraint clause; sealing clause; witness clause.

911.6 Add MSS 3021, fol. 253d (iii)

Quitclaim by Geoffrey son of Richard de Deping clerk for the houses late of Hugh vicar of Makeseia situated in Stanford in the parish of St Michael in Cornstal, which I held at a rent of 10s p.a. Sealing clause; witness clause.

911.7 Add MSS 3021, fol. 254 (i)

Memo: I Margerie daughter of Petronilla de Champeine in my virginity and over my seal confirm to Master Henry son of Master Sampson of Stanford, my master, while I am residing with the said Master Henry, that I agree to the following indenture:

Indenture by Master Henry son of Master Sampson de Stanford to Margerie daughter of Petronilla de Campaine for her marriage of my houses with appurtenances in the parish of St Peter of Stanford between the house of Herbert serjant (*servientis*) west and the house of James the Jew (*Jacobi Judei*) east; and also for her marriage my houses and garden etc in the parish of Holy Trinity outside the east gate of Stanford between the house of Walter son of Hugh son of Reiner east and the house of Elye de Langetoft west, rendering to me 40d p.a. for my life, 28d at Easter and 12d at Michaelmas for all services and exactions; after my death, the customary fees are due to the lord. Warranty clause; distraint clause; Margerie cannot alienate these houses. Sealing and witness clauses.

911.8 Add MSS 3021, fol. 254 (ii)

Sale by Achard son of Ralph Beauner of Stanford with the assent of Ysabelle my wife and my heirs to Achard son of Richard mercer and Geoffrey son of Peter le Hedlere of Stanford of an annual rent of 2s 6d p.a. from that house with appurtenances in the parish of St Andrew between the house which was of Hugh Stute south and the house which was of Roger son of Margaret north and part on me south, to hold to Achard son of Richard and Geoffrey son of Peter and their heirs and assigns. They gave to me one mark silver. Warranty, distraint clauses.

[Heading describes it as a rent from a cellar]

911.9 Add MSS 3021, fol. 254d (i)

Sale by Achard son of Richard mercer and Geoffrey son of Peter de Hedlere of Stanford to Cecilie daughter of William son of Sigge de Stanford of rent of 2s 6d p.a. from a house with appurtenances situated in the parish of St Andrew of Stanford between the house of Hugh Stute south and the house of Roger son of Margaret north, which rent Achard son of Ralph Beauuer sold to us. For this Cecilie gave 9s argent. Warranty clause.

911.10 Add MSS 3021, fol. 254d (ii)

Grant by Cecily daughter of William Sigge of Stanford in my legitimate power and with the counsel of my heirs to celebrate twenty masses for the salvation of my soul and those of my ancestors and relations present and to come, of one cellar with appurtenances in the parish of St Andrew in Barmigate between the house of Hugh Stute south and the house of Roger son of Margaret north under my solar next to the road against the entry to the cemetery, in free alms. To hold of me and my heirs. Warranty clause.

911.11 Add MSS 3021, fol. 258 (i)   24 April 1315

Charter of John earl of Warenne confirming the liberties in Stanford of Thorney abbey; *inspeximus* of charter of king Edward son of Edward [Edward II] of their rents in Stanford. (French)

8s 1¼ d from the under-written tenements:

Robert de Newerk one messuage in Estgate 3d

John de Reppis one tenement in Colgate 5½d

Emma de Ketelthorp one messuage on Claymount 3d

The prior of St Leonards two cottages outside the east gate 5½ d

The Carmelite friars for one messuage called le Chekerstede 9d

Henry le Taillur one messuage on Cleymount 2d

John le Cunte one messuage, one solar and one schop in Briggegate 13d

Emma Bertlimeu one house in (*infra*) her manse there 1d

Henry de Piribrok one messuage in Westgate 9d

Henry Leche one messuage there 6¾d

The place opposite the church of St Peter which Richard Marmion once held 3 ½ d

John Waldeshef three messuages at the bridge of Maleroye 2s 3d

Roger Mychelove one messuage at Eastgate 4d

John Freches one messuage which Hemmyng Lickesnot held 5d

Witnesses: Doms Thomas de Sheffeld, John de Heselarton, Peter de Montefort, William de Bayons, knights, etc

Dated at Reygate 24 April 8 Edward II

Letter patent to the bailiffs and ministers of Stanford, Kennington 28 April .

911.12 Add MSS 3021, fol 261-261d

a) *Sale* by Eustace Rufus of Stanford with the assent of Beatrice my wife to Richard prior of Deeping for 10 marks silver given to me of my house with appurtenances in Cleymund in the parish of St Michael of Cornstall[32] [*sic*] in Stanford between the house of Richard Ode west and the house of Aurekin[?] son of Roger Gosenol east, to hold to Richard prior and his successors free of all secular services save services to the abbot of Thorney of 50d (2d *inserted*) per annum at Easter. Warranty clause. Sealing clause.

Witnesses: Henry then reeve (*prepositus*), Walter de Tykincote, Walter de Repinghale, Hugh son of Reyner, Gilbert le Noble, Richard son of Selove, Peter de Castreton and many others.

---

[32] This suggests the parish may be St Michael the Greater, since the parish of St Michael in Cornstall (St Leonards Street) did not reach into Claymont (Broad Street) while the parish of St Michael the Greater did; see 4.15 above and Hartley and Rogers

b) <u>*Indenture*</u> of lease: Richard prior of St James de Deping with the assent of the abbot and convent of Thorney to Eustace Ruffus of Stanford and Beatrice his wife of our houses in Stanford situated in Claymund between the houses of Richard Ode west and of Flurekin[?] son of Roger Gosenol east for life for 3s per annum, at Michaelmas (18d) and Easter (18d). Repair and maintenance clause. Sealing clause.

Witnesses: Henry then reeve, Walter Tykincote, Walter de Repinghale, Hugh son of Reyner, Gilbert le Noble, Richard son of Selive, Peter de Castreton and others.

911.13 Add MSS 3021, fol. 262
<u>*Sale*</u> by Agnes relict of Walter Kysk of Stanford in my free widowhood with full legitimate power to Ralph Fulstirte of Stanford butcher, for a certain sum of money which he has given to me by hand, of a certain vacant place with appurtenances in the parish of St John Stanford between the tenement of the said Ralph west and the public way (*viam puplicam*) east, containing 30 feet (*pedes*) in length and 14 feet in width, to hold to Ralph, his heirs and assigns free of all dues except service to the chief lord of the fee. Warranty against all comers to Ralph of vacant place with appurtenances and all buildings constructed there or to be constructed there. Sealing clause.

Witnesses: Alfred le Mercer, Walter de Tilton, Ralph de Reynham, Robert Kykeman, Peter Hod, William Hod, William Tappeden, Henry de Fyncham, Geoffrey de Briggestok, John de Castreton and others.

911.14 Add MSS 3021, fol. 262d(i)   11 July 1342
John de Warenne to his officials in Stanford concerning the rights of Thorney abbey in their tenements in Stanford with suit of court twice each year at Michaelmas and Easter and rights of aletol, bochelghild, wyndowegild, relefs, eschetes, offare and onffare – they can hold their accustomed courts.

Dated: 11 July 16 Edward III

911.15 Add MSS 3021, fol. 262d (ii)   12 July 1391
<u>*Inspeximus*</u> and confirmation by Edmund duke of York and lord of the town of Stanford of the royal charters and of the confirmation by John de Warenne earl of Surrey to Thorney Abbey of all their rents and possessions in Stanford free of all dues save two suits of court each year, for the souls of ourself and Isabelle our consort and Edward our beloved son and our ancestors and heirs

Dated: London 12 July 15 Richard II

911.16 Add MSS 3021, fol. 262d-263 (iii)   6 April 1315
<u>*Inquisition*</u> at Stanford 6 April 8 Edward II before John de Heselarton knight, Elias de Birton then steward of Stanford and Robert de Neuwerk commissioners of John de Warenne earl of Surrey of the possessions of the abbot and convent of Thorney in Stanford on the oath of Eustace de Malherbe, William Apethorpe, Roger de Scavelere, John Asplon, Hugh Averey, Gilbert de Redyngg, John de Knotteshale, Richard de

Baldeswell, William de Baldeswell, William Buntyngg, Henry de Kerbroke, and Henry de Helpiston including offace, onfare, relief, aletol, buchelyeld, wyndowyeld, and all other customs, subject to two suits of court.

911.17 Add MSS 3021, fol. 289
Sale and quitclaim by Robert Niger son of Peter Niger of Stanford to Guy (*Widoni*) Wake my lord, his heirs and assigns of all my rights in the houses and appurtenances which were once my property and which I held of Guy Wake in the parish of All Saints in the market of Stanford, for six marks silver paid to me to acquit these houses of the Jews (*de iudaismo*). Sealing clause.

Witnesses: Dom Peter de Weston knight, Walter de Tykincote, Theodoric de Colonia, Hugh son of Reyner, William son of Ode, Clement rector of St Michael in Cornstall of Stanford, Geoffrey clerk vinitar, Richard de Colstreworth, William le Petit, Peter son of Geoffrey, Nicholas son of Alexander and others
Marginal: re houses etc of Robert Niger of Stanford in the parish of All Saints given to the prior of Depyng

911.18 Add MSS 3021, fol. 289
Sale and quitclaim by Henry son of Henry son of David de Stanford to Dom Guy Wake of my houses with appurtenances in Stanford, namely those situated between the oven (*forn'*) of the town and the house of Meir Judei west, with the rents belonging to those houses, namely from the house which Jose holds 2s and certain other dues, from the house which Robert Niger holds 3s and certain other dues; I give to the church all the rights I and my heirs and assigns may have in those houses, saving service to the chief lord of the fee. Before this sale, Guy gave to me of his magnanimity to acquit me of the Jews 24 marks and 10 quarters. Warranty. Sealing clause.

Witnesses: Walter de Tykencote, Henry de Tykencote, Terricus de Colonia, Henry son of Alexander, Nicholas his brother, Hugh son of Reyner, Alexander his brother, Richard son of Selef, Richard and Henry his sons, David clerk and others.

911.19 Add MSS 3021, fol. 289-289d
Grant and confirmation by Guy Wake for the health of my soul and the soul of Mabil my wife and our ancestors and successors and all faithful in pure and perpetual alms to God and to the church of St James de Deping of an annual rent of 72s in Stanford from the houses which I bought from Henry son of Henry son of David and from Robert son of Peter in the parish of All Saints in the market of Stanford by the hands of Richard de Colsterwithe, which houses they held of me. Quitclaim to Deeping St James.

Witnesses: Reiner dean of Stanford, Clement rector of St Michael de Cornstall, William de Pappele chaplain, Hugh son of Reiner, Alexander his brother, Walter de Tykencote, Tericus de Colonia, Henry son of Alexander, Nicholas his brother, Henry Scibeci and others

911.20 Add MSS 3021, fol. 289d

Agreement between Guy Wake and Gilbert de Northfolk tailor (*Cissorem*) of Stanford of a grant by Guy Wake to Gilbert de Northfolk and his heirs and assigns in fee farm all those houses and rents with appurtenances which Guy bought from Henry son of Henry son of David situated in the parish of All Saints in the market in Stanford and the houses with appurtenances which were of Peter Niger, to hold to Gilbert and his heirs and assigns (other than religious and Jews), rendering to Guy and his heirs £4 sterling at the four terms of the year; also 6d at Easter for steps to the door of the solar (*pro grade ad hostium solarii*). By this agreement, Gilbert bound himself to Guy to build on these houses in the first year buildingsto the estimated value of six marks silver and to maintain these houses and appurtenances in the same or better condition as he received them. Default clause. Warranty

Witnesses. Dom John Gubaud, Dom Robert de Colevile, Dom Peter de Welton , Hugh son of Reiner, Terricus Theonico, Henry son of Alexander, Robert de Norton, Henry Scibeci, William son of David, Robert son of Ysaac and others.

911.21 Add MSS 3021, fol. 289d-290

Grant by Guy Wake [to Deeping St James as ... above] of an annual rent of £4 sterling and 6d p.a. in Stanford from those houses which I bought of Henry son of Henry son of David and from Robert son of Peter in the parish of All Saints in the market by the hand of Gilbert le taylour and his heirs and assigns, which rent they took from those houses at the four terms of the year as by a charter which Gilbert had of me. Quitclaim to God and to the church of Deping St James of all rights I and my heirs have in these rents. Also paying to the chief lord of the town 6d annually for some steps built to the head of a certain chamber opposite the said church [All Saints in Stamford] (*pro gradibus firmatis ad caput cuidam camere versus prescriptam ecclesiam vj denarios*). Sealing clause. Warranty

Witnesses. Master Henry dean of Stanford, Clement rector of St Michael de Cornstall, Hugh son of Reiner, Alexander his son, Tericus de Colonia, Henry son of Alexander, Nicholas his brother, Henry Scibeci, Alexander le seriant, Walter le Flemeng, David clerk, Richard son of Richard, Henry his brother, Herebert Ferrano and others

911.22 Add MSS 3021, fol. 290

Charter by Alexander son and heir of Gilbert Cissor of Stanford to God and the church of St James of Depyng all my houses with rents and appurtenances in the parish of All Saints in the market of Stanford which Gilbert my father purchased from Guy Wake as is more fully contained in a charter which my father had from Guy which charter is retained by the religious[i.e. the priory] by my agreement (*ex tradicione mea propria*); rendering to the chief lord of Stanford 6d p.a. on Palm Sunday (*Pascha Florida*) for the stairs to the head of a certain chamber opposite the church there [i.e. All Saints church in Stamford]. Warranty. Sealing clause.

Witnesses. Walter Dragun then steward of Stanford, William de Notingham, Andrew Arketel, Alexander Lucas, Robert son of Ysaac, Hugh de Welledon, Hugh Bunting then reeve, John le Flemang of Clipshil, Reynour de Strandeby [*sic*], Robert Brond, Henry his

son, Hugh le mercer, William his brother, Bartholomew Allucarius [shoemaker[33]], John s
on of John de Castreton clerk and others.

911.23 Add MSS 3021, fol. 438

<u>Grant</u> by David abbot of Thorney in fee and inheritance to Geoffrey son of Richard de
Deping clerk those houses in Stanford in the parish of St Michael in Cornstall which we
had by grant of Hugh vicar of Makeseia at a rent of 10s payable to him and his heirs, 5s
at Michaelmas and 5s at Easter, saving to us and to the members of our house (*familie
nostra*) special easement (*speciali aisiamento hospicium*) as we have had before; saving service
to the chief lord of the town. Warranty.

Witnesses: Dom John de Folkworth, Master Adam de Ludon, Richard de Brampton then
steward and others

912 BRITISH LIBRARY HARLEIAN MSS 3658: CARTULARY OF THE PRIORY OF DEEPING ST JAMES *(dated approximately 1331 but containing items much earlier. All charters are undated).*

912.1 Harl 3658 fol 19v

Note: The prior of St James in Depyng used to receive rents of 60s p.a. from
tenements in Stanford in the parish of All Saints in the market; but he must maintain a
chaplain to sing prayers at 5 marks p.a. [i.e. £3 6s 8d]. There is nothing else in Stanford.

912.2 Harl 3658 fol 49 (i)

<u>Sale and quitclaim</u> by Robert Niger son of Peter Niger of Stanford to Guy (*Wido*) Wake
my lord of all my rights in the houses cp once belonging to me and held of Guy Wake in
the parish of All Saints in the market of Stanford for six marks silver to acquit these
houses of the Jews. Sealing clause.

Witnesses Dom Peter de Weston knight and others
[*See above 911.17*]

912.3 Harl 3658 fol 49 (ii)

<u>Sale and quitclaim</u> by Henry son of Henry son of David de Stanford to Guy Wake all my
rights in my houses cp in Stanford, namely those situated between the oven (*forn'*) and
the house of Meyr Judei with the rents belonging to these houses, namely from the
house which Jose holds 2s and certain other dues, and from the house which Robert
Niger holds 3s and certain other dues; saving service to the chief lord. Guy Wake of my

---

[33] ALLUCARIUS. Sutor qui facit calceos de aluta [shoemaker using soft leather]: du
Cange, *et al., Glossarium mediae et infimae latinitatis*, éd. augm., Niort : L. Favre, 1883-1887,
http://ducange.enc.sorbonne.fr/ALLUCARIUS accessed 14 April 2012

great necessity has paid to me 24 marks and ten quarters to acquit me of the Jews. Sealing clause.

Witnesses: Walter de Tikincote and others

912.4 Harl 3658 fol 49-49v (iii)

Grant and confirmation by Guy Wake for a chantry and the health of my soul and that of Amabilia my wife and our ancestors and successors and all faithful dead in free and perpetual alms to God and the church of St James in Depyng of a rent of 72s in Stanford from the houses which I bought from Henry son of Henry son of David and from Robert son of Peter in the parish of All Saints in the market of Stanford by the hand of Richard de Colstreworthe, his heirs and assigns, which houses are bound to pay this rent at the four terms of the year, as by my charter is fully expressed. Quitclaim of all rights. Sealing clause.

Witnesses Reyner dean of Stamford and others
Marginal note: Guy Wake knight gave the said houses to Richard de Colstreworthe and his heirs at an annual rent of 72s and he gave the said rent of 72s to the said church of EaDepyng.

912.5 Harl 3658 fol 49v (iiii)

Agreement of lease between Guy Wake and Gilbert de Northfolk *cissor* [tailor] of Stanford for all those houses and rents which Guy bought from Henry son of Henry son of David in the parish of All Saints in the market of Stanford with the houses which were of Peter Niger; grant to Gilbert and his heirs and assigns (except religious and the Jews) rendering annually to Guy Wake and his heirs and assigns £4 sterling at four terms of the year; also 6d on Palm Sunday to the lord of the town for steps to the door of the solar. Gilbert by this writing has freely bound himself to Guy in the first year to build buildings on the said houses and rents to the value of six marks and maintain them in such condition or better than he received them. Default and distraint clauses. Warranty. Sealing clause to this chirograph.

Witnesses: Dom John Gobaud and others
Marginal note: Guy Wake leased to Gilbert Cissor of Stanford and his heirs the tenements cp for £4 (and 6d inserted) sterling.

912.6 Harl 3658 fol 50 (v)

Grant and confirmation by Guy Wake of his full charity and for the health of the souls of himself and his wife Amabilia etc [*as in 912.4*] in pure and perpetual alms to God and the church of St James in Depyng the annual rent of £4 sterling and 6d in Stanford from the houses which I bought from Henry son of Henry son of David and from Robert son of Peter in the parish of All Saints in the market Stanford by the hand of Gilbert le Taylour and his heirs and assigns, which houses are burdened with a rent of £4 at four terms of the year as by my charter etc and 6d to the chief lord of the fee for steps to the head of a certain chamber against (*versus*) the said church. Quitclaim of all my rights. Sealing clause.

Witnesses: Master Henry dean of Stanford.

912.7 Harl 3658 fol 50-50v (vi)

Grant by Alexander son and heir of Gilbert Cissor of Stanford to God and to the church of St James at Depyng of all my houses and rents in the parish of All Saints in the market Stanford which Gilbert my father held of Guy Wake by a charter which at my request remains with the said religious to have and to hold the said houses and rents cp rendering annually to the chief lord of the fee 6d at Palm Sunday for steps etc as above. Warranty and sealing clauses.

Witnesses: Walter Dragoun then steward of Stanford and others.
Marginal note: *Memorandum that the said tenements were leased in the time of abbot Odo to Walter de Apethorpe and Alice his wife and Walter their son for life in the 28ᵗʰ year of Edward [I] for 40s p.a.*

912.8 Harl 3658 fol 53v-54   24 April 1315
Copy of 911.11 but with some variations as follows:
Robert de Newerk one messuage in Estgate 3d
John de Reppes one tenement in Colgate 5½d
Emma de Ketelthorp one messuage on Cleymund 3d
The prior of St Leonards two cottages outside Estgate 5½ d
The Carmelite friars for one messuage called le Chekerstede 9d
Henry le Taylour one messuage on Cleymund 2d
John earl Warenne one messuage, one cellar and one schop in the parish of St Mary at the bridge 13d
Emma Bertlimeu one house in (*infra*) her manse in the same parish 1d
Henry de Piribrok one messuage in Westgate 9d
Henry Leche one messuage in Westgate 6¾d
William de Baldeswelle and John Waldeschef three messuages at the bridge of Maleroie 2s 3d
The place opposite the church of St Peter which Richard Marmium once held 3½ d
Roger Mechelove one messuage at Westgate (*ad portam orientalem*) 4d
John Fresche one messuage which Hemming Likkesnot held 5d

Witnesses: Doms Thomas de Schefeld, John de Heselarton, Peter de Montefort, William de Bayhuse, knights, Dom William de Cusance, Mr John de Nevile clerks, Robert de Newerk, Richard de Frekenberg and others.

Dated: Reigate 24 April 8 Edward son of Edward: this was enrolled in the court of the lord [Warenne] in the castle at Stanford by Elyas de Birton steward, Eustace Malherbe and Henry de Sylton and others of the court, Thursday after Trinity 8 Edward son of Edward [22 May 1315]

912.9 Harl 3658 fol 54v-55   18 June 1351
Lease by William abbot of Thorney to Walter de Apethorp in Stanford and Cecil [*sic*] his wife and Richard their son of the houses in Stanford situated in the parish of All Saints in the market in the street of Byhyndebask for the life of each, rendering to the prior of St James at Depyng 30s at the four terms of the year; they shall build, repair and maintain buildings on the site. Warranty.

Witnesses: John de Chestre, William de Schylingthon, Thomas de Pountfreyt, Reginald Salteby, Elkshath [?] Assewell, Robert Talyngthon, William Gentyl burgesses of Stanford and others.

Dated : Thorney Saturday after the feast of St Botolph abbot 25 Edward III

912.10 Harl 3658 fol 56v
Note: In the year 1231 Guy Wake gave to the abbot and convent of Thorney and the church of St James in Depyng in pure alms his tenements in Stanford in the parish of All Saints in the market as by charters of Guy Wake and Alexander son of Gilbert Cissor made 16 Henry III.

913 SPALDING GENTLEMEN'S SOCIETY, WREST PARK CARTULARY (CROWLAND ABBEY) FOLIOS 185-189. *Most deeds are undated and without witness lists. They are numbered as in the cartulary.* [34]

913. 1 fol 185r
Sale by Geoffrey de Bodeneye and Hawys daughter of Roger Palmer wife of Geoffrey nephew (*nepos*) of Geoffrey dean in their dire penury (*dira penuria constenti*) to Peter chaplain parson of St Michael the Greater (*maioris*) of Staunford for 40s, of all our houses without retaining any in the parish of St Andrew by the cemetery on the south, namely those which Geoffrey the dean once held, which my brother gave to me [*sic*], to have and to hold to the said Peter and his heirs and assigns freely in inheritance in perpetuity, saving service to the chief lord of the fee. Warranty by us to Peter and his heirs. Sealing clause. Witnesses [no names]

913.2
Grant and confirmation by Peter chaplain rector of St Michael the Greater of Staunford for the health of my soul and my parents and kinsmen (*amicorum*) to God, St Mary, St Bartholomew and St Guthlac of Croiland and the monks serving God there, of my house in Staunford in the parish of St Andrew by the cemetery south with possession free of all secular services save to the chief lord of the fee. Witnesses.

913.3   30 March 1251
Recognisance by Geoffrey de Thornhawe burgess of Staunford and Matilda [35]his wife of an annual rent to the abbot of Croiland and convent, of 12s for the houses which were of Peter former rector of St Michael the Greater in the parish of St Andrew in Staunford – i.e. 3s at the feast of Nativity of St John the Baptist, Michaelmas, the Nativity and Easter. Distraint clause for this farm on our goods anywhere or the seizure of these houses; we

---

[34] I am grateful to Tom Grimes of Spalding Gentlemen's Society for help with this section

[35] This may be an error for Issabella mother of Matilda; see 913. 4, 5 and index

promise we shall not alienate these houses to religious, Jews or any other to the prejudice or damage of the abbot or convent of Croiland. Sealing clause. Witnesses

Dated: Croiland Thursday after the Annunciation of the Blessed Mary anno incarnation 1250

913.4 fol 185r-185v

Release and quitclaim by Matilda daughter of Issabella formerly the wife of Geoffrey de Thornhawe to the abbot of Croiland and convent, of those houses formerly of Peter rector of the church of St Michael the Greater of Staunford situated in the parish of St Andrew Staunford between the houses once of lady Greta [Grete/Grece?] and the cemetery of St Andrew, of which houses I the said Matilda was enfeoffed with Simon son of Robert de Bixer by the Issabella my mother in her free widowhood. Surrender of all rights and claims in those properties. I have surrendered those charters which I had by the feoffment by Issabella my mother with the charters of feoffment which Geoffrey de Thornhawe had of the abbot of Croiland and the convent and which Issabella had of Geoffrey de Thornhawe in full court of Staunford before the steward and others present there. Sealing clause

913.5

Grant and confirmation by Issabella formerly the wife of Geoffrey de Thornhawe in my free widowhood to Simon son of Robert de Bix of Thornhawe and to Matilda my daughter of those houses cp situated in Barmigate in the parish of St Andrew of Staunford to hold to Simon and his heirs and assigns freely by inheritance rendering annually to the abbot and convent of Croiland 12s at the four terms of the year. Warranty by Issabella and her heirs to Simon and Matilda my daughter and their heirs. Sealing clause.

913.6

Quitclaim by William earl Warenne for the health of my soul and my father and mother, my ancestors and successors to God, St Mary, St Bartholomew and St Guthlac of Croiland and the monks there of that house cp which they [the monks] had in the parish of St Andrew next to the cemetery south by the gift of Peter chaplain rector of St Michael the Greater and the houses which they bought from Thomas son of Hakun of Staunford in the said parish of St Michael in Claymount, namely those which Thomas son of Hakun took in exchange with Roger son of Mabil for those houses which were of Hakun his father, to hold to the abbot and convent in free and perpetual alms free of all secular services and exactions to me and my successors. Sealing clause. Witnesses.

913.7 fol 186r

Grant and confirmation by Philip parson of Carleby for the health of my soul and my successors to God and St Guthlac of Croiland of those houses cp which Hugh son of Reyner Maysent of Staunford sold to me in the parish of St Paul of Staunford which formerly were of Reginald Lambesheved situated between the church of St Paul east and the houses of Peter Kempe west in pure and perpetual alms free and quit of all services save the services belonging to those houses as by the charter of the said Hugh is more fully witnessed. Sealing clause. Witnesses.

913.8

Grant and confirmation by Henry abbot of Croiland and the convent to William le Petyt of Theford and his heirs of those houses cp which Philip dean of Carleby sold to us in the parish of St Paul of Staunford which once were of Reginald Lambesheved situated between the church of St Paul east and the houses of Peter Kempe west. William and his heirs shall have the said houses free of all services rendering to us 18s p.a. for all services save service to the chief lord at the four terms of the year. Warranty as Philip warranted to us. Sealing clause. Witnesses.

913.9

Sale and confirmation by Hugh son of Reyner Maysent of Staunford with the assent of my heirs and my other kinsmen to Philip parson of the church of Carleby son of dom Richard de Cotes of his houses cp in the parish of St Paul of Staunford which once were of Reginald Lambesheved situated between the church of St Paul of Staunford east and the houses of Peter Kempe west to hold to Philip or those to whom he may give, sell or assign them freely, quit of me and my heirs for 32 marks silver which Philip gave to me save the services of those houses. Warranty by Hugh in all appurtenances in the walls of the town of Staunford to the said Philip and his assigns. Sealing clause. Witnesses (no names).

913.10 fol 186r-186v

Quitclaim by Alexander son of Reyner Maysent of Staunford to Philip parson of Carleby son of dom Richard de Cotes of those houses cp in parish of St Paul Staunford which were of Reginald Lambheved situated between the church of St Paul east and the houses of Peter Kempe west, with all rights and claims which Alexander and his heirs had or could have, which Hugh my brother sold to Philip for 32 marks. For this confirmation, Philip gave to me one mark silver. Warranty. Sealing clause. Witnesses (no names).

913.11

Quitclaim by Simon son of William le Petyt of Theford to God and St Guthlac of Croiland of all his rights and claims in the houses in the parish of St Paul of Staunford which my father William had by grant of Henry abbot of Croiland, situated between the church of St Paul of Staunford east and the houses formerly of Peter Kempe west. So that neither I nor my heirs can sell any right or claim in the said houses cp. Sealing clause. Witnesses.

913.12 fol 186v-187r   3 April 1258

Lease in fee farm by the abbot and convent of Croiland to William de Pippes burgess of Staunford of those houses cp in the town of Staunford situated in the parish of St Paul between the houses once of Simon Kempe west and the church of St Paul east, to be held of the abbot and convent free of all services rendering one silver mark at the four terms of the year. If he shall owe suit of court for these houses, he and his heirs shall make suit [i.e. in person]. William and his heirs shall not alienate them to any Christian, Jew or any alien person. Default and distraint clauses with provision for re-entry. He shall maintain the property in as good or better condition as he received them, as by a special agreement (*pacto*) between the parties appended to this agreement. Warranty by Ralph the abbot and convent for these houses cp to William and his heirs as much as is possible. In witness those present in the convent have appended their sign (*alternatim signa sua apposuerunt*). Witnesses (no names).

Dated: Croiland 3 April 47 Henry son of John [Henry III]

913.13

Sale by Peter son of Ysaac of the great arches (*de Archia magna*) compelled by my necessity with the assent and counsel of Outhilda my wife to Reginald son of Gilbert de Berc of my messuage cp in Staunford situated between the house once of Geoffrey son of Reiner west and the house of Ralph son of Acard east in the parish of St John for 15 marks silver paid to me to maintain me and Outhilda in our great poverty and principally to free and acquit the said messuage taken into the king's hands because of debts to the Jews, to have and to hold the messuage to Reginald and his heirs and assigns free of all services save service to the chief lord. Warranty to Reginald, his heirs and assigns. Sealing clause. Witnesses (no names).

913.14a

Grant and confirmation by Reginald son of Gilbert de Berch for the health of his soul and those of his ancestors and heirs to God and St Guthlac of Croiland and the monks serving there, of that messuage with oven (*furnum*) cp in Staunford which I bought of Peter son of Ysaac de Archia magna situated between the house of Ralph son of Acard east and the house once of Reyner west in the parish of St John free of all secular services belonging to me save service to the chief lord ; for this grant the monks will give me 28 marks sterling. Warranty by Reginald to the monks. Sealing clause. Witnesses (no names).

913.14b fol 187r-187v [36]

Grant by Henry abbot of Croiland to Reginald Palmer and his heirs of that messuage in Staunford except the oven with free entry and exit to the oven which we retain in our hands, namely that messuage which Reginald de Berch gave to us situated between the house of Ralph son of Acard east and the house of Reyner west in the parish of St John, to hold to us quit of services rendering to us 20s annually at the four terms of the year. Warranty to Reginald and his heirs for the messuage against all as Reginald de Berch and his heirs gave warranty to us. Sealing clause. Witnesses (no names).

913.15

Grant and confirmation by Geoffrey son of Robert de Torpell and Alienora his wife the daughter of Robert Meirym of Helpeston for the health of the soul of Robert Meirym my ancestors and successors, to God and St Guthlac and the abbot of Croiland of his

[36] This deed is unnumbered in the cartulary

houses in the parish of St Mary at the bridge of Staunford cp situated between the house of Henry Hare south and the house of Thomas clerk north in pure and perpetual alms free of all secular services and exactions save service to the chief lord. Sealing clause. Witnesses (no names).

913.16

Grant and confirmation by Alianora the daughter of Robert Meirym of Helpeston for the health of my soul and the soul of Robert Meirym my father and Maude my mother to God, St Bartholomew and St Guthlac and the abbot of Croiland and the monks there, of my houses cp in the parish of St Mary at the bridge of Staunford situated between the house of Thomas clerk north and the house of Henry Hare south, in free and perpetual alms free of secular services save service to the chief lord. Sealing clause.

913.17

Grant and confirmation by Peter chaplain son of Robert Meirym of Helpeston to God, St Bartholomew and St Guthlac of Croiland and the monks there, of those houses cp in the parish of St Mary at the bridge which Alienora my sister the wife of Geoffrey Bulhernes gave to the monks situated between the house of Thomas clerk north and the house of Henry Hare south in free and perpetual alms freely of all secular services save service to the chief lord. Sealing clause. Witnesses (no names).

913.18 fol 187v-188r

Indenture of lease at fee farm by [Ralph] abbot and convent of Croiland to Richard le Escot of Staunford of his houses cp in Staunford situated in the parish of St Mary between the houses of Thomas clerk north and the house of Geoffrey seriente [serjeant] south to hold of the abbot and convent to Richard and Helewyse his wife and their heirs free of services rendering annually to the abbot and his successors 12s silver at the four terms of the year for all secular services save foreign (*forinsec*) service to the lord of the fee. Richard and his heirs shall not alienate it to anyone as above. Re-entry clause; they are to maintain it in as good or better condition as they received it as by a special agreement (*ex speciali pacto*) between the parties as above. Warranty. Sealing clause. Witnesses (no names).

913.19a

Grant and confirmation by John de Staunford son of Sampson le Chivaler to God and St Guthlac of Croiland of one stall (*solda*) in the parish of St George between the house of Geoffrey le Coupere which he holds of the nuns of St Michael in Staunford and another stall of my own in free and perpetual alms for the health of my soul and my ancestors and heirs. Witnesses (no names).

913.19b[37]

Grant and confirmation by Ralph abbot of Croiland to Robert Maidenlove of Staunford for his service (*pro servicio suo*) of a stall in Staunford in the parish of St George, namely that

---

[37] This deed is unnumbered in the cartulary; it may be combined with the previous entry as relating to the same stall.

which we have by gift of John son of Sampson as his charters shows, to hold to him and his heirs rendering 5s at four times a year for all services and demands. The said stall cannot be alienated without notifying us and our successors. Warranty to Robert and his heirs as far as belongs to us. Sealing clause. Witnesses (no names).

913.20 folio 188r-188v
a) *Grant and confirmation* by Thomas son of Eustace to God, St Mary, St Bartholomew and St Guthlac of Croiland and the monks there of a rent of 8s and four capons due to them for the land in Staunford, that is the rent which is paid to me by the hand of his bailiff or their attorney by Ralph son of Fulcon of Staunford and his heirs for the land which Ralph held of me in Staunford of the fee which Pampoke [?] held, namely at Easter 4s and two capons and at Michaelmas 4s and two capons. Distraint clause including the arable and meadow which Ralph holds by, but limited to the 8s rent and capons. Warranty to the monks. Sealing clause to this page (*presentem paginam*). Witnesses (no names).

913.21
Quitclaim by Thomas son of Thomas son of Eustace for the health of my soul and my ancestors and heirs to God and St Guthlac of Croiland and the monks there, of the homage and service of Thomas de Marham and his wife Avice and their heirs for the land which Ralph son of Fulcon once held of me in the town of Staunford and in the territory of the same town, both in homage and service and in relief and courts and all liberties belonging to that fee in the town and outside. The monks to have and to hold it all in free and perpetual alms completely freely without retaining anything to me and my heirs. Warranty by me and my heirs. Witnesses (no names).

ANY AMENDMENTS AND ANY FURTHER TITLE DEEDS RELATING TO MEDIEVAL STAMFORD IDENTIFIED WILL BE CALENDARED ON THE STAMFORD SURVEY GROUP WEBSITE

www.stamfordhistory.org.uk

reeve 628; the tailor 196, 214; son of Baldwin 447; son of Bu[...]lt 423; son of Burnild 483; son of David 242, 450, 583, 640; son of Luke 501; son of Reyner 149.2, 149.4, 209; son of Richard 403, 761; son of Richard son of Seluve de Stanford 559; son of Stanford 224; brother of David 157.1; brother of Hugh son of Reiner 559; Avice wife of 218; Cecily wife of Henry son of 558; Henry son of 152, 166, 183, 204, 211, 216-8, 245, 330, 339, 345, 367, 374, 414, 422, 447, 459, 476, 480, 484, 499, 502, 548, 558, 584, 639, 644, 911.18, 19, 20, 21; Hugh brother of 339; Matilda wife of 224, 226, 407, 654; Michael brother of Henry son of 211; Nicholas son of 217, 245, 339, 367, 447, 502, 579.2, 654, 657, 911.17,18, 19, 21; Nicholas brother of Henry son of 183; Reiner son of 412, 419; Simon son of 216, 506, 548, 654

Aleyn, Alen John 670, 767.6, 776

Alfred Hugh 460; Alfred the mercer 585;

Alfric the baker of Bradecroft 223, 442

Alice prioress of St Michael's 579.2, 592; *see* Andrew

Allcock John 758.146, 758.159

Allocarius Bartholomew shoemaker 911.22

Almer the smith 167

Almerton Cecily 4.3

Alpeisa daughter of Geoffrey 338, 507

Alriche, Alrych Hugh 230, 359; *see* Aylriche

Alrith, Alryth 657; Hugh 441

Alstan monk 263, 437

Alsy Hugh 297; William 297; *see* Aylcy

Aluerton, Alvertone Hugh de 29, 115, 147, 305, 378, 430, 713, 808

Alumpnus Robert 499; *see* Peter

Alver, *see* Halver

Alwether Margaret 694

Amabilia prioress of St Michael 600

Amfelisia, *see* Casewik

Amicia daughter of Geoffrey son of Outhild' 145; Amicia prioress of St Michael's 153, 241, 292, 328, 519

Anable John 235

Andrew Alice prioress of St Michael's 395, 571

Andrew the clerk 219, 478; Andrew rector of St Clement 400; monk 263, 597; prior of St Fromond 575; Andrew the palmer 221, 224, 339, 450, 583; Andrew *in venella* 518; son of Matilda 507; son of Peter 477; son of Stanewi 482, 489; Emma wife of 482; Henry son of Andrew 339; John 350, 449

Andrews 767.1, 767.3

Ang'lo William son of 437

Angelin William 310

Angelina 655; *see* Bulbals

Angelus 179; *see* Stanford

Annor 657

Ansex Thurstan de 292; *see* Bisex

Apethorpe, Abethorp, Aepthorpe ... de 200 ; Elizabeth daughter of John 754; Joan wife of John 112b, 128-9; John de 112b, 128-9, 731, 737, 739, 758.57, 758.71, 758.111, 758.128, 758.142, 758.148, 758.191, 758.193, 759, 772; John son of William 537; Robert de 1.3, 415, 758.71; Walter de 7, 8, 150, 252, 410, 465, 555; Walter son of William de 758.30; William de 1.2-3, 4.5, 7, 8, 150, 173, 230, 252, 273, 274, 278, 305-6, 311, 382, 391, 406, 410, 430, 441, 463, 472, 537, 553, 554.1-2, 555, 598, 648, 707, 713-4, 729, 740, 744, 758.22, 758.30, 758.58, 758.68, 911.16; William de senior 746, 748; William de junior 170, 188, 385, 388, 454, 456, 462, 746; William son of John 758.71

App' Henry 844

Apsat son of Simon 448; Gilbert brother of Apsat 448

aquario John 154; *see* Atwater

Arch *(ad arcam)*, Archam Robert 341, 451, 461, 496; *see* Larche

Arches Ysaac of the (great) 913.13, 14a, see Ysaac

Archetel, *see* Arketel

Ardekin William son of Roger 383

Ardenne Sarra wife of Thomas de 51;

Thomas de 51

Ardern Richard de 1.3, 79, 317, 699, 758.72, 758.84, 758.103, 753.107

Argrim 655

Arketel, Archetel, Arket' cordwainer 484; Andrew 145, 157.2, 177, 182, 196, 201, 205, 209, 215, 223, 241, 247, 255, 280, 292, 307, 352, 389, 392, 396, 408, 428, 432, 434, 442, 485, 496, 506, 509, 514, 522, 546, 560, 911.22; Andrew son of 245; James 199, 281

Armstone W 758.187, 758.192, 759, 772

Arnald William 518

Arnale John 59; Matilda wife of John 59

Arnewi 657; Robert son of Arnewi 657

Asard priest 578; see Acard

Ascelin Henry son of 336

Asciria sister of Acard 523

Ashbourn Robert de 758.50

Asheby, see Assheby

Aslekston Peter de 149.7

Asplon, see Absalon

Assewell, Asshewell, Aissewell, Ashwell Alice 271, 531; Eustace de 1.2, 146, 173, 469, 827; Henry de 42, 56, 184, 283, 758.29; Isabel wife of Henry de 42; John de 36, 526, 530; Roger de 1.2

Assheby, Asseby James de 76; Joan wife of James de 76; Nicholas de 149.3; William 758.146

Aston(a) ….. de 660; Alianora wife of Robert de 44; Robert de 44; see Aiston

At the bridge, see Absalon, Bridge

At Water Emma 548, 558; Geoffrey 152, 226, 231, 515; Henry 231; see aquario

Athelokston Richard de 354

Atteneston Richard de 521

Aubry Hugh 911.14

Aug[nes?], see Agnes

Aurifaber, see Goldsmith

Avegaya the Jew 513

Averey, Auerey Agnes wife of Hugh 820; Hugh 430, 713, 820, 911.16;

Margery wife of Walter 707, 740; Walter 707, 714, 740,746, 748

Aylcy Alan 333, 568; Hugh 333 ; see Alsy

Aylington Katherine daughter of Walter de 729; Walter de 729; see Elton

Aylrich of Bradcroft 758.21; Matilda wife of Aylrich 758.21; see Alriche

Azelinus the priest 407

B[….] Reginald de 265

Ba[loff] William bailiff 298

Babyngton Norman 108

Bachun William 157.1

Badburgham John 758.158

Badyngton Geoffrey de parson of church of Wardeboys 62; William de 258

Baillif Cecily wife of John 89a; John of Casewyk 89a

Baker Robert 657; William of Papley 674; see … Henry, Alfric, Henry P…, Richard, Waleran

Balcock' 506, 510

Baldeswel Emma de 758.48; Emma wife of Richard de 758.41; Richard de 305, 555, 758.14, 758.29, 758.33, 758.41, 814, 911.16; Richard son of Richard 555; Walter de 729, 758.74, 758.84, 758.107, 824; William de 4.18, 911.16

Baldwin son of Gilbert 682; Alexander son of 447; Gilbert son of 403, 418, 504; Alexander brother of Gilbert 504

Ball(e) Christiana wife of William 24; Richard 141; Robert 873; William 24

Ballard, Ballart Simon 266, 336, 548, 557-8, 560

Banduney, Baunduney Geoffrey 216, 459

Barbier Richard 729

Barbour Edmund 236; John 743; Thomas 679.1, 758.116

Bardern Richard 648

Barentyn Cecily wife of William 68; William 68

Barewe John 759, 772

Barford John junior 670

Barham, Berham, Berwham Alan de

294, 361, 363; Matilda de, nun of St
Michael's 437

Barker(e) Henry 834; John 723;
Richard *alias* Tyler 758.175; Thomas
111, 299, 758.117, 758.141, 758.161

Barnack, Bernak, Bernech Geoffrey de
621; Gervase de 250, 443 ; Gilbert
de 307; Hugh de 216, 245, 255, 337-
8, 343, 422, 545, 591, 621; John de
563 ; Nicholas son of William de
4.16; Richard de 206, 640; Thomas de
464, 758.52-3, 758.67; Thomas de
vicar of Soterton 173; William de
4.16, 173

Baron Joan wife of Richard 758.126;
Richard 758.74, 758.126; Robert
758.143

Barr John 759, 772

Barsham Geoffrey de 305, 320

Bartholomew, Bartholomeu the clerk
586, 758.6; the preacher 758.18; the
goldsmith 495; son of William 400;
Emma 859, 911.11; John 4.5, 44,
369, 388, 470, 707, 714, 740, 748;
Peter chaplain 454, 456; Richard 48,
295-6, 329, 347, 370, 387, 440, 456,
462, 525, 527

Barton Henry de 158, 732; Richard,
prior of St Leonard's 679.1-2

Bartye Katherine wife of Richard 691;
Richard 691

Basham Alice 767.2-4

Basset Alice 677; Emma wife of
Gilbert 823; Gilbert 823; Stephen
157.1; Thomas 109, 110, 321, 661,
678, 710, 719, 724, 726, 728, 731,
737, 739, 745, 758.155, 758.157,
758.159, 758.165, 758.169, 766.1,
835-6

Bassingburne John de 609

Baston Geoffrey de son of Robert 610,
621; Robert de 610, 621; Simon de
154; Waleran de 469, 758.44

Bate John 1.2, 80 [2], 465, 469, 472,
475, 729

Bateman Henry 534, 722

Baunduney, *see* Banduney

Bauntre Robert 743

Bayarde Thomas 750

Baynbrigge Henry 89a

Bayons William de kt 911.11

Bazule Peter de 530; William son of
530

Bealsby Robert 881

Beamond Robert 674

Beatrice 179, 655

Beaufitz Margaret wife of William 121;
Robert 121; William 7, 8, 121, 555

Beaufo Ralph senior 873-4

Beauner Achard 911.8, 9 ; Ralph 911.8,
9; Ysabell 911.8

Beaver, Beauuer Achard 911.9; Richard
911.9

Bedeford John de 463; Ralph de 4.16;
Thomas de 184, 274, 369, 390, 406 ,
470, 475, 527, 692, 765.2-3

Beever John 670

Bek, Beck Ralph 170, 440

Bekyngham John 672

Belbraz, Beubraz Hugh 231; Roger
492; William 407, 450, 654

Beldesby, Belesby, *see* Billesby

Bellamy Helena 670

Bellegetere John le 347

Belleweyer Reginald 154

Belme John de 229, 569

Belmesthorpe William de 171, 347,
382, 440, 527

Belte William 260

Belton John de 832

Belue Emma wife of John 333; John
de 333

Bemfeld Geoffrey 758.127

Bendow Robert 661, 706, 711, 715,
719, 726

Benedict abbot of Peterborough 263,
409

Benet William 713

Benson William 649

Ber(e)ford Robert de 279; Thomas de
parson 69; William de 457

Ber(e)ham, *see* Barham

Berage, Berege Robert 652; William
135

Berc, Berch, Berk

Berc, Berch Gilbert de 913.13, 14a ;
Reginald son of Gilbert 913.13, 14a,
b; Hildana wife of William 805;
Richard son of William de 183, 446;
William de 183, 446-7, 643, 805;

William son of 643; *see* Achard

Bere William 8

Berkec William de 522

Bernake, *see* Barnack

Bernard the priest 167; Bernard Alice wife of Geoffrey 38; Geoffrey 38; William 670

Bernardeshil John de 176; Richard de 246; Robert de 355, 362, 493, 505 ; Thomas son of John de 176

Berne Hugh de 910.5; Reiner 910.5; *see* Bourne

Bernevill Roger de 497

Bertelmeu, Bertilmeu, *see* Bartholomew

Berth, Berthi Hugh de 587; Richard 758.32; Thomas son of Hugh de 587

Berugh Thomas de 692, 765.2

Berwedon David de 175

Betrefare Roger 151, 400

Beubras, *see* Belbraz

Beverage Richard 130

Bewscher, Bewshire, Buschyr Thomas 156, 161, 165, 235; William 774

Beyll Roger 776

Beymond Robert 845

Bigod, Bigot Hugh le 241; William le 663

Biham Gilbert de 341; *see* Bytham

Bikeden Henry de 306; *see* Buckeden

Bilkes, Bilkesle William son of Geoffrey the clerk 4.9-10, 214; Bilkes, William 237, 286, 334, 356

Billesby, Byllesby, Beldesby, Belesby John 649; John of Wothop 193; John of Colyweston 193; John son of William 431; Margaret wife of Richard 350; Nicholas 649; Richard 350, 449; Robert de 562, 573; William 193, 232, 359, 431, 449

Billesdon Nicholas 844

Billesfeld Geoffrey de 166, 207, 625, 634; Geoffrey son of Robert de 614, 623; Robert de 466, 612, 623; Peter son of Geoffrey de 634

Billingburgh Cristiana wife of William 39; Isolda de 39; William son of Isolda de 39

Binewerc Roger de clerk 363

Biri, *see* Byri

Birthorp William de 171, 296, 329, 347, 359, 382, 440, 525, 527, 529, 758.61; *see* Wirthorp

Birton, *see* Burton

Birun Richard 400

Bisex Thurstan de 522; *see* Ansex

Biterhingge Richard de 557

Bitham, *see* Bytham

Bix, Bixer Robert de 913.4, 5 ; Simon son of Robert de 913.4, 5; Matilda wife of 913.4, 5

Blackman John 758.33; John the elder 758.49

Blanchard John 460

Blarew Richard de 583

Blatherwyk Reyner de 149.6

Bledelawe Hugh de 911.3, 4, 5, 6

Blewyt Gregory 694

Blogwyn Richard 737, 758.181, 758.186-7, 767.1, 771

Bloston Thomas 706, 708

Blound, Bloundes, Blund(us) Hugh 207, 242; Robert le 260, 713; Richard le 550; Roger 455; Thomas 4.10

Bocher, *see* Butcher

Bocli Turstan 663

Bodin Tostenus 659

Bodeneye Geoffrey de 913.1; Hawise wife of 913.1

Boge, Bogy Joan 540; John 302, 539;

Bohun, *see* Northampton

Bol(e)wyk Cecily/Celia wife of Gilbert de 185, 364; Gilbert de 185, 364, 390; William de 469; *see* Bulwick

Bol(l)e Alice wife of Simon 528, 574; Eustace 369, 470; Robert 4.16; Simon burgess 528, 574; Simon senior 369, 470; William chaplain 254; William son of Eustace 369, 470

Bolde John 758.179

Boltham Katherine wife of Thomas 862; Thomas 862

Bolton Robert de 190, 665; Roger rector of St Peters 590

Bond(e) Agnes 358; Bernard 248, 256, 270, 276, 282, 284, 295-6, 312, 323, 325, 329, 359, 364, 370, 382, 388, 425, 438, 440, 456, 462, 474, 508, 525, 551-2, 565; John 171, 529,

758.81-3, 758.98; John parson of St
Mary Bynwerk 758.115; John rector
of St Mary at the bridge 758.114;
John senior 306, 314; John alias
Marchaunt 358; Ralph 189, 234, 537,
542, 758.144, 835; Simon 314, 464,
532; William 248, 270, 295, 364,
370, 425, 546
Bondone, *see* Boudon
Bonet John 92, 340
Boneton William 724
Bonevile Roger de 443
Bonhomine chaplain 187
Boni, *see* Bonus
Boniface the clerk 248
Bonne William 326
Bonus, Boni, Bony Damisona wife of
Roger 398, 492, 548, 557-8, 560;
Roger 492, 548, 557-8, 560
Borehard Symon 443
Boresworth Richard 272
Borw William de, vicar of Moltoun 390
Bosesworthe John de 827
Bosse John 141; Thomas 657
Bosswel Thomas 156
Boston William prior of Fynneshead
236
Boteler Robert 672
Bottai, Bottay 179; Emma mother of
Juliana 405, 413; John 151, 178, 202,
210, 212-3, 225, 243, 245, 255, 310,
315, 330, 337-8, 343, 346, 351, 353,
383, 400, 405, 412-3, 418-9, 422-4,
433, 447, 479, 482-3, 488, 511-2,
516, 544-5, 579.1, 586, 654-5; Juliana
daughter of John 151, 337, 405; Sarah
(Sarre) sister of Juliana 337
Botterwyk Henry 819
Bottesford, Botelesford William de
252, 254, 465, 675-6, 758.100
Boudon, Bondone, Budone,
Buwedone Agnes wife of Thomas 21;
Hugh de 181, 280; Ingald de 212,
337, 349; Thomas de 21
Bourle, *see* Burley
Bourne abbot of 909; Hugh de 910.5
Bourne, *see* Berne
Bove Alice wife of Thomas 537;
Thomas chaundler 537
Bowes Agnes prioress of Wothorpe

priory 253
Bowman Ralph 845
Boysse Alard 853
Brab[...] John 146; Braban John 147,
278, 758.14, 758.15, 758.19
Bracy Henry 672; William 672
Bradecroft Alan de 427; Aylric de 439;
Alice wife of Thomas 427; Emma de
170; Margery daughter of William
758.189; Martin de 639, 642;
Richard de 152; Thomas de 337, 427;
Walter de 152; Walter son of William
de 639, 642; William de 489,
758.142, 758.189; William son of
Martin de 639, 642; *see* Fissher
Braibruc Henry de 892
Brake John 697
Brakenbergh Agnes de prioress 333,
648
Bram(p)ton Benedict de 325; John de
429, 465, 472; Richard de steward
911.23
Brassingburg Alice wife of Simon de
758.38; Simon de 758.36, 758.38
Brasyers Richard 758.84
Braunston Simon de 25; Wymarca wife
of Simon 25
Bray Simon 4.17
Brereste Thomas 832
Brerle Thomas 696, 697; Thomas son
of Thomas 697
Bressere William 751
Bret John 862
Bretevile Robert de 221
Bretun Reginald le 201, 521
Brid W 758.78, 758.87, 758.89, 758.90,
758.179, 758.180; *see* Byrde
Bride Agnes 423; Marieria wife of
William 344; William 344
Bridge (*ad pontem*) Absalon at the 292,
346; Absalon son of Simon at the
293; Apsal 459; Gilbert brother of
Apsal 459; Juliana wife of Absalon
son of Simon at the 293; Matthew at
the 518; Nicholas son of Absalon
293; Simon at/of the 293, 149.5,
578; Thomas son of Absalon at the
292; *see* Absalon, Gilbert, Samson
Brig(e)stok Geoffrey de 911.13;
Richard de 387, 758.31; Robert de

469, 648; Walter de 361

Briggs John 758.173; *see* Bryg

Brighton, *see* Bryghton

Briselaunce Geoffrey 324, 369, 470,
475, 765.3; Richard 281; Richard
son of Roger 181; Robert 15, 181,
391, 406, 553, 554.2, 598; Roger 4.13,
181, 197, 281, 307, 377, 489, 510,
556; William 258, 551, 556

Broc, Broke Miles 804; Reginald de
643

Brokendissh Richard 4.16

Brond(s) 578; Brond ...... 354; Henry
286, 376, 399, 758.43, 758.72, 758.74;
Richard 185, 270, 364, 370, 425, 519,
557; Robert son of 398, 548; Robert
911.22; Henry son of Robert 911.22

Bronne, *see* Brun

Brotherhous Alan 229, 333, 569;
Robert 229, 313, 569, 573

Browe John 661, 706, 708, 711, 715,
722; Robert 564, 672, 758.168,
758.170, 758.179, 837

Browne, Broune Alice wife of Robert
41; Anice 758.132; Anthony 776;
Christopher 130, 162, 386, 673, 694,
725; Edmund 131, 896; Edward 132;
Elena wife of Robert 771; Francis
131, 896; Humphrey 138; Joan wife
of Robert 771; John 128-9, 306, 317,
321, 536-7, 564, 658, 661, 672, 675,
699, 706, 708-9, 711, 715, 717, 722,
724, 726, 732, 737, 745, 758.80,
758.82, 758.86, 758.101, 758.113,
758.116, 758.143, 758.159, 758.161,
758.163, 758.166, 758.171, 758.186,
758.192, 765.5, 766.1, 771; John
draper 321, 537; John the elder
758.182; John glasyer 169; Maud
wife of John 758.113; Robert 7, 41,
131, 143, 758.183-4; Robert clerk
283, 296; Robert glover 239, 717,
724, 730, 741, 771; Robert
husbandman 704, 726, 743, 745;
Simon 463 ; William 128-9, 366, 564,
670, 673, 680-1, 688, 701, 703, 705,
707, 709-11, 717, 736-8, 749, 750,
752, 758.174, 758.178, 758.182,
758.190, 758.196, 758.199, 758.200,
758.202, 765.6-7, 765.9, 771; William

son of John 758.171; *see* Brun

Broy Hugh de 892

Brucelaunce, *see* Briselaunce

Brudenell Robert 673, 674, 694;
Thomas senior 141

Bruenchurt Ralph de 486

Brun, Brunne Alexander son of Osbert
de 560; Anabel de 4.8; Geoffrey de
693; Jocelyn 241; John de 459, 768;
Osbert de 379, 560 ; Ralph de 698 ;
Walter de 145, 151, 205, 219, 241,
245, 292-3, 337, 341, 346, 392, 448,
459, 478, 491, 496, 501, 514; William
220

Brundissh John de 24

Brunham, *see* Burnham

Bryan Ralph 840

Bryd, *see* Brid, Byrde

Bryden, Byrden John clerk 700, 702

Bryg, Brygge John 672, 758.164,
758.184, 854, 881; *see* Briggs

Bryggesthorp William de 648

Bryghton *alias* Rychardson Alice 727,
755; Alice wife of Nicholas 709, 734;
Nicholas 709, 727, 734; Roger 734;
William 734

Brynkhill Agnes wife of Richard de 84;
Richard de 84

Bryselaunce, *see* Briselaunce

Bu[...]lt Alexander son of 423

Buck William 670

Buckeby Richard de 155

Buckeden, Bugden, Bukeden Henry
234, 758.91, 758.93, 758.108, 768;
Hugh 769, 770; *see* Bikeden

Buckmynstr' Richard de 149.7

Bude Agnes 512

Budone, *see* Boudone

Bueles John de 892

Bugh John 852

Bukerel Andrew mayor of London 641

Bulbals Angelina 655

Bulhernes Geoffrey 911.2, 3; 913.17;
Alienora wife of 913.17

Bulkyngham William de 149.7

Bullock William draper 670

Bulwike Margaret wife of Richard
758.155; Richard 758.125, 758.144,
758.155, 865-8, 870

Buncheklot Richard 477

Bunne William 364

Bunting, Bonting, Buntie Agnes wife of Hugh 296; Bunting Hugh reeve 911.22; Hugh 176, 196, 214, 237, 267, 296, 334, 356, 378, 380, 384, 399, 467, 490, 558, 560, 585, 650; Hugh senior 398; Hugh son of Hugh 399, 467, 490, 558, 560; Robert 294, 361, 363, 378, 397; W 758.33; William 417, 911.16

Burbach John 549

Burden Richard 220

Burford John de 55; Roesia wife of John de 55

Burghley, *see* Burley

Burgo Benedict de 491; Gamel de 605, 622; Cecilia daughter of Matilda 622; Matilda daughter of Gamel de 602, 605, 622; Richard de 660; Thomas de 342; William de 419, 479, 488, 516

Burgoyn, Burgon John 673, 792

Buril' Roger de 227

Burley, Bourle, Burgele(a), Burle(e) lord of 848; Evermerus de 626, 629, 632; Henry 688, 758.184, 758.190, 854; Hugh de 4.17; John de 157.2, 432, 758.179, 432, 862; Peter de 307, 850; Robert de 189, 535, 758.81, 758.98; Roger de 442; Sampson de 227; Walter de 657; Walter heir to Evermere de 632; William de 626, 629, 632

Burnby John prior of Durham 679.1, 679.2

Burnel(d), Burnild Alexander 343, 482; Alexander son of 483, 512; Beatrice wife of William 565; Reiner son of 482-3; Walter 255, 342; William 198, 222, 257, 276, 309, 312, 364, 368, 393, 438, 508, 565

Burnham, Brunham Cecily wife of William de 50, 569; William de 50, 388, 456, 462, 569

Bursar Reginald de 618, 631, 633; Quinelda wife of Reginald the bursar 618; Richard son of Reginald the bursar 168, 214, 286, 467, 618, 633

Burton, Birton Cecily wife of Nicholas 113b; Elias de steward 911.16; Ellen

wife of Gilbert de 21; Geoffrey de 281; Gilbert de 21; John de 181, 280, 380; Hugh son of Roger de 312, 552; Nicholas de 113b, 275, 278, 281, 453, 550, 758.28; Richard 590; Robert de 4.4, 726, 745, 758.172, 759, 772; Roger de 312, 552; Thomas de 744; William de 549, 758.41, 758.49, 777; William de, rector of Easton by Stamford 306, 308, 344

Bury John 322, 561; Robert de 758.82; *see* Byri

Buschyr, *see* Bewscher

Bussh, Busches, Bushy John 350, 449, 562, 875, 886-8, 890-1, 902; Margaret 890-1, 903-4; William 190

Bustard William vicar of St Martins 568

Butcher, Bocher Hugh the 524; W 758.197; *see* Abraham, Heine, Hugh, Walkelin

Buttle Thomas alderman 366

Buwedon, *see* Boudone

Byllesby, *see* Billesby

Byllings John 758.191

Byrde John 765.9

Byrden, *see* Bryden

Byri, Biri Walter de 293, 404, 452

Byrthorp, *see* Birthorp

Bytham, Bitham Richard de 124; Robert de 53 ; Sarra wife of Robert de 53; William de 59, 68, 69; *see* Biham

Cagge Alice wife of Robert 91; Robert 91

Calabre John 202

Caldecote Michael de 439; Nicholas 717, 724, 730

Caldon John de 113c

Callewithe Richard de 644

Calve Richard 342

Cambridge earl of 317

Camera Amabilia/Orabilia wife of William de 304, 498; John son of William de 304; Richard de 157.1; Sibilie daughter of Orabilia 498; William de 304, 498

Campeine, *see* Champaine

Campeden Robert de chaplain 89b

Canell Richard 162, 700, 720, 725, 742,

767.3-4

Canon Simon 717; William 854

Capella Robert de, canon of Lincoln 263

Capp Hugh 210, 479

Capper Adam 758.72; Agnes wife of Alan 758.85; Alan 758.84, 758.85

Capron John 758.196, 767.1

Cardonvilla Hugh de 663

Care John 743

Caretarius Brihtine wife of Roger 618; Roger 618; see Carter

Carlton, Carelton, Carleton Henry de 72-3, 758.44; Lora wife of Henry de 72-3; William de 49

Carpenter Ada 634; Agnes de 281 ; Geoffrey of Corby 693; Margaret daughter of Ada 634; Roger le 340, 381; William le 269, 281 ; see Henry

Carter Brihtina 633; Roger 631, 633; Simon (le) 230 ; see Caretarius

Cas John 450, 654; see Cassus, Cays

Casche John 226

Casewik, Kasewik Ailrich/Alfric/Alric de 196, 345, 352, 414; Amfelisia ward of Richard 414; Richard son of Alric rector of St Mary at the bridge 414; Richard brother of Warner 345; Robert de 187, 243, 413, 423, 512, 544; Warner son of Alfric de 345; Warner brother of Richard 414

Cassus, Cassi John 407, 654 ; see Cas, Cays

Casterton, Cesterton, Chastrethone Accard de 187; Alice widow of Gilbert de 394; Clement de 113c; Emma wife of John 860; Ernald de textor 911.1, 2, 3; Geoffrey de 911.3; Gilbert de 223, 283, 307, 318, 349, 384, 504, 551,758.102; Henry de 686; John de 304, 380, 397, 399, 585, 650, 860, 911.13; Hugh de 4.19, 4.20; Ivetta wife of Reginald de 13; John de 201, 911.22; John son of John 860; John son of John de clerk 911.22; Margery wife of Clement 113c; de Peter de 199, 330, 346, 392, 500, 543, 547, 560, 911.12; Ralph de 758.13; Reginald de 13; Richard de 201, 304, 457, 643; Robert son of

Accard de 187; Thomas de 118, 184, 535, 758.39; Walter de 113c; William de 180, 269; see Magna

Castreton John de;

Castr', see Chestre

Castro Bernardi Cecily wife of William de 26; William de 26

Cat William 668

Catarall Thomas clerk 564

Catesby Philip de, parson of Grafton 190

Catworth Thomas 758.115

Caunce William 705, 718, 728, 733

Cay Avice wife of Walter 567; Walter 567

Cayleflete Joan wife of Robert 291, 373; Robert 291, 373

Cays John 654; see Cas

Cecil, Cecell, Cicell, Cissyll, Cycill land of 896; David 767.5, 799, 800-1, 844, 895; David senior 138-9; Richard 669, 767.6, 785, 793-4, 796, 900, 907; William 899

Cecily daughter of Matilda 436; Cecily duchess of York 743; Hugh son of Cecily 243; see Cicely

Cestertone, see Casterton

Cestre, see Chestre

Chaffare Hugh 256

Chalon(i)er John 317, 765.5

Chamberlain Ralph the 157.2, 432; Ralph of Empingham 168; Richard 98

Chambers Henry 138; Henry alias Hamport 139; Margaret wife of Henry 138

Champaine Petronilla de 911.7; Margerie 911.7

Chandeler John 758.145; Richard 766.1

Chapeleyn John 244, 297; Joseph 668; Thomas 838

Chapman George 710; Walter 75, 648

charcoalburner, see John

Chastrethone, see Casterton

Chaundeler, see Chandeler

Chaworth Thomas 108

Chenecourt, see Chevercourt

Chenet Nicholas de 609

Cherl Henry 154

Chester Ralph earl of 157.1

Chesterfeld Richard de 732

Chesterton, *see* Casterton

Chestre, Castre, Cestre Alice wife of John 95, 536; Bernard de 256; John de 1.1-3, 71, 150, 317, 536, 699, 729, 732, 744, 758.64, 758.105, 758.117; John 95; Lora wife of John de 71, 744; Margaret wife of John de 732; Robert de 441 ; William de 58

Chevercourt John 109, 110, 112a, 758.165, 758.173, 758.184, 854; Margaret wife of John 109, 110, 758.165

Cheyne Laurence 758.164, 758.167

Child, Chyld ..... burgess 758.8; Agnes wife of Simon 758.31; Hugh 361, 399, 485, 557, 758.3; Sampson 485; Simon 417, 758.6, 758.17, 758.31; Simon son of Hugh 758.3

Chirchefeld William de 604

Chitt (or Chut) Hugh 422

chivaler Sampson le 913.19a (see Sampson)

Chlive Peter de 201 ; *see* Clive

Christemnes John de 758.34-5

Chubbock, *see* Corby

Churchgate, Chirchegate, Churgayt, Chyrchegate John 888, 890, 891, 902-5

Cibici *see* Sibeci

Cicely de ... 354; *see* Cecily

Cissor Gilbert 911.22; Alexander son of 911.22 (*see* Northfolk; Taylour)

Cisterna Agnes wife of Hugh de 558, 560; Hugh de 558, 560

Clari Theobald de 198

Clay, *see* Cley

Claypole, Cleypole John 700, 720, 734, 742, 767.3-4, 845

Clement 654, 657; Clement chaplain 547; rector of St Michael Cornstall 911.2, 3, 4, 17, 19,21; Clement the vintner 207-8, 221, 242, 245, 250, 337, 345, 375, 414, 422, 437, 447, 523, 544, 584, 910.5; Clement son of Michael 683, 684; John 142; Thomas 142; Walter son-in-law of Clement the vintner 375; *see* Vintner

Clerc, Clerke David the 447-8, 451; Geoffrey the 579.1, 911.18, 21;

Isaac the 245; Isabell wife of Robert 758.183-4; John 449, 711, 715, 730, 840, 844; John of Talyngtone chapman 704, 717, 724, 726, 745, 757; John son of Peter 19; Matilda/Maude wife of John 19; Matthew the 452; Peter the 19, 245, 447; Richard (le) 138, 758.17, 894; Robert 758.183-4, 843; Roger 758.77; Simon the 447-8, 450; Thomas the 450, 913.15, 16, 17; Walter 443; William the 251, 563; see Ivo, Staunford

Clevebert Hugh 583

Cley, Clay Beatrice daughter of William 816; Emma 816; William del 41, 376, 463, 526, 758.48, 816

Cleypole, *see* Claypole

Clidlowe William 564

Cliff Roger 758.151

Clinton Joan wife of John de 124; John de 124

Clive, Cliva, Clyve Gilbert de 354, 911.2, 3; Isabel wife of Robert de 226; John 529, 758.152; Robert de 226 ; Simon de 181, 280

Clockematin 657

Cloket(t) John 50, 270, 295-6, 311, 329, 370, 382, 425, 529, 525; William 171, 252

Clonne Roger de, rector of the church of St Peter 576

Cloperton Agnes wife of Roger de 230; Roger de 230

Clopton Thomas 735, 743

Clyde Geoffrey 4.8

Clyve, *see* Clive

Cnotteshale, *see* Knotteshale

Cobbe Reginald barber 767.6

Cobbets John of Ryall 107

Cockerel, *see* Cokerel

Coife William 480

Coifer Robert 447

Cok, Cokke the Jew 250, 513; Beatrice 765.9; Henry 105, 158, 193, 703, 705, 709, 710, 718, 727, 733-4, 738, 749, 758.158, 758.196, 765.8, 834, 854; John 4.14; John son of Richard 758.200; Richard 661, 717, 706, 708, 711, 715, 722, 758.167, 758.181,

758.184, 758.192, 758.196, 758.198, 758.200, 840; Robert 862; Roger 892; Thomas 5, 93, 758.104; William 673; *see* Cooke

Cokerel Alice daughter of Richard 758.76; Joan wife of Simon 758.102-3; John 76, 279, 475, 714, 744, 758.49; Richard 758.76; Simon 317, 699, 758.102-3

Cokkesnol Peter 336

Cokla Roger 758.2; Samson son of Roger 758.2

Colbe Eve 297

Colemer John de, seneschal of Stamford 494, 584

Colestewrthe *see* Colsterworth

Colevill John de 220 ; Philip de 217-8, 579.1-2, 640; Philip son of Robert de 636; Robert de 523, 636, 911.20; William de 157.1, 523

Colonia Terricus de

Colewyk Emma wife of William de 40; William de 40

Colice 654; Colicia daughter of Fredegill' 494

Colier Griffin 141

Colin William 363

Colltewrthe, *see* Colsterworth

Collum Thomas de 862

Cologne, Colonia, Teutonicus Beatrice widow of Terricus 548; Terricus, Tedricus, Tehodricus, Thericus, Thierry de 152, 183, 216-7, 245, 288, 346, 375, 398, 447, 459, 500, 548, 559, 579.1-2, 601-6, 609, 611-2, 614-22, 624-8, 630, 632-4, 636-45, 657; 911.17, 18, 19, 20, 21 ; *see* Stanford, Terricus, Thierry, Tieis

Colson Henry 539; John senior 141

Colsterw(o)rthe, Colstewrth, Colltewrthe Agnes wife of Nicholas de 228, 416; Nicholas de 176, 228, 397, 416; Richard de 911.17, 19

Colston John 673, 674

Colton Roger de 648

Combe William 578

Compton William 138, 796

Cook(e) Avicia 757; Hugh the 583; Ralph 306; William 674; *see* Cok

Corby Henry de 517; Joan wife of John

senior 541; John 156, 161, 163, 165, 189, 706, 708, 711, 715, 722, 758.147, 882-3; John senior 541; Katherine wife of John 882-3; Marioun de 282 ; Richard de 258, 282, 318, 349, 368, 394, 539; Robert de 186, 219, 227, 241, 341, 496, 546; Sarah wife of Henry 517; Thomas 302, 533, 758.117, 758.168, 833; William de 173, 487; William *alias* Chubbok 542; William vicar of Corby 464

Corby Thomas 533;

Cordale, Cordel Geoffrey 697; John 193, 872-3, 906; Richard 885; Thomas 193, 885

Cordewaner Arketil 484; John son of Peter le 22; Matilda/Maude wife of John 22; Peter le 22; Robert the 455

Cormoraunt William 91

Cornel, Cornil Hugh 423, 512, 516

Corner Hugh at 398

Cornestal Andrew de 354, 500

Cornwall, Cornwayle Alueredus de 122; Christiana de wife of Alueredus de 122; Richard earl of 513

Corszoun Joan 1.3

Cotes dom Richard de 806, 913.9, 10

Cotesmore, Cotismor, Cottesmor Geoffrey de 278, 309, 417, 453, 758.7; Gilbert de 32, 47, 810; Joan wife of Gilbert de 32, 47, 810; Richard at 175; Richard de 181, 269, 279, 281, 428, 458, 514; Robert de 219, 478; William de 269, 279, 281; *see also* Gotesmore

Cothanke Geoffrey 635

Coton John 670

Cotyngham Andrew 104

Counte, Cunte John le 18, 198, 257, 276, 309, 368, 381, 438, 713, 753, 911.11; Robert (the) 437

Coupeldyk, Cupuldik Alice prioress of St Michael's 271, 322, 531-3, 535-6, 561, 567

Couper(e), Cowper Geoffrey le 913.19a; John 162 ; Richard le 758.31 ; Thomas (le) 4.20, 156, 735, 767.3-4

Coventre Richard 697; William de 355,

362, 446, 493, 505, 643
Cra... Geoffrey 241
Crane Robert 386, 720, 734, 742
Cranwell Katherine wife of Michael 108; Michael 108
Crauden Richard de 499
Craunford Robert de 148
Creton Robert de 381
Crik Thomas 4.7, 4.13
Cromwell Ralph (lord) 126-7, 758.187, 781
Crophill Ralph de 124
Cross William at the 168
Crouheft John 654
Croweheved Cecilia John son of 605; Geoffrey 605; John son of Geoffrey 605
Crowland, Crouland, Croyland Emma daughter of Richard 155; John de 758.83, 758.114, 758.132; Margery prioress of the house of St Michael 192, 541; Margot wife of John 758.114; Richard de 155
Crowland abbot of see Henry; Ralph
Croxtone Richard de 181
Crystoffer Thomas 906
Cunneur Peter le 26
Cunte, *see* Counte
Cuppere Alan 648, 699 *see* Couper
Cur... John de 241
Curtas Robert 873-4
Cusin Andrew 288
Cut(t) Hugh 315; William 236
Cycell, *see* Cecil

Dacus Jordan son of Oger 617; Oger 617
Dalby Geoffrey de 60; John 271; William de 387
Dalim Roger 758.146
Dallinge Peter de 154
Dalton John 767.5
Damien master 263
Damisel Peter 343
Damisoun Robert 518
Damlys Robert at 845
Danby William 97
Dans Richard de 220
Dansey Thomas 142

Danvers John 673; Robert 662
Darcy Henry of London 120; Margery wife of Henry 120
Darley, Derley Robert 717, 723, 750; William 743
Daubur Geoffrey le 337
David the clerk 204, 288, 375, 414, 447-8, 451, 543, 559, 911.18,21; the Jew 336; the scribe 379, 499; of Stanford 227; son of ......595; son of Leta 213; son of Roger 413; son of Simon 157.1; son of William 346; Alexander son of 166, 218, 242, 262, 450, 583, 640; Henry son of 262, 584, 668, 911.18, 19, 20, 21; William son of 145, 151, 186, 211-2, 219, 227, 255, 293, 310, 327, 330, 336-7, 341, 367, 375, 389, 404-5, 419, 422, 447, 459, 478, 480, 496, 502, 510, 515-6, 520, 545-6 , 586, 911.20; William son of William son of 408
Daykun the Jew 237
Decon, *see* Dycons
Deen Agnes wife of William de 66; Ivo de 220; John de 66; Margaret wife of John de 66; William de 66
Delenil Robert de 157.1
Denganye Henry son of Richard 555; Richard 555
Depe Robert 172
Depinge, Depyng Agnes de widow of William 251; Alfred de 385, 388, 454, 456, 465, 472; Geoffrey 911.4, 5, 6; Henry de 294, 363, 397; John 562; Matilda wife of William de 184; Philip of 893; Richard de 758.110, 911.4-6, 23; Geoffrey son of Richard de clerk 911.23; Thomas 566; William de 27, 175, 184, 251, 260, 282, 320, 713
Deppines Alfred de 909; Almedus 765.1
Derby John 420
Derebogh't Thomas 862
Derham Henry son of John de 274; John de 274
Derley, *see* Darley
Despenser lady le 469; Thomas le 758.97
Deynes Henry 758.63

Dicons, *see* Dycons
Dieulacres the Jew 910.5, 6
Digby Harry 581
Dingele Hugh de 220
Dionisius 635
Diston John de 421
Dixon 767.1, 767.3 ; Nicholas 126
doctor, *see* Leche, Walter
Dodus, Dod', Dodi, Doudas palmer
    578; David son of William son of
    Dodi palmer 578; Hugh son of 486;
    Letitia widow of William 411;
    Outhilda widow of William son of
    Dodus 166, 224; William 411;
    William son of 166, 210, 224, 578
Dodyngton Nicholas de 822
Doget Alice 203; Geoffrey 343, 545,
    657; Robert 220
Dorlot ... 573; Geoffrey 385, 429;
    Thomas 253
Douve, Duve Geoffrey 250; William
    361, 485
Dragun Walter steward 911.22
Draper Andrew 646, 661; Isabel wife
    of 646; Thomas 658
Drayton ..... 758.189; John 758.26;
    John son of Margery 758.189;
    Margery wife of ..... Drayton 758.189
Drie Hugh 226; Roger 289, 522
Drynckedregges Ranulf 815, 817, 820-1
Dudley Robert 670
Dufhouse Robert 758.133, 758.136
Dulle Hugh 459; *see* Ruffus
Dungund 657
Dunkotley Alice 445
Durante John 592, 790; William 703,
    705
Durbet William 157.1
Durea [?] Geoffrey de 647
Durham, Thomas Langley bishop of
    835
Duve, *see* Douve
Dycons, Dicons ... of Peterborough
    801; John 703, 705, 710, 727, 738,
    747, 750, 765.9, 844; Thomas 371
Dyer Adam son of Robert 479, 482,
    619; Clement son of Adam 619;
    Geoffrey son of Adam 619; Isabella
    wife of Adam 619; Peter the 186;
    Philip the 245, 255; Robert 354;

Roger 363, 622; William 619; *see*
    Adam, Henry, Peter, Philip, Richard,
    Roger, Tinctor
Dyester John 866
Dygby Henry 580, 581
Dygname Thomas 144
Dykeman Robert 911.12; W 758.197,
    758.199
Dyngele Robert de 758.41; W son of
    Robert 758.41; William de 1.2; 1.3
Dysk Agnes 911.12; Walter 911.12
Dyua Matilda de 660; William de 660

Easton, *see* Eston
Ebchester Robert prior of Durham
    680, 681
Eche Henry de 181
Edda Hugh son of 693
Edelyn W 758.20-22, 758.36; William
    230, 440-1
Edenham John 750
Edgose William 723, 756
Edows Thomas 697
Edward duke of York, *see* York
Edward Nicholas 162, 703, 705, 749;
    Thomas 700, 725
Edyngton Giles de 62
Effinton John de 394; Matilda de wife
    of John 394; *see* Uffington
Egilton William de 465, 472
Elias, Ellyas the clerk 393, 457; rector
    of the church of Holy Trinity 181;
    son of William 683-5; Nicholas de
    241
Elizabeth prioress of St Michael's 4.5,
    11, 215, 258, 334, 352
Ellerker John de, the elder 46, 117
Ellington Richard 758.77
Elmes, Elmys Edith wife of John 141;
    Elizabeth 129a, 673-4; John 141;
    John brother of William 674; Walter
    673; William 694, 767.5; William son
    of Elizabeth 129a, 674
Elton Richard de 187; Roger son of
    Richard de 187
Ely Sym[on] de 657
Elyas, *see* Elias
Elyss Henry 674
Empingham, Empyngham, Hempingh'
    Alcusa wife of William de 309; Henry

405

de 390, 460, 758.39; Hugh de 519;
John de 168, 173, 279, 324, 369, 470,
475, 573, 692, 765.2-3, 909; Michael
de 397; William de 309, 361
Engayne Henry 380, 758.62
Englyssh John 303, 348, 719; *see*
Hengleis
Enot William 828
Eringtona Stephen de 660
Erlistorp William de 269
Escher William 841
Escot Richard le 913.18; Helewyse wife
of 913.18
Esey Ralph 641
Estkyrke Simon parker of Eston 232
Eston Alice wife of Henry 439; Alice
daughter and heir of John de 466;
Andrew de 194, 300, 359, 466, 471;
Henry de 196; Henry son of Hugh
439; Hugh de 439; John de 82; John
son of Andrew de 194, 466, 471;
Matilda widow of Andrew de 300,
359; Matthew de 175, 199 ; Nicholas
de 61, 63, 77, 87, 173, 380, 469, 471,
648, 758.43, 758.68 ; Richard de 315,
339, 422, 631, 657, 857; Roger de
206, 212, 545; Roger son of Richard
de 631 ; William de 220, 377
Estwyk John 731, 733
Etegose, *see* Edgose
Ethell John 672, 835
Etton John 747
Eudo the tanner 209
Eustace Thomas son of 913.20, 21;
Thomas son of Thomas 913.21
Everard, Euerard Henry 399; John
726, 758.132, 758.140, 758.166, 835;
William 99, 758.65, 758.97
Evermere 626; *see* Burgele
Ewerby, see Ywareby
Exchequer William of the 157.2, 205;
see Scaccario
Exton Geoffrey de 355, 362, 493, 505;
Godwin de 463; Hugh de 377

Faber Baldewin 362
Faderman 268; Alice wife of William
(de) 35-7, 525; Edusa wife of
Richard 182; Henry 198, 203, 248,
257, 268, 275-6, 284-5, 295, 307,

309, 312, 323, 325, 334, 349, 364,
368, 393, 411, 481, 490, 517, 551-2,
565, 758.10, 848, 851; Richard 182,
186, 223, 342, 377; Sybil wife of
Henry 851; Thomas 248, 295, 552;
William 35-7, 177, 186, 197, 212, 215,
225, 227, 247, 323, 387, 400, 405,
474, 481, 519-20, 525, 527, 556;
William son of Henry 851; William
brother of Thomas 295; William
rector of Redemershill 174, 186
Fale Thomas 449
Fardon Geoffrey de 347
Farendon, Faryndon Robert de 181,
269, 390, 393, 460; Roger de 173 ;
Thomas de 269
Farndon Alice de 279
Fauer Geoffrey 647
Faukes John 804
Fauvel, Fauuel, Fawvel 453, 457;
Andrew 216; Hugh 153, 241; John
864; Marie wife of Robert 443;
Michael 4.7, 4.13, 292; Ralph 444;
Robert 443; William 858; *see* Sauvel
Fazakerly, *see* Fitzacreley
Fe[...] Roger le 269
Fenton John 775
Feraby William 635
Fernband Nicholas 436
Ferrario William 392
Ferrour, Ferrur Joseph le 758.20,
758.22; Beatrice wife of Joseph
758.20, 758.22; Roger le 585;
Thomas le 363
Ferrun, Ferrenn, Ferron Herbert 506;
Richard (le) 214, 357, 548, 758.6,
758.17; Richard the clerk son of
Richard 758.6, 758.17; Roger 548;
Ulmer 506, 548
Firmin, *see* Wodecroft
Fiskerton Henry de 502
Fissher, Fischer Alric 427; John 727;
Thomas 869; William 862; *see*
Bradcroft
Fitzacreley, Fazakyrley Nicholas 673;
Robert 670
Flamang, *see* Fleming
Flanders John 654; Robert son of 654
Flaxman William 724, 745
Fleming, Flammenc, Flandrens,

Flemang, Flemeng 354;
Andrew 265; Cecily wife of John le
16; Joan daughter and heir of Robert
410; John le 16, 180, 247, 279-81,
316, 334, 355, 362, 396, 434, 457-8,
493, 502, 505, 657, 758.24, 911.22;
John junior 356; John son of Walter
le 181, 199, 334, 372, 477; John son
of William le 14; John brother of
Walter 513; Nicholas son of John
758.24; Robert le 356, 359, 457,
758.34; Robert son of John (le) 367,
502; Robert son of Walter le 334;
Walter le 145, 177, 181, 183, 199,
215, 219, 241, 266, 280, 334, 336,
341, 346, 352, 389, 396, 403-4, 448,
452, 458, 477-8, 482, 485, 496, 501-2,
509, 513, 519, 521-2, 584, 629,
911.21; William le 4.5, 206, 210, 345,
374, 407, 414, 424, 433, 476, 480,
482, 707, 714, 740, 744, 746, 758.46,
758.47
Fletcher Joan wife of William 562;
Richard 844; William 562, 880-2, 885
Flete William (de) 549, 758.69, 758.70,
834; rector of St Pauls church 308;
rector of St Peters 233, 590
Fligisthorpe Robert de 693
Floode Noel 899
Flore Roger 239, 835
Flower Richard 592
Flurkin 452
Foderingeye William de 357
Folevyle John de 693
Folkelin, Folklyn, Folkelyn John
758.188; Robert 158, 164-5;
Thomas 158, 592
Folkworth John de 911.23
Folkyngham Alice wife of W 758.32,
758.37, 758.53; Cecily daughter of
Alice 758.37, 758.53; John de 347,
387, 529, 758.32, 758.52; John son of
Alice 758.37; Peter son of Alice
758.37; Peter son of Cecily 758.53;
Robert son of John de 758.52; W de
758.32, 758.37, 758.53; William de
284, 311-2, 411
Folvambe Godfrey 131
Footh Robert 438
For(e)ster, Forster, Foster Eustace le

393; John 767.5; Richard 193, 536,
758.87, 758.107, 853; Thomas 652
Forest Roger 580, 581
Fort Robert 1.2-3
Foscedame, see Fuscedame
Fosse Ralph de 217-8
Fosser John prior of Durham 675-6
Foster, see Forster
Fouldon Hamo de 707
Fox Thomas 661
Framton(a), Francton William de 176,
180, 209, 231, 266-7, 336, 392, 403,
451, 492, 501, 506, 510, 513-4, 519,
543, 560
Franceis John le 105, 355, 367, 381,
446-7, 461, 493, 502, 505, 537, 712,
725, 736, 738, 770, 875; John son of
John 355, 447, 493; John brother of
John 505; Jocelin 583; Robert 455;
W 657
Franciscus John 180
Francus John 362
Frankelein Thomas le 228, 416, 524
Frantona, Frantun, see Framton
Fraunceys, see Franceis
Frebarne John 112a, 386, 449, 700, 702,
712, 720, 725, 738, 742, 765.9, 797,
844, 869, 875, 884, 886, 890; Frebern
the weaver 208, 251; Margaret wife
of John 797-8
Fredegill', Fredegist Colicia daughter
of 262, 494
Freeman, Freman John le 328; Richard
172, 229, 246, 282, 297, 329, 333,
569, 864; Richard son of Ralph 246;
Thomas le 227, 249, 365, 384, 397,
442; Thomas son of John 328
Freine(y), Freyne William de 152, 209,
304, 403, 451, 498, 501, 543
Frenchman John the 476, 506; see
Franceis, Gallico
Frend John 171; John son of John 171
Freney, see Freiney
Fresches John 911.11
Freston Richard 758.147
Friseby John de 463, 526
Fulco, Fulcon Ralph son of 289, 613,
616, 624, 913.20, 21
Fulsham John 758.110
Fulstirte Ralph 911.13

Funne Stephen 460
Furner Henry le 507
Fuscedam, Foscedame, Futsadame
   Henry 266-7, 286; Hugh 560;
   Richard 346, 601-2, 622; Robert 367,
   414, 502
Fuscedo Richard 547
Fusse, Fusce Hugh 294, 361, 399, 548
Fyncham Henry de 911.13
Fynton John 906
Fyssher, see Fissher

Gabbegoky, Gabgoky, Galbegoky John
   45, 57; Matilda/Maude wife of
   William 22; William 22, 181, 269, 281
Galerus priest 179
Gallico John the 476; see Frenchman
Gallow Thomas *alias* Welles 883
Galun David 361
Gangy, see Gaugi
Garlemonger Adam 344
Gassale Thomas 758.170
Gate Geoffrey at the 166; Peter son of
   Geoffrey 166; Thomas son of
   Geoffrey 166; see Portam
Gatesby Philip de, parson of Grafton
   665
Gaugi, Gaugy Emma 227; Geoffrey
   227, 257, 318, 342, 489; Geoffrey
   son of Henry 196-7; Henry 197, 206,
   208, 225, 245, 251, 255, 288, 310,
   315, 327, 330, 337-8, 343, 346, 351,
   353, 412, 419, 422-3, 447, 479, 482-3,
   511-2, 520, 545, 579.1, 586, 657;
   Isaac brother of Henry 245, 337, 422;
   Philip 186, 258, 326, 334, 342, 349,
   377-8, 481, 489, 556, 758.3; Philip
   son of Emma 227; Roger 151, 515
Gaywode William 703, 710, 750, 875-
   6, 884
Gedney, Gedeneye Godfrey 758.141,
   758.150; Iveta wife of Stangrim de
   223; Stangrim de 223; Thomas 137,
   901
Geffron John 98, 758.186, 768
Gent William 869
Gentill, Gentilo, Gentyl Margery wife
   of William 314; William 159, 174,
   314, 324, 402, 464, 539, 568-9
Geoffrey 250, 578, 633, 758.63;

Geoffrey ... 167; at the water 152; the
   clerk 345, 457, 503; Geoffrey clerk
   vintner 911.17; Geoffrey dean 913.1;
   Geoffrey nephew of Geoffrey dean
   913.1; the chaplain 493, 505, 595;
   chaplain of St Andrew 523; the
   priest 167, 210, 213, 355, 413, 578,
   647; dean 263, 597, 683, 684, 685;
   prior of St Leonard 277; cellarer 647;
   the scribe 336; Geoffrey 'norrensi'
   207; the mercer 4.8, 510; the skinner
   207; the tanner 509; the vintner 380,
   501, 911.17; son of Godhue 628;
   son of Herlewin 207, 224, 242, 486,
   522-3, 583, 627; son of John 563;
   son of Outhilda 145, 219, 478 (*see*
   Ketene); son of Reiner 597; son of
   Roger 213, 413, 483; son of Waleran
   444; son of Walkelin de Keten 510;
   Alexander son of 264; Alpeisa
   daughter of 338, 507; Avice daughter
   of 219, 478; Christine wife of
   Geoffrey 483; Luice son of 523;
   Peter son of 204, 216, 288, 346, 367,
   374, 407, 451, 455, 461, 484, 499,
   502, 601, 614, 618, 623-4, 628, 633,
   764, 911.1, 17; Robert son of 206,
   443, 594; Simon son of 247, 428;
   William son of 292-3, 380, 457;
   William son of Geoffrey the vintner
   501; William brother of Alexander
   264
Gerard clerk 618, 631, 633, 657;
   Gerard priest 578, 647
Gere the miller 378
German, Terricus the, see Colonia
Gernet Richard vicar of St Martin's
   church 489; see Gerveth
Gernon Philip 832
Gerun Thomas de 421
Gervase lord 179; the stonecutter 338;
   the tailor 346, 458, 507; Aldusa wife
   of 458
Gervasii Geoffrey (*dictus Anglicus*) 572
Gerveth Richard vicar of St Martin's
   408; see Gernet
Geseling Geoffrey abbot of
   Peterborough 250, 654
Gibbes John 710, 738, 773, 843, 854
Giffard Katherine 758.152

Gilber son of [...] 151

Gilbert .....husb of Milicent 758.27; the clerk 437; chaplain of St Mary 523; dean of Barnack 202; dean of Stamford 231, 510; at the bridge 4.2, 216; ad pontem 507; the knight 166, 207, 627, 638; the marshal 459; the Noble 584; the tailor 266, 267, 316, 372, 428, 434; son of Baldwin 403, 418, 504; son of Ralph 563; son of William 583; brother of Alexander son of Baldwin 447; Alexander son of 316, 434; Baldwin son of 682; Henry son of 428; John 758.15; John son of John 758.15

Gilder Alice wife of John 758.134; John 234, 758.134

Gilmin called Norman 517; see Norman, William the

Girdler Peter 758.192

Gistun Godfrey de 209

Git Geoffrey son of 4.17

Githa Hugh son of 179

Glamford Robert de 263

Glatton Stephen de 4.18

Glenden Richard de 764

Glentworthe John de 198; Osanna wife of John de 198

Glint', Glinton, Glynton Geoffrey de 355, 493, 505 ; Geoffrey son of Richard de 355, 493, 505; John 673; Michael de 355, 493, 505 ; Richard de 355, 493, 505 ; Walter de 155, 294, 397, 399, 427

Gocelyn Stephen prior 320

God(e)felaghe Andrew 51, 184

Godchep Alice wife of Walter 203, 261; Margaret prioress 299, 360 ; Walter 203, 261

Godeman Robert 392, 414

Godemor Robert 345

Goderiche Alianora wife of John 124; John 124

Godfelaugh Andrew 283, 740, 748, 823; Emma widow of Andrew 823; Matilda 283; Thomas son of Andrew 823-4

Godfrey son of Godhue 601; Thomas 158

Godhue Geoffrey son of 628; Godfrey

son of 601

Godric, Godriche, Godriz 213, 655, 657; Abraham 361; Alexander 416; Hugh son of 657; Gilbert son of William 204; Margaret wife of Gilbert 204; Sampson son of 151, 208, 212-3, 221, 225, 245, 251, 255, 327, 337, 343, 351, 400, 412-3, 419, 422-4, 447, 479, 483, 488, 512, 516, 544; William 204; William son of 450, 583, 846

Godwyn John 290

Goilard Robert 187, 206, 591; Walter son of Robert of Wothorp 206

Goion Walter 4.9

Golafre John 662

Goldesworth, Goldysworth Alice daughter of Richard de 733; Katherine wife of Richard 718, 728, 758.194, 758.195, 767.1, 840; Margery wife of Richard 716, 733; Margery widow 703, 705; Richard 718, 728, 731, 733, 767.1, 840

Goldsmith Henry 910.2; Nicholas de 547; Peter 699, 758.85; see Bartholomew; Ralph

Goldston(e) Hugh 518; Robert 892

Goliardi, see Goilard

Gollok Robert 170; Simon 440

Goodloke Thomas 765.9

Goseberdkirke Nicholas de 411

Gosenel Aurekin 911.12; Roger 911.12; Walter 911.1

Gotesmore [?Cottesmore] Joan wife of Gilbert 27; Gilbert de 27

Graham Richard de 175; William de 527; see Grantham

Gralewald Robert 207

Grantham William de 174, 385, 429, 474 ; see Graham

Grat[er] Alfred le 340, 381, 490, 753 ; see Regrater

Grave Richard 601, 618, 624, 628, 633

Grecton, see Gretton

Gregory John 670, 710, 718, 727, 738, 750, 758.197, 773; Richard 765.7-9; Thomas 718, 731, 758.194, 767.1, 773, 853

Gren(e)ham ...... 758.124; Nicholas 101, 766.2; Thomas 837

Grendon John brother of William de 168; William de 168

Grene John 758.146, 759, 772 ; Robert 163, 833; William 871

Grenefeld William 735, 845, 894

Grensyde Thomas 791

Gresham William 127

Gressinghale, Grissinhale Robert 758.72, 758.74

Greta lady 913.4

Gretham Agnes wife of Walter de 208; Henry de 4.5 ; Philip de 230; Walter de 208

Grethed Adam 573; Margery wife of Adam 573

Gretton Norman de 145, 182, 186, 197, 219, 227, 257, 307, 405, 408, 478, 520, 546, 556; Robert de 340 ; Walter son of Norman de 378, 408 ; William de 859

Grey Elizabeth wife of Richard 127; Richard 127

Greywerk Margaret de 469; Roger 305, 320

Grofham Laurence 831; see Grosham

Grom Richard 412, 419

Grosham John de 252, 410; see Grofham

Grugon Lenthen 167

Grymes Robert 758.95

Grymston Henry 158, 162-4; John 158; Robert 162, 670, 767.4

Gryndere William 661

Guarles George 139 see Quarles

Gubaud Dom John 911.20

Gudchepe, see Godchep

Guero Richard 374

Gulson Humphrey 142; William 142

Gunby Thomas 747

Gunnild Henry son of 504

Gurlewald Robert 166

Gurram Roger 343

Gybbes, see Gibbes

Gybson John 670

Gydding William 726, 758.173, 758.198

Gygoure John 747

Gyldale Roland 879

Gylderr John 658

Ha[...]villa Henry de 206 ; Peter de 206 ; see Hawvell

Hacard son of Ivva 167; see Acard

Haconby Henry de 269

Haddestok Ailred de 199; Alfred de 304

Haketya Geoffrey de 227

Hakun Thomas son of 913.6

Halame Thomas prior of Newstead 775

Hale Henry de 33; William de 672

Hall(e) Agnes 777; Robert 907; Thomas (at) 409, 804; William 854; see Hawlle

Hallestead Walter de 758.52

Hallof Richard 583

Halom alias Milner Richard 321

Halstan priest 179, 597, 647

Halver Alver John son of Walter 758.45, 758.55; Ralph (le) 341, 496, 500, 543, 547; Walter (le) 406, 460, 526, 758.45, 758.55, 758.92, 813

Halyday John 706, 758.167, 758.171, 758.196

Hambleton 767.1, 767.3

Hameldon, Hamelton, Hamilton, Hamulton Robert 885; Walter de 8; William 193, 872, 885

Hamerton Joan wife of William de 85; W 758.84; William de 85

Hamo dean of Lincoln 263

Hampden John 662, 667

Hamport Henry alias Chambers 139; Margaret wife of Henry 139

Hampton Elyas de 354 ; Geoffrey 158, 164, 703, 720, 742, 750, 765.9

Hanford W 758.188, 758.194

Hangynghoughton William of 889

Hanneby Ralph de 314; Hanneby Ralph de vicar of All Saints by the bridge 314; Thomas son of Ralph de 314

Hans Robert 193, 360, 653, 670, 709, 710, 718, 723, 733, 738, 750, 774, 844

Hanuill Thomas de 11; see Hawvell

Hanworth Thomas 804

Har(e)court Robert 673-4; William 84

Har(r)yngton John 134, 777

Hardegrave, Hartgrave, Herdegrave Master 371; John 592, 767.6, 799

Hardekin Roger son of 213, 413;

William 518

Hare Henry 187, 657, 913.15, 16, 17;
Robert brother of Henry 187; *see*
Here

Hareby Simon 195; William 653

Haringworth Robert de 410, 527

Harleston Thomas 107

Harpele Alice de 287; Emma de 287;
Robert de 287

Harrison, Harryson Agnes wife of
Richard 878; Richard *alias* Johnson
878; William 907

Harstan Richard de 648

Hartgrave, *see* Hardegrave

Harwedon John de 474

Harwode Nicholas of Boston 94

Haseley Thomas 662, 667

Hasteinvill William de 659, 663

Hasteuel Thomas 713

Hastmel W 758.110

Hastolf the weaver 149.3

Hastynel Cecily widow of John 4.6

Hauboys Parva Margaret wife of Walter
de 274, 391; Walter de 274, 391, 553,
554.2, 598, 909

Haukyshey William 485

Haus, *see* Hans

Hauvill, *see* Hawvell

Haver Agnes wife of Robert 897;
Robert 589, 897

Hawe John 189, 322, 561, 758.114;
Sybil wife of John 189; Richard 652

Hawise *hatertera?* 212

Hawkyns William 670

Hawkys William 709

Hawlle William 128-9

Hawnell William 189

Hawvell, Hauville John 758.97,
758.142; John son of Richard 758.92;
Laurence 758.132, 758.139, 758.140,
758.147 ; Richard 758.40, 758.55,
758.92; *see* Hanuill

Haydy John 670

Hayter Robert 790

Hayward, Heywort Simon 322, 561;
William 159, 172, 229, 253, 333, 402,
568-9

Hebbys William 743

Hede Agnes 360

Hedlere Peter le 911.8-9; Geoffrey son
of 911.8-9

Hedo the butler 157.1

Heie Reiner 911.3 ; Clement son of
911.3

Heine the butcher 583

Hekeham, *see* Hykeham

Helpest(on), Helpistun... 248; Elis de
563; Helen wife of Waleran 444;
Henry de 911.16; Maxiena daughter
of 444; Pag'/Pain de 264, 443, 563;
Ralph de 444; Roger (de) 264, 292-3;
Roger son of Elis de 563; Simon de
270, 284-5, 295, 364, 370, 508;
Waleran son of Ralph 444

Hendle Walter 141

Heneseye Sampson de 55

Hengleis Simon le 563; *see* English

Henrison 865; Emma daughter of
Henrison 865

Henry 166, 486, 578; chaplain 911.2-3;
Henry (the) clerk 427; rector of
church of St John 149.5, 494-5;
dean of Stanford 255, 265, 330, 338,
911.21; master of St. John 636;
bishop of Whithorn 588; Henry the
carpenter 400; the dyer 495; the
physician 758.31; the reeve 911.12;
the spicer 501; son of Alexander
152, 204, 211, 216-8, 262, 330, 339,
345, 367, 374, 414, 422, 447, 459,
476, 480, 484, 499, 502, 548, 559,
584, 639, 644; son of Andrew the
palmer 339; son of Ascelin 336; son
of David 584, 668; son of Gilbert
the tailor 372, 428; son of Gunnild
504; son of Isaac 206, 210, 213, 346,
383, 407, 413, 423-4, 433, 476, 479,
482-3, 512, 544; son of Peter 545;
son of Reyner 451, 500; son of
Richard 447; son of Roger 516, 544;
son of Roger son of Lece 424; son
of Sampson 421, 547, 764; son of
William 846; Geoffrey brother of
Henry 424; Henry Henry son of
911.18, 19, 20, 21; Hodierna wife of
Henry 422; Isaac son of 412, 419,
424, 545; Nicholas brother of Henry
459; Richard son of 421, 644, 668;
Richard brother of Henry son of

Richard 447; Simon son of 266, 267
Henry abbot of Crowland 913.8, 11, 14b
Her... William 758.63
Herbert 355, 493, 505; Herbert the sergeant 152, 218, 251, 316, 367, 461, 480, 484, 505, 579.1-2, 640, 657; William son of 220
Herbi, Herdeby Henry de 758.106, 758.116, 758.128; John 758.186
Herbrand 345
Herbrok Emma wife of Thomas de 54; Thomas de 54
Herdegrave, *see* Hardegrave
Here Alice wife of Robert le 641; Ralph son of Robert le 641; Robert le 641; *see* Hare
Hereward, Herward 455, 461, 494, 630; Colicia wife of 494; Ralph 835; Reiner son of 204, 484, 499; Robert son of 480, 494, 612, 630
Herlewin 623, 628; Geoffrey son of 166, 207, 221, 224, 242, 250, 262, 486, 522-3, 583, 623, 628; Peter son of Geoffrey son of Herlewin 623, 628
Herlington John de 101, 758.124
Heron John of London merchant 767.5
Herryes, Herreys, Harres, Harreys, Harris Agnes wife of Thomas 887; Alice heir of 889; Thomas *alias* Saddyngton 872, 875-6, 884, 886-7, 889
Hersaldoun Richard de 551
Hert Agnes 758.87; John son of Agnes 758.87; John 758.87
Hervy Agnes (le) 305, 320, 381; William 662, 667
Herward, *see* Hereward
Heselarton John de kt 911.11, 16
Hesward John 652
Heton John de 100; William 126
Heyn Kate wife of Robert 191; Ralph de 911.12; Robert 191
Heyrer Simon le 304
Heyward, *see* Hayward
Hickson Nicholas 758.13
Hikeham, *see* Hykeham
Hilil priest 578
Hill Robert 313, 562; *see* Othe hill

Hingemund Achard son of 483; *see* Yncmund
Hingetorp William de 152; *see* Ingthorp
Hipetoft Alexander de 58; John son of Alexander de 58; Mabilla wife of John 58
Hirne Andrew son of Matilda in le 507; Matilda in le 507
Hirnham Hugh de 400; *see* Irnham
Hobson Thomas of London 767.5
Hochon John 771; Margaret wife of John 771
Hod Hugh 758.8-9, 758.16; Letitia daughter of Hugh 758.16; Nicholas 393, 758.16; Peter 911.13; William 361, 911.13; *see* Hode, Hood
Hoddesson William 804
Hode Agnes 653 ; *see* Hod, Hood
Hodiern Henry 251, 446
Hoklei Simon de 476
Holand Ralph 743
Holdierd Henry 211
Hollebeche Amy wife of Laurence de 58 ; Laurence de 58 ; Ralph de 58
Holme Bartholomew 670
Holton Thomas 723, 773, 843
Holyngton John 674
Honyman Reginald 306
Hoo Thomas 667
Hood Nicholas 256; *see* Hode
Hopkyns Henry 703, 705, 733, 854
Horbire Thomas de 207
Horbling William de 114
Horspate John 862
Horspole John clerk 108
Hotot Hugh de 29, 30; Robert 526
Houre Joan wife of John 142; John 142
Houton John de archdeacon of Northampton 157.2, 168, 432; Ralph de nephew of John 168
Howys Thomas 743
Hoyland William de prior 182
Huff' Ralph de 444
Huffinct, Huffington, *see* Uffington
Hufford, *see* Ufford
Hugh of Avalon bishop of Lincoln 262
Hugh the chaplain 455, 544; the priest 179, 213, 221, 224, 383, 413, 437,

Westminster 138; John the
apothecary 309; the charcoalburner
(*carbonario*) 498; the spicer 498, 506;
the tailor 380; John son of Maurice
491; son of Sampson 216, 346, 375,
448, 461, 484, 521, 687; son of
Walter 809; Geoffrey son of 563;
William son of 157.1-2

Johnson Agnes wife of Richard 878;
Jane wife of Maurice 651; Maurice
651; Richard *alias* Harryson 878;
Robert 670

Jolyvet John 868

Jones Constance 897; Jasper son of
Constance 897; William 897

Jordan, Jurdon John 879, 880; Oger
son of 595

Jose 434

Josep(h) Joan daughter of Robert 317;
John 170, 235, 369, 402, 692, 765.2;
Laura/Lora wife of Robert 90, 99,
317; Robert 90, 99, 317; William
274, 287, 312, 463, 475, 553, 554.1-2,
555, 598, 707, 714, 740

Joslan 655; Asceria daughter of 655

Jouy Avicia wife of Richard 98;
Richard 98

Joynour Alice wife of Robert 158;
Robert 158;

Juge William 436

Jurdon, *see* Jordan

Kasewik, *see* Casewik

Kastirton, *see* Casterton

Kec(k) Nicholas 439; Walter son of
Nicholas 399, 427, 439

Kelby W 758.182

Keling Reginald 654

Kelmingworthe Roger 851

Kempe Peter 913.7, 9, 10, 11; Simon
913.12

Kent, Kyent Athelina/Atthelena de,
widow of John de Brampton 254,
324, 385, 388, 429, 465, 472-3

Kerbroc Henry de 287, 911.16

Kesteven, Kesten Thomas 670, 709,
710, 712, 720, 725, 738, 742, 843

Ketel, Ketil 439, 634; Ketle the
woolmerchant 625; Walter 152, 266,
491, 507, 509, 548, 558, 560, 634;

Walter son of 183, 346, 461; *see*
Kotel

Ketelthorp Emma de 911.11

Keten(e) Alice de widow of Geoffrey
467; Amicia wife of William 145;
Andrew de 339; Avice widow of
William de 219, 478; Geoffrey de
467, 506; Henry de 209, 584, 617;
John de 153, 241; Roger de 319;
Simon de 521; Walkelin de 510;
William de 145, 219, 478; William
son of Wymund de 585; Wymund de
585

Keueton James de 732

Kikil Hugh 497

Kilham Thomas 789

Killyngworth Joan wife of John 386;
John 386; Thomas son of John 386;
William son of John 386

Kirkeby, Kyrkeby Alan de 124;
Eustace de 220 ; Gilbert de 481, 556;
Henry de 722, 827; Ingald de 220,
389; John 564 ; Margaret wife of
Henry de 827; Sibyl daughter of
Ingoldus de 389, 404

Kirkeman John 86; Margaret wife of
John 86

Kirkestede William 308, 549

Knight John esq 672; Richard son of
the, 168; W 758.186; *see* Gilbert,
Peter, Samson

Kno(t)t John 1.2, 750, 758.58, 831;
Richard 759, 771-2, 837; Robert 771;
Thomas 158, 853

Knocker Edmund 769, 770; Henry le
758.36, 756.38; Reymund le 758.57,
758.97

Knolkere Henry 170

Knotteshale Agatha, wife of John de
34, 42; Geoffrey son of John de 34;
John de 34, 42, 758.29, 758.33,
911.16; Peter de 63; *see* Cnotteshale

Knyvet Alianora wife of John 123;
John 123, 271, 533, 648; John son of
Richard 699, 893; Richard 699;
Richard junior 893; Robert son of
John 123

Kokerell John 273, 465

Kokke, *see* Cok

Kotel son of Ralph 224; *see* Ketel

Kupper Adam 306; John son of Adam 306
Kydenoth Geoffrey 519
Kylham John 784
Kynwolmerssh William senior 697
Kyrkeby, *see* Kirkeby
Kysk Agnes wife of Walter 15, 911.13; Walter 15, 911.13

Laay Robert de 157.1
Lacy Henry 136, 652; John de 16; Robert 136; Thomas 767.5-6
Lamare Galerus de 179
Lambard, Lambart John 360, 649; Nigel de 698; Osbert son of Nigel 698
Lambe Robert 670
Lambeshead, Lambsheved Reginald 913.7, 8, 9, 10 ; Thomas 447
Lambethest Reginald 806
Lancastr(e) Agnes wife of William 158, 164-5; John 158; William 158, 164-5
Lanceleve Pain brother of Richard 497, 563; Richard 497
Lane (*ad venellam*) Andrew in the 518; Emma wife of Michael 491; Michael at/of the 392, 513; Michael son of William 491; William de 491, 583
Lang(e)ton John 703; Simon de parson of St George 306, 768
Langar(d) Thomas 767.3-5
Langetoft Elye de 911.7
Langham Agnes wife of William 449; Emma wife of Henry 17; Henry de 17; John de parson St Michael the Greater 89b; William 449
Langley Thomas bishop of Durham 835
Lannator Toke 848
Larche Robert de 455; *see* Arch
Laurence the tanner 226, 361, 397; Joan wife of Thomas 130; Thomas 130
Laver Thok le 311
Lawson William 652
Lay John 696, 697; William 697
leatherworker, *see* Thurstan
Lecchelid Geoffrey of, canon of Lincoln 263
Lece, Lecia 655; Henry son of 516;

Peter son of 447, 517; Roger son of 250, 413, 424, 437, 483, 545, 655; *see* Lize
Lecha Roger le 826
Leche Henry le 8, 911.11; John 719, 835; Walter (le) 268, 323, 489; *see* Leke
Ledys William 678, 679.1, 758.175, 758.185
Lee Richard (o'the), wright 661, 688, 718-9, 724, 728, 737, 751, 758.167, 758.171, 758.173, 758.178, 758.184, 758.190, 758.196; Robert 719, 737; William 895; *see* Ley
Leef John 190, 665
Leek, *see* Leke
Leggepeny William 556
Legh Gunfrey de 113a; Alice wife of 113a
Lehaum, Leheum Geoffrey de 497, 577
Leicestre, Leycestr Agatha de 391, 406; Geoffrey de 225 ; Henry de 390, 406, 460; Hugh de 485; Margaret wife of Henry de 274, 390, 406; Philip de 363; William de 583
Leke, Leche, Leyke Agnes prioress 232, 239-40, 272, 302, 321, 358, 420, 538-9, 646
Lekisheuit Emma 805
Len(ne), Leune Adam de 198; Alan de 654; Matilda de prioress 155, 198, 203, 257, 259, 261, 309, 320, 340, 394, 425, 427, 438, 550-1, 565, 761
Lendone Simon de 249
Lenford Richard de 631
Lennes Robert 758.2
Lepere, Lopere John 124
Lescrop Richard 190
Leswin son of Segrim 655
Leta David and Roger sons of 213
Levenod 654
Levina 424, 483, 655
Levot, Lenot Robert 870
Lewin 637; Thomas son of 637; Inga sister of Thomas 637; Thomas monk, 679.2
Lewys William 758.185
Ley John 652, 735; *see* Lee
Leycestr, *see* Leicestre
Leyke, *see* Leke

Leyne Margery wife of Richard de 100; Richard de 100

Lichefelde, Lychefelde Agnes wife of Richard 887, 889; Agnes wife of Robert 877; Richard 887, 889; Robert 877

Lickesnot Hemmyng 911.11

Linc(oln) Nicholle Richard de 188, 472, 475, 692, 714, 758.68, 765.2; Thomas 4.5; William 769, 770

Lincoln John bishop of 126, 756, 825; official/officer of 25;

Lindesey John 758.152, 758.183, 767.1, 840, 854; Serlo de 178, 315, 379, 418

Lindon(e), Alan de 591 ; Ralph de 282; Simon de 153, 228, 416, 524; William de 229, 282, 650

Litstere Adam le 471; Richard 731, 739; Robert 189; Simon 831; W 758.54; William le 387

Little John the 547; John son of John 547; William the 559

Lize Roger son of 587; see Lece

Locksmith, Lokessmyth Robert 272, 758.121, 768, 852

Loghthorp [Longthorpe?] John 562

Lomb Robert 260; Thomas 363

London John de 585

Long(e) Elizabeth wife of John 401; John (le) 272, 401, 658, 706, 708, 710, 713, 732, 758.31, 758.94, 758.103-5, 753.107, 758.120, 758.122, 758.126, 758.133, 758.138, 758.143, 758.146, 758.158-9, 766.1, 768-9, 770; John the elder 758.138; John le skinner 305; John junior 321; Warin the 545

Longman William 283

Lorem Geoffrey 375

Lorimer Geoffrey 459

Loryng Robert 128-9

Lothtoplon Alan 269

Lovell Thomas 797-9

Lowick Robert 758.197

Lowthorp Joh 350

Lucas, Luke, Luk, Luke the skinner 338; son of Richard 507; Alexander 145, 157.2, 177, 180, 203, 237, 280, 286, 292, 304, 309, 316, 352, 393, 432, 434, 485, 492, 498, 517, 550, 758.7, 911.22; Alexander son of 501; Alexander brother of Isaac 196, 199, 201, 215; Alice daughter of Elizabeth 889; Amice widow of Alexander 550; Auota sister and coheir of Lucas 417; Elizabeth 889; Isaac 20, 145, 196, 201, 237, 280, 292, 316, 372, 408, 417, 428, 434, 477; John 891; Juliana wife of Isaac 20, 417; Phelicia sister and coheir of Lucas 417; Richard 299

Ludon Adam de master 911.23

Luffenham Henry de 325; Margaret wife of Nicholas 634; Nicholas de 625, 634; Richard de 149.6, 361 ; Thomas de 342, 377, 408; Walter de 342; Walter de brother of Thomas 408; William de 4.21

Luice the clerk son of Geoffrey 523

Luke, see Lucas

Lunderthorp Isabel wife of Roger de 48; Roger de 48

Lundr' Herbert de 523

Luneday mother of Henry son of Ralph 336

Lung, see Longe

Lurley John 758.146

Luscote John prior of the London Charterhouse 575

Luterel Robert 114, 693

Lutipati Thomas 526

Lutte William 661

Luue Acard son of 412

Luvel Andrew 168

Luwe, see Stanford

Lychefeld, see Lichefeld

Lydle Ripemund de 640

Lye William 371

Lymbergh Mabilla wife of Robert de 43; Robert de 43, 391, 692, 765.1-2

Lymbrenner Ralph le 171, 174, 244, 270, 314, 347, 370, 429, 529; Richard le 181, 329, 377; Thomas le 171, 270, 347, 370, 382, 429, 529, 758.69; W son of Thomas 758.69

Lymeborwe Robert de 909

Lyncoln, see Lincoln

Lyndesay, see Lindesey

Lyndon, see Lindon

Lyster, see Litstere

Lytell, Lyttyl John 134; William 758.146

Lyttler John 767.6

Mabel Roger son of 913.6
Mabel prioress of St Michael 290, 296, 357, 382, 425, 761
Mace Walter 758.102
Machon John 758.105
Madding Nigel 758.2
Madewell, *see* Maydnwell
Mage Robert son of 216
Magna Casterton Clement de 441; Walter son of Clement de 441
Maidenlove Robert 913.19b
Maisent', Meissentus 476, 654; Maisent Reiner 221, 806, 913.7, 9, 10; Reiner son of 262, 476, 486, 584, 654; Alexander son of Reiner 806, 913.10; Hugh son of 913.7, 9; Margaret wife of Reiner 654; *see* Reiner
Makeseye Agnes wife of Robert 477; Geoffrey de 460, 475, 553, 598; Geoffrey son of Geoffrey 475, 553, 554.1-2, 598; Makeseye John 674; Margery 420, 766.1; Robert de 361, 453, 457, 477; Roger de 71, 198, 323, 517; Simon de 101, 492; Stephen 758.124, 758.135-6; W 758.89, 758.90; Walter de 317, 531, 732; William (de) 6, 96, 125, 271, 532, 534, 692, 707, 714, 765.2
Makurneys John 277-8; *see* Mancourneys, Maturneys
Mal(h)erbe ...... 758.61 ; Adomar 758.81 ; Eustace/Stacy 39, 116, 147, 274, 278, 283, 311, 324, 369, 390-1, 406, 430, 460, 475, 553, 554.1-2, 598, 713, 748, 758.34, 761, 808, 909, 911.16; Lora wife of Eustace 39, 116; Peter 252;
Malpas David 670
Maltby Isabel de prioress 313
Man Stephen 758.130; W 758.51
Mancourneys John 713; *see* Makurneys
Manlyster Stephen 758.130
Manners, Maneris Richard (de) 609, 689; Thomas earl of Rutland 580, 581
Mar, *see* Mare
March Peter 328; Thomas son of Peter 328

Marchall, *see* Marshall
Marcham John 765.6
Marchaunt, *see* Bonde
Marche Peter 657, 758.1; Thomas son of Peter 758.1
Marchefeld John 758.116; Margery 758.82
Marcheford Geoffrey de 744; John 661
Mare, Mar Brian de la 206; Geoffrey de la 758.63; Joan wife of Geoffrey 758.63
Margaret prioress 566; daughter of Outhilda 480, 494, 499; Roger son of 617, 911.8-10
Margery prioress of Wothorp priory 365, 387
Marham Avice wife of Thomas de 459, 913.21; Thomas de 459, 913.21
Mariner Nicholas le 339
Mariscall, *see* Marshall
Mariun Nicholas 506
Markam John 898
Markeby John 709
Marmion Richard 911.11
Marra Thomas de 375
Marshall, Marchall, Mariscall Gilbert 375; John 672; *see* Gilbert; Simon
Martel William 682
Martin(e), Martyn monk 497; the apothecary 316; Gilbert 276; John 279
Martindale, Martyndale Robert 298
Martinwast Peter de 686
Masone, Masoun, Mazoun Hugh the 4.21; John (le) 67, 70, 758.44, 780; Matilda/Maude wife of Simon 97, 532; Simon 97, 532; *see* Hugh
Masthorp John 106; Robert 106
Mathews John 131
Matilda, Mathilda 179, 655; prioress of St Michael's 222, 325, 758.10; widow of Alexander son of Stanf[ord]166, 224; Cecily daughter of 436; Hugh son of 758.21; Reyner son of 451, 500, 543; Simon son of 183, 209, 217-8, 288, 447
Matthew, Mathew 657; chaplain 250, 444, 595; clerk 452; priest 179, 263, 587, 597; priest of St Martin 242, 437, 486, 523, 654; Matthew *ad pontem*

518; Robert son of 523

Maturneys Cecily wife of John 441; John 441; *see* Makurneys

Mauger 657; the weaver 511

Maurice 167; John son of 491; *see* Morys

Maurus Alan son of 288; *see* Mor

Mavan Peter esq 672

Maxey vicar of 911.3, 4, 5, 6 ; Hugh vicar of 911.23

Maxsey, *see* Makesey

May John 839; Margaret wife of John 839

Maydeford Geoffrey de 209

Maydenston Alan de 49; Alice wife of Alan de 49

Maydnwell Maydwell Thomas 649, 891, 906

Maymund(t) John 404, 713; Thomas 389

Maysent, *see* Maissent

Mazoun, *see* Mason

Megucer Alexander le 498; Osbert le 304; Osbert son of Alexander 498

Meir the Jew 911.18

Meirym Robert of Helpston 913.15, 16, 17; Alienora daughter of wife of Robert de Torpell 913.15, 16; Alienora sister of Peter and wife of Geoffrey Bulhernes 913.17; Maude mother of Alienora 913.16; Peter son of Robert chaplain 913.17

Meissentus, *see* Maisent

Melemakere Richard 146

Meltone, Meutone Milthon, Myllton Agnes 758.168; Clement de 147, 278, 287, 430, 453, 460, 713 , 753, 758.24; Henry 710; John de 156, 158, 274, 287, 713, 758.150, 853; Laurence 717, 728; William de 90, 758.58, 758.82, 893; William de parson of Holy Trinity 317, 765.5; *see* Molton, Taillour

Mercer Achard 911. 8, 9; Aldusa wife of Herbert son of William le 753; Alexander 537, 706, 708, 711, 715, 752; Alfred/Alured le 20, 309, 357, 393, 417, 550, 650, 911.13; Elizabeth 706, 708, 758.192; Elizabeth daughter of Henry Kirkeby 722;

Geoffrey le 334, 438, 489; Herbert son of William le 753; Hugh the 548, 557, 911.22; Joan daughter of Hugh 548; Margery wife of Alured le 20; Margery wife of Geoffrey le 438; Randulph 362; Reginald 758.126; Richard 758.143, 911.8-9; William le 154, 286, 548, 557-8, 560, 753; William brother of Hugh le 911.22; *see* Cisterna

Merch John de la 648

Merentishale Nicholas de 29; Robert son of Nicholas de 29; Sarra wife of Robert 29

Mering William 898

Merle Roger de 328

Merssh Edusa wife of John de 83; John de 83

Messager Matilda wife of Randolph 336; Randolph le 336; Richard 713; *see* Ralph

Messore Henry 442

Meuton, *see* Melton

Michael vicar of St Martin 330, 332, 338, 353, 419; *de la venele* 513; the tanner 363; brother of Henry son of Alexander 339; Clement son of 683-4

Micheloune Roger called 427

Middleton Thomas 705, 718, 733

Midedo, Mideto Reiner 480, 547, 583

Milisaund, Milisent Richard 4.20, 226

Miller, Mylner Alice wife of Edward 889, 890; Edward 792, 877, 889, 890-1; John 792; Matilda wife of Reymund le 60; Reymund le 60; Robert 657; Thomas 906; William 889; *see* Gere

Milner *alias* Halom Richard 321

Milton, *see* Melton

Mindham, *see* Mundham

Moigne Robert le 758.41; Thomas 134

Molle Alice wife of John 731; Elizabeth daughter of John 737; John 703, 705, 718, 728, 731, 733, 737, 739, 749-51, 754

Molton Clement de 4.18; *see* Melton

Monke, Munke John clerk 711, 715, 752; Roger 564; Thomas 804

Montefort Peter de (kt) 113a, 911.11

Mor(e) Alan 509 ; Alan son of Mor 346, 367, 414, 486, 502, 514; John of Okeham 366; *see* Maurus

Mor(e)ton Joan wife of Thomas de 290, 463; Peter de 698 ; Robert de 732; Thomas de 290, 430, 463, 688; Walter son of Joan 290, 463

Morchore Simon de 758.10

Morcote, Morkote Alexander de 306; Alice wife of William 360, 653; Henry de 47; Richard de 155, 653; William 360, 529, 653

Mordyt Henry 844

Morecrofte Agnes wife of Richard 133, 135, 776; Richard 133, 135, 776

Moreley John 661

Moresby, Morysby John 777; Margaret wife of John 777; Richard 127

Morewode, Morwood Margaret wife of William 797; Margaret daughter of William 797; W 758.166, 758.169; William 302, 539, 540, 562, 797

Morgan Elena wife of Philip 767.5; Philip 767.5;

Morin Henry 758.2

Morlond William de 477

Mortayn Roger de 693

Mortemer, Mortuo Mari Bartholomew de 663; John de clerk 278; Ralph de 497, 563; Thomas 834

Morwood, *see* Morewode

Moryng Henry 149.1

Morys, Moryce Nicholas 672, 866; Robert 866; Walter James 801; *see* Maurice

Morysby, *see* Moresby

Mott John 758.197; William 410

Mountegen Thomas 673

Mous W 758.65

Mousedale Robert 140

Mower John 670; Richard 674

Moyne Juliana wife of Robert le 61; Robert le 61

Mundeham Roger de 1.2-3, 81, 159, 402, 474, 534, 729, 826

Munke, *see* Monke

Murdok John 755

Musca Matthew 187

Musgrave Robert 11

Muston John 669

Mychell Isaac 599

Mychelove Roger 911.11

Myller, Myllner *see* Miller

Myllton, *see* Melton

Nassyngton Hugh de 4.19

Navenby, Naunby John de 100

Ne(o)uill Robert de 263 ; *see* Nevill

Nee Reiner 846; Henry son of Reiner 846; Ingusa 846; Clement brother of Henry 846

Negh Andrew 24

Nele Agnes wife of John 767.1; John 710, 731, 750, 767.1-2, 767.5; John senior 767.3-4

Nerford Walter de 146

Netlam John 580-1

Neue John 713

Neukirke Ralph de 171, 347

Neull John de 203

Nevill, Nevyll Alice de 339, 502; Alice widow of John de 190, 664-6; John de 147, 190, 664-6; Nicholas de 591 ; Roger de 591; Theobald de 693; Thomas 108

Nevour Robert 703, 705, 718, 728, 731, 733, 739, 750, 767.1

Newerk, Neuwerk Matilda wife of Robert 46, 117, 812; Robert de 46, 117, 812, 911.11, 16

Newesel[n] Peter 4.19

Neweton Cristian wife of William de 43; William de 43

Newstead, Novo Loco Geoffrey son of Stephen 326, 342; John de 325; Stephen de 222, 326, 342

Neye, Nye Andrew 199, 203, 214, 276, 340, 356, 381, 427, 490, 517, 753

Nicholas son of Absolon 341; son of Alexander 217, 339, 367, 447, 459, 502, 579.2; son of Thomas the clerk 448; the goldsmith 547; the messenger 513; brother of Henry son of Alexander 559; Amabil mother of Nicholas 448

Nicholle, *see* Lincoln

Niger Peter 911.17, 20 ; Robert 911.17, 18

Noble Geoffrey l(e) 228, 280, 390, 396, 416, 428, 476, 524; Geoffrey son of

Geoffrey 372; Gilbert the 521,
911.12; Hugh le 173, 279, 391, 765.3;
John 372; Thomas 475, 765.3; Walter
le 173, 324
Nodel John 1.2, 765.3-4
Noel Geoffrey 595
Nonnes, Nunnes atte Joan wife of
Walter atte 71, 714; Walter atte/de
71, 170, 188, 273, 369, 470, 475, 707,
714, 729, 740, 746, 748, 815, 817,
821; see Skillington Walter de
Noppe John 833
Noreis, Noreys Geoffrey 375; William
le 247
Noreman, see Norman(d)
Norens Geoffrey 459; John 211 ;
'norrensi', see Geoffrey
Norfolk, Norff', Norfolch, Northfolk'
Augustine de 287, 340, 381;
Katherine de 287; Peter de 13, 198,
222, 326, 508, 565
Norman, Normand Geoffrey le 396,
438; Gilmin called 517; John 311,
641; Reginald 185, 268, 284, 295,
312, 325, 393, 508, 565; Walter 19,
222, 237, 316, 334, 356, 368, 434;
Walter son of 198, 307, 377, 848;
William le 182, 223, 258, 316, 377,
385, 408, 429, 434, 474, 489 520, 546,
556
Normantoun Adam de 758.42 ; Robert
de 406, 909
Normanville Ralph de 601-2, 654, 687;
Ralph son of Ralph of 687
Nort(h)folk, see Norfolk
Northampton, Norh't' archdeacon of
432; Bohun William de earl of 1.3,
150, 469; Bartholomew de 490 ;
Hugh son of Robert de 310 ; Robert
de 310
Northborough, Norburc, Norburg',
Norhburg Geoffrey de 443; Galerus
de 179; Gilbert de 520; Hugh de 335;
Ralph de 222
Northfolk Gilbert de tailor 911.20 (see
Taylour; Cissor)
Northorp John 722
Norton, Nortune, Northona Richard
de 448; Robert de 216, 266, 506,
911.20

Norwiche Robert 138
Notingham Amice daughter of
Reymund 758.43; Hugh de 286;
Hugh son of William 154, 214; Joan
wife of Remund 765.4; Remund
758.43, 765.4; Thomas son of
Remund 765.4; Walter de 275, 397;
William de 231, 237, 266, 267, 275,
286, 911.22; William son of William
de 145, 154, 157.2, 182, 196, 201,
214-5, 223, 237, 292, 352, 361, 363,
365, 428, 432, 442, 458, 467, 485,
501, 504
Nousle Peter de 758.26; Agnes wife of
Peter de 758.26
Novo Loco, see Newstead
Nunnes, see Nonnes
Nye, see Neye

Obbethorp Geoffrey son of Gilbert de
28; Gilbert de 28; Mary wife of
Gilbert de 28
Obys John 395, 882-3
Ocle Henry de 372
Ode Richard 911.12; William de 911.17
Odo 654; clerk 486; William son of
617
Offinton Roger de 910.5; William
910.5
Offord, see Ufford
Offyngton, Ofyngton, see Uffington
Ofnemaiden Geoffrey 416
Oger son of Jordan 595, 617
Okeham John son of Nicholas de
758.51; Nicholas de 758.51
Okele Henry de 477, 514, 670
Ole W 758.201
Olier John of Depyngate 192
Orewyn Robert 111, 236
Osbert the janitor 498; the porter 524
Oseberneby Henry de 460
Oselstone Hugh de 439
Osward 663
Othe hille Robert 871; see Hill
Ottle Henry de 280
Ouerton Henry de 352; William de 283
Ouneby John de 150
Ouresby Roger de parson of church of
St George 719
Outhilda daughter of Sparrus 262, 480,

494, 499; wife of William Dodus
166, 224; Geoffrey son of 145, 219,
478; Margaret daughter of 480, 494;
Richilda daughter of 480, 494

Ovys, see Obys

Owen William 592

Oxenford, Oxon William de, prior of
St Michael 230, 244, 290, 296, 382

Oyler Isabel wife of Walter 531; Walter
531

Oyltone Henry de 713

P… Henry baker 660

Pacewell, see Pateshull

Pagan, see Pain

Page Beatrice 4.11; Hawisia wife of
Richard 4.12; John 366, 386, 648,
688, 711, 715, 728, 731, 737; Richard
4.12

Pain the chaplain 544; Pain master 511;
Pain priest 210, 379, 383, 407, 433,
476; rector of St Clement 217-8, 310,
330, 338, 418, 579.1, 636; Roger son
of 444; Sampson chaplain 547;
William son of 225; see Peyn

Pake William 307; see Peck

Pakington Robert de 54, 273, 692, 714,
744, 765.2

Palady John 756

Palefrer Christiana daughter of Peter de
Wakerley 627; Thomas 627

Palfrey John senior 189; William 189,
234

Palfreyman Christopher 738, 743; John
704, 706, 708, 719, 722, 726, 745,
758.138-9, 758.142, 758.150,
758.192, 766.1, 770, 776, 835-6; John
the younger 758.130; Roger 758.115

Palmer Andrew the 450; Cecily 4.10;
Hawise daughter of Roger 913.1
Hugh 578; John the 439; Geoffrey
son of John 439; Reginald 913.14b;
Palmer Roger 913.1; Thomas 126-7,
758.187; William (le) 354, 439, 556,
805; see Andrew, Dodus, Roger

Pampoke [?]913.20

Paneterie Thomas de la 147

Panetrie John de la 532, 696, 758.82

Pappele Adam de 519; Pappele John
de 400, 405, 515; Richard de 1.2,

4.16, 470, 744, 758.39, 860; William
de 152, 178, 217-8, 310, 315, 330,
337-8, 343, 379, 418, 423, 451, 461,
489, 503, 511, 515, 519, 543, 545,
579.1, 586, 591, 654; Pappele William
de chaplain 911.19; William de,
parson of St Mary of Binnewere 353,
400; William son of William de 545

Parcer John le 260 ; see Parker

Parchmener Geoffrey le 758.30; see
Parmenter

Parent 179; Alexander son of Gilbert
255; Geoffrey 167, 208, 212-3, 647;
Gilbert 225, 243, 251, 255, 262, 315,
327, 383, 413, 423-4, 437, 479, 482-
3, 503, 516, 544, 655, 657; Matilda
wife of Gilbert 503

Parker John 718, 728; Robert 758.144

Parmenter Acard 459; Denise daughter
of Acard 459; Peter le 320; William
184, 748; see Parchmener

Parnell Robert 709, 727, 734

Parsons Robert 161, 165, 371

Parteneye Reiner son of Robert de 175;
Robert de 175

Pateshull Sir 910.5; Simon de 910.4, 7;
Walter de 910.7; William de 910.6

Paumer, see Palmer

Paunton Philip de 693

Paynell John 679.2; William 147

Paynton Richard alias Ramsey 758.141

Pechel John 350, 449

Peck, Pekke Alice wife of Richard 245,
447; Marie 336; Ralph 4.4; Richard
145, 205-6, 208-11, 217, 219, 241,
243, 245, 251, 255, 262, 327, 336,
339, 341, 345, 367, 374, 383, 389,
392, 403-4, 407, 414, 422, 424, 433,
447-8, 451, 455, 458-9, 461, 476, 478-
80, 482, 484, 488, 494, 496, 502, 506,
509, 513-5, 516, 521-2, 559, 560, 583-
4, 602, 610-1, 613-4, 620, 623, 625,
627, 629, 630, 634, 638, 655, 687,
911.1; Richard senior 446; Richard
son of Richard 288, 421, 521, 543-4,
546, 668

Pedyngton Alan 240; Joan wife of Alan
240

Pekebriggs John de 758.44

Perce Hugh 427

Percesvil William 892

Perch William de 379

Percy Henry 862

Person Robert 592

Personric Richard 758.63

Pert, Peert Hugh 758.20, 758.22;
Nicholas 196, 352, 398, 439, 442;
Nicholas son of William 557; Robert
son of Simon 758.36; Simon 758.36;
William (le) 398, 548, 557-8, 560, 639,
642

Peryman Thomas 670

Petard Geoffrey of Talyngtone 724, 730

Peter 167; chaplain 497; clerk 245, 422,
447, 484, 494, 545, 578, 654; rector
of Pickworth 654; prior/parson,
rector of St Michael's 437, 683-5,
913.1, 2, 3, 4, 6; pupil of Reiner 204,
341, 461, 496, 499, 500, 503, 543;
Peter the knight 166, 207, 627, 638,
683, 684; Peter lord of Burley 312;
Peter the dyer 307, 342, 370, 408,
419, 515, 546; the skinner 380; the
stonecutter 262; the tailor 204, 484,
494, 499, 500; the tallowman 638;
Peter son of Geoffrey 204, 216, 346,
367, 374, 407, 451, 455, 461, 484,
499, 502, 522, 601, 614, 618, 624,
764; son of Geoffrey son of
Herlewin 623; son of Gervase 583;
son of Lecia 447, 517; son of
Richard 522, 560; son of Richard
son of Selove 152; son of William
545; Andrew son of Peter 477;
Henry son of 545; John son of 187;
Reginald son of 451, 543; Robert
son of 484, 494, 499, 500, 911.19, 21;
Sarah daughter of 517

Petit John 657; Robert 4.20, William le
216, 446-7; William le 911.17; of
Theford 913.8, 11; Simon son of
913.11

Petitprudom Richard 657

Petronila prioress 353

Pettismoch Gilbert 260

Peverel Robert of Peterborough 409

Peykirke William 314; William de
junior 568

Peyn Margaret wife of Ralph 570;
Ralph miller 570; see Pain

Phelipp, Phelyppe, Philipp, Philyppys
David 844; Hugh 717, 721, 723;
Katherine wife of Hugh 717, 721,
723; Katherine wife of Thomas 723;
Thomas 144, 162, 298, 375, 700, 702-
3, 705, 720, 727, 734-5, 742, 749, 750,
756, 765.9, 767.3-4; Thomas son of
Hugh 723; Thomas clerk son of
Thomas 735

Philip 657; dean, parson of Carleby 806,
913.7, 8, 9, 10; son of Richard de
Cotes 913.9; of Deeping chaplain
893; chaplain of Leicester 231; Philip
the dyer 245, 255, 337, 353, 412, 419

Philip dean/parson of Carleby

Phillippot John 190

Pickard, Pichard, Pykard Annoricus 25;
Henry 145, 219, 478

Pickworthe, Picwrze, Pykworth John
464; William de 181, 280, 514

Pilloc Geoffrey 152

Pilsgate, Pilesgate, Pilesiate Adam de
227; Alexander de 343; Geoffrey de
655; Ralph son of Geoffrey de 655

Pincebek Richard de 214

Pinkil Roger son of 219; Roger son of
William 145, 478; William 145, 219,
478

Pippes William de burgess 913.12

Piribrok, Pirbrok Dameta daughter of
Henry 826; Henry de 357, 463, 813-
4, 826, 911.11

Pitt, Pite, Pyte Beatrice wife of Richard
33; John of/in the 160, 758.136,
758.142, 758.144; Richard 33, 45,
748, ; Thomas 292

Pium Henry priest 221, 450

Plateni Henry lord of fee of 518

Plays John 190

Plomer Henry 765.5

Plouman Adam le 495, 506; John le
175, 467, 809 ; see Adam

Plowham Adam 149.1; John 4.14

Plumbton Nicholas de 648

Pod, see Poth

Poke Fulco 624; Ralph son of 624

Pole Edmund/Esmund de la 190, 664-
6; Pole Michael de la senior 190, 664-
6; William de la, earl of Suffolk 667

Pomerey John 873-4, 876

Poncyn, *see* Poucyn

Pont' Hugh de 595; Symone de 595

Pontefract R[.....] de 268 ; John de 54; Robert de 45, 758.10 ; Thomas de 1.2-3, 73, 273, 729, 826

Ponyngg Thomas de 147

Pope Thomas 711, 715; W 758.201

Portam John ad of Bernardshill 231; Thomas son of John 231; *see* Gate

Porter Adam 367, 414, 461, 502; Osbert le 228, 416, 524; Roger le 758.17-8; Richard son of Roger le 758.18 ; *see* Adam; Hugh

Portesmouth, Pottesmouth Alexander 149.3; Cecilia 275, 357, 814

Pot Henry 228; Nicholas 380

Poth (Pod) Richard 428; Thomas called 517

Potter Joan wife of Richard 135; Richard 135, 776

Potton Idonea/Idoneaugh wife of Robert de 28; Robert de 28; William 672

Poucyn, Poncyn, Pouncyn, Pucyn, Puncyn Alice wife of William 57; William 57, 185, 198, 203, 222, 256-7, 261, 275-6, 282, 284, 311-2, 323, 325-6, 356, 364, 368, 490, 508, 517, 550-2, 565

Pounceby John 712; William 750

Pounfrayt, *see* Pontefract

Power Richard 873-4

Prat Henry 197, 307, 318, 349, 356, 556, 848; John 303, 348, 537; Robert 6, 317, 531-2, 536, 758.88, 769

Predicas Reginald 216, 453, 457

Preston Gilbert de 513; John 661; William de vicar of All Saints by the Bridge 325

Prowet Alexander 332

Prudum Gilbert 379; Robert 379

Prysot John 128.2

Pucyn, *see* Poucyn

Pudelprest John 361

Pulte Alan 269

Puncyn, *see* Poucyn

Puntdelarches, Punchelard John 226, 758.13

Punteis Peter 339

Purser John 758.127

Puttok Henry 203

Pykard, *see* Pickard

Pykworth, *see* Pickworthe

Pynkyl, *see* Pinkil

Pyribrok, *see* Pirbrok

Pyth Richard 758.35

Pytte, *see* Pitt

Quappelad Alexander de 205, 458, 574; Constance wife of Alexander de 458; Henry son of Alexander de 458; Peter de 225; Thomas son of Alexander de 205

Quenton Graciana de wife of William 12; William de 12

Queurecheyo John de monk 572

Quichors William 419

Raas William barbour 769

Radcliff, Ratclyff, Rauclyff William 161-2, 165, 235, 652, 669, 694, 767.2-5, 765.9, 891, 895, 902-4

Ralph 500; rector of St Mary at the bridge 758.5; the chamberlain 157.2, 585; the goldsmith 495; the messenger 285; son of [...] 637; son of Acard 157.1, 207, 208, 210, 211, 242, 339, 345, 355, 362, 367, 374, 383, 407, 414, 424, 433, 480, 484, 486, 493-4, 502, 505, 516, 544, 583, 584, 601-2, 605, 612-3, 616, 620, 622-3, 625, 627, 683-4; son of Fulco 613, 616; son of Henry son of Ascelin 336; Adrian son of 375, 459; Emma daughter of Ralph 687; Joan wife of Ralph the messenger 285; Gilbert son of 563; Kotel son of 224

Ralph abbot of Crowland 913.12, 18, 19b

Ramsey Walter de 826; *see* Paynton

Randolf Richard 758.42; Robert 758.118

Rankell William 651, 775; William junior 894

Ranle, *see* Rauele

Rannes William 653

Rathwell Thomas 672

Rauclyff, *see* Radclyffe

Rauele, Raule John 106; Thomas de

188, 252, 359, 385, 388, 410, 429, 456, 465, 474, 526, 758.41; Thomas de senior 462

Raundes Robert de 388, 429, 454, 456, 462, 474

Rawceby, *see* Rouceby

Red, *see* Ruffus

Redberd Henry 384; Peter 282

Rede Hugh le 758.40, 818; John 767.6; Nicholas le 252, 254, 465

Redmild Robert de 457

Redyngges, Gilbert son of Henry de 807, 911.16; Henry de 807; Margaret prioress of St Michael 160, 233-4, 308, 401, 445, 534, 549, 596

Reest(e) Agnes wife of Jeffrey 765.6; Isabella wife of William 765.8; Jeffrey 765.6; William 765.7-9

Reginald, Reynald 249; chaplain of St Paul 686; the bursar 618; the dyer 149.8; the tanner 328; son of Peter 451, 543; Hugh son of 495; Joan wife of William 111; John junior 111; William son of John junior 111

Regrater Alfred de 650; *see* Grater

Reiner 911.7; Hugh son of 911.7

Reiner, Reymer, Reyner 149.2, 149.4, 177, 476, 647, 657, 911.7, 913.14a, b; chaplain 494, 683-4; chaplain of St Andrew 577 ; clerk 578; deacon 263, 597; dean 217-8, 221, 310, 341, 379, 418, 451, 500, 511, 543, 579.1, 584, 647, 911.19; priest 167, 210, 217-8, 221, 407, 421, 423, 433, 476, 484, 512, 578; son of Hereward 484; rector of Holy Trinity 226; Reiner Maisent 221, 806; Reiner the smith 167; Reiner son of Burnild 483; son of Alexander 412, 419; son of Hereward 204, 455, 461, 484, 499; son of Hugh 177, 215, 509; son of Maisent 262, 476, 486, 584, 654; son of Matilda 451, 500, 543; Reiner sons of 343; Alexander 911.19; Alexander son of Reyner 149.2, 149.4, 209, 289, 336, 375, 657, 911.18, 19; Geoffrey son of 263, 338, 597, 913.13; Henry son of 451, 500, 543; Hugh son of 145, 177, 208-11, 215-6, 219, 228, 245, 247, 251, 265, 289, 327, 330,

336-7, 339, 341, 345-6, 354, 367, 375, 389, 396, 403-4, 407, 409, 414, 416, 447, 459, 476, 478, 480, 484, 491, 494, 496, 500, 502, 510-1, 513-5, 521-2, 524, 546, 559, 579.1, 586, 911.7, 12, 17, 18, 19, 20, 21; 913.7, 9, 10; Peter son of 288; Peter pupil of 451, 461, 543; Agnes daughter of William 377; Alexander brother of Hugh son of Reiner 447, 459, 559; Henry son of Alexander 447, 559; Juliana wife of Hugh 586; Margaret wife of Reiner 476; Nicholas brother of Henry 447, 559; Sampson 258, 326, 334, 377; William 12, 145, 177, 186, 196-7, 215, 227, 258, 307, 318, 326, 334, 342, 349, 377-8, 384, 396, 408, 481, 489, 492, 514, 556; *see* Blatherwyk, Maisent, Midedo

Repinghale, Reppinchall Walter de 211, 289, 414, 911.12

Reppis John de 911.11

Restwold Richard 662

Reve Robert 193, 875, 885; Roger 384

Reynald, *see* Reginald

Reyner, *see* Reiner

Reynham Agatha de 758.33; Cecily wife of Godfrey de 34; Geoffrey de 149.4; Godfrey de 34, 286, 585

Reynhawe Ralph de 911.13

Richalde William de 626

Richard 167, 587, 596, 657; chaplain 345, 493; clerk 356, 457, 758.17; priest 355, 379; priest of Hengiston 660; rector of St Mary at the Bridge 392; vicar of All Saints beyond the bridge 758.81, 758.98; vicar of Ecton/Etton 202, 497; vicar of St Martin 400, 496; vicar of St Mary Binnewerch 339; Richard the baker 375, 459; of the chamber [*de camera*] 157.1; the dyer 467; the smith 510; seneschal of Stamford 486; serjeant of Brunne 149.3; son of Aldus 197, 412, 419, 515, 546; son of Emma of Wirthorpe 244; son of Henry 421, 644, 668; son of Richard 197, 377, 501, 556; son of Seluve 152, 207, 221, 242, 288, 403, 486, 559, 584; son of Ursi 682; son of Wolm' 490;

Alexander son of 288, 403, 761;
Henry son of 255, 288, 447, 911.18,
21; Luke son of 507; Peter son of
522; Richard Richard son of 911.18,
21

Richeman Barnard 767.3-4

Richemond John 767.6

Richilda daughter of Outhilda 480, 494,
499

Rick(e) Ralph 389, 404, 452

Ridell, *see* Rydell

Rihale, Ryhale Cecily wife of Robert de
585; Robert de 585; William de 307,
315, 591

Rikeman Robert 380

Ringesdon, Ryngusdon Alan de 474;
Geoffrey de 344

Ringestede Roger de 312

Rippel, Rippele, Ryppele Hugh de 211,
367, 502, 605, 619, 622, 635

Rippengale William 758.152

Rippes, Rippis Henry de 552 ; John de
323, 517, 526 ; William de 149.4, 558

Risbek John 658

Risinges Aunger de 400

Riston Stephen de 477

Robert 647, 657; Robert alumpnus
499; clerk 623; clerk of Haxstun'
444; master 647; chaplain 250, 486,
657, 684, 698; parson 362; priest 167,
179, 437, 587, 597; priest of
Scoftegate 242; rector of All Saints
210, 221, 224, 383, 407, 433, 450,
476, 584; vicar of St Andrew 400;
archdeacon of Huntingdon 263;
abbot 651; abbot of Peterborough
426, 600; the bursar 758.15; the
carter 504; the dyer 354, 602; the
physician 758.32; the smith 154,
758.35; the tailor 228, 416, 524; le
tanner 650; the white 365; son of
Adam of Spalding 807; son of Agnes
151, 223, 403, 442, 447, 485, 496,
546; son of Albinus 242, 367, 502,
617, 623; son of Alice 620; son of
Brond 398, 548; son of Geoffrey
206, 443, 594, 610; son of Hereward
480, 494, 612; son of Hugh 486; son
of Isaac 361, 396, 558, 560; son of
Mage 216; son of Matthew 523; son

of Peter the tailor 204, 484, 494, 499;
son of Robert 504; son of Stenketel
683, 684; Robert brother of Reiner
484; Thomas son of 241; Thurlstan
son of 493

Robin nephew of the monk 167

Roger 655; clerk 285; chaplain of the
church of St Mary at the bridge 293;
master 647; priest 647; archdeacon
of Leicester 263; the carpenter 199;
the dyer 294, 363; the palmer 183,
583; the porter 758.17-18; the reeve
167; son of Hardekin 213, 413; son
of Lece 213, 413, 424, 483, 516, 655;
son of Lize 587; son of Margaret
617; son of Pain 444; son of
Sparcolf 413; son of Ulfric 609;
brother of Wlmer 398; David son of
413; Geoffrey son of 213, 413, 483,
655; Henry son of 655, 516, 544;
Isaac son of 383, 545; James son of
187; Peter son of William son of 310;
William son of 213, 310, 413, 423,
483, 512, 544, 655, 686

Rol(le)stone William 758.172, 758.174

Rolond, *see* Rowland

Rome Geoffrey 214

Rondes Robert de 64, 593

Roose Robert 652

Rosby William 679.2

Rosewale Richard 667

Rothwel Agnes wife of Richard 758.42;
Richard de 758.42

Rouceby William 717, 724, 726, 730,
741, 758.152

Rouland, *see* Rowland

Rous Thomas le 393

Rove Roger 753

Roversby William 765.6; *see* Rouceby

Rowe Henry 171; John 172, 568; Ralph
326; Robert 171, 333, 464

Rowland, Rolond, Rouland John 481;
Robert 609; William 758.70, 758.117,
758.134

Ruffus, Red Alice widow of Geoffrey
de Withorp 249; Beatrice wife of
Eustace 911.12; Beatrice wife of
Robert 613; Eustace 911.12; Hugh
222, 326; Isaac (the) 375, 459, 687;
John 389, 404; John (the Red) son of

Hugh Dulle 375, 452, 459; Richard
  657; Richard son of Hugh 222, 326;
  Robert 613, 624; Yngusa wife of
  John the Red 452, 459
Rus Cecily wife of Ralph le 9; Ralph le
  9; Thomas le 276
Rusca Robert 421
Russel(l) Agnes 257; Agnes wife of
  John 520; Hugh 342; Geoffrey 153,
  328; Geoffrey steward of
  Peterborough 409; John 520, 556,
  829, 862; Katherine 331; Richard
  342; Richard son of Hugh 342;
  Robert 174, 297
Rutland, Roteland Thomas Manners
  earl of 580-1
Ruys Henry le 247
Rychardson *alias* Bryghton John 709,
  734; Roger of Tychmarsh 734;
  William 734
Rydel(l), Ridell 607; Hugh 272; Ivette
  wife of Nicholas 770; Nicholas 303,
  348, 770
Ryhale, *see* Rihale
Rykeman Robert de 149.4
Ryley John 789; Margaret 789
Ryngusdon, *see* Ringesdon
Ryppes, *see* Rippes
Ryvers Richard brother of William
  157.1; William de 157.1;

Sabeci, *see* Sibeci
Sabyn John 670
Saddyng Saul 342
Saddyngton, Sadyngton Agnes
  daughter of John 873, 874, 878, 884;
  Agnes wife of Thomas 887, 889;
  Amicia wife of John 873-4; John
  873-4, 878; Thomas *alias* Herryes
  872, 875-6, 884, 886-7; Thomas son
  of Agnes 873, 874, 884
Sadeler Agnes wife of Thomas 445;
  Thomas 445; W 758.69; William 1.2,
  4.5
Sae Henry de, brother of William 659;
  William de 659, 663
Saham William de 320, 758.8, 758.9
Salendin 657
Salett Robert 894
Salso Marisco Ennardus/Elnard 40;

Thomas de 40
Saltby Emma 539, 719, 766.1-2;
  Reginald de 1.3, 324, 410, 831;
  Richard 719; W 758.158; William
  son of Reginald 831
Saluagius 659; David son of Saluagius
  659
Sampson Henry 911.7; Master 911.7
Sampson, Samson 242, 250, 263, 383,
  476, 486, 587, 597, 911.7; the knight
  /chivaler 166, 207, 616, 683-4, 686,
  913.19a,b; 'ultra pontem' 355, 493,
  505; son of Godric 151, 208, 212-3,
  221, 245, 255, 327, 337, 343, 351,
  400, 412-3, 419, 422-4, 447, 479, 483,
  488, 512, 516, 544; son of Roger
  Cokla 758.2; Emma wife of John 77;
  Henry 228, 416, 524, 911.7; Henry
  rector of Easton 328; Henry son of
  421, 547, 764, 911.7; John 77, 183,
  199, 205, 214, 268, 276, 448, 459,
  461, 517, 522, 713, 717, 753; John
  son of 183, 216, 346, 375, 484, 521,
  687; Richard 37, 57, 184, 283;
  Robert 184; William 222, 270, 287,
  326, 342, 364, 370, 425
Samuel the Jew of Stanford 910.5,6
Sancto, *see* St
Sandwath Robert 735, 775
Sapcote 371; Anne wife of Richard
  804; Edward 395, 592, 791-2, 899;
  Francis 898; Francis son of Thomas
  856; Joan 542; John 539, 758.188;
  Katherine 804; Richard 162, 541,
  804, 898; Thomas 360, 783, 856
Sarah daughter of Peter son of Lecia
  517; Geoffrey son of 196; William
  son of 423, 512
Sarazin John 443
Saunford William de 147
Saunson John 356
Sauvel John 610, 621; *see* Fauvel
Savage, Sauvage Isabel prioress 653;
  James le 763 ; John 758.63, 758.68,
  758.78 ; Robert 412; Thomas 467,
  556
Sawnder Elizabeth 371; Roger 371
sawyer, *see* Ingerammus
Sayree Geoffrey 4.7
Scaccario Robert de 220; William de

432, 458, 514, 650; *see* Exchequer

Scanclerc Roger le 758.31, 758.40

Scarburgh William of North Luffenham 670

Scaveler, Scaueler, Schavelere, Staveler Alexander son of Luke le 372; Gilbert le 255; Gilbert son of Luke 255; Isaac son of Luke 255; John le 334, 380, 501; Luke son of Gilbert le 255; Robert le 391; Roger le 8, 121, 188, 274, 305, 311, 406, 463, 526, 553, 554.1-2, 555, 598, 707, 713, 740, 748, 810-2, 911.16 ; Roger le senior 822 ; Sampson 609

Scerr Robert 279

Schalonner Robert 324

Schavelere, *see* Scaveler

Schefeld Robert de 223

Scheldingtorp William de 183, 204, 330, 414, 447, 499; *see* Seldingthorpe

Schelford John 538

Schelington William de 324; *see* Skilington

Schepey Robert 350, 562, 885

Scherewynd Alice wife of John 533, 852; John 533, 852

Scherman, *see* Sherman

Schilton, see Silton

Schiluyngton, *see* Shilvington

Schirlond Thomas de 324

Schot William 441; *see* Scot

Schrobesbiri William de 7

Schyllington, *see* Skilington

Scibeci, *see* Sibeci

Sclater Simon 758.173

Sclefford, *see* Sleford

Scolicia 657; *see* Colice, Fredegill, Hereward

Scot(t) Richard the, 180; Richard 408; William 230, 758.21

Scotelthorp Margaret wife of Walter de 38; Richard son of 152; Robert de 758.48; Roger de 463, 526; Walter de 38

Scrope Richard le 665

Scute Hugh 628; Idonea wife of Walter 628; Walter son of Hugh 628

See Margaret atte/del prioress of St Michael 415, 466

Segrim 655; Leswin son of 655

Seint Waryn le 269

Seldingthorp William de 617; *see* Scheldingtorp

Seled Robert son of Walter 400; Walter 400; *see* Seluf

Seler John le 753

Selleware Richard 342, 515

Selona, *see* Seluf

Seluf, Selef, Selof, Selona, Selove, Seluve 245, 447, 546, 657; Alexander son of Richard son of Seluf 245, 418, 447, 546, 559, 657; John son of Peter 384; Peter son of Richard 372; Peter son of Richard son of 560; Richard son of 152, 166, 207, 221, 242, 245, 262, 289, 403, 418, 447, 486, 546, 559, 560, 584, 657, 761, 911.12, 18; Richard son of Richard son of 288; *see* Stanford

Semark Thomas 758.170

Semer William 148; William son of William 148

Sempingham Robert de 440, 527

Sergant, Seriant, Serjeant Alexander the 168, 204, 208, 217, 245, 251, 447, 480, 499, 559, 628, 911.21; Geoffrey 913.18; Henry le 217; Herbert le 152, 218, 251, 316, 367, 461, 480, 484, 505, 579.1-2, 640, 657, 911.7 ; Margaret 910.1, 3; Nicholas 910.1; Robert 910.1, 3

Serle John 872; William 885

Sessyl, *see* Cecil

Shardelowe John 667

Sharp Henry 758.186

Shauelere, *see* Scaveler

Sheffeld Thomas de kt 911.11

Shelyington, Sheluynton, *see* Shilvington

Shepe John 137

Shepherd Henry 1.3; Ralph 652

Sher(e)man, Scherman Agnes wife of William 112a; Henry 728; John 112a, 526, 670; Robert 758.193; William 112a

Shilvington, Shelyington, Scheluynton William de 1.2, 72, 146, 173, 279

Shordich, Shordych Isolda wife of Thomas de 82; Thomas de 82-3

Sibeci, Cibici, Sabeci, Scibeci, Sybecey,

Sybeti Henry de 145, 152, 182, 211, 216-9, 226, 245, 265, 288, 346, 367, 392, 403, 446-7, 451, 459, 461, 478, 491, 502, 506-7, 509, 515, 522, 543, 559, 635, 657, 668, 911.19, 20, 21; Ralph 486

Sibily, Sybely Henry 642; John 539, 758.188

Sibston John 758.140; William 758.140

Sigge Cecily 911.9, 10; William 911.9, 10

Silkerton Henry de prior of St Michael's 339

Silton, Schilton, Sylton Henry de 287, 430, 441, 469, 758.44; Robert 743

Simon burgess 236; chaplain of Eston 591; the clerk 152, 176, 231, 443, 447-8, 450; prior of Fineshade 386; the marshal 198, 517; the smith 525; son of Alexander 216, 506, 548; son of Alice 620; son of Geoffrey 428; son of Matilda 209, 217-8, 447; at the bridge 149.5; Abselon son of 149.5, 255, 293; Alexander son of 237; Apsat son of 448; David son of 157.1; Gilbert son of 255, 448; Peter 894; see Stanford

Skanclerc, see Scanclerc

Skaveler, see Scaveler

Skelton W de 758.49

Skelyngton, Skilington Joan wife of Walter de 707; W de 758.61; Walter de 260, 554.1-2, 598, 692, 707, 765.1-2, 909; see Nonnes

Skinner, Skynner Acard the 620; Alice wife of Acard 620; Alice daughter of Alice 620; Robert 750, 758.199, 759, 772; Robert son of Alice 620; Simon son of Alice 620; William the skinner 267; see Geoffrey, Peter

Skirbek Margaret wife of William de 94; William de 94

Skryvener William 711, 715

Skuns Matilda wife of Thomas de 48; Thomas de 48

Skyppewyth William 190

Sleford Nicholas (de) 536, 829; Stephen de 387, 758.27, 758.32, 758.152

Smalpoke Matilda 654

Smarte Richard 873-4

Smereman Reginald 758.18, 758.23

Smith, Smyth, smith Agnes wife of Walter 102, 908; Alice wife of Robert le 82; Elizabeth wife of William 136; Geoffrey 160; Hugh the 197, 349, 556, 657; Ivetta wife of Richard 95; John 103, 323, 706, 708, 711, 715, 758.129, 758.159, 758.175, 758.178, 758.179n, 758.180, 758.182, 758.185, 835; Richard 95, 255, 560; Richard son of William 136; Robert le 82, 154, 322, 561, 573, 661, 758.35; Simon the 525; Thomas the 447; Walter 102, 758.127, of Exton 908; William (the) 136, 212, 315, 337, 349, 356, 371, 422, 649, 869; William brother of Hugh 556; see Almer, Hugh, Jocelin, Reiner, Richard, Robert, Simon, William

Smyth Agnes 908; Walter of Exton 908

Snartford Adam 271

Snoo William 735

Soalgrave Richard 190

Soalworth William 190

Solfa 657; Alexander 577

Somerby, Someredeby Henry 271; John de 692, 765.2-3; Robert de 285, 296

Somercote, Sumercote, Sumerkotis William de 178, 225, 310, 315, 319, 337, 351, 379, 400, 418, 489, 545, 579.1, 586, 591

Sotico Gilbert 586

Sowe Margery wife of Roger 514; Roger de 514

Sowresby, Soureby John de 758.109; Margaret wife of Thomas 105; Thomas 105

Sowtere Peter 750

Soyles John 190

Spalding Adam de 397; Asselina wife of John 322, 561; John 322, 561; Richard de 4.5; Robert son of John 322, 561; Thomas 573

Spandeford John 832

Sparcolf, Sparkoll ...... 288; Roger son of 413

Sparrus 204, 499; Emma daughter of

262, 494; Outhilda daughter of 262, 480, 494, 499

Spencer, Spenser Robert 863, 866-8; William 360, 653, 734, 765.9, 788

Sperlyng Andrew 662

Sperneton, Sperveton Lewen 167; Robert de 655; Robert son of Lewen 167; Simon nephew of Lewen 167

Spicer, Specer, Spycer Alice wife of John 89b, 123; Edda wife of Raymond le 8; Henry le 334, 340; Joan wife of Reimund 758.72, 765.5; John (le) 89b, 123, 176, 196, 231, 317, 389, 510, 531-2, 536, 658, 699, 732, 758.81, 758.98-99, 758.112, 758.130-1, 768-71; John son of Reymund 765.5; Raymond/Reimund le 7, 8, 758.72, 765.5; Thomas 239, 321, 420, 537, 661, 706, 708, 719, 722, 745, 829, 835; William 409; see Henry, John

Spicier Raymond le 317

Spirgournell, Spygurnel Margaret wife of William 172; William 159, 172, 229, 253, 402

Spiritus William 683

Spofford John de 331, 830, 893

Sprigg John 812

Spycer, see Spicer

St Albans William de 419

St Andrew (Sancto Andrea) Geoffrey de 242

St Denis (Sancto Dionisio) Simon de 353, 500

St Edmund Emma daughter of Walter 758.4-5, 758.7; Richard de 176, 341, 496, 546; Richard son of Walter de 294, 451, 461; Walter 176, 231, 294, 448, 758.4;

St Feriolo Bartholomew de 758.5, 758.7, 758.11, 758.25; Emma wife of Bartholomew de 758.5, 758.7, 758.11-12; John son of Bartholomew 758.25

St Fromond Alexander prior of 572, 576; Andrew prior of 575

St Ives Thomas de 758.79, 758.96

St John Roger de 762

St Laud (Sancto Laudo) Ralph de 693

St Mark (Sancto Marco) William de 173

St Medard (Sancto Medardo) Geoffrey de 153, 241, 249 ; Geoffrey brother of Robert de 178; Robert de, parson of Norton 178

Stable Thomas 747

Stabley John 758.137

Stacy William 99, 189, 272, 758.103, 758.126, 758.196, 768-70, 852

Stainby, Staindeby, Standeby, Stenby, Stiandeby, Steandeby, Styandeby Achard 910.2; Agnes wife of William de 1.1, 150; Hugh de 327, 367, 374, 502, 601, 618, 624, 628, 633; John 239, 272, 302, 321, 420, 537-8, 722, 758.146, 766.1; Reyner de 336; William de 1.1, 86, 88, 150, 234, 271, 415, 531, 532, 533, 536, 648, 671, 699, 729, 732, 758.60-1, 758.75, 758.97, 758.104, 758.153-4, 768, 835

Stake Amie/Amy wife of Richard 102-4 ; Anna 908; Richard 102-4, 758.127, 758.129, 908

Staleham, Stoleham Robert 99, 189, 234, 658, 722, 758.123, 758.127, 758.129, 758.139, 758.147-8; W 758.159, 758.188, 769, 770; William 835

Stamford Samuel de, see Samuel

Standeford Robert de 606-7; see Stanford

Staneburne Philip de 316

Staneland Roger 32

Stanewi, Stanwin(e) 167, 655; Andrew son of 482, 489, 655

Stanf[ord], Staumford, Staunford (de) 166 ; Absalon de 496; Achard son of Luwe de 545; Adam de 341, 496, 543; Adam son of Achard 545; Agnes de 491, 657; Alexander de 255, 446, 450, 668; Alexander son of 166; Alexander son of David de 560, 579.1; Alexander son of Richard 255; Alice daughter of Wakelin de 330; Alice wife of Alexander son of David de 579.1; Alice widow of Robert de 764; Alice Gilbert son of 547; Alpeisa sister of Simon son of Geoffrey de 346; Andrew de 31, alias Tikencote 911.2; Angelinus de 647; Cecilia daughter of Matilda de 381;

David de 227, 400, 560, 579.1; Dodi de 224; Fulco de 616, 655, 913.20 (*see* Fulcon); Geoffrey de 346, 847; Gilbert son of Baldwin de 504; Gilbert son of Ywen de 547; Gunilda widow of Ketel de 623; Harbin de 654; Henry de 500, 534, 654; Henry son of Alexander 668; Hereward/Herward de 455, 461; Hugh de 332; Hugh son of Reiner de 586; Hugh son of Wimund de 544; John son of Geoffrey 847; John son of Peter de 18; Staunford John de son of Sampson le chivaler 913.19a, b; Jordan de 545; Juliana sister of Reginald de 495; Ketel de 623; Leviva wife of Hugh 544; ; Luwe de 545; Matilda de 381; Matilda wife of Alexander de 450; Matilda wife of Henry de 654; Matilda/Maude wife of John 18; Matilda wife of Robert de 645; Miles de 892; Nicholas de 53, 205; Nicholas son of Absolon 496; Peter de 18, 337; Peter son of Reginald de 495; Peter son of Richard 498, 558; Ralph son of Fulco de 616, 655; Reginald de 495, 515; Reyner de 522, 586; Richard de 198, 222, 368, 438, 498, 517, 558; Richard son of Selowe/Seluf de 255, 447; Robert de 606-7, 732, 764; Robert son of Agnes 491; Roger son of Harbin de 654; Samuel de 910.5; Selowe de 255; Sigge of 911.9, 10; Simon son of Geoffrey de 346; Stephen son of Reginald de 9; Symon de 895; Thericus de 579.2; Thomas de 370, 376 ; Wakelin de 330; Walter de 758.4-11; William de 222; William son of David de 400; William son of Harbin de 654; William son of Henry de 534; William son of Yoselin de 645; Wimund de 544; Yoselin de 645; Ywen de 547

Stanhowe, Stanhough Thomas de 259, 282, 376

Stanlowe William 126

Stanwick Andrew son of 319

Stanwine, *see* Stanewi

Stapelford Robert de 758.40; Thomas son of Robert 758.40; William de 349

Staunford, *see* Stanford

Staunton Richard 758.139

Stavelere, *see* Scaveler

Staynbury Margaret prioress 570

Steanby, *see* Stainby

Stede Anabel wife of John 703, 705, 716; John 162, 700, 702-3, 705, 712, 716, 720, 725, 736, 738, 742, 747, 774

Stelyngton Robert 674

Stenby, *see* Stainby

Stenketel Robert son of 683-4

Stephen the clerk 404; parson St Peter 217-8, 579.1; prior of Peterborough 259; son of Reginald 261

Ster Alice wife of Hugh 87; Hugh 87

Stiandebi, *see* Stainby

Stikeling, Stykeling Agnes daughter of John 180; John 180, 547, 758.13

Stile Letitia atte 174

Stob... William de 758.10

Stockton, Stocton John 758.161; Robert de 453

Stodard Andrew 734

Stok(es) Stok, Stokys, Stouk(es) Amice de 485; Christina wife of Ralph de 10; Felicia de 654; John de 713; Ralph de 10, 145, 181, 280, 372, 399, 428, 452, 477; Robert de 594; Thomas clerk 670, 712, 720, 725, 742; Walter 718, 728; William de 155, 198, 222, 261, 309, 340, 368, 394, 427, 438

Stokyll Robert 144

Stoleham, *see* Staleham

Stontandgay Robert 387

Storeton Elizabeth wife of William 701, 709, 715, 727, 734, 755; John 758.191; William 661, 688, 701, 709, 711, 715, 734, 752, 758.195, 758.202

Storm Thomas 758.107, 758.158

Stourborn Margaret prioress 571

Stoyle Agnes wife of William 378; William 378

Strakar Robert 298

Strandeby Reynour de 911.22 (*see* Stainby)

Strauley Robert de 7

Stretton William de 361

Strykeswold Robert 706, 708, 711, 715, 752, 837

Stubley John 833

Stude Walter 345

Stuklee John parson of St John the Baptist 769, 770

Sturri Robert 524; Rose 524; Rose daughter of Gilbert 365

Stute Hugh 523, 911.8, 9, 10; William son of Hugh 523

Styandeby, *see* Stainby

Stykeling, *see* Stikeling

Stynour (Styvour) Geoffrey le 713

Styward Reginald 768

Subbyri William 364

Sudbir(i), Sudbury, Sutbyris John de 404, 452; John brother of William 501; William de 149.3, 458, 495, 501

Suffolk Alice wife of William earl of 126; Charles duke of 690, 691; earl of 710; William earl of 126; *see* Pole

Suleny Henry de 241

Sumercotes, *see* Somercote

Surrey earls of, *see* Warenne

Suthluffenham Agnes de 354

Suthorp Geoffrey de 621; Robert son of Geoffrey de 621 ; William de 33

Suttoc Walter 226

Sutton Beatrice wife of William de 119; Joan wife of William de 52; John 758.192; Margaret 758.171; Simon de 119; Thomas de 119, 894; William de 52, 119, 688, 750, 771

Swafeld Andrew de 583; Hugh 92; Margaret wife of Hugh 92

Swafend Hugh de 453

Swalewecliva Richard of 263

Swatbon Anne wife of Robert 582; Robert 582

Swayn Juliana wife of William 4.2; William 4.2

Swynestede John son of Geoffrey de 40; Geoffrey de 40

Sybbeston William 758.130, 758.132

Sybecey, *see* Sibeci

Sybely, *see* Sibily

Sybeston William 322, 561

Sybil prioress of St Michael 319, 419

Sybton Henry de 294

Sylton, *see* Silton

Symon, *see* Simon

Syngalday William 677

Sysyll, *see* Cecil

Taillour, Taliour, Talur, Taylyor Adam le 385; Aldus wife of Gervase le 528, 574; Alexander (le) 31, 283, 286, 316, 399; Andrew son of Stanwi 210, 433; Gervase le 528, 574; Gilbert the 372, 428, 911.21; Henry le 911.11; John (le) 108, 156, 161, 165, 454, 456, 462, 670, 673-4, 796; John *alias* Milton 781; John son of Thomas 146; Katherine daughter of Richard 159, 402; Laurence 366, 711, 715; Margaret daughter of Richard 159, 402; Peter le 455, 543, 547, 654; Ralph 758.139-40, 758.147, 758.151; Richard 159, 229, 283, 402, 569, 670; Robert le 228, 286, 556, 863; Robert son of Peter 451, 499, 500 543, 654; Stanwi 210, 433; Thomas 146; William le 910.7; *see* Acard, Alexander, Cissor, Gervase, Gilbert, John, Northfolk, Peter, Robert , *see* Talliator

Tal[...]t Hugh de 583

Taleboth John 168

Tales Robert 894

Talingtone Peter de 171, 527, 529; Simon de 171

Talliator William 910 .4; *see* Taillur

tallowman, *see* Peter

Talmur Peter 627

Talun Hugh 220

Talyngton, *see* Talington

Tame John son of Walter de 78; Walter de 78

Tannar Henry 231

Tanner, Tanour, Thanore Laurence the 226, 361; Thomas 895; *see* Eudo, Geoffrey, Laurence, Michael, Reginald, Robert, Taverner, Wace

Tappeden William 911.13

Tastard, Tastard/ton, Testard Richard 200, 352, 427, 440

Tatte Hugh 292

Taverner Alexander 652; John 88, 758.82; Maud daughter of Sara 758.113; Sara 758.113; Sarra wife of

John 88

Taylboys John 126

Tayllur, Taylor, Taylyor, *see* Taillour

Tekencote, *see* Tikencote

Templer John 62, 74, 758.68, 758.78;
Matilda wife of John 62, 74; Thomas
clerk 649

Tenche Peter 613, 624

Tendale, *see* Tyndale

Terricus, Thericus 610; *see* Cologne,
Stanford, Tieis

Testard, *see* Tastard

Teutonicus, *see* Colonia

Thanore, *see* Tanner

Thikencot, *see* Tickencote

Thirnyng William 401

Thistillton John 156, 670; John son of
John 156; John junior husbandman
161; Thomas de 473, 487; Walter
de 480, 482; *see* Twisylton

Thomas 758.63; the clerk 166, 224,
242, 262, 352, 374-5, 448, 450, 459,
480, 523, 583, 913.15-7; the priest
167; priest of Westone 249; vicar of
St Andrew 330; called Poth 517; the
barber 154; the franklin 524; the
freeman of Wothorp 384; son of
John 363; son of Robert 241; son of
Walter 365; Amabil mother of
Nicholas son of 448; John 894;
Nicholas son of 448; W 758.97; *see*
Freeman

Thornhawe Geoffrey de burgess 913.3,
4, 5; Matilda wife of 913.3; Issabella
wife of 913.4, 5; Matilda daughter of
Issabella wife of Simon son of
Robert de Bix(er) 913.4, 5

Thomasson John 420

Thorleby, *see* Thurlby

Thornef John 592; Katherine wife of
Richard 107; Richard 107, 724

Thorney David abbot of 911.23

Thornhawe Geoffrey de 392, 911.1;
Henry de 304, 911.1; John 911.1;
Sybil wife of Henry de 304

Thorp John 804; Walter de 396;
William de 471; William de, son of
Walter de 396

Thorpel, *see* Torpel

Threkingham John de 698

Thron, Throu Richard 398, 557

Thurlby, Thorleby, Thurleby, Turlebi
Geoffrey de clerk 178, 217-8, 315,
353, 418; Geoffrey serjeant 353;
Hugh de 42-3, 50-1, 54, 56, 526, 553,
554.1-2, 555, 598, 707, 740, 758.45,
818; Margaret de 822; Margaret wife
of Hugh de 526, 758.45, 818; Ranulf
de 276; William de 184, 369, 746

Thurlstan son of Robert 493; William
son of 506, 548

Thurstan, Thurston the leatherworker
645; son of Robert 355; Richard de
147; Robert 581; William son of 176;
see Trurton, Turstan

Thwayt Christiana/Christine wife of
Roger 58; John de 58; Roger son of
John de 58

Thystilthon, *see* Thistleton

Tichemers, *see* Titchmarsh

Tickencote, Tekencote, Thicincothe,
Tichincote, Tikencot, Tykencote
Alexander de 4.3, 23, 278, 453; Alice
widow of Hugh de 551; Andrew son
of Henry de 410, 911.1-3; Beatrice de
389, 404, 452, 911.2-3; Henry de,
149.6, 205, 210, 221, 224, 286, 292,
345, 379, 398-9, 414, 459, 558, 584,
611-2, 616, 635, 640, 657, 805, 911.1-
3, 18; Henry brother of Walter de
375, 383, 407, 433, 450, 476, 910.2-3;
Henry son of Walter 522; Hugh de
4.15, 175, 223, 267, 286, 334, 368,
396, 446, 490, 504, 510, 514, 551,
560; Hugh de senior 237, 807; Hugh
son of Henry de 149.6, 201, 292,
399, 558; Hugh son of Walter de
4.12, 182, 186, 292, 389, 404, 428,
452; John de 650; Juliana wife of
William 805; Walter de 4.12, 182,
186, 204-6, 208, 210-1, 216, 221,
224, 245, 251, 286, 289, 292, 327,
337, 339, 345, 367, 375, 383, 407,
414, 422, 424, 428, 433, 447, 450,
455, 459, 461, 476, 479, 484, 486,
488, 490, 494, 499, 502, 511, 516,
522, 544, 579.1, 584, 602, 605, 611-4,
616, 620, 622-3, 625, 627, 629, 630,
633, 634-7, 645, 910.2-3, 911.12, 17-
19; Walter son of Henry 216;

Walter son of Walter de 205, 490; William de 4.3, 201, 267, 288, 365, 374, 380, 389, 399, 404, 452, 492, 548, 639, 642, 849; William son of Henry 805

Tiddeswell , Tyddiswell Emma wife of Henry de 55; Henry de 1.2-3, 4.5, 52, 55, 59, 65, 188, 252, 274, 324, 369, 465, 468, 472, 554.1, 692, 707, 714-5, 729, 740, 746, 765.2, 780; Richard de 758.40

Tieis, Tyeis Terri le 521, 635 ; *see* Terricus

Tilton, Tylton Walter de 237, 361, 434, 911.13

Tinctor, Tinturer Robert 221, 601, 654; *see* Dyer

Tinwel, Tynwel .... 758.166; Emma widow of Walter de 170; Richard de 177, 196, 215, 223, 237, 316, 318, 377, 434, 442, 467, 481; Walter de 170, 230, 758.20-1, 758.26; Walter son of Walter 758.26; *see* Tunnewell

Titchmarsh, Tichemers Beatrice de 4.21; Bricthva wife of Hugh de 584; Hugh de 584, 654; Leticia wife of Robert de 221, 602; Ralph de 660; Robert de 221, 601-2, 654; Robert brother of Hugh de 584

Toche (?) Robert 653

Toft Amfalisia wife of Henry de 392; Henry de 392; Robert 766.1; *see* Tost

Tokes Walter son of Robert 377

Toky Henry 670

Tolethorp Gilbert de 207, 242, 608, 615; Henry de 603, 608; Henry son of Gilbert de 615; Ivette daughter of Robert de 486; Robert de 486; Thomas de 631

Tonley, *see* Tounley

Toon John 771

Tornah(am) Geoffrey de 345, 414

Torp John de 220; Peter brother of John de 220; Walter de 545, 586, 655; *see* Thorp, Torpel

Torpel, Thorpel Hugh 495; Hugh son of William de 451; Robert de 913.15; Alienora wife of 913.15; Roger de 250, 443, 563, 577; William de 221, 451, 455, 523

Tossewold Agnes wife of John 571; John 571

Tost Robert 661 ; *see* Toft

Toucestr Nicholas de 184

Touke Michael 518

Tounley, Tonley, Townley Harry 371; Henry 161, 165, 298

Tovy John 703

Towyn Robert 765.5

Toyton Robert 549

Tredegold Agnes 199

Tredflour Hugh 74, 146

Trenchepayn John 758.87, 758.89, 758.157

Tresham William 126

Trewe William 723; *see* Trou

Trigg, *see* Trygge

Trihampton John de 273

Trille Agnes daughter of Henry 440; Henry 440

Trive Robert 455

Trou(w)e Reginald 225; Richard 176, 231, 363, 448, 492

Trurton, Thurston Robert 580-1; *see* Thurstan

Trussell John 834, 862

Trye John 691

Trygge, Trigg Nicholas 767.3-5; Thomas 767.3

Tundur W 758.201

Tunnewell Walter de 427; *see* Tinwell

Turbert, Turburt chaplain of All Saints 310, 351, 503; priest of All Saints beyond the bridge 418; Peter ward of 418

Turgisi 654

Turlebi, *see* Thurlby

Turstan 655; Wimund son of Turstan 655; *see* Thurstan

Twisylton John de 279; *see* Thistleton

Tyard Agnes daughter of John 135; Alexander 703, 705, 733, 750, 839; Joan wife of John 135; John 135; William 724;

Tychemerssh, *see* Titchmarsh

Tydde Thomas 907

Tyddeswell *see* Tiddeswell

Tyeis, see Tieis

Tykencote, *see* Tickencote

433

Tyler John 226, 758.77, 758.105;
  Richard *alias* Barker 758.175
Tylton, *see* Tilton
Tyndale, Tendale John 272, 862
Tynewell, *see* Tinwell
Tynton Robert de, rector of Uffington
  308
Tyrwhyt Robert 401

Uffington, Offinton, Huffinct' 243;
  Henry de 585; Hugh de 25, 208, 213,
  245, 251, 327, 383, 413, 422, 424,
  479, 482, 516, 655; Isabella wife of
  Henry 585; Joan wife of Roger de
  113b, 115; John de 86, 324, 369,
  765.3; Juliana wife of Roger de 30;
  Matilda wife of Hugh de 213, 351,
  422, 479, 655; Roger de 29, 30,
  113b, 242, 686, 758.4, 758.12, 910.5;
  Roger son of Simon de 115, 753;
  Sarra daughter of Roger de 23, 29;
  Simon de 115, 189, 753, 835; Simon
  son of Roger de 30; William 910.5;
  William son of Roger de 242, 686
Ufford, Hufford, Wfford Adam de
  178, 206, 208, 212, 225, 245, 251,
  255, 310, 315, 327, 330, 337-8, 351,
  353, 379, 400, 412, 418-9, 422-4,
  479, 482-3, 488, 511-2, 516, 544-5,
  657; Alan de 586 ; *see* Upford
Ulfric Roger son of 609
Ulmer the farrier 510; *see also* Ferrun,
  Wolmer
Underbrok Alice 297
Unwin, Wnwine 654; Walter 437
Upford Adam de 628; Geoffrey de
  660; Gunnore wife of Adam 628;
  Hugh de 440; John 661; *see* Ufford
Urmeston Roger 694
Ursi Richard son of 682

Vaghhan Robert 765.9
Valle Gilbert de 659, 663
Vawsher Thomas 592
venellam ad, *see* Lane
Venour, Venur Amabil le prioress of St
  Michael 230; Mabel le prioress 285,
  305, 370, 376
Verney John 673-4
Vernon Elizabeth wife of Richard 127;

Richard 127
Vffington, *see* Uffington
Vfford, *see* Ufford
Vicary Nicholas 193
Vife William 645
Villain Geoffrey the 435; Richild sister
  of Geoffrey 435; Mathilda sister of
  Geoffrey 435
Vintner Clement 9 10.5
Vintner, Vineter Aldusa wife of
  Clement the 250; Clement the 207-8,
  221, 242, 245, 262, 459, 577, 910.5;
  Clement son of Michael 250;
  Geoffrey le 23, 911.17; Michael the
  250; William son of Geoffrey le 23;
  see Clement, Geoffrey
Virsop, see Wirsop
Viyil 263
Vowe John 758.165, 758.196
Vpex Thomas 163
Vylur Benedict le 10
Vyncent David 795
Vyne Andrew 567

W(o)decroft Emma widow of Roger
  de 202; Firmin de 178; Hugh son of
  Richard 178; Gilbert de 342, 377;
  Gilbert son of Reginald de 14; Isabel
  wife of Reginald de 14; Mary
  daughter of Ralph 178; Pain de 202;
  Ralph son of Firmin de 178;
  Reginald de 14; Richard de 178;
  Roger de 202
W(o)defoul Robert 342; William 4.6,
  292-3
W[o]lneth Matilda 316
Wac, *see* Wake
Wace the tanner 403, 418; Walter 658;
  see Wase
Wacrile Richard de 172; *see* Wakerley
Wade Henry 568
Wadingtoun Thomas de 758.82
Wake, Wac Agnes wife of William 898;
  Baudewin 663; Guy 911.17, 18, 19,
  20, 21; Mabil wife of 911.19; William
  898
Wakefeld Emma wife of William de 79;
  William de 79
Wakelin prior of Land 263
Wakerley, Wakyrl' Agnes wife of

Bernard de 248; Alice de 247, 282;
Alice wife of Henry de 177, 186;
Bernard son of John de 248; Henry
de 186, 197, 227, 255, 315, 337-8,
400, 405, 422, 496, 515, 520, 545-6;
Hugh son of Henry 496; Joan wife
of John de 33, 284; John de 33, 93,
146, 248, 284, 317, 323, 438, 565,
765.5; John son of Bernard de 248;
Juliana wife of John de 93; Margery
widow of Richard de 384; Matilda de
657; Peter de 157.2, 270, 425, 432,
627; Ralph de 24, 282, 411; Richard
de 329, 384, 686 ; Robert de 249;
Thomas de 397; William de 270, 405;
William son of Peter 425
Walbeeff, Walbyeff Anne wife of
Robert 140; James 140; John 911.11;
Richard 900; Robert 140, 143, 592; *see*
Walleff
Walcot(e) Agnes wife of John de 56;
John de 56, John 386; Nicholas de
487; Richard de 257-8
Waldebef, *see* Walbeef
Walentru John 559
Waleran priest 437; the baker 455;
Geoffrey son of 444
Walg' Geoffrey 846
Walington Hugh de 324; Richard 719,
758.152, 835; Thomas de 534, 722
Walkelin the butcher 583
Walker Alice le 527; Thomas 895
Walle William 171
Walleff Robert 767.6; *see* Walbeeff
Walles, Wallis, Waulles William in the
359, 378, 388, 456, 462, 758.48; *see*
Walle, William
Walmuford Mabel de 629
Walsh Geoffrey 758.158
Walsyngham Thomas 662, 667
Walter 657, 758.1; the chaplain 654,
683-4, 686; the clerk 497; the priest
221, 263, 619; rector of Nettleham
153; the doctor 489, 517; the
physician 758.4-12, 758.23, 758.25;
the plumber 809; son of Ketil 346;
son of Norman 198, 349, 377, 848
Waltham Richard de 758.59
Walton John 313
Walyngton, *see* Walington

Ward(e) Henry 758.188; John 236, 652,
688, 758.152; Nicholas 758.170;
Thomas 717, 724, 726, 730, 741,
745
Wardale Agnes wife of William 658;
William 658
Wardon Alvas de 892
Waren, Warin, Waryn clerk 497; 'longi'
396; Emma 765.5; James 131; John
696
Warenne earl 758.10, 758.43, 811-2;
John de earl of Surrey 147, 177, 196,
200, 207, 215, 311, 374, 427, 434,
440-1, 472, 499, 526, 911.11, 14, 16;
Matilda countess of 609; William earl
of 913.6
Warner John 706, 708, 711, 715, 724,
752, 758.172, 758.174; William vicar
of Lilford 674
Warr(e), Ware lord la 678, 835;
Elizabeth wife of Roger la 1.1; Joan
de la 150; Joan wife of John la 1.1;
John la 1.1; John son of John la 1.1;
Margaret wife of John la 1.1; Roger la
1.1; Thomas de la 835
Waryn, *see* Waren
Wasclan, *see* Wastlen
Wase Walter 832; *see* Wace
Wasteney William le 241
Wastlen Elizabeth 767.5; Richard 298,
735
Wat' (?er/ir) John 890
watchman, *see* Ivo
Waters, Watir, Waturs John 872, 875,
884-6; William 885
Watervill, Wautervile Acel/Atel de
629, 632; William son of Acel/Atel
de 629, 632; William de, abbot of
Peterborough 238
Watgott Henry 674
Watson Joan widow 895; John 895;
Thomas 133, 906
Watts William 767.6, 907
Waulles, *see* Walles
Wayte, Whayte Alice wife of Robert le
80-1; Robert le 80-1, 819; William le
176, 231
Wdecroft, *see* Wodecroft
Wdeful, *see* Wodefoul
weaver, *see* Frebarne

Webster John 674

Weldon, Welledon Conrad de 729;
Elizabeth prioress 195, 291, 303, 540,
542; Hugh de 176, 180, 266-7, 348,
366, 373, 492, 513, 560, 911.22; John
(de) 89b, 98, 125, 127, 322, 531-2,
561, 732, 864; Robert de 145, 477; W
758.182

Wele John 665

Well Thomas at the 411

Welleby Adam son of Robert de 40;
Margaret wife of William de 40;
Robert de 40; William de 40; William
son of William de 40

Welles, Wylles John 673; Thomas 833,
891, 902-5; Thomas *alias* Gallow
883; *see* Wilys

Wellowe Alice wife of John 106; John
106

Welton Peter de 911.20; Robert de 676,
see Weldon, Weston

Weng, *see* Wyng

Wermington, Wermyngton John de
256, 309, 311, 380, 393, 417, 427,
550, 713; Peter de 758.45

Wermouth Richard 738, 767.4

Werymle John de 29

Wessington John 677-8

West Richard 658, 834

Westby Henry son of Roger 847; Roger
de 847

Weston John de 75; Margaret wife of
John de 75; Nicholas de 153, 228,
416, 524; Peter de 591; Peter de
knight 911.17; Ralph de 207, 910.4;
Richard de 204, 245, 446-7, 461, 499,
500, 506, 559, 668; William de 157.1,
357, 631, 910.4; William son of Ralph
de 207 (*see* Welton)

Westrense Adam 304

Wfford, *see* Ufford

Whayte, *see* Wayte, Whyte

Whiston Thomas clerk 697

White, *see* Whyte

Whitewell John 869

Whithed, Whiteheved Henry 758.163;
Juliana 767.1, 840

Whithorn bishop of 588

Whitley John 875, 884

Whitton, Whytton John 895

Whyte, Whayte, White, Wyte Hugh (le)
216, 453, 457; Ralph le 4.4

Whytesyde John 661, 708, 719, 758.161

Wido son of Wimund 612; son of
Wydo 630

Wiggele, Wygele Reg[inald] de 342;
Roger de 203; Stephen de 222, 257,
326; Stephen son of Roger de 203;
see Wyggesle

Wike Robert de 279; *see* Wykes

Wikilsey Simon de 535

Wilcoks Richard 758.168, 758.170

Wilek Peter de 638; Christiana
daughter of Peter de 638

Wilkes William 352

William 179, 185, 657, 663, 758.1;
chaplain of St. Peter's church 221,
584; chaplain of Weston 591; the
clerk 208, 217-8, 260, 276, 364, 460,
483-4, 551, 586, 663; rector of All
Saints 668; rector of St Mary
Bynnewerk 758.119; vicar of All
Saints 508; dean of Helpeston 153;
monk 263, 597; dean of
Peterborough 249; prior 353; prior
of St Fromond 577; abbot of
Peterborough 784; marquis of
Winchester 691; the mercer 154, 286,
548, 557-8, 560, 753; the Norman
182, 223, 258, 316, 377, 385, 408,
429, 434, 474, 489, 520, 546, 556; the
palmer 354, 439, 556, 805; the
skinner 267; the smith 136, 212, 315,
337, 349, 356, 371, 422, 649, 869; of
Hangynghoughton 889; son of
Ang'lo 437; son of Acard 447, 583,
683-5; son of Adam 507; son of
David 145, 151, 197, 211-2, 219, 227,
255, 327, 330, 336-7, 341, 346, 367,
375, 389, 404-5, 419, 422, 447, 459,
478, 480, 496, 502, 510, 515-6, 520,
545-6, 559, 586; son of Dodus 224;
son of Geoffrey 380, 457, 501; son of
Godric 450, 583, 846; son of Herbert
220; son of Hugh the smith 349; son
of Iolan 432, 585; son of John 157.1-
2; son of Odo 617; son of Reiner
151; son of Roger 213, 413, 423, 483,
512, 544, 686; son of Sarah 423,
512; son of Thurstan 506, 548; son

of William son of Acard 686; son of
William son of David 341, 408; son
of William the smith 349; son of
Wymund 157; Outhilda wife of 224;
Bartholomew son of 400; Elias son
of 683-5; Gilbert son of 583; Peter
son of 310
William, Williams, Willyams, Willyames
Agnes, wife of Thomas 161, 165;
Willyams dame 298; David 161, 165;
George 161, 165; Henry 161, 165;
Thomas 161, 163-5, 767.5, 786, 856,
898, 906; Thomas senior 138, 156,
796; Thomas 47, 235, 298, 395, 591;
William 138, 161, 165, 592, 796
Willmeford Mabel de 632
Willobye Henry 898
Willowyndere John 909
Willy Joan wife of John 125; John 125,
533
Wilton Eustace de 263
Wilys Richard 309; see Welles
Wimar 657
Wime Geoffrey de 205, 216
Wimund, Wymund 157.1, 167, 179,
655; clerk 578; Clemencia wife of
Hugh son of 423, 512, 655; Hugh
son of 423, 512, 655; Levina wife of
Hugh son of Wimund 512; William
son of Wymund 157.1
Wimundeham, see Wymondham
Winat 657
Winchester, William marquis of 691
Winer archdeacon of Northampton 263
Wion Ralph de 523
Wirfo Alan 154
Wirsop, Virsop Matthew de 197
Wirthorp, [Wir]thorp, Wittorp,
Wo(r)thorpe, Wretorp, Wrythorp,
Wyrthorp Adam de 329, 861; Alan
de 80-1, 159, 172, 253, 313, 385, 402;
Albreda wife of Richard de 65; Alice
wife of Nicholas de 397, 492; Alice
wife of Simon de 64, 474, 593;
Emma de 322, 524, 561, 865;
Geoffrey son of William de 187, 249;
Henry de 520; Inga wife of William
de 212; John de 153, 657; John son
of Peter de 206; Katherine daughter
of Alan 861; Matthew de 149.8, 405,

519-20; Michael de 149.5; Nicholas
de 397, 492; Peter de 206; Reginald
de 187, 857; Richard de 1.2, 65, 221,
243, 297, 729, 744; Richard son of
Emma de 244; Robert son of
Reginald de 857; Simon de 64, 474,
593; Thomas de 200; Thomas son of
John de 153; William de 212, 249,
297; William son of Reginald de 187;
see Birthorpe, Wyrthir'
Wiseman, see Wyseman
Wissynden, Wyssenden John de 342;
Thomas de 326, 342; Walter de 753
Witham, see Wytham
Wither Hugh 438
Wittering, Wyteryng John de 758.83;
Richard de 398; Walter de 185, 565;
William de 364
Wiyer William 312
Wlmer, see Wolmer
Wlneth, see Wolneth
Wnwyne, see Unwin
Wod(e) Margaret wife of William 797;
William 743, 797
Wodehous John 835
Wodeslade, Wodeschlade Geoffrey de
35, 67, 324, 369, 475, 525, 765.3;
Joan sister of Geoffrey de 35;
Margery wife of Geoffrey de 67
Wollewynder John le 390, 469
Wolm[er], Wlmer Richard son of 490;
Roger brother of 398; see Ulmer
Woodcroft, see Wodecroft
Worminton, see Wermington
Worthen Martin 750
Wortyn(g) John 314, 464, 568-9, 717,
724, 726, 730, 741
Woston Robert de 842
Wothorpe, Writhorp, see Wirthorp
Wryght, Wright John 445; Richard 366,
672; Robert 856
Wrythe Geoffrey le 253; William son
of Geoffrey le 253
Wulston Guy 673-4
Wurdeler John 743
Wyberton Alice wife of John de 85;
John de 85
Wych Hugh 295; Sarah wife of Hugh
295; W 758.102
Wycher Hugh 364

INDEX OF PLACE NAMES

The pre-1974 counties have been used to locate places. Uncertain locations are in italics.

Aldawe, Aldehaue ditch beside 149.5, 149.7, 482

Aleseler le inn 272

All Saints 351, 450, 503; All Saints in the town [sic] 758.196; All Saints in the Market 224, 263, 314, 325, 383, 407, 418, 420, 433, 476, 486, 508, 575, 577, 584, 597, 612, 657, 668, 758.81, 758.98, 758.132, 758.140, 758.142, 758.147, 758.167, 758.196; mass of St Mary in 4.9, 188, 278, 472, 648, 758.41, 758.58; parishioners 648; parsonage 168; tithes 308

All Saints beyond the bridge 156, 210, 221, 314, 325, 343, 418, 565, 657, 758.81, 758.98, 758.114, 758.132, 758.140, 758.147; All Saints, chaplain of (named) 503

Almshouse of Staunford 767.6; bedehouse in Stamford 669, 767.6

Angel (Aungel) of the hope (Mary) 670, 758.28, 758.181, 758.200

Angelondes (SB) 245

Antelope (Mary) 747, 777

Baker street (Mary) 1, 260, 465, 472-3, 487; Baxtergate 768

Barmigate 911.10, 913.5

Barngate 201; Baronngate 286

Beere inn de la 844

Behinde the bak, Behindebach, Behyndbak, Bihindebak, behyndeyebak street, Byhindebak (ASM) 149.3, 278, 434, 537, 758.43, 758.51, 758.58, 758.72, 758.74, 758.84, 758.103, 758.107, 758.126, 758.143, 758.159, 758.171, 758.192,

Belle La (Mary) 703, 705, 718, 728, 733, 748

Belmangoret arable 896

Bermergores arable 758.160

Bernardishil 231, 363

Blakemilde meadow 443

Blandford 599

Bornle [?Burle?] Sik 438; Bornle wood 438

Borough-gate (SB) 758.69

bowdyslane 775

Bradcroft, Bradecroft, Breadcroft 128-9, 557, 758.20, 758.21-22, 758.26, 758.36, 758.38; mill dam of 758.20;

castle demesne in 439; crofts 427, 441, 561, 758.26, 758.22, 758.142; cross 223, 439, 442; meadow in 439-41, 639; pond 441

Brakenell, Brakenhil, Brakenhyl 468, 520, 592

Braudeswro (Wo) 350

Brictrimeholm meadow 242

bridge 4.16, 149.8, 162, 205, 243, 256, 426, 467, 516, 546, 556, 777, 853; chapel on 758.156; see St Thomas hospital; see Mallory, Smale, Uffington

Bridge Strete, Briggate, Brigstrete, Brigstrette 291, 373, 678, 911.11

Broadheng, Brodeeng meadow 399, 526, 639, 642, 673-4, 758.104, 758.183

Bulepit, Bulpite (SB) 535, 655.12

Bulgate (Wo) 449

Burgons house 792

Butcher Street (ASM, JB, Mary, MG) 149.1, 149.6, 250, 330, 361, 654.8-9, 654.13, 758.152

Bynwerk, Binnewerc, Bynnewerk St Mary 4.21, 7, 8, 155, 176, 209, 228, 231, 294, 306, 330, 344, 361, 363, 369, 397, 400, 410, 448, 470, 475, 524, 554-5, 598, 654.4, 675-6, 679, 683-5, 704, 717, 723, 745, 758.42, 758.95, 758.100, 758.115, 758.118-9, 758.162, 758.193, 895

Castle 183, 204, 262, 471, 480, 484, 494, 499, 622, 648, 654.11, 654.17, 657, 758.184, 831; Dyke, ditch of 133, 341, 496, 500, 543, 635, 651, 758.19, 758.30, 758.58; demesne, lands 379, 421, 434, 439, 519, 548, 557, 616, 630; Castle lane 822; meadow 399, 639, 642; tithes 575

chapel of St Mary Sempringham manor in Stamford 114, 693; of St Thomas at the bridge, see hospital

chapter land in Wothorpe 907

Chardiacre, Charedic (Kar'dik) 377, 423, 512

Chekeracre (SB) 307

Chekerstede 911.11

Cheyne lane, Chynelane 677, 758.169

Chinemeresenge 655.13; see

Kilmershenge

churchyards, *see* cemetery

Clarimont (MG) 628

Claymond, Cleymond, Cleymont (ASM, And, MG) 4.15, 485, 668-9, 671, 758.45, 817-8, 820, 823-4, 828, 831, 911.11, 12, 913.6 ; see Clarimont, Clementslane

Clementeslane (MG) 536

Clippessil, Clyppeshull, Clypshyll waye (ASM) 506, 844, 896, 911.22

Colgate, Colegat street, Collegate lane (MG) 286, 330, 491, 513, 758.5, 758.11-2, 758.18, 758.25, 758.87, 758.116, 758.125, 758.186, 911.11

Corewensty street, Cornewelsty, Corwansty lane, Corwensty, Covensty street (MG and Mary) 4.11-2, 392, 509, 677, 758.44, 758.82, 758.157

corn market 316

Cornstall 334, 428, 434, 514, 559, 710, 758.138, 758.158, 758.161, 758.181, 758.196, 758.200; church 289, 325; parish 4.15, 149.7, 184, 283, 354, 758.29; gate 184, 283, 354; street 652, 658, 701, 706, 708-9, 711, 721, 727, 734

Corpus Christi altar of in church of St Mary at the bridge 150; Corpus Christi and BVM, *see* gild

Cressaunt inn (Mary) 736

croft common (Wo) 322; see St Martins croft; St Michael's croft; nuns croft, Bradcroft croft, West Croft

cross, *see* Bradcroft; Burley; Dames; High; Maydenes; Pertes; Ryhall; Spitulcrosse; Stumpe; Wothorpe; wooden in fields 758.66

Damesarescros 282

Deepdale, Depedale 172, 655.22, 758.160

Derebowyth 371

ditch, dyke, fosse 149.5, 152, 166, 224, 546, 848 ; castle 133, 341, 496, 500, 543, 635, 651, 758.19, 758.30, 758.58; great ditch 245, 479, 482; green 271, 393, 420, 560, 750, 758.73; high dyke 532; old 444; town ditch 311, 469,

617;

douvacre (Wo) 384

E(a)stgate 173, 470,701, 706, 708-9, 711, 722, 727, 734, 828, 910.1, 911.7,11; East gates 146

East-by-the-water, Est-by-the-water street (SB) 162, 377, 670, 758.83, 758.115, 758.132, 758.139, 758.147, 758.168

Empingham ditch 166, 224; road to Empyngham, Empyngate 420, 548, 750, 758.176, 814

End of the town 758.172

Erleslane (in Cornstall) 710

Estholm 758.104

Estmedewe 670

Etrowe mill of 846

Feldhofne 416; Feldovensty lane in MG 758.4, 758.9, 758.11, 758.16, 758.23, 758.31

fish market (MG) 236

Fisher[s] Street 292

Fisslepes 4.1

flax market (ASM) 651

fosse, see ditch

Friars: Carmelite 582, 675-6, 911.11; Franciscan 675-6; Greyfriars 690-1; Sack site of 147

Fullers Street 209 (Peter), 226 (Bin)

furlong, *see* Middle

Gannoc street, Gannok le 306 (Bin, Westgate) 758.71, 758.79, 758.95

gates 4.1, 4.19, 146, 272-3, 276, 291, 316, 326, 373, 442, 474, 554.1-2, 592, 653, 675-6; Cornstall gate 184, 283, 354; East gate 173, 269, 279, 347, 470, 514, 675-6, 758.24, 911.7; North gate 758.172, 759, 772; postern gate 342, 775; Scotgate gate 146, 447, 504, 614, 712, 738, 758.41, 758.49; West gate 147, 235, 365, 522, 680; *see* Westgate

George inn 791, 855

Gildhous toft (Wo) 159, 229, 402, 569

Gledegate 228 (Bin, Peter) 228, 233, 397

Goddeshous (Eastgate) 701, 706, 708-9, 711, 722, 727, 734

Gorebrod Halfaker 634; goryd acre 371

Graves le (land in Wo) 350, 449

house of 154, 913.19a; brother of 154; chapter 160, 241, 319, 331, 339, 502; chapterhouse 160, 172, 192, 233-4, 240, 244, 259, 261, 285, 290-1, 297, 303, 320-1, 331, 348, 357, 360, 366, 373, 376, 394, 420, 445, 473, 487, 531-2, 535, 539, 541-2, 567, 576-7, 596, 646, 653; church of 154; altar of Holy Trinity in church 336; altar of St Mary Magdalene in church 336; commons in 657; courtyard 327; guest house 442; infirmary 657; kitchen in 657; lay sisters house of 442; martyrology 331; pension 325, 332; pittance 145, 219, 226, 293, 338, 396, 437, 443, 478, 654.13; **prior of St Michael's nunnery** 238; Henry de Fiskerton 339, 502; Stephen Gocelyn 320; William de Hoyland 182; John 519; John de Ketene 153, 241; Roger de Ketene 319; Hugh de Leycestre 485; Henry de Overton 352; William de Oxenford 230, 244, 290, 296, 382; Peter 437, 683-5; Stephen of Peterborough 259; John Roland 481; William de St Albans 419; Thomas de Staunford 285, 370, 376; William 353; William de Stob.. 758.10; William de Stokys 155, 198, 222, 261, 309, 340, 368, 394, 427, 438; William de Weston 357; **prioress of nunnery of St Michael** 4.5, 172, 174, 191, 195, 199, 214, 238, 242, 244, 252, 254-5, 257, 265, 268-70, 273, 275, 280, 286, 295, 297, 300-1, 311, 314, 323, 332, 335, 344, 347, 350, 356, 364, 368, 371, 374, 380-1, 387, 396, 399, 408, 410, 417, 436-7, 440, 463-4, 468-9, 471-3, 487, 490, 494, 501, 507-8, 517-8, 527, 552, 555, 773, 850, 855, 898; Alice 579.1-2; Amice 153, 241, 292, 328, 352; Alice Andrew 395, 592, 571; Agnes de Brakenburgh 333, 585, 648; Alice Copuldyk 271, 322, 531-3, 535-6, 561, 567; Margaret Croyland 192, 541; Elizabeth 11, 215, 258, 334, 352; Margaret Godechepe 299, 360; Isabel 169; Agnes Leke 232, 239, 240, 272, 302, 321, 358, 420, 538-9,

646; Matilda (de) Lenn 155, 185, 198, 203, 222, 259, 261, 309, 320, 325, 340, 394, 425, 427, 438, 550-1, 565, 761; Mabel 290, 296, 357, 382, 425, 761; Isabel de Maltby 313; Margaret 566; Margery, Marjorie 365, 397; Matilda 758.10; Alice de Neville 339, 502; Petronilla 353; Margaret Reddinges 160, 233-4, 308, 401, 445, 534, 549, 596; Katherine Russell 331; Isabel Savage 653; Margaret atte See 415, 466; Margaret Steynbury 570; Amice de Stokes 485; Margaret Stourborn 571; Sybil 319, 419; Amabilia le Venur 230, 285, 305, 370, 376, 585, 600 (*see* Mabel); Elizabeth Weldon 195, 291, 303, 348, 366, 373, 540, 542; sacristy in 657; vestry in 657; union with Wothorpe convent 782; Nunnesyerde 321, 366; *see* Nonne Croft, Syster gate

Nuns Style 541
oldebolepyt [SB] 256
Ovensty, Hovensty (MG, JB) 758.2-3, 758.6, 758.8, 758.17, 768
Paradise, Paradys Lyttyl 773
Pecksall, Pekesall yard 758.158, 767.1-5
Pertes cross 758.103
Peterborough (Burg) road to 516, 758.147
Pilsgate road to 248
Pinfold, Pynnefold 843; (SB) 758.83
Pitacre (Bradcroft) 152; (SB) 402
Pittes 220
Plateni fee of 518
poor house near bridge 149.8
Portesgate 468
Puntdelarchsty, Punchelardsty lane (Peter) 758.13, 758.19
Quarell Close 855
Quichorsberne 508
Racon-rowe street 758.191
rectory: Holy Trinity 5; St Clement 712, 738; St Mary Bynnewerk 324, 369, 475, 554, 598, 717, 724, 726, 730, 741, 745, *see* St Peter; St Michael the Greater 236; St Peter 743, 750
road to St Michael's nunnery 225, 474, 479, 481

Roberdesdale 282

Rogeford, Rogford 297, 329, 518

Ruskhill (Wo) 244

Ryhall cross 353

Salegate 629, 632, 849; Saltergate (Wo) 297, 449, 573

Saracen's Head, Sarsynneshed inn (Mary) 838

Sawces acre (SB) 371

Scardic 516

Schepcoteslane (SB) 535, 541; Schepisgate Lane (SB) 256

Schord 655.12

Scobothes (ASM) 758.159

Scotgate, Scoffegate, Schoftegate, Scoftgate Gate, Scofthegathe, Skoftgate 4.18-20, 154, 160, 242, 463, 504, 614, 670, 731, 737, 739, 758.33, 758.35, 758.172, 759, 772; gates of 446-7, 712, 738, 758.41, 758.49

Sempringham, Sempryngham, Sempyngham, tenement of in Stamford, manor of in Stamford, chapel at, prior of 114, 239, 648, 693, 758.71, 758.79, 758.95, 822

Sevenwellis 327; Sevenewellesty [SB] 177, 215, 247

shortlands 371

Silver Street, Selverstrete 758.105, 758.186

Smale Brigges 670

Sme(h)thil 274, 447, 559, 634

Spitell (Wo) 360, 653; Spitulcrosse 371; Spiteldic (SB) 368; Spitelhendland, Spitelhevedlond (Wo) 229, 569

spring in Bradecroft 758.26; spring on Claymond 758.45

Spycers Lane (Peter) 776

St Andrew parish 911.8-10; 913.3, 4, 5; cemetery 913.1, 2, 4, 6

St Clement 4.18-9, 101, 123,154, 217-8, 308, 310, 331, 338, 355, 400, 418, 420, 430, 493, 504-5, 579.1, 636, 657, 712, 731, 736-9, 758.33, 758.35, 758.40, 758.58, 758.90, 758.105, 758.124, 758.160, 758.164, 758.172, 759, 772, 819, 841, 896; altar/chantry of St Nicholas in 101, 123, 420, 758.90, 758.105, 758.124, 758.160, 759, 772; rectory 712, 738;

see subjects: chantry

St Cuthbert's fee 375, 677-8

St George 306, 572, 719, 768, 788, 910.2, 913.19a, b

St Giles, *see* Hospital

St John the Baptist 149.5, 469, 494.5, 547, 572, 636, 750, 758.137, 769, 770, 788, 833, 910.4,7, 911.13, 913.13, 14a, b; St Johns bakehouse 770; St Johns oven 768, 910.4,7 (*see* oven); St Johns Well 775; St John Baptist and St Thomas, *see* Hospital

St Leonard 7-8, 177, 215, 234, 268-9, 274, 277, 353, 375, 459, 531, 617, 626, 655.5, 677-8, 679.1-2, 681, 683, 685-7, 758.10, 758.34, 758.158, 758.160, 774, 911.11; grange of prior of 758.158; land of prior of 758.160

St Leonardsford 774

St Martin 98, 242, 276, 317, 330, 338-9, 351, 353, 400, 408, 418-9, 437, 481, 488, 496, 503, 511, 523, 568, 579.1, 632, 654.6, 654.12, 788; cemetery 419, 539, 657; church 426, 657; churchwardens 161; churchyard 792; gild of 298; parishioners 592; pension from church of 426; rectory 793; vicarage 332, 445; *see* croft, Martinscroft

St Mary 523, 682; St Mary at the bridge 1, 249, 293, 392, 414, 683-5, 758.5, 758.114, 788, 913.15, 16, 17, 18; altar of corpus Christi 1.1, 150; gild of corpus Christi 162; gild of St Mary 3, 4.1-21, 149.1-8, 234, 758.113; mass of 149.3-5, 149.7-8, 758.58; proctor of mass 149.7-8

St Mary Bynnewerk 758.162; cemetery 7; church of 330, 338; churchwardens 361; rectory of 324, 369, 475, 554, 598, 717; *see* Binwerk

St Mary convent at Wothorpe 153,170, 228, 249, 253, 329, 365, 416, 504, 518, 524, 585; union with St Michael's nunnery 782

St Michael at Arches 135

St Michael Cornstall 289, 325, 758.29, 911.1-6, 12, 17; *see* Cornstall

St Michael the Greater 89b, 758.106, 910.5-6, 911.12, 913.1, 2, 6; cemetery

304, 498, 910.6; churchyard 729
St Michael's, *see* nunnery
St Michaels croft 295
St Nicholas, see St Clements
St Paul church 572, 575-6, 686, 758.82, 758.146, 758.158, 909, 913.7-12; altar of St Mary 288; lamp before the altar 288; parsonage of 897; rector 308, 477; tithes 308
St Peter 170, 183, 217-8, 221, 233, 548-9, 557, 560, 572, 576, 584, 590, 619, 635, 679, 686, 758.67, 758.105, 758.156, 762, 911.7,11; Firm (or Farm) of 758.102; land 152, 758.103; rectory 750; tithes 590
St Thomas Hospital, *see* Hospital
Star Lane, Sterlane 669, 692, 765.1-3, 765.5, 765.8-9, 828, 909
Staunford Style 252
Stonefeld 497
Stump Crosse (Wo) 907; stone commonly called Stumpe(d)ston, Stumpestan 210, 433, 647, 655.4, 655.7,
Suelisheved 655.18; *see* Sevenwellis
Sundersok, Sundersoken (Bradcroft) 152, 398, 421, 548, 557-8, 560, (Peter) 636, 640, 644, 758.27, 758.198, 813-4
Swal.... Stede (SB) 758.54
Swyneyard 896
Syster gate of the nunnery 360
Tabard, Taberd le (Mary) 126, 747
Tenteryard 255, 655.1, 657
Thwertdykes 758.73
Tolthorpsty 469
Tunge the 758.73
Tunkeacre (Bradcroft) 379
Uffington bridge 668, 687
Vaudey 477, 773
vicarage ASM 758.182; St Martin 332, 445
walls 527, 597; town walls 7, 8, 183-4, 269, 283, 609, 758.29, 758.44-5, 758.141, 758.161, 758.182, 775-6, 897
Warden yarde (Wo) 360, 653
Watergalle (Wo) 449; Watergate le (Peter) 233; Watergate Lane (George) 767.6
Webestergate street 268, 349, 445, 525, 542-3, 758.10, 758.201,

Welland river, water, Weland, Wylland 156, 159, 162, 177, 185, 208, 215, 222, 229, 241, 251, 270, 298, 326, 343, 364, 370, 377, 399, 402, 425, 471, 526, 539, 549, 571, 590, 639, 642, 758.1, 758.26, 758.42, 758.83, 758.114-5, 758.132, 758.139, 758.147, 758.188, 774-5, 844, 855
wells 775; *see* Sevenwellis, St Johns, Westwelles
Wes(t)crofte (Wo) 172, 313, 449, 567
Westewelles (Bin) 410;
Westwellelane (Bin) 344
Westgate 365, 628, 758.71, 895, 911.11
Westrawe (Bridge Street) 678
Wintes 297
Wolle-rowe, Wolrowe (ASM) 188, 256, 648, 758.48, 758.127, 758.152, 758.166, 758.199
wooden cross 758.66
end of Stamford entries

Stapleford Leics 580-1
Stixwould Lincs 690
Stoneleigh, Stoneley Warws 691
Stowe by Deeping Lincs 107, 140, 143, 563
Stradbroke Suffolk 662
Stretton Rutland 670; Stretton on the Fosse Warws 758.52, 758.54
Sturton Lincs 691
Sutterton, Soterton, Sutirton Lincs 173, 758.54
Swannes 662
Swayfield Lincs 670, 687
Swineshead, Swynesheved Lincs 1.1, 469
Swinestead, Swynested, Swynsted Lincs 40, 129a, 141, 670, 673-4
Swinthorpe Lincs 691
Swynfen Staffs 580-1
Tallington Lincs 140, 142, 704, 717, 724, 726, 730, 745, 757, 758.51, 828
Tansor, Tansoner Northants 672
Temple Bruer Lincs 691
Thetford 913.8, 11
Thorn Gobaud Yorks 124
Thornaugh, Thornhawe Northants 115
Thorney Cambs 651-2, 758.58, 758.141, 758.158, 911

Thornholm Lincs 691

Thorpe Achurch, Achirche Northants 673, 674

Thre(c)kyngham Lincs 58

Tickincote Rutland 113b

Tinwell, Tynwell Rutland 230, 750, 758.166, 758.198, 783, 794, 814, 826, 837, 898; gallows 758.176; gate 758.103; heath 758.176; mere 758.156

Titchmarsh, Tychemersh Northants 734

Tol(e)thorpe Rutland 580-1, 758.28

Torpel in Barnack Northants 801

Twyford 670

Uffington, Wffyngton Lincs 29, 30, 86, 177, 308, 549, 590, 686, 689, 832; bridge 668, 687; road to 215

Ufford Northants 144, 294, 443, 497

Upton Northants 118; chapel of 660

Upwell Norfolk 580-1

Vaudey abbey Lincs 477, 773

W[oo]decroft Northants 178, 202

Wakerley, Wakerle Northants 119, 873-4

Walceteholm, Walkoteholm 610, 621

Walcot 864; Walcote Lincs 124, 687; Walcote by Barnack Northants 125, 670, 795

Warboys, Wardeboys Hunts 62

Warmington, Wermyngton Northants 670, 672-4

Waterfulford Yorks 580-1

Watlington Hill Oxon 673

Welby, Welleby Lincs 40, 48

Weldon, Welledon Northants 304, 498, 775

Wenton by Cottesmore Rutland 360, 653, 656

Westminster 9-12, 16-25, 30-49, 52-58, 65-109, 114-9, 121-5, 138, 150, 763

Weston 249, 591, 862

Wffington, see Uffington

Whaplode, Quappelade Lincs 58, 522

Whithorn bishop of 588

Whitwell, Wytewell Rutland 109, 110, 157.2, 432, 758.165

Wigsthorpe, Wiggesthorp, Wyxsthorpp in Lilford Northants 673-4

Wilbarstoke, Wilberdstoke Wilbarstuk Northants 509

Wilsford, Willesford Lincs 40

Wilsthorpe, Willesthorp, Wylsthorp Lincs 670, 758.74, 758.84, 758.143

Wing Rutland 113a

Wingfield, Wyngfeld Suffolk 190, 662; almshouse 665; see Oldwyngefeldhall

Witham, Withome, Wytham Lincs 107, 128, 129a, 141, 670, 673, 674, 675; North Witham 758.56; South Witham 127, 670

Wittering, Wetring, Withering, Wyteringg Northants 115, 203, 261, 606, 758.170, 770

Wodeston 95

Wolfehouse Rutland 673-4

Woodstock, Wodestock 758.179, 758.185

Woolsthorpe, Woollesthorpe Lincs 670

Worton in Cassington Oxon 673

Wothorpe, Werthrop, Wirthorp, Wyrthorp Northants 105, 159, 172, 187, 193, 227, 229, 232, 240, 244, 246, 249, 282, 297, 313, 321-2, 328, 333, 350, 360, 365-6, 402, 411, 416, 431, 449, 561-2, 567-9, 573, 591, 649, 653, 670, 758.1, 782, 793, 804, 854, 857-90, 898, 901-7; cemetery 153, 253; church of 793, 885; common croft of 322; convent 153, 170, 228, 249, 253, 329, 365, 416, 504, 518, 524, 585, 782; cross 322, 561; prioress of convent of Wothorpe 246, 249, 329; Isabel prioress 153, 170; mill 321, 366, 566, 570; oven 249; rectory of 793; road to 326, 351, 544; village 431; watercourse 229, 321, 402, 569

Wotton by Wodestock Oxon 758.179W

Wymondham Leicestershire 580-1

Yarwell Northants 800

Yaxley, Yakesle Cambs 101, 758.124, 869

York 26-9, 50-1, 57, 59-64, 114, 120, 580-1, 588, 593

758.193, 854; seal of 359

chivaler, *see* Sampson

Cistercian order 296, 299

cloth, *see* burnet, burrel

croft 200, 213, 310, 332, 351, 359, 413, 424, 441, 446-7, 449, 483, 541, 560, 567, 655.3, 655.16, 655.26

cross 168, 223, 322, 353, 371, 442, 546, 561, 758.2, 758.66, 758.103, 758.197, 907

deanery, see chapter

dower 467, 503, 514, 548, 550, 551, 558, 565, 602, 764

easement 911.23

fosse, *see* ditch *in Stamford placenames index*

gallows 623, 625, 758.176

garden 8, 113, 117, 158, 161, 163-5, 170, 189, 232-3, 240, 253, 296, 313, 322, 386, 395, 460, 470, 530, 539, 542, 561, 651-2, 658, 669, 670, 677, 679.2, 689, 701, 706, 708-12, 722, 726-7, 731, 734, 736-40, 745, 752, 758.38, 758.41, 758.49, 758.57, 758.65, 758.69, 758.70, 758.81, 758.95, 758.97-8, 758.110, 758.116-7, 758.134, 758.138, 758.141, 758.144, 758.147, 758.158, 758.161, 758.181, 758.191, 758.193, 758.196, 758.200-1, 765.3, 765.6-9, 766.1-2, 767.6, 773, 776, 789, 843, 868, 895-6, 900, 903, 911.7; *see* orchards

gild of Corpus Christi 1.1-3, 162, 191-2, 758.196; of Corpus Christi and St Mary 162; gild of St Martin 2, 298; gild of St Mary 3, 234, 758.105; gild of the Holy Trinity 709; gild of St Mary 149.1-2, 149.6-7; alderman of gild 149.7; proctor 4.9, 4.11, 4.14, 4.16, 149.8, 472, 648; *see* mass

holm 444, 589, 758.104

Jews 237, 250, 288, 319, 336, 339, 343, 419, 479, 500, 513, 603, 616, 619, 624, 627, 634-5, 638, 910.5, 911.7, 913.3, 12, 13

landgable (tax) 342, 370, 515, 600

leper 124, 784, 789

library 238

malt 360, 653

mass 210, 331, 865; of BVM 3, 4.1-21,

114, 149.1-8, 278, 472, 648, 699, 758.41, 758.58, 911.16; mass of St Mary in All Saints church 758.58; *see also* chantry, gild

obit, *see* anniversary

occupations (*see also name index*)

apothecary 188, 309, 316, 758.8, 758.9, 758.43

baker/baxter 4.4, 71, 200, 223, 236, 284, 375, 442, 459, 660, 711, 715, 758.170, 758.195, 758.68

barber 150, 154, 472, 473, 487, 712, 731, 738, 758.15, 767.6, 769, 860

barker 162, 842

butcher/bocher 228, 231, 256, 309, 387, 416, 524, 529, 583, 750, 758.27, 758.144, 758.152, 758.163, 758.199, 759, 772, 865, 911.13; *see* 485

butler 157.1

carbonario (charcoal burner or collier) 498

carpenter 96, 199, 400, 535, 717, 724, 730, 741

carter 504

chandler/chandeler/chaundler 537, 767.6

chapman 704, 758.107

clothier 758.32, 758.37, 758.53

cook 152, 583

cooper/coupere 758.31

cordwainer/cordewaner 75, 455, 484, 538

corviser 758.161

doctor 489, 517; *see* physician

draper 236, 321, 366, 537, 661, 670, 700, 702, 706, 708, 711, 720, 722, 724, 726, 735, 742, 745, 752, 758.143, 758.159, 758.166, 758.171, 758.192, 766.1

dyer 149.8, 186, 245, 255, 284, 294, 307, 337, 341, 342, 353, 354, 363, 370, 377, 408, 412, 419, 438, 467, 479, 482, 495, 496, 500, 515, 543, 546, 602, 651, 894

farrier 510

ferrour 751,

fisher 184, 427, 713

fishmonger 4.5, 184, 713, 758.39

flaxman 726

fuller 411, 515

furbisher 324, 843

glasier 169

glover 239, 616, 717, 724, 730, 741, 771

goldsmith 495, 547, 719, 758.51

harper 52

husbandman 156, 161, 704, 723, 726, 745, 758.186, 906

innholder/innkeeper 856, 897

ironmonger 750,

janitor 315, 330, 338, 353, 498, 503; *see* porter

leather dresser 645, 758.38

locksmith 303, 348

litster/lyster 471, 758.130

master chanter 189

mercer 4.8, 20, 298, 320, 398, 417, 506, 510, 548, 557, 558, 560, 585, 723, 749, 750, 758.133, 758.136, 758.199, 911.8-9

merchant/mercator 162, 188, 386, 564, 624, 670, 674, 681, 701, 703, 705, 710, 725, 738, 746, 749, 758.14, 758.50, 758.155, 758.174, 758.198, 758.199, 758.200, 758.202, 765.7, 765.9, 767.5, 804, 808

messenger 285, 513

miller 60, 230, 344, 366, 378, 570

notary public 159, 402, 680, 767.3, 767.4

osteler 769, 770

palmer 183, 221, 224, 339, 354, 439, 450, 578, 583

parchemyner 758.97

parker 232, 758.180

patynner 670

pewterer 162

physician 758.4-11, 758.23, 758.25, 758.31, 758.32; *see* doctor

plasterer 750

plouman/ploughman 495, 500

plumber 410, 809

porter 178, 204, 228, 379, 416, 418, 499, 524, 758.17-18; *see* janitor

roofer 481, 556,

saddler/sadeler 95, 536, 737, 739, 751, 758.117, 758.188

sawyer 411

scribe 231, 336, 379, 499

shepherd 200, 360, 653

shoemaker 180, 562, 670, 911.22

skinner 4.5 , 207, 267, 305, 338, 380, 620, 713, 758.115, 818

slater/sclatter 759, 772

smith 154, 167, 197, 212, 255, 315, 323, 337, 349, 356, 394, 400, 422, 447, 510, 520, 525, 556, 560, 719, 758.35, 777

spicer 409, 498, 501, 506, 819

stapler 162, 670, 674, 725; *see* woolmerchant

stonecutter 262, 338

tailor 87, 177, 196, 204, 214-5, 228, 260, 266-7, 316, 322, 346, 372, 380, 416, 428, 434, 439, 451, 458, 484, 494, 499, 500, 507, 524, 543, 545, 553, 556, 561, 655.7, 670, 678, 758.175, 834

tallowman 638

tanner 4.21, 13, 171, 209, 244, 270, 296, 328, 343, 361, 363-4, 370, 382, 397, 403, 418, 509, 517, 525, 527

taverner 648, 758.116

tawyer 390

tiler 283, 758.192, 880, 882

vintner 23, 207, 250, 334, 356, 380, 501, 718, 728,

walker 758.147

weaver 149.3, 149.7, 208, 251, 511, 911.1

wolman 771

wool merchant 340, 364, 625, 758.33; *see* stapler

wright 567, 661, 719, 724, 726, 758.170, 758.190

officials:

Alderman of Stamford 5, 158, 162, 173, 189, 235, 279, 298, 306, 317, 366, 531-2, 536, 648, 658, 670, 688, 699, 700, 703, 705-6, 708-711, 717-8, 720, 722-3, 725-8, 731, 733-6, 738, 742, 744, 750, 758.41, 758.46-47, 758.60-1, 758.64, 758.75, 758.80, 758.86, 758.88, 758.91, 758.93-4, 758.97, 758.99, 758.101, 758.104-5, 758.109, 758.109, 758.111-2, 758.120-3, 758.126, 758.128, 758.131, 758.133, 758.135-6, 758.142, 758.144-6,

758.148, 758.153-4, 758.159, 758.171,
758.178, 758.183-4, 758.190, 758.194,
758.197, 759.199, 759, 765.9, 766.1,
767.3-4, 769, 770—4, 777, 787, 843;
of gild 1-3, 4.7, 4.13, 4.18, 4.20,
149.1-2, 149.7, 298, 707, 708
bailiff 176, 186, 284, 295, 298, 325,
370, 377, 529, 552, 565, 600, 619,
758.32, 764, 788, 794, 913.20
chamberlain 585, 773-5, 843
churchwardens 161, 885
constable 587, 643, 659
dean 153, 166, 202, 217-8, 221, 231,
242, 255, 263, 310, 318, 327, 330,
338-9, 341, 359, 379, 418, 421, 423,
451, 455, 481, 494, 496-7, 500, 510-2,
543, 547, 577, 578, 584, 590-1, 597,
647-8, 758.17, 683-5, 854; dean
911.19, 21, 913.1; of Carleby 913.8;
of Lincoln 263; of Peterborough
178, 249
literatus 648, 758.175
marshall 198, 459, 517
president and scholars [college
unknown] 144
prior; *see* nunnery, *named monastic houses
e.g.* Durham
receiver 460
reeve 151, 166-7, 207, 213, 250, 288,
327, 405, 412-3, 437, 480, 495, 500,
506, 583, 601, 618, 624, 628, 633,
911.12, 911.22
serjeant, sergeant 152, 168, 245, 251,
353, 367, 447, 461, 480, 502, 559,
657, 913.18; at law 138, 694; of
Bourne 149.3; of St Leonards 269;
see name index
steward /seneschal 158, 207, 211, 328,

367, 409, 453, 486, 502, 584, 631,
812, 911.22-23; of Peterborough 153,
223, 328
warden 4.9, 153, 238, 253, 353, 478,
573, 648, 669, 758.90, 758.105, 759,
772, 789
watchman 480
yeoman 758.180, 895, 897

oratory private 825
orchards 689, 758.138; *see* gardens
pension 238, 263, 332, 426, 572, 577,
597
pilgrimage (to Holy Land) 187, 488,
613, 618, 633
pinfold 758.83
poverty, penury, indebtedness,
creditors, necessity 166, 209, 336,
343, 425, 447, 467, 495, 497, 517,
583, 603, 605, 611, 616, 618-9, 622,
624, 627, 633, 637, 645, 758.13,
913.1, 13
pupil (*alumpnus*, ward) 204, 341, 451,
461, 484, 494, 496, 499, 500, 543,
654.17 ; *see* Peter pupil of Reiner
requiem 188
saltpans 58
sheepfold 657
sparrowhawk 17-19, 21-22, 24, 39, 41,
113b
tithes 308, 332, 335, 360, 421, 549, 575,
590, 653, 849, 850
watercourse, aquaduct 229, 241, 321,
402, 569
windowgeld 911.14, 16

Lightning Source UK Ltd.
Milton Keynes UK
UKOW010214170612

194529UK00001B/3/P